Communications
in Computer and Information Science   220

T0092714

Maria Manuela Cruz-Cunha
João Varajão
Philip Powell
Ricardo Martinho (Eds.)

ENTERprise Information Systems

International Conference, CENTERIS 2011
Vilamoura, Portugal, October 5-7, 2011
Proceedings, Part II

 Springer

Volume Editors

Maria Manuela Cruz-Cunha
Polytechnic Institute of Cávado e Ave
4750-810 Vila Frescainha S. Martinho BCL, Portugal
E-mail: mcunha@ipca.pt

João Varajão
University of Trás-os-Montes e Alto Douro
5001-801 Vila Real, Portugal
E-mail: jvarajao@utad.pt

Philip Powell
Birkbeck, University of London
London, WC1E 7HX, UK
E-mail: beidean@bbk.ac.uk

Ricardo Martinho
Polytechnic Institute of Leiria
2411-901 Leiria, Portugal
E-mail: ricardo.martinho@ipleiria.pt

ISSN 1865-0929   e-ISSN 1865-0937
ISBN 978-3-642-24354-7   e-ISBN 978-3-642-24355-4
DOI 10.1007/978-3-642-24355-4
Springer Heidelberg Dordrecht London New York

Library of Congress Control Number: 2011936643

CR Subject Classification (1998): H.3, H.4, H.2, J.1, H.5, D.2, K.4.4

Typesetting: Camera-ready by author, data conversion by Scientific Publishing Services, Chennai, India

Printed on acid-free paper

Springer is part of Springer Science+Business Media (www.springer.com)

Preface

CENTERIS – Conference on Enterprise Information Systems—is an international conference addressing the largely multidisciplinary field embraced by the enterprise information systems (EIS), from the social, organizational and technological perspectives.

The CENTERIS 2011 edition, focused on *aligning technology, organizations and people*, and was held in Vilamoura, Algarve, Portugal. This was the place where during October 5–7, 2011, under the *leitmotiv* of enterprise information systems, academics, scientists, information technologies/information systems professionals, managers and solution providers from all over the world had the opportunity to share experiences, present new ideas, debate issues, and introduce the latest developments, from the social, organizational and technological perspectives.

More than 180 manuscripts were submitted to CENTERIS, coming from all over the world. There were about 120 papers selected for presentation and inclusion in the conference proceedings. The selected papers represent more than 350 authors from academia, research institutions and industry, representing around 30 countries.

These proceedings are intended for use by academics and practitioners that want to be aware of what is currently in the EIS agenda, from research to everyday business practice. We believe that the high quality and interest of the contributions presented at the CENTERIS 2011 edition makes this an important book in the EIS field.

Please enjoy your reading!

October 2011

Manuela Cunha
João Varajão
Philip Powell
Ricardo Martinho

Organization

CENTERIS 2011 was organized by the Polytechnic Institute of Cávado and Ave and the University of Trás-os-Montes e Alto Douro, Portugal.

General Chairs

Maria Manuela Cruz Cunha   Polytechnic Institute of Cávado and Ave, Portugal

João Eduardo Quintela Varajão University of Trás-os-Montes e Alto Douro, Portugal

Program Chair

Philip Powell   University of London, UK

Organization Chair

Ricardo Martinho   Polytechnic Institute of Leiria, Portugal

Organizing Committee

António Tavares	Polytechnic Institute of Cavado and Ave, Portugal
António Trigo	Polytechnic Institute of Coimbra, Portugal
Catarina Reis	Polytechnic Institute of Leiria, Portugal
Dulce Gonçalves	Polytechnic Institute of Leiria, Portugal
Emanuel Peres	University of Trás-os-Montes e Alto Douro, Portugal
João Varajão	University of Trás-os-Montes e Alto Douro, Portugal
Maria Manuela Cunha	Polytechnic Institute of Cavado and Ave, Portugal
Ricardo Martinho	Polytechnic Institute of Leiria, Portugal
Rui Rijo	Polytechnic Institute of Leiria, Portugal
Vitor Fernandes	Polytechnic Institute of Leiria, Portugal
Rita Ascenso	Polytechnic Institute of Leiria, Portugal

Scientific Committee

Adamantios Koumpis	Research Programmes Division, ALTEC S.A, Greece
Ahmed Elragal	German University in Cairo, Egypt
Albert Boonstra	University of Groningen, The Netherlands
Alberto Arroyo	Orienta, Spain
Alexandra Klen	Universidade Federal de Santa Catarina, Brazil
Álvaro Manuel Rocha	University Fernando Pessoa, Portugal
Américo Azevedo	University of Porto, Portugal
Ana Maria Fermoso Garcia	Pontifical University of Salamanca, Spain
Anca Draghici	Politehnica University of Timisoara, Romania
Andrew Targowski	Western Michigan University, USA
António Cunha	University of Trás-os-Montes e Alto Douro, Portugal
Antonio José Balloni	CTI, Brazil
Bart H.M. Gerritsen	TNO Netherlands Organization for Applied Scientific Research, The Netherlands
Bernard Grabot	École Nationale d'Ingénieurs de Tarbes (ENIT), France
Calin Gurau	GSCM – Montpellier Business School, France
Carmen de Pablos	Rey Juan Carlos University, Spain
Carola Jones	Universidad Nacional de Córdoba, Argentina
Carrillo Verdún	Universidad Politécnica de Madrid, Spain
David Romero	Tecnológico de Monterrey, Mexico
Diane Poulin	Université Laval, Canada
Dimitrios Koufopoulos	Brunel University, UK
Dirk Werth	Institut für Wirtschaftsinformatik, Germany
Dulce Domingos	University of Lisbon, Portugal
Emad Abu-Shanab	Yarmouk University, Jordan
Esra Tekez	Sakarya University, Turkey
Ethel Mokotoff	Alcalá University, Spain
Fernando Moreira	Universidade Portucalense, Portugal
George Jamil	Universidade FUMEC, Brazil
Gilliean Lee	Lander University, USA
Giorgio Bruno	Politecnico di Torino, Italy
Goran Putnik	University of Minho, Portugal
Hans-Henrik Hvolby	Aalborg University, Denmark
Heiko Duin	BIBA Bremer Institut für Produktion und Logistik GmbH, Germany
Henrique O'Neill	ISCTE, Portugal
Jaideep Motwani	Grand Valley State University, USA
Jens Eschenbächer	BIBA Bremer Institut für Produktion und Logistik, Germany

Jonatan Jelen	Parsons The New School for Design, USA
Jorge Marx Gómez	Oldenburg University, Germany
Jose L. Caro	University of Malaga, Spain
José L. Leiva Olivenca	University of Malaga, Spain
José Tribolet	INOV - INESC Inovação, Portugal
Kam Hou Vat	University of Macau, Macau
Klara Antlova	Technical University of Liberec, Czech Republic
Laura Ripamonti	Università degli Studi di Milano, Italy
Leonardo Soto	University of Guadalajara, Mexico
Leonel Morgado	University of Trás-os-Montes e Alto Douro, Portugal
Leonel Santos	University of Minho, Portugal
Ljubo Vlacic	Griffith University, Australia
Lorna Uden	Staffordshire University, UK
Luis Amaral	University of Minho, Portugal
Luís Borges Gouveia	Universidade Fernando Pessoa, Portugal
Mahesh S. Raisinghani	Texas Woman's University, USA
Manuel Cabral	University of Trás-os-Montes e Alto Douro, Portugal
Manuel Mora	Autonomous University of Aguascalientes, Mexico
Manuel Pérez Cota	Universidad de Vigo, Spain
Marco Khrmann	Brunel University, UK
Marilisa Oliveira	UEPG/UNAM, Brazil
Mário Caldeira	Technical University of Lisbon, Portugal
Marko Kolakovic	University of Zagreb, Croatia
Masakazu Ohashi	Chuo University, Japan
Matjaz Mulej	University of Maribor, Slovenia
Mayumi Hori	Hakuoh University, Japan
Maximino Bessa	University of Trás-os-Montes e Alto Douro, Portugal
Meira Levy	Ben-Gurion University of the Negev, Israel
Michal Žemlicka	Charles University, Czech Republic
Miguel Mira da Silva	Instituto Superior Técnico, Portugal
Nicolaos Protogeros	University of Macedonia, Greece
Nuno Lopes	Polytechnic Institute of Cávado e Ave, Portugal
Nuno Rodrigues	Polytechnic Institute of Cávado e Ave, Portugal
Patrícia Gonçalves	Polytechnic Institute of Cávado and Ave, Portugal
Paulo Garrido	University of Minho, Portugal
Paulo Tomé	Polytechnic Institute of Viseu, Portugal
Pedro Anunciação	Polytechnic Institute of Setúbal, Portugal

Pedro Quelhas de Brito	University of Porto, Portugal
Pedro Soto Acosta	Universidad de Murcia, Spain
Philip Powell	Birkbeck, University of London, UK
Raul Morais	University of Trás-os-Montes e Alto Douro, Portugal
Rémy Glardon	Swiss Federal Institute of Technology at Lausanne, Switzerland
Ricardo Colomo Palacios	University Carlos III of Madrid, Spain
Rinaldo Michelini	PMAR Lab of the University of Genoa, Italy
Roberto Razzoli	PMAR Lab of the University of Genoa, Italy
Rossi Setchi	Cardiff University , UK
Rui Dinis Sousa	University of Minho, Portugal
Rui Gomes	Polytechnic Institute of Viana do Castelo, Portugal
Samo Bobek	University of Maribor, Slovenia
Sanja Vranes	The Mihajlo Pupin Institute, Serbia
Snezana Pantelic	The Mihajlo Pupin Institute, Serbia
Thomas Schlegel	University of Stuttgart, Germany
Tor Guimaraes	Tennessee Tech University, USA
Valentina Janev	The Mihajlo Pupin Institute, Serbia
Vitor Carvalho	Polytechnic Institute of Cávado e Ave, Portugal
Vladimír Modrák	Technical University of Kosice, Slovakia
Vojko Potocan	University of Maribor, Slovenia
Wai Ming Cheung	Northumbria University, UK
William Lawless	Paine College, USA

Supporting Entities

Polytechnic Institute of Cávado e do Ave
University of Trás-os-Montes e Alto Douro
Polytechnic Institute of Leiria
GESITI/CTI/MCT

Table of Contents – Part II

EIS Applications

Cost Per Flying Hour – Use of Information from the Integrated
Management System 1
   Carlos Páscoa, Pedro Santos, and José Tribolet

Hybrid GA-Based Improvement Heuristic with Makespan Criterion for
Flow-Shop Scheduling Problems 11
   Pavol Semančo and Vladimír Modrák

Framework for Collaborative 3D Urban Environments 19
   Miguel Melo, Maximino Bessa, Tânia Rocha, José Sousa,
   Emanuel Peres, João Varajão, and Luís Magalhães

Evaluating an Enterprise Content Management for the Macao
Government Agency 29
   F. Pong, R. Whitfield, and J. Negreiros

Interactive Models Supporting Construction Planning 40
   A.Z. Sampaio and J.P. Santos

Foundations for a Mobile Context-Aware Advertising System 51
   Guilherme Alexandre, Telmo Adão, Martinho Gonçalves,
   Luís Magalhães, Maximino Bessa, Emanuel Peres, and João Varajão

Virtual Fitting Room Augmented Reality Techniques for
e-Commerce 62
   Francisco Pereira, Catarina Silva, and Mário Alves

Towards an Enterprise Information Subsystem for Measuring
(Perceived) Landside Accessibility of Airports 72
   Maarten Janssen, Jan van den Berg, Mohsen Davarynejad, and
   Vincent Marchau

AEMS: Towards an Advanced Event Management System 82
   Paulo Cristo and Ricardo Martinho

Technical Aspects and Emerging Technologies

Cloud Computing: A Platform of Services for Services 91
   Nuno Sénica, Cláudio Teixeira, and Joaquim Sousa Pinto

Cloud Computing to Support the Evolution of Massive Multiplayer
Online Games 101
   Dario Maggiorini and Laura Anna Ripamonti

Quality Evaluation Methods to Improve Enterprise VoIP
Communications   111
    Filipe Neves, Salviano Soares, Pedro Assuncao, Filipe Tavares, and
    Simão Cardeal

Survey on Anti-spam Single and Multi-objective Optimization   120
    Iryna Yevseyeva, Vitor Basto-Fernandes, and José R. Méndez

Location-Based Service for a Social Network with Time and Space
Information   130
    Ana Filipa Nogueira and Catarina Silva

Citizens@City Mobile Application for Urban Problem Reporting   141
    António Miguel Ribeiro, Rui Pedro Costa, Luís Marcelino, and
    Catarina Silva

Mobile Multimedia Visiting Guide to Knowledge and Experiences
Sharing   151
    Diogo Lopes, Miguel Pragosa, Catarina Silva, and Luis Marcelino

Mobile Application Webservice Performance Analysis: Restful Services
with JSON and XML   162
    Carlos Rodrigues, José Afonso, and Paulo Tomé

Error-Detection in Enterprise Application Integration Solutions   170
    Rafael Z. Frantz, Rafael Corchuelo, and Carlos Molina-Jiménez

Back-Propagation Artificial Neural Network for ERP Adoption Cost
Estimation   180
    Mohamed T. Kotb, Moutaz Haddara, and Yehia T. Kotb

TCP, UDP and FTP Performances of Laboratory Wi-Fi IEEE 802.11g
WEP Point-to-Point Links   188
    J.A.R. Pacheco de Carvalho, H. Veiga, N. Marques,
    C.F. Ribeiro Pacheco, and António D. Reis

Systems of Synchronism in Optical Digital Communications   196
    António D. Reis, José F. Rocha, Atílio S. Gameiro, and
    José P. Carvalho

Social Aspects and IS in Education

Emphasizing Human Tasks and Decisions in Business Process
Models   206
    Giorgio Bruno

Technology Readiness Index (TRI) Factors as Differentiating Elements
between Users and Non Users of Internet Banking, and as Antecedents
of the Technology Acceptance Model (TAM) 215
    *Péricles José Pires, Bento Alves da Costa Filho, and
    João Carlos da Cunha*

Developing an Instrument to Assess Information Technology Staff
Motivation 230
    Fernando Belfo and Rui Dinis Sousa

Analysing People's Work in Organizations and Its Relationship with
Technology 240
    António Gonçalves, Marielba Zacarias, and Pedro Sousa

Autonomic Arousal during Group Decision Making Consensus Rules
versus Majority Rules: Pilot Study 260
    *Alana Enslein, Chelsea Hodges, Kelsey Zuchegno, Tadd Patton,
    Reeves Robert, Stephen H. Hobbs, Joseph C. Wood, and W.F. Lawless*

Exploring a Framework for a New Focus in Information and
Communications Technology Education 270
    Arturo Serrano Santoyo

Interoperability on e-Learning 2.0: The PEACE Case Study 276
    Ricardo Queirós, Lino Oliveira, Cândida Silva, and Mário Pinto

IT/IS Management

ALBIS - ALigning Business Processes and Information Systems:
A Case Study 286
    Lerina Aversano, Carmine Grasso, and Maria Tortorella

Challenges of Teams Management: Using Agile Methods to Solve the
Common Problems 297
    *Mariana de Azevedo Santos, Paulo Henrique de Souza Bermejo,
    Adriano Olímpio Tonelli, and André Luiz Zambalde*

Risk Management Model in ITIL 306
    Sarah Vilarinho and Miguel Mira da Silva

What Service? 315
    *Ana Cardoso, Isabel Ferreira, João Álvaro Carvalho, and
    Leonel Santos*

Enterprise Information Systems - Managing I.T. Human Resources
from 18 to 70 Years Old (Living with the Conflict of Generations) 325
    Joel Mana Gonçalves and Rejane Pereira da Silva Gonçalves

An Analysis of MoReq2010 from the Perspective of TOGAF   335
   Ricardo Vieira, Francisco Valdez, and José Borbinha

Strategic Alignment: Comparison of Approaches   345
   Karim Doumi, Salah Baïna, and Karim Baïna

Experimenting a Modeling Approach for Modeling Enterprise Strategy
in the Context of Strategic Alignment   356
   Karim Doumi, Salah Baïna, and Karim Baïna

How and Why Do Top Managers Support or Not Support Strategic IS
Projects?   369
   Albert Boonstra

Defining a Process Framework for Corporate Governance of IT   380
   Alberto Arroyo and José D. Carrillo Verdún

Assessing Information Technology Use in Organizations: Developing a
Framework   388
   Emre Sezgin and Sevgi Özkan

Information Systems Planning - How to Enhance Creativity?   398
   Vitor Santos, Luís Amaral, and Henrique Mamede

Software Solutions Construction According to Information Systems
Architecture Principles   408
   Sana Guetat and Salem Ben Dhaou Dakhli

Author Index   419

Cost Per Flying Hour – Use of Information from the Integrated Management System

Carlos Páscoa[1,2], Pedro Santos[1], and José Tribolet[2,3]

[1] Department of University Education, Portuguese Air Force Academy, Sintra, Portugal
[2] Department of Information Systems and Computer Science, Instituto Superior Técnico,
Technical University of Lisbon, Portugal
[3] CODE - Center for Organizational Design & Engineering, INOV,
Rua Alves Redol 9, Lisbon, Portugal
{cjpascoa,ptrs1988}@gmail.com, jose.tribolet@inesc.pt

Abstract. An organization cannot function without knowing how much it produces and how much each product costs. The Portuguese Air Force is no exception, and so, determining the Cost per Flying Hour is essential for decision-making.

Information concerning the Cost Factors included in the Cost per Flying Hour used to be stored in various Information Systems, but with the implementation of the Defense Integrated Management System in Portuguese Air Force, these Information Systems became obsolete, as the Integrated Management System now concentrates all the information about the Cost Factors. However it did not have the ability to calculate the Cost per Flying Hour because some of its modules were not yet implemented. Thus the Cost per Flying Hour began to be calculated using inflation. In 2010 a Model in which the Cost Factors were obtained directly from sources was proposed.

In this investigation work, it is recommended that the new Model start to use the Integrated Management System data, being the main source of information. Thus, it is defined and proposed a Calculation's Model of Cost per Flying Hour, presenting its formula and the method of obtaining the information for it.

Keywords: Organizational Engineering, Information Systems, Cost per Flying Hour, Self-Awareness.

1 Introduction

Over the years, the organizations, including non-profit ones, are subject to constant changes to keep operating at the cutting edge and not be overcome by other organizations.

When changes occur, there is always an adaptation period in which problems due to inadequate or incomplete implementations are often detected. The Portuguese Air Force (PoAF) had specific software applications for calculating the Cost per Flying Hour (CPFH) that would seek Cost Factors (FC) in various Information Systems (IS). The Defense Integrated Management System (SIG) implementation made those IS to be discontinued and caused the impossibility for CPFH calculation. To solve the problem

M.M. Cruz-Cunha et al. (Eds.): CENTERIS 2011, Part II, CCIS 220, pp. 1–10, 2011.
© Springer-Verlag Berlin Heidelberg 2011

CPFH started to be calculated according to the annual inflation. This was done for the last four years.

In order to link investigation to the operational side, the Air Force Academy begun to address real organizational problems in a new master thesis scientific area called Organizational Engineering (OE). In 2010, to overcome the various limitations caused by using only inflation, SOARES et al. (2010) [1] developed a Model that allowed obtaining a CPFH from scratch, getting FC values directly from the responsible entities. In 2011, CPFH was addressed, again, in order to try to solve the need for calculating the CPFH from SIG. This paper describes the adaptation of the Model developed in [1] to SIG, presenting the formula and the method of obtaining the information for it.

The Flying Hour (FH) is directly attached to PoAF's operational product. Although it is a governmental and non-profit organization, it is necessary to determine its cost in order to optimize the budget allocated by the Government with the purpose of improving management and operation. CPFH is, therefore, a powerful management indicator for decision making. Additionally, it also defines what the Organization does, who does it and how it is done. It can be said that the CPFH is part of a very important organizational concept: self-awareness, which allows for a better organizational understanding from the stakeholders point of view.

Following a social science research methodology, an initial question is proposed: "How to get the CPFH through SIG?". This question is decomposed into auxiliary questions and hypotheses (each related to one question):

- Q1: What organizational benefits might come from CPFH being calculated through SIG?
- H1: Easy access to centralized data, using fewer human resources, allowing for the visualization of CPFH by all entities who require this information in a faster, easier and updated way will bring enormous organizational benefits.
- Q2: Having in mind the current limitations, how can SIG be improved in order to provide accurate CPFH?
- H2: Given the economical limitations (number of licenses) associated to using an Enterprise Resource Planning (ERP), adapting a (Excel) spreadsheet to retrieve SIG data, in a timely manner, could provide the needed situational awareness.
- Q3: Who inserts the values to calculate the CPFH, and when and where are they inserted?
- H3: The introduction of values is done by the responsible entities in the SIG at the earliest opportunity.

2   Concepts and Application

This chapter contains essential ideas to the elaboration of this article, including what OE is, what SIG is and, finally, what has already been done on the CPFH subject.

2.1   Organizational Engineering

OE comes as a set of principles and practices that aim to answer the following question: "How to draw and improve on a holistic approach, all elements associated *with a company using analysis methods and tools to better achieve that the organization meets its strategic objectives."*[2].

The aim of OE is to increase efficiency, effectiveness, communication and coordination, and it should be able to be possible to apply it to any type of organization and to all areas that need an improvement in their performance [3].

Concepts such as self-awareness and agility are essential to the success of the organization.

The notion of self-awareness as a concept of OE is of extreme importance to the organization. People must know who they (and others) are in the organization and what and how they (and others) are doing things [4]. Thus, if the organization has a strong self-awareness, it will know its strengths, limitations, values and motivations [5] and the employees will be directed by common objectives.

OE strives for agility, which represents the ability to act quickly with a management effort in the accurate response to change. It also represents the ability to initiate changes in order to achieve business advantage [6].

2.2 Integrated Management System

There are currently two main projects in PoAF, an older one, the Integrated System for Management Support of the Air Force (SIAGFA), and a newer one, SIG. While the first is exclusive to the management of PoAF, the second one manages the various branches of the Ministry of National Defense (MND), being imposed by it.

This project applies Business Process Management (BPM) concepts *"aligning the Information Systems with the organization strategy and involving several distinct entities like the Ministry of Defense, the Army, the Navy and the Air Force that had to focus on identifying common processes and adapt to a unified concepts, procedures and applications"* [6]. SIG has the objective of integrating the Financial, Logistic and Human Resource's information produced in the Defense's organisms, to implement the Official Plan of Public Accounting (OPPA) and to be able to do their accounting organized by branch and produce reliable, timely and useful management information for decision making. This optimizes resources, gains efficiency and reduces operating costs. It has its structure based on Software Systems Applications and Products (SAP), which is the SIG's ERP. It is in this program that the data is inserted by the responsible entities.

However, with the implementation of SIG in PoAF, there was an enormous amount of problems that resulted in the loss of information, namely the impossibility of calculating the CPFH. This happened due to the fact that part of the information necessary to calculate the CPFH was now in SIG, which made SIAGFA unable to access the required information. Thus, as said before, PoAF started to update CPFH through inflation, which produces only an approximate value of the real CPFH and does not account for changes in the various components.

Currently, SIG has the Financial and Logistic modules almost fully implemented, and the Human Resources (HR) module is in the process of being implemented as well. For the time being, PoAF has decided not to implement the Maintenance module in SIG. This has happened because SIG does not have the specific requirements for the PoAF's various weapons systems, due to the large number of different existing aircraft types. Also the Operational module is not going to be integrated into the SIG for now. Thus, in the near future, SIG will handle PoAF's management areas of Finance, Logistics and HR, but the Operational and Maintenance areas will continue to be handled at SIAGFA.

2.3 CPFH Typification

In 2004, a Directive (DIR) was created to explicitly state how CPFH should be calculated. Although most of the used IS are discontinued, the document is still in force. In practice, it has no application in the present scenario. However, the associated formulae are still valid.

The operational CPFH, for each weapon system, is defined as the sum of the CF's values that directly contribute to the support of the weapons system divided by the Number of Flying Hours (NFH). CF can be classified as:

- Fixed Costs, that include the Structure Costs and Amortized Costs, which contain operational and maintenance staff cost, depreciation of inventory equipment and aircraft Inspections outside PoAF;
- Variable Costs, that contains costs associated with aircraft fuel and lubricants, material consumption, as well as the costs of repairs / maintenance carried out in the Organization.

This form of Automatic Calculation of CPFH used IS as a means to collect information of the various CF, i.e., these applications contained data from the Flying Units, which resulted in a final output, the CPFH. Each of the applications was independent and had an EPR assigned to ensure its smooth function.

Due to the inclusion of SIG in PoAF and to the changes that came from the restructuring that has undergone (for example, some CF absorbed others previously under the responsibility of other entities), CPFH DIR became useless. So, the CPFH had to be calculated by adding the inflation rate to the previous year's CPFH.

However, [1] did not use SIG as an information source. Instead, the information was obtained directly from the Directions through Excel files filled by these.

In [1], there were some changes regarding what was written in the DIR CPFH. The costs associated with aircraft fuel and lubricants and unit material began to be included in the Variable Costs. The costs with staff (remuneration of operational and maintenance staff), as well as costs related to various repairs / maintenances carried out began to be included in the Fixed Costs.

However, the definition remains the same: fixed costs are CF's which do not vary with the NFH, while variable costs are CF's that are directly related to the NFH.

However, since these various CF were introduced by only three distinct Entities / Directions, a new division was made into three types of costs: Direction of Maintenance Weapon Systems (DMSA); Costs (costs associated with repairs / maintenance, as well as the Unit material); Direction of Supply and Transports (DAT) Costs (costs associated with aircraft fuel and lubricant) and Direction of Personnel (DP) Costs (costs associated with remuneration of operational and maintenance staff).

Generally one can define the CPFH as the sum of different values / costs introduced by the authorities, divided by the NFH.

The Automatic Calculation of the Cost per Flying Hour (ACCPFH) can be explained as follows: DAT is responsible for entering data into the DAT Excel file, the same goes for the DMSA that inserts it into the DMSA Excel file and DP in the DP Excel File. After entering all the data, this information goes to the core file, CPFH TOTAL, in which the data is processed obtaining the CPFH. Note that the DP Costs may also be obtained through Air Units Personnel (AUP) DIR (which contains information about the number of staff needed for each Flying Unit) and the Direction of Finances of the Air Force (DFFA) pay table (which contains the remunerations of the various ranks of PoAF).

Despite the changes, the truth is that the developed formula will be the same for the CPFH DIR as for [1], thus validating this Model.

3 Model Adaptation

Given the need to create a Model to obtain the CPFH through SIG, as previously mentioned, the Model described in section 3 was created.

This Model is an adaptation of [1] to SIG. In this chapter, the information available in SIG is described, as well as the method used to obtain it. The method to obtain information not available in SIG is also mentioned.

3.1 Definition and Calculation Formulae of the Operational CPFH

In this Model, intended to calculate the Operational CPFH, i.e., the CPFH whose costs are directly associated with air operations (which contains the cost of remuneration of operational staff plus fuel and lubricants) and costs associated with maintenance (which includes the costs of remuneration of maintenance staff and weapons systems maintenance) is considered.

As this essay intends to use SIG to determine CPFH, there must be a new definition that fits this system, where the new CF must be specified with SIG's designations, to be obtained more easily.

So these costs can be divided depending on who is responsible for them. Thus, the costs of weapons systems maintenance will be defined as DMSA Costs. The costs of the fuel and lubricant will be defined as DAT Costs. And the costs related to the remuneration of operational and maintenance staff will be defined as DP Costs.

The general formula of Operational CPFH is the sum of the different values of these three costs, divided by the NFH.

In turn, each of these three Costs has different CF related to. However, SIG does not follow the description given by CPFH DIR (and updated by [1]), to the various CF. What this program does is to give a Control Code and an associated Economic Expenditure to the various costs of the various entities. Thus, if the cost of this information can be obtained through SIG, in addition to its definition, it is necessary to specify its designation found in the SIG, which translates into a corresponding Control Code and an associated Economic Expenditure.

For example, CF related to DAT Costs can be defined as follows:

- Costs of Fuels and lubricants - POL.
  These costs are in SIG and are defined there as follows:
- Fuels and lubricants - 02.01.02;
- Fuels and lubricants - Previous Years - 02.01.02.A0.09.

The developed formula of the Operational CPFH with the CPFH DIR designations is the following:

$$\text{Operational CPFH} = \frac{POL + MIL + MCU + RDMSA + RRA + POR + PMR}{NFH}$$

In turn, if what is required is the formula of Operational CPFH with the SIG designations, the formula is as follows:

$$\text{Operational CPFH} = \frac{02.01.02 + 02.01.02.A0.09 + 02.01.14 + 02.01.03 + 02.01.14 + 07.01.14 + POR + PMR}{NFH}$$

3.2 Information Available in SIG

To calculate the Operational CPFH the following values are needed:

- Maintenance Costs of aircraft;
- Fuels and lubricants Costs;
- Remuneration of operational and maintenance staff;
- NFH.
  Through the SIG planning tool (SEM-BW), it is only possible to obtain:
- Maintenance costs, i.e., DMSA Costs, specified by Flying Unit. It is possible to access the system and retrieve this information;
- Costs for fuels, i.e., the DAT Cost, which is also specified by Flying Units.

This is because SIG has still not implemented all the modules. The information available in either case depends on the accuracy of the information provided by the Directions and its insertion into the computer system. However there are problems in the execution (fleet results). The fuels are purchased by DAT in large quantities allocated to an air base unit and stored in a warehouse. The computer system only allows each received bill to match only one Element of Action. If there is only one facture for the unit, but several Activities / Elements of Action (fleets of the same unit), those responsible for this insertion place that cost only on a single Element of Action (fleet), and when there is a need for more fuel, they put this new cost in another Element of Action.

This way, it can be verified that the various Flying Units have fuel costs associated in the SIG, but this information is not properly attributed to the fleet and as such this information cannot be retrieved from SIG.

As for the remuneration of operational and maintenance staff, its associated SIG module is still under development and now it only shows the total remuneration of PoAF, which means that SIG cannot be used to retrieve this formation because the total remuneration in SIG contains not only the operational and maintenance staff but also all the rest of the PoAF staff, and it is not possible to isolate operational and maintenance staff.

SIG cannot be used to obtain the NFH either, since it does not have the operational component of PoAF implemented (this one is still active in SIAGFA). It will then be necessary to use this system to get the NFH of each weapon system.

It can be concluded that it is currently impossible to use SIG (SEM-BW) only to obtain the CPFH. There is the possibility of using another SIG tool, the Analytic

Accounting (CO) that is not being exploited. In the past, a query was created to automatically provide this calculation but it was never validated and tested, falling into disuse.

In the maintenance component, SIG has all the necessary information available, specified both by Flying Unit and as total. In the fuel component, the SIG contains inaccurate information regarding the specific cost per Flying Unit. As for the remuneration component, SIG is now useless. For NFH, SIG is also useless because the operational module is still associated with SIAGFA.

3.3   General Scheme for Obtaining CPFH Information

As mentioned before, due to the implementation of SIG in PoAF, much of the information required for the CPFH calculation moved to this system and therefore the old CPFH calculation Model has become obsolete. This has led to a need for a reformulation of the previous scheme for obtaining the information. So the following diagram was created with information concerning what is necessary for the calculation of CPFH, the information stored in SIG, as well as the one that is missing and finally where to obtain all the necessary information.

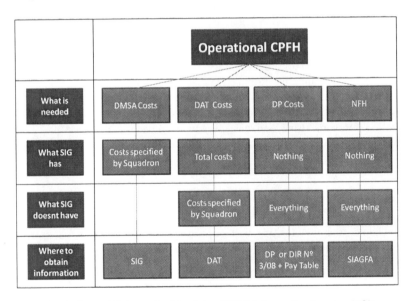

Fig. 1. General Scheme for Obtaining CPFH Information (source: [12])

3.4   Obtaining CPFH Information

DMSA Costs are obtained through SIG, starting the SEM-BW application and filtering the information depending on what is wanted. DAT Costs are obtained requesting directly the information from DAT. Soon, these costs will be obtained through SIG since its problem is being solved. NFH are obtained through SIAGFA. It is only necessary to access the program and filter the required information (per Flying

Unit and time period). DP Costs can be obtained in two ways: the same way as DAT Costs, (requesting the information directly to DP) or through AUP DIR and DFFA pay table (which contains the remunerations of the various ranks).

3.5 Validation of the CPFH Calculation Model

The values in [1] and this Model adaption are similar. Since [1] has been validated (by comparison with the values obtained with the Model which was used until 2004) it would be sufficient to validate this new way of calculating CPFH. However, there is another way to do that, which is by validating cost by cost.

For DP Costs, since the DFFA pay table and the AUP DIR change annually, these are accepted as certain. If the method chosen consist of requesting this value directly from DP, then the information is automatically validated by the Direction, as in others CPFH Models in which these values that are used.

As for DAT Costs, they are directly obtained from DAT, which are already validated by the Direction itself, which makes the DAT Costs used in this Model automatically validated.

DMSA Costs are the ones whose validation is not supported by other Models, because this is the only Model that currently uses SIG to obtain the CPFH. However, DMSA validates the information it gets from SIG, and the entities responsible for SIG have to verify the information recorded there. It can also be mentioned that the values obtained from SIG do not differ much from the values of the other Models, and that the small variation is due to the fact that these do not get the information automatically, but manually. So the DMSA Costs obtained from this Model are validated.

Finally, the NFH is validated because it is used in a IS that has been already in the organization for some time and has already been validated. Since the method of obtaining NFH is by consulting this system, the information is considered to be true and trustworthy.

4 Conclusion

In this chapter the conclusions will be presented through answers given to the questions initially made at the beginning of this work.

- Q1-Since SIG provides direct access to information, there is an easier access to data and less use of human resources. As SIG is available for the entire organization, anyone can access it and retrieve the data necessary to calculate CPFH in a faster, easier, and updated way, than if they had to request them from the various Directions. The hypothesis is subsequently validated.
- Q2 - It is still necessary to adapt a document because SIG has not yet explored the CO tool, making it impossible to use SIG to gather information and to do the calculations automatically. As such, it is necessary to explore this tool to obtain the CPFH directly through SIG. The hypothesis is validated.
- Q3 - The various entities already have systems for registration and verification of information, such as DMSA and DAT (this one is already correcting the problem of correct value introducing by Flying Unit in SIG). As for other costs, since its

modules are not yet implemented in SIG, they cannot be introduced there. But these costs can be obtained by any member of the organization by other means. The hypothesis is then not validated.

Finally, the answer to the initial question is: Since SIG has not implemented HR and operational modules yet, it is impossible to obtain the DP Costs and NFH through SIG, making the use of others IS who hold this information essential, such as SIAGFA for NFH and AUP DIR with DFFA pay table (or DP itself) for the DP Costs. Concerning DAT Costs, given that they contain inaccurate values, they cannot be retrieved from SIG (but this problem is already being solved and eventually it will be possible to use SIG to obtain these costs). DMSA Costs may be retrieved from SIG, requiring only that they will be filtered.

While performing this investigation work, problems relating to the CPFH calculation through SIG were found, which made it impossible to calculate CPFH using only SIG. The following recommendations point towards the correction of those problems:

- Implementation of the HR module in order to get the DP Costs;
- Exploration of the CO tool to be able to calculate the ACCPFH using only SIG as an IS;
- Implementation of the Maintenance module to gain a more specific control of maintenance costs;
- Implementation of the Operational module to obtain the NFH of each aircraft and thus disable SIAGFA, which is an old IS;
- Solve the problem of DAT Costs (already in progress);
- Create the opportunity to view the costs per mission;
- Create the opportunity to view the costs with National Forces Stationed in Foreign Countries, included in the cost of their fleets;
- Include in SIG costs paid by the State, (as the costs of maintenance contracts) to get an idea of how much it will cost to maintain the aircraft when PoAF has to pay for such costs.

It is also proposed that further research is carried out on the definition and calculation formula of Organizational CPFH and Life Cycle CPFH through SIG, when the HR and Operational modules have been implemented. It is also suggested that work should be done to get the Automatic calculation of the three types of CPFH using the CO tool when it is further explored.

References

1. Soares, J., Tribolet, J., Páscoa, C.: Definição de um Modelo de Cálculo do Custo da Hora de Voo dos Sistemas de Armas da Força Aérea Portuguesa, Master Thesis, Portuguese Air Force Academy, Sintra, Portugal (2010)
2. Macedo, P., Zacarias, M., Tribolet, J.: Técnicas e métodos de investigação em Engenharia Organizacional: Projecto de Investigação em Modelação de Processos de Produção. Bragança, 6ª Conferência da Associação Portuguesa de Sistemas de Informação (2005)
3. Organizational Engineering Institute: What is Organizational Engineering (2009), http://www.oeinstitute.org/what-is-oe.html (Consult. 27 Out. 2010)

4. Vicente, D., Tribolet, J.: Towards Organizational Self-awareness: A Methodological Approach to Capture and Represent Individual and Inter-Personal Work Practices, Master Thesis, Instituto Superior Técnico, Lisboa (2007)
5. Northup, T.: Awareness: The key Insight for Organizational Change, http://www.lmgsuccess.com/documents/awareness.pdf (Consult. 27 Out. 2010)
6. Allen, P.: Service Orientation: Winning Strategies and Best Practices, 1st edn. Cambridge University Press, New York (2006)
7. Páscoa, C.: The BMP Concept in the Actual Structure of the Military Organization. Technical University of Lisbon, Lisboa (2007)
8. Portuguese Air Force: Cálculo Automático do Custo da Hora de Voo, Chefe do Estado-Maior da Força Aérea, Lisboa, Portugal (2004)
9. Portuguese Air Force: Módulos de Pessoal para operação e Manutenção dos Sistemas de Armas, Chefe do Estado-Maior da Força Aérea, Lisboa, Portugal (2008)
10. Tribolet, J., Páscoa, C.: Organizational Engineering I Lecture Notes 2008/09. Portuguese Air Force Academy, Sintra (2008)
11. Portuguese Air Force; Sistema Integrado de Gestão da Defesa Nacional (SIG) - PONTO DE SITUAÇÃO, Logistics Command, Lisboa, Portugal (2010)
12. Santos, P.: O Custo da Hora de Voo – Aproveitamento da Informação do SIG, Master Thesis, Portuguese Air Force Academy, Sintra, Portugal (2011)

Hybrid GA-Based Improvement Heuristic with Makespan Criterion for Flow-Shop Scheduling Problems

Pavol Semančo and Vladimír Modrák

Faculty of Manufacturing Technologies of Technical University of Kosice, Bayerova 1,
08001 Presov, Slovakia, Slovak Republic
{pavol.semanco,vladimir.modrak}@tuke.sk

Abstract. In the paper, we proposed a hybrid improvement heuristic for permutation flow-shop problem based on the idea of evolutionary algorithm. The approach also employs constructive heuristic that gives a good initial solution. Hybrid GA-based improvement heuristic is applied in conjunction with three well-known constructive heuristics, namely CDS, Gupta's algorithm and Palmer's Slope Index. We tested our approach on Reeves' benchmark set of 21 problem instances range from 20 to 75 jobs and 5 to 20 machines. Subsequently, we compared obtained results to the best-known upper-bound solutions.

Keywords: flow shop, scheduling, genetic algorithm, heuristic, metaheuristic.

1 Introduction

A flow-shop production introduces a manufacturing system where n jobs are processed by m machines in the same order. The problem of finding an optimal schedule is referred to as flow-shop scheduling problem (FSSP). In a permutation flow-shop scheduling problem, denoted as PFSSP, the same sequence, or permutation, of jobs is maintained throughout [1]. The objective of the flow-shop scheduling problem is to meet optimality criterion of minimizing the makespan, total flow time or total weighted flow time. This paper investigates an optimal job sequence for flow-shop scheduling benchmark problem with objective to minimize the makespan. The general scheduling problem for a classical flow shop gives rise to $(n!)^m$ possible schedules [2]. For flow-shop scheduling problem Johnson proposed algorithm that optimally solves a 2-machine flow-shop problem [3]. It was later demonstrated that m-machine flow-shop scheduling problem (FSSP) is strongly NP-hard for $m \geq 3$ [4]. Permutation FSSP also has to meet standard requirements like a job cannot be processed by two or more machines at a time and a machine cannot process two or more jobs at the same time.

The optimization of FSSP employs the three major types of scheduling algorithm (exact, approximation and heuristic). However, the most common type of scheduling algorithms for NP-hard FSSP is heuristic that produces near-optimal or optimal solutions in reasonable time. The heuristics can be further classified as constructive

M.M. Cruz-Cunha et al. (Eds.): CENTERIS 2011, Part II, CCIS 220, pp. 11–18, 2011.
© Springer-Verlag Berlin Heidelberg 2011

heuristic and improvement heuristic (or meta-heuristic). The improvement heuristic in contrast to constructive heuristic starts with a initial schedule trying to find an improved schedule. In this paper, the improvement-heuristic approach is proposed incorporating the idea of evolution. If no improvement occurs for a certain number of iterations, the algorithm backtracks to the last best result. Hybrid GA-based improvement heuristic is performed by predetermined number of iterations and report of the best result.

The rest of the paper is organized as follows. The next section reviews the relevant scheduling literature for the flow-shop scheduling heuristics algorithms. In the section, namely hybrid GA-based improvement heuristic, the formal description of GA approach is covered. The Section, "Computational Experiments," discusses results obtained from the experiment. The summary of the paper and possible future research ideas are presented in the section, namely Summary and Conclusions.

2 Research Background

The model of flow-shop scheduling problem with makespan (C_{max}) as an objective function can be specified according to 3-filed classification ($\alpha/\beta/\gamma$). The first filed, namely α, stands for machine environment. For the flow-shop scheduling the machine environment is denoted as Fm, where m is the number of the machines. The β-field specifies the job constraints like for permutation of jobs the *prmu* abbreviation is used. The last field determines the optimally criterion like makespan (C_{max}). Based on this 3-field classification the general flow-shop scheduling problem can be denoted as $Fm/prmu/C_{max}$. This notation was firstly suggested by Conway and until now is handy [5].

Hejazi and Saghafian introduced a comprehensive review of algorithms for flow-shop scheduling problems with makespan criterion [6]. Approaches solving flow-shop scheduling problem range from heuristics, developed, for example, by Palmer [7], Campbell [8], Dannenbring [9] to more complex techniques such as Branch and Bound [10], Tabu Search [11], Genetic Algorithm [12], Shifting Bottleneck procedure by Balas and Vazacopoulos [13], Ant Colony Algorithm by Blum and Sampels [14] and others.

The flow-shop sequencing problem is one of the most well-known classic production scheduling problems. Focusing on the PFSSP with C_{max} objective function, first classical heuristics was proposed by Page [15]. Palmer adopted his idea and proposed the slope index to be utilized for the m-machine n-job permutation flow shop sequencing problem. A simple heuristic extension of Johnson's rule to m-machine flow shop problem has been proposed by Campbell. This extension is known in the literature as the CDS (Campbell, Dudek, and Smith) heuristic. Another method to obtain a minimum makespan is presented Gupta [16]. A significant approach to solving the FSSP proposed Nawaz [17], in which they point out that a job with larger total processing time should have higher priority in the sequence.

One of the important factors that are quite frequently discussed in FSSP is the setup time (see reference [18]). The setup time represents the time required to shift from one job to another on the given machine. In the flow-shop environment, the setup time is included in the processing times of each job [19].

Modern approaches designated for larger instances are known as meta-heuristics. Approaches that combine different concepts or components of more than one meta-heuristic are named as hybrid meta-heuristic algorithms [20]. Heuristic methods for make-span minimization have been applied, for example, by Ogbu [21] using Simulated Annealing (SA) and by Taillard [22] applying Tabu Search (TS) algorithm. Nagar et al. proposed a combined Branch-and-Bound (BB) and Genetic Algorithm (GA) based procedure for a flow shop scheduling problem with objectives of mean flow time and make-span minimization [23]. Similarly, Neppalli were used genetic algorithms in their approach to solve the 2-machine flow shop problem with objectives of minimizing make-span and total flow time [24]. An atypical method based on an Artificial Immune System (AIS) approach, which was inspired from vertebrate immune system, has been presented by Engin and Doyen [25]. They used the proposed method for solving the hybrid flow shop scheduling problem with minimizing C_{max}. Obviously, there are plenty of other related approaches to this problem that are identified in survey studies, such as that of Ribas [26].

3 Hybrid GA-Based Improvement Heuristic (HGI)

Genetic algorithm (GA) forms one of the categories of local search method that operate with a set of solutions. GA is inspired by well-known Darvin's theory about the evolution. GA-based heuristic is started with a set of solutions, also referred to as population. Solutions (or in terms of genetic algorithm, chromosomes) from initial population are taken to form a new population with hope that the new population will be better than the old one. The selection of solutions is performed by a "survival of the fittest" principle to ensure that the overall quality of solutions increases from one generation to the next. This is repeated until some condition (for example number of generations or improvement of the best solution) is satisfied. The framework of proposed HGI algorithm is introduced below.

3.1 Notation of HGI Algorithm

The following notation was used for proposed genetic algorithm:

G	number of generations
P	population size
$F(s)$	fitness function
s_i	initial solution
p_c	crossover probability parameter
p_m	mutation probability parameter
c	chromosome string

3.2 HGI Operators

The most important parts of the genetic algorithm are genetic operators, referred to as encoding, selection, crossover and mutation operator that impact the whole performance.

Proposed hybrid GA-based improvement heuristic employs permutation encoding of chromosomes, where each chromosome is a string of numbers (genes), which represents number in a sequence.

For the selection of best chromosomes the roulette wheel method was used. Proposed HGI employs also a method, called elitism, before roulette wheel selection to ensure that at least one best solution is copied without changes to a new population, so the best solution found can survive to end of run.

The crossover operator is carried out with a crossover probability. Crossover selects genes from parent chromosomes and creates a new offspring. It randomly selects a crossover point and everything before this point is copied from the first parent. Then the second parent is scanned and if the scanned gene is not yet in the offspring, it is appended. This method is also called as Single point crossover.

Mutation is also done randomly for each gene and it depends upon another parameter called mutation probability. In this method inversion mutation is adopted where one gene is selected at random and exchanged with another gene mutually. Basically it is an order changing where two numbers are exchanged.

3.3 Pseudo Code of HGI Algorithm with Makespan Criterion

In the paper HGI is used to search for solution of minimal make-span. Figure 1 introduces the pseudo code of proposed hybrid GA-based improvement heuristic in conjunction with constructive heuristic. The constructive heuristic gives a good initial solution to be improved by GA-based heuristic. The objective of the fitness function is to minimize a makespan. The best solution is represented by minimal makespan.

Step 1   Find s_i by selected constructive heuristic
Step 2   Generate initial P based on s_i and randomness
Step 3   Apply selection with elitism
Step 4   Apply crossover with p_c
Step 5   Apply mutation with p_m
Step 6   Compute the fitness value for new offspring
Step 7   Evaluate and save the best chromosome
Step 8   Go to Step 2 until the generation value reaches G

Fig. 1. Pseudo code for hybrid GA-based Improvement heuristic algorithm

4 Computational Experiments

The experiment was run with objective of minimizing makespan on benchmark dataset that has 10 instances. The dataset ranges from 20 to 500 jobs and 5 to 20 machines. The CDS, Palmer's Slope Index, Gupta's algorithms and HGI were coded in PHP script, running on a PC with 1.6 GHz Intel Atom and 1GB of RAM. All PHP-coded algorithms has user friendly interface with eventuality to select whether to run each heuristic itself or all together. It has also an option to draw a Gantt chart. Table 1 contains the input parameters of HGI approach for the experiment purposes.

Table 1. Constraints for HGI algorithm

Parameter	Value
P	20
G	100
p_c	0.6
p_m	0.05
$F(s)$	makespan

4.1 Results

Results of hybrid GA-based heuristic are represented by use of percentage improvement from solution of constructive heuristic and gap from upper-bound solution (UB). The paper will refer to the 3-heuristic HGI versions, namely P-HGI (Palmer-HGI), C-HGI (CDS-HGI) and G-HGI (Gupta-HGI). Average computational times (CPU) for each size of the problem are summarized and depicted in Figure 2. The computation times of course vary by the size of the problem. The variance, within three versions of HGI was not significant.

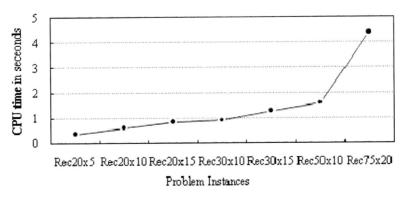

Fig. 2. Average CPU time for each of 3 HGI algorithm versions

Table 2 summarizes the results for all 21 instances and also shows average percentage improvement of HGI over constructive heuristic. Table 2 also introduces the upper bounds and percentage gap from the best-known bound for the best HGI result. The results are displayed for P-HGI, C-HGI and G-HGI.

Table 2. Makespans and average percentage improvements for Reeves' benchmark problems for flow-shop scheduling

	Problem Instance	Size	UB	G-HGI	C-HGI	P-HGI	Best HGI	% Gap from UB
1	Rec01	20x5	1260	1289	1306	1310	1289	2.30
2	Rec03	20x5	1114	1164	1150	1117	1117	0.27
3	Rec05	20x5	1285	1281	1281	1271	1271	-1.09
Average % Imprv HGI				11.76	11.52	4.89		
Average % Gap from UB								0.49
4	Rec07	20x10	1626	1608	1595	1665	1595	-1.91
5	Rec09	20x10	1592	1638	1627	1607	1607	0.94
6	Rec11	20x10	1552	1539	1563	1517	1517	-2.26
Average % Imprv HGI				8.72	9.08	8.77		
Average % Gap from UB								-1.07
7	Rec13	20x15	2002	2076	2070	1999	1999	-0.15
8	Rec15	20x15	2008	2046	2070	1995	1995	-0.65
9	Rec17	20x15	2038	2061	2091	2009	2009	-1.42
Average % Imprv HGI				14.25	7.83	7.25		
Average % Gap from UB								-0.74
10	Rec19	30x10	2191	2241	2290	2201	2201	0.46
11	Rec21	30x10	2060	2246	2210	2203	2203	6.94
12	Rec23	30x10	2101	2251	2173	2170	2170	3.28
Average % Imprv HGI				9.48	9.69	8.09		
Average % Gap from UB								3.56
13	Rec25	30x15	2676	2743	2861	2751	2743	2.50
14	Rec27	30x15	2478	2558	2566	2517	2517	1.57
15	Rec29	30x15	2387	2554	2547	2557	2547	6.70
Average % Imprv HGI				12.14	10.04	4.90		
Average % Gap from UB								3.59
16	Rec31	50x10	3179	3279	3305	3309	3279	3.15
17	Rec33	50x10	3231	3324	3388	3264	3264	1.02
18	Rec35	50x10	3338	3403	3388	3393	3388	1.50
Average % Imprv HGI				6.93	11.21	6.60		
Average % Gap from UB								1.89
19	Rec37	75x20	5268	5651	5725	5538	5538	5.13
20	Rec39	75x20	5336	5793	5645	5589	5589	4.74
21	Rec41	75x20	5317	5710	5670	5656	5656	6.38
Average % Imprv HGI				8.93	9.94	4.54		
Average % Gap from UB								5.41

Overall neither of 3-heuristic HGI versions performed significantly better, although all of them gave feasible improved solutions. For flow-shop scheduling problem sizes range from 5 to 15 machines and 20 jobs, HGI found new upper bound solutions. For 24 of the 30 problems and found a new upper bound for one problem. HGI improved initial solutions for all problem instances, on average, by 6.43%.

5 Summary and Conclusions

In presented study, the scheduling problem with sequence-dependent operations was dealt. The main idea is to minimize the make-span time and thereby reducing the idle time of both jobs and machines since these criteria are often applied for operational decision-making in scheduling. Under above mentioned consideration an hybrid improvement heuristic based on evolutionary algorithm (HGI) is proposed and applied to the permutation flow-shop scheduling problem. The GA-based heuristic approach uses a constructive heuristic to get an initial solution that tries to find improvements iteratively.

The HGI algorithm was used to improve upon heuristics, namely, Palmer, CDS and Gupta. For all three heuristics, HGI showed significant improvements. The best improvements were compared well with the upper bounds. The average gap from the upper bound was 1.88% for all 21 problems.

Future research should look at this heuristic for the more difficult flow-shop scheduling problems involving sequence-dependent setup times. Different objective functions can also be tested.

Acknowledgement. This work has been supported by the Grant Agency of the Ministry of Education of the Slovak Republic and Slovak Academy of Sciences (VEGA project No. 1/4153/07 "Development and application of heuristics methods and genetic algorithms for scheduling and sequencing of production flow lines").

References

1. Pinedo, M.: Scheduling: Theory, Algorithms and Systems. Springer, New Jersey (2008)
2. Gupta, J.N.D.: Analysis of Combinatorial Approach to Flowshop Scheduling Problems (1975)
3. Johnson, S.M.: Optimal Two and Three Stage Production Schedules with Set-Up Times. Naval Research Logistics Quarterly 1, 61–68 (1954)
4. Garey, M.R.D., Johnson, D.S., Sethi, R.: The Complexity of Flowshop and Jobshop Scheduling. Mathematics of Operations Research 1, 117–129 (1976)
5. Conway, R.W., Maxwell, W.L., Miller, L.W.: Theory of Scheduling. Addison-Wesley, Reading (1967)
6. Hejazi, S.R., Saghafian, S.: Flowshop Scheduling Problems with Makespan Criterion: A Review. International Journal of Production Research 43(14), 2895–2929 (2005)
7. Palmer, D.S.: Sequencing Jobs through a Multi-Stage Process in the Minimum Total Time - A Quick Method of Obtaining a Near Optimum. Opers. Res. Q 16, 101–107 (1965)
8. Campbell, H.G., Dudek, R.A., Smith, M.L.: A Heuristic Algorithm for the n Job, m Machine Sequencing Problem. Management Science 16(10), 630–637 (1970)

9. Dannenbring, D.G.: An Evaluation of Flow Shop Sequencing Heuristics. Management Science 23(11), 1174–1182 (1977)
10. Brucker, P., Jurisch, B., Sievers, B.: A Branch and Bound Algorithm for the Job Shop Scheduling Problem. Discrete Applied Mathematics 49(1), 109–127 (1994)
11. Gendreau, M., Laporte, G., Semet, F.: A Tabu Search Heuristic for the Undirected Selective Travelling Salesman Problem. European Journal of Operational Research 106 (2-3), 539–545 (1998)
12. Murata, T., Ishibuchi, H., Tanaka, H.: Genetic algorithms for flowshop scheduling problems. Computers & Industrial Engineering 30(4), 1061–1071 (1996)
13. Balas, E., Vazacopoulos, A.: Guided Local Search with Shifting Bottleneck for Job Shop Scheduling. Management Science 44(2), 262–275 (1998)
14. Blum, C., Sampels, M.: An Ant Colony Optimization Algorithm for Shop Scheduling Problems. Journal of Mathematical Modelling and Algorithms 3(3), 285–308 (2004)
15. Page, E.S.: An approach to scheduling of jobs on the machines. J. Royal Stat. Soc. 23, 484–492 (1961)
16. Gupta, J.N.D.: Heuristic Algorithms for Multistage Flowshop Scheduling Problem. AIIE Transactions 4(1), 11–18 (1972)
17. Nawaz, M.E., Enscore, I., Ham, I.: A Heuristic Algorithm for the m Machine, n Job Flow Shop Sequence Problem. OMEGA 11(1), 91–95 (1983)
18. Allahverdi, A., Ng, C.T., Cheng, T.C.E., Kovalyov, M.Y.: A Survey of Scheduling Problems with Setup Times or Costs. European Journal of Operational Research 187, 985–1032 (2008)
19. Hendizadeh, S.H., ElMekkawy, T.Y., Wang, G.G.: Bi-Criteria Scheduling of a Flowshop Manufacturing Cell with Sequence Dependent Setup Time. European Journal of Industrial Engineering 1, 391–413 (2007)
20. Zobolas, G.I., Tarantilis, C.D., Ioannou, G.: Minimizing Makespan in Permutation Flow Shop Scheduling Problems Using a Hybrid Metaheuristic Algorithm. Computers and Operations Research 36(4), 1249–1267 (2009)
21. Ogbu, F.A., Smith, D.K.: The Application of the Simulated Annealing Algorithm to the Solution of the n/m/Cmax Flowshop Problem. Computers & Operations Research 17, 3243–3253 (1990)
22. Taillard, E.: Benchmarks for basic scheduling problems. European Journal of Operational Research 64, 278–285 (1993)
23. Nagar, A., Heragu, S.S., Haddock, J.: A Combined Branch-and-Bound and Genetic Algorithm Based Approach for a Flowshop-Scheduling Problem. Annal. Oper. Res. 63, 397–414 (1996)
24. Neppalli, V.R., Chen, C.L., Gupta, J.N.D.: Genetic Algorithms for the Two-Stage Bicriteria Flowshop Problem. Eur. J. Oper. Res. 95, 356–373 (1996)
25. Engin, O., Doyen, A.: A New Approach to Solve Hybrid Flow Shop Scheduling Problems by Artificial Immune System. Future Generation Computer Systems 20, 1083–1095 (2004)
26. Ribas, R., Leisten, J.M.: Review and Classification of Hybrid Flow Shop Scheduling Problems from a Production System and a Solutions Procedure Perspective. Computers and Operations Research 37(8), 1439–1454 (2010)

Framework for Collaborative 3D Urban Environments

Miguel Melo[1,2], Maximino Bessa[1,2], Tânia Rocha[1], José Sousa[1], Emanuel Peres[1,3], João Varajão[1,4], and Luís Magalhães[1,2]

[1] Universidade de Trás-os-Montes e Alto Douro, Apartado 1013,
5001-801 Vila Real, Portugal
[2] INESC PORTO, Rua Dr. Roberto Frias, s/n 4200-465, Porto, Portugal
[3] CITAB – Centro de Investigações em Tecnologias Agro-Ambientais e Biológicas,
Universidade de Trás-os-Montes e Alto Douro, Apartado 1013,
5001-801 Vila Real, Portugal
[4] Centro Algoritmi, Universidade do Minho, Guimarães, Portugal
emekapa@sapo.pt, {maxbessa,trocha,jmsousa,eperes,
jvarajao,lmagalha}@utad.pt

Abstract. With Virtual Reality (VR) systems it is possible to visualize three-dimensional environments with a high level of detail and visual fidelity. The users can manipulate and interact with those virtual environments in an intuitive way, close to reality. The VR systems enable the access to digital services that can promote, amongst others, collaborative work, data sharing or e-commerce. In this paper, we present a multidisciplinary solution that can offer added value to users through a collaborative environment with an intuitive interface. This environment will use geo-referenced databases to replicate urban environments and represent real world problems in a virtual way, making possible a better and more flexible approach in order to solve them. It is also proposed an architecture and some digital services are illustrated to show its potential.

Keywords: Collaborative work, Virtual urban environments, Digital services.

1 Introduction

There are several areas where the Virtual Reality (VR) systems are currently explored, such as: videogames, remote education, virtual tourism, urban planning or remote education. In this paper we use a VR system to explore applications on citizenship and e-commerce. The objective is to have a collaborative environment that recreates urban areas with high levels of visual fidelity, capable of offering digital services. The collaborative environment should offer an intuitive interface where the user will be able to navigate remotely through an urban area, having access to services like if he was there physically. One of the motivations behind this project is to bring an added value to citizens of the urban areas covered by our VR system, through the supply of pertinent digital services. Those digital services should allow the user to remotely acquire or access services available in a determined urban place, bringing him a more flexible and comfortable way to enjoy the services or goods that he wants.

M.M. Cruz-Cunha et al. (Eds.): CENTERIS 2011, Part II, CCIS 220, pp. 19–28, 2011.
© Springer-Verlag Berlin Heidelberg 2011

They also bring an opportunity to people that cannot go to the physical places due to, for example, mobility handicaps.

Other reason that led us to this project is related with collaborative work. Our platform intends to bring a collaborative component so the users can cooperate and enhance their virtual urban environment together. The users will also be capable of proposing or reporting issues that need some attention by the local authorities. These aspects will allow them to create social ties and motivate all the users to the enrichment of their social life, building a strong and united community with civic duty awareness.

The collaborative work can promote the concept of citizenship, which we intend to explore, giving the users a set of digital services in order to accomplish that. Other area that we intend to boost is e-commerce due to the possibility of the user acquire goods or services in a remote way with the advantage, when available, of personalizing their requests.

For this paper we propose a collaborative environment, so it will be explored the "wiki" concept where the users can contribute with information collectively with the particularity of not requiring that the contents are reviewed or approved before publication. Our project also intends to extend this concept to the 3D universe, creating a "3D wiki". The "3D wiki" concept will allow the users to contribute for the visual fidelity of the virtual urban environment as they will be able to contribute with information related with elements that make part of real urban environment recreated. The information can vary from the feedback given on certain digital services to the visual aspects of certain buildings, parks, streets, etc.

In the next section we will explore some tools that are, somehow, related to the platform that we intend to develop. In third section it will be presented the proposed architecture for the collaborative 3D urban environments. The last section is about the conclusions and future work planned.

2 Related Work

It is intended to develop a tool capable of recreating urban environments in a collaborative way and associate digital services to them. There are two kinds of tools that can be related to this kind of project. The first kind is capable of making available a collaborative virtual environment, such as Google Earth [1], Second Life [2] or OpenSim [3]. The second kind provides services associated to an urban environment. Examples are foursquare [4], Gowalla [4] and "A minha rua" [5].

Google Earth, Second Life or OpenSim offer interactivity and collaborative work to their users. Google Earth [1] is an application provided by Google, which has the purpose of representing the whole world virtually. In order to accomplish that, the application uses satellite images, aerial images and geographical information. The majority of the represented places are in 2D but, in certain areas, 3D representation is available. The visualization is made from the top, and the users, in a first stage, see a flat image of a vast terrestrial area. As the user zooms in, the flat image becomes more detailed and gives him more detailed information about a specific region. When the user uses a bigger zoom, a more oblique view of the region is offered so the user can have a better perception of how that place looks like. In the areas where 3D is available, it is offered to the users a frontal view so they can see the buildings as they are, therefore enhancing the users' experiences. This tool can be used for entertainment or with scientific purposes, bringing a lot of advantages and opportunities in research areas.

Second Life [2], from Linden Lab, is a collaborative virtual environment that intends to be a simulator of the real life. To have access to this virtual environment, the user just has to register and download a viewer from the official website. This viewer provides an intuitive interface with a high level of interactivity where the user can customize all the aspects of his avatar and profile [7]. Besides that, the user can build almost every kind of objects and associate textures and/or scripts to them. The scripts allow programming the objects behavior (for example, an object that follows an avatar), send messages, and communicate with Web services, amongst others. Linden Scripting Language (LSL) is the language used for programming objects, which intends to be an intuitive language so everyone can use it with no major difficulties.

OpenSim [3] shares many aspects with the Second Life. The big difference between both is that with OpenSim the user has complete access to the server-side aspects. Besides that, this tool is open-source so who uses it can extend it according to their needs. Another advantage is that the server can be hosted locally and that can bring more flexibility on development.

Regarding to foursquare and Gowalla [4], they share the same concept: they are social networks based on location. The users use mobile devices to check in, meaning that they share their location and, additionally, they can give some feedback about that same location. With Gowalla, for example, the user has a virtual passport and when he checks in at some place, he collects a stamp. There is the possibility of receiving rewards that can be awarded spontaneously or according to the number of times that the user checks in at a specific place. The rewards can be, for example, virtual items that the user can keep or discard. The user can also leave virtual items as a reward for other users [6]. Real rewards can also be awarded such as discount coupons, movie tickets, etc. To have access to these services the user just needs to register and install the proper application that can be found in the respective websites.

The project "A minha rua" (meaning "My street" in English) is directed to local authorities. This project promotes the civic duty giving to the citizens of one determined place the possibility of expressing their dissatisfaction or reporting issues related to the public spaces [5]. The adherent local authorities have, in their website, a space reserved for this service, where the citizens can fill up a form to report the anomalous situations. The user just has to identify the issue and, optionally, can attach some photos or even propose a solution for that issue. At any time, the users can view all the reported situations and check how the process is being handled. This project intends to foment the citizenship activities, giving one more active paper for all the citizens of a certain region and, at the same time, improve the urban environments management.

All the analyzed tools provide a set of interesting features over urban environments. The project that we are developing contemplates all this features and combines them in a single platform, where the users can have access, through an intuitive and natural interface, to a set of digital services. Due to the collaborative nature of the project, the platform offers to the users the possibility of contributing for a higher level of visual fidelity. The users will be able to, for example, edit the visual appearance of the elements that constitute the virtual urban environments or share any kind of information related with them.

3 Technical Approach

The concept of collaboration consists in operate or execute an action in a joint way, having a mutual aid in the execution of tasks without having any hierarchical relation or obligation between the collaborators [8][9]. The spontaneous collaboration of users in order to achieve a common goal can result in social and cognitive gains [10], thus, we can stimulate these gains to all the users of this project through collaboration and, at the same time, promotion of citizenship and civic duty awareness.

The creation of the elements that will constitute those environments could be modeled individually but with that procedure a lot of resources would be consumed and that would significantly delay the project. The use of procedural modeling is the solution to this problem as it allows building 3D models from a set of rules that are processed using computer graphics techniques [11]. The collaborative environment will be built based on OpenSim, which will be extended to enable import urban elements produced by a procedural modeling system. These procedures will be followed by the implementation of digital services.

3.1 Architecture

Like it was said before, this paper is focused on the tasks related with the development of a collaborative virtual urban environment and the services associated with it. So, in this section, we give more emphasis on the client-side architecture. A scheme of the general architecture is presented in Fig. 1.

The application is based on client-server architecture. In the client side we have the "Collaborative Urban Environment" that is the users' entry point. The access to the collaborative environment is made through a client application that will recreate the urban environments based on interaction with the system's server. The "Procedural Modeling System" contains all the necessary mechanisms for collecting and processing information associated with the urban environments. The information associated to the models that constitute the virtual urban environment is stored in a database called "GIS/Urban Information". Depending on the service that the user requests, it can communicate with the server and retrieve information from the "External services" database when it is requested information about external services or it can be processed by external Web services. The "Administrator" is the only one that has direct access to the system so he can solve possible problems and make the maintenance of the system with no restrictions.

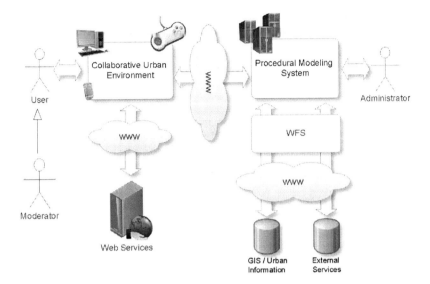

Fig. 1. General Architecture of the collaborative environment

This project will be divided in two modules developed by different teams: the first team will be responsible for creating a unified model of information in order to create set of rules and process them. The second team will be responsible for processing those set of rules and create the virtual urban environment and all the services associated to them. The following sections are more directed for the second module, since it will be the work done by the authors.

3.2 Actors

There are stipulated three types of users: the "Mobile Device User", the "OpenSim User" and the "Administrator". To use the platform all users must be registered. Once users are registered, they will have access to their login credentials and to their own profile, which can be fully customized.

The main difference between the "Mobile Device User" and the "OpenSim User" is in the way they connect to the platform. Like the names suggest, the "Mobile User Device" uses mobile devices to have access to the platform and the "OpenSim User" uses a desktop or a laptop (with OpenSim installed). In terms of functionalities the difference resides in the fact that the "Mobile Device User" can only view images of the virtual urban environment while the "OpenSim User" can explore and discover the virtual urban environment through an intuitive 3D interface.

The "Administrator" is responsible for supervising the whole system and guarantee that the whole system is running properly. He have the power to act directly on the platform if some problematic situation arises.

3.3 Collaborative Virtual Environment

To have a better perception of how the system works in terms of functionalities available from the point of view of the user, a use-case diagram has been built and is presented in Fig. 2.

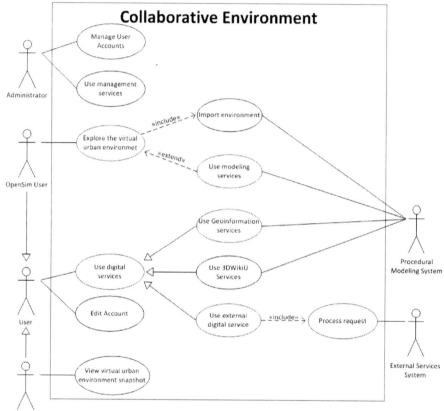

Fig. 2. System use-cases

This diagram presents the users that are registered in the platform. These users have the possibility of editing their account details or to use the digital services available. There are three types of services that can be used at any time by any user: the geoinformation services, the 3DWikiU services and the external services. The geoinformation services are related to the information associated to the elements that are represented by the 3D models that populate the virtual environments; the 3DWikiU services are the original services of the platform like the service similar to "A minha rua" that is intended to develop (it has not been set yet which services will definitely integrate the collaborative environment but the selected ones will be designated by 3DWikiU Services). These two are processed by the "Procedural Modeling System" (presented in Fig. 1). If the user uses the third type of service, it will be processed by an external services system that provides the functionality required to execute the service requested. Two possible examples of external services are: a hotel reservation or the purchase of an item in some store through the platform.

In Fig. 2 it is not represented the direct access that the "Administrator" has to the system because the diagram only contemplates the functionalities available for the users through the collaborative environment.

3.4 Digital Services

This project intends to explore, essentially, two main areas: citizenship and e-commerce. The citizenship concept can be promoted by the offer of public services in a collaborative way to the community, i. e., by the offer of public services where the citizens can work in a cooperative way and improve the quality of life in their community. It is intended to develop a project similar to the project "A minha rua" where users can report situations that need the attention of the local authorities and, at the same time, give the possibility of the users propose a more clarified solution due to the nature of our platform that allows a collaborative work with visual results. Other situations that can be here explored are polls to decide how and what to build in certain places, monitoring functions to preview the traffic or to take a look at the weather forecast.

E-commerce can stimulate local businesses due to the possibility of the user acquire goods or services in a remote way through the collaborative environment that is intended to develop. The system should accept orders, reservations or any other kind of service that allows to the users get the products that they want remotely.

The social aspect is also important to build a strong community with civic duty awareness. An aspect that can promote the cooperation between citizens is related with urban planning services. It is also expected that it can be provided to the user a reliable 3D replica of the real urban environment, built based on geographical data, where he can navigate on it and have a perception of how the real urban environment looks like. But the added value that we intend to give our platform is the possibility of collaborative edition, meaning that, at the same time the user navigates, he can modify any building in order to make it more similar to the real one. These modifications can be done on floors, textures, houses, streets, parks or any other urban environment related object. The users will also have the possibility of communicate between them via chat or voice.

4 System Prototype

The project that is here presented has the intention to be a collaborative environment that recreates virtual urban environments with a set of digital services associated. For testing, purposes OpenSim has been installed and some buildings were created there, in order to make an approximate simulation of a virtual urban environment. This task was performed to have a better understanding of the requirements and procedures that are required to successfully accomplish the objectives proposed. The Fig. 3 illustrates the general aspect of the environment created.

To access the virtual world, the use of a viewer was needed and, in this case, the viewer used was Hippo OpenSim Viewer [12]. Around 30 buildings were created so the virtual environment could resemble an urban environment in order to evaluate the level of visual fidelity that OpenSim can offer.

Fig. 3. Overview of the environment created with OpenSim

After having one collaborative environment configured and running without any problems, it is intended to associate digital services with the objects that recreate urban environments elements. That will make those objects an extension of the real ones and offer to the user a new set of advantages with remote access to their services. In order to test this aspect with OpenSim, a script has been created to be possible such integration. The script is associated to each object and, when an object is touched, it detects the UUID (Universal Unique Identifier) of that object and opens a media browser that is built in on the viewer. In that browser it is possible to open webpages, so the script is set to open one particular PHP webpage that gets the UUID of the object and gives information about it. The architecture is shown in Fig. 4.

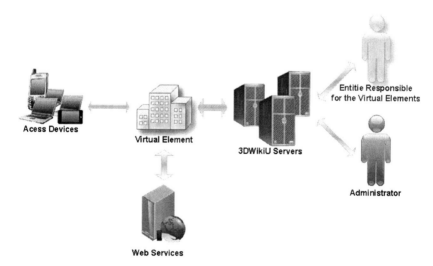

Fig. 4. Architecture of the access to the digital services

So, from an entry point (which can be a desktop or a mobile device) the user has access to the urban environment where are located all the virtual elements that recreate the urban environment. When a user touches one of those elements, that element will communicate with the 3DWikiU servers to retrieve the desired information. This can be done based on Web Services or through the 3DWikiU Servers. The entities responsible for that data are the entities responsible for the real world elements represented and the administrators. The first ones are responsible for information about the products or services available and the administrators are responsible for all kind of information that can be associated with that same element.

OpenSim can be an interesting tool to this project judging by the preliminary tests that have been here documented. Also, OpenSim has a lot of functionalities that promote collaborative work and the interface of the viewers (in this case the Hippo OpenSim Viewer) is intuitive. Regarding the OpenSim browser, he can be valuable to offer digital services since it is possible to communicate with Web servers without any problems. Further tests will be made to test the real capabilities of the OpenSim and to see how it will react when dealing with a considerable amount of data. With these preliminary tests OpenSim has shown to be a tool with the quality needed to accomplish the objectives proposed in this project.

5   Conclusion and Future Work

Some tests have been made using OpenSim to simulate the urban environments and the results were good but a set of more demanding tests have to be done in order to determine definitely if the OpenSim will be used to implement the proposed architecture. After the proper choice of the tool that we will use to recreate urban environments, it will be developed the necessary mechanisms to allow the generation of the elements that will recreate the urban environments in the virtual world. That process will be made recurring to procedural modeling.

It will be also made a study of potential digital services that are relevant to the collaborative environment that we intend to develop. After this study is complete, the most interesting and relevant digital services will be selected. The aspects that will be important to determine either to select or discard a digital service are related with the importance and added value that they can bring to the collaborative environment users.

At last, the selected services will be implemented and integrated in the collaborative environment. The digital services will have their basis on the 3D objects that are part of the virtual urban environment.

Acknowledgments. This work is partially supported by the Portuguese government, through the National Foundation for Science and Technology – FCT (Fundação para a Ciência e Tecnologia) and the European Union (COMPETE, QREN and FEDER) through the project PTDC/EIA-EIA/108982/2008 entitled "3DWikiU – 3D Wiki for Urban Environments".

References

1. Miller, M.: Using Google Maps and Google Earth. Pearson Professional Computing, London (2010)
2. Rymaszewski, M., Au, W.J., Wallace, M., Winters, C., Ondrejka, C., Batstone-Cunningham, B., Rosedale, P.: Second Life: The Official Guide. SYBEX Inc., Alameda (2006)
3. Zhao, H., Sun, B., Wu, H., Hu, X.H.: Study on building a 3D interactive virtual learning environment based on OpenSim platform. In: 2010 International Conference on Audio Language and Image Processing (ICALIP), pp. 1407–1411, 23–25 (2010)
4. Ebling, M.R., Cáceres, R.: Gaming and Augmented Reality Come to Location-Based Services. IEEE Pervasive Computing 9(1), 5–6 (2010)
5. Agência para a Modernização Administrativa IP. A minha rua, http://www.portaldocidadao.pt/portal/aminharua/
6. Hendaoui, A., Limayem, C., Thompson, C.W.: 3D Social Virtual Worlds: Research Issues and Challenges. IEEE Internet Computing 12, 88–92 (2008)
7. Cuddy, C., Glassman, N.R.: Location-Based Services: Foursquare and Gowalla, Should Libraries Play? Journal of Electronic Resources in Medical Libraries, 336–343 (2010)
8. Damiani, M.F.: Entendendo o trabalho colaborativo em educação e revelando seus benefícios. Educ. Rev. (31), 213–230 (2008)
9. Schmidt, K., Simone, C.: Coordination mechanisms: Towards a conceptual foundation of CSCW system design. Computer Supported Cooperative Work 5, 155–200 (1996)
10. Tolmie, A.K., Topping, J.T., Christie, D., Donaldson, C., Howe, C., Jessiman, E., Livingston, K., Thurston, A.: Social effects of collaborative learning in primary schools. Learning and Instruction 20(3), 177–191 (2010)
11. Fletcher, D., Yue, Y., Al Kader, M.: Challenges and Perspectives of Procedural Modelling and Effects. In: 14th International Conference on Information Visualisation (IV), pp. 543–550 (2010)
12. Hippo OpenSim Viewer, http://mjm-labs.com/viewer/

Evaluating an Enterprise Content Management for the Macao Government Agency

F. Pong, R. Whitfield, and J. Negreiros

USJ – University of Saint Joseph, Rua de Londres (NAPE), Macau, ROC
fpong@esigntrust.com, {rcw,joao.garrot}@usj.edu.mo

Abstract. Information contained within documents is an essential ingredient of any office operation. A content management application (CMA) is an organization plan for the conception, use, retention, disposal and selective preservation of its data. Using an appropriate CMA framework can greatly help Macao Government agencies, for instance, that are increasingly using electronic means to create, exchange and store a major variety of records daily. By definition, a record is information, in whatever form, for government functions, activities, decisions and other important transactions. As expected, as the volume of electronic information increases, so does the complexity of managing electronic records. This project goal was to evaluate the software capabilities of the Alfresco© Enterprise Content Management (ECM) against a set of functional requirements, aimed by the Macao Government agency. Drawing on the results of this evaluation, the present analysis concludes that Alfresco© ECM is capable of supporting an entire agency needs related to the management of its records content.

Keywords: Enterprise Content Management, Alfresco©, Open Source Software, Macao Government.

1 Preamble

As Macao undergoes rapid economical and technological changes, the public as well as the private sector are increasingly relying on information technology (IT) to manage work, make decisions, and perform business processes and as critical means of communication. Much of this change is prompted largely by the government that needs to streamline their operations while sustaining high-quality levels of service, despite staff reductions depleted by current on human resources high demand from the emerging and established businesses. Consequentially, some business transactions, that were traditionally paper-based, are now being performed electronically. While the government still continues to use large amount of paper, increasingly records are being created electronically and it will remain in an electronic format for most of their life cycle. This shift trend from a paper to an electronic environment requires a practical solution to manage large quantity of computer-based information, in accordance with today's increasingly strict regulatory environment.

The current Macao Government administration had pledge to be transparent and accountable in its functions and decision-making. With inadequate records management,

M.M. Cruz-Cunha et al. (Eds.): CENTERIS 2011, Part II, CCIS 220, pp. 29–39, 2011.
© Springer-Verlag Berlin Heidelberg 2011

compliance to this goal becomes quite complex. Therefore, good record-keeping is one of the most critical issues in every government. Having in place an open mechanism for DM will improve public access to information which will improve transparency, leading to a decline or corruption or the perception of corruption. The government must also comply with the newly enacted 2010 Personal Data Protection law, which in part deals with protecting personal data held by the government and other specific laws agencies.

The DM importance is highlighted by the fact that, according to Price Waterhouse Coopers (PWC), its study reports that the average worker spends 40% of their time managing non-essential documents while International Data Corporation (IDC) estimates that employees spend 20% of each day looking for information in hardcopy documents and that, 50% of the time, they can't find what they need [1,2]. It is estimated that the average office makes nineteen copies of each document, spends US$20 on labor to file each document, loses one out of twenty office documents, consumes US$120 searching for every misfiled document and waste US$250 recreating each lost document.

The Macao agency has five major business divisions and some areas of those divisions include inter-governmental exchanges, operational management, financial services, point of sales, professional and public services. Unavoidably, each area has multiple business processes which follow different protocols. Thus, in any given day, few thousands of transactions occur as an execution result of various business processes.

The research main objective here is to evaluate Enterprise Document Management (ECM) software for the Macao Government agency, which provides a comprehensive set of tools with the potential to significantly improve DM efficiency. This project has been initiated recently because it has been recognized that ECM deployment can deliver substantial benefits to the private and public sector. Considerable workload reduction can be achieved through streamlining and automating existing business processes, for instance. It is expected that business documentation control will improve legislative compliance, reduce risk and deliver productivity to the organization. Other benefits include the internal and external communication improvement and knowledge value maximization.

Henceforth, the main document management requirements for this governmental body are as follows: Is it low cost? Is technical support and developer available? Are patches ongoing? Can users publish a static page? Is social networking plug-ins available? Are search logs available? Is this product a portal and can be integrated with another one? Can users customize the site? Can users check in and out digital assets to a centralized library? Can users customize workflow? Are content analytical tools available? Are there metadata tags available for content?

This paper is divided into four other sections. The background, deliverables and report outline are discussed in section 2 while the following one includes basic concepts discussion such as the methodology for selection and software testing. This includes the functional evaluation approach and criteria selection for some individual ECM components. As well, a testing techniques discussion and proof of concepts practices are highlighted. Within section 4, Alfresco© ECM is presented and the appraisal findings are listed. Deriving conclusions and highlight main implementation concerns of ECM software, in general, are identified in the last section..

2 Background

Any basic ECM comprises the following components [3]: Document Management for check-in/check-out, version control, security and library services for business documents; Document Imaging for capturing, transforming and managing images within paper documents; Record Management for long-term archiving, automation of diverse policies, ensuring legal, regulatory and industry compliance; Workflow for supporting business processes, routing content, assigning work tasks and states audit trails; Web Content Management (WCM) for Website controlling; Collaboration Suite for document sharing and project teams supporting.

In their latest study about the ECM industry state, [4] concluded that ECM is good for business. By bringing together a combination of technology, policy and process, ECM provides good information governance and improved compliance. More recently, Microsoft©, Oracle© and IBM© are steadily establishing themselves in this ECM market by acquiring smaller players and bringing new technology with broader suite functionality, better process control, improved ease of use and a stronger focus on reliability.

Open Source Software (OSS) are just like any Commercial-Off-The-Shelf (COTS) software but are made available in source code form for which the source code and certain other rights are provided under a software license that permits users to study, change and improve the software [5]. This concept has existed for more than twenty-five years and, during this period, applications like Apache© and Linux© has been phenomenally successfully in providing real business value [6]. Many of today's Internet applications are almost completely based on OSS such as Email/Application/DNS/Web servers, browsers, office productivity suites and databases. A study sponsored by the Swedish Agency for Public Management concluded that OSS is not any makeshift phenomenon, but instead a fully adequate and dependable competitor to existing proprietary products and solutions [7]. Positively, OSS continues to make inroads into the corporate environment embraced by most of the top tiers corporation in the world [6].

According to [8], there is also a lot of myth and misconceptions around OSS such as: (A) There Is No Support for Open Source: There's quite a lot of support for OSS but some of its functions are differently from commercial software. Effectively, OSS gives you more options for support because there more experts familiar with the software. (B) Open Source is Less Functional: Many OSS exceeds the functionality of equivalent commercial software. Apache© is the leading Web server while PostgreSQL© and MySQL© are used by thousands of companies to support sophisticated applications. (C) OSS is Less Secure: Since source code is freely distributed with the applications, anyone can report and even fix bugs. A lot of people do it and tends to happen very quickly. With commercial software, it may take the company weeks to admit there is a hole, much less fix it. On the other hand, there is no guarantee that an open source package is secure, too. (D) OSS Is Free: It may be available for free, but that's not the same as saying there's no cost to use it. Its real cost is supporting and customization that is optionally provided by the software company. (E) Open Source is Hard to Use: The first OSS wave was mostly written by experts, and oriented toward programmers and network administrators and not toward individual users. That has changed radically as the open-source community has developed.

Regarding OSS for ECM solutions, [9] in its ECM Magic Quadrant framework, positions all vendors by intersecting their ability to execute (YY axis) with their completeness of vision (XX axis). Curiously, it considers Alfresco© to be a visionary in its field, as shown in Figure 1 (left). As well, Forrester Research© states that Alfresco© challenges the proprietary players by providing a low cost alternative solution. It ranked as contender (Figure 1, right) due to its strength in core documents/records management and providing functionality and content services in a unified repository.

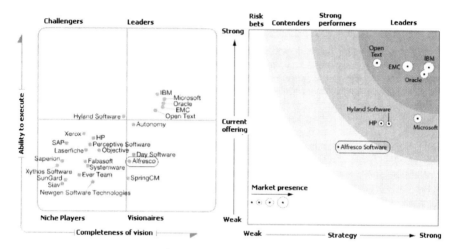

Fig. 1. ECM Magic Quadrant by Gartner© (left) and the Forrester WaveECM Suites (right)

Based on those reports, it can be observed that Alfresco© COTS have demonstrated its presence and effectiveness in this ECM marketplace. Broadly, Alfresco© uses a packaged strategy, instead of developing a custom solution for any specific client. This approach has been proven effective since this software packaging method is currently a common practice for software acquisition in both private and public sectors. Alfresco© became, than, the choice for this Macau Agency project. Concerning its Total Cost of Ownership (TCO), the table 1 summarizes the comparison pricing options for one thousand users.

Table 1. ECM TOC in US Dollars for 1000 users for a high availability enterprise configuration [10]

Vendors	Configuration	ECM Cost	Combined Stack Cost	Total Year Cost	Alfresco Year 1 Saving	% Year Saving
Alfresco	Red Hat + MySQL	$46,250	$3,798	$50,048		
Documental	Oracle + Windows	$863,937	$61,151	$925,088	$875,040	95%
Open Text	Oracle + Windows	$637,304	$61,151	$698,455	$648,407	93%
MS SharePoint	2 SQL Server + 3 Windows	$20,411	$339,149	$339,149	$289,101	85%

3 Research Methodology

The approach employed for this ECM testing regarding individual functionalities was to use functional testing techniques (Proof of Concept), that is, the system under test is viewed as a black-box while the test cases selections are based on a specific software requirements that meet the business ones [11]. Notice that any test scenario case is a set of conditions or variables under which a tester will determine if a requirement upon an application is partially or fully satisfied. In order to fully test all these requirements, there must be at least one test case for each requirement, unless a requirement has sub-requirements.

To demonstrate ECM capabilities, the blue application print was created in the PoC environment. By definition, the blue print is a skeleton application build in the ECM system, but initially without any actual content. It is composed of a security framework, the folder structure within the content repository and the categories for classification. In later stages, the workflow, business rules and other advanced modules was added.

In addition, an Intranet workspace was built to test each ECM component (management of workflow, records and documents, users, web content, search and browse capabilities) requirements. Notice that each of the business area has its own users, space, documents repositories, security privileges and so on. The organization chart, shown in Figure 2, illustrates the relationship between each business area in the Intranet. The PoC aim is to demonstrate that all business divisions can collaborate on creating an effective environment to manage all of its documents in a consistent and logical manner. Unsurprisingly, members belonging to each specific business area (ECM administrators, executives and directors, information technology, finance and accounting, public relations, marketing, human resources and sales) should be included in this diagram chart.

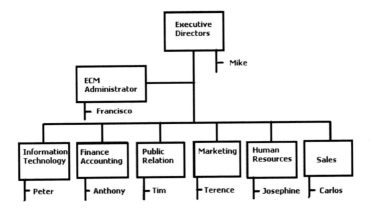

Fig. 2. Proof of Concept organization chart

As part of its expanding business, the Government Agency built and operates a Data Center (DC) to facilitate E-commerce development of the Macao region. The services provided by this DC is a process element aimed to instill electronic transactions trust with security and integrity. As a result, this operation is subjected to periodic assessments by independent assessors and other regulatory conformities, which include keeping records for, at least, fifteen years. To address these specific needs and to test the flexibility of Alfresco© ECM, the workflow for the Incident Management process includes all these restrictions. Certainly, the ECM implementation scope must always be aligned with the enterprise level goals and business initiatives, as well as with the mission statement defined by the ECM strategy.

4 Analysis of Results

The evaluation results show that Alfresco© is an integrated services suite able to provide comprehensive content management and search. Alfresco© supports intranet, extranet and Web applications across the organization using one integrated platform (see Figure 3). As well, it uses some of the open standards like Java Content Repository, AIFS Support for Windows© Files Sharing, NFS and FTP, Spring Aspect-Oriented Framework, Hibernate, Lucene Text Search Engine and JBPM Business Process Management. It can easily be integrated with external business applications using J2EE based framework, Kofax©, Quark©, Facebook©, iPhone©, Joomla© and Drupal©. Regarding security, Alfresco© applies permission to folder level or it can be set to individual content items by supporting external identity systems such as LDAP, NTLM, Kerberos and Active Directory.

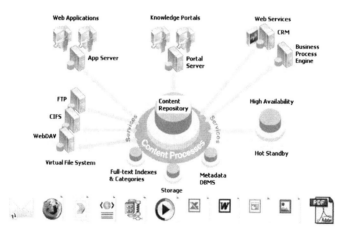

Fig. 3. Alfresco© content repository

Alfresco© Explorer is a Web client interface that uses any standard browser to automatically display easy, comprehensive and personalized navigation. The main page sets the functional areas together and serves as the access point for many of the most commonly used daily tasks (according to our results, this system can handle up to twenty-seven requests per second with good performance). As shown in Figure 4, each item can be accessed, for instance, by clicking the corresponding link on the left side of the page which follows a hierarchical framework.

Fig. 4. Alfresco© site navigation

The evaluation test results of the DM module shows that contents are displayed easily and intuitively, providing many enhancements for document management flow, including the ability to check-in and check-out documents, locally or remotely. It also provides integration capabilities for Microsoft Office© and Open Office©. Additional functionalities includes major and minor version numbering and tracking, support for multiple content types, policy enhancements, workflow integration and tree view support. Still, a lack of central control to ensure the quality and accuracy of each copy produced can be found, leading to contradictions across the all platform. Unfortunately, this issue can only be resolved by somebody with experience in editing online copy and has the authority to remove inappropriate material.

Alfresco© includes two types of build-in workflows: Simple and Advanced. The first one involves documents flow through various spaces/folders. Depending on the task, a content item is moved/copied to a new space at which point a new workflow instance is started. In the second one, a task is created by attaching to documents to be reviewed and assigned to the appropriate reviewers. The same workflow capabilities are available with Document Management (DM), Records Management (RM) and Web Content Management (WCM) modules. Custom advanced workflow supports complex business requirements.

Another particular module of Alfresco© is the User Management, only available for administrators personnel. It includes the ability to provide and assign access privileges to users, define security categories, control data user access and system functions and, optionally, can maintain audit users trails. Yet, these audit logs at Macau government agency shows that WCM go quite unused except for by a few individuals, that is, the belief that content management can be easily decentralized is false. Quite probably, training courses on how to use it and content contributors (by providing basic templates) as a mandatory task for each employee is part of the solution. But more does not mean better because the more they put in line, the harder it is for the users to find the content they want (in spite of the Alfresco© Search functionality provides an intuitive and flexible user interface to search unstructured and structured information by including the ability to control the query scope). Henceforth, it crucial to answer "is the posted content essential for helping those users complete their objectives?" Once again, the dilemma is technological but a planning one by setting up clear rules on how to use the WCM.

Implementing an EMS with multi-lingual support is easy. Creating a multi-lingual website is quite hard since the organization needs to find a translator over the long term. It happens that this issue is quite pertinent in Macau due to presence of four current languages: Putonghua, Cantonese, English and Portuguese. So, the Macau government must think twice before requesting multi-lingual support [12].

Table 2. Examples of content creation (top) and adding a business rule (bottom)

As well, Alfresco© is fully customized, so users can become productive on the platform more quickly. Table 2, for instance, illustrates the construction for behaviors (creation of a draft document) and workflows (conversion to PDF format) using common sense wizards. Indeed, it is key to avoid leaving the user with no obvious next step because at no stage is the user left without a next action.

5 Final Thoughts

Electronic document management (DM) can facilitate the migration from paper to electronic format and alleviate the burden of creating and maintaining paper archives. Hence, a complete DM must contain business process management, collaboration tools and be capable of integration with existing legacy systems.

This study evaluates Alfresco© ECM application against the criteria discussed previously. It shows strengths in document, records and Web content management, includes advanced workflow capability, capable of control the entire storage needs and can be easily integrated with Microsoft Office© and large OSS community applications. Alfresco© is a complete ECM in the sense that can surely improves employees productivity who works mainly with text documents. Furthermore, it is especially capable for deployment in Government agencies due to the need to process large amount of documents on a daily basis (see Table 3). It is also a ready to use application with no additional cost for most environments. On its own, Alfresco© is capable of running as an isolated system but also can be integrated and communicate with external systems that need to share information.

Table 3. Generic example of a Web site life cycle. Electronic Content Management (ECM) tries to gain more control over content and presentation by keeping its content timely and accurate, alleviate Webmaster bottleneck and eliminate the file forest [13].

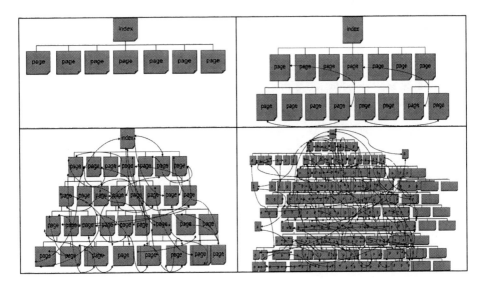

Nevertheless, the success keystone of any ECM implementation is planning, primarily, not the software itself. Developing the ECM strategic arrangement begins with understanding of the organization current business processes, the existing content and the users. Initially, the deployment scope should be moderate, that is, its phase's implementation must be smooth so as to not drastically affect the staff working environment all at once. Independently of the content management application (CMA) choice, agencies and organizations should adjust its procedures and steps to fit their individual needs in a step-by-step strategy. Furthermore, governments should not start by researching the ECM technical features but, instead, conduct a proper requirement analysis to match the institution set of needs. Of the eight major reasons software development projects fail, five relate to requirements errors, that is, this account for just over 50% of software project failures [14]. Once again, stating [13], (A) requirements are needs, as seen from the system user's perspective; (B) requirements deal with what a system must do, not on how the system will do it; (C) requirements definition means to surface, understand and document every required capability for every user of the system.

As a future work, some real performance parameters must be covered such as the number of documents that can be stored or time needed for loading/indexing 1GB of document that information should be documented and presented to the audience.

At last, ten golden rules are presented next and to have in mind: 1) No one should assume the content will be written by the ECM itself; 2) Misplaced and redundant information is not checked by the ECM, too; 3) Statistically, there is a tendency of high turnover in content managers during its life cycle; 4) There is a tendency to delegate content management to newest employees; 5) According to [13], of just under 100 companies, only 27 of companies surveyed planned to continue using their ECM as they do now; 6) ECMs and organizations are complex, dynamic and fuzzy; 7) Depict graphs to model documents workflow; 8) Perform gap analysis (the difference between the "as is" and the "desired") constantly; 9) Identify all user types and how each type interact with the system; 10) Keep in mind non-functional requirements such as ECM performance.

References

1. Muehlen, M.: Workflow-Based Process Controlling, p. 281. Logos Verlag Berlin (2002) ISBN 3-8325-0388-9
2. Laserfiche: Document Management Overview for Financial Services, p. 85. Compulink Management Center Inc. (2007),
   http://www.laserfiche.com/~/media/Files/
   Resource%20Library/DMO/DocumentManageOver_FS.ashx
   (retrieved in July 2010) ISBN 0-9726861-1-8
3. Shegda, K., Gilbert, M.: Key Issues for Enterprise Content Management Initiatives, Gartner Inc. (2009),
   http://www.gartner.com/it/content/787300/
   787313/key_issues_for_enterprise_cm.pdf (retrieved in July 2010)
4. AIIM, State of the ECM Industry (2010),
   http://www.aiim.org/Research/Industry-Watch/
   ECM-State-of-Industry-2010 (retrieved in July 2010)

5. Wikipedia, Open Source Software (2010),
   http://en.wikipedia.org/wiki/Open_Source_Software
   (retrieved in June 2010)
6. Stephens, T.: Open Source Software: Governance and the Open Source Repository, p. 480.
   US IGI Global, BellSouth Corporation, USA (2007) ISBN 978-1-59140-892-5
7. Andersson, I., Laurell, T.: Free and Open Source Software - A Feasibility Study, p. 24.
   Swedish Agency for Public Management (2003),
   http://www.campussource.de/org/opensource/
   docs/schwed.studie.pdf (retrieved in May 2010)
8. Cook, R.: Ten Misconceptions About Open Source Software Inside CRM (2008),
   http://www.insidecrm.com/features/10-misconceptions-012408/
   (last retrieved in October 2010)
9. Gartner: Key Issues for Enterprise Content Management Initiatives, p. 7, Gartner Inc., ID
   G00166575 (2009),
   http://www.gartner.com/it/content/787300/
   787313/key_issues_for_enterprise_cm.pdf (retrieved in July 2010)
10. Alfresco: Total Cost of ownership for Enterprise Content Management, White paper, p. 16
    (2010),
    http://www.aiimhost.com/Infonomics/July/
    AlfrescoWhitePaper.pdf (retrieved in July 2010)
11. Desikan, S., Ramesh, G.: Software Testing: Principles and Practice, p. 485. US Pearson
    Education, London (2006) ISBN 817758295X
12. Boag, P.: 10 Problems Your Content Management System Will Not Solve And How To
    Overcome Them. White Paper (2009), http://boagworld.com/technology/
    10-problems-your-content-management-system
    -will-not-solve-and-how-to-overcome-them/
    (retrieved in December 2010)
13. Rose, B., Pruyne, R.: Content Management Best Practices, Penn State University (2004),
    http://blogs.das.psu.edu/webcontent/
    wp-content/uploads/CMSRequirements101104.ppt
    (retrieved in September 2010)
14. Standish Group, Chaos, p. 8 (1995),
    http://www.projectsmart.co.uk/docs/chaos-report.pdf
    (retrieved in July 2010)

Interactive Models Supporting Construction Planning

A.Z. Sampaio and J.P. Santos

TU Lisbon, Dep. of Civil Engineering and Architecture
Av. Rovisco Pais 1049-001 Lisbon, Portugal
zita@civil.ist.utl.pt, jo.p@sapo.pt

Abstract. The construction of a building has been traditionally supported on the timeline schedules of the construction activities established in each case, and on technical drawings of the project. A prototype based on Virtual Reality (VR) technology with application to construction planning, was implemented. This interactive virtual model intends to present the project in a three-dimensional (3D) way, connected to construction planning schedule, resulting in a valuable asset in monitoring the development of the construction activity, based on the construction planning designed. The 4D application considers the time factor showing the 3D geometry of the distinct steps of the construction activity, according to the plan establish to the construction. The 4D model offers a detailed analysis of the construction project. Additionally, VR technology is used and presented as an innovative visual tool. It allows the visualization of different stages of the construction and the interaction with the construction activity. This application clearly shows the constructive process, avoiding inaccuracies and building errors, and so improving the communication between partners in the construction process. This tool is an important support in project conception and application.

Keywords: Virtual Reality, Civil Engineering, 4D model, Integration.

1 Introduction

In construction management, technical drawings have had, throughout times, a crucial role in communication between the numerous partners in a project. Generally, drawings represent formal solutions, and often incompatibility mistakes are only detected in advance stadium, on site, with additional costs.

In this field, 4D models, where the time factor is added to the three-dimensional (3D) model, promote the interaction between the geometric model and the construction activity planning, allowing immediate perception of the work evolution. With planning, correct evaluation and adequacy to intervenient needs, 4D models are a positive contribution decisions-maker when establishing planning strategies [1]. Moreover, Virtual Reality (VR) technology makes possible the interaction and the visualization of the construction work evolution, both immersive and interactively.

The main aim of a research project, now in progress at the Department of Civil Engineering of the Technical University of Lisbon, is to develop virtual models as tools to support decision-making in the planning of construction management and maintenance. A first prototype concerning the lighting system has already been

M.M. Cruz-Cunha et al. (Eds.): CENTERIS 2011, Part II, CCIS 220, pp. 40–50, 2011.
© Springer-Verlag Berlin Heidelberg 2011

completed [2]. A second prototype concerning the maintenance of the closure of walls, both interior walls and façades, was also developed [3]. The present prototype was implemented, supported on Virtual Reality (VR) technology, where the construction of a building and the related sequence of activities are used [4].

Actually information technology namely 4D modeling (3D+time) and VR technics has been used in the construction activity and in education [5]. At the Dep. Civil Engineering of TU Lisbon, some didactic models were generated. The research project, presented in this paper, follows a this previous work concerning education: Two 3D geometric models were created to help the rehabilitation of buildings activity [6]; and three VR models were developed to support classes (construction of a wall, of a bridge and of a roof), of Technical Drawing, Construction and Bridge disciplines, concerning Civil Engineering educational field [7]. The didactic VR models are usually presented in both face-to-face classes and in a e-learning platform.

2   Construction Planning

Construction management can be defined as *the planning, co-ordination and control of a project from conception to completion (including commissioning) on behalf of a client requiring the identification of the client's objectives in terms of utility, function, quality, time and cost, and the establishment of relationships between resources, integrating, monitoring and controlling the contributors to the project and their output, and evaluating and selecting alternatives in pursuit of the client's satisfaction with the project outcome* [8].

Therefore, it is essential the project designer comprise the knowledge to correctly identify the different stages of the construction planning, as well as take into consideration the logistics and resources involved in the project. The construction management and its planning depends on the target, while the people in the construction site have the need for a more detailed presentation, the client may want something more general and wide-ranging.

Hadju, in *Network Scheduling for Construction Project Management*, define the steps to create a good planning [9]:

- Task definition and description, considering the detail required;
- Task interdependencies definition and creation of a list of predecessors and successors;
- Network design, considering tasks' interdependencies;
- Resources and time estimation;
- Base calculations, including total project length;
- Advanced calculations, aiming a more efficient project, considering, cost, resources and task duration;
- Project control throughout its implementation;
- Project revision, considering the tasks, their duration and the necessary resources, with the intention of presenting alternatives to the established planning.

The steps one through five comprise the initial stage, six and seven consist of the scheduling stage, and the last is the project stage. There are several different factors to consider in the process of *planning*:

- Workscope
- time;
- resources;
- costs;
- quality;
- communication;
- risk;
- contracts and procurement.

Levine, about the project management, mentions *that the function involved in planning and control of projects (...) are just a part of the scope of project management. Add to this some of the soft skills, such as managing resources who report to other managers, using temporary or outsourced personnel, communication with a wide span of involved or concerned individuals, on several levels, and satisfying multiple stakeholders, the task becomes rather large and specialized* [10].

When going through the other factors, the stress is, most of the times, put on the triangle time-resources-costs [11]. These three factors are interconnected and interdependent. Time has a great significance in planning, as the tasks' length must converge to project duration compatible with the deadline. In defining the duration of a task the available resources must be considered. And this availability is intrinsically connected to the costs associated with the project.

On the present work, a prototype was developed supported on VR technology, where the construction of a building and the related sequence of activities are used. The construction planning used in the implemented prototype is realistic and considers the designed and written documentation, measurements and quantities map, specifications and regulations with relevance to the project.

3 VR in Construction

Virtual Reality technology is often considered a way to simulate reality through graphics projection, allowing the user to interact with their surroundings. In construction industry, from the conception to the actual implementation, project designs are presented mostly on paper, even though the two dimensional reading is often not enough, as mistakes can be introduced in early stages of conception or elements misunderstood on the construction site. 3D models present an alternative to avoid inaccuracies, as all the information can be included with the necessary detail [12].

These models can be separated into two categories: the operations level and the project level. The operations level, yet in an early and theoretical stage, can be described as the integration between the virtual model and the planning, the equipment, the temporary structures and any other resources needed in the construction process, and its conception is a difficult task, although the final result can be really positive. The project level is easier to implement and is the core of this paper.

Computer systems used in construction for graphic representation have experienced a vast evolution, allowing new ways of creating and presenting projects. 4D models, also labeled as 3D evolutionary models, permit a better comprehension of the project throughout its life, minimizing the information loss through the chain of events. The 4D virtual models have been studied for their applications, and one example is the project developed in Columbia University which presents, using Virtual Reality technology, a step-by-step guide in assembling complex structures.

One of the benefits of VR in construction is the possibility of a virtual scenario being visited by the different specialists, exchanging ideas and correcting mistakes. Some applications are already offering the possibility of communication between different specialties while developing a mutual project [13].

The concept of Building Information Modeling (BIM), considers the integration of 3D models with the planning of all aspects of the project, including resource management and logistics, with the purpose of reducing errors, and therefore costs, by using software to generate a accurate model of the final product, containing all the information needed to everyone involved in construction and maintenance. A BIM application is not only used to create the elements, but also as a manager of all the designs, uncovering construction errors when merging the different specialties. Applications like *Autodesk's AutoCAD Revit Architecture Suite*, *AutoCAD Revit Structure Suite* and *AutoCAD Revit MEP Suite* offer the possibility of different specialist working on the same project in different files and then combining then efficiently [14]. One drawback of these 4D models is the amount of time needed to create them, as well as the lack of trained personnel to do it.

Other applications offer a different kind of communication, being more focused on manipulating than creating the model. *EON Studio* is one of these applications where, by programming actions associated with different objects within the model, the final user can experience the interaction and the virtual reality in the presentation [15].

4   Implementation of VR Model

A prototype concerning the management of the construction activity was created with the purpose to present a three-dimensional model integrated with its construction planning schedule [3]. The application was developed in three stages: the planning, the modeling, and the integration of the first two stages.

- The **planning** has to consider the final purpose of the presentation, and the definition of the tasks and its detail has to be done according to this idea. Using *Microsoft Project 2007*, the tasks are introduced and the relations between them defined;
- The geometric **modeling** needs to relate correctly with the tasks defined in the planning stage. Using *AutoCAD 2010* as a modeling tool, the layers do the distinction between the different tasks and the elements are creating considering the detail necessary to the correct comprehension. The application also presents a real-time illustration of the construction evolution through **photographs** from the site, taken at specific points in time;

- The third stage, the **integration**, makes use of two programs: *EON Studio 5.0* and *Microsoft Visual C# 2008 Express Edition*, where the first takes the 3D model created with *AutoCAD* and introduces it in the application developed using the second.

The application, developed in C#, integrates all the components described with the interface presented in

Fig. 1. The application has the following organization:

- Virtual model (1);
- Pictures of construction site (2);
- Planning task list (3);
- Gantt map (4).

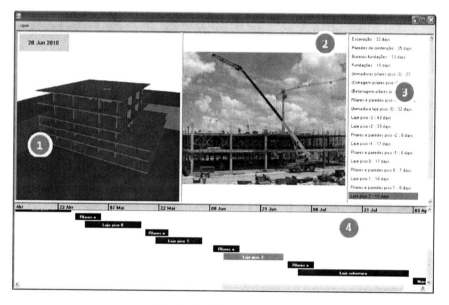

Fig. 1. Application interface

The interaction with the application is made through 3 and 4. Both the task list items and Gantt map bars are buttons that when pressed send the information to the *EON* about the task selected, and in return *EON* presents the model in the current state, this meaning that it shows and hides specific elements considering the construction's current stage.

EON can interact with the model in a number of different ways. In this prototype only the state of elements and position of camera is changed. The state of an element is presented by its Hidden property, whether it is selected or not, whilst the camera position is determined by translation and rotation coordinates. *EON Studio* also offers the possibility to change the material associated with each element, creating a more realistic model.

Any new objects can be introduced in the application, just by modeling the new elements considering their position relatively to the ones already in the simulation and programming the associated action in *EON Studio*.

Likewise, the application accepts any kind of construction project, as long as the imperatives of their implementation are met. Additionally, and with the appropriate models, it can also be used in construction site management.

There are some limitations in the prototype, like the static position of the model. This was established to provide an easier interaction with the 3D model, and to focus the attention of the user on the important sections on each task, guiding them correctly through the development of the construction.

5 Programming Details

This prototype's weakness is the time needed to make the preparation for the actual interaction with the application. Modeling a building may not be much extended. However, the programming of the actions in *EON Studio* can be time-consuming.

In the application, the geometric model of the building is presented in sequence simulating the construction activity. For that, each modeled component of the building is connected to the programming instruction: hidden and unhidden (Fig. 2.). This is one of the capacities allowed by the *EON software*. The command of unhide is linked to each step (label of the list of activities and bar of the *Gant* map) and to each geometric model. The identification both in the list/map and the related geometric model is established by a number. The number corresponds to the sequence defined in the design project. An action will begin when the user click over a label or a bar.

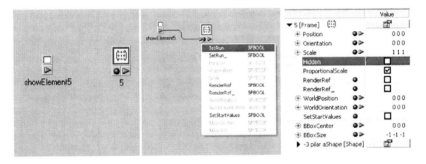

Fig. 2. Hidden and unhidden instruction

Fig. 3. presents a tree of links connecting the command of interaction (executed by the user) and the instruction show of the respective element (see the instruction *showelement_n* linked to the geometric model identified by the n number). In addition the control of the position and orientation of a camera (position, zoom and orientation of the model in relation to the observer) must be defined in accordance with the selected construction step. The position of the camera is controlled within the EON software as shown in Fig. 3.

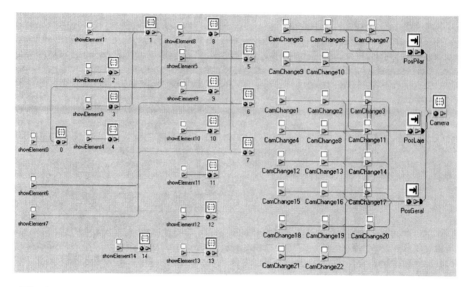

Fig. 3. Diagram of actions hidden and unhidden for each element and Control of the camera

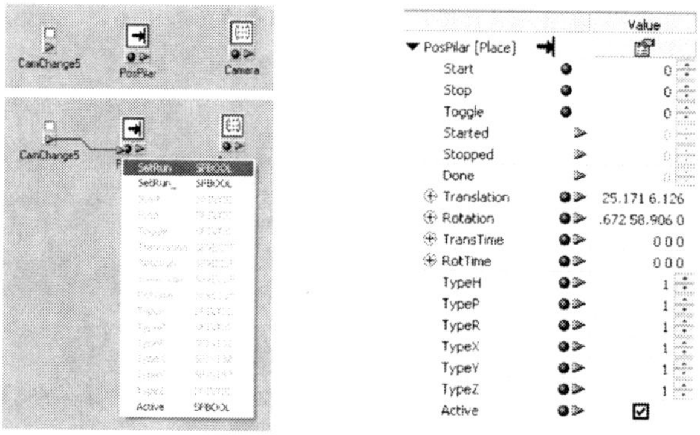

Fig. 4. Control of the translation and rotation movements of the model

6   Testing the Prototype

As a method of testing the application, a construction project was implemented, particularly the structure of a building, using its graphic documentation, such as architectural and structural blueprints, the project description and construction planning (Fig. 5).

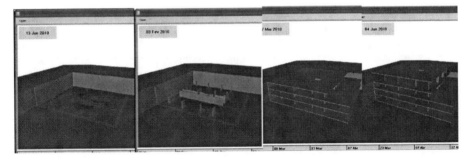

	Name	Duration	Start	Finish
1	Excavation	25 days	Mon 23-11-09	Fri 25-12-09
2	Retaining walls	26 days	Wed 25-11-09	Wed 30-12-09
3	Foundation holes	10 days	Fri 25-12-09	Thu 07-01-10
4	Foundations	12 days	Tue 29-12-09	Wed 13-01-10
5	(Column reinforcement level -3)	20 days	Thu 07-01-10	Wed 03-02-10
6	(Column formwork level -3)	20 days	Thu 07-01-10	Wed 03-02-10
7	(Column concreting level -3)	20 days	Thu 07-01-10	Wed 03-02-10
8	Columns and walls level -3	20 days	Thu 07-01-10	Wed 03-02-10
9	(Slab reinforcement level -3)	23 days	Thu 14-01-10	Mon 15-02-10
10	Slab level -3	32 days	Thu 14-01-10	Fri 26-02-10
11	Slab level -2	24 days	Wed 03-03-10	Mon 05-04-10
12	Columns and walls level -2	7 days	Tue 06-04-10	Wed 14-04-10
13	Slab level -1	12 days	Fri 09-04-10	Mon 26-04-10
14	Columns and walls level -1	7 days	Tue 27-04-10	Wed 05-05-10
15	Slab level 0	12 days	Fri 30-04-10	Mon 17-05-10
16	Columns and walls level 0	6 days	Tue 18-05-10	Tue 25-05-10
17	Slab level 1	11 days	Fri 21-05-10	Fri 04-06-10
18	Columns and walls level 1	7 days	Mon 07-06-10	Tue 15-06-10
19	Slab level 2	13 days	Thu 10-06-10	Mon 28-06-10
20	Columns and walls level 2	7 days	Tue 29-06-10	Wed 07-07-10
21	Slab roof	24 days	Fri 02-07-10	Wed 04-08-10
22	Walls roof	9 days	Thu 05-08-10	Tue 17-08-10

Fig. 5. Construction planning, the Gantt map and the 3D model of the building structure

The whole project was simplified to meet this paper's academic purposes, and the list of tasks was defined considering the more characteristic stages in a construction process, and also a few tasks focused in construction details of certain elements. As a result, *AutoCAD* layers were created for each task defined and the 3D model assembled. When finished, the 3D model is exported to *EON Studio*, where a diagram of events is created, after what the application is ready to be used. As explained before, the task list and the virtual model are connected. When selecting a task, the relevant construction stage is presented (Fig. 6).

Fig. 6. Application's virtual model

The first scenario concerns the landscape and then the foundation work began. In this example, some construction details were modeled, including one column progress. This progress is presented in Fig. 7 throughout three stages. A detail of the reinforcement and the concentration of a slab are also presented in the figure.

When constructing a building, the planning sometimes needs to be changed due to unexpected contingencies. Implementing these changes in the prototype is actually very simple, as the user just have got to change the tasks new start and finish dates in *MS Project* and load the new file into the application. When a task is selected in the construction planning chart a static position of the model is presented.

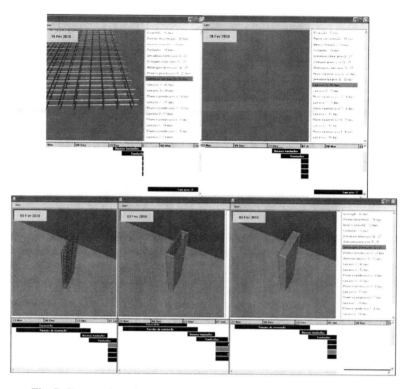

Fig. 7. Construction of a slab and a column: reinforcements and concreting

A first view is always linked to a task. This was established to provide an easier interaction with the 3D model, and to focus the attention of the user on the important sections on each task, guiding them correctly through the development of the construction. Next, in order to obtain the same point of view of the photo, the user can manipulate the virtual model, choosing an identical perspective. So, visualizing what is planned and what was done in the real place, the construction work is better compared and analyzed (Fig. 8). In addition the user can manipulate the model walking through the virtual building observing any construction detail he wants to compare.

Fig. 8. Rotation applied to the virtual model

All steps were modeled and linked to the planning chart. Details of the construction work are presented in Fig. 9. The data concerning each visualized task is shown in the upper left corner of the virtual model window.

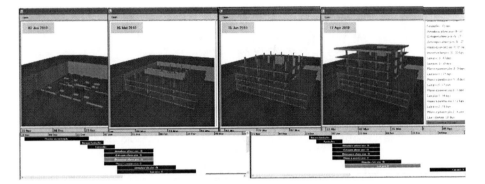

Fig. 9. Sequence of the construction process

7 Conclusions

Technical drawings and explanatory texts often have little detail and are frequently insufficient in fully comprehending the object.

Virtual Reality technology and its capability of interaction and connectivity between elements were employed in the prototype's implementation, offering several benefits both in presenting and developing projects. Mistakes can easily be caught before construction a start, which translates in time and cost reduction.

In this paper was introduced a prototype which purpose is to ease the control of construction planning throughout project's development. It can be used with any kind of construction project and, being a flexible application, accepts new data when necessary, allowing for a comparison between the planned and the constructed.

The prototype can also be expanded to include other aspects of construction management, such as resource administration, or to have a real-time access to the construction, through the use of cameras installed on site. The use of new mobile technologies could move the application to the construction site, clarifying any doubts about location or position of each component.

Acknowledgments. The authors gratefully acknowledge the financial support of the Foundation for Science and Technology, a Governmental Organization for the research project, *Virtual Reality Technology applied as a support tool to the planning of construction maintenance-* PTDC/ ECM/67748/ 2006, now in progress.

References

1. Yerrapathruni, S., Messner, J.I., Baratta, A.J., Horman, M.J.: Using 4D CAD and Immersive Virtual Environments to Improve Construction Planning. In: CONVR 2003, Conference on Construction Applications of Virtual Reality, Blacksburg, VA, pp. 179–192 (2003)

2. Sampaio, A.Z., Ferreira, M.M., Rosário, D.P.: Interaction and Maintenance in Civil Engineering within Virtual Environments. In: ANT 2010 International Conference on Ambient Systems, Networks and Technologies, Paris, France, November 8-10, pp. 238–248 (2010)
3. Gomes, A.R.: Virtual Reality technology applied to the maintenance of façades, Integrated Master Degree Thesis in Construction, TU Lisbon, Portugal (2010)
4. Santos, J.P.: Construction Planning using 4D Virtual Models, Integrated Master Degree Thesis in Construction, TU Lisbon, Portugal (2010)
5. Mohammed, E.H.: n-D Virtual Environment in Construction Education. In: The 2nd International Conference on Virtual Learning, ICVL 2007, pp. 1–6 (2007)
6. Sampaio, A.Z., Henriques, P.G., Ferreira, P.S.: Virtual Reality Models Used in Civil Engineering. In: IMSA 2006 Proceedings of the 24th IASTED International Conference on Internet and Multimedia Systems and Applications Education. ACTA pres Anaheim, CA (2006), http://portal.acm.org/citation.cfm?id=1169188
7. Sampaio, A.Z., Ferreira, M.M., Rosário, D.P., Martins, O.P.: 3D and VR models in Civil Engineering education: Construction, rehabilitation and maintenance. Automation in Construction 19, 819–828 (2010)
8. Walker, A.: Project Management in Construction, 4th edn. Blachweel Publishing, Oxford (2002)
9. Hadju, M.: Network Scheduling Techniques for Construction Project Management. Kluwer Academic Publishers, Dordrecht (1997)
10. Levine, H.A.: Practical Project Management: Tips, Tactics, and Tools. John Wiley & Sons, New York (2002) ISBN 0-471-20303-3
11. Casimiro, J.: Planeamento Integrado de Prazos e Custos nas PMEs, Civil Engineering Final Report, TU Lisbon, IST (2006)
12. Grilo, L., Monice, S., Santos, E.T., Melhado, S.: A Realidade Virtual e a possibilidade de aplicação na construção: do projecto colaborativo à realidade ampliada. In: II Simpósio Brasileiro de Gestão da Qualidade e Organização do Trabalho na Construção Civil, Sibragec 2001, Fortaleza, Brasil (2001)
13. Webb, R.M., Haupt, T.C.: The Potential of 4D CAD as a Tool for Construction Management. In: 7th Int. Conf. on Construction Application of Virtual Reality, USA (2003)
14. Autodesk AutoCAD Architecture 2010/Civil3D/Revit (2010), http://images.autodesk.com/ (accessed on March 2010)
15. EON, EON Studio (2010), http://www.eonreality.com/ (accessed on September 2010)

Foundations for a Mobile Context-Aware Advertising System

Guilherme Alexandre[1], Telmo Adão[1], Martinho Gonçalves[1,2], Luís Magalhães[1,2], Maximino Bessa[1,2], Emanuel Peres[1,3], and João Varajão[1,4]

[1] Universidade de Trás-os-Montes e Alto Douro,
5001-801 Vila Real, Portugal
[2] Instituto de Engenharia de Sistemas e Computadores do Porto,
4200-465 Porto, Portugal
[3] Centro de Investigação e de Tecnologias Agroambientais e Biológicas,
5001-801 Vila Real, Portugal
[4] Centro Algoritmi, Universidade do Minho,
4800 Guimarães, Portugal
{galexandre.jacob,telmo.adao,martinhofg}@gmail.com,
{lmagalha,maxbessa,eperes,jvarajao}@utad.pt

Abstract. Advertisers struggle to reach effectively and efficiently to their customers, continuously seeking to influence them and simultaneously reduce the overall publicity costs. Business areas like the mobile devices industry, together with wireless technologies and interactive environments, bring an huge opportunity for marketing purposes, supporting the chance to turn advertising into a convenient and easily accessible source of information by letting marketers communicate with costumers in a more direct, personal and contextualized way. This paper presents some foundations for the development of a system that will allow context-aware personalized profile-based advertising delivery, by using Bluetooth technology to identify and communicate with customers in a given geographic area, through their mobile devices.

Keywords: Advertising, Context-aware, Personalization, Mobile, Bluetooth.

1 Introduction

Advertising is defined as the non-personal presentation of ideas, products and services, where the identifiable source entity has to pay for it [1]. Also, as the main medium for organizational promotional communication [2], it is constantly morphing in an effort to achieve efficiency gains by maintaining customers or reaching new ones, while using lesser resources. Recently the advertising industry has suffered a major change, especially if taken into consideration the paradigm in which ads were intended to reach as many consumers as possible [3], with low concern about the cost/efficiency ratio. Nowadays, being a profitable business [4] and as technology advances, advertisers can choose between a wide range of communication channels - being the most popular the Internet [3] - in which profits can be optimized, thus improving the advertising cost/efficiency ratio.

M.M. Cruz-Cunha et al. (Eds.): CENTERIS 2011, Part II, CCIS 220, pp. 51–61, 2011.
© Springer-Verlag Berlin Heidelberg 2011

The most obvious example of an advertising paradigm change is television: as users achieve more and more control over the contents they want to watch, which means in some cases that they do not have to waste time watching commercials between them [5], advertisers were forced to look for other ways to communicate with them while trying to maintain the advertising overall costs, like using careful product placement in television contents.

This paper proposes a Bluetooth advertising system, which allows basic context data assembly, such as location, time and day, for advertising differentiation and costumer targeting purposes. The system pushes sought advertising to the users' personal mobile device, using the devices' Bluetooth support. This work intends initially to describe and analyze the background literature information referring to mobile advertising efficiency and related work, in order to scientifically support an advertising delivery system proposal, further described and tested on this paper.

2 Background

As this new marketing era forms its groundings, there are some environments that impose themselves as more viable and attractive to both marketers and technology promoters, such as the Internet and the mobile market [2] [3], which try to respond to some of the previously referred issues. M-advertising can be defined as the business of encouraging people to buy products and services by using mobile communications as the medium to deliver the advertisement message. This industry is already taking advantage of the mobile devices proliferation. However, there is a gap between the hardware and software capabilities of mobile devices and the actual use of their features, which can be partially explained by their heterogeneous characteristics. In fact, as mobile devices have many manufacturers and each one has their market segments, approaches and options, there is not a hardware/software standard to use, which hinders the development of applications intended to reach a wider audience. Vatanparast [6] states that todays' development in information technology is helping marketers to keep track of customers and to provide new venues by reaching smaller customer segments more cost effectively and with more personalized messages, even though the global mobile advertising industry is in its early years. It is also important to refer that forecasts concerning the growth of mobile advertising are providing enthusiastic information.

Komulainen [7] referred to the potential relevance that mobile advertising could have in the future, underlining some supporting reasons, such as: the high penetration rate of mobile devices which almost totally sets aside the concerns about leaving some costumers out of advertisement campaigns when choosing only the mobile market; mobile devices are personal communication devices and individually addressable, thus ensuring advertisers that by addressing one device, they are addressing the individual that owns it and not someone else, almost 24 hours a day; mobile devices are capable of receiving multimedia and interactive content, which provides a creative potential to marketers and makes feedback analysis more trustworthy. In [6], Vatanparast suggests that mobile advertising, when compared to the existing advertising channels, holds strong promises to become the most powerful targeted one-to-one digital advertising medium by means of offering new and better ways to take advertising messages to users.

Ubiquitous computing is related to smart environments, in which embedded sensors or devices interact and respond individually to a specific user and situation by analyzing and acquiring context data. Ubiquitous computing can be combined with mobile advertising to create opportunities for both users and companies. This can exponentially increase advertisers' targeting efficiency, as sensors tell them who are and where are their customers. However, customers also have the advantage of choosing when, where and how frequently they are willing to be exposed to advertising information, through their mobile devices [3].

This type of context-aware advertising can be a solution for the need of a more effective and efficient use of resources when delivering advertising, through the use of environmental contextualization data, as time, day and geographical location, together with an user typical profile information, like age, name, gender and personal preferences. By relying on this contextualization data, users can be provided with convenient, compelling and useful advertising [4]. This can also means that contextualized advertising messages will be perceived by users more as information and not as much as promotional content, endorsing relationship marketing strategies and fidelity approaches, which can lead to good viral and word-of-mouth marketing campaigns [8]. However, a one-to-one personalized marketing campaign suggests a previously acquired knowledge about the targeted individual with the purpose of correctly select which information should be presented. Logistic issues come to hand when using this approach as companies cannot profile effectively a large number of individuals with limited resources when considering the quantity and variety of information needed to correctly segment the population. Nowadays, with the widespread and use of social networks, profiling information is already shared widely between users. This shifts the challenge from finding information to gaining access to it, while regarding privacy and permission concerns.

There are some technologies and services available which can be used in M-advertising and ubiquitous computing, such as Bluetooth, Radio-Frequency IDentification (RFID), Near-Field Communication (NFC) and wireless networks (IEEE 802.11), as well as location-based services (LBS) through Global Positioning System (GPS) technologies [2] [4]. Leo Bhebhe in [9] defines LBS as wireless mobile content services that provide location-specific information to mobile devices users moving from one location to another. That kind of information is crucial when knowing what products or services to announce at a given time and based on the users' location. In [10], John Krumm predicts that many ubiquitous computing applications will eventually be supported by advertising.

3 Related Work

Previously referred as a profitable business, advertising is an attractive industry due to the efforts made in many distinct research areas such as sociology, statistics and technology. The main contribution of this work is centered in the technology area, by arguing the use of free and widely spread mobile wireless communication technologies, namely Bluetooth, as the basis of a one-to-one mobile advertising delivery system. Today, Bluetooth can be considered as a common communication technology, supported in the majority of mobile devices, as stated in [11]: "Almost everyone today has his or her mobile phone, and Bluetooth has already become a standard inclusion on most mobile phones, laptops and PDAs".

Previous studies conducted as tests for M-advertising commercial applications have been analyzed when preparing this work. B-MAD system [12][13][14] is an example and consists on WAP Push advertising content delivery, which is made by pushing advertising contents to any discovered and connected device, using Bluetooth. An Ad-Server selects the specific advertising to be sent to a given device, by examining the connected device advertising content reception history. B-MAD has some limitations namely Bluetooth's low communication speed, which endangers contextualization by the users' location and the absence of contextualization data sources, which makes harder segmenting and targeting users.

Studies related to M-advertising efficiency factors were examined and taken into account when designing the proposed system [15][16][17][18]. Next, some of the most meaningful are highlighted:

3.1 Contextualization through Time and Geographic Location

Location and time context data for advertising are known to be of great value for improving efficiency in segmentation and targeting operations, as they could support the increase of convenience and usefulness of ads being presented and consequently improve the impact made in the users buying decision process.

The previously referred studies underlined the importance of users location data, not only for enhancing the user capability to know which products/services are available in his current geographic area, but also as a tool to respond to an important M-advertising challenge which is improving efficiency and efficacy results: the "right place, right time" rule [19].

3.2 Incentive to Potential Costumers

When asking for users attention there is the possibility of creating distractions or even of interrupting the task/action that they are undergoing, which can increase their irritation or frustration.

There is also the need to stimulate service trial and use, which cannot be done without offering the users some type of compensation. This is also a characteristic of todays' marketing strategies, as the advertising paradigm shifts between invasive, uninformative and standardized advertising to one-to-one informational and useful content. As stated in [18], "Nine out of ten (86 percent) of the respondents to a Nokia-sponsored survey, conducted by HPI Research Group, on mobile marketing agreed that there should be a trade-off for accepting ads on their mobile devices".

3.3 Advertising Source Credibility

Credibility is related to users' perception about the advertising message content and increases as the message reliability, power and attractiveness grow, which is known in the studied literature as a crucial factor to determine users' attitude regarding M-advertising [18]. As stated in [20], "Credibility refers to the public's attitude towards the source of information. This reaction to media content is expressed at the mental perception level, and takes the form of trust or distrust in the message". Consumers' credibility perception about a specific advertising will influence their value assessment of not only that advertising, but also the associated brand and company credibility.

3.4 Advertising Content Length and Dimension

"Individuals will have to go through the message before determining if it is of any value", [18]. Short and succinct messages do not take much from the users' attention, avoiding previously referred unwanted behaviors and attitudes. By using short and informative advertising it is possible to stimulate the "instinct buying" - again influencing the buying decision process – and also to promote the users' curiosity and interest. As a useful analogy, it is known that there is a negative relation between Internet banners' size and the users' response to it.

3.5 Concrete versus Abstract Advertising Content

Based on the studied literature, an informative content, which is not vulnerable to different interpretations, is considered as concrete advertising. On the contrary, contents with higher ambiguity levels, susceptible to have different interpretations, are considered as abstract advertising. In an M-advertising scenario, users are more willing to attribute value to an informative message. However, there are exceptions in which more general contents should be considered, such as brand awareness advertising, for example.

4 Mobile Context-Aware Advertising Delivery System Proposal

When analyzing this kind of technologies for commercial purposes, it is important to focus on the perspectives of each and every system player, to better understand their role. The proposed advertising system consists in the delivery of personal advertising contents based on multiple contextualization data - which is obtained from various sources - to mobile device users. This is done by using strategically placed Bluetooth access points. Depicted in Fig. 1 is the proposed general mobile context-aware advertising delivery system architecture, where three main actors can be identified: user, store and promoter.

4.1 User

The user is located at the end point of the communication channel, where a one-to-one personalized promotional and informative message is intended to be delivered. The communication channel starts off with the promoter, who owns the advertising system and is followed by the store, Fig. 1, which will be detailed further on this paper. The main mobile context-aware advertising system features are: contextualization, device adaptation, personalization, legal rights, privacy and security.

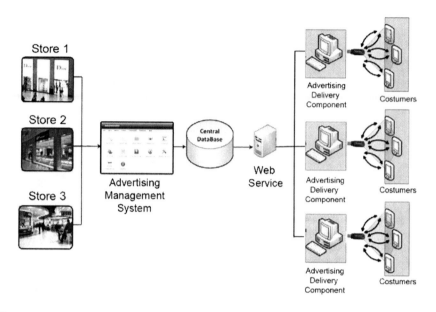

Fig. 1. General mobile context-aware advertising system architecture proposal, which is composed by stores or regions connected to a central database, through an Advertising Management System. A web service receives information requests from the existing Advertising Delivery Component, based on the clients' context data and then fetches the according advertising content from the central database, returning and delivering it to the user. Finally, the Advertising Delivery Component is constantly inquiring the surrounding environment, searching for users.

4.1.1 Contextualization

Data gathering concerning to the user's personal context - demographic and preferences- and searching for the best efficiency/cost ratio can be done by one of two ways:

a) User's profile from social networks accounts: This type of connection would give users the opportunity to receive information based on their personnel profile data such as name, age, birthday, relationship status, as well as their preferences like online friends and local networks, depending on the data made available by the users' profile. It can also benefit from the existing applications made for geographic location discovery, as well as other LBS and location-based social networks, like for instance Foursquare. Using social networks accounts profiles does not imply previous registry in the advertisement system and could benefit from the social networks marketing capability and potential. However and as it involves a number of personnel data access permissions, it can encounter resistance from some users.

b) An online web platform supported by the mobile context-aware advertising systems' promoter, in which users can beforehand provide the context data: it has the advantage of not having to obtain the users' permission in order to collect personal data, since that would be done previously, together with the user/mobile device association, by registering on the web platform. Information provided by users can be more detailed, like for instance store or brand preferences, as well as clothes size or budget limits. However, a mandatory registry process can be annoying and time consuming to some users, depending on other promotion efforts in order to be successful.

Time and geographic location contextualization data can be processed as previously stated by a social network connection or through a decision system application, which is responsible for determining the hour, day, month and year, along with important calendar events, like for instances holidays. This latter application also determines the Bluetooth access-point identification (geographic location), gathers information and proceeds to database queries, in order to decide which advertising message contents should be sent to the user, according to the context data. This context inquire is crucial to the advertising system efficiency, as it brings closer advertising contents delivered and users real needs, discarding any other content that based on the available contextualization information, does not make sense.

4.1.2 Device Adaption
The advertising content to be delivered has to be adapted to mobile devices software and hardware parameters. Given the previously referred mobile devices market heterogeneity, this is achieved by using minimum common denominator values, such as screen size, contrast or resolution.

4.1.3 Personalization
Content personalization refers to the advertising capability to address an individual using his specific and unique identifying information, thus differentiating the content from other individuals. Message personalization can be achieved by using a profile name (which is associated with the user registry on social networks like Facebook, Twitter or Windows Live), through users Bluetooth device identification, by means of the online platform username and by using users' preferences and advertising system delivery log data.

4.1.4 Legal Rights, Privacy and Security
The advertising system is guided by the existing policies in use on the various platforms it accesses, obtaining users' permission when required, namely on the Bluetooth connection and on any data collection requirement.

4.2 Store

Any physical small/medium location with the purpose to develop commercial transactions and which is situated inside a commercial space - the promoter - is considered a store. Each promoter can have several stores coexisting. The store's role in the mobile context-aware advertising system is to provide ads and choose the parameters - among the context data available variables - used by the advertising system to determine when they should be presented to the user.

The mobile context-aware advertising system promoter provides the store with access to an Advertising Management System, which in turn enables it with the capability to manage and control the advertising content (ads) to be sent, the frequency and the context parameters. Ads are then stored in the central database (which is owned by the system provider), along with the associated context parameters information. Later they can be filtered by the advertising system based on context information and can finally be delivered to the user.

4.3 Promoter

The promoter can be represented by different entities depending on the situation, which accounts the mobile context-aware advertising system flexibility. Until now, the promoter was considered to be a shopping mall. However and further in this paper, another scenario will be presented in which the promoter is considered to be a university.

A given promoter is the owner, controls and maintains the mobile context-aware advertising system, which includes the advertising management system and Bluetooth devices, along with its information flow. It is further responsible to make it available to the stores as a service. The advertising delivery component is centralized and common for all the remaining components.

The proposed mobile context-aware advertising system operation, designed to function in commercial surfaces, starts interacting with a user when the application responsible for environment enquiring produces a Bluetooth-connection acceptance signal. Then, a response signal sent by a user mobile device is returned to a Bluetooth receiver module, triggering a system request to collect user profile information and context data, such as day and time. Finally, the collected information is used when searching the central database for convenient advertising ads, which generates a response and triggers the delivery of an advertising result to a users' mobile device.

5 Pilot Test

In order to test the feasibility of the proposed mobile context-aware advertising system, a field experiment involving 32 randomly picked owners of a mobile device with Bluetooth support was conducted. Also established were some control parameters considered important for corroboration purposes, such as: Bluetooth push-based advertising system, advertising images differentiation, context data (location, time and day) acquisition and its qualitative relevance for the user. Complementary responses were also obtained about the test subjects' Bluetooth using habits, privacy concerns and personal data sharing opinion for social network platforms interaction.

In order to accurately develop and implement the pilot test, advertisements were designed according to the expected context data acquisition, location (store), time and day. The tested individuals were asked to turn on their mobile device Bluetooth support and then to travel through a pre-determined course. Rooms equipped with computers were used to simulate stores. When users pass within a given room surrounding area, their mobile devices are caught by the constant Bluetooth enquiring process made by the computer in the room and an application choses the proper advertising and sends it to those users who chose to connect to the system. This application is a Bluetooth push-deliver service, supported on Object Exchange profile (OBEX). It runs at the store level and is permanently inquiring the environment in order to detect devices with active Bluetooth support. Subsequently, the application inquires each device found to know about the available OBEX profile. This last inquire tries to obtain an URL connection where to send the context aware advertising contents. Based on day, hour and location data the application enquiries the central database to select which advertising file should be sent to the users.

Through a quantitative and qualitative inquire, participants have provided enough data to conclude about the mobile context-aware advertising system viability, usability and efficiency. So, about the participants Bluetooth using habits, while 31% of the users said that they use their mobile device Bluetooth support "very often", only 6% of them admitted to use Bluetooth in a regular basis, being the most common response, with 44%, "never" use Bluetooth. Participants were also asked to evaluate the task on a scale from 1 to 5, being 1 very uncomfortable and 5 very comfortable. While 63% of participants felt always comfortable when completing the requested task, 31% acknowledged to have felt comfortable and only 3% of participants were uncomfortable with the advertising contents reception on their mobile devices. A great majority - 72% - of the participants considered the demonstrated method to be important in a commercial space, with only 3% thinking that the prototype would be of small value to that purpose. Almost all of the test participants - 97% - experienced good or excellent advertising contents visualization and screen adaptation on their mobile device.

During the pilot test two of the participants have failed to complete the requested tasks, in different process stages. One of the individuals could not receive the advertising contents on his mobile device, as well as establishing the Bluetooth connection due to an OBEX incompatibility. As for the second individual, a device software problem occurred which made impossible to visualize the advertising content received.

Although some issues were found, such as device compatibility and environment enquire speed, issues that demand system improvements, the main objectives earlier stated for this field experiment were successfully achieved. The context (location, time and day) data acquisition for advertising delivery adapting was also proven, along with the users' success in completing the task needed to receive the advertising.

6   Conclusions and Future Work

The main purpose of this work was to propose some foundations for a mobile context-aware advertising delivery system that could allow future development and research, using wider system architecture as guide and performing a pilot experiment as a concept model.

In the pilot test that took place it was possible to correctly deliver the advertising content with relevance within the context in which the users were inserted. All of the enquired participants have considered the delivered advertising as being convenient for the time and place in case.

The major percentage - 75% - of the enquired individuals has admitted that they never or rarely had used their mobile device Bluetooth support, which led to the conclusion that an effort would have to be done to incite that behavior. On the other hand, users felt comfortable when using the prototype, which means that privacy limits were not crossed or security bounds breached. This might be due to the advertising source credibility, the pilot test location (a university building) or the low experiment requirements. The obtained results justify further research in this area, such as compatibility tests with all mainly used mobile devices and improved application for smart phones and other mobile devices.

For future work purposes it will be also important to perform a field experiment to test the complete architecture, as well as the mobile context-aware advertising system functioning on a commercial area and a business model which considers the implementation and maintenance costs estimations.

References

1. Bulander, R., Decker, M., Schiefer, G., Kölmel, B.: Comparison of Different Approaches for Mobile Advertising. In: Proceedings of the Second IEEE International Workshop on Mobile Commerce and Services (WMCS 2005), pp. 174–182. IEEE Computer Society, Washington, DC, USA (2005), http://dx.doi.org/10.1109/-WMCS.2005.8, doi:10.1109/WMCS.2005.8
2. Bulander, R., Decker, M., Schiefer, G., Kölmel, B.: Enabling Personalized And Context Sensitive Mobile Advertising While Guaranteeing Data Protection. In: Proceedings of the EURO-mGOV (2005)
3. Eriksson, C.I., Akesson, M.: Ubiquitous Advertising Challenges. In: 7th International Conference on Mobile Business, ICMB 2008, July 7-8, pp. 9–18 (2008), http://ieeexplore.ieee.org/stamp/ stamp.jsp?tp=&arnumber=-4570159&isnumber=4570141, doi:10.1109/ICMB.2008.19
4. Simoes, J.: A generic enabler framework for contextualized advertising within interactive multimedia services. In: IEEE International Symposium on a World of Wireless, Mobile and Multimedia Networks & Workshops, WoWMoM 2009, June 15-19, pp. 1–3 (2009), http://ieeexplore.ieee.org/ stamp/-stamp.jsp?tp=&arnumber=5282399&isnumber=5282393, doi:10.1109/WOWMOM.2009.5282399
5. Urban, G.L.: Customer Advocacy: A New Era in Marketing? Journal of Public Policy & Marketing 24, 155–159 (2005)
6. Vatanparast, R.: Piercing the Fog of Mobile Advertising. In: International Conference on the Management of Mobile Business, ICMB 2007, July 9-11, p. 19 (2007), http://ieeexplore.ieee.org/stamp/ stamp.jsp?tp=&arnumber-=4278563&isnumber=4278535, doi:10.1109/ICMB.2007.52
7. Komulainen, H., Ristola, A., Still, J.: Mobile advertising in the eyes of retailers and consumers - empirical evidence from a real-life experiment. In: 2006 International Conference on Mobile Business, ICMB, p. 37 (2006)
8. Simoes, J., Lamorte, L., Boris, M., Criminisi, C., Magedanz, T.: Enhanced Advertising for next generation networks. In: 2009 ITU-T Kaleidoscope Academic Conference (2009)
9. Bhebhe, L.: Location Service for Restaurants. In: TKK T-110.5190 Seminar on Internetworking (2008)
10. Krumm, J.: Ubiquitous Advertising: The Killer Application for the 21st Century. IEEE Pervasive Computing 10(1), 66–73 (2011), http://ieeexplore.ieee.org/stamp/stamp.jsp?tp=&arnumber=5396 316&isnumber=5676140, doi:10.1109/MPRV.2010.21

11. Chen, Y., Chou, H., Lin, C., Lin, H., Yuan, S.: A System Implementation of Pushing Advertisement to Handheld Devices via Bluetooth. In: Fourth International Conference on Networked Computing and Advanced Information Management, NCM 2008, September 2-4, pp. 133–136 (2008),
    http://ieeexplore-.ieee.org/stamp/stamp.
    jsp?tp=&arnumber=4623992&isnumber=4623958, doi:10.1109/NCM.2008.168
12. Aalto, L., Göthlin, N., Korhonen, J., Ojala, T.: Bluetooth and WAP push based location-aware mobile advertising system. In: Proceedings of the 2nd International Conference on Mobile Systems, Applications, and Services (MobiSys 2004), pp. 49–58. ACM, New York (2004),
    http://doi.acm.org/10.1145/990064.99-0073, doi:10.1145/990064.990073
13. Ojala, T.: Case studies on context-aware mobile multimedia services. Journal on Digital Information Management 8, 3–14 (2010)
14. Halim, A.H., Fauzi, A.H., Tarmizi, S.: Bluetooth mobile advertising system using pull-based approach. In: International Symposium on Information Technology, ITSim 2008, August 26-28, vol. 4, pp. 1–4 (2008),
    http://ieeexplore.ieee.org/stamp/stamp.jsp?tp=&arnumber=4631
    881&isnumber=4631845, doi:10.1109/ITSIM.2008.4631881
15. Haghirian, P., Madlberger, M., Tanuskova, A.: Increasing Advertising Value of Mobile Marketing - An Empirical Study of Antecedents. In: Proceedings of the 38th Annual Hawaii International Conference on System Sciences (HICSS 2005) - Track 1, vol. 1, p. 32c (2005)
16. Vatanparast, R., Butt, A.H.: Factors Affecting Use of Mobile Advertising: A Quantitative Study. In: 42nd Hawaii International Conference on System Sciences, HICSS 2009, January 5-8, pp. 1–8, (2009),
    http://ieeexplore.-ieee.org/stamp/stamp.jsp?
    tp=&arnumber=4755447&isnumber=4755314, doi:10.1109/HICSS.2009.214
17. Drossos, D., Giaglis, G.M.: Mobile Advertising Effectiveness: an Exploratory Study. In: International Conference on Mobile Business, ICMB 2006, June 26-27, p. 2 (2006),
    http://ieeexplore.ieee.org/stamp/sta-mp.jsp?tp=&ar-
    number=4124097&isnumber=4124089, doi:10.1109/ICM-B.2006.30
18. Drossos, D., Giaglis, G.M., Lekakos, G.: An Empirical Assessment of Factors that Influence the Effectiveness of SMS Advertising. In: 40th Annual Hawaii International Conference on System Sciences, HICSS 2007, p. 58c (2007)
19. Ranganathan, A., Campbell, R.H.: Advertising in a pervasive computing environment. In: Proceedings of the 2nd International Workshop on Mobile Commerce, WMC 2002, pp. 10–14. ACM, New York (2002),
    http://doi.acm.org-/10.1145/570705.570708, doi:10.1145/570705.570708
20. Lee, C., Hsieh, M.: The Influence of Mobile Self-Efficacy on Attitude towards Mobile Advertising. In: New Trends in International Conference on Information and Service Science, NISS 2009, June 30-July 2, pp. 1231–1236 (2009),
    http://ieeexplore.ieee.org/stamp/stamp.
    jsp?tp=&arnum-ber=5260506&isnumber=5260409, doi:10.1109/NISS.2009.91
21. Haghirian, P., Madlberger, M., Inoue, A.: Mobile Advertising in Different Stages of Development: A Cross-Country Comparison of Consumer Attitudes. In: Proceedings of the 41st Annual Hawaii International Conference on System Sciences, January 7-10, p. 48 (2008),
    http://ieeexplore.ieee.org/stamp/
    stamp.jsp-?tp=&arnumber=4438752&isnumber=4438696,
    doi:10.1109/HICSS.2008.318

Virtual Fitting Room
Augmented Reality Techniques for e-Commerce

Francisco Pereira[1,2], Catarina Silva[1], and Mário Alves[2]

[1] Computer Science and Communication Research Centre
School of Technology and Management, Polytechnic Institute of Leiria, Portugal
[2] Redcats Portugal, SA
2091763@my.ipleiria.pt, catarina@ipleiria.pt,
mjalves@redoute.pt

Abstract. The area of augmented reality in e-commerce has become a reality in some companies and has great potential to spread. This paper focus on providing augmented reality solutions for e-commerce. We show that it is possible to define a strong platform for marketing products and for advertising promotions. Our approach is based on introducing computer vision in a hands-free augmented reality setting. The proposed framework is prepared to operate in two different environments: personal computers and public street marketing places.

Keywords: Augmented Reality, Computer Vision, E-Commerce.

1 Introduction

E-commerce is a strong application field of augmented reality applications. Specifically in the area of clothing sales, the inability of users to foresee how particular clothing will fit them when shopping online has always been a significant weakness. It was therefore naturally that people began to associate the area of augmented reality with electronic sale of clothing. This step allowed to overcome a difficult hurdle and raised the quality level and competitiveness of this business to new levels.

Augmented reality can be defined as an interactive combination of real and virtual in real time, registered in 3D [1]. The use of augmented reality in the retail market is being used by several companies like La Redoute[1] and Springfield[2]. In this context, different applications will be presented to define a background on the state-of-the-art in this field. The research of this work aims to understand the limitations and also to provide some augmented reality solutions in the sale of textile in e-commerce. The main limitations of current solutions include the need of additional localization aids or complex hardware, which can be difficult to deploy in different working environments, such as personal computers and public street marketing places.

---

[1] http://www.laredoute.pt
[2] http://spf.com

M.M. Cruz-Cunha et al. (Eds.): CENTERIS 2011, Part II, CCIS 220, pp. 62–71, 2011.

The rest of the paper is organized as follows. Section 2 introduces the background of the research, where we analyze two types of augmented reality applications and two projects with computer vision. In Section 3 we present the proposed solution and the possibility to use it in "street marketing". Section 4 finalizes the paper with the conclusions and possible lines of future work.

2   Background

In this section we will describe two applications of augmented reality in e-Commerce and explain with examples the advantages and disadvantages associated with each one. Specifically we present two different models of augmented reality that allow virtually dressing: "Augmented Reality with markers" and "Augmented Reality with silhouettes". These two models have in common the use of a digital camera to capture images in real time and the use of gestures instead of a mouse or a keyboard.

2.1   Augmented Reality with Markers

Augmented reality with markers is an application that can detect a marker in a paper and substitute it for a virtual object. For the application to detect the symbol printed on the paper, it will need to use a mechanism called image segmentation "Threshold". In a simplified form, this method converts each pixel color in white or black (respectively 0 or 1) depending on the level of image brightness. This need is due to the speed factor, because computers work better with '0 's and '1' s. The creation of markers is accomplished normally printing in black and white for the same reason.

By applying the filter, the application seeks the position of the marker in three dimensions (x, y and z) for the camera and also its orientation (e.g., if the symbol is in the front or on the side). After applying the filter and proceeding to detection, the software checks and detects the marker and after that the marker it is constantly replaced by a 3D object (this process is called rendering).

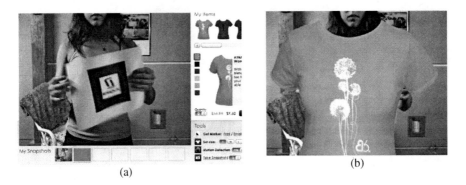

(a)

(b)

Fig. 1. Augmented Reality with markers. (a) Application search for the marker. (b) Marker replacement with a virtual object. (Adapted from http://www.zugara.com)

Figure 1 was taken from a video made available by Zugara[3] [2], which shows a web application of augmented reality that uses a digital camera to capture frames. Over the course of iterative capture of frames by the camera, each frame that "enters" the application is processed and analyzed in order to find a marker that is subsequently designed as clothes. Briefly, the application is constantly looking for a marker (Figure 1-a) on a white sheet so it can be replaced with a virtual object (Figure 1-b).

This process is rather unnatural to the user, especially together with constantly holding a sheet of paper with a symbol in front of a computer. Another limitation is the inconvenience to the user of this having to print the symbol for each application that uses this technology.

2.2 Augmented Reality with Silhouettes

Augmented reality with silhouettes is a type of augmented reality application that does not need any paper or marker, but rather obligates a person to be situated always in the same place. The silhouette can be seen as a blank person's (see Figure 2-a) and it must be placed at the center of the application window. The objective of this technique it is to help users to be placed at the right position. After the user places himself in the right position, the silhouette it is substituted by virtual clothes (Figure 2-b). The following example is taken from a video released by "Seventeen.com" [3] where the functioning modes are explained.

          (a)   (b)

Fig. 2. Augmented Reality with silhouettes. (a) Placement of the user in the silhouette. (b) Substitution of the silhouette for the clothes. (Adapted from "Seventeen.com")

After correct positioning of the user, she can freely manipulate the application through gestures. Those gestures may be: change clothes, photography, product information and product evaluation.

---

[3] http://www.zugara.com

2.3 Using Computer Vision for Head Tracking

The type of application "Augmented Reality with markers" requires the printing of a special symbol on a blank sheet and obligates the users to constantly hold the printed sheet so that the virtual image moves. On the other hand, Augmented Reality with silhouettes does not need any markers, but has the great disadvantage of requiring the users to be located in the same place when they are experimenting with virtual clothing.

To have a solution that does not use any type of markers, silhouettes or avatars, a survey was carried out to find ways to know how we can detect a person in real time and then put clothes virtually on, allowing the user the ability to be placed freely where he wants. To solve this problem, we resorted to the area of computer vision more specifically to head tracking systems.

Computer vision, according to Dana Ballard and Christopher Brown [4], is the construction of explicit, meaningful descriptions of physical objects from images. This area is designed to allow computers to be able to analyze, interpret and extract information about objects contained in images. These may vary from image sequences, view of multiple cameras or digital images released.

There is a wide range of applications using computer vision for detection a person in the area of augmented reality but in the following we will detail two specific paradigmatic research projects.

2.3.1 Application for Head Tracking

This application was developed by Daniel Baggio [5] (Figure 3) and is called "6 degrees of freedom head tracking"[4]. It has the ability to detect a person's face and superimpose it with masks or other virtual objects. This mask has the ability to move according to the movements of the head of the users. In technological terms, it only uses open source software: OpenCV [6] and OpenGL/GLUT [7]. OpenCV is a tool for image processing and computer vision algorithms; this includes how to detect the human body, faces, eyes, nose, upper body, among others. OpenGL/GLUT behaves as a graphical design tool such as DirectX.

In sum, the application finds a person's face with OpenCV and projects on it with a 3D format mask over his face with OpenGL, after which it follows the movements of the face again with OpenCV.

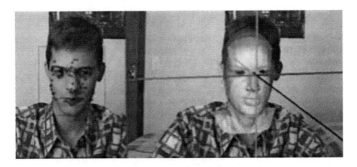

Fig. 3. "Head Tracking" application [5]

---

[4] http://code.google.com/p/ehci/wiki/6dofhead

2.3.2 YDreams Solution

YDreams[5] is a Portuguese company that works in several interesting applications in the area of augmented reality. The applications developed by YDreams allow the user to create an interactive environment and mixed between real and virtual. Figure 4-a shows an application in which a person is in front of a webcam and a monitor. The application detects the person and puts a virtual animated balloon in the top of his head simulating what the person is thinking. Another application is to put a virtual doll to play a game with a person. The doll walks after the person that it detects. This placement of the virtual doll along the ground it is possible by detection of the environment that surrounds.

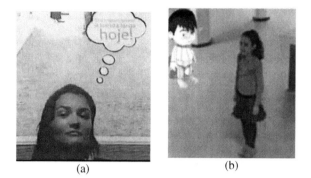

(a)   (b)

Fig. 4. Different augmented reality applications [8]

This application was developed using a proprietary platform, YVision created by YDreams. This platform aims to enable easy creation of modular interactive environments using augmented reality, image processing, computer vision and mobile technologies, among others.

This computing platform also uses the following open source tools: OpenCV, the Ogre3D and Open Dynamics Engine (ODE). The Ogre3D is a 3D library for OpenGL and/or Direct3D. This tool is widely used in video games and rendering of 3D objects. The ODE is an engine that has as main features the ability to simulate the drive mechanism of objects and collision handling. The OpenCV is, as mentioned before, a computer vision tool for image processing.

3 Proposed Approach

After the analysis of the two previously presented models of augmented reality and also of the two projects that include augmented reality and computer vision with head tracking, we reached the stage of creating a Virtual Fitting Room (VFR) framework for developing a solution for personal computer and for street marketing.

The base of this work was developed with C++ because it is a portable language, fast and free to use and develop. Like the last two projects (YVision and "6 degrees of

---

[5] http://www.ydreams.com

freedom head tracking") this application also uses OpenCV and OpenGL. The architecture was separated in three areas: Augmented Reality, Computer Vision and Image processing, as is depicted in Figure 5.

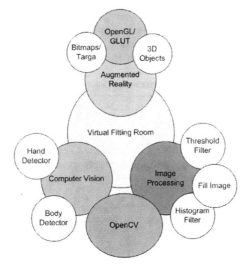

Fig. 5. Virtual Fitting Room context

For augmented reality we used OpenGL to put the virtual objects and for the Computer Vision and Image Processing we used only OpenCV. With OpenGL we use clothes with 2D images but it is possible to use 3D objects in the future. With OpenCV we adapted an algorithm created by Andol Li [9] to detect the human body color (Figure 6). In this algorithm we use a range in RGB color format (min (0,30,80) ->max (20, 150, 255)) to detect the color and if the image has any pixel that is in that range it will turn it to white other wise to black. This was used to detect the action on the buttons if a button finds that more then 1/3 of his size was occupied with white it accepts the detection.

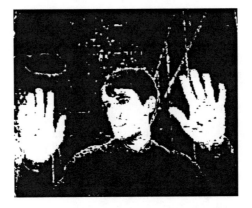

Fig. 6. Hand detector algorithm

For detection of the human body or head tracking we use a Haar classifier from OpenCV. These functions were originally developed by Viola & Jones in 2001 [10] only to detect faces. This classifier uses artificial intelligence for detection of any object that we train; fortunately OpenCV has many classifiers that we can use like upper body and head (Figure 7). In your case we chose to detect the upper body because it is faster and more accurate then only for the head. This upper body we use was "train" by Hannes Kruppa and Modesto Castrill [11].

Fig. 7. Virtual Fitting Room setup

The histogram filter equilibrates the light of the image. This is important, since the light is one of the main limitations of this kind of applications. If we do not put the image too much darker or shiner we usually have better results. We are using this filter for every frame that is captured.

Figure 8 presents a flowchart of the application. For every new frame that it is captured it will pass through all the process. The histogram filter will help the "Upper Body Detector" and the "Hand Detector". The result of the detector case it finds anybody will be two points that we can use to make a rectangle. This detector may not be run on every frame, making the program faster but, at the same time, loosing same precision in the detection. After the detection, the OpenGL reproduces the dress and places them down the neck. The "Hand Detector" tries to find in all the buttons more than 1/3 of skin color in them if it finds in any button it will process the action of that button. All of this process will be repeated over and over again always starting with a new frame.

3.1 Solution for Personal Computer

With the application presented in the last section, we can import it to a Web server. Unfortunately it is not possible to also import it directly but we can use the ideas of the presented work to implement a solution in Adobe Flash with OpenCV. For the server side with this idea we can make the consumers happier making the application exhibit more natural movements then the actual ones. The requirements for use on the client side are: VGA digital camera, internet connection and a browser that allows the use of Adobe Flash technology.

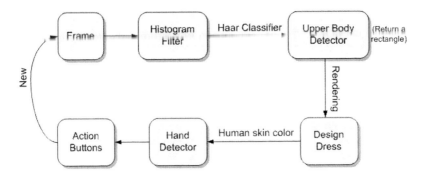

Fig. 8. Flowchart of the Virtual Fitting Room

3.2 Solution Environment "Street Marketing"

For "Street Marketing" for instance in a shopping mall or even in the street, we developed a real solution that is prepared to be used (Figure 9). In this solution we can select the gender of the person to specify the catalogue, the size of the clothes (S;M;L;XL), choose lots of different clothes, take a photo and publish it on Facebook. To publish on Facebook it was created an application where we have to login and give permission to create an album and post a photo in it.

Fig. 9. Virtual Fitting Room for Street Marketing

3.3 Environmental Constraints

Throughout this study, we concluded that there were four major problems for the use of such applications with gestures and body probes, these are: lighting conditions, camera positioning, ability to measure the size of the people and the "noise" of the environment.

The lighting condition that the digital camera receives may have serious problems in using this type of applications. The ideal conditions for the operation are: having a lighted space and not have a glowing light to the camera. There are algorithms used to "balance" playing with the brightness of the image brightness and contrast, for example, changing the image histogram.

Normally the cameras have VGA resolution with 640 by 480 pixels, which makes a difference of a quarter of its size. This dimension would be ideal if we were only interested in detecting the upper body and not the entire body. If the goal is to detect and "play" with the clothes with the whole body, the ideal scenario would be that the resolution be the reverse, more vertical and less horizontal.

A major difficulty that a person usually has to choose what clothes will buy in this type of market is to know exactly what the ideal size is. Unfortunately it is impossible to know people geometric measurements when using only a VGA camera. However, y using more than one camera it is already possible to measure the distance from which a person lies to the cameras. The simplest solution is to use this case with the Kinect[6], that in addition of using a digital camera, comes with two infrared cameras known as 3D depth sensors to grasp the depth of the environment.

Finally, the last limitation is the ambient noise. A practical example of this limitation occurred when an algorithm has been tested for the detection of a person's entire body around a pillar. When a person stood near that pillar when the algorithm was working, the person was not detected. If the person starts to deviate from the pillar, the probe was already done so and the noise disappeared.

4 Conclusions and Future Work

In this paper we presented a virtual fitting room framework with augmented reality techniques for e-commerce. Different approaches were analyzed and tested. The use of face detectors in this kind of applications opposing to not having to use both markers as silhouettes creates a friendlier environment between the user and machine. In addition to this analysis, an application was developed to test the technology with OpenCV and OpenGL, based on the proposed six degrees of freedom head tracking. The work was developed and designed to street marketing and the environmental test was very promising.

Possible lines of future include alternatives to common webcams, using for instance the Kinect, which could be advantageous by grasping a perception of the environment in three dimensions. Yet another possibility of future work is using augmented reality with computer vision to detect pages of a fashion catalogue, through a mobile application and further information or to place multimedia elements.

References

1. Azuma, R.: A Survey of Augmented Reality Presence: Teleoperators and Virtual Environments (1997)
2. Zugara: Zugara's Augmented Reality & Motion Capture Shopping App., http://www.youtube.com/watch?v=NxQZuo6pFUw (accessed March 30, 2011)

---

[6] http://www.xbox.com/kinect

3. Seventeen.com. Augmented Reality Online Shopping,
   http://www.youtube.com/watch?v=fhjuSMDJ4-U (accessed March 30, 2011)
4. Ballard, D., Brown, C.: Computer Vision. Prentice Hall, Englewood Cliffs (1982)
5. Oficial site of OpenCV, http://opencv.willowgarage.com/wiki/
   (accessed March 30, 2011)
6. OpenGL, http://www.opengl.org/ (accessed March 30, 2011)
7. Baggio, D.: EHCI 0.6 - Ransac, more robust,
   http://www.youtube.com/watch?v=BovphSjw_tI (accessed March 30, 2011)
8. YDreams. YDreams - About us, http://www.ydreams.com/#/en/aboutus/
9. Li, A.: Hands detection demonstration (July 27, 2009),
   http://www.andol.info/hci/1116.htm (accessed March 29, 2011)
10. Viola, Jones: IJCV See pages 1,3. Robust Real-time Object Detection. In: Second
    International Workshop on Statistical and Computational Theories of Vision – Modelling,
    Learning, Computing, Computing and Sampling, Canada (January 3, 2001)
11. Kruppa, H., Castrill, M., Schiele, B.: Fast and Robust Face Finding via Local Context. In:
    Proceedings of the Joint IEEE International Workshop on Visual Surveillance and
    Performance Evaluation of Tracking and Surveillance (2003)

Towards an Enterprise Information Subsystem for Measuring (Perceived) Landside Accessibility of Airports

Maarten Janssen, Jan van den Berg, Mohsen Davarynejad, and Vincent Marchau

Delft University of Technology, Faculty of Technology,
Policy and Management Jaffalaan 5, 2628 BX Delft, The Netherlands
mail@maartenjanssen.com,
{J.vandenberg,M.Davarynejad,V.A.W.J.Marchau}@tudelft.nl

Abstract. For modern airports that daily receive up to a hundred thousand or more passengers, visitors and workers, easy accessibility is key in order to become the preferred multi-modal hub. To achieve high-quality accessibility by means of all kinds of transport modalities, an Enterprise Information Subsystem (EIS) that measures the quality of the provided airport accessibility is a conditio sine qua non. This paper takes up the challenge for designing such an information system while taking the landside perspective. The main contribution concerns a *performance measurement framework* in which clients' demands can be related to the transport services offered by means of a measurable set of accessibility indicators. Based on this, an overall picture on the airport accessibility quality can be created. To illustrate the feasibility of the framework, the results of three (partial) implementation steps towards an EIS are shown. The first one relates to client profiling; the other two to performance measuring dashboards. We finalize by reflecting on the use of the performance measurement system for improved decision-making and by drawing conclusions.

Keywords: airport accessibility, transport modalities, performance framework, dashboard, enterprise information subsystem.

1 Introduction

The bigger airports of today usually service hundreds of connections to worldwide airports in many different countries [1]. As a consequence, thousands of people are daily travelling to such an airport, including travellers, visitors, and workers. All these actors prefer to have fast and easy access to the airport. It is now recognized that airport accessibility is a major determinant of airport choice [2]. This in fact concerns the *perceived* accessibility, i.e., the amount of accessibility travellers and workers experience when travelling to the airport. Evidently, the preferences of different traveller groups towards airport accessibility might vary.

Usually, travelling to an airport can be done by using different transport modalities including public transport (like train, bus and metro), transport by taxi, and transport by (private) cars. The variety in the supply of the transport modalities as well as their

M.M. Cruz-Cunha et al. (Eds.): CENTERIS 2011, Part II, CCIS 220, pp. 72–81, 2011.

quality is supposed to strongly influence the perceived airport accessibility of the various traveller groups. Based on these arguments, a matching problem between demand for high-quality transport services and supply of all kind of transport modalities is identified. This matching problem is the central focus of this paper. Since both supply and demand are likely to vary in time, the matching problem to be solved is considered to be dynamic.

The literature on this subject shows awareness of the fact that accessibility of an airport is a considerable factor on the total airport valuation [2], [3], [4]. However, literature describing a solution for the identified matching problem was not found. For solving the problem, measuring the accessibility quality of an airport (as perceived by various groups of visitors) seems to be key as is underpinned by the following view: 'The ability to measure performance of operations can be seen as an important prerequisite for improvement.' [5]. Moreover, a case study among traffic workers at a major airport in the Netherlands (results of this case study are used throughout this article) revealed that although various necessary performance data sets are available, these data and the information that they contain are insufficiently used for strategic decision-making. Or, to express this in words as used by one of the airport workers: 'We just don't know how well we are doing our job.' [1].

Based on these observations, it is argued that there is a need for a method and system to measure accessibility performance, as a starting point to optimise the accessibility of international airports. As a first step into fulfilling this need, the *aim of this paper* is to introduce a performance measurement framework that identifies (*i*) the various airport clients and their demands, (*ii*) the various transport services and their characteristics, and (*iii*) a way the clients' demands can be related to the transport services offered. In addition, some implementation examples are given showing the way the framework can be used to create a complete performance measurement Enterprise Information Subsystem (EIS).

The remainder of this paper is structured as follows. In section 2, the accessibility challenges of modern airports are specified and the notion of accessibility performance is discussed. Next, in section 3, it is shown how client accessibility needs and transport services offered can be related to each other by means of a basic set of quality factors. This paves the way for designing the performance measurement framework. Section 4 shows the result of some first explorations on implementing the framework in a performance measurement EIS. In section 5, a reflection is provided on the obtained results and upon the possibilities to use the system. Finally conclusions are drawn in section 6. For more details, reference [1] is recommended.

2   Landside Accessibility Performance of Airports

2.1   Airport Accessibility Performance

Performance on quality to the client in the service industry can be described as: 'The degree in which a company is able to offer service solutions that meet the client's demands' [9]. Here, the service solutions concern the different transport modalities to access an airport. Basically, accessibility can be seen as the capability to reach a desired destination. The term accessibility in transportation planning is often used with a relatively vague definition like 'the ease and convenience of access to spatially distributed opportunities with a choice of travel' [6], [7]. According to Shriner and Hoel [8], the main function of the airport-landside access system is to provide service to airport passengers and visitors. Superimposed on this continuous activity, it also concerns the travel conducted by airport workers and cargo transporters. The accessibility services offered by an airport must focus on furnishing circulation, distribution, and storage of vehicles. The same authors also state that the capabilities of the available infrastructure are most of the time limited and the possibilities to quickly provide new facilities unlikely. Therefore the basic challenge for the people who are responsible for airport accessibility is to operate existing facilities more efficiently.

A first step to analyze the quality of accessibility is to operationalise the term into a set of concrete and relevant outcomes of interest, i.e. criteria/factors that form the basis for decisions of travelers towards airports. Accessibility here concerns accessibility as enabled by the available transport services towards the airport. In addition, the factors to be chosen should be measurable quantities, either directly or indirectly. In short, a basic set of measurable accessibility indicators is needed that enables assessing accessibility to an airport as made available by means of various transport services.

Table 1. List of six basic accessibility performance indicators and their decomposition into 34 transport performance characteristics (further explanation is given below)

COST	TRANSPORT COSTS	PRICE TRANSPARAN-CY	PARKING COST				
TIME	TRANSFER/ WAITING TIME	TRAVEL DISTANCE	AMOUNT OF TRANSFERS	DISTANCE ARRIVAL AND TERMINAL/ OFFICE	TOTAL TRAVELTIME	FEELING OF EFFICIENCY (DISTANCE/ TIME)	WAITING TIME ON EGRESS
RELIABILITY	CHANCE ON CANCELLA-TION	TRAVEL ALTERNATIVES	DELAY DUE TO UNCLEAR SIGN POSTING	DELAY ON AIRORT GROUNDS	CHANCE ON DELAY	DELAY (IN TIME)	
QUALITY	WAITING COMFORT ON AIRPORT	LUGGAGE SPACE DURING TRANSPORT	SAFETY MODALITY	DRIVING QUALITY OF CHAUFFEUR	WORK/ ENTERTAIN-MENT DURING TRANSPORT	SEAT COMFORT	CLEANLI-NESS INTERIOR
	ATTITUDE STAFF MODALITY	FINDABILITY TERMINAL	ATTITUDE AIRPORT TRAFFIC OPERATION PERSONELL	CURBSIDE SAFETY ON AIRPORT GROUNDS	FINDABILITY MODALITY		
CONVE-NIENCE	INCREASED WAITING DUE TO UNDERCA-PACITY	TRAVEL FREQUENCY	OPERATIO-NAL TIMES MODALITY				
INFORMA-TION	TRAVEL INFORMATI-ON IN MODALITY AND STOP	REAL TIME INFORMATION ON DEVATIONS	PRICE INFORMATI ON IN MODALITY AND STOP				

Inspection of literature for useful performance measures of perceived airport accessibility by travelers yielded a useful starting point in reference [8]. It identifies 12 measures to evaluate landside access for airports. It turned out however that for the purpose of this paper not all of them are relevant [1]. Therefore it was decided to organize a few sessions with transport experts working at our case study airport. As a result of those activities, six relevant basic *performance indicators* have been identified, namely, *cost, time, quality, reliability, convenience,* and *information.* In order to make the overall performance measurable, these 6 identified indicators have next been decomposed in 34 different, detailed, and measurable *transport performance characteristics* (see table 1). The precise way of how the performance characteristics determine the 6 performance indicators and, based on those, the overall performance needs a dedicated analysis but this topic is outside scope of this paper (for some explorations on this, see [1] where a 'weighted tree' approach is proposed).

2.2 Landside Transport Modalities

In this subsection, we focus on the other side of the matching problem by considering some characteristics of the different available transport modalities at the supply side. Continuing our case study, we found out that quite a number of transport facilities is present. An overview of these is provided in figure 1.

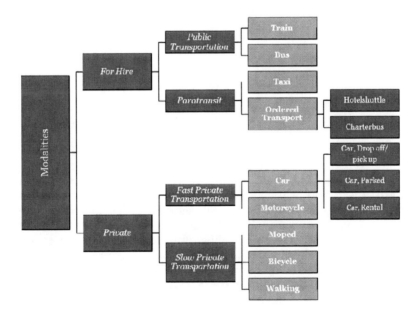

Fig. 1. Example of available transport facilities towards an airport

The next challenge is the design of a performance measurement framework for matching supply and demand. This will be undertaken in the next section.

3   Designing the Performance Measurement Framework

The design challenge is a matching problem. The outcome of it should be a quantified performance measure. A first step here is to investigate whether different client groups have indeed different demands. Actually, a confirmation for the posed hypothesis was found based on the content of figure 2: it can easily be seen that the two different actors identified, being airport workers and airport travelers, show a different distribution of the use of different transport modalities. Based on this idea, several demand profiles need to be defined, each of which corresponds to a specific client group.

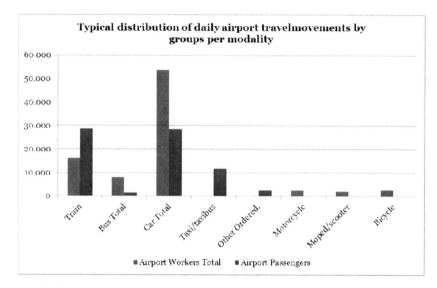

Fig. 2. Distribution of the use of transport modalities by different client groups

Based on the above-given analysis, we designed the contours of the performance framework that is shown in figure 3. It shows how, in principle, each client demand profile on the left hand side can be used to select the best mix of transport modalities on the right hand side, vice versa. *Demand profiles* can be determined based on client characteristics: clients can be just visitors of the airport or people who arrive or depart by plane, they may be airport workers, first class business people, holiday backpackers, etc. It is clear that their demand profiles differ with respect to cost, time, reliability, convenience and other airport accessibility quality factors. The numbers in the figures show the number of clients of that type per day. On the right hand side of the figure some information is given on the way the travel & transport department of the airport can control, guide or influence the *performance characteristics* of the various transport modalities. To find an optimal match, the performance characteristics of the transport modalities should also be expressed in terms of the accessibility quality factors cost, time, reliability, convenience, etc. The extent to which the airport can control, guide or influence each transport modality was investigated in more detail by means of a responsibility analysis of all transport stakeholders involved [1]. Instead of elaborating on that, we prefer here to add some information on implementation issues of the framework in the next section.

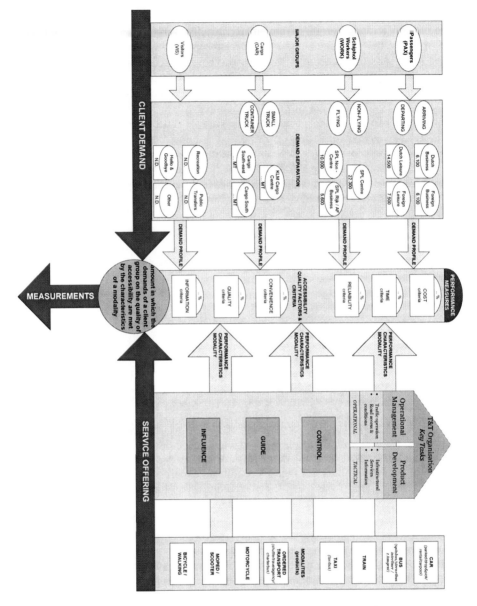

Fig. 3. Generic framework for measuring airport accessibility performance

4 On Implementing the Performance Measurement System

Client Profiles. From the information given in figure 2, it was concluded that different traveler groups do have different transport quality needs. These needs have been specified in more detail by conducting an experiment focusing on the two biggest client groups being passengers and airport workers. To get feedback from members of these groups, the 34 criteria mentioned in table 1 were put onto separate post-it notes and collected in random order in containers. Different colors were used for the post-it notes in a way that criteria belonging to the same quality factor (cost, time, etc.) were put on notes with the same color. Next, two types of large posters were created, one for each client group. On each poster a horizontal axis was drawn with values going from 'no influence' via 'some influence' to 'great influence'. The posters were placed on different locations at the airport and people were asked to put one (randomly selected) post-it note on the poster at a location that, according their perception as either a passenger or an airport worker, corresponds to its influence on airport accessibility. The experiment was 8 times repeated per client group (16 times in total). Based on careful visual inspections of the various experiments evidence was found for the hypothesis that different client groups have different demand profiles [1].

Actually, the posters can also be used to link weights to the different criteria by putting a grid of 5 cells on the poster, with weight values 1, 2, 3, 4 and 5. By adding up the various weight values of all criteria, a weight per quality factor can be defined for all different client groups. In this way, each profile corresponds to a set of *weighted* quality factors. An example of a poster with weights is shown here:

Fig. 4. Example of a segmented poster with post-it notes showing weights values from 1 till 5

Differentiation scores. As said, demand profiles can be determined based on the position of the post-it notes from the 16 conducted experiments. To do so, the average score of each criterion has been calculated together with the standard deviation, modus and median [1]. The criteria that belonged to the same performance indicator (color) were also averaged to get a weight score at factor level. When the combined indicator scores are compared between the two client groups of airport workers and airport passengers, the differences in demands become clear. As can be seen from the results shown in table 2 (next page), there is a significant difference in the quality demands towards accessibility between these two traveler groups. Especially the weights of cost, reliability and information show a high difference in valuation.

Table 2. Resulting performance indicator weights of two traveler groups as calculated from the collected data

Factor	Cost	Time	Reliability	Quality	Convenience	Information
Passenger	3,9	3,6	4,6	3,3	4,1	1,4
Worker	1,8	4,2	3,2	2,4	4,3	2,7

Dashboards' development. Measuring accessibility performance in practice using the framework developed above requires quite a lot of data sources since, according to our design, this involves 34 performance values (remember table 1). If these values would be available from an enterprise information subsystem, a weighted scheme can be used to get an estimation of the overall accessibility performance as perceived by the different client groups. As weights, the weights as found in our experiment described above can be used. The final results could be made available by means a dashboard, like in other business intelligence-inspired applications.

Unfortunately, an investigation revealed that many of the necessary data sources are not yet available at airports. However, some of them are available and based on those it was quite easy to create a dashboard [13] that is able to show over time the (un-weighted) values of several key performance indicators including volumes of passengers per transport modality, day and month, and trends on client satisfaction on airport accessibility [1]. This first, simple dashboard can be seen as a first step in developing a dashboard that calculates the full accessibility performance of an airport based on which operational, tactical and strategic decisions can be prepared.

An important missing link of the sketched approach is that the *perception* of the different traveler groups is not considered. For that purpose, another experiment was set up where - based on tweets (short messages) collected from the social network sites like Twitter [10] - data were collected to measure real-time sentiments on the accessibility of the airport. In the implementation, the data collection service of Socialmention [11] has been used. In this service, different social media can first be real-time queried and the incoming data next sorted, processed, and normalized. A simple system was set up where, for each half an hour, the data collected by Socialmention were put in an excel sheet that can be considered as a first version of a second dashboard. To measure the sentiment of travelers about the transport service they use, the number of times a selected group of words occur in the data were calculated. Some words have a positive connotation like 'nice, 'fast' and contribute to a positive sentiment, while other words like 'disruption', 'delay', 'failure' represent a negative sentiment. Aggregation of the sentiment data yields an indication of the perceived transport quality and how this changes over time. For more details of this first version dashboard system, we refer to [1]. To gain better insight in perceived accessibility of travelers based on social network sites' data, more sophisticated web and text mining approaches should be applied [14]. This is part of future research.

5   Reflecting on the Next Steps

Measuring perceived airport accessibility in practice is no sinecure. By using the generic framework for measuring airport accessibility performance, we have shown that there exist various ways to realize a concrete implementation. Our explorations however, are just initial experiments. Evidently, these experiments should be further developed along the following lines:

1. First start thinking and deciding on what models and methods are applicable in measuring perceived accessibility of client groups.
   (the introduced 'weighted quality factor approach' may be chosen here, next to the social network site-based approach, among others[1]);
2. Knowing in detail the methods to be used, corresponding data collection and storage in an EIS can start;
3. Next, several experiments should be executed, the outcomes of which should be validated;
4. Having developed and implemented these methods according accepted standards, decision makers can be trained on how to interpret the data and information as collected in the several dashboards.

6 Conclusions

In this paper, the challenge has been to design an Enterprise Information Subsystem (EIS) that measures the accessibility quality as perceived by people traveling to an airport. For all kinds of reasons, this is a complex matter. For example, different people in practice do have different travel demands. In practice, many different transport modalities are often present. Aggregating data into information assumes the availability of data. For aggregating data into relevant information, we need the right mathematical models that have been validated in practice.

After having explored and analyzed various aspects of different client demands and several transport modalities yielding a list of six basic *accessibility performance indicators* and their decomposition into 34 transport performance characteristics, we have designed a *generic framework for measuring airport accessibility performance*. This concerns the main outcomes of our research. In the remainder of the text, several ways to use the framework in order to realize an implementation of a concrete enterprise information subsystem have been explored. This results obtained relate to client profiling and to the implementation of two dashboards on measuring accessibility performance. These experiments have shown that the framework contains all kinds of points of contact that support the work towards a concrete implementation.

We are aware of the fact that still much work is needed to come to a fully operational and validated EIS for measuring airport accessibility that is truly useful in practice. A 4-steps approach has been recommended to develop and deploy such an EIS.

References

1. Janssen, M.J.: A Performance Measurement System for Schiphol's Traffic & Transportiation, Measuring Perceived Landside Accessibility of Multimodal Airports. Master's Thesis, Delft University of Technology, Faculty of Technology, Policy and Management, The Netherlands (2011)

---

[1] In current research, a multi-criteria decision-making (MCDM) method has been chosen to integrate the aforementioned performance indicators (table 1) in a structured way. The Analytic Hierarchy Process (AHP) (first introduced by Saaty [12]) is one of the most commonly used MCDM methods in such a situation. Because of the inherently vagueness of human judgment, a fuzzy version of AHP is preferred here.

2. Transportation Research Board: Airport Cooperative Research Program, Airport Ground Access Mode Choice Models. Techical Report, Synthesis 5, 151 (2008)
3. Gosling, G.D.: Predictive reliability of airport ground access mode choice models. Airlines, Airports, and Airspace: Economic and Infrastructure Analysis, Technical Report, pp. 69–75 (2006)
4. Humphreys, I., Ison, S.: Changing airport employee travel behaviour: the role of airport surface access strategies. Trans. Pol. 12, 1–9 (2005)
5. Lohman, C., Fortuin, L., Wouters, M.: Designing a performance measurement system: a case study. European J. of Oper. Res. 156, 267–286 (2004)
6. Dong, X., Ben-Akiva, M.E., Bowmann, J.L., Walker, J.L.: Moving from trip-based to activity-based measures of accessibility. Trans. Res. Part A: Pol. and Pract. 40, 163–180 (2006)
7. Shi, J., Ying, X.: Accessibility of a Destination-Based Transportation System: A Large Airport Study. Tsinghua Sc. and Techn. 13, 211–219 (2008)
8. Shriner, H.W., Hoel, L.A.: Evaluating improvements in landside access for airports. Trans. Res. Record 1662, 32–40 (1999)
9. Abe, M., Jeng, J.J., Li, Y.: A tool framework for KPI application development. In: Proceedings of the IEEE International Conference on e-Business Engineering (ICEBE 2007), Hong Kong, China, pp. 22–29 (2007)
10. Twitter, http://twitter.com/
11. SocialMention, http://urlinformatie.nl/www.socialmention.com
12. Saaty, T.L.: The Analytic Hierarchy Process. McGraw-Hill, New York (1980)
13. Turban, E., Sharda, R., Delen, D.: Decision Support Systems and Business Intelligence Systems, 9th edn. Pearson Prentice Hall (2011)
14. Nasraoui, O., Zaiane, O., Spiliopoulou, M., Mobasher, B., Yu, P., Masand, B. (eds.): WebKDD 2005. LNCS (LNAI), vol. 4198. Springer, Heidelberg (2006)
15. Azofra, V., Prieto, B., Santidrian, A.: The usefulness of a performance measurement system in the daily life of an organisation: a note on a case study. British Acc. Rev. 35, 367–384 (2006)
16. Bourne, M., Neely, A., Mills, J., Platts, K.: Implementing performance measurement systems: a literature review. Int. J. of Buss. Perf. Mgt. 5, 1–24 (2003)
17. Correia, A.R., Wirasinghe, S.C., De Barros, A.G.: A global index for level of service evaluation at airport passenger terminals. Trans. Res. Part E: Logistics and Transportation Review 44, 607–620 (2008)
18. Folan, P., Browne, J.: A review of performance measurement: towards performance management. Computers in Industry 56, 663–680 (2005)
19. Jehanfo, S., Dissanayake, D.: Modeling surface access mode choice of air passengers. Proceedings of the Institution of Civil Engineers: Transport 162, 87–95 (2009)
20. Neely, A., Mills, J., Platts, K., Richards, H., Gregory, M., Bourne, M., Kennerley, M.: Performance measurement system design: developing and testing a process-based approach. Int. J. of Op. and Pr. Mgt. 20, 1119–1145 (2000)

AEMS: Towards an Advanced Event Management System

Paulo Cristo[1] and Ricardo Martinho[1,2]

[1] School of Technology and Management, Polytechnic Insitute of Leiria
[2] Computer Science Communication and Research Centre, Polytechnic Institute of Leiria
Morro do Lena, Alto do Vieiro, 2411-901 Leiria, Portugal
cristo.paulo@gmail.com, ricardo.martinho@ipleiria.pt

Abstract. Open source event management systems such as OpenConf, Easychair and CiviCRM do not foresee the activities, resource allocation and costs management features necessary to each programmed event item. In this paper we present AEMS – an advanced event management system with project management like features. We present the requirements for such features, based on a case study carried out with a real-world customer. Then, we describe the development of AEMS and discuss its data model, architecture and the developed prototype. With AEMS, our customer will be able to manage all activities, resources and costs associated with an event. The results from applying our development to our real-world customer will allow us to derive AEMS to a generic software product.

Keywords: Event management, project management, registration, activities, participants, tasks and assignments, schedules, calendar, notifications, access levels, reporting, dashboards, teams, open source.

1 Introduction

Event management is the process by which an event is planned, prepared and produced. Like any other form of management, it involves the assessment, definition, acquisition, allocation, direction, control and analysis of time, finances, people, products, services, and other resources, in order to achieve objectives [2]. An event can also be described as an "organized occasion such as a meeting, convention, exhibition, special event, gala dinner, etc. An event is often composed of several different yet related functions" [3].

When we are referring to events, we are including a broad range of genres, like workshops, presentations, conferences, seminaries, fairs and festivals, business and corporate events, government and civic events, sports events, etc. Current approaches to Event Management Systems (EMS) cover a range of these kinds of events, but lack support for registering associated managing activities. For example, a conference program has sessions (program items), which in turn have a range of managing activities (management items) such has room preparations, scheduling and session chair assignments.

The most common features that we can find in current EMSs are: Attendee´s registration; Event scheduling; Contact management; Automatic notifications; Event publishing (event info page) and Invoice and payment functionalities.

M.M. Cruz-Cunha et al. (Eds.): CENTERIS 2011, Part II, CCIS 220, pp. 82–90, 2011.
© Springer-Verlag Berlin Heidelberg 2011

In this paper, we propose AEMS: an event management system which, besides considering these common features, adds the following ones (detailed further in section 3): management items (tasks) associated with event program items; participant's management and role assignment to each management/program items, and schedule management; cost management for both management/program items. We named our project "advanced" due to the inclusion of such features. Our approach includes Project Management Body of Knowledge [1] best practices regarding the scope management (presentation of work breakdown structures), time and cost management (scheduling and cost estimation processes). As a proof of concept, we also present a prototype for AEMS. For this implementation, we used scenarios from a real customer company, which events are mostly related with cultural and educational activities at a museum. Its main event kinds include guided visits, conferences, exhibitions, theater events and workshops.

Although we may have similar events occurring along the year (recurrence), each single event has very specific characteristics, so we felt the need for a generic tool that could, at the same time, not only accommodate the singularity of every event, but also respond efficiently to the identified common requirements.

This paper is organized as follows: the next section refers to most prominent related work on EMS solutions and approaches. Section 3 describes the overall architecture for our AEMS event management prototype, and section 4 presents an application example for this architecture. Section 5 concludes the paper and presents further developments.

2   Related Work

During our study, we tried to understand more about the EMSs available on the market. There are many commercial solutions out there, with huge differences in what concerns to the quality of the product itself and the number and relevance of the features included. Unfortunately, in almost every single case it is barely impossible for a common user to get in touch with the product, since there is no trial or demo version freely available. Most of the companies only provide a features list [8 11] that we have to rely on, and the possibility to request a demo meeting via a sales representative. Most of these tools are also extremely expensive for small businesses or individuals.

From what we were able to realize from publicly disposed information, the majority of these solutions are somewhat poor in terms of functionalities that we consider to be key features, especially in what concerns to project management capabilities for events. On the other hand, a few of them have so many "extra" features that they become extremely confusing from the user's point of view, making them inappropriate for non-skilled users [9,10].

Due to the difficulties on deeply studying any commercial software, we focused more on the open source market, were the offer is extremely shorter and fragmented, despite the existing demand that we can realize just by spending some time browsing the terms on the Internet. The existing projects are particularly oriented to a specific type of event, and they normally target the group formed by conferences [24] and seminaries and online ticket selling [7]. From the open source systems we analyzed, we found no EMS solution that could address the management activities of events.

Following is a short presentation of the open source tools that we took in special consideration either by its popularity or functionalities.

OpenConf [14] is a system that is used to manage online conferences, allowing paper and program submission, and reviewing features by other members. It is available in two versions; the community and the professional edition. OpenConf is used specifically for conferences, workshops and seminaries. It has no project management features and it is not suitable for other type of events. Its main features are: proposal submission, file upload, documents reviewing, email notifications, data export (SQL E CSV) and reporting, build online programs, offers and reviewing proposals.

EasyChair [15] is another free and widely spread conference management system, being used in more than 4000 conferences in 2011, according to information available on the project site. Like OpenConf, it is entirely designed to the same specific types of events and does not offer support for others. Its main capabilities are: automatic paper submission, paper assignment based on the preferences of PC members, list of the latest events, submission of reviews, sending email to PC members, referees and authors, monitoring email, online discussion of papers, automatic preparation of conference proceedings.

CiviCRM [16] is a totally different tool. It includes a Customer Relationship Management (CRM) set of modules, specially focused on fulfilling the needs of small, non-governmental, non-profitable and cooperative organizations. It is designed to allow data management about volunteers, activists and downers, as well as the handling of more generic contact types, like employees, customers and sales people. It integrates the CiviEvent module, which has some event management features. CiviCRM can be installed on top of a Content Management System (CMS), like Drupal [17] or Joomla [18]. This is the open source tool that we found more close to any commercial software, in terms of features, which include:• custom event types,• online registration for paid and free events, contacts management, automatic registration confirmations, Import and export participant data from other systems (CSV files), event data exporting features (iCal files).

Although CiviEvent has some of the capabilities we were looking for on an EMS, it is just a small subset of the CiviCRM application, and not purposely designed for event management. Therefore, it lacks all the project management aspects we are looking for, as well as some basic event related features we need, like the concept of event items (or sub-events), team assignments or any sort of visual agenda scheduling.

Storm [19] was another free tool that got our attention. Unlike the others mentioned in this paper, Storm is not an EMS at all, but a project management solution, with some interesting features that we would like to see on our AEMS system, especially in what concerns to organizing human resources, distributing them along the tasks/projects, and also because it has the possibility to create work tickets and manage execution times. It is also possible to create a few reports and do expenses control (costs management). Storm has a big part of the management features that we want to build for events, and because of that it was very helpful in clarifying our concept. Storm also integrates with the Drupal platform.

At first, we thought that these last two projects could be a perfect match if they could be integrated. Therefore, our first efforts were driven to the integration, customization and the extension of CiviCRM and Storm in one single application. However, we soon realized that a process involving tree different data models (Drupal, CiviCRM and Storm) designed with such different purposes, even if sharing the same core platform, would result in a bigger development effort than developing our EMS from scratch.

3   AEMS Requirements, Domain Model and Architecture

In this section we will present the requirements for our own EMS, as well as present a brief overview over the data model and the architecture of the system.

The main requirements for our system (customer´s and derived ones) are:

- Event and participant types. (we introduced the concept of "active" and "passive" participants)
- Participant   roles (attendee, presenter, host...)
- Event items (Our approach breaks down events into management items and program items)
- Contacts management
- Costs and budget control
- Team building and personal   time tables (worker time sheets)
- Automatic program building and file upload features
- Visual calendar scheduling
- Internationalization support (English and Portuguese)
- Participant's profile (with events list and activities)
- Dashboard and custom reports (for instance, monthly activities, type and number of attendees, budget/expenses tracking) with drill down features)
- Automatic email notifications
- Online payment features (credit card, bank transfer and paypal)
- Invoice and confirmation receipts
- Mailing lists and email marketing campaigns
- Tickets and badges printing
- Wait lists
- Registration management (participants, limits, groups)
- Different application   access levels (user roles based)
- Data import, export, and synchronization features (for contacts and events) with desktop (Outlook) and mobile client
- Publishing of an event profile (event website), with view and registration functionalities
- Social media networking
- Service layer for mobile applications

In the following figure we have a very brief overview of our core domain model. Events have participants (that can be of two types; active or passive, and have different roles assigned). Each event can have several event items (program or management). Every participant should be on our contact list. If the participant is internal to the company he belongs to a team and is associated with one department.

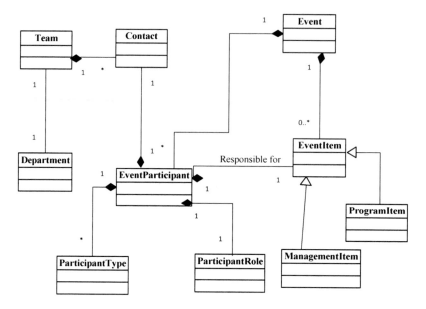

Fig. 1. Brief overview of the AEMS domain model

The domain model of Figure 1 is implemented by following the architecture illustrated in Figure 2.

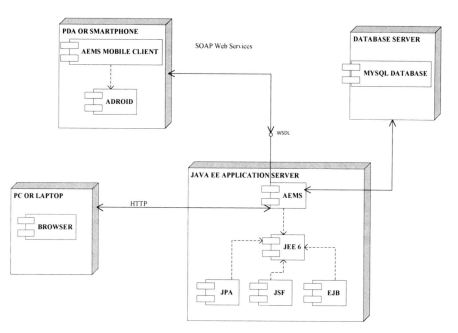

Fig. 2. AEMS architecture

It basically depicts a three layer architectural pattern implementation [15]. The core platform is Java EE 6 [20] and the application is built mainly using EJB's (Enterprise Java Beans), JPA (Java Persistence API) and JSF (Java Server Faces – Model-View-Controller MVC-based [5]) technologies deployed on a JEE application server. We use MySQL [21] server as backend database and we provide a web services layer (SOAP) [22] for interfacing with mobile clients.

4 Application Example

Following we show some screenshots of the application on earlier stages of the development process. They are result of use cases and acceptance tests carried out derived from regular meetings with customer. Figure 3 shows the main screen of the application where we have an agenda to easily view/edit any current event or act as a shortcut to create new ones. The main sections navigation menu is on top of the page and on the left corner we have relevant information about current or upcoming events, there is also a list of common tasks, actions or "todos" waiting for input. The main screen "widgets" may also vary according to login roles.

Fig. 3. Main page of AEMS

Figure 4 shows the employees work scales design page. In our customer´s case employees do not work the normal "Monday to Friday" week so we need to know who is available to work on a given day or week and who is not, in order to assign them tasks/events. In this page we can easily choose a person from a team/department (the person is identified by name and with a different color in the calendar) and then pick any date on the agenda to automatically inform the system that the person in question is working on that time period. At the bottom of the page the full year view calendar is also updated with the same information. We have other views where we can see the employee entire profile, regarding the events where he was involved (participant and events will be identified by the same color).

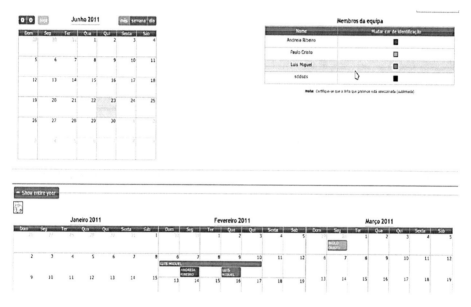

Fig. 4. Work scales design page

The next figure shows the event items edition page. We can edit an event and create self-contained sub-events (event items). These event items can be of two types: program items and management items. Program items are part of the event program itself and are visible to everyone (except if the event is not public), while management items are internal management activities that are not visible to the public in general. Each event item can also contain other event items. Event items are organized in hierarquical order inside an event. Every event item will have assigned a responsible person (an active participant) and a cost (can be zero). At the end we have a complete tree of all the tasks and activities that are part of the event and we can automatically build an event program from the program items information.

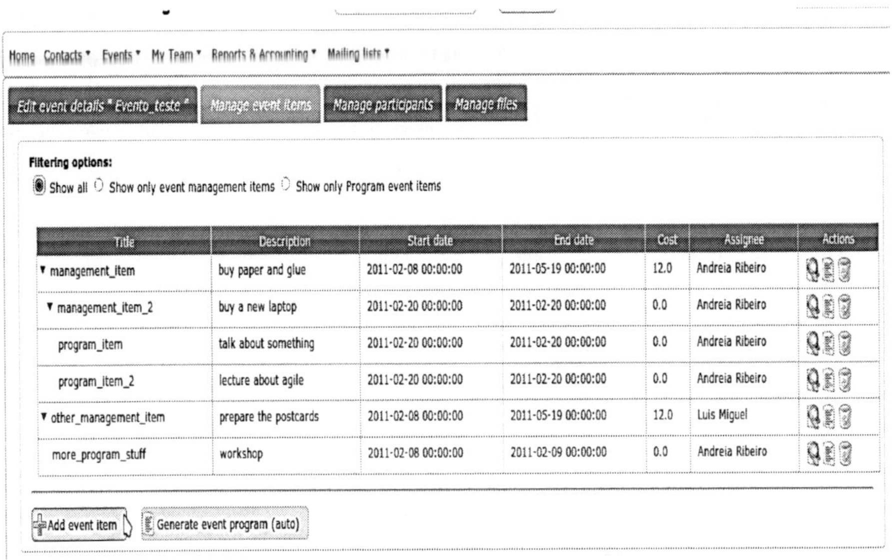

Fig. 5. Edit event / add event items

5   Conclusions and Future Work

We have developed a tool that allows end users to easily integrate and attach project management tasks and activities to events life cycle, from configuration to planning and management processes. We have presented the architecture, the domain model, and a functional prototype based on a real customer´s request. By performing several iterations and acceptance tests [6], we are validating each of the common and advanced features proposed.

As future work we are going to develop a mobile client for the android platform and add a service layer for other future clients. We are also considering the integration of a data synchronization server (Funambol [23] DS Server), that would allow synchronization of contacts and events between our web application and our mobile client(s), and also with Microsoft Outlook, therefore providing a support for exchanging updated and real time data with other systems, at the same time that can work as a backup system for events and contacts data.

References

1. Project Management Institute. A Guide to the Project Management Body of Knowledge (PMBoK). Project Management Institute, PMI (2008)
2. Silvers, Rutherford, J.: Event management Body of Knowledge (2003),
   http://www.juliasilvers.com/embok.htm
3. Accepted Practices Exchange (APEX) Industry Glossary of terms CIC (2003)
4. Fowler, M.: Patterns of Enterprise Applications Architecture (2002)

5. Reenska, T.: MVC XEROX PARC (1978), -79,
   http://heim.ifi.uio.no/~trygver/themes/mvc/mvc-index.html
6. Tito, D.V.: Avaliação da usabilidade do JEMS - Journal and Event Management System - através de avaliação heurística, ensaios de interacção e questionários de satisfação (IHC 2006)
7. Solaris, J.: The quest for an open source, free, complete event management software,
   http://www.eventmanagerblog.com/open-source/
   open-source-free-complete-event-management-software
8. Online Registration Center, Symphony Event Management Software,
   http://www.onlineregistrationcenter.com/features.asp,
   http://www.symphonyem.co.uk/Product/Features/
9. EventPro Event Management Software,
   http://www.eventpro.net/features/General.pdf
10. MISION Event Software,
    http://event-master.com/regis_key_features.html
11. Ennect Web Marketing Tools,
    http://www.ennect.com/Event/features.aspx
12. Online event registration, http://www.eventbrite.com
13. Event registration and ticketing, http://www.amiando.com/
14. OpenConf Peer Review & Conference Management System,
    http://www.openconf.org
15. EasyChair Conference System, http://www.easychair.org
16. CiviCrm Community Site, http://civicrm.org/civievent
17. Drupal CMS, http://drupal.org
18. Joomla CMS, http://www.joomla.org
19. Storm project, http://drupal.org/project/storm
20. JAVA Enterprise Edition,
    http://www.oracle.com/technetwork/java/javaee/
    overview/index.html
21. MySQL database, http://www.mysql.com
22. SOAP Simple Object Access Protocol version 1.2, W3C,
    http://www.w3.org/TR/soap/
23. Funambol Open Source Mobile Cloud Sync, http://www.funambol.com
24. Herceg, D., Marcicevic, Ž.: A lightweight conference management system in ASP.NET. Novi Sad J. Math. 39(1), 111–121 (2009)

Cloud Computing: A Platform of Services for Services

Nuno Sénica, Cláudio Teixeira, and Joaquim Sousa Pinto

DETI, University of Aveiro
{njs,claudio,jsp}@ua.pt

Abstract. This article describes the state of the art of cloud computing, focusing on its features and on the variety of services and applications that can be placed inside a cloud system, such as databases, processing, cloud gaming, storage and backup, etc.. This article also assesses and highlights the advantages and disadvantages of using cloud computing by companies and provides an overview of cloud computing trends and solutions currently available.

Keywords: Cloud Computing, IaaS, PaaS, DaaS, SaaS.

1 Introduction

The computing world is moving towards a new paradigm, where home computers (which have seen its processing power and capabilities exponentially increased in the last decades) are being replaced with small devices with low processing power and less capable of performing heavy tasks such as high definition video playback, 3D image rendering or heavy duty servers.

Nowadays, home computers have the ability to perform such tasks and also the required specifications to run them in parallel, either by the use of virtualization techniques, which may include several instances of several operating systems, or by using multiple applications/servers within the same operating system. These kind of applications usually require dedicated servers for intensive tasks and high speed broadband access for traffic intensive applications such as video streaming or online gaming, even though this configuration may not be available to the end user at a reasonable and affordable price. A new business opportunity has set which intends to provide storage space, internet bandwidth and a shared/dedicated server cluster where users are able to deploy their applications and make them available on the internet.

Companies like Amazon, Microsoft and Google (among others) are providing a mechanism and a business model in which the usage of their infrastructure is charged according to the used processing power and space allocation in a platform of services based on a cloud computing paradigm.

New applications and trends are now being studied and made available to the public. One of the major trends is related to cloud gaming where frame processing is done on a cloud environment and only video is sent to the client which interacts

M.M. Cruz-Cunha et al. (Eds.): CENTERIS 2011, Part II, CCIS 220, pp. 91–100, 2011.

as usual with the game. Also, the usage of mobile devices is exploding and, although those devices are quite powerful in terms of computational resources, they are battery powered making complex computations consume a large amount of battery resources due to the intense cpu utilization. [11] presents a study on how to use cloud computing to save energy on mobile systems, by offloading computational power in order to save energy.

There is currently no consensus on the definition of cloud computing [21], [4], however it is commonly agreed that the definition made by [13] is the closest and the more accurate. [13] defines cloud computing as "a model for enabling convenient, on-demand network access to a shared pool of configurable computing resources (e.g., networks, servers, storage, applications, and services) that can be rapidly provisioned and released with minimal management effort or service provider interaction.".

The term cloud computing, also known as cloud, appeared after the usage of a cloud to depict the internet or a network, thus abstracting its real components. In the case of cloud computing, the main goal is to take that abstraction to the next level, representing a large network, the way it works and is deployed to provide its services. Neither how it works, how it is deployed or even how it scales have to be clear to their users as long as it fulfills the users' needs, which only need to take into account: 1) how to use it and 2) how much it costs. Nevertheless, a question is always posed at this point: "Is Cloud Computing really ready to be taken into use ?" [12] covers this topic in detail by presenting cloud computing, its advantages and challenges and its future according to several analysts.

The questions raised in this last paragraph are covered in the next sections.

In the first part of this paper, we present how a cloud can be deployed in terms of ownership and also how it works. Then, we will go through the services that are made available on a cloud computing solution and the added value of each of the business segment to its users. The available solutions currently on the market, with its pros and cons are then presented. We conclude this article with a brief assessment of the cloud computing paradigm.

2   Overview

In order to implement and fully understand why cloud computing is a valid paradigm, we need to analyze the current capabilities and drawbacks of other computing systems.

Personal computing refers to the computing capabilities of desktops and mobile devices, such as smart phones, PDAs, laptops and tablets. These devices are owned and used by a single user, although some of them might have more processing power than needed by its user, they are always limited to the device itself, preventing it to scale. Usually these devices do not provide any mechanism to automatically install new resources, services or applications, lacking an on-demand provisioning. Although the available bandwidth for personal consumers is increasing very fast, it is still not enough to provide services to the global community, these connections are intended for personal use only.

Parallel computing is an area that has been gaining momentum in the last decades, aiming at having symmetric multi processor and multicore systems which can provide time and space sharing. These types of environments are mostly used within an organization, which limits in terms of infrastructure and broad access. Parallel computing is scalable but is limited to the current technologies in terms of hardware to support it, thus affecting the resources and on-demand provisioning. Nevertheless, it is a great advantage, also more expensive, when compared to personal computing environments, in terms of allowing several processes to run in a real parallel environment (not only multi-threaded) without noticing any service degradation in concurrent processes.

Cluster computing is an extension of parallel computing. The advantage to use this kind of environments is that it is not only a multi-processor and multicore system, but several instances of those which are interconnected and working as a single computing resource optimized for parallel processing. This kind of environments provides good scalability, although on-demand provisioning is still limited to the existing resources.

Grid Computing has proven to be a highly scalable and performant environment, greatly optimized for distributed and parallel processing, although used mainly for scientific applications. One of the main reasons blocking the evolution of the previous computing models was that it only belong to one organization, which were not willing to share their infrastructure, resources and services with other companies. However on-demand provisioning is not guaranteed [13] since it still requires the agreement and action on the organization providing their resources, which also limits any guarantee on service contracts. Even if not guaranteed on-demand resources allocation is possible and can be tightly coupled with the user's profile and account.

Cloud computing is taking the benefits and limitations of the previous environments into consideration, and is designed to offer such capabilities to their customers by means of virtualization, cluster and grid techniques, data center management and its ubiquitous access. Each of these item allows the cloud to provide on-demand services such as automatic service composition; broad network access by providing a service oriented architecture, interoperable APIs in actual internet technologies; high scalability and elasticity (which is often considered to have infinite processing power) and since its large data centers and powerful servers are distributed it is easy to upgrade without any service interruption; contractual services including resource management, performance monitoring, service level monitoring, accountability and billing. Due to its versatility and business model, cloud computing is also considered as an utility model, since its pay per use model resembles any other utility service we use everyday [6].

To the customer, the advantages of using a cloud computing infrastructure can be evaluated simply by the lack of physical infrastructure, maintenance and upgrades that were previously needed to support their operations. This clearly reduces IT management complexity, lowering the running costs and avoiding expenses with capital expenditure, software licenses, implementation of services, operational costs with the IT and HR support or even with electricity and physical conditions required to maintain these hardware on its premises.

As stated before, the cloud infrastructure is highly scalable. One of the reasons is its ability to break complex workloads into smaller pieces which are sent to be processed to a distributed infrastructure which can be expanded by adding new physical machines. In order to split the workload and then merge the results back and send it to the requester, a technique named MapReduce [8] is used. MapReduce is a programming model and implementation to perform such tasks, one of the most used implementations is Apache Hadoop [3], which besides mapping the operations into key/value pairs to be processed in parallel and then merged back, also provides a distributed file system to be used within the cloud. Each customer is allocated a virtual set of resources. The customer doesn't need to know the details of the underlying infrastructure, therefore customers can share the same physical resources, although a problem affecting one customer will not affect the others since the virtualization software provides that kind of isolation. Once problems occur in the cloud, its distributed architecture and monitoring applications are able to detect any fault and with little or no service disruption, totally transparent to the user, the workload is rescheduled, restarted or moved, providing the means to repair itself and keeping the services going, thus being elastic and fault tolerant. In other environments, faults may cause problems on fulfilling the agreed service level agreement (SLA), but as previously described the ability to dynamically adjust to problems will make the cloud meet the defined goals.

Cloud computing has faced a dramatic growth in popularity in the last years, mainly due to the fact that it uses the internet and web to be accessed. Its high bandwidth and low cost of network capacity enabled the use of remote computing and storage. The use of rich web applications boosted the use of cloud by exploring Software as a Service deployment, which will be explained in the next section. This usage, along with the increasing number of smart mobile phones and tablets using these technologies, contributed to its growth and will continue to contribute, since network enabled low powered devices can serve as a doorway for bigger resources.

Thus, the current tendency and the future reality is to have virtually everything running inside a cloud system. Internet access bandwidth is increasing very fast, becoming more ubiquitous and computing devices are more portable. This increases user's mobility, as devices tend to have less processing power leaving that capabilities to a cloud computing system.

3   Deployment Model

A cloud computing as stated in the previous sections is a virtually infinite infrastructure with virtually unlimited resources. Although desirable, it is not always true, since different applications and business model can have a significative impact depending on the deployment type or nature of each cloud. In this section, we will describe the several deployment models available for cloud computing environments.

Private clouds, as its name points out, private cloud are infrastructures operated exclusively by an organization to serve their purpose. Although it is usually collocated within the organization's premises, it might be placed outside the organizations but used only by a specific organization.

Community Clouds are intended to be used and shared by several organizations as the cloud provides them with common contents and services using the cloud infrastructure. [13] identifies the mission, security requirements, policy, compliance consideration and examples of its usage. Another form of community clouds has been proposed in [18] in which the cloud is extended using home and personal computers, so that their idle processing power can be considered a cloud resource to be made available to the cloud infrastructure, with the possibility of being rewarded by its usage.

Public Clouds are available to the general public or a large industry group and it is usually owned by a single organization which utilizes their infrastructure to sell cloud services. e.g. Amazon webservices, salesforce, etc.

Hybrid Clouds are a mixture of two or more types of clouds, either private, community or public. [13], again, states that although each piece of the cloud remains as unique entities, they are bound together by standardized or proprietary technology enabling data and application portability (e.g., cloud bursting for load-balancing between clouds).

Sky Computing [10], although not commonly accepted, has into consideration that the sky is the limit, and having multiple and hybrid clouds working all together across multiple domains is the ultimate cloud deployment. It consists of interconnecting several cloud infrastructures using interoperability protocols for multiple level of abstractions. Although this is envisioned, there are still some issues to resolve in terms of standardization, complexity of billing and monitoring, as well as data governance and security and service contracts fulfillment.

4 Delivery Models - Layers

Cloud computing provides several services whose main goals are to serve a large amount of business models that will be used by 3rd parties or end users. All these models share a similar approach: storage resources and servers are virtualized and management and provisioning mechanisms are set in place to make the resources available (and accounted for) to the customers. Figure 1 depicts the layered structure of cloud computing showing some examples of services provided in each layer. Cluster and super computing models can be combined in order to form a grid. In these grid environments, utility computing, as referred above, can be deployed originating the deployment of cloud computing on top of the computing platform. From this layer above, there is a list of services provided by a cloud computing environment, representing the four delivery models that this paper covers: Data as a Service (DaaS), Infrastructure as a Service (IaaS), Plaftform as a Service (PaaS) and Software as a Service (SaaS).

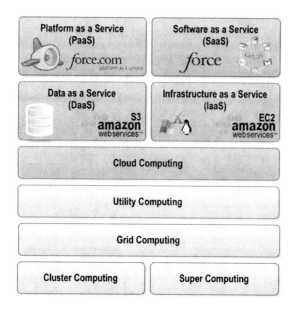

Fig. 1. Layered representation of Cloud Computing

The IaaS layer provides virtual servers where users can load their own software. This is the lower level (software wise) service provided in the cloud, and it is achieved by utilizing virtualization concepts to provide CPU, storage and networks where the users can install and execute their software, whether an application or an operating system. Scaling the cloud at this point is very simple, since additional elements can be added to overcome computing needs (scale up), being dismissed when that extra processing power is not needed anymore (scale down). Management and control of this layer is provided and it is not done by the user, which only has control on the virtualized services provided, eventhough he may finetune the rules used to decide the scaling.

The DaaS layer provides virtually unlimited storage capacity at high speed data transfer. The basic understanding of a cloud system that doesn't do anything else apart from saving data and providing data when requested can be considered as a service to be provided by a cloud infrastructure. Security constraints need to be taken care of [19], concerning the way that information is stored in the cloud and exchanged between the cloud and its users.

The PaaS layer provides a internet-accessible application programming interfaces (APIs) for cloud application developers. This allows the user (developer) to deploy on the cloud infrastructure any application built upon tools or programming languages supported by the infrastructure owner which offer a service for on-demand application deployment, composition and execution. In order to develop an application using the cloud's supported features, the infrastructure owner must make available a software development kit (SDK). Currently there's no standard SDK for broad use, being specific for each cloud environment, which will tightly couple and make a complete dependency from the developer to the provider [16], since the applications would need to be refactored when moving away from one provider to another (vendor lock-in effect). Management and control is only available on the deployed applications, providing no other control on the underlaying infrastructure, such as storage and operating systems used.

The SaaS layer presents to users applications running on a cloud. These applications are usually accessed using a web-browser but can be also accessed using other client applications provided by the platform. Web services or rich internet applications are the common enablers of this layer, which allow the user to manage and control only specific aspects of the application to be used. SaaS is the most common usage of cloud computing and has been described in [20] and [9] on how to make it available on the cloud, although it is regularly confused as both representing the same thing. Typical usage of SaaS provides software multi-tenancy, enabling the same core software to be fully customized and used by different users, with all the maintenance (dis)advantages that such solutions imply.

All these services can be combined and the business case can be applied to each of the models independently. For instance, a company can contract a IaaS model which is then contracted to other company to develop some platform (PaaS) which by its own resells to a third company that provides some software service (SaaS) to costumers. This SaaS application can also make use of another company's DaaS product.

5   Available Solutions

Currently the market is being flooded with different solutions for the several models of cloud computing services. Table 1 provides a brief overview of the different solutions supported by the cloud's major players.

Amazon provides a storage and virtualization solution, Amazon S3 (Simple Storage Service) [2] provides a service with virtually unlimited storage that can be accessed using a web service interface and Amazon EC2 [1] (Elastic Compute Cloud) as a rental service of virtualized computers accessible by web services where customers are able to run, manage and deploy their own applications. Both services claim to be scalable, elastic, inexpensive and simple to use. Prices vary between 0.093 Eur to 0.14 Eur per GB on the S3 storage service and 0.085 Eur to 2.10 Eur per hour on the EC2 instances. Google offers Google Base for storage, and Google App Engine for application deployment. Google App Engine is a web oriented service, allowing users to run their Python or Java web applications. It is limited to the web environment although it is free to use up to 1GB of storage and 5 million page views per month. While Amazon provides full control of both operating system and running software levels (proving a Infrastructure as a Service model), Google only provides access to their platform for web applications, which can be considered as a Platform as a Service model. Other solutions, such as Microsoft Azure's and Sun Grid also provide such kind of services. Microsoft Azure [14] provides an intermediate solution between Google App Engine and Amazon EC2, so that it provides an SDK to develop .NET

Table 1. Comparison between available solutions

Service	Type	Price	Features
Amazon S3	DaaS	0.093-0.14 Eur / GB	Pay per use
Amazon S3	DaaS	Free	5 GB Storage 15 GB in/out data transfer per month
Amazon EC2	IaaS	0.085-2.10 Eur / Hr	Pay per use
Amazon EC2	PaaS	Free	750h on Linux 15 GB in/out data transfer per month
Google Base	PaaS	Free	1GB storage 5M Page Views / month Python or Java
Microsoft Azure	IaaS	0.05-0.96 USD / Hr	.Net application support Pay-as-you-go
Microsoft Azure	IaaS	Free	.Net application support 500MB Storage 500MB in/out data transfer per month
Sun Grid	PaaS	from 1 USD / Hr	Solaris OS Java, C C++ and Fortran
Google Apps	SaaS	Free	Mail, Maps, Search, Docs,....

applications but still allows the users to choose storage model and application structure as in Amazon EC2. Sun Grid   [17] is a "simple to use and simple to access data center on-demand". Sun claims that Sun Grid is the only true compute utility in the world, with prices from 1 USD/CPU-hour, as a pay per use model, supporting applications based on Solaris OS, Java, C, C++ and Fortran. Solutions from IBM, Nimbus and Eucalyptus are also available, providing the user a huge variety of solutions and options to choose from.

One other interesting aspect when analyzing Table 1, is that there is a free solution for each type of deployment but also the above commercial solutions are available for a more professional and intensive usage. This way there is hardly any good excuse for not trying cloud computing.

In the market of SaaS, Google is leading the way with almost every one of its available applications running on a browser, for instance, Google Mail, Google Maps, Google Search, Google Docs, etc... Several other players, salesforce, Telstra T-Suite, BT - SaaS for SMEs provide their own products and applications.

Apart from the industry, there are also solutions available for the research areas, for instance Open Cirrus [7] which, according to the project's website, "is an open cloud-computing research testbed designed to support research into the design, provisioning, and management of services at a global, multi-datacenter scale.". The project aims to provide other research projects with the facilities to develop and research new trends applicable to cloud computing, in an open environment ready to use. According to [5], Open Cirrus is a joint initiative sponsored by major companies like HP, Yahoo and Intel, working in a collaborative way with several institutes and universities around the world. The testbed is spread around 10 heterogeneous locations concerning North America, Europe and Asia. The testbed is composed by at least 1000 cores per site and storage, a cloud stack implemented on physical and virtual machines and also global services across sites such as single sign-on, monitoring and storage. This testbed provides direct access to physical resources, which is prevented by any of the above described solutions, and this was also a motivation for the Open Cirrus project. [5] describes Open Cirrus' architecture, design and implementation and also the economical model of the project.

OnLive [15] is one of the first companies in the world providing high definition cloud gaming. OnLive provides gaming on-demand without the need of having super computers to process information. The client just needs a computer capable of playing video, all game processing and 3D rendering is done on game servers. The image is processed and sent as a video stream to the user, which interacts in the same way with the game engine as a regular console, the difference here is that the whole gaming processing is done somewhere in the cloud. OnLive is capable of providing high definition at 720p format, although a fast internet connection (around 6Mbit/s) is required to be able to play without any interruption. Triple play (internet, television and telephone) operators, such as the Portuguese MEO, are also adopting this technology, allowing their customers to play graphic intensive and online games using just a game controller and the set top box.

6   Summary and Conclusion

This article provided an introduction regarding the needs for cloud computing infrastructure. A brief overview to the cloud system was presented as well as a detailed explanation on what cloud computing really is, its pros and cons. If on one hand, cloud users do not have to worry about hardware, maintenance, electricity, housing, air conditioning, etc., on the other hand they may have to compromise data security (location and access wise), intellectual property and vender lock in, etc..

Cloud computing is still evolving, but it has assured a place in the internet of the future. More and more applications and services are moving to the cloud. It represents a key driver to new business models in the Internet and drives the development of several new techniques to provide customers with the best solution possible. Its layered infrastructure and business models permits a wide range of solutions to be offered, expanding and opening new application opportunities, paving the way to new technology trends.

Nevertheless, cloud computing still has to mature: each cloud is currently isolated and locks-in the customer to that specific infrastructure, which limits the customer's ability to select the best option at any time. Cloud computing is lacking standardization, either for APIs between cloud layers (e.g. between PaaS and IaaS), interoperability with and across clouds, or between public clouds and enterprise systems. Standardization efforts are in place but still away from a clear result.

Despite the long way to go, cloud computing is already mature enough with plenty of solutions available and ready to be used, as illustrated in the last section of the article.

References

1. Amazon: Amazon ec2, http://aws.amazon.com/ec2/
2. Amazon: Amazon s3, http://aws.amazon.com/s3/
3. Apache: Apache hadoop, http://hadoop.apache.org/
4. Armbrust, M., Fox, A., Griffith, R., Joseph, A.D., Katz, R., Konwinski, A., Lee, G., Patterson, D., Rabkin, A., Stoica, I., Zaharia, M.: A view of cloud computing. Commun. ACM 53, 50–58 (2010)
5. Avetisyan, A., Campbell, R., Gupta, I., Heath, M., Ko, S., Ganger, G., Kozuch, M., O'Hallaron, D., Kunze, M., Kwan, T., Lai, K., Lyons, M.: Open cirrus: A global cloud computing testbed. Computer 43(4) (April 2010)
6. Buyya, R., Yeo, C.S., Venugopal, S., Broberg, J., Brandic, I.: Cloud computing and emerging it platforms: Vision, hype, and reality for delivering computing as the 5th utility. Future Generation Computer Systems 25(6), 599–616 (2009)
7. Cirrus, O.: Open cirrus (March 2011), http://www.opencirrus.org
8. Dean, J., Ghemawat, S.: Mapreduce: simplified data processing on large clusters. Commun. ACM 51, 107–113 (2008)
9. Dubey, A., Wagle, D.: Delivering software as a service. The McKinsey Quarterly (2007)
10. Keahey, K., Tsugawa, M., Matsunaga, A., Fortes, J.: Sky computing. IEEE Internet Computing 13(5), 43–51 (2009)
11. Kumar, K., Lu, Y.H.: Cloud computing for mobile users: Can offloading computation save energy? Computer 43(4), 51–56 (2010)
12. Leavitt, N.: Is cloud computing really ready for prime time? Computer 42(1), 15–20 (2009), http://dx.doi.org/10.1109/MC.2009.20
13. Mell, P., Grance, T.: Cloud Computing Definition. Tech. rep., National Institute of Standards and Technology (June 2009)
14. Microsoft: Microsoft azure, http://www.microsoft.com/windowsazure/
15. OnLive: Onlive, http://www.onlive.com/
16. O'Reilly, T.: Is google app engine a lock-in play? (October 2009), http://radar.oreilly.com/archives/2008/04/is-google-app-engine-a-lockin.html
17. Sun: Sun grid, http://www.sun.com/service/sungrid/
18. Teixeira, C., Azevedo, R., Pinto, J.S., Batista, T.: User provided cloud computing. In: Proceedings of the 2010 10th IEEE/ACM International Conference on Cluster, Cloud and Grid Computing, CCGRID 2010, pp. 727–732. IEEE Computer Society, Washington, DC, USA (2010)
19. Truong, H.L., Dustdar, S.: On analyzing and specifying concerns for data as a service. IEEE Asia-Pacific Services Computing Conference, APSCC 2009, pp. 87–94 (December 2009)
20. Turner, M., Budgen, D., Brereton, P.: Turning software into a service. Computer 36(10), 38–44 (2003)
21. Wang, L., von Laszewski, G., Younge, A., He, X., Kunze, M., Tao, J., Fu, C.: Cloud computing: a perspective study. New Generation Computing 28, 137–146 (2010), doi:10.1007/s00354-008-0081-5

Cloud Computing to Support the Evolution of Massive Multiplayer Online Games

Dario Maggiorini and Laura Anna Ripamonti

University of Milano, via Comelico 39,
I-20135 Milano, Italy
{dario.maggiorini,laura.ripamonti}@unimi.it

Abstract. In these recent years, with the gain in popularity of online games, we are witnessing a progressive increment in the number of massive multiplayer online games available over the Internet. Given the scalability requirements imposed by a huge population of users over an extended length of time, game providers face the major challenge of long-term IT infrastructures dimensioning. In particular, the risks are over-allocation (wasting resource and money) or non-timely upgrades (loosing subscribers and revenues.) In this paper we advocate Cloud Computing as a viable solution to dynamically allocate resource for a massive game service infrastructure in order to satisfy users' needs while minimizing maintenance costs. To this extent we envision a mid-term future where game provisioning will be performed by means of a three-tier architecture: the users, the game provider, and the cloud provider. We believe that many medium/small game providers may benefit from the on-demand resources allocation infrastructure offered by the cloud, due to shorter deployment time and reduced total cost of ownership.

Keywords: Cloud computing, Massive Multiplayer Online Games, Scalability.

1 Introduction

In these recent years, with the gain in popularity of online games, and massive online game in particular, we are witnessing a progressive increment in the number of Massive Multiplayer Online Games (MMOGs) available over the Internet, as reported by [1]. A MMOG is a game where a huge number of users in a shared virtual environment can interact in real time and build social relations. The evolution of every MMOG, in terms of active subscriptions and - as a consequence - workload, is usually characterized by a linear growth up to hundred of thousands or even millions of users, a relatively brief steady state, and a linear decrease until going out of service. An analysis of active subscriptions for some very popular (and fairly long lasting) MMOGs is reported in Fig. 1; as we can see there is a considerable variation in usage (and resources allocation) between peak and final periods. With a few notable exceptions, such as World of Warcraft (WoW) [2] and EverQuest (EQ) [3], this duty cycle may take from a few months to a few years, depending on popularity; in the average, a product from a small publisher may foresee a lifespan of two years. Some long-lasting cases have been well analyzed by [4].

M.M. Cruz-Cunha et al. (Eds.): CENTERIS 2011, Part II, CCIS 220, pp. 101–110, 2011.

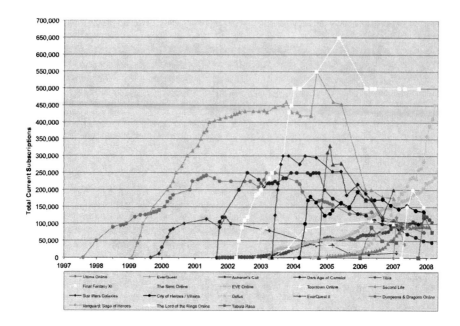

Fig. 1. MMOG active over time subscriptions for MMOG in the range of 70,000 to 700,000 users (source: http://www.mmogchart.com/)

Given the scalability requirements imposed by the huge number of players over an extended length of time (see Fig. 2), game providers face the main challenge of long-term IT infrastructures dimensioning. Currently, the usual approach to address the scalability problems is to adopt a clustered architecture on the server side. While this approach has the advantage to be easily deployed and provide protection from hardware failures, it also needs a careful and detailed planning, in order to be effectively extended.

In the MMOGs market, performing a correct prediction is very difficult, also due to a number of non-technical factors; IT managers usually plan infrastructures based on previous experiences, while constrained by the available budget and hoping for the best. In particular, they may decide to over-allocate servers for peak usage, wasting resources and money, or to target a lower users population planning upgrades, which may not be timely, with the risk to lose subscribers.

In recent times, Cloud Computing (CC) [5] has been proposed as an alternative to local computation by means of a software infrastructure providing resources on demand via a computer network. These resources can be provided at any traditional layer: software, platform, and infrastructure with minimal deployment time and reduced Total Cost of Ownership (TCO) thanks to an on-demand, self-service, and pay-per-use model.

In this paper we advocate CC as a viable solution to dynamically allocate resource to a MMOG infrastructure, in order to satisfy gaming needs for a huge number of users, while minimizing maintenance costs. Many medium/small game providers may benefit from the on-demand resources allocation infrastructure offered by CC, due to shorter deployment time and reduced TCO.

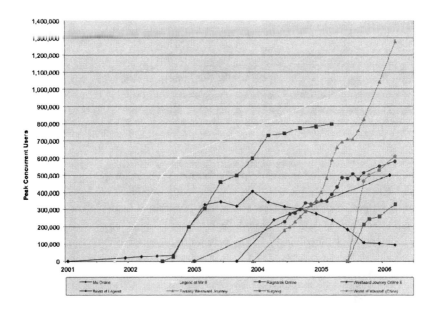

Fig. 2. Asian market: MMOG peak concurrent users (source: http://www.mmogchart.com/)

The structure of the paper is organized as follows: §2 and §3 provide respectively a brief overview on CC and online games, while §4 and §5 dig into technical benefits and issues of adopting CC as an infrastructure for MMOGs. Finally, §6 and §7 analyze related works and draws conclusions.

2 Cloud Computing

Cloud Computing (CC) [5] proposed itself as a completely new approach to distributed computing and has been defined as a pool of easily usable and accessible virtualized resources, which can be dynamically reconfigured to adjust to a variable scale and load, in order to allow for optimal resource utilization [6]. A cloud is a hardware and software infrastructure which is able to provide service at any traditional IT layer: software, platform, and infrastructure, with minimal deployment time and reduced costs, thanks to an on-demand, self-service, and pay-per-use model. A high-performance web application can be easily deployed in a remotely virtualized server running on a distributed hardware infrastructure, and everything will be charged only for the resources affectively used, while sharing the cloud infrastructure with other users. Due to its strong service orientation, all functionalities in a cloud are decomposed in primitives, which will be assembled as required by the user. For this reason, the three service levels mentioned above are usually referred to as: *Software as a Service* (SaaS), *Platform as a Service* (PaaS), and *Infrastructure as a Service* (IaaS). IaaS provides a mechanism to access hardware or other physical resources without any investment in physical assets or physical administrative requirement.

PaaS virtualizes operating systems and offers traditional client-server environments where to run legacy infrastructure services. While IaaS and PaaS provide services which are meaningful only to system administrators and developers, SaaS provides a service which is directly accessible by end-users: it will present the full stack of cloud services in the same way users expect to use their applications.

As for accessing the cloud services there are two models: if a cloud is made available on a pay-as-you-go basis, it is usually called *Public Cloud* and the service takes the name of *Utility Computing*. Well known examples of Utility computing are AmazonWeb Services [7], Google AppEngine [8], and Windows Azure [9]. On the other hand, *Private Cloud* is the term used for datacenters which are internal to some organization and not made available to the public. Cloud Computing is the sum of SaaS and Utility Computing, but does not normally include Private Clouds. Cloud Computing offers to application providers the possibility to deploy a product as a SaaS (and to scale it on demand) without building or provisioning a datacenter. Fig. 3 depicts the general idea behind the Cloud Computing layered architecture.

Fig. 3. Users and Providers in Cloud Computing

As an example of existing service, Elastic Compute Cloud (EC2) from Amazon Web Services sells 1.0-GHz x86 ISA virtual machines (slices) for $0.10 per hour, a new slice can be added in 2 to 5 minutes. Amazon's Scalable Storage Service (S3) charges $0.12 to $0.15 per gigabyte-month, with additional bandwidth charges of $0.10 to $0.15 per gigabyte to move data in to and out of the storage cloud.

The decision to make available a service as a SaaS depends on expected traffic and computational time. In the case of a MMOG traffic is usually low, since content gets typically deployed on the user machine; this is usually done to avoid excessive fees from the ISP and to improve performances on narrow-band local loops. In-game traffic may be, in the case of WoW, as low as 48 Kbps or even less; in terms of S3 this means roughly 300 hours (12 days) of uninterrupted play with one dollar per user. Computational power requirements depend on actual game implementation, but, since game server machines main tasks are physical simulation and managing players interaction, it is usually possible to assign a fair number of players to the same server. In the case of Second Life [10], up to 50 players may sit on the same server with a reasonable system performance, this means with EC2 an average expense of $1.44 per month per user. After the above considerations, and throwing in the picture that the average connection fee in a MMOG is around $20 per user per month, moving to the cloud should be a significant economical advantage.

For a detailed discussion about CC including economics on distributed systems see [11].

3 Architecture of Online Games

Commercial MMOGs are services provided by companies charging user for connection time. As such, they must satisfy the same requirements as other mission-critical 7/24 services. This means, they must be secure, scalable, and fault tolerant. We are not going into the details of the whole IT infrastructure needed to provide such a service, which includes, among other things, customer support over phone, trouble ticketing, many firewalls, and payment and charging systems. In this paper we are going to focus on the actual game server subsystem, providing the game and representing the most significant part in term of management and investment. An overall architecture for a generic game server subsystem is depicted in Fig. 4, while a most general discussion can be found in [12].

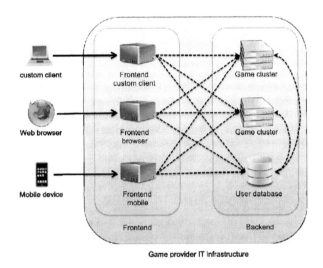

Fig. 4. Overall architecture of an online game service

In order to provide the service, the game provider sets up a number of frontend machines, which will be contacted by the players via different kind of devices. Each frontend machine is usually in charge for a specific kind of client. We may have custom clients implemented ad-hoc for the game (like in WoW), web browsers generic clients (as for FarmVille [13]) or a mobile device (as in Armada Galactic War [14]). It is worth noting that these channels are not mutually exclusive, as the same game may provide access to different in-game services by means of different devices.

The frontend servers will take care to authenticate the user using a *User database* and then will redirect the connection to the backend, taking care to balance the load in the backend tier.

In the backend, on the side of the User database, sits the actual machines providing the game experience. These machines are built as clusters of sub-server and each cluster runs an independent and autonomous copy of the virtual world offered to the users. Figure 5 reports a possible internal setup for a game cluster.

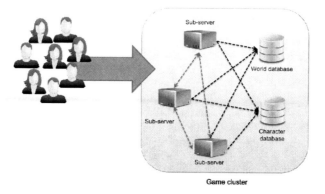

Fig. 5. Architecture of a game cluster

Inside a game cluster there are many sub-servers, taking care of the actual virtual world simulation and databases specific to the world instance. The *World database* holds information about environment configuration and objects, while the *Character database* manages everything related to in-game players representations.

Each sub-server is usually assigned to a geographical zone and players move from one sub-serve to another while playing. Communication among servers is required only for players handoff and "long-range" communications between users.

Scalability inside game clusters becomes an issue in two situations: when designers want to extend the game map, and when all players collapse in the same location (e.g., due to some in-game event). Map expansion may be a big problem, because it will require hardware intervention to add other machines (one per cluster) and extend the connectivity grid. Moreover, hardware issues might constrain the game design process and vice versa. The problem caused by a lot of players gathering in the same place (e.g., to perform a siege) is inherent in the architecture: since the sub-servers are geographically located, one is getting the entire load, while the others sit idle. Changing strategy and performing load balancing by distributing players is not an option: since players interact with each other most of the time, synchronization messages between servers will grow exponentially, with a severe loss of performance.

By adopting a CC approach, the above scalability problems will be remarkably mitigated. Adding a machine will require the allocation of a new slice, while the IaaS level will take care to ensure optimized communication between sub-server slices. If the situation goes critical, having all player meeting at the same point, the workload may be transferred temporarily on a more powerful slice or the zone can get split into two subzones by means of a new slice. As an added benefit, CC will avoid the game provider getting charged for empty zones, whit an additional money saving during low usage periods.

4   Putting an Online Game in the Cloud

We already discussed in Sec. 2 and 3 that there are economical and technical benefits in deploying in a cloud a service infrastructure with massive gaming requirements. Being able to put game clusters in a cloud will open a completely new perspective for

MMOGs provisioning: a massive game, as a service, may be built using resources from the cloud and offered to players.

The easiest way to move the game service into the cloud is by relocating the game clusters there, as depicted in Fig. 6. In the picture we can see that the backend tier shrunk to the User database alone and, after authentication, frontend servers will just forward players to the cloud service.

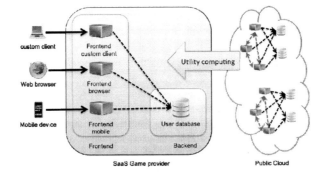

Fig. 6. Backend deployment using SaaS

It is unlikely that the User database can be moved inside a Public Cloud due to its extremely critical content: user passwords and billing information. For the same reason, the frontend servers should remain in the game provider network: they need authentication information from the User database. If frontend would be deployed in the cloud, a way to reach the User database would be needed (from the cloud as a whole), resulting in a major security weakness. On the other hand, frontend servers may be efficiently clustered and authentication is performed infrequently; thus, this is not going to be a severe limitation to the system.

The only way to move the remaining pieces to the cloud is by using a Private Cloud. While this is feasible in theory, there is a couple of point against it. Firstly, the game provider must own and manage the Private Cloud infrastructure (and pay for it), thus keeping the scalability and flexibility, but potentially loosing most of the cost reduction. Secondly, service virtualization will be effective only if there are many world instances or more than one game running, which is not the case for many companies. In general, small game service providers will find more fruitful to manage authentication internally and demand game clusters operations.

Despite the limitation imposed by Utility Computing architecture, there is one more major advantage in cloud deployment: if the PaaS layer can be tailored to gaming needs, we can build a real *Cloud Gaming* infrastructure. Inside a gaming cloud, basic gaming services might be already available to provide building blocks for online games providers. These basic services will take care to implement common functionalities, commonly deployed inside gaming clusters, e.g., character management, instant messaging, game physic simulation, in-game database management, and client software update. By using these services from the cloud, game developers may just deploy an MMOG with a sensible reduction of development time and cost. The gaming cloud provider, on the other hand, may provide value-added services to customer such as inter-world messaging (even if the worlds belong to different providers), a common shared virtual currency or seamless character migration between different MMOGs.

5 Cloud Gaming Issues

Unfortunately, from a technical standpoint, there are a number of requirements from Cloud Gaming, which are only partially addressed by current CC infrastructures. In order to be functional to a MMOG, a gaming cloud must efficiently handle (*i*) real time communication and Quality of Service (QoS), (*ii*) content protection, and (*iii*) users privacy.

As already address in [15], gaming quality of experience is closely related to communication delay and jitter, and MMOGs are no exception. Network technology and resources over-provisioning are the usual approach to grant real time communications in network infrastructures. This is a reasonable solution in a protected environment, but in a competitive one, with resource allocated on demand and a cloud shared with other providers, this approach may no longer be reliable. QoS solutions at link layer (e.g., MultiProtocol Label Switching - MPLS [16]) or network layer (e.g., Int-Serv [17] or Diff-Serv [18]) must be integrated in the cloud IaaS layer. APIs for virtual services provisioning must be designed to support call admission mechanisms and explicit service deadlines in order to request the needed Quality of Gaming and monitor network conditions.

In massive virtual environments (e.g., Second Life [10]) it is now possible for players to contribute their own content. Beside the obvious enormous space requirement, this feature raises the question about who is responsible to protect Intellectual Properties (IP). The added tier of virtualization forward data storage to a third party, which may not be trusted, and must not be known to the SaaP user. Moreover, IP on game content is a valuable asset for the game provider; storing it on an external cloud shared with competitors is an ill desired option, if a strong protection mechanism is not available.

Privacy is a hot topic lately, and users really do care about it. Forwarding all user actions to the cloud provider is required in order to compute an updated game state, nevertheless, anonymity must be ensured through a robust and reliable mechanism. The cloud provider must be unable to link actions to accounts and vice versa.

6 Related Work

While MMOGs scalability has already been widely addressed in literature, as summarized by [19], research has been mainly focused on improving scalability limitations of the client-server model by switching to a peer-to-peer approach [20].

In [21] a peer-to-peer architecture is defined to distribute messages among players and share the network load on a broad area by prioritizing messages and shaping traffic. In [22] a scalable publication-subscription (pub-sub) infrastructure is proposed: each player subscribes to a region in the game in order to be notified about events; a Distributed Hash Table (DHT) structure takes care to organize locations in a map. Finally, in [23] a hybrid approach is proposed to increase security by means of coordinators in the regions.

The closest work, to the best of our knowledge, with what we presented here is [24], where an improvement over [21] and [22] is proposed. messages are distributed on a peer-to-peer network following a bandwidth-savvy approach and the DHT has been embedded into the cloud. Authors of [24] deploy a First Person Shooter game in a cloud environment and perform measurements proving a real performance improvement.

Regarding the scalability, the aforementioned works are mainly focused on the sheer number of players and not on the extensibility of the overall architecture, while our contribution is more concerned about ensuring a limitless expansion to storage and computational load, while trying to be design-agnostic. In particular, [24] perform analysis over a FPS, which has specific constraints such as a (very) limited map and a short lifespan, if compared to a MMOG. Moreover, authors assume the game provider is using a Private Cloud, which we argued has some considerable drawbacks in a real commercial environment.

Outside the academic world, several companies claim to be using CC to provide game services; among them we can find Zynga (the producer of FarmVille [13]) and Onlive [25]. Onlive has a Private Cloud only for sake of internal scalability, while Zynga's Farmville – as a browser game – exploits Facebook's cloud, sharing it with other web-based applications. Unfortunately, FarmVille cannot be classified among the MMOGs, because of the limited interactions between users taking place inside the game.

7 Conclusions and Future Work

In this paper we discussed the combination of Massive Multiplayer Online Games with the Cloud Computing approach. During the presentation a number of benefits have been outlined, indicating that CC can be a viable solution to extend boundaries of current MMOGs deployment. In particular, CC can help to improve scalability, to lower TCO, to reduce development time, and to increase interoperability.

Currently, CC is already available on many platforms, both commercial [7-9, 26, 27] and open [28]; what is still missing is a clear definition of the basic building blocks to be provided from a Gaming Cloud in order to create a massive game. Once base services will be identified, the problem will shift to improve technical functionalities of the cloud regarding QoS and call admission.

In the future we are planning to define a functional model of a Gaming Cloud and to perform a prototype deployment in our department network.

References

1. MMORPG Community, http://www.mmorpg.com/ (last visited March 27, 2011)
2. World of Warcraft, http://www.battle.net/wow/ (last visited March 27, 2011)
3. EverQuest, http://www.everquest.com/ (last visited March 27, 2011)
4. Bruce, W.: Charting the future of the MMOG industry (2008), http://www.mmogchart.com/ (last visited March 27, 2011)
5. Hayes, B.: Cloud computing. Communications of the ACM 51(7), 9 (2008)
6. Vaquero, L.M., Rodero-Merino, L., Caceres, J., Lindner, M.: A break in the clouds: towards a cloud definition. SIGCOMM Comput. Commun. Rev. 39(1), 50–55 (2008)
7. Amazon Web Services, http://aws.amazon.com/ (last visited March 27, 2011)

8. Google App Engine, http://code.google.com/appengine/ (last visited March 27, 2011)
9. Windows Azure, http://www.microsoft.com/windowsazure/ (last visited March 27, 2011)
10. Second life, http://www.secondlife.com/ (last visited March 27, 2011)
11. Armbrust, M., Fox, A., Rean, A., Joseph, A.D., Katz, R., Konwinski, A., Gunho, L., Patterson, D.A., Rabkin, A., Stoica, I., Zaharia, M.: Above the Clouds: A Berkeley View of Cloud Computing, Technical Report EECS Department, University of California, Berkeley, UCB/EECS-2009-28 (2009)
12. Megler, V.: Online game infrastructures, Part 1: Develop a high-level business description and identify patterns. IBM developerworks, http://www.ibm.com/developerworks/ibm/library/wa-games1/ (last visited March 27, 2011)
13. Zynga: FarmVille, http://www.farmville.com/ (last visited March 27, 2011)
14. Armada - Galactic War: http://www.jumpthestream.com/ (last visited March 27, 2011)
15. Kaiser, A., Maggiorini, D., Achir, N., Boussetta, K.: On the objective evaluation of real-time networked games. In: Proceedings of the 28th IEEE Conference on Global Telecommunications. IEEE Press, Los Alamitos (2009)
16. Rosen, E., Viswanathan, A., Callon, R.: Multiprotocol label switching architecture. IETF RFC 3031 (2001)
17. Braden, R., Clark, D., Shenker, S.: Integrated services in the internet architecture: an overview. IETF RFC 1633 (1994)
18. Blake, S., Black, D., Carlson, M., Davies, E., Wang, Z., Weiss, W.: An architecture for differentiated services. IETF RFC 2475 (1998)
19. Gil, R., Tavares, J.P., Roque, L.: Architecting Scalability for Massively Multiplayer Online Gaming Experiences. Presented at the International DiGRA Conference (2005)
20. Knutsson, B., Honghui, L., Wei, X., Hopkins, B.: Peer-to-peer support for massively multiplayer games. In: Twenty-Third Annual Joint Conference of the IEEE Computer and Communications (2004)
21. Bharambe, A., Douceur, J.R., Lorch, J.R., Moscibroda, T., Pang, J., Seshan, S., Zhuang, X.: Donnybrook: enabling large-scale, highspeed, peer-to-peer games. In: Proc. of the ACM SIGCOMM 2008 Conference on Data Communication (2008)
22. Bharambe, A., Pang, J., Seshan, S.: Colyseus: a distributed architecture for online multiplayer games. In: Proc. of the 3rd Conference on Networked Systems Design & Implementation (2006)
23. Jardine, J., Zappala, D.: A hybrid architecture for massively multiplayer online games. In: Proc. 7th Annual Workshop on Network and Systems Support for Games (2008)
24. Najaran, M.T., Krasic, C.: Scaling online games with adaptive interest management in the cloud. In: Proc. 9th Annual Workshop on Network and Systems Support for Games (2010)
25. Onlive game service portal, http://www.onlive.com/ (last visited March 27, 2011)
26. IBM Corporation: Cloud computing overview, http://www.ibm.com/ibm/cloud/ (last visited March 27, 2011)
27. Oracle/Sun Corporation: Cloud computing overview, http://www.oracle.com/technology/tech/cloud/index.html (last visited March 27, 2011)
28. IBM Corporation: Cloud computing with linux, http://www.ibm.com/developerworks/linux/library/l-cloud-computing/ (last visited March 27, 2011)

Quality Evaluation Methods to Improve Enterprise VoIP Communications

Filipe Neves[1], Salviano Soares[2], Pedro Assuncao[1],
Filipe Tavares[3], and Simão Cardeal[3]

[1] Polytechnic Institute of Leiria/ESTG – Telecommunications Institute
Apartado 4163, 2411-901 Leiria, Portugal
[2] Universidade de Trás-os-Montes e Alto Douro – IEETA ,
Apartado 1013, 5001-801 Vila Real, Portugal – Aveiro
[3] Portugal Telecom Inovação,
R. Eng. José F. Pinto Basto, 3810-106 Aveiro, Portugal
fneves@ipleiria.pt, salblues@utad.pt, paassunc@ieee.org,
filipe-t-tavares@ptinovacao.pt, simaovertigo@gmail.com

Abstract. In the last few years there has been a dramatic development in voice communications technology with a significant move towards Voice over the Internet Protocol (VoIP). Since the Internet was primarily designed as a best-effort technology, good quality conversation and intelligibility are not guaranteed. In this paper we address quality evaluation of voice communications in the context of modern enterprises using VoIP as an emerging technology with impact in their activity. Relevant factors for service providers and enterprises using VoIP technology are described, such as those related to measurement of intelligibility and evaluation of overall voice communications quality. Also, the most relevant voice quality evaluation methods recommended by the ITU-T are described along with the main features that can be used to improve voice communications. Fundamental concepts are presented, such as intrusive, non intrusive, objective, subjective and parametric methods. Mastering the concepts of such emerging technology, has recently lead to research and development of a model-based voice quality monitor for VoIP services. After its successful implementation, it is now fully operational in a Portuguese telecom operator.

Keywords: MOS, Voice quality, QoE, Enterprise voice communications.

1 Introduction

Nowadays it is quite evident that a technological revolution was happening in the last few years, spreading over many areas of daily life, which are currently supported by digital technologies. In the telecommunications world, the emergence of the packet-switching technology was one the most important factors responsible for the success of the current digital telecommunications world of services and applications. The widespread use of the Internet Protocol (IP) has reached traditional telephony communications in a global scale and Voice over IP (VoIP) is rapidly taking over

M.M. Cruz-Cunha et al. (Eds.): CENTERIS 2011, Part II, CCIS 220, pp. 111–119, 2011.
© Springer-Verlag Berlin Heidelberg 2011

legacy technologies. Indeed, the existing IP infrastructure soon appeared suitable for transporting telephony voice signals because of its low cost associated to the flexibility and richness of possible services. Call center integration, directory services over telephones, IP video conferencing, fax over IP and Radio/TV broadcasting are among an ever increasing number of services and applications [1].

According to statistics from the Organization for Economic Co-operation and Development (OECD), the use of VoIP services has been steadily increasing [2]. For example, the French *Autorité de Régulation des Communications Électroniques et des Postes* (ARCEP)[1] unveils that, from the third quarter of 2006 to the corresponding quarter of 2010, the use of the Public Switched Telephone Network (PSTN) exclusively for VoIP services rose from 5% to 37% [3]. According to [4], it is expected that VoIP will replace conventional telephony in a couple of decades. Analysts predict that the number of VoIP consumers is increasing from 70 million in the second quarter of 2008 to nearly 200 million by 2012 [5]. Perspectives outlined by [6] state that the emerging VoIP traffic over the cellular network will represent 23% of the total voice traffic time by 2015 in occidental Europe. There is also a current evolution of voice services towards VoIP over WiFi (VoWiFi) which has recently emerged as promising technology [7].

On the one hand, there is still margin for the VoIP market to grow. On the other hand, this is conditioned by the quality of the technology which results in better services and eases wide acceptance [8], [9]. In fact, since the IP technology was originally designed for data traffic, it implements a best-effort network which does not ensure Quality of Service (QoS) because the available resources are shared among all users. Therefore, in IP telephony, some traffic key parameters such as bandwidth, delays, packet delivering and packet priority are not guaranteed by the communications network, resulting in multiple impairment factors. Moreover, analog/digital and digital/analog conversions, high compression codecs and heterogeneous technology along the transmitting path introduce additional impairment factors such as distortion, echo and delays which are harmful, especially in the two-way communication. If double-talks and mutual silence periods increase, then lower interactivity is obtained [10]. A practical use case was evaluated in [7], where the strong impact of packet losses in VoIP performance is minimized by a packet loss concealment strategy.

Despite of the potential problems, VoIP services should be able to achieve comparable voice quality to that of legacy PSTN networks in order to be competitive [7]. Although VoIP services often offer much cheaper solutions than PSTN, what really matters is essentially the user perception of the service quality. Therefore it is of great importance for service providers to establish benchmarks for the QoS of their services and to have universal metrics and procedures that quantify how users experience such quality, i.e., the Quality of Experience (QoE). For this purpose the International Telecommunication Union (ITU), through its Telecommunication Standardization Sector (ITU-T) has released a set of recommendations to standardize metrics and methods to carry out proper evaluation of telephony voice quality. In the following sections, the most relevant aspects related to voice quality evaluation are described. A technological background is provided with a level of detail that makes it useful for engineers and technical managers in different types of enterprises.

---

[1] www.arcep.fr/eng

This paper is organized as follows. After this introductory section, section 2 defines concepts and classifies the most relevant voice quality evaluation methods ranging from subjective, objective and parametric. Section 3 defines the Mean Opinion Score (MOS) as a voice quality metric and describes various types of subjective evaluation methods. Section 4 establishes objective quality evaluation methods and presents the PESQ algorithm, while section 5 presents the E-Model as the most relevant parametric method. Finally section 6 concludes the paper.

2   Voice Quality Evaluation Metrics and Methods

The quality measurement in voice services comprises both the QoE and QoS. While MOS is main metric used in QoE evaluation, network quality factors, such as packet loss and throughput are used in QoS [11]. The most classical and perhaps the easiest way to evaluate the voice quality relies on the calculation of physical values that affect the respective signal. Such physical values include parameters like the Signal to Noise Ratio (SNR), the signal level, the Root Mean Square Error (RMSE), the delay and delay variation or packet loss rate [12]. Although these metrics seem to be attractive due to their determinism and objectiveness, they do not provide, *per si*, a reliable evaluation metric about the communication intelligibility. Even taking into account these metrics, voice quality evaluation is primarily a subjective task. In fact, it depends on the evaluator subject, its humor, hear reliability, expectations and auditory tastes. For the same subject, the perceived quality even varies along the time. Therefore, to be sufficiently reliable, voice quality assessment must take into account its inherent subjective nature.

Subjective assessment of voice communications is characterized by obtaining scores from users that reflect, in a natural way, the characteristics of the human hearing. Subjective evaluation resorts to people specifically recruited to provide their opinions. In this context, the ITU-T Rec. P.800 defines a set of methods and procedures to carry out subjective evaluation [13]. Since these methods are very onerous, time-consuming and difficult to repeat, subjective evaluation may be performed by using computational algorithms that model the *average* human hear. Since their repeatability, under the same test conditions, gives invariable results, these are called *objective methods*. Such methods are also necessary to measure the accuracy of voice concealment algorithms by enabling easy computation of the signal distortion [14].

In order to perform voice quality assessment, processed voice samples (degraded or improved) are used for evaluation. For either subjective or objective methods, there are methods where only the voice sample under evaluation is needed, avoiding a reference signal for comparison. However, there are other quality evaluation methods where a reference signal or sample is used for comparison. In the particular case of objective methods, these are called intrusive methods because they interfere with the normal operation of the system under evaluation. Another class of voice quality evaluation methods, known as parametric methods, does not use any reference signal, but a set of parameters characterizing the voice communication system under evaluation. Fig. 1 illustrates this classification of voice quality methods.

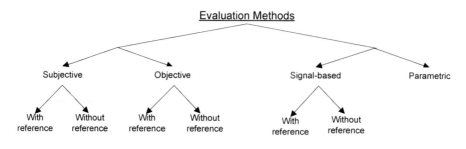

Fig. 1. Classification of voice quality evaluation methods

3 Subjective Methods

Subjective methods for voice quality evaluation described in ITU-T Rec. P.800 are known as MOS-based methods [13]. This ITU-T recommendation contains the definition of the standard procedures that must be followed in order to carry out valid assessment of voice quality in communication systems. The voice signals are presented to each listener and their individual opinions comprise the respective contributions to the MOS. The *MOS* value can be obtained by the following expression,

$$MOS = \sum_{i}^{N} p_i \bigg/ N \ , \tag{1}$$

where p_i represents the score given by each subject in experiment i, N represents the number of experimental tests and *MOS* represents the average of the scores.

As mentioned above, the ITU-T Rec. P.800 establishes a set of mandatory procedural requirements to be met on executing the evaluation tests. Some of the most relevant requirements are the following: 1) Physical conditions of the room; 2) Monitoring the progress of the experiments; 3) Criterion for selecting subjects; 4) Procedures for recording sentences and talks; 5) Hearing procedures; 6) Characteristics of the recording and monitoring equipment; 7) Gathering results and their statistical processing. Each type of test has its own kind of opinion scale. Next sections describe the various types of subjective methods and their opinion scales.

3.1 Conversation-Opinion Tests

Conversation tests are characterized by two-way vocal interaction between two subjects, where each one alternates the role of speaker and listener. Two opinion scales are used in this type of quality evaluation.

The conversational quality scale contains five levels to rank the *Opinion of the connection [the subject] have just been using*, from Bad (level=1) to Excellent (level=5). Based on the individual quality levels, the quantitative scores are recorded and an average value is obtained by using expression (1), which corresponds to a Mean Conversation-Opinion Score represented by MOS_C.

The other opinion scale is the difficulty scale, which allows either "yes" or "no" as possible user opinions. These are the answers to be given to the following question, by the subject at the end of each conversation: *Did you or your partner have any difficulty in talking or hearing over the connection?*. This procedure leads to the Percentage Difficulty scale, represented by the symbol %D.

3.2 Listening-Opinion Tests

In listening tests, the subjects just listen to a set of sentences and provide their opinions about the perceived quality. This kind of tests encompasses a set of methods described below.

Absolute Category Rating (ACR): this method uses three opinion scales: the Listen-Quality scale, the Listening-Effort scale and the Loudness-Preference scale.

The Listen-Quality scale contains five levels for the *quality of the speech* from Bad (level=1) to Excellent (level=5). The Mean listening-quality Opinion Score is represented by the symbol MOS.

The Listening-Effort scale represents the *effort required to understand the meaning of the played sentences* that led to the previous scores. These opinions go from "No meaning understood with any feasible effort" (level=1) to "Complete relaxation possible; no effort required" (level=5). The resulting average quality is represented by the symbol MOS_{LE}.

The Loudness-Preference scale takes into account the perceptual level of the listened speech signal. The *loudness preference opinion* ranges from "Much quieter than preferred" " (level=1) to "Much louder than preferred" " (level=5). The resulting average quality is represented by the symbol MOS_{LP}.

The vocal material used shall consist of simple, short sentences, meaningful and randomly chosen from non-technical literature as defined in the ITU-T Rec. P.800.

Degradation Category Rating (DCR): this method is derived from the ACR method and improves its sensitivity to differentiate quality when applied to communication links of good quality. The DCR method uses a reference signal (signal A), ideally with a MOS score of 5, passed through a degradation system to obtain the lower quality signal (signal B). Both voice samples are presented to listeners either as simple pairs (A-B) or in pairs with repetition (A-B-A-B). The *Level of Annoying* opinions range from "Degradation is very annoying" (level=1) to "Degradation is inaudible" (level=5). The evaluated Degradation Mean Opinion Score is represented by the symbol DMOS.

Comparison Category Rating (CCR): this method is similar to the DCR method: in each experiment one pair of voice samples is presented to the listener. However, in the CCR method, both the processed and unprocessed samples are randomly chosen in each test. In half of the experiments, the processed sample follows the unprocessed one, whereas in the remaining half, this order is reversed. Also, in the CCR method, the processed sample can be either degraded or improved. The subject listeners use a Comparison Scale of opinion whose opinions range from "Much Worse" (level=-1), through "About the Same" (level=0) to "Much Better" (level=3). The resulting MOS score is represented by the symbol CMOS.

Continuous Evaluation of Time Varying Speech Quality (CETVSQ): this method is defined in ITU-T Rec. P.880 [15]. It is particularly useful to assess the impact of temporal fluctuations of voice quality. By taking into account both the instantaneous and the overall perceptual quality, this method is a useful tool to diagnose degradations due to either packet loss in VoIP or handover in mobile networks. It is composed by two parts: 1) formulation, at a given instant, of an opinion in a continuous scale with sliding during the speech sequence and 2) formulation, at the end of the sequence, of a global opinion, on a standard scale of five categories.

4 Objective Methods

To be effective, subjective methods require both, precise testing procedures and a significant number of opinions to make them representative. These requirements make such methods very time consuming and expensive. Therefore, a more practical and quick solution is to use objective methods to assess the subjective quality. Their repetition under the same conditions always leads to the same final MOS scores [16]. These methods evaluate the subjective quality based on mathematical models of the psycho-physical system of an *average* human ear, considered representative of the existing human diversity. Herein, an objective method of subjective evaluation is presented.

Perceptual Evaluation of Speech Quality (PESQ): this method is based on the PESQ algorithm, described in the ITU-T Rec. P.862 [17]. It permits evaluation of narrow-band telephony codecs and end-to-end telephone systems. PESQ compares an original signal, $x(t)$, with its degraded version, $y(t)$, that results from transmitting $x(t)$ through the system under evaluation. The output given by PESQ is a MOS prediction of the perceived quality, i.e., an estimate of the result of actual subjective testing. The key process is the transformation of both the original and degraded signals into an internal representation of audio signals, similar to that of psychophysical human hearing system, taking into account the perceptual frequency (Bark) and loudness (Sone). Fig. 2 shows the basic operational framework of PESQ and its relationship with subjective MOS.

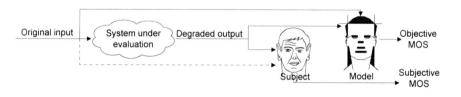

Fig. 2. Overview of the basic philosophy used in PESQ

PESQ takes into account the real effects of telephone systems, like filtering, delay variation or distortion. Currently this is the main reference on telephony voice quality evaluation. ITU-T Rec. P.862 defines test factors, coding technologies and applications for which this method proved to have acceptable accuracy. Since PESQ revealed to be inaccurate to test some factors, such as delay, it does not provide a comprehensive assessment of the overall quality of transmission. Thus, it is possible to obtain high PESQ scores with a poor call quality that includes impairment factors not relevant to PESQ. Most of the PESQ information comes from subjective experiments using the listening-quality method ACR. This recommendation should therefore be considered as referring to the opinion scale ACR_{LQ}.

5 Parametric Methods

The most relevant parametric method is the E-Model, described in the ITU-T Rec. G.107 [18]. It is presented as a planning tool to evaluate the combined effect of several parameters affecting the quality of a 3.1 kHz bandwidth telephony conversation. This model can predict the transmission quality from objective parametric values concerning physical characteristics of the subsystems involved in the acquisition, transmission, switching and delivery of voice signal. It provides an estimation for the quality of voice transmission from the mouth of the speaker to the ear of the listener, as it would be perceived by an *average* user positioned on the receiving side.

The output of the E-Model is a rate factor, R, which represents the overall quality of a two-way communication. According to its value, the ITU-T Rec. G.109 defines five categories of speech transmission quality, as shown in Table 1 [19].

Table 1. Definition of categories of speech transmission quality

R-value range	100-90	90-80	80-70	70-60	60-0
Quality category	Best	High	Medium	Low	Poor

From the R-factor, it is possible to infer an estimated conversational MOS score from the expression[2] [18]:

$$\text{MOS}_{CQE} = \begin{cases} 1; & R < 0 \\ 1 + 0.035R + R(R-60)(100-R)7\text{x}10^{-6}; & 0 < R < 100 \\ 4.5; & R > 100 \end{cases} \quad (2)$$

There is a large number of parameters inherent to transmission systems that represent degradation factors for the voice quality, thus influencing the overall voice quality in an end-to-end system. The E-Model relies on the concept that psychological factors on the psychological scale are additive. So, the R-factor combines all relevant transmission parameters. It is given by:

$$R = R_0 - I_s - I_d - I_{e\text{-}eff} + A . \quad (3)$$

In expression (3), R_0 is the basic SNR, including circuit noise and room noise. *Is* represents the degradation caused by noise that occurs simultaneously with the signal. *Id* represents the degradation due to delays. *Ie-eff* is the degradation caused by low-bandwidth codecs (i. e. compression) and caused by random packet loss. A is an

---

[2] MOS_{CQE} stands for Estimated Mean Conversation-Opinion Score.

advantage factor that allows for compensation of impairment factors when there are other advantages of access to the user. For example, a user of Global System for Mobile communications (GSM) technology is more tolerant to lower experienced quality than he would be on using PSTN. Thus, such user may tend to score with the same value two telephone sessions with objective difference of quality.

6 Conclusions and Future Work

In the voice communications context, we highlighted the importance of packet switching technology in emerging VoIP technologies along with the challenges posed by the non-guaranteed QoS. We described the most relevant issues concerning the quality of VoIP communications and how they affect intelligibility. The level of technical detail is adequate to be understood by both managers and engineers of modern enterprises. Overall, useful insight about voice quality evaluation methods was given in the paper, which is of utmost importance for service providers and application developers of such emerging technology. As future work we are studying voice signal reconstruction methods to enhance QoE in VoIP. We are designing optimized algorithms to increase customer satisfaction with VoIP services and to minimise the impact of technology limitations on user perceived quality.

References

[1] Al-Akhras, M., Momani, I.A.: VoIP Quality Assessment Technologies. Intech. VoIP Technologies (February 2011) ISBN: 978-953-307-549-5
[2] Borges, I.: VoIP Interconnection Challenges. Workshop do Plano Inovação 2008-2010. Portugal Telecom Inovação, S. A., Aveiro (March 13, 2009)
[3] Autorité de Régulation des Communications Électroniques et des Postes, "Observatoire trimestriel des marchés des communications électroniques en France; 3ème trimestre 2010; résultats définitifs." Website (January 16, 2011), http://www.arcep.fr (acceded on March 2011)
[4] EntirelyVoIP - Everything VoIP Related, "EntirelyVoIP." Website (April 16, 2008), http://entirelyvoip.com (acceded on September 2009)
[5] Point Topic Ltd., "Broadband Money Makers" Website, http://point-topic.com (acceded on September 2009)
[6] www.3G.co.uk, Cellular VoIP will generate more revenue than all fixed VoIP services. Website (September 18, 2006), http://www.3g.co.uk (acceded on April 2009)
[7] Mondal, A., Huang, C., Li, J., Jain, M., Kuzmanovic, A.: A Case for WiFi Relay: Improving VoIP Quality for WiFi Users, pp. 1 –5 (May 2010)
[8] Chu, C.-H.K., Pant, H., Richman, S.H., Wu, P.: Enterprise VoIP Reliability. In: 12th International Telecommunications Network Strategy and Planning Symposium, Networks 2006 (November 2006)
[9] Stephen, M.S., Sacker, M., Spence, C.: The Business Case for Enterprise VoIP. White Paper, Intel Information Technology. Computer Manufacturing VoIP/SoIP (February 2006)
[10] Guéguin, M., Bouquin-Jeannès, R.L., Gautier-Turbin, V., Faucon, G., Barriac, V.: On the evaluation of the conversational speech quality in telecommunications. EURASIP Journal on Advances in Signal Processing 2008 (2008)

[11] Hoßfeld, T., Binzenhöfer, A.: Analysis of Skype VoIP traffic in UMTS: End-to-end QoS and QoE measurements. Computer Networks 52(3), 650 666 (2008)

[12] Falk, T.H., Chan, W.-Y.: Performance study of objective speech quality measurement for modern wireless-voip communications (2009)

[13] ITU-T, P.800: Methods for subjective determination of transmission quality, tech. rep., ITU-T (1996)

[14] Neves, F., Soares, S., Reis, M., Tavares, F., Assuncao, P.: VoIP reconstruction under a minimum interpolation algorithm. In: IEEE International Symposium on Consumer Electronics, ISCE 2008, pp. 1–3 (April 2008)

[15] ITU-T, P.880: Continuous evaluation of time varying speech quality, Mai (2004)

[16] Rix, A., Beerends, J., Kim, D.-S., Kroon, P., Ghitza, O.: Objective assessment of speech and audio quality - technology and applications. IEEE Transactions on Audio, Speech, and Language Processing 14, 1890–1901 (2006)

[17] ITU-T, P.862: Perceptual Evaluation of Speech Quality (PESQ): An objective method for end-to-end speech quality assessment of narrow-band telephone networks and speech codecs (February 2001)

[18] ITU-T, G.107: The E-Model, a computational model for use in transmission planning (March 2005)

[19] ITU-T, G.109: Definition of categories of speech transmission quality (September 1999)

Survey on Anti-spam Single and Multi-objective Optimization

Iryna Yevseyeva[1], Vitor Basto-Fernandes[2], and José R. Méndez[3]

[1] INESC Porto, Campus FEUP, Rua Dr. Roberto Frias n.º 378,
4200-465 Porto, Portugal
iyevseyeva@inescporto.pt
[2] CIIC, Institute Polythecnic of Leiria, 2411-901 Leiria, Portugal
vitor.fernandes@ipleiria.pt
[3] University of Vigo, Campus As Lagoas S/N, 32004 – Ourense, Spain
moncho.mendez@uvigo.es

Abstract. In this paper anti-spam filtering is presented as a cumbersome service, as opposing to a software product perspective. The human effort for setting up, adaptation, maintenance and tuning of filters for spam detection is stressed. Because choosing the proper scores (relevance) for the spam filters is essential to the accuracy of the anti-spam system and one of the biggest challenges for the Apache SpamAssassin project (the most widely adopted anti-spam open-source software), we present a survey on single and multi-objective optimization studies for this purpose. Our survey constitutes a contribution and a stimulus for further research on this open research topic, with particular emphasis on evolutionary multi-objective approaches.

Keywords: Anti-spam, optimization, multi-objective.

1 Introduction

Email and Web applications were responsible for the massive adoption of the Internet for personal, business and governmental usage in the last two decades.

Malicious usage of electronic data distribution and all other forms of unsolicited communications, also designated as spam, has reached scales never seen before. Every day e-mail users receive lots of messages containing unsolicited, unwanted, legal and illegal offers for commercial products, drugs, fake investments, etc. Spam traffic has increased exponentially in the last few years. During September 2010, the percentage of spam deliveries accounted for about 92% of all Internet e-mail traffic [1]. The number of messages arriving to a mail server can easily reach the order of a million per month for small organizations or be in the order of a million per day for a medium/big organization. Estimates on worldwide cost of spam in each of the last few years are of hundreds of billions US dollars [2], mainly due to lost of productivity for users and costs of setting up and maintaining anti-spam systems.

Although e-mail has represented the main distribution channel of spam contents due to its low cost and fast delivery characteristics, Web became recently also a target

M.M. Cruz-Cunha et al. (Eds.): CENTERIS 2011, Part II, CCIS 220, pp. 120–129, 2011.
© Springer-Verlag Berlin Heidelberg 2011

for spam distribution. The change of the strict publishing-consumer approach of Web 1.0 to the collaborative approach of web 2.0, adopted by CMS (Content Management Systems), where every user is able and stimulated to produce, publish and share data, made it attractive for spam to be spread through Weblog posts, Wikis, social networks, virtual communities, etc., in addition to SMS (Short Messaging System) advertising.

The traditional e-mail services have been modified, with varying degrees of success, to adapt to this type of attacks that are able to block email servers completely. The cost of transmitted messages bandwidth, processing time, storage and specially time spent by users to manually identify and remove spam messages is alarmingly high (reaching several days a year devoted to spam sorting [2]) and follows the growth trend of spam traffic growth. The problem becomes critical in recent fast growth communities of mobile device users (*e.g.* Android, Blackberry, etc.), mainly because of mobile devices considerable reduced resources.

Current solutions for filtering spam are often based on centralized or distributed trusted and untrusted servers lists. There are also solutions for message content analysis, but these apply only to a limited scope (only text, neither images nor PDF). They introduce probabilistic uncertainty in the processing of mail and require a comprehensive maintenance for the filters to properly identify the types of messages that must be accepted or not. Methods of sending spam are continuously refined and adapted to most common and up to date filters, forcing anti-spam system administrators to constantly react and upgrade their system in a permanent race against spammers.

Several hundreds of complex filters are used in initial distributions of anti-spam systems and more filters are added in a regular basis. Importance and tuning of each of them depends on system, type of organization, business domain and requires heavy manual configuration and maintenance. Anti-spam filters are also context (location, language, culture) dependent and anti-spam tools based on the analysis of messages need to be tuned to local, specific contexts. Most popular and general anti-spam tools are optimized primarily for the spam in United States of America, being not so effective for spam filtering messages in other languages.

Anti-spam systems aim for manual work reduction on spam-filters tuning, configuration, maintenance and filters adaptation to the context or operation domain.

Due to the very high amount of messages to be classified in very short time by anti-spam systems, high performance algorithms for filters processing are need in order to minimize classification processing time.

2 Spam Filtering Approaches

Due to the high complexity of spam classification, current solutions are based on the combination of multiple techniques of different types, namely collaborative, content-based and domain authentication techniques.

Collaborative filtering is based on the use of different protocols and tools, which allow exchange of information on spam messages and source servers (spam emails or servers that have been used to distribute spam). The flexibility of the Domain Name System (DNS) protocol allows sharing information on whether a server is a source of spam or not. This gave rise to two well know techniques named white lists (i.e. dnswl.org [3]) and black lists (i.e. SpamHaus lists [4]), DNSWL and DNSBL, respectively. Peer-to-peer (P2P) complex systems were also created to share spam messages signatures among users. The most well-known among them are Pyzor [5] and Vipul's Razor [6] projects that use Nilsimsa algorithm signatures.

Content-based techniques are based on data mining and artificial intelligence approaches (Naïve Bayes, Support Vector Machines and Latent Semantic Information) that analyze the textual contents and structure of the messages and determine their legitimacy with respect to known patterns. Currently, this approach still face open research problems related to processing of images and binary files in e-mail attachments, for determining their legitimacy. Due to low performance issues, only the Naïve Bayes algorithm has been used in actual mail servers. Content based techniques success depends on context centered (language, location, business activity), extensive machine learning training and specific filters for each type of e-mail to be processed.

Domain authentication techniques identify the e-mail servers authorized to sending e-mails from different domains. These techniques use DNS service intensively to publish authorization information. In the last years Sender Policy Framework (SPF) [7] has become a *de facto* standard for the authentication domain. However, due to the limitations of this authentication scheme (especially for message forwarding), a new standard protocol Domain Keys Identified Mail (DKIM) [8] was created based on the use of digital signatures. Among other alternative popular techniques of this type, DMTP (Differentiated Mail Transfer Protocol) [9] can also be mentioned.

Collaborative techniques are only useful once a user has rated a particular email as spam, provided that it matches a known signature or corresponds to some information criteria about the e-mail. Authentication schemes are useful only when mail is sent through non-authorized mail servers. If the spammer gets an account on an authorized email server to send emails from a specific domain (which is not uncommon), these schemes are completely ineffective. Finally, content based techniques are prone to wrong classification, but they are a good complement for the emails not captured by other techniques.

Finally, we highlight the usage of regular expression matching in order to handle spam messages that are not correctly detected while using the above mentioned techniques. Regular expressions are included by hand in filters every time a new kind of spam messages is detected (for instance spam about potassium iodide pills after Fukushima nuclear disaster).

The success of each of the existing techniques, when used in isolation, is usually low. In practice, all effective anti-spam services are based on combinations of these techniques. The optimal combination of filters and their importance (or weights) depends on the context (language, user profile, business and social domain) of the e-mail sender, receiver and message. The proper choice of filter scores (or weights) and performed tests fully determines the effectiveness of spam filters.

3   Spam Filtering Problem Formulation

Optimization of the scores of filters may be formulated as both the single objective and multi-objective optimization problems. For instance, one may wish to reduce the number of spam messages arriving to mail box without losing any legitimate messages (single objective formulation with constraint), or minimize both the number of spam messages not caught by filters and the number of legitimate messages classified as spam (two objectives formulation).

For the moment few solutions have been found in the literature on optimization of scores of filters for spam classification.

SpamAssassin, the most widely used open source anti-spam system, uses either a single-objective genetic algorithm or a simple Neural Network Perceptron to set scores [10], depending on versions and software distributions. While the genetic algorithm version can take hours to run, the Perceptron is able to set scores in minutes, not producing so good results. Although genetic algorithms can achieve better results, processing time needs to be highly reduced to allow more frequent re-scoring, keeping the filter updated. By now, SpamAssassin generates scores rarely, approximately at each major release. Recently, a new single-objective genetic algorithm named Grindstone4Spam has been released at University of Vigo in order to optimize SpamAssassin filters [11].

In addition to processing time concerns, another important challenge is to face several objectives/criteria simultaneously instead of a single objective approach. In section 4 we address and compare research contributions adopting those approaches.

3.1 Objectives and Metrics

As an ensemble of classifiers problem formulation, objectives and accuracy can be measured by the amount of correct and wrong classified messages. In other words, amount of false positive (FP) and false negative (FN) classifications. False positive classifications are understood as being messages classified as spam, but they are legitimate messages, and false negatives, messages classified wrongly as legitimate when they are spam. Most widely used performance metrics in the context of spam classification are related to false positive and false negative ratios. TCR (Total Cost Ratio) is one of the most used metric, it is formulated as the ratio of false negatives and false positives, takes into account the relative importance of false positives and false negatives and allows for the single objective problem formulation. TCR is described in Equation 1, where *fn* and *fp* represent the number of false negative and false positive message classifications respectively, *nspam* represents the total amount of spam messages in the testing corpus and *k* the relative importance of legitimate messages loss compared to the non detection of spam messages. Typical values for *k* are 1, 9 and 999.

$$TCR = \frac{nspam}{k \cdot fp + fn} . \tag{1}$$

Another two important performance measures in the context of spam filtering systems are precision and recall, defined in equation (2) and (3) respectively.

$$precision = \frac{nspam\text{-}fn}{nspam\text{-}fn + fp} . \tag{2}$$

$$recall = \frac{nspam\text{-}fn}{nspam} . \tag{3}$$

Recall computes the ability of classifying spam e-mails (higher values imply more spam detected). Precision calculates the quality of a filter to generating low false positives (higher values imply lower false positives rate).

For multi-objective problem formulation, false negatives and false positives must be taken as individual, independent and conflicting objectives, meaning that improving one of the objectives leads to degrading the other one.

3.2 Testing Corpora

To generate scores for SpamAssassin large testing sets of data are need (known as *corpora*). *Corpora* means, for the current purpose, public data sets of spam and legitimate messages with known characteristics (user profile, language, type of business activity, etc.). Representative collections of email messages were made publicly available for the purpose of spam filtering research and benchmarking. The most widely used public spam data sets are LingSpam [12], Spambase [13], SpamAssassin [14], PU1 [15,16] and TREC 2005 Spam Track Public Corpus [17]. These data sets are constituted by email messages labeled as spam or legitimate, allowing for spam classifiers quality assessment.

SpamAssassin supports a process to collect testing data, made available by a community of volunteers worldwide that run the *mass-check* script on their known local legitimate and spam messages. This script processes each message and outputs the spam status (spam or legitimate), the list of rules hit, and some extra data useful for anti-spam tools analysis.

For more realistic, objective performance evaluation and to check against specialization effects, training and test sets are usually defined. Data are split into training set for score generation (typically 90% in most of published studies) and validation set (typically 10%) for scores quality evaluation.

3.3 SpamAssassin Scores Calculation

Scores calculation is done in current SpamAssassin software distributions by the following processing sequence:

- *mass-check* is run to check spam and legitimate messages each rule hits;
- *mass-check* results are used to define each rule score-range. Rules hitting more legitimate messages are restricted to negative scores, and the ones hitting more spam are restricted to positive scores. Those contributing to high discrimination legitimate vs spam are given larger score-ranges, up to the threshold limit;
- As an open-source project, rules and scores are publicly available and spammers can create messages to avoid or hit specific rules. Rules with negative scores should not be exploitable by spammers (*e.g.* spammers should not be able to fake whitelist messages);
- Due to the high (user, business, etc.) context dependence classification of messages, limits/range should be set on what is an acceptable score for each rule in order to prevent a single rule hit to be responsible for the message classification (*e.g.* 4.5 for the 5.0 default threshold);
- If a rule with positive score matches too many legitimate messages or too few spam, its maximum score is decreased. This "score ranges" calculation is done by the SpamAssassin *score-ranges-from-freqs* script;

- Some rules have hard-coded scores ("immutable rules"), not automatically generated. For instance "whitelists" have hard-coded scores, don't match many messages and would be given a very small "score range". "Bayes" rules are also immutable in order to prevent illogical scores among rules from the same family (*e.g.* BAYES_99 must have higher score than BAYES_95). "Immutable" rules have scores set to 0, if they don't hit enough messages in the training set. SpamAssassin software ignores rules with a score of 0.

A possible improvement on processing time to be introduced in the SpamAssassin optimization process can be the identification and deletion of rules having little contribution to the classification process.

4 Applied Optimization Techniques

Anti-spam systems filters score setting and tuning is, like many system administration tasks, a "traditional" manual process, based on system administrators experience, following a try and error approach.

To simplify this task, some single and multi-objective optimization techniques have recently been applied for the automatic setting of anti-spam filters scores. These experiments haven't revealed yet very convincing results. In this section we describe these techniques, their characteristics and known results.

Table 1 shows the optimization techniques that were applied to the most widely used open source anti-spam system (SpamAssassin). In addition of being the most popular open source anti-spam system, SpamAssassin is also known as the base/trunk of many commercial anti-spam software distributions.

Table 1. Optimization techniques applied to SpamAssassin

Project	Algorithm type	Characteristics
SAGA (SpamAssassin Genetic Algorithm)	Genetic algorithm	Single-objective
Perceptron	Neural network	Prediction/Class ification
Grindstone4Spam	Genetic Algorithm	Single-objective
Logistic Regression	Statistical	Multi-objective
MOSF (Multi-Objective Spam Filtering)	Evolutionary algorithm (NSGA II)	Multi-objective
SPAM-NSGA-II-GP	Genetic programming (adapted NSGA II)	Multi-objective

An initial analysis of the presented optimization techniques allows us to state generically that single objective techniques present very limited application scope, they don't allow for tradeoff settings in scenarios where false positive and false negatives are to be achieved through a fine grain multi-objective customized process, leaded by specific user profile needs (reflected in the input *corpus*). While it is expected that a business email anti-spam system setup and tuning doesn't cause loss of legitimate messages (at the expenses of higher false negative classifications), in some Blog anti-spam scenarios it is expected that spam (insultuous or offensive) messages are not allowed to enter or be published into Blog public access areas, eventually at the expenses of legitimate messages loss. In between these two extreme examples, it is possible to find a variety of examples that cover the complete spectrum of needed tradeoffs to be set by a fine tune multi-objective optimization technique.

The use of scalarization techniques, modeling multi-objective problems as single objective problems, either by summing up the objectives in a weighted sum and optimizing (minimizing/maximizing) the weight sum of objectives, or by aggregating the objectives into a single objective "utility function" (like in the TCR metric), may lead to the lost of flexibility. Scalarization techniques may limit the solution space search to convex problems only and prevents the exploration of all optimal solutions throughout the optimization process.

SAGA (SpamAssassin Genetic Algorithm) and Grindstone4Spam [11] projects belong to the type of single objective approaches described above and suffer therefore from the previously mentioned drawbacks.

While SAGA and Perceptron are delivered together with SpamAssassin software distributions (therefore, scores generation and feedback from their usage can be analyzed easily), Grindstone4Spam, Logistic Regression [18] and MOSF [19] were tested via simulation and exploratory testing. SAGA and Perceptron have been extensively referred by the anti-spam system administrators community in technical foruns. Analysis of those references leads to the conclusion that SAGA is not providing the best results in all situations when compared to other techniques (*e.g.* Logistic regression) and it is too slow (run duration of hours) for dynamic operation of spam filtering, if frequent updating of filters and corresponding scores are needed. Perceptron uses the stochastic gradient descent method for training a neural network with a linear transfer function and logarithmic sigmoid activation function. Technical/implementation problems make it unable to produce good scores, revealing also instability and incompatibilities among software distributions.

Logistic regression study in [18] presents two different algorithms, IRLS-LARS - Iteratively Re-weighted Least Squares Least Angle Regression and TR-IRLS - Truncated Regularized Iteratively Reweighted Least Squares, to perform the logistic regression calculations and shows that TR-IRLS algorithm (the best of the two) is as fast as Perceptron, very fast compared to the GA and superior to GA for scores set 0 (Bayes and network tests disabled) and scores set 1 (Bayes disabled and network tests enabled). The reference messages data set (*corpora*) used in the study was the data collected for the SpamAssassin 3.2.0 release made of 1,681,081 messages, split into training (90%) and testing set (10%).

While SAGA and Perceptron fully handle score ranges and immutable rules (mentioned in section 3.3), Logistic regression and Grindstone4Spam did not present full exploitation of those relevant pre-processing features.

In [19] MOSF - Multi-Objective Spam Filtering is presented. MOSF is based on NSGA II [20] and is used for the purpose of SpamAssassin scores multi-objective optimization. In multi-objective optimization many solutions are incomparable using the fitness function approach. For the evolutionary algorithm selection implementation two widely used schemes are available, Fonseca and Fleming [21] and Goldberg [22]. The first is adopted in the MOSF study (where the rank of a solution x is equal to the number of solutions in the population that dominate x) together with crowding distance (when solutions of the same rank have to be distinguished) to preserve population diversity. In this study gene mutation probability is set to 1%, mutation value is random, taken from a normal distribution with mean 0 and standard deviation 5 and recombination is done by n-point crossover with five parents. MOSF is run as an (n+n)-evolutionary strategy, with population size 200 for 40,000 fitness evaluations. MOSF uses TREC 2005 Spam Track Public Corpus [17], composed by 52,790 spam and 39,399 legitimate, split into 90% and 10% of the *corpura* for training and testing respectively. However MOSF initial stage results lack behind SAGA results, it produces better (dominant) solutions rapidly after the initial stage, along the same (SAGA) number of function evaluations. It beats SpamAssassin setup in classifying both spam and legitimate messages, also reducing processing time by the means of ignoring low impact/contribution rules with no loss in performance.

In SPAM-NSGA-II-GP study [23] the spam filtering problem is formulated as a specific information retrieval problem. Spam and legitimate messages are seen as non-relevant and relevant documents respectively, and the information retrieval query definition seen as analogous to rules definition for spam filtering (a query is used to get relevant documents, a rule is defined to block spam messages). SPAM-NSGA-II-GP follows an Inductive Query by Example (IQBE) approach. IQBE techniques are known as processes in which searchers provide sample of (relevant and optionally non-relevant) documents and the algorithms induce/learn the key concepts in order to find other/new relevant documents [23]. In SPAM-NSGA-II-GP an IQBE evolutionary approach is presented, based on genetic programming, with queries represented by expression syntax trees and algorithms using classic operators (crossover, mutation, and selection). Boolean rules are encoded in expression trees, subtrees are randomly selected and crossed-over, randomly selected terms or operators are changed in a randomly selected tree and first generation is created with all terms in spam messages. The approach is guided by a weighted fitness function combining *precision* and *recall* criteria. SPAM-NSGA-II-GP was tested using the public spam data set - PU1 dataset [15], consisting of a mixture of 481 spam and 618 legitimate messages, showing the benefits of multi-objective evolutionary approaches in spam filtering under the IQBE parading. SPAM-NSGA-II-GP also provides flexibility to set profiles for the user to select higher false negatives or false positives avoidance preferences.

The proposed SPAM-NSGA-II-GP algorithm is based on the well known NSGA-II algorithm, adapting NSGA-II to use genetic programming components. It falls aside of the scope of the previous techniques presented in this section, in the sense that it is focused on artificial intelligence techniques for rules creation and not in scores optimization, like the previous techniques. It is therefore difficult to set comparison references with this last method and the former ones.

5   Conclusions and Future Work

As a large scale major Internet service, under intense and permanent attack by advanced spammers software, email service requires anti-spam systems with increasing complexity and continuous improvements on optimization algorithms and processes for spam filtering purposes.

Due to the high cost of (human) maintenance of network support services, including email service, it is expected that a future generation of techniques are to be introduced in order to make these services more self-protected, self-adaptive, self-configurable and self-optimized, to get the best from any situation, to meet users needs in diverse situation with low or without explicit human intervention.

Spam filter design problem is intrinsically multi-objective, given a spam filter, stopping as many spam e-mails as possible is in direct conflict with preventing the loss of legitimate e-mails.

Statistical approaches, neural networks, single and multi-objective evolutionary algorithms proposals were presented and discussed in this paper. From both the theoretical studies and implemented techniques for the most widely used anti-spam open source software (SpamAssassin), we concluded that: results can and need to be improved; more extensive testing and comparison needs to be performed for existing multi-objective optimization techniques; indepth study on multi-objective evolutionary algorithms customization for the purpose of spam filters score tuning is needed.

The presented studies have shown the potential of optimization that can be achieved but not yet fully explored. Although other ambitious approaches could be studied and mentioned in our study (advanced genetic programming, swarm, immunitary approaches, etc.), we kept focused on the most promising, immediate, applicable, by the moment most effective approaches of dealing with the open research topic of setting optimal scores/weights for spam filters – multi-objective evolutionary optimization.

From the perspective of autonomic computing self-management features for the email anti-spam service, we can clearly state that the journey toward a fully autonomic anti-spam service is still at the early stage. Important milestones along the path are worth to mention, namely, improvement of automated functions to collect and aggregate email messages information, scores optimized/automatic/dynamic settings, automatic filters/rules construction, etc.

References

1. MessageLabs Ltd., MessageLabs Intelligence,
   http://www.messagelabs.co.uk/intelligence.aspx
2. Schryen, G.: Anti-Measures: Analysis and Design. Springer, Heidelberg (2007)
3. Dnswl.org, http://www.dnswl.org/
4. SpamHaus Project Organization, The SpamHaus Project, http://www.spamhaus.org/
5. Geeknet Inc.: Pyzor, http://pyzor.sf.net/
6. Prakash, V.V.: Vipul's Razor, http://razor.sf.net/
7. Sender Policy Framework (SPF) for Authorizing Use of Domains in E-Mail - version 1,
   http://www.ietf.org/rfc/rfc4408.txt
8. DomainKeys Identified Mail (DKIM) Signatures,
   http://www.ietf.org/rfc/rfc4871.txt
9. Duan, Z., Dong, Y., Gopalan, K.: DMTP: Controlling spam through message delivery differentiation. Computer Networks 51, 2616–2630 (2007)
10. Apache SpamAssassin Project, http://spamassassin.apache.org/

11. Grindstone for SPAM, `http://sing.ei.uvigo.es/grindstone4spam`
12. LingSpam dataset,
    `http://www.aueb.gr/users/ion/data/lingspam/public.tar.gz`
13. Spambase dataset, `http://www.ics.uci.edu/~mlearn/`
    `MLRepository.html`
14. SpamAssasin dataset, `http://spamassassin.apache.org/publiccorpus/`
15. PU1 dataset,
    `http://www.iit.demokritos.gr/skel/`
    `i-config/downloads/pu1_encoded.tar.gz`
16. Androutsopoulos, I., Koutsias, J., Chandrinos, K., Spyropoulos, C.: An experimental comparison of naive Bayesian and keyword-based anti-spam filtering with personal e-mail messages. In: 23rd Annual International ACM SIGIR Conference on Research and Development in Information Retrieval, pp. 160–167 (2000)
17. TREC 2005 Spam Track Public Corpus, plg.uwaterloo.ca/gvcormac/treccorpus (2005)
18. Findlay, D., Birk, S.: Logistic Regression and Spam Filtering. Master Thesis (2007)
19. Dudley, J., Barone, L., While, L.: Multi-objective spam filtering using an evolutionary algorithm Evolutionary Computation. In: IEEE World Congress on Computational Intelligence (CEC 2008), pp. 123 -130 (2008)
20. Deb, K., Pratap, A., Agrawal, S., Meyarivan, T.: A fast and elitist multiobjective genetic algorithm: NSGA-II. IEEE Transactions on Evolutionary Computation 6, 182–197 (2002)
21. Fonseca, C., Fleming, P.: Genetic algorithms for multi-objective optimisation: formulation, discussion, and generalisation. In: Fifth International Conference on Genetic Algorithms, pp. 416–423 (1993)
22. Goldberg, D.: Genetic Algorithms in Search, Optimization, and Machine Learning. Addison-Wesley Professional, Reading (1989)
23. López-Herrera, A., Herrera-Viedma, E., Herrera, F.: A Multiobjective Evolutionary Algorithm for Spam E-mail Filtering. In: 3rd International Conference on Intelligent System and Knowledge Engineering (2008)

Location-Based Service for a Social Network with Time and Space Information

Ana Filipa Nogueira[1] and Catarina Silva[1,2]

[1] School of Technology and Management, Polytechnic Institute of Leiria; Portugal
[2] Computer Science Communication and Research Centre, Polytechnic Institute of Leiria; Portugal
{ana.nogueira,catarina}@ipleiria.pt

Abstract. The proliferation of social networking and sharing of all kinds of information, including location information, triggered the emergence of new services, including location-based services. In this paper we enhance location-based services by adding a temporal component, allowing information about past and future locations to be considered.

Such services may be important for those who want other know their locations, for personal or professional reasons, for example allowing others to have knowledge of ones agenda, including locations and times, without need to establish personal contact.

We defined an architecture that provides location-based services to users of social networks, including information about time and space, which can be accessed through the social network or a mobile application.

To assert the validity of the proposed framework, we defined case studies to evaluate the system, where real situations were considered.

Keywords: Location-Based Services, Social Networks.

1 Introduction

The appearance of Web 2.0 provided a new way of social interaction, the Social Network Sites. Nowadays, there are many social networks with various available services, that are also available for mobile devices. In this paper, we discuss the Location-Based Services (LBS) that allow the user to have access to information that is location dependent. The main goal of the proposed work is the addition of a temporal component into a set of location-based services. Thus, a user may know the past and future locations of social network users who allow it.

A social network can be defined as a Web-based service that allows individuals to construct a public or semi-public profile within a bounded system, articulate a list of other users with whom they share a connection, and view and traverse their list of connections and those made by others within the system [1]. Some examples of social networks include Facebook, Orkut, Foursquare, hi5, MySpace, YouTube, Twitter and LinkedIn. According to Vincenzo Cosenza [2], the social networking site Facebook is the most used worldwide.

M.M. Cruz-Cunha et al. (Eds.): CENTERIS 2011, Part II, CCIS 220, pp. 130–140, 2011.
© Springer-Verlag Berlin Heidelberg 2011

Apart from personal information, comments and private messages between users, social networks allow sharing other types of information namely, the location. There are currently some applications in a few generic social networks, which allow their members to access the location of other users. For example, Facebook provides Locaccino [3] and Friends on Fire [4], and Orkut provides Nanonavi [5] and LiveContacts [6].

Rapleaf conducted a study [7], covering 49.3 million people, which focuses on the age and gender of social network users. This study covered people who are at least on one social network and have public information about their age. Contrary to expectations, female users are the majority on social networks. The female presence is stronger in the ages between 14 to 34 years, but from the age of 35 years up, the number of male users is slightly higher. In general, users use the social networks to stay connected to family and close friends and perhaps this is why most of social networks users have between 2 and 25 friends [7].

Social networks are used by individuals in their personal life, but also by institutions seeking to publicize their work. The Nonprofit Social Network Survey Report [8], released in April 2009, describes a study conducted in a sample of 980 professionals on the use of social networks by their organizations. Only non-profit institutions were covered. This report concluded that the trends regarding the use of social networks are similar to trends for personal use. Facebook, YouTube and Twitter are the most used social networks with 74%, 47% and 43% respectively. The main purpose of the use of social networks by these institutions is the marketing, typically to promote brands, programs, events or services of the institution.

One of the trends is the integration of social networks with LBS, since the sharing of location is almost a requirement among users of social networks. Thus, location-based social networks began to emerge, where people can track and share location information with others, whether via mobile device or desktop computers. Since location is an important aspect in people's lives, there are several real applications that can be supported by this type of social networks [9], such as applications for navigation or entertainment. Section 3 presents some of these applications as case studies of this work. Such services may be important for those who want other know their locations, for personal or professional reasons, for example allowing others to have knowledge of one's agenda, including locations and times, without need to establish personal contact.

Here, we propose the creation of a LBS that provides location-based services with time and space information available for users of a social network, in this case, Facebook. The proposed services are also conveniently available via mobile device.

The rest of this paper is organized as follows. Section 2 presents the background and technologies related with location-based services. Section 3 describes the case studies for this work, which will test the proposed services. Section 4 presents the proposed solution, available services, architecture and implemented prototypes. Finally, Section 5 concludes with the results and future work.

2   Background

In this section, we present the background of the proposed work related to the current location-based services and technologies that enable their development.

2.1   Location-Based Services

Social networks simplify communication because they add a set of social data on the Internet and also because they influence the development of new types of applications for mobile devices [10]. Presently, the trend is the extension of social networking applications to mobile devices, allowing the creation of diversified LBS. Location-based services are services that provide a set of information that is dependent on the user's location information [11]. Currently, the LBS can be characterized as [12]:

- Proactive: are automatically initiated when a predefined event occurs.
- Cross-referencing: Self-referencing LBSs are services in which the user and target coincide, while cross-referencing LBSs exploit the target location for service-provisioning of another user.
- Multi-target: the focus is on interrelating the locations of several targets among each other.
- Application-oriented: offer applications tailored to the user and delivered dynamically on the basis of current location and execution context.

There are two broad categories of LBS services considering the way information is sought [13], namely Pull services and Push services. In the Pull services, the user directly requests the information, which may include the location. In the Push services the user intervention is indirect or nonexistent, since these services attempt to get information when a particular event occurs.

2.2   Examples of LBS

The evolution of technology associated to mobile devices and the consequent growth of software development tools has provided the appearance of various LBS. We highlight the following services: Locaccino [3], Latitude [14], TripIt [15] and Dopplr [16].

The application Locaccino, available for the Facebook, allows sharing locations among its members by controlling their visibility to other members of the social network. The control of privacy settings belongs to the user. The Google Latitude is a LBS service that stores the user's location history. TripIt and Dopplr are social networks that provide services for disclosure of a user's travel plans, thus providing information about his future locations.

Although the described services permit a user to access the location information of others, the temporal component is very limited or nonexistent. Existing services do not allow access to all periods (current, past and future) of the temporal component.

2.3 Technologies

In this section, we introduce the technologies used to implement the work presented in this paper. The work consists of a mobile application and a web application (available on Facebook). There are many development platforms for handheld devices, including Native environments (Symbian, iPhone or Palm OS) and Runtime environments (Java ME or .NET Compact Framework). Native applications need to be compiled for a particular operating system and therefore are not as portable as the applications deployed to runtime environments [17]. For this reason, we chose a platform that allows the execution in runtime environments. We have chosen the Java ME, because there is a wide variety of mobile devices that have integrated Java Runtime Environment (JRE) [18].

The web application is integrated into the social network Facebook and its development is conditioned by it. The Facebook Open Platform provides a set of technologies, among which, PHP (Hypertext Preprocessor), that was chosen because it allows the creation of dynamic web pages [19].

3 Case Studies

Here, we discuss the case studies defined for evaluating the system, representing real application scenarios for the proposed work. The case studies for this project are: Students of Computer Engineering, Geocaching, Biclis and Carpooling.

3.1 Students

The first case study focuses on a group of students of Computer Engineering and provides an application to locate colleagues, for example, for seeking a partner to form a study group, forming groups to participate in meetings or organize extra-curricular activities. This is a case study that can be easily implemented due to the proximity and responsiveness of the students of Computer Engineering with regard to new technologies. The group of participants could be extended to include teachers. This case study, despite being very specific, can be generalized to other groups of students belonging to different courses and institutions.

3.2 Geocaching

Geocaching is a treasure hunt game in which participants (geocachers) are equipped with Global Positioning System (GPS) equipment. The main goal of the game is to locate containers hidden outdoors, called geocaches, and then share (online) the experiences lived during the search. This new form of treasure hunting is enjoyed by people of all ages and from all over the world [20]. The most common geocaches (traditional) are placed by a participant in a particular location. Subsequently, the user accesses the website and publishes the GPS coordinates of the geocache. In addition to the GPS coordinates, the users also post images and information about the caches' locations.

The proposed work can be used to group a set of geocachers and to disseminate information related to the location of the geocaches, which may include the physical location and any time information associated.

3.3   Biclis - A Bicycle Sharing System

The Biclis is a system of public bicycle sharing of Leiria. This system was developed under an European project [21], a partnership between several Portuguese entities: the City of Leiria, the School of Technology and Management of the Polytechnic Institute of Leiria and ENERDURA - Regional Energy Agency of Alta Estremadura [22] [23].

The proposed work could help the Biclis service through social network that would support users' information, allowing online registration instead of by paper. Also, through the system we could identify the locations of requisition or delivery of bicycles, plus it would be easy to insert a new location. The system would also allow employees to locate Biclis cyclists.

3.4   Carpooling

The Carpooling is the shared use of a car by the driver and one or more passengers, usually for travel between workplace and residence. In carpooling applications, a user can register itself as a carpooler, set schedules, set up his personal data, set the current location and find other carpoolers. Additionally, we propose to add other services such as: define routes between two locations and meeting points between carpoolers and also access to useful information and services of the social network.

3.5   Conclusion

In all case studies the users/participants involved share common interests and intend to disclose or access information from other users. Thus, we can justify the need to use and integrate user information in a social network. The analysis of case studies led us to identify some common requirements, including: determine the current location of a user; schedule events by setting a time and place; invite other members to events; share interesting places; communicate with other users; create a calendar or schedule from future activities; consult future locations (through schedules) from other users; access information about places where we or other members have been; access profile information of a member of our community and set a status message and disclose that status to other members of the social network.

4   Proposed Approach

In this section, we present the proposed approach to develop a location-based service for a social network with time and space information.

4.1 Introduction

The proposed solution allows users of a social network to have knowledge of the location of other users, taking into account the temporal component. For example, a user can share his agenda or location history with others. The availability of current, past and future information will be the differentiating factor from the existing services. This work uses a social network as support system to provide LBS. The main objectives of the proposed system are:

- Create location-based services with time and space information;
- Implement services that are available in mobile applications and Facebook;
- Evaluate and define the most appropriate mechanisms to ensure the privacy of users, taking into account the available services;
- Assert the viability of the location-based services with time and space information through the use of these in a real scenario.

Given these objectives, the system was divided into two subsystems: a mobile application and a web application.

4.2 Services

Table 1 shows the mapping done for some of the functional requirements of the system, namely online/offline availability and push/pull services. One of the most important services in the system is the access to information of the user locations (current, past and future) and from other users. Available services include the management and sharing of user schedules as well as consult the schedules of other users (if they allow it). Another group of system services includes management, consultation and sharing of points of interest (created by the user or other users). It is also possible to do event management, disclosure and sending invitations to other users (depending on the event).

The user can restrict the presented information by defining a perimeter or route between two points. The system has the ability to send alerts about the proximity of other users and points of interest and also about the proximity

Table 1. Examples of functional requirements

Requirement	Mobile Online	Mobile Offline	Web	Information Pull services	Information Push services
Show on map the system users, depending on the settings of each one.	x	x	x	x	x
Enable and disable the logging of the locations' history.	x	x	x	x	–
Estimate the future location of a user based on his history and/or combinations of future schedules.	x	–	x	x	x
Create rules for sharing of information.	x	x	x	x	–

(geographical or temporal) of an event. The user can search and view detailed information of other members and also organize them into groups depending on the type of relationship existing between them. The system enables communication with other users, depending on the client used (web or mobile), via e-mail, Short Message Service (SMS) or phone calls. Apart from location and communication services, it is possible to access external services such as weather forecast or a list of open pharmacies.

Privacy is very important in the context of location-based services and for this reason the user must have the highest possible control over the disclosure of his data. Thus, the presented work allows the user to configure: when, where and to whom, his locations are available (current, past and future); his personal data and status message (away, busy, etc.); the detail level of his location (GPS coordinates, etc.); the frequency of registration of current location and alerts on the proximity of other users, points of interest or events.

4.3   Architecture

The proposed architecture (Fig. 1) was designed according to the architectural pattern Model-View-Controller (MVC). It is constituted by a server (LBS Server) and two client applications: a mobile client and a web client.

The LBS Server is the component responsible for the availability of system services, consisting of six modules. The different services are the responsibility of the modules: LBS Services module is responsible for location-based services with time and space Information; Facebook Services module provides specific social network services and External Services module that is responsible for handling

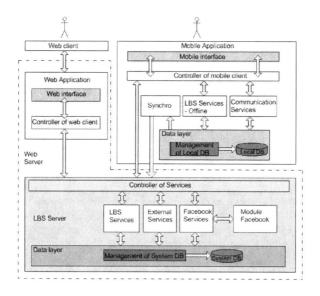

Fig. 1. Architecture

requests related with outside services. The Controller of Services module is responsible for delegating responsibilities to the three previous modules and module Module Facebook allows the access to information of social network users. Finally, there is the Management of System DB module, which is responsible for operations related to access to the system database.

The Mobile Application is also composed of six modules. LBS Services - Offline module is responsible for the availability of location-based services with time and space information, which should be available when there is no Internet connection. The mechanisms that enable communication with other users are the responsibility of the Communication Services module. The Synchro module handles all data synchronization operations between the local database and the system database. The module Mobile Interface defines the interface of the mobile application, and the Controller of mobile client implements the handlers related to the visual component. In the data layer, the module Management of Local DB was defined, that is in charge of operations related to local data storage.

The Web Application is composed of two modules: Web interface, the module responsible for the application interface and Controller of web client, the module that implements the handlers related to the visual component.

4.4 Prototypes

In this section, we present some of the prototypes of the mobile application. After authentication, the system displays a home screen (Fig. 2(a)), where a map is available showing the mobile device user's current location. The mechanism that will permit to move forward or backward in time is available. This screen also includes, at the bottom, the buttons that allow the access to the system options: My Info, People, Events, Points of Interest, Routes, Alerts, External Services and Settings.

My Info There are four tabs (Fig. 2(b)) that allow access to information about the current location, location history, the agenda and the user's personal data. In addition, we can configure the properties related to each of these items, which include the rules of visibility.

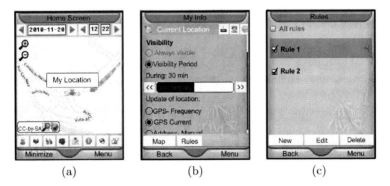

(a)   (b)   (c)

Fig. 2. (a) Home Screen; (b) My Info - Settings; (c) My Info - Visibility

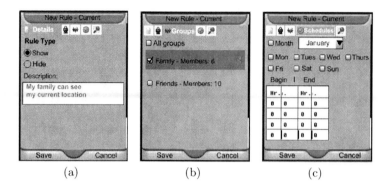

(a)   (b)   (c)

Fig. 3. Rules: (a) Visibility rules; (b) Group rules; (c) Schedule rules

In the "Current location" , "Location History" and "Schedule" tabs there is the option "Rules" that allows the configuration of the visibility rules associated with the selected item (see Fig.2(c)). In Fig. 3 the creation of a visibility rule is illustrated for the current location, where the user must specify: the type of rule (hide or show the information), a name for the rule, the friends and the groups (Fig. 3(b)) to which the rule is applied. The user can also specify the schedules (Fig. 3(c)) and location where the rule applies.

Friends Here, we can get information about friends from Facebook, which use the system to share their locations. A list of groups created by the user is also provided, allowing him to manage those groups. The user can select friends and groups and view their locations on the map. We can access the details of each friend and depending on the rules of visibility, access their locations (current, past and/or future). The user can control the requests for friendship, through: the creation of new friend requests and viewing of incoming and outgoing requests.

Events The user has the possibility to create, view, edit and delete his events. Events can be disseminated to all or part of the community and may sometimes require confirmation by the guests. The user has access to the events that were created and also to the received invitations. The user has the ability to accept or refuse invitations and even include a message in reply. An event is associated with a location and a time period, and this information can be viewed on the map.

Points of interest The user has access to the points of interest that created and those that were shared by his friends. It is also possible to manage this information and to access the details of each point of interest.

Routes The user has the possibility to enter two locations and display information that is available along this route. The available information may be: the locations of friends, events or points of interest. The user can also manage and view the details of his routes.

Alerts Provides a list of all the alerts received in the current day and the user can view the alerts received on any day. As in other contexts, the user can view detailed information about the alert and also remove the selected alert.

External Services The user can access the weather forecast, the open pharmacies and the information about post offices. Thus, the user must indicate the address or GPS coordinates as well as the day for which he wants to get the information.

Settings The user has access to a set of configuration options, such as setting up personal data and to manage groups and users.

5   Conclusions and Future Work

The popularity of social networks and the evolution of mobile technologies have led to the migration of social networks to mobile devices, increasing the importance of location information. Thus, some location-based services have appeared in social networks, which have been increasing importance.

The work presented in this paper proposes to use the infrastructure of Facebook to support a system that provides location-based services in space and time. In addition to the specific social networking services, the user should have access via mobile device or Web services system.

One of the main objectives of this work, beyond the implementation of the system, was to make it possible for it to be used in various contexts. We presented different case studies proving the usefulness and generality of the system. The case studies for this project were: Students of Computer Engineering, Geocaching, Biclis and Carpooling.

From the case studies analysis, it was established that the spatial and temporal information is something that the participants would like or need to disclose. For example, in the case study Students of Computer Engineering, the users publish their locations in order to interact socially with colleagues. On the other hand, in the Carpooling case study, the access to other users' locations and schedules may be a need for those without cars.

The defined case studies allow, in addition to determining the real situations where the system can be tested, the identification of the various user profiles that use the system features. From the interaction of different users, information can be extracted about the user profile of the location-based services with time and space information and the restrictions of each one related to the sharing of their locations.

Future work includes the provisioning of all the services specified in the architecture and the testing in a real context, by applying the system to the defined case studies. Based on the real use of the system we'll be able to verify, in practice, the usability of the system, applied to each case study. After using the system for some time, by social network users, we can analyze the information that they shared. Another suggestion, that could also prove interesting, would be the implementation of the mobile prototype in the Android's platform, because currently there are several devices that support this operating system.

References

1. Boyd, D., Ellison, N.B.: Social network sites: Definition, history, and scholarship. J. Computer-Mediated Communication 13(1) (2007)
2. Cosenza, V.: World map of social networks (2009), http://www.vincos.it/world-map-of-social-networks/
3. Locaccino - Mobile Commerce Lab Carnegie Mellon University (2010), http://locaccino.org
4. Friends on fire (2010), http://apps.facebook.com/on-fire/
5. Nanovi (2010), http://www.nanonavi.com/en_products.php
6. Live Contacts (2010), http://www.livecontacts.com/Public/DefaultIntro.aspx
7. Rapleaf, Inc.: Rapleaf Study Reveals Gender and Age Data of Social Network Users (2010), http://www.rapleaf.com/business/press_release/gender_age
8. NTEN, Common Knowledge, ThePort: Nonprofit Social Network Survey Report: Technical report (2009)
9. Knies, R.: Location-Based Social Networks Take Off (2010), http://research.microsoft.com/en-us/news/features/lbsn-120909.aspx
10. Rana, J., Kristiansson, J., Hallberg, J., Synnes, K.: Challenges for Mobile Social Networking Applications. In: International Conference on Communications Infrastructure. Systems and Applications in Europe, vol. 16, pp. 275–285 (2009)
11. Küpper, A.: Location-based Services: Fundamentals and Operation. John Wiley & Sons, Chichester (2005)
12. Bellavista, P., Küpper, A., Helal, S.: Location-Based Services: Back to the Future. IEEE Pervasive Computing 7, 85–89 (2008)
13. Steiniger, S., Neun, M., Edwardes, A.: Foundations of Location Based Services (2009), http://www.e-cartouche.ch/content_reg/cartouche/LBSbasics/en/html/index.html
14. Google Latitude (2010), http://www.google.com/intl/en_us/mobile/latitude/
15. Tripit (2010), http://www.tripit.com/
16. Dopplr (2010), http://www.dopplr.com/
17. Blom, S., Book, M., Gruhn, V., Hrushchak, R., Köhler, A.: Write once, run anywhere - a survey of mobile runtime environments. In: Proceedings of the 2008 The 3rd International Conference on Grid and Pervasive Computing - Workshops, pp. 132–137. IEEE Computer Society, Washington (2008)
18. Asakura, Y., Okuyama, G., Nakayama, Y., Usui, K., Nakamoto, Y.: Multi-Application Platform for Mobile Phones. In: IEEE Workshop on Software Technologies for Future Embedded and Ubiquitous Systems (WSTFEUS 2004), pp. 139–143 (2004)
19. Facebook Open Platform (2010), http://developers.facebook.com/fbopen/
20. Geocaching - The Official Global GPS Cache Hunt Site (2010), http://www.geocaching.com/
21. Tat-project - Students Today, Citizens Tomorrow (2010), http://www.tat-project.eu/
22. Regional Energy Agency of Alta Estremadura (2010), http://www.enerdura.pt/
23. City of Leiria: Leiria has free bycicles (2010) (in Portuguese), http://www.cm-leiria.pt/pagegen.asp?SYS_PAGE_ID=856987

Citizens@City
Mobile Application for Urban Problem Reporting

António Miguel Ribeiro, Rui Pedro Costa, Luís Marcelino, and Catarina Silva

School of Technology and Management
Polytechnic Institute of Leiria, Portugal
{2100044,2100048}@my.ipleiria.pt,
{luis.marcelino,catarina}@ipleiria.pt

Abstract. Urban problems, such as holes in the pavement, poor accesses to wheelchairs or lack of public lighting, are becoming pervasive. Despite the fact that most of these problems directly affect life quality and sometimes even safety, not everyone has the readiness or initiative to report them to the proper authorities. This fact makes these "black spots" difficult to identify and the repairing process slow. Citizens@City is an Android mobile application that allows the general population to play a more active role in the identification of these problems by reporting them to the proper authorities in a simple and fast way. Moreover, citizens will have the possibility to follow the identification and repairing processes, and know at a given moment its status (e.g. identified, repairing scheduled, solved). Additionally, it will also allow the proper authorities to identify and manage the reported problems, from their identification until they are solved.

Keywords: Mobile Applications, Urban Problem Reporting, Android.

1 Introduction

Current urban problems, e.g. missing or eroded crosswalks, holes in the pavement, poor accesses to serve handicapped citizens or lack of public lighting, are becoming a general concern, since they affect citizens' life quality. Despite the potential impact, not everyone is ready to take the initiative to collaborate with the proper authorities in the identification and repairing of these problems. Hence, these "black spots" may cause avoidable accidents and may become more severe if remain unsolved. For instance, the light outage on some streets may increase criminal actions on those areas, or leaving a hole opened may cause someone to fall in.

This paper presents a different way to report the mentioned problems other than filling paper forms in the City Hall, for instance. Citizens@City is intended to mobilize the citizens to help on this management and keep the urban area as safe and clean as possible in a short time frame. The best way found to do this is letting citizens carry their own reporting tool, so we propose a mobile application running on a smartphone.

M.M. Cruz-Cunha et al. (Eds.): CENTERIS 2011, Part II, CCIS 220, pp. 141–150, 2011.

Urban problem reporting is a worldwide issue. Most common approaches are based on manual reporting or emailing. There exists limited information on available applications. The most relevant is PDX reporter (http://www.portlandonline.com/), an application for iPhone and Android platforms developed for the city of Portland. PDX allows citizens to interact with the city concerning problems or issues with publicly maintained infrastructure. PDX Reporter requires a permanently active internet connection and does not permit the citizens to follow the identification and repairing processes, or know at a given moment its status.

Another application with a similar purpose is "My Street", a web application made available by the Portuguese Government to all citizens that can report problems on registered City Halls (http://www.portaldocidadao.pt). The users may report a problem exclusively from a web browser, selecting its location on a map and providing its basic information, consisting on a category, subject, description, image and the user contact. Limitations of web applications for the purpose of reporting urban problems include limited availability, no automatic geo-referencing and relying on the memory of citizens to report problems at a later time.

In this work we propose a different way to report the mentioned problems other than filling paper forms or using web interfaces. Citizens@City is an Android mobile application to mobilize the citizens to help on this management to keep the urban area as safe and clean as possible in a short time frame.

The rest of the paper is organized as follows. In Section 2, we describe the proposed approach, including the different working contexts, communication and security issues. In Section 3 we present the proposed architecture and in Section 4 we explain the development and deployment options. Section 5 details the tests carried out and finally, in the last section we conclude the paper and describe possible lines of future work.

2 Proposed Approach

In this section, we start by introducing the main goals of Citizens@City, including different contexts, and proceed by presenting and explaining communication and security issues.

2.1 Introduction

The main functionality of Citizens@City is to allow citizens to report urban problems. Anyone can run the application and report points of interest (urban problems expressed by subject, description, location, and an optional picture of the spot). The location can be inserted specifying an address, selecting a point on a map or retrieving GPS coordinates automatically from the mobile device. Only registered users have access to the full functionality of the service. A paradigmatic example of registered user functionality is the possibility of following up the repairing process of the problems submitted, otherwise impossible when points are submitted anonymously. There can be two roles for registered users: administrator and general user.

The system allows users to browse the reported spots in a list or, alternatively, view them in a map. It also permits that the user filters and searches points using keywords or subcategories. When the user selects a point, he is presented with the point's detail, including comments and observations. Users may, at this point, submit comments, whether he is registered or not. A point observation consists in a feedback given by a privileged user. Privileged (administrator) users may also change a point status, which is visible to everyone and moderate the comments submitted by registered or anonymous users.

The mobile application has the ability receive updates (i.e., new points added, categories renamed, subcategories deleted, etc.) in order to keep the information synchronized.

2.2 Communication and Security

Communication and security issues are of extreme importance in mobile applications. Users must be aware of communication needs and possible security breaches. When installing the application on a smartphone, users are usually informed about these settings, but sometimes fail to take notice. Citizens@City does not force the use of an Internet connection. It is indeed possible to use the application without an Internet connection, however, only the point's basic information is presented to the user. This basic information includes the category, subcategory, subject and localization. If the user had also downloaded other information earlier, the point's picture for instance, it will also be available.

In this context, online and offline modes were defined. The online mode requires an internet connection to exchange data with the server, and can be either a Wi-Fi or a 3G connection. On the other hand, the offline mode does not require an internet connection, since the points created by the user can be uploaded to the server later. In any of the previous modes, the geographic coordinates can be obtained by the mobile device using GPS, which allows the points' location to be automatically filled in. This system does not use Bluetooth communication since the data exchange with the server will always be based on the internet, and not on this type of technology. However, the user can provide a data connection to the device by Bluetooth. The offline mode allows the access to a part of the services provided by the system. These services use information previously downloaded and also information created by the user. The main features of the offline mode are:

- Show and search/filter the points previously downloaded (which are being kept in the device database) in the form of a list, allowing the user to access its basic information.
- Maintain (create, remove, edit) a list of points identified by the user for later submission.

The online mode allows a user to interact with all the system's features, among which stand out the following:

- Register or authenticate
- Submit all the points previously created by the user which have not already been uploaded to the server.
- Receive new points and categories updates.
- Obtain detailed information of the points.
- Possibility to see all points over a map interface.
- User registration and authentication with the system

In what concerns security, a system token is provided so that unauthorized users cannot access services restricted to registered users. Since the user can choose to sign in or not, he is given the possibility to store a password that will be used in the authentication process. The password is not kept in plain text, but its hash is stored. Since there are two roles acting within the system, it is also necessary to store which user belongs to which role to prevent general users to perform administrative actions.

The communication between the devices with the REST web service is done over HTTP. To be possible to keep sessions between calls to the server, tokens that identify a user in the server are used. These tokens consist in an alphanumeric string and expire after an idle time.

The user can control his level of privacy. For example, when inserting a point, the user is asked to input his location; however, three different scenarios may happen (i) the address is written by the user; (ii) the user selects a point on the map; and (iii) localization is obtained via GPS. In the first and second scenarios it is not guaranteed that the user was actually at that sight when he inserted the point. In the last scenario it is possible to know, through point's insertion time if the user's location at a given time. However, registration is not mandatory and, even an authenticated user can log off and send the point anonymously. Even if he sends the point while signed in, only little information is needed for registration: username, password and email. The system also allows the users to comment the points. These comments can be submitted with user information or anonymously.

3   Proposed Architecture

Citizens@City consists of a mobile application that communicates with a remote webservice, which is responsible for processing the clients' requests, accessing to a central database installed in the same machine, and returning the requested information. Part of this information (point's lightweight information such as name, location, description, subject, and category and subcategory information) is kept locally on the client's own database. Figure 1 illustrates the system's high level overview.

As already mentioned, registered users are associated with one of two roles, regular user or privileged user. Users in the latter role should be properly authorized and have the power to manage all the available points on system. Regular users should not have that capability.

Despite the fact that there are two different types of users, both use the same application, since it allows them to properly authenticate.

Fig. 1. System's high level overview

The mobile client architecture is depicted in Figure 2. It consists of several layers, starting with the SQLite database embedded in Android. Next there are several components communicating with the database. Each of these implements the CRUD (Create, Retrieve, Update, Delete) operations for each logic component (points, subcategories, categories, status, comments and observations). The layer on top of these is a database facade that provides an entry point for the persisted data manipulation. Above the database facade there are three components that communicate with it: the update service, the webservice gateway and the business logic. The first provides the service watching for updates to be downloaded to the client. The second one offers a common way to communicate with the webservice in order to send or retrieve data. The last one is used by the interface controllers in order to present the data properly to the user.

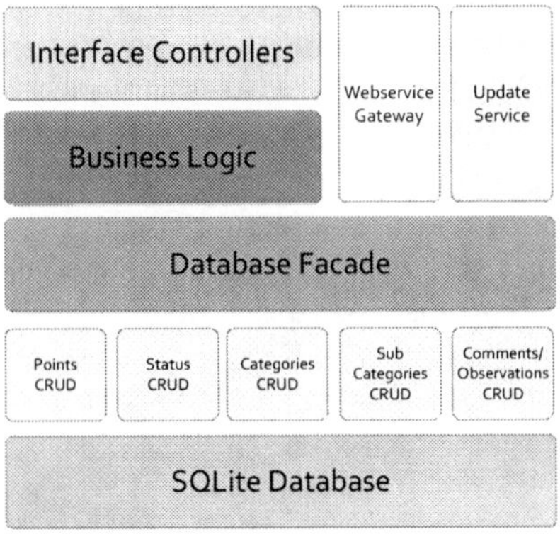

Fig. 2. System's architecture

The database management system used to maintain data on the server side was PostgreSQL, since it is free, stable and has a good support [13]. The webservice was developed using Java Enterprise Edition 6 based on REST model and running on a Glassfish Server 3. This model is lighter than the SOAP webservices since it generates less communication overhead [9], making response parsing on both sides lighter, saving processing time on the mobile device and reducing battery drain.

4 Development and Deployment

Although this application targets a specific problem (identify problems on the public streets), the proposed architecture allows an easy adaptation to other types of point marking system, just by including different categories and sub-categories.

In this section we will discuss the development and deployment options, namely the mobile platform, types of services and user interface.

4.1 Android Platform

Android was chosen as the application environment due to its extraordinary and constant growth in the smartphone market. Despite the fact that there is a wide price range for these devices, the updates are manufacturers' responsibility. The Android platform was also chosen since all Android terminals share common features (used by this application) and the quality/price relation that makes them more accessible than others with the similar features.

4.2 Push and Pull Services

The interaction between mobile client and server can be carried out under push and/or pull models whether communication is initiated by the client (pull) or the server (push). Citizens@City uses both types of interaction.

When the points list is asked to the server, it sends all that exists. The server sends only basic information about the points list and, in other to receive more complete records like comments and observations, another specific request must be done. This two level pull service gives more control to the users.

The server contains a database with all the information provided by the system. In turn, the mobile application maintains a database with simple and light information in order not to compromise the device's performance. However, the user may choose to download the complete information of a certain point. For the points saved for further submission, all of its information is saved until it is sent.

Categories, subcategories and its images are also stored on the device because this information is always used together with the points.

4.3 User Interface

The graphical user interface should be the simplest possible. The information should be pulled and presented to the user only when requested. The different screens should also be coherent so that the user do not have to learn the different menus and can use them in an intuitive way.

To develop the user interface several metaphors were used to help the user feel more comfortable and familiar with the application. The metaphor used on the point submission screen was a paper form where the user fills in the fields in order to report a problem. To the list of points, comments and observations the metaphor used was an archive of identified problems where the user can browse, select and consult the files To the comments and observations screens was also used the billboard metaphor where a user can post comments and the proper authorities can post observations. The metaphor used for the map screen was maps with geographically organized information to better visualize the reported problems [4].

The user interface itself was studied to keep it simple and intuitive so the user does not need to stop and stare to the screen trying to understand what he may be able to do or how to do it. On the main screen list information that is on the local database and only when the user presses the "MENU" button on the device more options are shown. This is the standard behaviour on the Android platform. Also, the application inherits its theme from the system and the icons used are the ones provided by the Android platform.

Figure 3 shows the application's initial screen, presenting the point list, with the menu open.

Fig. 3. Application's initial screen showing the menu

The decision to make the first screen as a list was based on suggestions from the surveys used to gather the functional requirements. The main opinion was that the user should be presented with useful information since the beginning rather than having to navigate across menus and screens to do something basic as access the existing points and see their details.

A special attention was given to colors in the application. The light font color over the dark background facilitates the visually impaired and the color blind people to read the text. Another aspect concerning accessibility is the way that the points are shown. Since a visually impaired person may have difficulty interacting with the map, it would be easier to interact with a list [10].

5 Tests, Evaluation and Results

In this section we will describe the tests carried out and infer some conclusions on the results analysis.

5.1 Introduction

In order to develop a system resilient to failure, it must be exhaustively tested. There are several types of tests that can be done by different types of users. In this case three types of testers were considered: programmers, independent testers and the customer. Programmers are the system development team responsible to implement the requirements. Independent testers are people who know the system but did not develop it. They are comfortable with technology and area in which the system works. The customer is for whom the application is being developed and it is not necessarily the final user but fits the same profile. The customer does not need to be comfortable with technology. In this case, the customers to test the application will eventually be City Hall workers.

Independent testers helped to ensure that the previously defined requirements were satisfied. The defined system tests included using the application like a normally user would use it daily basis, namely: create and submit points; filter and consult points; insert comments and observations; comment moderation; use of GPS; use of camera; use in offline and online mode; update points; and test stress the application to verify its behaviour.

5.2 Method

Despite the fact that there are several ways to execute usability tests, it was decided to follow the "10 cents" approach [1]. Four random persons were selected [6] aged between 20 and 50 years old because, ages when people care and take the initiative on the world they live in and are somewhat comfortable with technology (they are not experts but are familiar with it). Within this age range are selected: a younger and technology experienced person that may be a student that uses computers every day; a person who barely interacts with computers, only uses them when at the ATM but asks for help to get something from the internet; another person that use computers to play or browse social networks; and a middle aged person, without deep knowledge about computers but use them to execute routine tasks like using home banking, email or text processing.

It was asked the users to register on the application and log in. After this, it was proposed to create and submit a point, where the location should be selected on the map. It was also proposed to the users to perform the same task without a data connection. After re-establishing the data connection, the users were asked to update the points list and, after the update and on a previously submitted point, they were defied to see its details, comment it and see its observations. Finally, it was asked to search and filter the points list, in order to find the point the user submitted earlier.

5.3 Evaluation and Results

During the implementation process, a heuristic evaluation [5] was performed by an independent tester. The feedback received suggested four amendments to the user interface. The first was to simplify the point submission screen by creating a wizard. However, in order to keep the user from navigating through several screens to perform a task, this suggestion was not pursued. The second one suggested that the user should not be restricted to perform authentication only in the first screen. It was proposed to create a button displayed in every application's screen. Since the is no more than three levels of depth, returning to the first screen is a quick and intuitive operation and the user may not even be interested to log in while using the application. The third suggestion requested the creation of a button to reset the filter applied. This one was implemented since it makes perfectly sense that the user filters the points and intends to see them all again in a fast way.

5.4 Results

During the development phase, it was observed that the application, when running for the first time, took a little too much time to show some feedback to the user. This fact can lead users to think that the application crashed. This could be improved by showing the user some image that indicated that there was work in progress. Also, when the application is starting, the first thing that is done is loading the points from database. If there are a lot of points persisted, the application startup can be slow.

The results obtained from the several tests were useful to improve the application to turn it faster and more usable. First of all, most of the users was not familiar with the Android platform and took some time to learn how to access the options through the "MENU" key. Concerning the application itself, most of the users revealed problems accessing the register option. Also, half of the users did not realized at first what was the purpose of the buttons (the ones with the compass and map) on the submission point screen. All users did not understand at first the difference between a comment and an observation.

6 Conclusions and Future Work

With the proposed architecture, citizens can now report problems that may encounter while crossing the city. Hence, they are given the opportunity to participate actively in preserving the urban area. Also, it allows helping the proper authorities to identify and repair these "black spots". In short, Citizens@City has the potential to help keep the city clean and free of unnecessary problems, while increasing in a short-medium time frame, the quality of life for residents.

Citizens@City main achievements, overcoming prior limitations of existing approaches, include ubiquitous availability, automatic geo-referencing, possibility of off-line service, and possibility of the citizens following up the identification and repairing processes, or knowing at a given moment its status.

Future work directions may consist of developing more robust registration processes, implementing a more flexible backoffice and extending filtering capabilities.

As a final note, it is important to mention that the application was designed to be adaptable to several scenarios. In this case it was deployed in an urban problem reporting scenario but, for instance, it could be used by mobile operators to track the strength of GSM signal in a city.

Acknowledgements. We would like to thank the City Council of Leiria for their cooperation in this project.

References

1. Krug, S.: Section 9 - Usability testing on 10 cents a day. Don't Make Me Think! A Common Sense Approach to Web Usability (2000)
2. Open Handset Alliance, http://www.openhandsetalliance.com/
3. Chen, G., Kotz, D.: A Survey of Context-Aware Mobile Computing Research. Dartmouth Computer Science Technical Report
4. Krug, S.: Section 2 - How we really use the Web. Don't Make Me Think! A Common Sense Approach to Web Usability (2005)
5. Nielson, J.: Heuristic Evaluation (2005),
http://www.useit.com/papers/heuristic/

6. Tohidi, M., et al.: Getting the Right Design and the Design Right: Testing Many Is Better Than One. Montréal (2006)
7. Google Inc. Designing for Performance. Android Developers. Google Inc. (2011), http://developer.android.com/guide/practices/design/performance.html
8. Richardson, L., Ruby, S.: RESTful Web Services. O'Reilly Media, Sebastopol (2007)
9. Snell, J., Tidwell, D., Kulchenko, P.: Programming Web Services with SOAP. O'Reilly Media, Sebastopol (2001)
10. How People with Disabilities Use the Web. World Wide Web Consortium (W3C) (May 5, 2004), http://www.w3.org/WAI/EO/Drafts/PWD-Use-Web/
11. IEEE Guide for Developing System Requirements Specifications. IEEE (1998)
12. Google Inc. Platform Versions. Android Versions. Google Inc. (January de 2011), http://developer.android.com/resources/dashboard/platform-versions.html
13. PostgreSQL Global Development Group. About. PostgreSQL, http://www.postgresql.org/about/

Mobile Multimedia Visiting Guide to Knowledge and Experiences Sharing

Diogo Lopes[1], Miguel Pragosa[1], Catarina Silva[1,2], and Luis Marcelino[1,2]

[1] Polytechnic Institute of Leiria, School of Technology and Management, Campus 2,
2411-901 Leiria, Portugal
[2] Computer Science and Communication Research Centre (CIIC)
School of Technology and Management, Polytechnic Institute of Leiria
Leiria Portugal
{2100818,2100046}@my.ipleiria.pt,
{catarina,luis.marcelino}@ipleiria.pt

Abstract. The increasing search for applications that enable the sharing of experiences and the absence of applications that motivate the sharing of local knowledge prompted the development of Visit-M. It is a mobile application that allows residents and visitors of a city to share their experiences and knowledge as a community. Visit-M stimulates a strong social participation, enabling contributions of users alongside with contributions of local authorities. This paper presents a mobile and collaborative digital agenda for local events, places and routes capable of triggering a "social network" effect, generating continuous interest to create a dynamic community. To assess the integration of the developed application into the local community, local authorities were involved and potential users were invited to test the application with encouraging preliminary results.

Keywords: multimedia guide, knowledge sharing, mobile computing, social communities.

1 Introduction

Mobile devices are powerful personal computers that can replace the traditional and somewhat limited multimedia guides with more rich and up to date content. However, applications for these devices are usually targeted for a global market and there is no multimedia guide for local residents to share knowledge both with the local community and with visitors that usually value local knowledge.

The developed application focuses on this knowledge share, being a useful tool to assist visitors through the city. The Visit-M application works on a distributed scenario, allowing local authorities, local businesses and users to share a common data repository where all the community members can insert their own information. Visit-M could also be very important to local leisure resources enhancement, since it promotes public events, places and routes and allow users to evaluate them.

The application was named after its main purposes, since it is a Mobile Multimedia visiting guide for locals and outsiders: Visit-M. The "M" stands for those two words:

M.M. Cruz-Cunha et al. (Eds.): CENTERIS 2011, Part II, CCIS 220, pp. 151–161, 2011.
© Springer-Verlag Berlin Heidelberg 2011

"Multimedia" and "Mobile", which are two of the most important features of the application.

In this paper, we first address the city guides background as well as its main strengths and weaknesses, illustrated by Leiria's case study. The following section presents related work that was considered during the development of this project. Section 3 describes the proposed approach and section 4 the developed work. Section 5 evaluates the implemented system and section 6 concludes this paper.

2 Related Work

Many of the guides available are still in the form of traditional pocket books, which are usually sold or freely distributed in kiosks, public institutions and some other city points with large turnout. The city council of Leiria has its own free guide, which is called "Leiriagenda" and is monthly available to everyone.

Although everyone can easily access traditional handbooks, they may not be available at anytime or place. Furthermore, with a monthly agenda it is not possible to fix publishing mistakes or even update the published information.

The second kind of solutions is the already existing multimedia guides, which could be divided into mobile and web applications. The "Trip advisor"[1] is an example of a worldwide known web application, which also has mobile clients on different platforms. However, it is a platform that is targeted to comments from outside visitors on specific services such as accommodation or restaurants. It is uncommon to find information from local residents about services or events, so visitors often only have comments from other visitors.

There are also one other kind of applications, which focuses on the location-based communities at the expense of the application's global scope [1]. These applications come closer to our purpose, since the developed application aims to serve its users with the most valuable information available.

In contrast to the traditional handbooks, Visit-M is dynamic and allows the main authority to fix possible publishing mistakes simply by accessing a remote web site with all the back office tools needed.

Another advantage of our application is that it allows its users to share multimedia content that may present realistically events and locals, alongside with institutional content that may be more elaborated and more reliable.

After the topics above, we will show that our application could be an asset to residents that may evaluate services and events within the community and visitors who travel to the town, since it reflects the local reality.

3 Proposed Approach

This section introduces the proposed approach, focusing in three main topics: the system requirements, gathered from the study of existing guides and from meetings with City Hall representatives; the study of applicable interaction metaphors, based on real world objects; and the architecture, where the application structure is discussed in detail.

---

[1] http://www.tripadvisor.com

3.1 System Requirements

The system analysis is one of the most important subjects in the software development phase, since it allows developers to identify the features that the application should offer to its users. In this context we applied techniques, such as the storyboard and low fidelity prototypes to identify the application requirements and use cases [2][3].

The key model entities for this system are places, events and routes. A place is a geographic location that is time invariant. An event is an activity within a period of time and with a location. A route is a sequence of places or events that defines a trajectory. All these entities are associated with categories, such as Historic, Religious or Leisure, etc.

A critical requirement is the ability to list existing places, events and routes and filter them according to the user's preferences. Details of these places would make such lists unmanageable, so an event short presentation is also required and the details of an event, local or route is only showed upon request.

A user should be able to insert new events, places and even routes, or comment on existing ones. This collaborative production of contents requires the platform to be mediated. The town's administration would be a natural candidate to this role, which Leiria's administration accepted.

The application should also allow users to bookmark their favorite items, to share them with their friends and also to manage internet access over the mobile network and automatic updates when connected to the Internet.

The geo-reference of all items is also paramount to this application. Taking advantage of the device's GPS capabilities, it would be possible to guide users towards their points of interest.

Additional features that were identified but are not yet implemented are (1) the ability for a user to search content by the user that introduced or commented on an item and (2) relate multimedia content already available on the Web to a place, event or route. Feature (1) would allow the creation of "virtual guide": someone to follow and feature (2) would integrate the platform with other social networks.

The addition of context awareness to the application could be a further improvement to this application. For example, weather conditions or time of day could be taken into account when filtering events, places or routes [4].

3.2 System Metaphor

Correctly mapping the system behavior with the system mental model created by the user is imperative to achieve an intuitive interface [5]. Thus, we identified useful metaphors based day-to-day objects to guide the system development [6].

The first metaphor identified is the tourist guide, simply because it is a easy to use object that shared its purpose with the developed application.

The opinion sharing system available has the guestbook as a reference, since it allows the users to insert their own opinions about a place, an event or even a route.

A widely available multimedia library could also be used as a metaphor on the developed application, since it allows its users to combine multimedia data like videos, audios or pictures with a single item.

Finally it is also possible to compare the Visit-M application with a map showing its information geographically sorted. The application is enhanced by the GPS service, and it could turn the application into a location-based tool capable to show its users the nearest places.

3.3 Architecture

This work consists on a distributed application based on a remote application, a web service provider and the back-office application, which share the same central database through a remote information server.

A remote application was implemented on the Android platform and is able to store the user's personal information locally. The web server provides content to the client platform and receives content from authenticated users. The back-office application manages all information items, monitoring and supervising all insertions, deletions and updates to the information on the central database. The back-office tool must also allow the mediating entity to deny or to temporarily block system users.

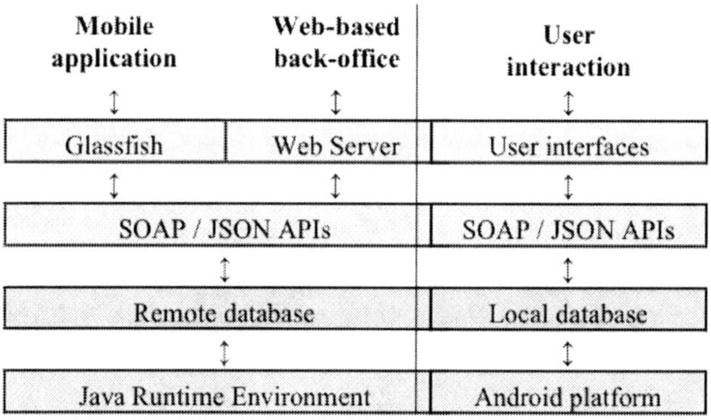

Mobile application	Web-based back-office	User interaction
↕	↕	↕
Glassfish	Web Server	User interfaces
↕	↕	↕
SOAP / JSON APIs		SOAP / JSON APIs
↕		↕
Remote database		Local database
↕		↕
Java Runtime Environment		Android platform

Fig. 1. A graphical representation of the proposed architecture

As it can be seen through the figure above, the remote information server provides two external interfaces in order to allow both the mobile and the back-office applications to share the same central database.

The information sharing one of the system's components and the central database could be done through any kind of Internet connection, such as a third generation mobile data connection, or simply a Wi-Fi infrastructure.

Since the application targets a large audience, it is expected that situations like an abrupt traffic rate growth could occur. In this case our application takes advantage of the high availability system provided by the Glassfish Application Server [7].

4 Developed Work

This section presents the decisions taken during the development phase of Visit-M. First, we will describe the mobile platform and the communication technologies chosen. Then we will detail the online and offline modes of Visit-M functioning, the privacy and security requirements defined and also the way the application accesses the information. The performance, battery lifetime and memory requirements will also be described, since they are one of the most important topics on the mobile software development field.

4.1 Development Platform

The first step taken on the application development phase was the choice for the most advantageous mobile platform. This is clearly a very important matter, since it has a strong influence on the final result of our application, as well as on the public it focuses on. In this section we will present all the conclusions taken about this context.

The Android OS is also one of the most widely used mobile operating systems, with a particular growing community, what sometimes makes the difference on the programmers' life. The huge growths on the Android's market [8] as well as the rising number of applications available on the official market are clearly two great examples of that. Facing the features and the goals of the developed application, it should be planned to have a large lifetime as well as to be available to a large number of users, so the points above identified become even more important.

The selected operating system is also based on the Java programming language, what becomes a great advantage for the programmers, since it is a well-known language. It strongly reduces the learning time that would be necessary to start programming over an unknown language. Beside this, all the development tools needed are freely available to everyone. Finally, there is also a wide and free documental support available to all the developers.

4.2 Communication Technology

The communication technologies usage also has a great importance on the performed work, because the main advantage of creating a mobile application is the chance to make use of the several communication technologies available on the today's world.

The social side of our application could only be accessed when an Internet connection is available on the mobile device. However the mobile data plans are still expensive, which led to the creation of two different Internet profiles. The first one is applied when the user accesses the Internet through a Wi-Fi access-point, and the second one is applied only when the user disposes of a mobile Internet connection. These profiles allow the application users to set more tightly the way their Internet connection should be used only by changing an option on the settings interface.

Without a valid Internet connection the application will be limited to its local features only, with no updates or social interaction available.

The Global Positioning System (GPS) network is also used by our application in order to identify the exact position of a device when its user decides to create a new point of interest using its coordinates. If the user disables his GPS device or it is not available, this service is not available, but the application still functions. We also take into account the usage of the Bluetooth technology allowing the users to share information between them, since the usage of a central data storage server made it unfeasible otherwise.

4.3 Online and Offline Modes

Since the application is to be used on the day-by-day life, and the user may not always have an available Internet connection, this project was planned to offer its users a graceful degradation state. This means we applied all the features needed to provide the user the most possible amount of resources even when not all the external application's requirements are available.

When the user does not have any available data connection, he will not be able to check the item's location on the maps, to access any multimedia content or even to insert new items on the central database. However, the application allows the user to store the inserted items locally, uploading them as soon as an Internet connection becomes available. This interaction is performed over the SOAP Web Service presented in section 3.3, "Architecture".

The application scalability level could naturally be affected by unusual user behaviors, such as an intensive usage of the application's offline mode. However, the local database uses the SQLite lightweight platform, which let the programmers to tune its settings according to the performance and efficiency requirements [9].

4.4 Privacy and Security

The private data protection is always a critical point when dealing with the user privacy and security [10]. In our application we tried to ensure our users privacy delimiting their private data visibility. In this context, one of the main measures taken about the sensible user data says the users will never receive more personal information about the community users than their usernames. A second measure applied says the application will never store de remote user's information, even if it is non-private data.

The security of the whole system is also a critical point of our application, since it trusts on the user's data insertion. To fix this problem we applied an authentication system, which users will have to complete every time they try to insert data onto the central server. The application also allows the users to store their own credentials in order to not be disturbed again. This way the major entity has a stricter control over the application's users, since it becomes possible to block users with an improper behavior.

When transferring the users' credentials over the network we are also aware of their privacy by sending the secret password masked over the MD5 digest algorithm.

4.5 Services and Persistence

One of the most often raised paradigms on the mobile computing is the way the users access the information [11]. Our scenario uses a distributed architecture where all the information is remotely stored on a central server, what makes it even more important.

Since we could ensure the data persistence on our application, it was also necessary to create two independent databases. The first one, placed on the central server, must be able to store all the public data inserted plus some system information. The second one, placed on each mobile device, must be able to store the private information inserted by each user plus some more public items downloaded. The Visit-M application lets the user choose what classes of items to synchronize, and if it should be automatically done or not.

4.6 Performance and Battery Life

One of the most important paradigms of today's mobile computing relates to the relationship between the autonomy and the performance levels achieved. In most cases a great performance may offer a better user interaction experience, but on the other hand, it usually causes an unwanted degradation of the battery lifetime. When relating to the developed application, we can identify some traffic bottlenecks that may be a critical point on the user's interaction process.

Data synchronization between the mobile devices and the central server is perhaps the most critical point when it comes to the application's performance, since it forces the user to be limited by his Internet connection and also by the amount of items to be transferred. Besides this, it is also important to avoid the excessive energy resources consumption.

In order to overcome these problems Visit-M provides a settings interface where the user can specify under what circumstances the data synchronization should be performed, and what kind of items should be synchronized. Further, the synchronization process runs over an asynchronous task, allowing the user to perform other tasks during this time.

The accesses to the multimedia resources available may have a significant impact on the user interaction, since it depends on the quality of the Internet connection available as well as on the size of files to transfer. In this context, all the resources are accessed over external applications, so nothing could be done in order to mitigate these consequences except of alerting the user for possible excessive battery consumption.

The GPS usage could also limit the device resources not only by the battery consumption but also by the network coverage required to show the map. In order to handle these behaviors, the settings panel available also allows the user to disable all the GPS-related features.

Accesses to the local database were also taken into account, since they represent a challenge for the device's computational power. In this context we tried to avoid any unnecessary database access. For instance, instead of fetching the user settings every time the application needs it, we perform a startup access to the local database, and make these values available during all the application lifetime.

Finally, there is another interface restriction based on the item listing, since its size depends on the amount of items inserted by the whole community. This means the application could be forced to fetch a huge amount of items from its database and to show all of them on a simple user interface. To solve this problem we decided to implement a dynamic system capable of listing all the items on an iterative way.

4.7 User Interaction

The interaction between the mobile application and its users may define the success of the implemented system. Thus, a significant effort focused on the development of the user interface and the identification of features that could increase the user's experience.

Several small-scale usability tests were performed during the project development to provide a qualitative evaluation of the implemented features [12][13]. The initial trials identified several layout problems caused mainly by the overlap from the virtual keyboard over form components.

Fig. 2. The "No items found" interface   **Fig. 3.** The main interface screen

Beyond other common usability features, Visit-M ensures the application's state remain the same even when the device stops the application's execution. For instance, if the user changes his device's orientation, all the screen content will be properly restored, including the user's position on a long list of items.

To support devices with different specifications, different image resolutions were prepared for low, medium or high definition screen and the application was tested on different mobile phone models and on a tablet.

If the user tried to filter the item's listing by the item's type but nothing was returned, instead of showing the user a blank screen, the application will show another screen suggesting the addition of a new item (Fig. 2). This interface is also shown every time the user tries to check for an item's opinions that do not exist.

Applications build for community participation must be inclusive and should foster universal access. The first measure taken on this way was the usage of an Android XML attribute called "content description". This field briefly describes the content of a view, what becomes really useful when using screen reader software over views without any textual representation.

In order to favor the identification of the truly important information, we also decided to build each application screen with a simple and minimalist design, using large elements and high contrast colors (Fig. 3).

The application screens are also be hierarchically ordered, to provide an easier surfing to the user. The title bar is used as a visual mnemonic that presents the user current position on the application's structure (Fig. 4). This aid may be valuable in the real world context, where the user is easily distracted from the application. This visual standard was applied throughout the entire user interface.

Additionally, images such as the main menu items are always supported with a textual description, in order to help users identifying its contents.

Fig. 4. A contextualization title bar

5   Evaluation

To verify the usability of the implemented application, its basic features were tested with potential users: authentication, add comments and introduce new points of interest. For this evaluation a test script was created that defined the tasks to perform.

5.1   Users Profiles

The script was presented to six individuals (four males and two females) with ages from 19 to 28 years old. All users were students in higher education but were not enrolled on computer science courses nor were users of the Android platform. The option to select users with no affinity with the Android platform or with average knowledge about computer systems was an attempt to present the system to potential "regular" users.

These participants are individuals that are not frequent users of technological communication tools such as Facebook or messaging platforms. Half of these users do not access the Internet from their phones while the others do so frequently. It is also worth mention that these users are not regular readers of the town's paper guide, which content is included in the developed application.

5.2   Tests Execution

Users followed the scripts individually, assisted by at least one team member. The application was installed on an Android phone LG Maximus with all resources configured (internet access, GPS, etc.). During the execution, users were asked to think aloud and verbalize both their thinking and their actions so that the observer could follow their logics.

Each task was performed separately so that the difficulty on one of them could not jeopardize the execution of the remaining tasks.

The first task required the participant to register herself/himself as a new user. This involves accessing the application menu (using the device's physical menu button), choose to "Create User" and enter a user name, e-mail address and password.

The second task consisted in the introduction of a comment about a defined "Place of interest". For this task the user would have to choose a list of places of interest, select the location to show more detail, followed by selection of comments and then just enter a new comment.

The third task was to introduce a new event. For this the user would have to choose the event list and choose the option in the menu system (using the system menu button) to "Add Event ".

5.3 Tests Results

Only half of the participants successfully finished the first task and all considered inappropriate to use the menu button on the system. Since none of these participants use an Android device on a daily basis, it is reasonable to assume that this adaptation is part of the learning process.

All users completed the second task successfully. This task did not require access to the system options menu button, as the required options were all on screen. Table 1 shows the average time and average number of errors related to this task.

Table 1. Average execution time of successful trials

Task	Average time (s)	Number of trials until success
Task 1	120	3
Task 2	62	6
Task 3	154	4

The third task was completed by 4 of the 6 users. Both users who have not completed this task also had not completed the first task. However, one of the users that had not completed the first task has now finished this. The reduced number of users in these circumstances (failing the first task but performing the third) may indicate a high learning curve for this platform.

The tests show a high success rate in the use of the application. Only the lack of knowledge of the platform was a barrier to successful use of the application on the Android platform.

6 Conclusions and Future Work

This paper presents a collaborative social multimedia guide that is a different approach to the traditional production of content from municipal governments. This change in the paradigm of content production associated with the ability of the population to evaluate events, places and routes may significantly alter the planning of activities and the way those activities are presented.

Having participated on the definition of the system, the representatives from the City Hall of Leiria recognize the potential of social networking on local communities. To make this possible, a simple and intuitive mobile application was implemented and tested. Apart from the natural barriers caused by a platform change, users could easily achieve the tasks' objectives.

The Visit-M application is a local platform that can be used as an aid to visitors from small and medium tourist locations. Once adopted by a large community of users, this solution can easily become a great advantage not only for those visiting the locality, but also for the local entities directly or indirectly dependent on tourism.

Given the constant changing world of mobile computing, it becomes simple to identify new areas of research in both the medium and long terms. The development of features sensitive to the external environment (also known as "context awareness features") would surely prove to be a great asset in the user interaction. Therefore, we plan to develop the application in this direction during a future phase of development.

Also, the use of GPS device could be optimized through the implementation of a monitoring device in real time. Thus, the application would be able to deal not only with local events or thematic routes, but also with actual routes.

Acknowledgments. We would like to thank the City Council of Leiria for their cooperation in this project.

References

1. Conde, T., Marcelino, L., Fonseca, B.: Implementing a System for Collaborative Search of Local Services. In: Briggs, R.O., Antunes, P., de Vreede, G.-J., Read, A.S. (eds.) CRIWG 2008. LNCS, vol. 5411, pp. 17–24. Springer, Heidelberg (2008)
2. Buxton, W., Baecker, R., Tohidi, M., Sellen, A.: User Sketches: A Quick, Inexpensive, and Effective way to Elicit More Reflective User Feedback. In: NordiCHI (2006)
3. Buxton, B.: Sketching User Experiences: Getting the Design Right and the Right Design. Morgan Kaufmann Publishers, San Francisco (2007)
4. Gellersen, H., Schmidt, A., Beigl, M.: Multi-Sensor Context-Awareness in Mobile Devices and Smart Artefacts. Mobilie Networks and Applications Journal (2002)
5. Norman, D.: The Design of Everyday Things. Doubleday Business, New York (1988)
6. Han, S., Yang, H., Park, J.: User interface metaphors for a PDA operating system. International Journal of Industrial Ergonomics 40, 517–529 (2010)
7. Oracle Corporation: Oracle GlassFish Server 3.1 High Availability Administration Guide, http://download.oracle.com/docs/cd/E18930_01/html/821-2426/index.html (accessed March 2011)
8. Canalys: Canalys press release 2010/081, http://www.canalys.com/pr/2010/r2010081.html
9. Song, T., Gao, T.: Performance Optimization for Flash Memory Database in Mobile Embedded System. In: Second International Workshop on Education Technology and Computer Science (2010)
10. Reagle, J., Ackerman, M., Cranor, L.: Beyond Concern: Understanding Net Users' Attitudes About Online Privacy. In: The Internet Upheaval: Raising Questions, Seeking Answers in Communications Policy (1999)
11. Harmon, R., Unni, R.: Perceived Effectiveness of Push vs. Pull Mobile Location-Based Advertising. Journal of Interactive Advertising (2007)
12. Buxton, W., Baecker, R., Tohidi, M., Sellen, A.: Getting the Right Design and the Design Right: Testing Many Is Better Than One. In: CHI, Canada (2006)
13. Krug, S.: Usability tests on 10 cents a day. In: Don't Make Me Think! A Common Sense Approach to Web Usability. 9, New Riders Publishing, Indianapolis (2000)

Mobile Application Webservice Performance Analysis: Restful Services with JSON and XML

Carlos Rodrigues, José Afonso, and Paulo Tomé

Escola Superior de Tecnologia e Gestão de Viseu,
Campus Politécnico de Repeses
3504-510 Viseu, Portugal
{cmatosr,caracas4921}@gmail.com,
ptome@di.estv.ipv.pt

Abstract. Mobile devices are growing on a pace without precedents. It is estimated that by 2013 there will be about 1.1 Billion Smartphones on use. This quick growth on Smartphone numbers and the appearance of marketplaces where mobile applications can easily be bought or downloaded is turning mobile development into a big market. As the number of users grows in a fast pace, so does the demand for new applications, leading to faster development cycles in order to produce faster results. In many cases, mobile applications are connected to pre-existing systems and it is necessary to find a quick, but stable, secure and light way to establish a communication between the mobile application and the pre-existing background system. This article aims to show how restful Webservices, combined with JSON, may help developers to fill this gap while keeping security, stability and speed.

Keywords: Mobile Applications, Webservices, XML, JSON, Performance, Android.

1 Introduction

Computer applications always had the need to communicate and interact with external systems. Technologies like CORBA – Common Request Broker Architecture, RMI – Remote Method Invocation and RPC – Remote Procedure Call, were and are still used in order to allow applications to share data and to interact [2, 5]. Those technologies had limitations such as complexity, lack of interoperability with different technologies and different systems, lack of standards, among many others drawbacks. Webservices are a set of standards and methods that allows different applications to share Data and interact. As Webservices have well defined interfaces and as they are independent of hardware, operating system and of the technology underneath, the problems faced by older technologies do not affect them. The interoperability of Webservices comes from its use of XML standards, allowing different environments to share data, and since XML is text-based and self-describing, there are no conversion issues.

Now, with Webservices being called from, not only computers, but also from mobile devices, with reduced bandwidth, sometimes with tiny data plafonds, and

M.M. Cruz-Cunha et al. (Eds.): CENTERIS 2011, Part II, CCIS 220, pp. 162–169, 2011.
© Springer-Verlag Berlin Heidelberg 2011

reduced processing power, Webservices must be analyzed to see if they need some adjustment for this new paradigm. It is important to keep in mind that the way Webservices are called and how their response is consumed, must be as light as possible, not only to save bandwidth, but also to improve battery life, by consuming less power decoding and de-serializing the Webservice response.

This paper aims to analyze data-exchange formats and how they behave when used in mobile applications. This will be done by reviewing the State of Art on this field and by producing a benchmark application in order to analyze its results.

2   State of Art

New mobile applications are released every day in a very fast pace. Some aspects in mobile communication and the way mobile applications call Webservices have already been analyzed. This kind of analyses always provides a good starting point.

2.1   REST Webservices

REST (REpresentational State Transfer) defines a set of architectural principles for designing Webservices that focus on system resources, including how resource states are addressed and transferred over HTTP by a wide range of clients, which may be written in different languages.

Basically, in a REST architecture, data and functionality are considered resources, and URIs (Uniform Resource Identifier) are used as representations to access any resource [8].

Despite of REST not being a standard, it works under several principles, such as client and server being fully identified, separated and stateless [6]. Each HTTP message contains all the information needed to make a request. This means that neither the client nor the server needs to write any state of communications between messages. In practice, many HTTP-based applications use cookies and other mechanisms to maintain session state such as rewriting URLs, which are not allowed by the REST principles. REST also uses well defined operations applied to these resources, by taking advantage of HTTP well known verbs like GET, POST, PUT or DELETE, which may be directly mapped to CRUD operations (Create, Remove, Update and Delete).   Universal syntax is used to identify resources, exposing structure-like URI's, leading to each action being identified by its URI. Rest principles say as well that it must be possible to retrieve data as XML, JSON or both, since with these two formats it is possible to have more power and flexibility [4].

Restful services implementation offers a set of advantages, including scalability of components, its stateless approach, its lightness, due to the low overhead, human readable results, several interfaces, it is easy to build with no toolkits being required, it is independent from technology, programming language, and operating system, and allows and encourages the use of XML, JSON or both [7].

2.2   SOAP Webservices

A SOAP Webservice [1] has well-defined standards, allowing it to be supported by different types of tools and systems, but by using it, the developer has to be concerned about the creation of the WSDL specification and wrap the result into a simple bulky SOAP message.

On the other hand a REST service is simple to develop, easy to use and introduces less delay between the client and the service provider, and depends entirely on the HTTP protocol. The main problem on REST development is the lack of development toolkits [9]. Tests already made [5] prove that Restful services are more suitable for mobile applications. They are faster, providing smaller and faster responses, due to its less overhead, when compared to conventional SOAP Webservices.

2.3 Data-Exchange Formats

Although XML is a great data-interchange format, which does its part greatly, there is a lot of overhead just to describe and identify the data. Mobile applications often run on mobile devices with wireless and 3G connectivity, and most of the time there is a limit bandwidth and a small data plafond. Reducing communications overhead as much as possible without compromising performance and without increasing the need for computing power is a great way to improve mobile applications efficiency and effectiveness.

XML is not the only data-interchange format used to share data between applications. Data can also be interchanged, per instance, as CSV (comma separated values) although this format is not self-describing. This leads to a reduced overhead (only one byte between each field for the separator), but this format is not self-describing and those unaware of the response format may not be able to read it properly.

JSON (JavaScript Object Notation) is a light and free data-interchange format [3]. It is easy for applications to parse and generate, as it is easy for humans to read. Since it is self-describing, theoretically all programming languages are able to parse and generate JSON. Below, on Figure1 it is possible to see a JSON object and a JSON Array:

Object: { field1:"value1",field2:"value2"}

Array: [
        {field1:"value1" , field2:"value2"},
        {field1:"value3" , field2:"value4"}
        ]

As the previous code snippet shows, a JSON object is delimited by brackets ({ }) and may contain several fields, separated by a comma (,). Every field has a text identifier, followed by a colon (:) and then by its value. An array is delimited by square brackets ([]).

A JSON value can simply be a string in double quotes, but it can also be a number, a Boolean, an array or even another JSON object. JSON also accepts null values.

A JSON string is a sequence of zero or more Unicode Characters inside double quotes and accepts escape characters like most programming languages. JSON does not allow hexadecimal or octal numbers, but decimal numbers are declared like on any programming language.

JSON offers several advantages on its implementation, such as its lightness, being easy to parse and generate, being human readable and being easily integrated with webpages as it uses Javascript syntax. Some big sized API's already return JSON (e.g. Yahoo!).

Like every technology, JSON has some drawbacks too. It may not be as readable as XML or HTML, which implies that the user must understand the syntax clearly. Potentially problems with character encoding and escape characters may appear.

The choice between XML and JSON depends on the job that is being done. In situations like the current one, where there is a need for retrieving data from a Webservice and then parse it, JSON and XML are both perfectly capable. If there is a need to update specific parts of a document, JSON may not be the best option. Since this article intent to analyze and compare how JSON and XML behave when used on a mobile application, a mobile application was created for measuring some variables and provide useful information for a better decision between JSON and XML use on mobile applications.

3 The Benchmark

Several analyses have been made in order to test XML and JSON libraries performance. Mobile developers, more than desktop applications or web developers tend to develop faster, as the demand for mobile applications grows in a fast pace. It is important, though, to keep the quality of this kind of applications.

What is trying to be done here is a comparison using the default XML and JSON libraries included on the SDK. What is trying to be achieved is a comparison between libraries that are already included on the SDK, so developers do not need to include external libraries. External libraries may bring additional functionalities and performance, but that is not the purpose of this paper.

Mobile applications are supposed to be light and fast. One of the points that should be taken under consideration is the processing time for parsing both JSON and XML responses. A faster parsing means that the processor stays less time allocated to the processes responsible for parsing the information, so it consumes less power and provides faster results. That is why one of the perspectives under this benchmark was built on, is the ability to see the time consumed by every parsing operation.

The time for retrieving the data from the server is not measured on this benchmark because there are several external factors that may change the readings. The stopwatch starts right before the parsing beginning and stops when the parsing is complete.

Developers also have also to be aware that mobile operators offer plafond based rates, where traffic is measured. So it is also important to analyze the response size, since a smaller response size allows the users to maximize their traffic plafond usage.

3.1 The Webservice

In order to feed the benchmark application, it was create a Restful Webservice capable of returning a specific number of "person" type records, each one having an id, a name, an age and a telephone number. This Webservice is going to be called from a very simple Android application created only for this purpose, which is discussed below.

To create the Webservice the Code Igniter PHP Framework, was used. Since it implements the MVC (Model View Controller) pattern, the API usage is very easy to understand. The service may be found on the following URI: http://portavermelha.net/restserver/.

The request tells the server what is the output format (XML or JSON) and how many "persons" is it going to retrieve. There is no additional logic on this service, and the data is generated by a loop. In order to retrieve 100 people on JSON format, the request URI is http://portavermelha.net/restserver /index.php/benchmark/persons/count/100/format/json. If no format is specified, XML will be returned as default.

3.2 The Application

The code for this application may be found on the following GitHub Repository (https://github.com/CarlosRodrigues/RestfulBenchmark) and it can be downloaded for testing or any other purpose.

Fig. 1. Benchmark Application Running screenshot

The application, a screenshot is shown in Fig. 1, was built for Android Devices, using Android SDK and Eclipse. In order to run it, it is necessary an Android Device running Android 2.2 Froyo or having installed Eclipse with the Android ADP plugin and Android Device Manager with a virtual device with Android 2.2.

The goal is to collect the processing time and bandwidth used to process each request, so the information can be collected and then analyzed.

In order to get the results, a class named person was created with the same fields as the Webservice returns: id, name, age, phone number. This class will help storing the instances created when parsing the data. So if the request to be parsed brings 100 persons, at the end of the parsing there will be a collection (in this case, particularly a Java ArrayList) containing 100 instances of the person class.

The JSON parsing was done using JSONArray class, which is part of the Android API. XML parsing was also done using an Android API class called DocumentBuilder, and to get every node's information, the Node class.

After the parsing, a message box is shown in which are included the elapsed time and the request size. The results are below.

3.3   The Results

The test was made using an Android Virtual Device (AVD), running Android 2.2 (SDK 8) on a laptop with an Intel core i5 430 processor clocked at 2.27Ghz, so when running this test on different machines or even on real Android devices, the results will vary.

   The first purpose of this test is to analyze how the overhead of the data-exchange formats increases the bandwidth when calling Webservices from mobile applications. The following chart (Fig. 2) shows the response size (the bandwidth used), for both JSON and XML requests.

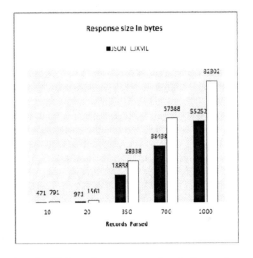

Fig. 2. Chart Representing the Webservice response size, in bytes, for several different record count

The vertical axis represents the response size in bytes and the horizontal axis represents the number of records parsed. In black are represented the readings for JSON requests and in white the readings for XML requests. It is possible to see that XML introduces more overhead than JSON, no matter how many records are returned.

   At this point, it is possible to see that the use of JSON instead if XML means a considerable reduction on the bandwidth necessary to call a Webservice, but that means nothing it implies consuming more processing time on the mobile application.

   So, it is also necessary to analyze the time (and thus the computing power) necessary to parse all the records. The elapsed time is calculated by evaluating the difference between two time stamps: just before the loop that parses the records starts, and soon after it ends. Below (Fig. 3) is a chart that shows the values.

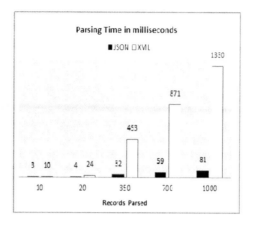

Fig. 3. Chart Representing the Webservice response parsing time, in milliseconds, converting the text response in Java Objects

Again, in this chart (Fig. 3), the horizontal axis represents the parsed record count for each test, but now the vertical axis is represents the time for each request. Smaller parsing times means that the process is faster, consumes less processing power, less energy and the user gets the results faster.

In white are represented the XML parsing times and in black JSON ones. It is possible to see that using the default parser for JSON and XML from the Android SDK, JSON is parser a lot faster than XML.

Combining the results of these two charts, it is possible to see that the use of JSON instead of XML, may reduce the bandwidth and the processing time for Webservices usage.

4   Conclusion

Developing applications for such devices with reduce processing power, limited battery duration and limited connectivity, means a more challenging task to developers, than computer application development. It is, tough, necessary to find ways to minimize these issues in order to ensure the quality of the developed applications.

Regarding the results obtained, it is possible to see that the use of JSON instead of XML as data-exchange format reduces considerably not only the bandwidth necessary but reduces also, the computing time necessary to parse the data.

JSON, like XML is auto-describing, it is easy to parse from an application and easy to read for humans. Despite of this test being built on Android, almost every programming language has at least a JSON parser class [5]. If that is not the case for one specific language, there is quite easy to build one or use one of the open source libraries available. This situation also means that there is work to be done on this field.

Each JSON parsing library provides a different approach to parsing Webservice responses. Even knowing that they all work with JSON, there are performance gaps among them. The next step is to make a comparison between the open source JSON parsers currently used on Mobile Application Development, in order to see, for specific situations, what is the most profitable approach. This way it will be possible to see how and why some parsers are faster than others, and, perhaps, combine the good parts of each one, maximizing performance.

References

1. Allamaraju, S.: RESTful Web Services Cookbook: Solutions for Improving Scalability and Simplicity. O'Reilly Media and Yahoo (2010)
2. Carneiro, L.: Sistemas distribuidos com RMI, CORBA e SOA. Consulted in 2 de, de Sistemas distribuidos com RMI, CORBA e SOA (2008)
3. Crockford, D.: JavaScript: The Good Parts, Unearthing the Excellence in JavaScript. O'Reilly Media / Yahoo Press (2008)
4. Freitag, P.: Rest vs Soap Webservices. Consulted in 2 de 2011, de (2005),
   http://www.petefreitag.com/item/431.cfm
5. Hamad, H., Saad, M., Abed, R.: Performance Evaluation of RESTful Webservices for Mobile Devices. International Arab Journal of e-Technology, 72–78 (2009)
6. Pereira, B.: Webservices Rest. Consulted in 2 de 2011, de Webservices Rest (2009):
   http://brunopereira.org/webservicesrest-indice/
7. Richardson, L., Ruby, S.: Restful Web Services. O'Reilly Media, Sebastopol (2008)
8. Rodriguez, A.: RESTful Webservices: The basics. Consulted in 1 de 3 de 2011, de IBM (6 de 2008):
   http://www.ibm.com/developerworks/webservices/
   library/ws-restful/
9. Weeber, J., Parastatidis, S., Robinson, I.: REST in Practice: Hypermedia and Systems Architecture. O'Reilly, Sebastopol (2010)

Error-Detection in Enterprise Application Integration Solutions

Rafael Z. Frantz[1], Rafael Corchuelo[2], and Carlos Molina-Jiménez[3]

[1] Dep. de Tecnologia, UNIJUÍ University
Rua do Comércio 3000, Ijuí 98700-000, RS, Brazil
rzfrantz@unijui.edu.br
[2] Dep. de Lenguajes y Sistemas Informáticos, Universidad de Sevilla
Avda. Reina Mercedes, s/n, Sevilla 41012, Spain
corchu@us.es
[3] School of Computing Science, University of Newcastle
Newcastle upon Tyne, NE1 7RU, United Kingdom
carlos.molina@ncl.ac.uk

Abstract. Enterprise Application Integration (EAI) is a field of Software Engineering. Its focus is on helping software engineers integrate existing applications at a sensible costs, so that they can easily implement and evolve business processes. EAI solutions are distributed in nature, which makes them inherently prone to failures. In this paper, we report on a proposal to address error detection in EAI solutions. The main contribution is that it can deal with both choreographies and orchestrations and that it is independent from the execution model used.

Keywords: Enterprise Application Integration; Error Monitoring; Error Detection; Dependability and Resilience.

1 Introduction

Companies are relying heavily on computer-based applications to run their businesses processes. Such processes must evolve and adapt as companies evolve and adapt to varying contextual conditions. Common problems include that the applications were not designed to facilitate integrating them with others, i.e., they do not provide a business level API, and that they were implemented using a variety of technologies that do not inter-operate easily [13]. The goal of Enterprise Application Integration (EAI) is to help reduce the costs of EAI solutions to facilitate the implementation and evolution of business processes.

Figure §1 sketches two sample EAI solutions that involve four applications and three integration processes. Note that a solution is only a logical means to organise a set of processes: different solutions can share the same processes, and a solution can contain another solution. The processes interact with the applications using the facilities they provide, e.g., an API in the best case, a user interface, a file, a database or other kinds of resources. They help implement message-based workflows to keep a number of applications' data in synchrony or

M.M. Cruz-Cunha et al. (Eds.): CENTERIS 2011, Part II, CCIS 220, pp. 170–179, 2011.

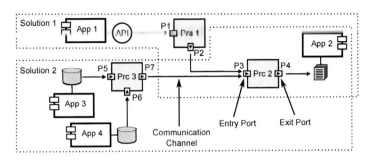

Fig. 1. Sample EAI solutions

to build new functionality on top of them. Processes use ports to communicate with each other or with applications over communication channels. Ports encapsulate reading from or writing to a resource, which helps abstract away from the details of the communication mechanism, which may range from an RPC-based protocol over HTTP to a document-based protocol implemented on a database.

The Service Oriented Architecture initiative has gained importance within the field of EAI, since it provides appropriate technologies to wrap applications and to implement message workflows. Centralised workflows, aka orchestrations, rely on a single process that helps co-ordinate a workflow of messages amongst a number of other processes and applications; contrarily, decentralised workflows, aka choreographies, do not rely on such a central co-ordinator. The tools used to implement workflows include conventional systems [8], others based on BPEL [15], and others like BizTalk [5], or Camel [10].

EAI solutions are distributed in nature, since they involve several applications and processes that may easily fail to communicate with each other [8], which argues for real-world EAI solutions to be fault-tolerant. There seems to be a general consensus that the provisioning fault-tolerance includes the following stages: event reporting, error monitoring, error diagnosing, and error recovery. Event reporting happens when processes report that they have read or written a message by means of a port; the goal of error monitoring is to analyse traces of events to find invalid correlations, i.e., anomalous sets of messages that have been processed together; such correlations must later be diagnosed to find the cause of the anomalies, and appropriate actions to recover from the error must be taken in the error recovery stage.

Orchestration workflows rely on an external mechanism that analyses inbound messages, correlates them, and starts a new instance of the orchestration whenever a correlation is found. The typical execution model is referred to as process-based since a thread must be allocated to run a process on a given correlation; contrarily, the task-based execution model relies on a pool of threads that are allocated to the tasks. Simply put, in the process-based model threads remain allocated to a process even if that process is waiting for the answer to a request to another process; contrarily, in the task-based model, no thread shall be idle as long as a task in a process is ready for execution.

In this paper, we report on a proposal to build an error monitor for EAI solutions. The key contribution is that it works with both orchestrations and choreographies, and that it is independent from the execution model used. In Section §2, we report on other proposals in the literature; in Section §3, we present an overview of our proposal; in Section §4, we delve into our proposal to detect errors; finally, we present our conclusions in Section §5.

2   Related Work

Error detection is relatively easy in orchestration systems because either correlations are found prior to starting an orchestration process and everything happens within the boundaries of this process. Contrarily, in choreographies, a correlation may typically involve several processes that run in total asynchrony, and there is not a single point of control; furthermore, EAI solutions may overlap since it is common that processes are reused across several business processes. This makes it more difficult to endow choreographies with fault-tolerance capabilities.

The research on fault tolerance that has been conducted by the workflow community is closely related to our work. Chiu and others [4] presented an abstract model for workflows with embedded fault-tolerance capabilities; it set the foundations for other proposals in this field. Hagen and Alonso [8] presented a proposal that builds on the two-phase commit protocol, and it is suitable for orchestrations in which the execution model is process-based. Alonso and others [1] provided additional details on the minimum requirements to deal with fault tolerance in orchestrated systems. Liu and others [12] discussed how to deal with fault tolerance in settings in which recovery actions are difficult or infeasible to implement; the authors also assume the existence of a centralised workflow engine, i.e., they also focus on orchestrations. Li and others [11] reported on a theoretical solution that is based on using Petri nets; they see processes as if they were controllers, and report on detecting some classes of errors by means of linear parity checks; the key is that they focus on systems in which a fault can involve an arbitrarily large number of correlated messages, which are consumed and produced by distributed processes, but are assume that they are choreographed by a central processor. An architecture for fault-tolerant workflows, based on finite state machines that recognise valid sequences of messages was discussed in [6]; this proposal is suitable for both orchestrated and choreographed processes; however it is aimed at process-based executions.

The study of fault tolerance in the context of choreographies has been paid less attention in the literature. Chen and others [3] presented a proposal that deviates from the previous ones in that their results can be applied to both orchestrations and choreographies. They assume that the system under consideration is organised into three logical layers (front-end, application server, and database server), plus an orthogonal layer (the logging system). Since they can deal with choreographies, they need to analyse message traces to detect errors. They assume that each message has a unique identifier that allows to trace it throughout the execution flow; unfortunately, they cannot deal with EAI solutions in which messages are split or aggregated, since this would require to find correlations amongst messages, which is not supported at all. Due to this limitation, it can easily deal with both process- and task-based execution models. Yan and Dague [16] suggested to re-use the body of knowledge about error detection in industrial discrete event systems, in error detection in web services applications; they discussed runtime error detection of orchestrated web services; a salient feature of this proposal is that, similarly to [14], the authors assume that failure events are not observable; the granularity of execution in this approach is at process level. Baresi and others [2] discussed some preliminary ideas for building an error monitor that can be used for both orchestrated and choreographed processes. No implementation or evaluation was provided.

Our analysis of the literature reveals most authors in the EAI field focus on orchestrations and the process-based execution model; choreographies and the task-based execution model have been paid little attention so far. Another conclusion is that the distinction amongst the stages required to provision fault tolerance is often blurred. The reason is that many proposals focus on error recovery since error detection or error diagnosing is quite a trivial task. In many proposals, the presence of an error can be derived from a single event. For instance, the conventional try-catch mechanism involves the notification of a single event to be caught by the exception mechanisms [7]. However, there is a large class of applications in which the presence of an error can only be deduced from the analysis of traces of events that are related to each other, e.g., by order, parent-child relationships, propagation, or causations. Error detection in these cases is a challenging problem, in particular, when the number of events is large.

3   Overview of Our Proposal

Our proposal builds on a monitor to which each port must report events, and a set of rules that help determine if correlations are valid or not. A monitor is composed of three modules called Registrar, Event Handler, and Error Detector, three databases called Descriptions Database, Graphs Database, and History Database, and a queue called Graphs Queue. Figure §2 presents the abstract model for them.

The Registrar module is responsible for maintaining the Descriptions Database up to date. This database provides the other modules a description of the solutions, processes, ports, and rules the monitor handles. (Note that we use term 'artefact' to refer to both solutions and processes.)

The Event Handler uses the events reported by ports to update the Graphs Database and the Graphs Queue. An event can be of type Reception, which happens at ports that read data from an application (either successfully or unsuccessfully) and other ports that fail to read data at all, Shipment, which occurs when a port writes information (either successfully or unsuccessfully), and Transfer, which happens when a port succeeds to read data that was written previously by another port. Every event has a target binding and zero, one, or more source bindings. We use this term to refer to the data involved in an event, namely: the instant when the event happened, the name of the port, the identifier of the message read or written, and a status, which can be either Status::OK to mean that

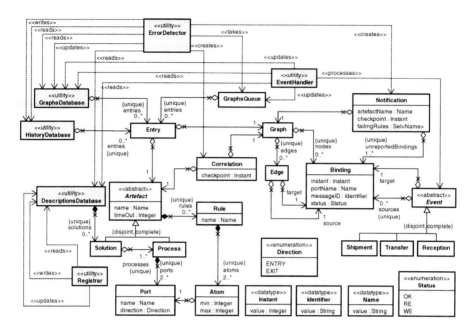

Fig. 2. Model for Registrar, Event Handler and Error Detector modules

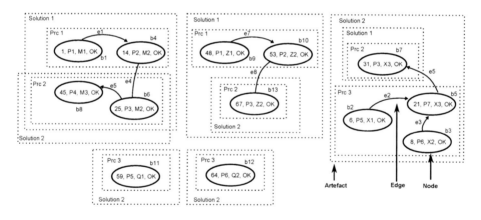

Fig. 3. Sample Graphs Database

no problem was detected, Status::RE to mean that there was a reading failure, or Status::WE to mean that there was a writing failure.

The Graphs Database stores an entry per artefact in the Descriptions Database; such entries contain a graph that the Event Handler builds incrementally, as it receives events. Figure §3 shows a sample Graphs Database for the EAI solution in Figure §1. For instance, let us focus on bindings b_6 and b_4: the former is involved in process Prc_2 and both solutions, and it denotes that port P_3 dealt with message M_2 at instant 25, and that the result was successful; the later is involved in process Prc_1 and $Solution_1$ only, and it indicates that port P_2 dealt with message M_2 at instant 14, and that the result was successful; besides, the edge between them both indicates that binding b_6 originates from binding b_4.

The Graphs Queue is used to refer to the entries in the Graphs Database that have changed since the database was analysed for the last time. This helps minimise the work performed by the Error Detector, whose abstract model is presented in Figure §2. Note that it is relatively easy to find correlations in a graph like the one in Figure §3 since this task amounts to finding the connected components of the graph [9]. Contrarily, verifying them depends completely on the semantics of the EAI solutions involved. This is why we assign each artefact an upper bound to the total amount of time it is expected to take to produce a valid correlation, i.e., a time out, and a set of rules of the following form, cf. Figure §2:

$$P_1[m_1..n_1], \ldots, P_p[m_p..n_p] \rightarrow Q_1[r_1..s_1], \ldots, Q_q[r_q..s_q],$$

where P_i and Q_j are port names and m_i, n_i, r_i, s_i denote the minimum and maximum number of messages a correlation allows in each port so that it can be considered valid. For instance, a rule like $P_5[1..1]$, $P_6[1..1] \rightarrow P_4[1..10]$ regarding $Solution_2$ in Figure §1 means that it is a requirement for a correlation to be considered valid that it has one message at port P_5, one message at port P_6 and then 1–10 messages at port P_4.

The correlations found by the Error Detector module are removed from the Graphs Database and stored in the History Database. This helps us complete them if new messages are reported later.

4   Detecting Errors

Due to space limitations, we do not provide additional details on the Registrar or the Event Handler modules. Instead, we focus on the Error Detector, which is the central module. Its algorithm is as follows:

```
1: to detectErrors() do
2:     repeat
3:         s = findCorrelations()
4:         for each correlation c in s do
5:             verifyCorrelation(c)
6:         end for
7:     end repeat
8: end
```

It runs continuously; in each iteration, it first finds a set of correlations and then verifies them sequentially. In the following subsections, we delve into the algorithms to find correlations and to verify them.

4.1   Finding Correlations

The algorithm to find correlations is as follows:

```
 1: to findCorrelations(): Set(Correlation) do
 2:     take entry f from the Graphs Queue
 3:     checkpoint = getTime()
 4:     s = find connected components of f.graph
 5:     result = ∅
 6:     for each graph g in s do
 7:         c = new Correlation(artefact = f.artefact, graph = g, checkpoint = checkpoint)
 8:         add c to result
 9:     end for
10: end
```

This algorithm starts by taking an entry f from the Graphs Queue at line §2; if there is not an entry available, then we assume that the algorithm blocks here until an entry is available. Note that the core of the algorithm is line §4, in which we find the connected components of the graphs that corresponds to the entry we have taken from the Graphs Queue.

4.2   Verifying Correlations

A correlation can be diagnosed as on-going, valid or invalid. A correlation is on-going if its deadline has not expired yet. Bear in mind that correlations are analysed within the context of an artefact, which must have an associated time out and set of rules. The deadline for a correlation is defined as the time of its earliest binding plus this time out. This provides a time frame within which all of the messages involved in the correlation are expected to be reported. A correlation is valid if all of the messages it involves were read or written by the expected deadline, there was no reading or writing failure, and all of the rules involved are passed; otherwise, it is considered invalid and a notification must be generated so that it can be diagnosed and appropriate recovery actions can be executed later. The algorithm to verify a correlation is as follows:

```
 1: to verifyCorrelation(in c: Correlation) do
 2:     findCompletion(c, out completedGraph, out unnotifiedBindings)
 3:     status = every binding b in completedGraph.nodes has status OK?
 4:     earliestInstant = minimum of completedGraph.nodes.instant
 5:     latestInstant = maximum of completedGraph.nodes.instant
 6:     deadline = earliestInstant + c.artefact.timeOut
 7:     notPassedRules = checkRules(completedGraph, c.artefact)
 8:     isValid  = deadline <= c.checkpoint and latestInstant <= deadline and
 9:                 status == true and notPassedRules == ∅
10:     isInvalid = (deadline < latestInstant) or
11:                 (deadline <= c.checkpoint and (not status or notPassedRules ≠ ∅))
12:     if isValid then
13:         f = find the entry for c.artefact in the Graphs Database
14:         remove c.graph from f.graph
```

```
15:         g = new Entry(artefact = c.artefact, graph = c.graph, isValid = true)
16:         add g to History database
17:    elsif isInvalid then
18:         f = find the entry for c.artefact in the Graphs Database
19:         remove c.graph from f.graph
20:         g = new Entry(artefact = c.artefact, graph = completedGraph, isValid = false)
21:
22:         add g to History database
23:         n = new Notification( artefactName = c.artefact.name, graph = completedGraph,
24:                       unnotifiedBindings = unnotifiedBindings, checkpoint = c.checkpoint,
25:                       notPassedRules = notPassedRules)
26:         send n to the notification port of the monitor
27:    elsif
28:         - Nothing to do, since c is an on-going correlation
29:    end if
30: end
```

The algorithm gets a Correlation c as input; the first thing it has to do is to complete it with the help of the History Database. Note that correlations that are not on-going are removed from the Graphs Database; due to the asynchronous nature of EAI solutions, that implies that a after a correlation is verified, additional correlated messages may be reported. This is also the reason why before verifying a correlation, it must be completed using the History Database. Algorithm findCompletion, which is explained later, performs this tasks; given a correlation c, it returns a graph that includes $c.graph$ and additional nodes and edges found in the History Database, as well the subset of bindings in the completed correlation that have not been notified, yet.

4.3   Completing Correlations

The algorithm to complete a correlation is as follows:

```
1: to findCompletion(in c: Correlation, out completedGraph: Graph,
2:                    out unnotifiedBindings: Set(Binding) ) do
3:    completedGraph = new Graph(nodes = shallow copy of c.graph.nodes,
4:                               edges = shallow copy of c.graph.edges)
5:    unnotifiedBindings = shallow copy of c.graph.nodes
6:    s = find all of the entries for c.artefact in the History database
7:    for each entry f in s do
8:        intersection = c.graph.nodes ∩ f.graph.nodes
9:        if intersection ≠ ∅ then
10:           merge f.graph into completedGraph
11:           if not f.isValid then
12:               remove intersection from unnotifiedBindings
13:           end if
14:       end if
15:   end for
16: end
```

This algorithm takes a correlation c as input and returns a graph that is a completed version of $c.graph$ and a set of bindings that have not been notified so far. It first creates an initial completed graph at line §3 from a shallow copy of the nodes and the edges of the graph of correlation c. A shallow copy is made because otherwise line §10 would modify the original graph in correlation c. The loop at lines §7–§15 discovers if there are common bindings between correlation c and an entry f. If common bindings are found they are merged into the resulting completed graph, and bindings that were detected to be already in the graph of entry f are removed from the set of unnotified bindings, leaving only new bindings that were not reported yet. Note that this is done only if graph f represents an invalid graph; otherwise all bindings are new.

4.4   Checking Rules

The algorithm to check rules is as follows:

```
 1: to checkRules(in g: Graph, in t: Artefact): Set(Name) do
 2:     result = ∅
 3:     for each rule r in t.rules do
 4:         for each atom a in r.atoms do
 5:             n = count bindings b in g.nodes such that b.portName == a.port.name
 6:             if n < a.min or n > a.max then
 7:                 add r.name to result
 8:             end if
 9:         end for
10:     end for
11: end
```

This algorithm takes a graph that represents a correlation and an artefact as input; it returns the subset of rules associated with the artefact that the correlation does not pass. The algorithm is simple since we just need to count the number of bindings that involve the port referenced in the atom; if this figure is not within the margins that the atom establishes, then it is added to the result of the algorithm since that rule is not passed.

5   Conclusions

In this paper, we have presented a proposal to detect errors in the context of EAI solutions. It is novel in that it is not bound to orchestrations or choreographies, neither to a process- nor a task-based execution model; it is totally independent. We have analysed the time complexity of our algorithm and we have proved that it is $O(b + c\,h)$, where b denotes the average number of bindings that have been reported by means of events since the last checkpoint, c denotes the average number of correlations found at each checkpoint, and h the average number of entries for an artefact in the History Database. Note that b and c are expected to vary within some margins as long as the Descriptions Database does not change; contrarily, h increases monotonically as time goes by. This implies that after a point in time, this complexity is dominated by h, i.e., the algorithm behaves linearly in the average number of entries per artefact in the History Database. Recall that the only purpose of this database is to complete correlations that are found in the Graphs Database, just in case a message is processed by a port after the deadline for the corresponding correlation expires. In practice, it makes sense to remove old information from the database periodically, say a week; this puts an upper bound to the size of the History Database, which, in turn, puts an upper bound to the total time the algorithm may take to detect errors.

References

[1] Alonso, G., Hagen, C., Divyakant, D., Abbadi, A.E., Mohan, C.: Enhancing the fault tolerance of workflow management systems. IEEE Concurrency 8(3), 74–81 (2000)

[2] Baresi, L., Guinea, S., Kazhamiakin, R., Pistore, M.: An Integrated Approach for the Run-Time Monitoring of BPEL Orchestrations. In: Mähönen, P., Pohl, K., Priol, T. (eds.) ServiceWave 2008. LNCS, vol. 5377, pp. 1–12. Springer, Heidelberg (2008)

[3] Chen, M., Accardi, A., Kiciman, E., Lloyd, J., Patterson, D., Fox, A., Brewer, E.: Path-based failure and evolution management. In: Int'l Symp. Netw. Syst. Des. and Impl., p. 23 (2004)

[4] Chiu, D., Li, Q., Karlapalem, K.: A meta modeling approach to workflow management systems supporting exception handling. Inf. Syst. 24(2), 159–184 (1999)

[5] Dunphy, G., Metwally, A.: Pro BizTalk 2006. Apress (2006)

[6] Ermagan, V., Kruger, I., Menarini, M.: A fault tolerance approach for enterprise applications. In: IEEE Int'l Conf. Serv. Comput., vol. 2, pp. 63–72 (2008)

[7] Goodenough, J.: Exception handling: Issues and proposed notation. Communications of the ACM 18(12), 683–696 (1975)

[8] Hagen, C., Alonso, G.: Exception handling in workflow management systems. IEEE Trans. Softw. Eng. 26(10), 943–958 (2000)

[9] Hopcroft, J.E., Tarjan, R.E.: Efficient algorithms for graph manipulation. Communications ofthe ACM 16(6), 372–378 (1973)

[10] Ibsen, C., Anstey, J.: Camel in Action. Manning Publications (2010)

[11] Li, L., Hadjicostis, C., Sreenivas, R.: Designs of bisimilar petri net controllers with fault tolerance capabilities. IEEE Trans. Syst. Man Cybern. Part A: Syst. Humans 38(1), 207–217 (2008)

[12] Liu, C., Orlowska, M., Lin, X., Zhou, X.: Improving backward recovery in workflow systems. In: Int'l Conf. Database Syst. Adv. Appl., p. 276 (2001)

[13] Messerschmitt, D., Szyperski, C.: Software Ecosystem: Understanding an Indispensable Technology and Industry. MIT Press, Cambridge (2003)

[14] Sampath, M., Sengupta, R., Lafortune, S.: Failure diagnosis using discrete-event models. IEEE Trans. on Control Syst. Technol. 4(2), 105–124 (1996)

[15] Wright, M., Reynolds, A.: Oracle SOA Suite Developer's Guide. Packt Publishing (2009)

[16] Yan, Y., Dague, P.: Modeling and diagnosing orchestrated web service processes. In: IEEE Int'l Conf. on Web Serv., pp. 51–59. IEEE Computer Society, Los Alamitos (2007)

Back-Propagation Artificial Neural Network for ERP Adoption Cost Estimation

Mohamed T. Kotb[1], Moutaz Haddara[2], and Yehia T. Kotb[3]

[1] Software Engineer, London, Ontario, Canada
[2] University of Agder, Norway
[3] University of Western Ontario, Canada
mthabet@gmail.com, moutaz.haddara@uia.no,
ykotb@csd.uwo.ca

Abstract. Small and medium size enterprises (SMEs) are greatly affected by cost escalations and overruns Reliable cost factors estimation and management is a key for the success of Enterprise Resource Planning (ERP) systems adoptions in enterprises generally and SMEs specifically. This research area is still immature and needs a considerable amount of research to seek solid and realistic cost factors estimation. Majority of research in this area targets the enhancement of estimates calculated by COCOMO family models. This research is the beginning of a series of models that would try to replace COCOMO with other models that could be more adequate and focused on ERP adoptions. This paper introduces a feed-forward back propagation artificial neural network model for cost factors estimation. We comment on results, merits and limitations of the model proposed. Although the model addresses SMEs, however, it could be extended and applied in various environments and contexts.

Keywords: ERP, cost estimation, neural networks, SMEs.

1 Introduction

Due to their large scale, complexity and substantial investments, ERP systems have been a center of attention from academia and practice. For various reasons, more and more SMEs are adopting ERP systems. SMEs are fundamentally different environments when compared to large enterprises [1]. SMEs are greatly affected and more sensitive to costs than large enterprises, as they have limited budgets and scarce resources [2]. ERP adoption projects are non trivial, and they require careful planning, budgeting, management, and execution. ERP adoptions research shows that cost overruns usually occur during the ERP adoptions, and companies cross their estimated budgets significantly [3-6]. Project budgeting and cost estimation are necessary in the preparation and planning phase for ERP systems' adoptions. They give an insight into the roadmap of the adoption project boundaries, as they highly contribute to project success and the prevention of cost overruns, and in some cases, cost overruns have driven the implementing companies to bankruptcy [5, 7, 8]. There is few research that targets ERP cost estimations in SMEs [2]. Thus the need for more reliable and realistic ERP cost estimation models persists [2, 7, 9-11].

M.M. Cruz-Cunha et al. (Eds.): CENTERIS 2011, Part II, CCIS 220, pp. 180–187, 2011.
© Springer-Verlag Berlin Heidelberg 2011

This paper aims at calculating weights for ERP cost factors using synthetic data coupled with artificial neural network technology (ANN). The objective of using the ANN technology is to calculate the weights based on real scenarios that represent successes and failures in industry. The advantage of using this technology is that whenever the parameters change, or a new parameters/perspective is added to the parameters profiles, all is needed is to have the ANN retrained. In future research, the proposed model will be fed with historical data.

The rest of this paper is organized as follows: Section 2 provides an overview of literature in the area of ERP cost estimation. Section 3 formulates the problem under discussion. Section 4 shows the chosen optimization method for cost factor estimation. Section 5 discusses the architecture and training phases of the artificial neural network. Section 6 illustrates the experiments and results, and finally section 7 concludes the work and highlights the proposed solution extensions and future work.

2 Study Background

In literature, very few studies address ERP costs identification and ex-ante evaluation in SMEs environments [2], as well as, there is an evident gap in ERP adoption cost management and estimation research areas [2, 5, 10, 12, 13]. The gap is partly because the ERP adoption cost identification and estimation is a complex chore [4, 5, 10, 14-19]; it requires attentive analysis of both direct and indirect (*usually hidden*) costs. Moreover, the established and extensively used software cost estimation models e.g. COCOMO (COnstructive COst MOdel) [20] are not adequate to an ERP setting [5, 10-12, 14, 21]. COCOMO and analogous models are primarily focused on estimating software development costs, and some of their considered cost factors might not be valid for ERP adoption projects, as lines of code (KLOC) and development time (D) are not pertinent factors in an ERP context [10, 14, 17, 21-23]. Nevertheless, these models could be relevant to ERP vendors when pricing their ERP packages.

As an effort to extend the application of COCOMO into ERP systems implementations, Maya Daneva [13] introduced a model that complements the classic COCOMO model [20] with Monte Carlo simulation to introduce errors that results in more realistic estimates. The model has been designed to take the management portfolio under consideration [24]. The model has been seen be one good alternative to ERP adopters as it does not need inputs from the ERP vendors or consultants. Other researchers have investigated software development cost estimation as a guide for package pricing, like [5, 20, 25, 26]. Another paper explored cost estimates for cross-organizational ERP projects [10], while Brocke, et al. [27] adopted a Transaction Costs theory in order to govern ERP costs in a service oriented architecture (SOA) implementation context. Moreover, another research focused on adoption long-term business opportunity costs in contrast to benefits [28].

Although it wasn't applied in ERP cost estimation for SMEs, however, the use of artificial neural network for cost estimation is not new. It has been used in different fields in industry [24, 29, 30]. On the other hand, the input variables values ranges in application domains in [24, 29, 30] can be predictable. This leads to a faster weight convergence. ERP cost factors estimator can receive inputs with a very large range of values. Data preprocessing is required to facilitate the training task on the training algorithm.

3 Problem Formulation

The cost factors estimation for ERP products adoption is an NP-Complete problem for its nature. NP-Complete problems are defined to be the set of problems where an accurate solution using the available processing time takes Millions or even billions of years. Solutions for this problem class is always approximate within an acceptable error range.

The Problems under discussion can be seen as a set of profiles, every profile is collected from a company that went through the ERP adoption process, costs that map to the set of profiles and a set of weights where every weight is associated to a factor. We will call the cost factors, the costs and the associated weights as ERP adoption cost components.

The relationship between the ERP adoption cost components is governed by the following equation:

$$
\begin{pmatrix}
P_{1,1} \cdots\cdots\cdots P_{1,m} \\
\cdots\cdots\cdots\cdots\cdots \\
\cdots\cdots\cdots\cdots\cdots \\
P_{n,1} \cdots\cdots\cdots P_{n,m}
\end{pmatrix}
\begin{pmatrix}
\omega_1 \\
\cdot \\
\cdot \\
\omega_m
\end{pmatrix}
=
\begin{pmatrix}
\phi_1 \\
\cdot \\
\cdot \\
\phi_m
\end{pmatrix},
\tag{1}
$$

Where $(P_{1,1}\cdots\cdots\cdots P_{1,m})$ are the cost factors for the first profile,
$\varnothing 1$ is the first profile associated cost and ω_1 is the weight associated to the cost factor.

The Weight vector ω is the unknown piece of equation. It is imperative to determine the weights values that minimize the following equation:

Minimize
$$
\sum_{k=1}^{m}\phi_k - \sum_{i=1}^{n}\sum_{j=1}^{m}P_{i,j}\omega_j
\tag{2}
$$

4 Optimization Method

The choice of the artificial neural network technique came as an answer for the following two questions:

1-   Are the equations simultaneous? Simultaneous equations are those that have the same unknowns and the same solutions. Some of the unknowns in cost factors equations are highly subjective. An example is giving a value that best represents the learning curve of the staff in the company. This means that there can be a lack of integrity and inconsistency between the same parameter collected from two different institutions. The other issue is that not always the same parameters types or numbers are collected.

2-   Are the collected parameters accurate? Like mentioned in the above paragraph, some parameters values are very subjective. Values that are given to those parameters are typically holding considerable errors when projected on the big picture. An example is comparing expertise in one company to another.

The answers to the above two questions favor optimization techniques that will traverse a solution surface and select, if the data is error free, the global minimum. If the data contain a considerable amount of errors, a local optimum is found. The vectors in Equation (1) are not simultaneous, so whether they are linear or nonlinear, there is no unique solution for vector ω values. The equations parameters are holding a considerable amount of errors due to human errors in estimation and sizing. The neural network with its inherent capability in generalization can overcome the challenging nature of the data.

5   Proposed Back-Propagation Artificial Neural Network Model

In section 3 the characteristics of the solution method is summarized as a method that is tolerant to errors and imposes a generalization behavior throughout the solution life cycle. Nevertheless, able to traverse solution surface and reach to an optimum solution. All those characteristics favor the artificial neural network solutions. Neural networks can be black boxes that do not need a neural network expert to train them. Profiles are introduced to these networks as inputs and classifications as outputs.

Neural networks training is either supervised (feed-forward back-propagation networks) or unsupervised (associative, competitive, etc.). Supervised training is the paradigm that is chosen in this research because the output during training is controlled. Basic principles of artificial neural network can be found in [31, 32].

The number of neurons in the input layer in the proposed architecture equals to the number of cost factors. The number of neurons in the hidden layer is chosen to be the number of input neurons. Optimum selection of the number of hidden layer neurons is explored in [33].

The number of neurons in the output layer is thirty six neurons, every neuron gives either 0 or one. Every four neurons represent the BCD coding for the set of numbers from 1 to 9. The Highest twelve neurons represent the billion range, where the lower twelve neurons represent the million range, and the lowest twelve represent the thousands. A cost of 1 billion, three hundred million and fifty thousands are represented as {0000 0000 0001 - 0011 0000 0000- 0000 0101 0000}.

Table 1 shows possible values for two independent parameters. Parameter 1 can be more effective to cost factors than parameter 2, and therefore its weights or cost factor should be more significant than those of parameter 2. It is a good practice to put both parameters in one domain, so that their values can be more comparable. This domain, we call it the normal form, should reflect how effective the rate if change is to the final total cost. The best representative of this is standard deviation. Comparing the standard deviation of every parameter values against the corresponding costs not actually normalized all data but gives indications about the sensitivity of the cost against every parameter.

Table 1. Abstraction of two independent variables possible values

Parameter 1	Parameter 2
0.1	500
0.3	300
0.5	1000

The training algorithm for the neural network is on two stages, feed-forward and back-propagation. Weights are given initial values all over the network. These initial weights can be of the same value or random. The input vectors are fed to the network and propagated though all the connections and the actual outputs are perceived. The forward propagation is governed by the following equations:

$$O_j = \sum I_i \omega_{ij} + \theta_j \tag{3}$$

Where O_j is the output of node j, I_i is the output of the input node I_i, ω_{ji} is the weight that links input node I_i with output node O_j and θ_j is the threshold on the activation function for output node j.

The sum square error of the outputs of the network on all patterns is:

$$\varepsilon = \frac{1}{2} \sum_{i=1}^{n} (d_i - O_i)^2 \tag{4}$$

ε is the SSE, d_i is the desired output on the output layer neuron I, and O_i is the actual output on the same neuron. The network weights update is governed by the equation:

$$\omega_{i+1} = \omega_i + (d - O)O(1 - O) \tag{5}$$

Equation (5) assumes that the activation functions on the output nodes are step functions (output is either 0 or 1). O in equation (5) is the actual output, d is the desired output and i is the iteration number.

6 Experiments and Discussions

Five hundred different patterns are used in training and five hundred patterns are used for testing. The testing results show that the success of cost estimation highly depends on the correlation between the input pattern and at least one of the training patterns. Estimation error is inversely proportional to the correlation. Figure 1 shows the relationship.

The experiments were conducted using synthetic data driven from both Gaussian and uniform distributions. Uniform distributions showed better success rate than the Gaussian. The difference in success rate depends on the standard deviation which the Gaussian variants are driven from. High standard deviations lead to higher failure rates. In general, the experiments indicate the necessity of having high population of data profiles in order to develop a robust kernel (neural network) for cost factors estimation. Moreover, it is expected that two data profiles that lead to the same cost will have high correlation.

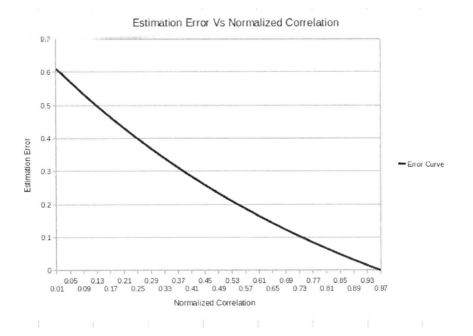

Fig. 1. Estimation error versus correlation between the input data and correlation data. X-Axis is the normalized correlation and Y-Axis is the estimation error.

7 Conclusion and Future Work

The proposed framework allows for cost factors estimation without the need of the involvement of architects or project managers to define function points as an input for systems such as COCOMO. The proposed framework is neural network based. A feed-forward back-propagation artificial neural network is proposed for cost factor estimation. The neural network is composed of an input layer with a number of neurons equals to the number of the data factors, a hidden network with a number of neurons equals to the number of input neurons and a thirty six output neurons that cover the cost ranges from thousands to billions. Every digit in this range is represented by four neurons, BCD encoding.

Figure 1 reveals the most obvious limitation to the model. The model is limited to its high noise and inaccuracy. The experiments show that the accuracy of data collection is a key factor for successful and accurate cost factor estimation. As a future work, data used for training should be grouped according to relevance and correlations. Inaccurate data should be identified and factored out.

An extension for this work is a correlation based technique that should identify dependencies and relations between factors. Input patterns should be classified according to correlation and training takes role on relevant data patterns separately. When an input pattern to be tested, it gets classified first and then propagated through the relevant network.

Another promising venue is building a case-based reasoning on the classified patterns. Once data is classified, it is much easier to be processed among closer and more relevant peers.

References

1. Welsh, J.A., White, J.F.: A small business is not a little big business. Harvard Business Review 59(4), 18–27 (1981)
2. Haddara, M., Zach, O.: ERP Systems in SMEs: A Literature Review. In: HICSS, Kauai, Hawaii, vol. 44 (2011)
3. Haddara, M., Päivärinta, T.: Why Benefits Realization from ERP in SMEs Doesn't Seem to Matter? In: HICSS, vol. 44. IEEE, Kauai (2011)
4. Holland, C.R., Light, B.: A critical success factors model for ERP implementation. IEEE Software 16(3), 30–36 (1999)
5. Jones, C.: Estimating software costs Bringing realism to estimating, 2nd edn. McGraw-Hill Companies, New York (2007)
6. Martin, M.H.: An ERP Strategy. In: Fortune, pp. 95–97 (1998)
7. Haddara, M.: ERP Adoption Cost Factors in SMEs. In: European and Mediterranean Conference on Information Systems (EMCIS 2011), Athens, Greece, June 30-31 (2011)
8. Newman, M., Zhao, Y.: The process of enterprise resource planning implementation and business process re-engineering: tales from two chinese small and medium-sized enterprises. Information Systems Journal 18(4), 405–426 (2008)
9. Daneva, M.: Approaching the ERP Project Cost Estimation Problem: an Experiment. In: Proceedings of the First International Symposium on Empirical Software Engineering and Measurement. IEEE Computer Society Press, Los Alamitos (2007)
10. Daneva, M., Wieringa, R.: Cost estimation for cross-organizational ERP projects: research perspectives. Software Quality Journal 16(3), 459–481 (2008)
11. Elragal, A., Haddara, M.: The Use of Experts Panels in ERP Cost Estimation Research. In: Quintela Varajão, J.E., Cruz-Cunha, M.M., Putnik, G.D., Trigo, A. (eds.) CENTERIS 2010. CCIS, vol. 110, pp. 97–108. Springer, Heidelberg (2010)
12. Al-Mashari, M.: Enterprise resource planning (ERP) systems: a research agenda. Industrial Management & Data Systems 102(3), 165–170 (2002)
13. Daneva, M.: Complementing approaches in ERP effort estimation practice: an industrial study. In: Proceedings of the 4th International Workshop on Predictor Models in Software Engineering. ACM, New York (2008)
14. Abdel-Hamid, T.K., Sengupta, K., Swett, C.: The impact of goals on software project management: an experimental investigation. MIS Q 23(4), 531–555 (1999)
15. Buonanno, G., et al.: Factors affecting ERP system adoption: a comparative analysis between SMEs and large companies. Journal of Enterprise Information Management 18(4), 384–426 (2005)
16. Fui-Hoon Nah, F., Lee-Shang Lau, J., Kuang, J.: Critical Factors for Successful Implementation of Enterprise Systems. Business Process Management Journal 7(3), 285–296 (2001)
17. Thayer, R.H., Fairley, R.: Project Management. In: Marciniak, J. (ed.) Encyclopedia of Software Engineering, pp. 900–923. John Wiley, New York (1994)
18. Vogt, C.: Intractable ERP: a comprehensive analysis of failed enterprise-resource-planning projects. SIGSOFT Softw. Eng. Notes 27(2), 62–68 (2002)

19. Stensrud, E.: Alternative Approaches to Effort Prediction of ERP Projects. Inf. & Soft. Techn. 43(7), 413–423 (2001)
20. Boehm, B.: Software Cost Estimation with COCOMO II. Prentice Hall, Upper Saddle River (2000)
21. Jorgensen, M., Shepperd, M.: A Systematic Review of Software Development Cost Estimation Studies. IEEE Trans. Softw. Eng. 33(1), 33–53 (2007)
22. Daneva, M.: ERP Requirements Engineering Practice: Lessons Learnt. IEEE Software 21(2), 26–33 (2004)
23. Myrtveit, I., Stensrud, E.: A Controlled Experiment to Assess the Benefits of Estimating with Analogy and Regression Models. IEEE Trans. Softw. Eng. 25(4), 510–525 (1999)
24. Fewster, R.M., Mendes, E.: Portfolio management method for deadline planning. In: Proceedings of METRICS 2003. IEEE, Los Alamitos (2003)
25. Boehm, B., Sullivan, K.J.: Software economics: a roadmap. In: Proceedings of the Conference on The Future of Software Engineering. ACM, Limerick (2000)
26. Boehm, B.: Software Engineering Economics. In: Advances in Computing Science & Technology, Prentice Hall, Upper Saddle River (1981)
27. van Brocke, J., Schenk, B., Sonnenberg, C.: Classification Criteria for Governing the Implementation Process of Service-Oriented ERP Systems - An Analysis Based on New Institutional Economics. In: AMCIS, San Francisco (2009)
28. Lindley, J.T., Topping, S., Lindley, L.T.: The hidden financial costs of ERP software. Managerial Finance 34(2), 78–90 (2008)
29. Kim, G., Seo, D., Kang, K.: Hybrid models of neural networks and genetic algorithms for predicting preliminary cost estimates. Journal of Computing in Civil Engineering 19, 208 (2005)
30. Rush, C., Roy, R.: Analysis of cost estimating processes used within a concurrent engineering environment throughout a product life cycle. In: International Conference on Concurrent Engineering: Research and Applications, p. 58. CRC, Boca Raton (2000)
31. Daniel, L.S., Robert, E.M.: Toward a Model of Consolidation: The Retention and Transfer of Neural Net Task Knowledge. In: Proceedings of the INNS World Congress on Neural Networks. Lawrence Erlbaun Assosciates, Mahwah (1995)
32. Towell, G., Shavlik, J.W.: Interpretation of artificial neural networks: Mapping knowledge-based neural networks into rules. In: Advances in Neural Information Processing Systems (1993)
33. Teoh, E.J., Tan, K.C., Xiang, C.: Estimating the Number of Hidden Neurons in a Feedforward Network Using the Singular Value Decomposition. IEEE Transaction on Neural Network 17, 1623–1629 (2006)

TCP, UDP and FTP Performances of Laboratory Wi-Fi IEEE 802.11g WEP Point-to-Point Links

J.A.R. Pacheco de Carvalho[1,2], H. Veiga[1,3], N. Marques[1,3],
C.F. Ribeiro Pacheco[1], and A.D. Reis[1,2,4]

[1] U. de Detecção Remota, [2] Dept. de Física, [3] Centro de Informática
Universidade da Beira Interior, 6201-001 Covilhã, Portugal
[4] Dept. de Electrónica e Telecomunicações / Instituto de Telecomunicações,
Universidade de Aveiro, 3810 Aveiro, Portugal
{pacheco,hveiga,nmarques,a17597,adreis}@ubi.pt

Abstract. Wireless communications, e.g. Wi-Fi, have been increasingly important in the context of networked and virtual organizations and enterprise information systems. Performance is an issue of fundamental importance, resulting in more reliable and efficient communications, therefore improving enterprise information system yield. Security is equally important. Laboratory measurements are made about several performance aspects of Wi-Fi IEEE 802.11g WEP point-to-point links. A contribution is given to performance evaluation of this technology under WEP encryption, using available access points from Enterasys Networks (RBT-4102). Detailed results are presented and discussed, namely at OSI levels 4 and 7, from TCP, UDP and FTP experiments, permitting measurements of TCP throughput, jitter, percentage datagram loss and FTP transfer rate. Comparisons are made to corresponding results obtained for open links. Conclusions are drawn about the comparative performance of the links..

Keywords: Wi-Fi, WLAN, WEP Point-to-Point Links, IEEE 802.11g, Wireless Network Laboratory Performance.

1 Introduction

Contactless communication techniques have been developed using mainly electromagnetic waves in several frequency ranges, propagating in the air. Examples of wireless communications technologies are Wi-Fi and FSO, using microwaves and laser light, respectively. Their importance and utilization have been growing.

Wireless communications are increasingly important for their versatility, mobility and favourable prices. It is the case of microwave based technologies, e.g. Wi-Fi. The importance and utilization of Wi-Fi have been growing for complementing traditional wired networks. Wi-Fi has been increasingly important in the context of networked and virtual organizations and enterprise information systems. Wi-Fi has been used both in ad hoc mode and infrastructure mode. In this case an access point, AP, permits communications of Wi-Fi devices with a wired based LAN, through a switch/router.

M.M. Cruz-Cunha et al. (Eds.): CENTERIS 2011, Part II, CCIS 220, pp. 188–195, 2011.

Thus a WLAN, based on the AP, is formed. Wi-Fi has reached the personal home, where a WPAN allows personal devices to communicate. Point-to-point and point-to-multipoint setups are used both indoors and outdoors, with specific directional and omnidirectional antennas. Wi-Fi uses microwaves in the 2.4 and 5 GHz frequency bands and IEEE 802.11a, 802.11b, 802.11g and 802.11n standards [1]. As the 2.4 GHz band becomes increasingly used interferences increase. There is a growing large base of installed equipments working in this band. The 5 GHz band has been receiving considerable attention, although absorption increases and ranges are shorter. Nominal transfer rates up to 11 (802.11b), 54 (802.11 a, g) and 600 Mbps (802.11n) are permitted. CSMA/CA is the medium access control. Wireless communications, wave propagation [2,3] and WLAN practical implementations [4] have been studied. Detailed information is available about the 802.11 architecture, where an optimum factor of 0.42 was presented for 802.11b point-to-point links at 11 Mbps[5]. Wi-Fi (802.11b) performance measurements are available for crowded indoor environments [6].

Performance has been a fundamentally important issue, giving more reliable and efficient communications and, therefore, improving enterprise information system yield. In comparison to traditional applications, new telematic applications are specially sensitive to performances. Requirements have been pointed out, such as: 1-10 ms jitter and 1-10 Mbps throughput for video on demand/moving images; jitter less than 1 ms and 0.1-1 Mbps throughputs for Hi Fi stereo audio [7].

Wi-Fi security is very important, as microwave radio signals travel through the air and can be easily captured. WEP is a security method for providing authentication. In spite of presenting weaknesses, it is still widely used in Wi-Fi networks for security reasons, mainly in point-to-point links. In WEP, the communicating devices use the same shared key to encrypt and decrypt radio signals.

Several measurements have been made for 2.4 and 5 GHz Wi-Fi open links [8-9], 5 GHz Wi-Fi WEP links [10]as well as very high speed FSO [11]. In the present work new Wi-Fi (IEEE 802.11 g) results arise, using WEP, through OSI levels 4 and 7. Performance is evaluated in laboratory measurements of WEP point-to-point links, using available equipments. Comparisons are made to corresponding results obtained for open links.

The rest of the paper is structured as follows: Chapter 2 presents the experimental details i.e. the measurement setup and procedure. Results and discussion are presented in Chapter 3. Conclusions are drawn in Chapter 4.

2   Experimental Details

The measurements used (Fig. 1) Enterasys RoamAbout RBT-4102 level 2/3/4 access points, equipped with 16-20 dBm IEEE 802.11 a/b/g transceivers and internal dual-band diversity antennas [12], and 100-Base-TX/10-Base-T Allied Telesis AT-8000S/16 level 2 switches [13]. The access points had transceivers based on the Atheros 5213A chipset, and firmware version 1.1.51. The configuration was for minimum transmitted power and equivalent to point-to-point, LAN to LAN mode, using the internal antenna. In every type of experiment, interference free communication channels were used. This was checked through a portable computer, equipped with a Wi-Fi 802.11 a/b/g adapter, running NetStumbler software [14]. WEP encryption was activated in the APs, using 128 bit encryption and a shared key for data encryption composed of 13 ASCII characters.

The experiments were made under far-field conditions. No power levels above 30 mW (15 dBm) were required, as the access points were close.

A laboratory setup has been planned and implemented for the measurements, as shown in Fig. 2. At OSI level 4 , measurements were made for TCP connections and UDP communications using Iperf software [15], permitting network performance results to be recorded. For a TCP connection, TCP throughput was obtained. For a UDP communication with a given bandwidth parameter, UDP throughput, jitter and percentage loss of datagrams were determined. TCP packets and UDP datagrams of 1470 bytes size were used. A window size of 8 kbytes and a buffer size of the same value were used for TCP and UDP, respectively. One PC, with IP 192.168.0.2 was the Iperf server and the other, with IP 192.168.0.6, was the Iperf client. Jitter, which indicates the smooth mean of differences between consecutive transit times, was continuously computed by the server, as specified by RTP in RFC 1889 [16]. The scheme of Fig. 2 was also used for FTP measurements, where FTP server and client applications were installed in the PCs with IPs 192.168.0.2 and 192.168.0.6, respectively.

The server and client PCs were HP nx9030 and nx9010 portable computers, respectively, running Windows XP. They were configured to maximize the resources available to the present work. Batch command files have been written to enable the TCP, UDP and FTP tests. The results were obtained in batch mode and written as data files to the client PC disk. Each PC had a second network adapter that permitted remote control from the official IP University network, via switch.

3   Results and Discussion

The access points were configured for IEEE 802.11 g with typical nominal transfer rates (6, 9, 12, 18, 24, 36, 48, 54 Mbps). Measurements were made for every nominal fixed transfer rate. In this way, data were obtained for comparison of the laboratory performance of the links, measured namely at OSI levels 1 (physical layer), 4 (transport layer) and 7 (application layer) using the setup of Fig. 2. For every nominal fixed transfer rate, an average TCP throughput was determined from several experiments. This value was used as the bandwidth parameter for every corresponding UDP test, giving average jitter and average percentage datagram loss.

At OSI level 1, noise levels (N, in dBm) and signal to noise ratios (SNR, in dB) were monitored.

The main TCP and UDP results are shown in Figs. 3-5. In Fig. 3 polynomial fits were made to the 802.11g TCP throughput data, where R^2 is the coefficient of determination. An average TCP throughput of 9.6 +- 0.3 Mbps was found. A reasonably good agreement was found with the data obtained for open links [9]. In Figs. 4-5, the data points representing jitter and percentage datagram loss were joined by smoothed lines. It was found that, on average, the best jitter performances were found for open links (2.4+- 0.1 ms versus 2.6+-0.1 ms for WEP). Concerning percentage datagram loss data (1.3+- % on average) no significant sensitivity was found, within the experimental error, to link type.

At OSI level 7 we measured FTP transfer rates versus nominal transfer rates configured in the access points for the IEEE 802.11g standard, as in [9]. The data are shown in Fig. 6, including polynomial fits. The results show the same trends found for TCP throughput.

Generally, the results measured for WEP links were not found as significantly different, within the experimental errors, from corresponding data obtained for open links. Except for jitter, where the best performances were found for open links.

Fig. 1. Access point (A) [12] and switch (B) [13]

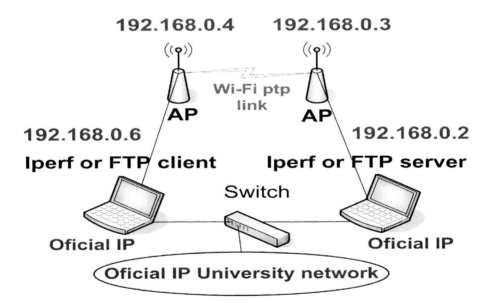

Fig. 2. Laboratory setup scheme

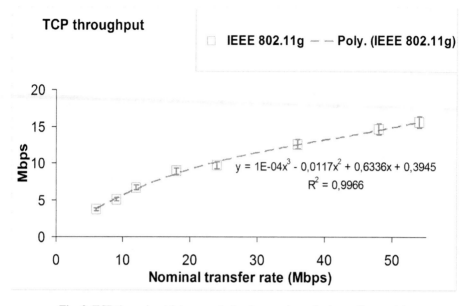

Fig. 3. TCP throughput (y) versus technology and nominal transfer rate (x)

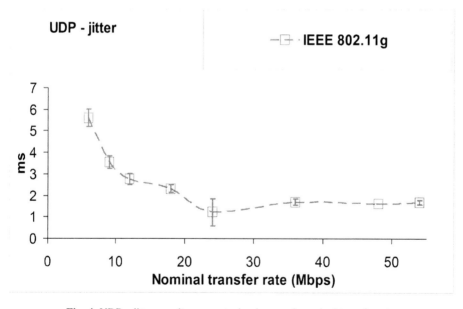

Fig. 4. UDP – jitter results versus technology and nominal transfer rate

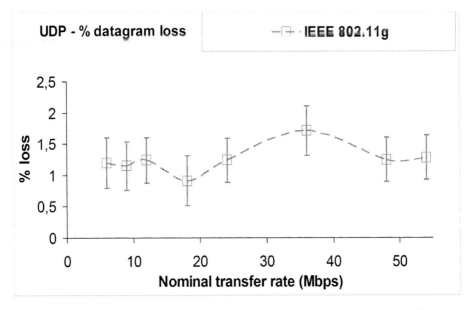

Fig. 5. UDP – percentage datagram loss results versus technology and nominal transfer rate

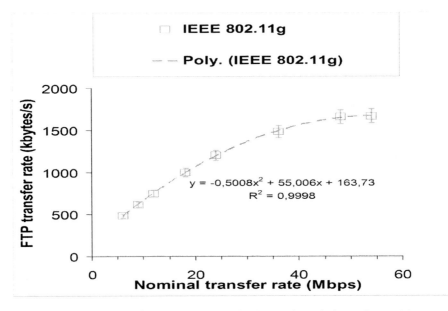

Fig. 6. FTP transfer rate (y) versus technology and nominal transfer rate (x)

4 Conclusions

A laboratory setup arrangement has been planned and implemented, that permitted systematic performance measurements of available wireless equipments (RBT-4102 access points from Enterasys Networks) for Wi-Fi (IEEE 802.11 g) in WEP point-to-point links.

Through OSI layer 4, TCP throughput, jitter and percentage datagram loss were measured and compared. For TCP throughput a reasonably good agreement was found, on average, between the data for WEP and open links. For jitter, it was found that, on average, the best performance was for open links. For percentage datagram loss, no significant sensitivities were found, within the experimental errors, to link type.

At OSI layer 7, the results show the same trends found for TCP throughput.

Generally, the results measured for WEP links were not found as significantly different, within the experimental errors, from corresponding data obtained for open links. Except for jitter, where the best performances were found for open links.

Additional performance measurements either started or are planned using several equipments and security settings, not only in laboratory but also in outdoor environments involving, mainly, medium range links.

Acknowledgments. Supports from the University of Beira Interior and FCT (Fundação para a Ciência e a Tecnologia)/POCI2010 (Programa Operacional Ciência e Inovação) are acknowledged. We acknowledge Enterasys Networks for their availability.

References

1. IEEE, IEEE Std 802.11-2007; IEEE Std 802.11n-2009,
    http://standards.ieee.org/getieee802
2. Mark, J.W., Zhuang, W.: Wireless Communications and Networking. Prentice-Hall, Inc., Upper Saddle River (2003)
3. Rappaport, T.S.: Wireless Communications Principles and Practice, 2nd edn. Prentice-Hall, Inc., Upper Saddle River (2002)
4. Bruce III, W.R., Gilster, R.: Wireless LANs End to End. Hungry Minds, Inc., NY (2002)
5. Schwartz, M.: Mobile Wireless Communications. Cambridge University Press, Cambridge (2005)
6. Sarkar, N., Sowerby, K.: High Performance Measurements in the Crowded Office Environment: a Case Study. In: Proc. ICCT 2006-International Conference on Communication Technology, Guilin, China, November 27-30, pp. 1–4 (2006)
7. Monteiro, E., Boavida, F.: Computer Networks Engineering, 4th edn. FCA-Editor of Informatics Ld., Lisbon (2002)
8. Pacheco de Carvalho, J.A.R., Gomes, P.A.J., Veiga, H., Reis, A.D.: Development of a University Networking Project. In: Putnik, G.D., Cunha, M.M. (eds.) Encyclopedia of Networked and Virtual Organizations, pp. 409–422. IGI Global, Hershey (2008)
9. Pacheco de Carvalho, J.A.R., Veiga, H., Gomes, P.A.J., Ribeiro Pacheco, C.F., Marques, N., Reis, A.D.: Wi-Fi Point-to-Point Links- Performance Aspects of IEEE 802.11 a,b,g Laboratory Links. In: Sio-Iong, A., Gelman, L. (eds.) Electronic Engineering and Computing Technology. LNEE, vol. 60, pp. 507–514. Springer, Netherlands (2010)

10. Pacheco de Carvalho, J.A.R., Veiga, H., Marques, N., Ribeiro Pacheco, C.F.F.P., Reis, A.D.: Comparative Studies of Equipment Performance in Laboratory Wi-Fi IEEE 802.11a WEP Point-to-Point Links. In: Proc. CENTERIS 2010 - Conference on Enterprise Information Systems, Viana do Castelo, Portugal, October 20-22, p. 33 (2010)
11. Pacheco de Carvalho, J.A.R., Marques, N., Veiga, H., Ribeiro Pacheco, C.F., Reis, A.D.: Experimental Performance Evaluation of a Gbps FSO Link: a Case Study. In: Proc. WINSYS 2010 - International Conference on Wireless Information Networks and Systems, Athens, Greece, July 26-28, pp. 123–128 (2010)
12. Enterasys Networks, RoamAbout RBT-4102 Access Point technical data, http://www.enterasys.com
13. Allied Telesis, AT-8000S/16 level 2 switch technical data, http://www.alliedtelesis.com
14. NetStumbler, NetStumbler software, http://www.netstumbler.com
15. NLANR, Iperf User Docs, http://dast.nlanr.net
16. Network Working Group, RFC 1889-RTP: A Transport Protocol for Real Time Applications, http://www.rfc-archive.org

Systems of Synchronism in Optical Digital Communications

António D. Reis[1,2], José F. Rocha[2], Atílio S. Gameiro[2], and José P. Carvalho[1]

[1] Dep. Física / U. D. Remota, Universidade da Beira Interior Covilhã, 6200 Covilhã, Portugal
[2] Dep. Electrónica e Telec. / Instituto Telec., Universidade de Aveiro, 3810 Aveiro, Portugal
{adreis,pacheco}@ubi.pt, {frocha,amg}@ua.pt

Abstract. To transmit fidelity the information, at long distances, was from the beginning, a great human dream. The information signal, when transmitted from the emitter to the receiver, suffers attenuation and distortion. Then, it is necessary to use frequently a regenerator to restore the original amplitude and also to retime the bit original period. The amplitude can be restored with an amplifier with AGC (Automatic Gain Control) and the bit duration can be retimed with a synchronizer with AFC (Automatic Frequency Control).

Keywords: Synchronism, Digital Telecommunications.

1 Introduction

To establish a communication between two remote points it is necessary an emitter, a communication channel and a receiver [1-3].

The emitter supplies an original strong and perfect signal, but the communication channel attenuates and distorts the signal, then the receiver receives a weak and distorted signal. The receiver regenerator, to restore the original signal format needs two main blocks which are the amplifier with AGC that compensates the attenuation and the synchronizer with AFC that recovers the distortion [4, 5].

Fig.1 shows the blocks diagram of a general communication system

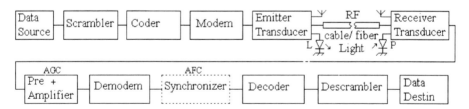

Fig. 1. Blocks diagram of a general communication system

Others secondary blocks can be added in order to improve the system quality. So, in the emitter, we can add the scrambler, coder and modem. On the other hand, in the receiver, we can add the demodem, decoder and descrambler [6, 7].

M.M. Cruz-Cunha et al. (Eds.): CENTERIS 2011, Part II, CCIS 220, pp. 196–205, 2011.
© Springer-Verlag Berlin Heidelberg 2011

In the emitter: the data source provides the data symbol sequence, the scrambler guarantees a data sequence same when the input is inactive, the coder prepares the data sequence with null DC to a good transmission, the modem makes a spectrum translation, the emitter transducer converts the electric energy in other form adapted to the communication channel [8-10].

In the receiver: the receiver transducer converts the travel input energy form in an electric signal, the amplifier AGC amplifies the signal controlled by the signal peak, the synchronizer with AFC recovers the clock to sample and to retime the data, the decoder makes the inverse of the coder, the descrambler the inverse of the scrambler, the demodem the inverse of the modem and the data destine processes the data.

This work presents a general communication system, in particular the regenerator, with special relevance for the synchronizer [11, 12].

2   Channel of Communication

The communication channel can be a cooper cable, an optic cable or same the atmosphere. In this case an optic cable designed as optic fibre.

The optic fibre is an alternative transmission medium that in the windows of wave length λ of minor attenuation (1-st in 850nm with attenuation 2 dB/km, 2-nd in 1310nm with attenuation of 0.25dB/km and 3-th in 1550nm with attenuation 0.25dB/km), transmits the signal with low attenuation, with a bandwidth 1000 times superior to the cooper cable and a transmission speed of various Gigabauds.

So, the signals reach great distances without repeaters (regenerators) and carries a great information density. One unique optic fibre carries multiservices of sound, image and data.

Fig.2 shows the blocks diagram of a general communication system

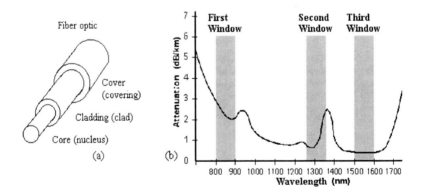

Fig. 2. Optic fibre (a) and its three windows of transmission (b)

The optic fibre is constituted essentially by silica, that exists in great quantity in the nature sands, whereas the nature cooper reserve is diminishing.

The optic signals have different nature, therefore they have great immunity to electric noises.

The optic fibre provides high bit rate, then is convenient to use the synchronous communication without redundancy and consequently 100% transmission efficiency.

However, the synchronous communication needs a clock in perfect data synchronism, what demands the synchronizer. Also, the data becomes attenuated with distance, what demands the amplifier.

3 The Amplifier with AGC

The amplifier with AGC (Automatic Gain Control) has two main blocks which are the preamplifier with controlled variable gain and the power amplifier with fixed gain.

The preamplifier has high voltage gain, but low output current. On other hand, the power amplifier has low gain, but high output current (Fig.3).

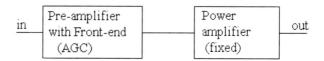

Fig. 3. Preamplifier with AGC (a) and power amplifier (b)

The AGC means that the preamplifier has a controlled variable gain so that the output signal peak be constant. The power amplifier has a fixed gain that can be implemented by an operational amplifier with a totem pole par - transistor (Fig.4)

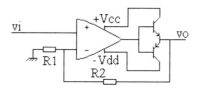

Fig. 4. Power amplifier

This block can be implemented only with the operational amplifier. This block for low current necessities can be dispensable.

3.1 The Preamplifier with AGC

The preamplifier with AGC has two parts which are the Front-end and the circuit of AGC (Automatic Gain Control). Fig.5 shows the AGC circuit

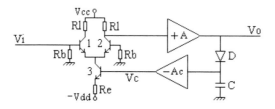

Fig. 5. AGC (Automatic Gain Control) circuit

The preamplifier has a Front-end (input part with a PIN / APD) that receives the light emitted by the emitter transducer (LED / LASER).

The Front-end has two types, namely the front-end of high impedance and the front-end of transimpedance.

A. Front-End of High Impedance

This amplifier has a great sensibility to the input signal, but on other hand has some signal integration what causes problems of dynamic range. Fig.6 shows the front-end of high impedance

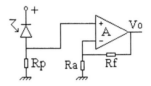

Fig. 6. Front-end of high impedance

The signal integration causes some distortion and limits the amplification value, so that the output be inside of the Dynamic Range.

B. Front-End of Transimpedance

This front-end has less sensibility to the input signal, but on other hand has no signal integration, what avoids some problems. Fig.7 shows the front-end of transimpedance.

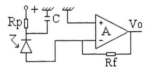

Fig. 7. Front-end of transimpedance

The lower input signal sensibility can be compensated, after, with an higher amplification.

4 Synchronizer with AFC

The synchronizer recovers the clock and after uses it to sample the data at the appropriate time (maximum opened eye diagram) in order to minimize the bit error rate and also retimes the bit period to its emitter original value. The AFC (Automatic Frequency Control) means that the synchronizer has a controlled block that is able to follow the input signal frequency. This block usually is the VCO.

Fig.8 shows the synchronizer, with their fundamental blocks which are: the input adapter circuit, the clock recover, the phase adjust and the output decision circuit.

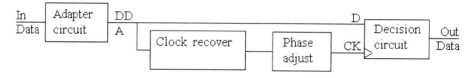

Fig. 8. Synchronizer with their main blocks

The input adapter provides the appropriate voltage level to excite the others blocks. The clock recover extracts the clock with an equal frequency to the input bit rate. The phase adjust shift the clock positive transition to the bit center (maximum opened eye diagram). The decision circuit samples and retimes the data.

There are a great diversity of synchronizers, but in general, we can consider three big categories, which are the open loop synchronizers, the mixed loop synchronizers and the closed loop synchronizers. In the open loop synchronizers there are no blocks inside the loop, in the mixed loop synchronizers there are some blocks inside the loop and in the closed loop synchronizers all the blocks are inside the loop.

Each category has various types of synchronizers, in the open loop, we consider the tank (coil and capacitor), the SAW (Surface Acoustic Wave), the monostable (digital circuit with feedback) and the astable (multivibrator). In the mixed loop, we consider the analog, the hybrid, the combinational and the sequential. In the closed loop, we consider the also the analog, the hybrid, the combinational and the sequential.

Following , we show the three categories each one represented only by one of their synchronizer types.

4.1 Open Loop Symbol Synchronizer

This synchronizer category has four types, namely the tank, the SAW, the monostable and the astable. However, here, we only present the tank as representation of this category.

A. The Tank (OL-t)

Fig.9 shows the tank open loop that consists of the input comparator (CMP1), the differentiator (RC circuit), the tuned tank (LC circuit), the adjust phase (delay circuit - not necessary) and the output comparator (CMP2).

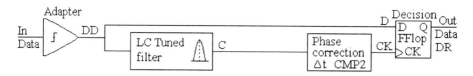

Fig. 9. Synchronizer of open loop tank (OL-t)

The input comparator converts the continuous signal into discrete signal. The differentiator concentrates the energy around the transitions. The current drive (transistor) applies current pulses to the tuned tank. The tuned tank produces a damped wave (analog clock) with frequency equal $1/(2\pi LC)$. The output comparator converts the analog clock into a digital clock.

4.2 Mixed Loop Symbol Synchronizer

This synchronizer category has four types, namely the analog, the hybrid, the combinational and the sequential. However, here, we only present the analog as representation of this category.

A. The Analog (ML-a)

Fig.10 shows the analog mixed loop that consists of the input tank LC followed of the analog carrier PLL (Phase Lock Loop). The analog carrier PLL (CPLL) has an analog phase comparator.

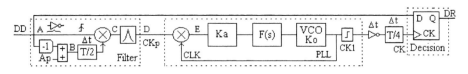

Fig. 10. Synchronizer of mixed loop analog (ML-a)

The tuned LC converts the input data transitions into an analog clock damped wave with limited quality. The PLL converts this analog clock into a digital clock of very good quality. The analog phase comparator compares the input phase with the VCO phase producing an error pulse that is filtered and then controls the VCO to follow the input signal phase. The output VCO is the system digital clock.

4.3 Closed Loop Symbol Synchronizer

This synchronizer category has also four types, namely the analog, the hybrid, the combinational and the sequential. However, here, we only present the analog as representation of this category.

A. The Analog (CL-a)

Fig.11 shows the analog closed loop that consists of a bit PLL (Phase Lock Loop) that extracts directly the clock from the input data sequence.

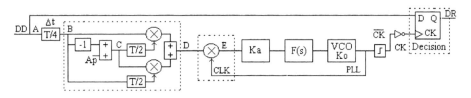

Fig. 11. Synchronizer of closed loop analog (CL-a)

The Bit PLL (BPLL) has a phase comparator that is able to synchronize directly the VCO (Voltage Controlled Oscillator) with the input data bits sequence. The analog phase comparator compares the VCO phase with the input phase and the difference error pulse is filtered (F(s)) and then forces the VCO output to follow the input signal phase. The VCO output is the system digital clock.

5 Design, Tests and Results

All the synchronizers have been designed with the same linearized transfer function and they were tested with equal conditions [5].

5.1 Design of the Parameters

To compare the various synchronizers in equal conditions, it is necessary to design all the loops with identical linearized transfer functions.

The loop gain is given by Kl=Kd.Ko=Ka.Kf.Ko, where Kf is the phase detector gain, Kd is the phase comparator gain, Ko is the VCO gain and Ka is the control parameter that acts in the root locus providing the desired characteristics.

To test the synchronizer, we used a normalized bit rate tx=1baud, that simplifies the analysis, giving normalized values for the others parameters. So, we used a clock frequency fck=1Hz, an extern noise bandwidth Bn=5Hz and a loop noise bandwidth Bl=0.002Hz. Ps=A^2_{ef} is the signal power and Pn= No.Bn is the noise power. No =$2\sigma n^2.\Delta\tau$ is the noise spectral density and $\Delta\tau$=1/fSamp is the sampling period.

The relation between SNR and noise variance σn^2 is SNR = Ps/Pn = A^2_{ef}/(No.Bn) = A^2_{ef}/($2\sigma n^2.\Delta\tau$.Bn) = 0.5^2/($2\sigma n^2*10^{-3}*5$)= $25/\sigma n^2$.

1-st order loop (the results are similar with the 2-nd order loop)
In the 1-st order loop, the filter F(s) = 0.5Hz eliminates the high frequencies, but mantains the loop characteristics. This cutoff frequency is 25 times greater than Bl=0.02Hz. The transfer function is

$$H(s)=\frac{G(s)}{1+G(s)}=\frac{KdKoF(s)}{s+KdKoF(s)}=\frac{KdKo}{s+KdKo} \tag{1}$$

and the loop noise bandwidth is

$$Bl=\frac{KdKo}{4}=Ka\frac{KfKo}{4}=0.02Hz \tag{2}$$

So, for the analog synchronizer (Km=1, A=1/2, B=1/2; Ko=2π), the loop bandwidth is

$$Bl=0.02=(Ka.Kf.Ko)/4 = (Ka.Km.A.B.Ko)/4 = 0.02 \text{ -> } Ka=0.08*2/\pi \tag{3}$$

For the hybrid synchronizers (Km=1, A=1/2, B=0.45; Ko=2π), the loop bandwidth is

$$Bl=0.02=(Ka.Kf.Ko)/4 = (Ka.Km.A.B.Ko)/4 = 0.02 \text{ -> } Ka=0.08*2.2/\pi \tag{4}$$

For the combinational synchronizers (Kf=1/π; Ko=2π), the loop bandwidth is

$$Bl=0.02=(Ka.Kf.Ko)/4 = (Ka*1/\pi*2\pi)/4 = 0.02 \text{ -> } Ka=0.04 \tag{5}$$

For the sequential synchronizers (Kf=1/2π; Ko=2π), the loop bandwidth is

$$Bl=0.02=(Ka.Kf.Ko)/4 = (Ka*1/2\pi*2\pi)/4 =0.02 -> Ka=0.08 \qquad (6)$$

The jitter depends on the signal Aef, noise No and loop noise bandwidth Bl.
    For analog PLL the jitter is

$$\sigma\phi^2=Bl.No/Aef^2=Bl.2.\sigma n^2.\Delta\tau=0.02*10^{-3}*2\sigma n^2/0.5^2=16*10^{-5}.\sigma n^2 \qquad (7)$$

For the others PLLs the jitter formula is more complicated.

- 2nd order loop:
The second order loop is not analised, but the results are identical to the first order.

5.2 Test Setup

To obtain the jitter noise curves of the various synchronizers, we used the following setup (Fig.12) [5].

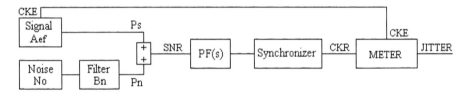

Fig. 12. Blocks diagram of the test setup

The signal noise ratio SNR is given by Ps/Pn, where Ps is the signal power and Pn is the noise power. They are defined as Ps=Aef^2 and Pn= No.Bn = 2σn^2.Δτ.Bn. Aef is the RMS amplitude, Bn is the extern noise bandwidth, No is the noise power spectral density, σn is the noise standard deviation and Δτ is the sampling period (inverse of samples per time unit). Here, we don't use the prefilter (PF(s)=1).

5.3 Jitter Measurer

Fig.13 shows the jitter measurer (M), which consists of a flip flop RS that detects the phase variation of the recovered clock (VCO) relatively to the fixed phase of the emitter clock. This random phase variation is the jitter of the recovered clock. [5].

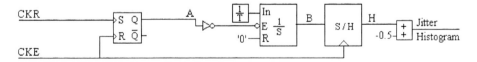

Fig. 13. The jitter measurer

The other blocks convert this phase variation into an amplitude variation which is the jitter histogram.

5.4 Results and Discussion

Fig.14 shows the jitter noise curves of the three categories, namely the open loop represented by the tank (OL-t), the mixed loop represented by the tank with analog CPLL (ML-a) and the closed loop represented by the analog BPLL (CL-a).

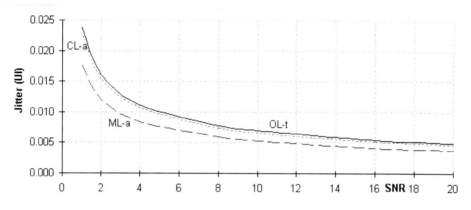

Fig. 14. Jitter-SNR curves of open loop(OL-t), mixed loop(ML-a) and closed loop(CL-a)

The three categories are represented by their synchronizers and are all analog types. So, they don't have noise margin and then all the noise is considered.

The three synchronizers have similar jitter performance curves, but we see that rigorously the tank is slightly the worst, the analog BPLL is the intermedium and the tank with CPLL is sligtly the best.

6 Conclusion and Future Work

We studied the symbol synchronizers of open loop (OL), mixed loop (ML) and closed loop (CL). We verified that the three analog synchronizers, with the same extern noise bandwidth and loop noise bandwidth, have similar jitter noise curves, although with a slightly advantage of the mixed loop due to its double tuning.

The three synchronizers are similar in terms of jitter, however they can be different in other evaluation characteristics parameters. So, for example in terms of capture and lock range the closed loop has the best performance, the mixed loop has an intermediate performance and the open loop has the worst performance. Also, in terms of stability the closed loop has the best stability, the mixed loop has intermediate stability and the open loop has the worst stability. In terms of speed, the open loop is advantageous.

Acknowledgments. The authors are thankful with the FCT (Foundation for sCience and Technology).

References

1. Imbeaux, J.C.: Performance of the delay-line multiplier circuit for clock and carrier synchronization in Digital Satellite Communications. IEEE Journal on Selected Areas in Communications, 82–95 (1983)
2. Rosenkranz, W.: Phase Locked Loops with limiter phase detectors in the presence of noise. IEEE Transactions on Communications com-30(10), 2297–2304 (1982)
3. Witte, H.H.: A Simple Clock Extraction Circuit Using a Self Sustaining Monostable Multivibrator Output Signal. Electronics Letters 19(21), 897–898 (1983)
4. Hogge, C.R.: A Self Correcting Clock Recovery Circuit. IEEE Transactions on Electron Devices, 2704–2706 (1985)
5. Reis, A.D., Rocha, J.F., Gameiro, A.S., Carvalho, J.P.: A New Technique to Measure the Jitter. In: Proc. III Conference on Telecommunications. Figueira Foz-PT, pp. 64–67 (2001)
6. Simon, M.K., Lindsey, W.C.: Tracking Performance of Symbol Synchronizers for Manchester Coded Data. IEEE Transactions on Communications com-2.5(4), 393–408 (1977)
7. Carruthers, J.B., Falconer, D.D., Sandler, H.M., Strawczynski, L.: Bit Synchronization in the Presence of Co-Channel Interference. In: Proc. Conf. on Electrical and Computer Engineering, Ottawa-CA, pp. 4.1.1–4.1.7. (1990)
8. Huber, J., Liu, W.: Data-Aided Synchronization of Coherent CPM-Receivers. IEEE Transactions on Communications 40(1), 178–189 (1992)
9. D'Amico, A.A., D'Andrea, A.N., Reggianni, R.: Efficient Non-Data-Aided Carrier and Clock Recovery for Satellite DVB at Very Low SNR. IEEE Jou. on Sattelite Areas in Comm. 19(12), 2320–2330 (2001)
10. Dobkin, R., Ginosar, R., Sotiriou, C.P.: Data Synchronization Issues in GALS SoCs. In: Proc. 10th International Symposium on Asynchronous Circuits and Systems, Crete - Greece, CD-Edition (2004)
11. Noels, N., Steendam, H., Moeneclaey, M.: Effectiveness Study of Code-Aided and Non-Code-Aided ML-Based Feedback Phase Synchronizers. In: Proc. IEEE Intern. Conference on Communications (ICC 2006), Istambul-TK, pp. 2946–2951 (2006)
12. Reis, A.D., Rocha, J.F., Gameiro, A.S., Carvalho, J.P.: Sequential Symbol Synchronizers based on Clock Sampling of Discrete Pulses. In: Proc. VIII Symposium on Enabling Optical Network and Sensors (SEONs), Porto-PT, CD-Edited (2010)

Emphasizing Human Tasks and Decisions in Business Process Models

Giorgio Bruno

Politecnico di Torino, Torino, Italy
giorgio.bruno@polito.it

Abstract. This paper focuses on decision points, which are a feature of knowledge-intensive processes; in particular, task selection and data selection are addressed. Task selection occurs when the same business entities can be handled with different tasks, and a choice has to be made; data selection takes place when the entities to be acted on have to be selected from among those available. A notation called Task-Oriented Modeling of business Processes (TOMP) is presented with the help of an example showing a number of decision points. This paper also discusses the impact of decision points on to-do lists.

Keywords: business process models, to-do lists, tasks, decision points.

1 Introduction

Business processes are a standard way of organizing work in a business context. They consist of a number of units of work (called tasks) designed to produce a product or service [1]. They cross functional boundaries in that they involve members of different departments; common examples are developing a new product, ordering goods from a supplier, and processing and paying an insurance claim [2].

Tasks fall into two categories: human tasks are those performed by human participants playing suitable roles (associated with the tasks), while automated ones are implemented by services.

In the context of Process-Aware Information Systems [3], tasks are meant to operate on the business entities residing in the underlying information system, and they are carried out by participants through graphical user interfaces, through which they can generate new business entities, retrieve and modify existing ones, as well as invoke external services.

Business processes are specified by means of diagrams (i.e. process descriptions) that establish precedence constraints among the constituent tasks. From a technological point of view, tasks and process descriptions need different implementation tools: process descriptions are handled by process engines, while tasks are mapped into enterprise application software. The contact point is provided by the to-do lists through which (human) participants receive work from the process engine.

When a participant clicks a to-do list entry, a suitable interface is displayed so that they can perform the work required. The details regarding the task implementation are not part of the process description, which only includes the information on the events exchanged between the process engine and the task implementation.

M.M. Cruz-Cunha et al. (Eds.): CENTERIS 2011, Part II, CCIS 220, pp. 206–214, 2011.
© Springer-Verlag Berlin Heidelberg 2011

In Business Process Model and Notation (BPMN) [4], there is a building block called user task which is actually an interface to a category of tasks meant to be activated on a single input event and to produce a single output event. As a matter of fact, these building blocks encompass two sequential interactions, i.e. a send action and a receive action: the first results in a new entry added to the to-do list of the intended participant, while the second waits for the arrival of the completion event from the task implementation.

Unfortunately, this simple task-interface pattern is not able to cope with all the relevant situations. A first example is the handling of back orders, which are generated when customer orders cannot be completely filled. Usually, purchasers do not handle one back order at a time, but they wait until the number of items needed enables them to take advantage of a quantity discount, and then they place a bulk order with a supplier: the corresponding task operates on a series of inputs before the output is emitted and which inputs have to be acted on are decided by the purchaser.

Another situation is when a participant can react to a given request in several ways each of them implying a different course of action. For example, upon receiving a request for quote from a customer, an account manager can react in three ways. They can: a) discard the request (and they have to give reasons for the rejection); b) provide a quote; c) start a reselling initiative by entering a request for quote for a seller. The decision in this case amounts to the selection of the proper task the incoming request will be handled with.

For those situations, BPMN provides no building blocks and therefore the interactions with the task implementations have to be explicitly represented through events along with send operations and receive ones.

A process description should be a road map that can be observed from different viewpoints; it has to be amenable for being interpreted by a process engine, nevertheless it has to be meaningful to the participants involved. Therefore, this paper emphasizes the need of placing human tasks and human decisions in the foreground and presents a notation called Task-Oriented Modeling of business Processes (TOMP) aimed at fulfilling this purpose.

This paper is organized as follows. Sections 2 and 3 present TOMP with the help of an example that emphasizes decisional situations, which are a feature of knowledge-intensive processes [5]. In particular, task selection and data selection are addressed: the former occurs when the same business entities can be handled with different tasks, and a choice has to be made, and the latter takes place when the entities to be acted on have to be selected from among those available. These sections also discuss the impact of decision points on to-do lists and propose the inclusion of decisional entries in addition to ordinary task entries.

Related work is illustrated in section 4, in which two major lines of research are considered, one on flexible processes [6-10] and the other on the connection between activity-centric models and data-centric ones [11] .

Another line of research, the one addressing to-do lists [12-15] in the domain of personal or collaborative work, is mentioned in the conclusion as a relevant stimulus to the next development of TOMP.

2 The Basics of TOMP

This section introduces the basics of TOMP with the help of an example that presents a situation of task selection driven by incoming requests. The example refers to participants belonging to three roles (customer, account manager and seller) involved in commercial transactions. A first set of requirements is as follows.

Customers enter requests for quote for a given product or service. A request for quote (rfq in short) is handed by the process engine to a suitable account manager (determined by means of a business rule, called amSR). Then, the account manager can select one option among three alternatives. They can: a) discard the request (and they have to give reasons for the rejection); b) provide a quote; c) start a reselling initiative by entering a request for quote for a number of sellers of their choice.

The task model is shown in Fig.1. The selection of participants will be addressed at the end of this section.

As to its graphical representation, TOMP draws on Petri nets and hence it is made up of places and transitions connected by oriented arcs. Transitions are oval and represent tasks; places are small circles and represent decision points; the oriented links define the data flow consisting of tokens that point to business entities.

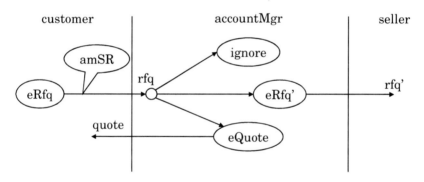

Fig. 1. An example of task selection

In the domain of Process-Aware Information Systems [3], participants, by taking decisions and performing tasks, are meant to operate on the business entities residing in the underlying information system.

Swim lanes group the tasks belonging to the same role.

Tasks are given simplified names, e.g. eRfq means enter rfq. Task eRfq produces an rfq, i.e., a business entity, as shown by the output link. The name of the link usually reflects the name of the class of the business entity: in general, the class name is equal to the link name with the initial in upper case. Link rfq enters a decision point (taking the same name) connected to three alternative tasks: the decision is in charge of an account manager, because the decision point and the tasks belong to the swim lane related to role accountMgr.

The entity that enters a decision point turns out to be a request for decision (RFD in short) for the intended recipient. A decision point is depicted as a small circle that is connected to a number of tasks representing the possible options. When one option is taken, the RFD is fulfilled.

If the account manager selects the reselling option, they have to enter a request for quote for a number of sellers selected from among those available. This new request for quote is called rfq' to set it apart from the one coming from the customer; its class is Rfq'. The selection of the sellers is made by the account manager with task eRfq'.

From an operational point of view, RFDs bring about an extension to the common notion of to-do list. Usually, a to-do list includes a number of task entries: when a participant clicks a task entry of their to-do list, the main window of the task GUI appears and they can perform the specific work related to the task.

RFDs are included in to-do lists as well (they are referred to as decisional entries); however, their handling is different in that it involves two steps. The first step consists in examining the RFD; if a participant clicks a decisional entry, a decisional view showing the appropriate details of the RFD as well as the list of the admissible tasks appears. When the participant selects one task, the main window of the task GUI appears as in the case of task entries.

Account managers may be dealing with several customer requests at the same time, and then their to-do lists may contain a number of entries related to such pending requests. An example is shown in Fig.2: the to-do list contains two decisional entries, referred to as rfq-1 and rfq-2. If the account manager clicks the eQuote option, after selecting rfq-1 from their to-do list, the main window for task eQuote appears. If, after some time, the task is suspended, a task entry is added to the to-do list so that the task can be resumed later on.

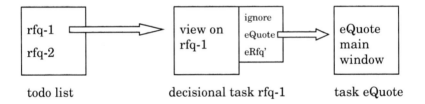

Fig. 2. The handling of decisional entries in the to-do lists of account managers

A task model in TOMP is mainly a behavioral model in that it shows what tasks the process is made up of and what their precedence relationships are; however, the data flow is also shown, in terms of the business entities acted on by the tasks.

The data flow provides a connection between the behavioral model and the information model. In fact, while the decisions on the business entities needed are taken in a separate business analysis phase, there are relationships that originate from behavioral issues. A companion information model can then be produced in which the behavioral relationships (those implied by the data flow) are emphasized with the help of association classes indicating the related tasks. In Fig.3 the companion information model of the example presented in Fig.1 is shown. Association classes appear as labels of relationships.

A quote is related to an rfq, because it is produced by task eQuote, which receives an rfq and produces a quote: by extension, class Rfq can be referred to as the input class of task eQuote, and class Quote as its output class. The relationship between class Rfq and class Quote is depicted as an oriented arc originating from the output class of the corresponding task and ending in the input class. For a similar reason, there is a relationship between class Rfq and class Rfq': it corresponds to task eRfq'.

An rfq is instead produced by a spontaneous task, i.e. a task whose execution depends on the will of its performer. Spontaneous tasks do not appear in to-do lists; they are typically activated via menus. In companion information models, such tasks are shown by relationships between the output classes and the roles of their performers.

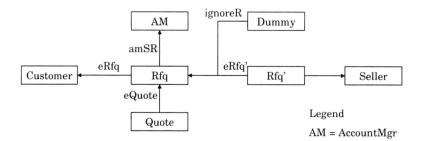

Fig. 3. The companion information model of the example shown in Fig.1

For the sake of simplicity, it is assumed that each role is mapped to a distinct class, e.g. Customer, AccountMgr (AM) and Seller.

A task producing no output, such as task ignoreR, is shown by a relationship between class Dummy and its input class.

A companion model only shows the classes and relationships related to a task model; it is to be considered as a part of the overall information model.

At this point, some considerations on the selection of the participants involved in tasks and decisions can be made.

When a customer enters a request for quote, the process engine adds a decisional entry to the to-do list of an account manager; but, which account manager will be involved? On the basis of the above-mentioned requirements, the process engine is to be supported by a business rule, called amSR: this is the reason why the name of this business rule is shown near the output link of task eRfq. The outcome of amSR is recorded by an association between the rfq and the entity representing the account manager selected; such associations are represented by the relationship between class Rfq and class AM, in Fig.3.

The account manager is then determined by the process on the fly, when the rfq is issued by task eRfq. In all the other cases, the process engine assumes that the intended participant has already been determined and hence there is an association between the business entity to be handled and the entity representing its handler.

The recipients of an rfq' are established by the performer of task eRfq': therefore, at the completion of this task, the process engine will take advantage of the associations (between the rfq' and the intended seller entities) that have been established by the task.

From a task model, on the basis of the considerations made so far, the companion information model can automatically be derived: as a matter of fact, it represents a data-centric view complementary to the activity-centric view provided by the corresponding task model. This a confirmation of the duality between the two views discussed in [11].

3   Data Selection

This section addresses data selections i.e. decisions to be taken on groups of entities. An example is given in Fig.4 and is a continuation of the example presented in Fig.1.

If an account manager decides to start a reselling initiative by selecting task eRfq', then they will receive the quotes provided by the sellers involved. The quote provided by a seller is called quote' in order to set it apart from a quote provided by an account manager (quote); the class of such quotes is Quote'.

Account managers receive the seller quotes and, at a certain point in time, they may select one of them on the basis of which they build the final quote (with task eQuote2) to be sent to the customer. However, they may also decide to ignore all the quotes received.

The handling of seller quotes deserves particular attention. These quotes must be grouped on the basis of the rfq they have been asked for. As a matter of fact, an account manager may be dealing with several customer requests at the same time, and hence they may be receiving quotes asked for different requests. Seller quotes do not bring about separate entries in the to-do list, because they will be examined collectively. For this reason, they are aggregated and presented as a single entry, called group decisional entry.

The decision point collecting seller quotes is not simply called quote'; it is instead called Σquote', where Σ is the group symbol, and, in addition, a grouping condition is indicated. Condition "same .rfq'.rfq" means that the quotes related to the same rfq, via an rfq', belong to the same group.

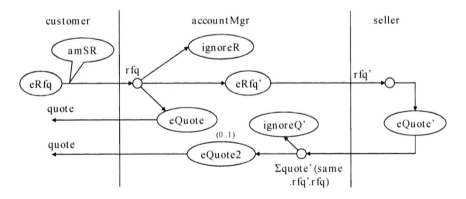

Fig. 4. An example of data selection

Group decisional entries are more complicated to handle than simple decisional entries, shown in Fig.2. The example shown in Fig.5 refers to an account manager who is handling two customer requests, say, rfq-1 and rfq-2. So far, they have received two seller quotes (say, q-1a and q-1b) for rfq-1; then the to-do list also includes a group decisional entry for this two quotes, say, Σquote'-1.

If the account manager clicks that entry, a window including three major sections appears: the left section shows the list of quotes, the right section displays a view on the quote selected from the list (e.g. q-1b), and the options available are presented in the section below.

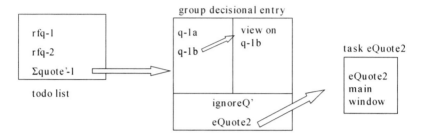

Fig. 5. The handling of group decisional entries in the to-do lists of account managers

If option eQuote2 is selected, the main window for task eQuote2 appears; then, only option ignoreQ' will be allowed for the remaining quotes in the list. Task eQuote2 can be selected at most once for the group of seller quotes: this constraint is shown in the task model by adding a multiplicity constraint (0..1) close to the oval symbol of the task.

Selecting one item out of a group involves a comparative evaluation of the group members and this can be facilitated by specific tools that can be added during the implementation of the task model. For example, a sorting tool that reorders the list of seller quotes by increasing prices could be invoked through an implementation-time option.

4 Related Work

TOMP is intended for knowledge-intensive processes, i.e. processes calling for some degree of creativity and adaptation to specific circumstances [5]. What distinguishes knowledge-intensive processes from processes aimed at repetitive, standardized work (i.e. routines), is the relevant presence of human decisions.

Human decisions call for a more flexible control flow. Several approaches have been proposed to improve flexibility in business processes [6]. In the case-handling approach [7], a stronger integration between control-flow issues and data-flow ones is pursued, because the process evolution is driven by the state of the case rather than by the completion of its activities [8].

BPMN provides the notion of ad hoc sub-process, which is a group of tasks to be carried out in any number and order as decided by their performers. This solution clearly provides too much flexibility and too little control. The Business Process Constraint Network (BPCN) approach [9] is an extension to ad hoc sub-processes in that it supplements them with a number of constraints (e.g. mandatory, prohibitive, inclusion and exclusion) which can be indicated graphically. When the workflow engine assigns an ad hoc sub-process to a certain performer, they have first to produce an actual sequence of steps conforming to the constraints, and then the workflow engine will proceed. In the Declare approach [10] there are ad hoc sub-processes with constraints similar to BPCN ones, but they are handled in a different way at run time. There is no need to define a complete variant in advance, but any task of the ad hoc sub-process can be performed as long as the mandatory constraints are not violated.

The major difference between TOMP and the above mentioned approaches is the presence of explicit decision points that are related to specific business entities. In the example illustrated in the previous sections, the account managers are able to make decisions for several cases at the same time (i.e. customer requests and seller quotes). Modeling the data flow makes it possible to accommodate several interrelated cases in the same model.

5   Conclusion and Future Work

TOMP pays particular attention to the practical implications of process models, i.e. to their impact on to-do lists. By looking at a process model, participants should be able to deduce how their to-do lists will look like. As illustrated in the previous sections, TOMP to-do lists include decisional entries corresponding to the decision points in the process models, and the options related to such entries are obtained from the tasks linked to the decision points.

A lot of research has been done on to-do lists outside the business process world and TOMP development can benefit from the results of this work as follows.

In a more general context, to-do lists [12] are the basis for organizing personal work. They are fed by personal tasks generated by their owners. Personal tasks come in a variety of forms [13] and their interface does not impose a specific implementation effort which, instead, is needed by business tasks. Several tools have been developed to automatically generate tasks from emails, e.g. [14]. This feature can be useful in TOMP in order to activate tasks that enable their performers to transform unstructured information into structured one and to inject it into a business process.

To-do lists can be used as a bridge between personal workspaces and collaborative ones: task delegation [15], which is based on the dynamic mutual assignment of pieces of work in a team, may be an effective means to come up with informal collaborative processes. Task delegation could be added to TOMP as a feature of decisions: for example, an account manager, instead of directly providing a quote, could delegate the accomplishment of this task to another participant (e.g. a sales representative).

Acknowledgments. The work presented in this paper has been partly supported by MIUR under the PRIN 2008 project "Documentation and processes".

References

1. Rummler, G.A., Brache, A.P.: Improving Performance: how to manage the white space on the organizational chart. Jossey-Bass, San Francisco (1995)
2. Davenport, T.H., Short, J.E.: The new industrial engineering: information technology and business process redesign. Sloan Management Review, 11–27 (Summer 1990)

3. Dumas, M., van der Aalst, W.M.P., ter Hofstede, A.H.M.: Process-Aware Information Systems: bridging people and software through process technology. Wiley, New York (2005)
4. BPMN, http://www.omg.org
5. Alvesson, M.: Knowledge work and knowledge-intensive firms. Oxford University Press, Oxford (2004)
6. Nurcan, S.: A survey on the flexibility requirements related to business processes and modeling artifacts. In: IEEE 41st Annual Hawaii International Conference on System Sciences. IEEE Press, New York (2008)
7. van der Aalst, W.M.P., Weske, M., Grünbauer, D.: Case handling: a new paradigm for business process support. Data & Knowledge Engineering 53(2), 129–162 (2005)
8. Künzle, V., Reichert, M.: Towards object-aware process management systems: Issues, challenges, benefits. In: Halpin, T., Krogstie, J., Nurcan, S., Proper, E., Schmidt, R., Soffer, P., Ukor, R. (eds.) Enterprise, Business-Process and Information Systems Modeling. LNBIP, vol. 29, pp. 197–210. Springer, Heidelberg (2009)
9. Lu, R., Sadiq, S., Governatori, G.: On managing business processes variants. Data & Knowledge Engineering 68, 642–664 (2009)
10. van der Aalst, W.M.P., Pesic, M., Schonenberg, H.: Declarative workflows: balancing between flexibility and support. Computer Science - Research and Development 23, 99–113 (2009)
11. Kumaran, S., Liu, R., Wu, F.Y.: On the duality of information-centric and activity-centric models of business processes. In: Bellahsène, Z., Léonard, M. (eds.) CAiSE 2008. LNCS, vol. 5074, pp. 32–47. Springer, Heidelberg (2008)
12. Riss, U.V., Rickayzen, A., Maus, H., van der Aalst, W.M.P.: Challenges for business process and task management. Journal of Universal Knowledge Management (2), 77–100 (2005)
13. Bellotti, V., Dalal, B., Good, N., Flynn, P., Bobrow, D.G., Ducheneaut, N.: What a to-do: studies of task management towards the design of a personal task list manager. In: SIGCHI Conference on Human Factors in Computing Systems, pp. 735–742. ACM, New York (2004)
14. Grebner, O., Riss, U.: Implicit metadata generation on the semantic desktop using task management as example. In: Conference on Formal Ontologies Meet Industry, pp. 33–44. IOS Press, Amsterdam (2008)
15. Stoitsev, T., Scheidl, S., Spahn, M.: A framework for light-weight composition and management of ad-hoc business processes. In: Winckler, M., Johnson, H. (eds.) TAMODIA 2007. LNCS, vol. 4849, pp. 213–226. Springer, Heidelberg (2007)

Technology Readiness Index (TRI) Factors as Differentiating Elements between Users and Non Users of Internet Banking, and as Antecedents of the Technology Acceptance Model (TAM)

Péricles José Pires[1], Bento Alves da Costa Filho[2], and João Carlos da Cunha[1]

[1] Universidade Federal do Paraná, Centro de Pesquisa e Pós-Graduação em Administração (UFPR/CEPPAD), Av. Pref. Lothário Meissner, 632, CEP 80.210.170 Curitiba, Paraná, Brazil
periclesjpires@gmail.com, jccunha@ufpr.br
[2] IBMEC Brasília, QRSW 2, bloco B4, AP. 103, CEP 70675-224 - DF e Faculdades Alfa Goiânia, GO, Brazil
costaf@uol.com.br

Abstract. The scope of this work covers the study of models developed for assessing critical aspects of consumer use and acceptance of technology-based products and services. We used the Technology Acceptance Model (TAM), and the Index of Readiness for the use of Technology (TRI) as theoretical references. We carried out field research on Internet banking users in order to: (1) evaluate the differences between the groups in terms of predisposition towards technology using the TRI model; and (2) test whether the influencing factors of this model could be antecedents to the main construct of the technology acceptance model (TAM). The analyses showed that for proposal (1), three of the four dimensions, - optimism, insecurity and discomfort, - presented significant differences between the groups; and for proposal (2), the factor ´optimism`, a positive view of technology, was observed to be a significant antecedent of the intention to use on-line services.

Keywords: Technology Acceptance Model (TAM), Technology Readiness Index (TRI), Internet banking users, intention of use.

1 Introduction

This research took as its theoretical framework the TRI and TAM scales, with the aim of assessing predisposition, use and acceptance of technology in an auto-service context such as Internet banking. Such models have been the object of research since publication of the original studies; TAM by Davis [1] and TRI by Parasuraman [2] and Parasuraman and Colby [3]. With regard specifically to the TAM model, several articles have been published on testing information systems interfaces as well as those proposing improvements to the basic model: [4-8]. In the case of the TRI model test results can be generalized for contexts such as insurance services, and industrial equipment [9]. Mention should be made of Souza and Luce's research in Brazil [10, 11]; they sought to validate the instrument using confirmatory factorial analysis, with

M.M. Cruz-Cunha et al. (Eds.): CENTERIS 2011, Part II, CCIS 220, pp. 215–229, 2011.

their results indicating that TRI may help to distinguish between users and non-users of technological products, and to predict adoption of these products.

We carried out this research study into users and non-users of Internet banking in two stages: (1) firstly, we made a comparison between the two groups to evaluate whether there were any differences in relation to predisposition to technology, with the aid of the TRI model; (2) following this, we analysed whether the formative factors of this model might help to explain the main dependent variable of the technology acceptance model (TAM), intention of use. To perform stage 1, we carried out exploratory factorial analyses and variance analyses, with results pointing to differences in terms of optimism and insecurity between users and non-users of internet banking. In stage 2, we carried out a statistical analysis using structural equation modelling and assessing the TRI model factors as antecedents of the main dependent variable of the TAM model, intention of use, which produced significant results for the optimism construct.

The remaining structure of the paper approaches the following subjects: in items 2 and 3 we present the fundamental concepts and models upon which we based our research arguments; the susceptibility of consumers to technology was discussed through the Technology Readiness Index (TRI). We also present the Technology Acceptance Model (TAM) which assesses a subjective probability of future use of technology. In items 4 and 5 we show how both models TRI and TAM could be combined into a third model with more power of explanation and statistically tested. In item 6 we bring the research design mentioning details of a sample of users and non users of internet banking service. In items 7 and 8 we discuss the results of the survey and finally on item 9 we did a synthesis of the concluding remarks of the paper.

2 Consumer Technology Readiness

The modern consumer is obliged to live with the dynamics of technology, whether through automation used in traditional commerce (automated cash terminals, bar codes, credit and debit cards), or through virtual services such as e-commerce, Internet banking, e-government or distance-learning, and is left with little alternative but **to face up to** the advance of technology. Parasuraman argues that the number of products and services based on technology (use at home, work, leisure, etc.) is growing quickly; but in spite of this growth in quantity, these apparatuses do not bring the benefits the customers expected. On the contrary, there is growing evidence of frustration when dealing with technological systems or apparatuses mainly in auto-service. These gadgets invite the customers to interact with machines and equipment instead of offering personal treatment, a form of service still very much sought after [11].

There is a tendency towards growth of technologically highly sophisticated products, resulting in fundamental transformations in the interaction of the company with the customer. This indicates the need for a broad study since academic research into the readiness of people to use such systems is still considered to be at early stage [2]. Mowen and Minor [42] argue that technological changes can significantly alter consumers' way of life. Mick and Fournier [27] noted that technology instead of always being positive is often paradoxical. At the same time as it generates positive feelings of control, freedom, novelty, competence, efficiency, satisfaction, association and engagement, it may also provokes feelings of chaos, enslavement, obsolescence, incompetence, inefficiency, dissatisfaction, isolation and disengagement.

We should point out that these paradoxes in many cases provoke strong negative emotions in the consumers who in their turn react with a number of defence mechanisms. Those could rang from ignoring the innovation to postponing the purchase. When referring to the eight paradoxes of technology presented by Mick and Fournier [27], Parasuraman [2] concluded that they reflect two facets: they are potential **stimulators** or **inhibitors** of readiness for technology. He also mentions other studies [1], [13], which identified this dichotomy in the beliefs and motivations of certain customers and which may increase or reduce the probability of adoption of new technology.

The works of Swinyard and Ghee [45] emphasized the importance of attitude in distinguishing between users and non-users of financial products and services. Customers with attitudes favorable to technology, computers and convenience are usually less dependent on service provided by people, preferring electronic auto-service channels like ATMs and Internet banking. Conversely, customers that do not like technology and do not feel comfortable with auto-service equipment tend to limit their interaction with this type of equipment to the minimum possible.

Banks have had long experience in introducing new technologies for interaction with customers (e.g. ATM's, touch-tone banking, telephone-service centers and on-line banking) [14, 15]. Banking by Internet represents an interesting subject for study in the field of innovation. It is an area in which many financial institutions have pursued strategies for reducing costs, increasing revenue and increasing customer retention. However, there are doubts as to whether these elements can be dealt with simultaneously [15]. Technology applied to banking services and materialized in electronic form may be an important means of customer retention. In research on customers of an on-line broker, Chen and Hitt [31] identified that heavy users showed a tendency to be more loyal to that company. Hitt and Frei [35] found out that frequent users of electronic banking are more profitable for the banks and acquire financial products and services more frequently than customers using traditional channels. In the study of Hitt and Frei [35] the results of the study did not point to the traditional demographic differences, which usually identify heavy users with segments of the population having better socio-economic conditions. Thus it is evident that there is room for studies that assess the influence of technological factors on the consumption of financial products and services, with important consequences in terms of customer loyalty and profitability.

3   Technology Acceptance Model (TAM)

The technology acceptance model (TAM) developed by Davis [1] is an adaptation of the TRA model, Theory of Reasoned Action, [16], specifically applied to the users of computers or information systems. The object of the model is to provide an explanation for the decisive causes of computer acceptance in general. It also seeks to explain user behavior when faced with various technologies linked to computer science by not only predicting but also explaining why one system can be accepted or rejected.

The essential purpose of the TAM model is to provide a basis for mapping the impact of external factors on the internal individual ones such as beliefs, attitudes and behavioral intentions. This model was formulated to measure these impacts by evaluating some fundamental variables suggested by previous research on cognitive and affective acceptance of computers. The TAM model is based on two main constructs linked to belief, **perceived usefulness and perceived ease of use** [1, 4, 17, 18]. For Meuter [12] these two constructs influence attitudes to auto-service machines, which in turn directly influence the intention of the individual to use technology [19, 20]. It is worth remembering that the two constructs were adapted from the innovation characteristics of Rogers [43], and are equivalent to the relative advantage (perceived usefulness) and perceived ease of use (complexity).

The **perceived usefulness construct PU** can be defined as the subjective probability that a user will adopt a certain technology such as an information or computer system; when confirmed, this may increase performance in relation to the object in use. Moore and Benbasat [41] define PU as relative advantage a construct originally proposed by Rogers [43], meaning how the apparatuses linked to the technological innovation are perceived as superior in comparison with traditional practice.

The second prominent concept in the TAM model is **perceived ease of use - PEOU**, which corresponds to the individual's expectations of having to make less physical or mental effort when using a certain system or technology. A series of studies has already examined the effect of the PU and PEOU constructs and revealed them as important determining factors in the use of interactive systems [21, 5, 22, 23, 12]. The studies of Moore and Benbasat [41] and Agarwal and Prasad [30] on initial adopting factors and evaluating innovation characteristics presented results that showed evidence of usefulness and perceived ease of use (along with compatibility) as the most influential constructs in the decision to continue using technology.

The first group of hypotheses we tested concerned the acceptance of the technology model itself as applied to users of Internet banking, as given below (see Figure 1):

H1: Ease of use perceived by the users of Internet banking influences perceived usefulness.

H2: Perceived usefulness influences Internet banking users' intention to continue using it.

H3: Perceived ease of use influences the Internet banking users´ intention to continue using it.

4   TRI Model (Technology Readiness Index)-Index of Readiness for the Use of Technology

The model developed by Parasuraman [2] and Parasuraman and Colby [3] is a measuring instrument for assessing the readiness of the North American consumer for technology. It was developed from a series of qualitative research programs (focus group) with consumers from several sectors of the economy (e.g., financial services, online services, e-commerce and telecommunications). It enjoyed the collaboration of Rockbridge Associates; a company based in Virginia, United States, specializing in service and technology research, and was formatted by NTRS (National Technology Readiness Survey), which generated several items and scales for the research. As the study progressed, a survey was developed with 1200 respondents which, after several trials, resulted in a highly consistent construct of four dimensions and 36 variables (items). The readiness-for-use constructs are divided into drivers and inhibitors for adoption of technology and are represented by optimism, innovativeness, discomfort and insecurity [2]. A brief description of each one follows below.

a.   **Optimism:** a positive vision of technology and the belief that it offers people more control, flexibility and efficiency in their lives.

b.   **Innovativeness:** the tendency towards being a pioneer in the use of technology, a leader or opinion-former.

c.   **Discomfort:** a perception of lack of control over technology and the feeling of being pressured or oppressed by it.

d.   **Insecurity:** distrust of technology and skepticism of one's own ability to use it properly.

We can see that the first two constructs optimism and innovativeness are drivers or positive inducers to the use of technology. The last two discomfort and insecurity are inhibitors or factors that may delay the adoption of new technology. Parasuraman [2] reinforces the importance of the constructs tested and indicates that the respondents of the research carried out were classified by scores in high, medium or low consumption potential accordingly. Each one of the four dimensions may differ in terms of use of high technology products and services. Thus the fact an individual may be led to adopt a certain technology in a specific area (e.g. high use potential) does not imply that he will adopt it in another situation [10].

We propose a series of tests which aim to verify if it is possible to differentiate, in terms of TRI factors, between Internet users in general and users of Internet banking in particular. This evaluation may be justified if we take into account the differentiated profile of the users of Internet services, supposed familiar with the information technology infrastructure of the global network. Considering these TRI factors as the differentiating elements between technology users and non-users, (see Figure 1), we put forward the following hypotheses.

H4: The optimism factor, defined as a positive vision of technology, and the belief that it offers greater control, flexibility and efficiency in people's lives, is a differentiating element between users and non-users of Internet banking.

H5: The innovativeness factor, defined as a tendency to be a pioneer, leader or opinion-former in the use of technology, is a differentiating element between users and non - users of Internet banking.

H6: The discomfort factor, defined as perception of lack of control over technology and the feeling of being pressured or oppressed by it, is a differentiating element between users and non-users of Internet banking.

H7: The insecurity factor, defined as distrust of technology and skepticism of one's own abilities to use it appropriately, is a differentiating element between users and non-users of Internet banking.

5   TRI Factors as Antecedents of the Technology Acceptance Model (TAM)

Parasuraman [2] suggested that models should be proposed to test several antecedents and consequences as much for consolidating the TRI model as for extending the four dimensions (optimism, innovativeness, discomfort and insecurity). Inclusion of the TRI factors in the Technology Acceptance Model (TAM) was due to interests common to both proposals: assessment of critical aspects regarding use and the ability of consumers and users to live with and relate easily to technologically based products and services. TRI is a model composed of constructs which both induce (optimism and innovativeness) and inhibit (discomfort and insecurity) in the use of technology. Hypotheses were tested aiming to assess the impact of each of the four TRI factors on intention of continued use, main dependent variable of the technology acceptance model, as seen in Figure 1. The hypotheses for influence of the TRI factors on the Technology Acceptance Model are the following:

H8: The optimism factor, defined as a positive view of technology and the belief that it offers greater control, flexibility and efficiency in people's lives, significantly influences the intention of continued use of Internet banking.

H9: The innovativeness factor, defined as the tendency to be a pioneer in use of technology, a leader or opinion-former, significantly influences the intention of continued use of Internet banking.

H10: The discomfort factor, defined as the perception of lack of control over technology and the feeling of being pressured or oppressed by it, significantly influences the intention of continued use of Internet banking.

H11: The insecurity factor, defined as distrust of technology and skepticism of one's own abilities to use it appropriately, significantly influences the intention of continued use of Internet banking.

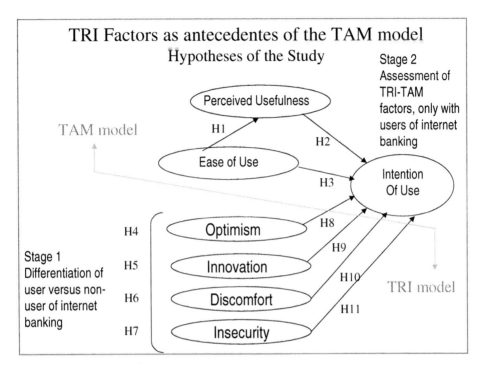

Fig. 1. Summary of proposed hypotheses of the study

6 Sample and Collection of Data

We carried out the field research with Internet users in the city of Curitiba (South of Brazil) in 2008, some of whom were users of Internet banking. We instructed the interviewees to answer questions on the use of technology-based products and services occurring in Parasuraman [2] ´s (2000) Index of Readiness for Technology (TRI).The respondents who besides accessing the Internet also used Internet banking, were requested to answer an extra group of questions concerning the Technology Acceptance Model (TAM).

We based the size of the sample on the number of indicators used in the statistical analyses of the study which were: exploratory factorial analysis, confirmatory factorial analysis and multiple regressions. For the factorial and multiple regression analyses, Hair et al. [24] recommend at least five cases per variable. In confirmatory factorial analysis, Bentler [25] suggests that the proportion of the size of the sample in relation to a free parameter should be at least five to one. We obtained a non-probabilistic judgement sample with 231 valid questionnaires, with 124 being users and 107 being non-users of Internet banking, whilst all were users of the Internet. According to Churchill [28], a judgement sample is one in which the elements are chosen because it is believed that they represent the population of interest. The data collection instrument used a seven point Likert scale, rangin from "I totally disagree" (1) to "I totally agree" (7). In this study, the Likert scale was considered as an interval scale, in accordance with the opinions of Aaker, Kumar and Day and Hair [19], Babin, Money and Samouel [24], although there are authors who consider it to be ordinal [26].

6.1 Treatment of the Data

The Kolmogorov-Smirnov test, with Lilliefors significance level for normality, showed significant statistical evidence for all the variables, refuting the nil hypotheses, and indicating that the data have non-normal distribution. However, the Levene test for variance homogeneity that is less sensitive to non normality of the data presented only eight significant statistics among the forty seven variables of the study. This indicates there is homocedasticity between the two Internet banking groups, users and non-users, for most of the variables. In addition to Levene, the Mann-Whitney test applied to the 47 variables showed significant statistical evidence (alpha equal to or less than 5%) for 18 variables. In fact, for 29 variables the results pointed to the two Internet banking groups, users and non-users, as originating from populations with the same variance. Aaker [28] and Churchill [19] argue that in t tests, the violation of normality is not as serious as the violation of homocedasticity. With regard to randomness and independence, it should be remembered that the sample is non-probabilistic. Therefore their elements were not chosen randomly. However, users and non-users of Internet banking constitute independent groups, there being a database control for this differentiation.

7 Technology Readiness Index - Mensuration Model

Considering that this scale had already been tested, we employed confirmatory analyses with the original constructs used by Parasuraman [2], translated into Portuguese [10]. The exploratory factorial analyses functioned only as an auxiliary to the initial evaluation of the factors predicted in the model.

We carried out confirmatory factorial analysis using the EQS structural equations program, version 6.1. The results presented in Table 1 show that the optimism and innovativeness factors are well adjusted to the sample data. NNFI, CFI and GFI indices are all above 0,9 and RMSEA within the interval recommended by Hair for the discomfort and insecurity constructs. NNFI and CFI indices are a little below the acceptable levels, except for RMSEA, which showed above the recommended limit of 0,08, indicating the need for adjustment of the factors mentioned. Values referring to chi-square are not shown in Table 1, since these tend to present significant results, thus not being an appropriate measure mainly for samples over 200 elements. The reliability of the internal coherence of the constructs is in any case shown to be good in accordance with Hair [33]. Cronbach alpha coefficients of the factors are all above 0,7, that is to say, all the factors showed acceptable **convergent validity**.

Of all the indicators used in the TRI model, we only needed to suppress one variable of the innovativeness factor whose factorial load was shown to be inadequate, well below the acceptable minimum of 0,4 in a sample of 200 to 250 respondents [24].

Table 1. Measures of adequacy

FACTOR	Measures of Adequacy				Reliability
	NNFI	CFI	GFI	RMSEA	Alfa Cronbach
Optimism	0,94	0,96	0,91	0,07	0,85
Innovativeness	0,96	0,97	0,96	0,08	0,75
Discomfort	0,81	0,85	0,90	0,09	0,74
Insecurity	0,79	0,86	0,90	0,12	0,75
Source: the authors' research.					

Regarding the **discriminating validity** of the constructs, Table 2 presents a correlation matrix of TRI factors, starting from factorial scores, in which a significant correlation between optimism and innovative aspects, 0,54, is identified, and between discomfort and insecurity, 0,53. These values are very close to those of the original study by Parasuraman [2]: 0,52 and 0,56 respectively. We may consider this an acceptable degree of association which does not invalidate the differentiation between the constructs. It is predictable because the pairs of factors mentioned represent respectively the inductors and the inhibitors which determine the predisposition of people to use of technology. These correlations of moderate intensity according to Hair [33] do not adversely affect the discriminating validity, since according to Churchill [28] only if one measure has a very high correlation with other measures in a model, will there be a risk of not evaluating distinct attributes.

Table 2. Correlation between TRI factors matrix

	Optimism	Innovativeness	Discomfort	Insecurity
Optimism	1,00			
Innovativeness	0,54**	1,00		
Discomfort	-0,10	-0,10	1,00	
Insecurity	-0,02	-0,02	0,53**	1
* * significant correlation for alpha = 1% Source: the authors' research.				

The TRI of the sample of this study was larger than the indices of previous research studies. In the inducer constructs optimism and innovativeness, the respondents were shown to be more positive in relation to technology, and in the inhibiting constructs discomfort and insecurity, the respondents were shown to be less negative. This meant that the average, 3.14, reflected a greater predisposition to the technology of the sample when compared with the other studies mentioned. The fact that the interviewees were all necessarily Internet navigators, and some of them were customers of Internet banking, possibly contributed to this result. The Internet user profile is still associated with people familiar with technology and innovation. In the previously mentioned studies, some of the sample did not use the Internet or any other technologically-based products and services.

8   The TRI Model Explains Differences between Users and Non-users of Technology

When submitted to variance analysis (ANOVA) to assess differences between users and non-users of Internet banking, two of the four TRI factors presented indicators with significant statistical differences; viz., optimism and insecurity (hypotheses H4 and H7, respectively). Of the 10 variables that compose the optimism construct, eight showed significance for alpha equal to 1%, suggesting that this factor is very helpful in explaining the differences between users and non-users of Internet banking. Users of the bank via Internet have a more positive vision with regard to subjects involving day-to-day contact, interaction, use and control related to technology. In the same way for the insecurity construct many of the indicators presented significant differences between the two groups. Of the seven variables that form the factor insecurity five exhibited statistical significance. This suggests that the users of Internet banking can deal with the risk of having privacy information violated.

Concerning the discomfort construct (hypothesis H6), of the 11 indicators only three presented statistically significant differences between the two groups. The items involved were those concerning the usefulness of help to the user by telephone or Internet. Difficulties encountered when a person does not know how to deal with high technology equipment, and when there is imminent possibility of failure of the latter. In the case of the innovativeness factor (hypothesis H5), there were no statistical differences between the segments under examination. We did not therefore perceive that the users of Internet banking were more predisposed to innovation than the non-users. In summary, of the four hypotheses concerning the TRI factors, two were confirmed - hypotheses H4 and H7 - suggesting that the specific use of a service(Internet banking) that involves interaction and trust in information technology differs by virtue of a greater optimism and less insecurity on the part of the users of the service.

8.1   TRI Factors as Antecedents of the TAM Model

We evaluated the technology readiness factors (TRI) in relation to the Technology Acceptance Model (TAM) by means of a hypotheses test which tried to verify whether the four TRI dimensions - optimism, innovativeness, discomfort and insecurity - were antecedents of the intention of continued use construct. Due to the limitation of size of the sample with 124 respondents and to the large amount of observable variables involving the two models, in a total of 47, we attempted to work with the factorial scores as a substitute for the group of variables that composed the original factor. In this second stage of the research, we considered only the 124 respondents who were users of Internet banking

Initially we carried out an analysis on the structural equations program to evaluate the relationships between the constructs of the TAM model separately, the results of which are in Table 3. We may see that the three relationships presented significant regression coefficients: (1) the impact of the ease of use construct (FPEOU) in the perceived usefulness construct (FPU), confirming hypothesis H1; (2) the impact of the perceived usefulness construct (FPU) on the intention of continued use (FIU), confirming hypothesis H2; and (3) the impact of ease of use construct (FPEOU) on the intention of continued use, confirming hypothesis H3. We should point out that the relationships with greater coefficients refer to hypotheses H2 and H1, with coefficients of 0,75 and 0,54 respectively. The regression coefficient, which represents hypothesis H3, with a value of 0,14, becomes non-significant when the TAM and TRI models are run simultaneously. The relationship between ease of use (FPEOU) and intention of continued use (FIU) has, historically, been the most unstable part of the TAM model, as seen in the meta-analysis carried out by Ma and Liu [39]. In any case, the technology acceptance model, originally proposed by Davis [1], has all the significant relationships, giving special attention to the high determination coefficient (R2) of 0,69 in the main regression, the one which has intention of continued use (FIU) as a dependent variable. This confirms that the concepts of ease of use and the perception of usefulness of a technologically based service such as Internet banking are good predictors of intention of continued use of the service.

Table 3. Structural equations with standardized coefficients

Equations	Determination Coef. -R2
FPU = 0,541 * * FPEOU + 0,841 ERROR	0,293
FIU = 0,752 * * FPU + 0,140 * FPEOU + 0,548 ERROR	0,699
* * Coefficient significant to level of 1% / * Coefficient significant to level of 5%.	

To assess the relationships of the TRI and TAM models simultaneously and in integrated fashion, we ran the structural equations program, as shown in table 4. We may thus see that of the seven hypotheses established for the model together (H1, H2, H3, H8, H9, H10 and H11), three were shown to be significant statistically: H2, H1 and H8, with regression coefficients of 0,75, 0,57 and 0,28 respectively. We draw attention to the fact that the regression coefficient of hypothesis H3, referring to the influence of the ease of use construct (FPEOU) in relation to intention of continued use (FIU), is no longer significant. However, the regression coefficient which represents hypothesis H8, referring to the influence of the optimism factor (OTIM), is shown to be significant, being the only factor of the TRI model to significantly influence the TAM model. It is worth emphasizing that joining the two models made a modest contribution to the explained variance, when the variation occurring in the determination coefficient (R2) of 0,69 to 0,72 is observed; in other words, an increase of only 3% in the capacity to explain intention of continued use.

Table 4. Structural equations with TRI versus TAM model standardized coefficients

Equations	Determination-Coef. R2
FPU = 0,565 * * FPEOU + 0,825 ERROR	0,320
FIU = 0,752 * * FPU + 0,75 FPEOU + 0,276 * * OTIM-0,099 INOV-0,007 DISC. + 0,057INSG + 0,525 ERROR	0,725
* * Coefficient Significant to level of 1% / * Coefficient significant to level of 5%	

9 Conclusions

This study attempted to evaluate separately and jointly two very well-known models in the literature: the Index of Readiness for Technology (TRI), developed by Parasuraman [2] and the Technology Acceptance Model (TAM), proposed by Fred Davis [1]. The hypotheses raised had two main objectives: (1) to evaluate the potential of the Index of Readiness for Technology in order to explain the differences between users and non-users of technology; and (2) to test whether the four factors that compose TRI - optimism, innovativeness, discomfort and insecurity - could be antecedents of the Technology Acceptance Model (TAM).

As for objective 1, in the research carried out with users and non-users of Internet banking, the results of the analyses indicated that three of the four TRI-forming constructs, - optimism, insecurity and discomfort, - showed significant differences between the two groups. The differences presented in the **optimism** factor translated into greater value for users of Internet banking in terms of convenience and practicality offered by technology. The differences in the **discomfort** factor, for their part, were linked to the perception of user help systems which do not help when some difficulty is encountered. In the case of the differences in averages registered by the **insecurity** factor, these referred mainly to the confidence (or lack of it) in carrying out transactions, giving confidential data such as credit card numbers and passwords; the possibility of confirmation in writing of these transactions is raised; thus reminding us of the value given to human contact in the relationship with a company. As for the **innovativeness** factor, no significant differences were detected, probably because the two groups were both users of Internet.

In relation to objective 2 on the other hand, the results presented only one of the four factors of the TRI model as statistically significant: optimism; that is, having a positive view of technology and a belief that it offers greater control, flexibility and efficiency in people's lives, which may partly explain the intention to continued use. We may call attention to the fact that the three other factors were not confirmed as antecedents of intention of use. Probably the variations in discomfort and insecurity were not reflected in intention of use because the sample was familiar with information technology. Also, perhaps the second inducing factor, innovativeness, did not offer any potential explanation due to the respondents' characteristics. Perhaps the variations were not sufficient in terms of innovative predisposition to affect the intention to continue using certain technology-based products or services.

One of the theoretical aims of this study was to evaluate the possibility of improving understanding of the unexplained part of the main dependent variable of the technology acceptance model: intention of use. The original work developed by Davis [1] and the subsequent studies of Venkatesh and Davis [7], on TAM 2, and the one by Venkatesh [46], on UTAUT (unified theory of acceptance and uses of technology), were able to obtain determination coefficients above 0,7. This means that a large part of the construct variance on screen may be explained by the independent variables, with emphasis on the perceived usefulness construct. In the sample used here, we obtained a determination coefficient (R^2) of 0,69 when the TAM model was analyzed in isolation, a result equivalent to the above mentioned studies. Incorporation of the constructs of the TRI model, - optimism, innovativeness, discomfort and insecurity, - into the TAM model increased R^2 by only 0,03, in other words, an increase of only 3% of explained variance in intention of use, which is assumed to be a small contribution.

In future works we intend to test the proposed model in other interactive interfaces such as electronic commerce and services in order to find out if results obtained here would persist in different web environments. This way we could verify the model consistency as much as proceed eventual modifications suggested by data collected in these forthcoming surveys.

References

1. Davis, F.D.: Perceived usefulness, perceived ease of use, and user acceptance of information technology. MIS Quarterly 13(3), 319–341 (1989)
2. Parasuraman, A.: Technology readiness index (TRI): a multiple-item scale to measure readiness to embrace new technologies. Journal of Service Research 2(4), 307–320 (2000)
3. Parasuraman, A., Colby, C.: Techno-ready marketing: how and why your customers adopt technology. The Free Press, New York (2001)
4. Davis, F.D., Bagozzi, R.P., Warshaw, P.R.: User acceptance of computer technology: a comparison of two theoretical models. Management Science 35(8), 982–1004 (1989)
5. Taylor, S., Todd, P.: Understanding information technology usage: a testing of competing models. Information Systems Research 6(2), 144–176 (1995)
6. Dasgupta, S., Granger, M., Mcgarry, N.: User acceptance of e-collaboration technology: an extension of the technology acceptance model. Group Decision and Negotiation, 87–100 (2002)
7. Venkatesh, V., Morris, M.G., Davis, G.B., Davis, F.D.: User acceptance of information technology: toward a unified view. MIS Quarterly 27(3), 425–478 (2003)
8. Keat, K.T., Mohan, A.: Integration of TAM based electronic commerce models for trust. Journal of American Academy of Business 5(1-2), 404–410 (2004)
9. Taylor, S.A., Goodwin, S., Celuch, K.: An exploratory investigation into the question of direct selling via the internet in industrial equipment markets. Journal of Business to Business Marketing 12(2), 39–54 (2005)
10. de Souza, R.V., Luce, F.B.: Assessment of applicability of TRI index for the adoption of technology-based products and services in Brazil. In: Anais do Encontro Nacional da Associação Nacional de Pós-Graduação e Pesquisa em Administração, Atibaia, SP, Brasil, vol. 27 (2003)
11. de Souza, R.V., Luce, F.B.: Assessment of applicability of TRI index for the adoption of technology-based products and services. Revista de Administração Contemporânea 9(3), 121–141 (2005)
12. Meuter, M.L., Ostrom, A.L., Roundtree, R.I., Bitner, M.J.: Self-service technologies: understanding customer satisfaction with technology-based service encounters. Journal of Marketing 64(3), 50–64 (2000)
13. Dabholkar, P.A.: Incorporating choice into an attitudinal framework: analyzing models of mental comparison processes. Journal of Consumer Research 21(1), 100–118 (1994)
14. Clemons, E.K., Hitt, L., Gu, B., Thatcher, M.E., Weber, B.W.: Impacts of e-commerce and enhanced information endowments on financial services: a quantitative analysis of transparency, differential pricing, and disintermediation. Journal of Financial Services Research 22(1-2), 73–90 (2002)
15. Frei, F., Harker, P.: Value creation and process management: evidence from retail banking. Working Paper (99-16). Wharton Financial Institutions Center, Philadelphia (1999)

16. Fishbein, M., Ajzen, I.: Belief, attitude, intention, and behavior: an introduction to theory and research. Addison-Wesley, Reading (1975)
17. Karahanna, E., Straub, D.W., Chervany, N.L.: Information technology adoption across time: a cross-sectional comparison of pre-adoption and post-adoption beliefs. MIS Quaterly 23(2), 183–218 (1999)
18. Gefen, D.: TAM or just plain habit: a look at experienced online shoppers. Journal of End User Computing 15(3), 1–13 (2003)
19. Aaker, D.A., Kumar, V., Day, G.S.: Marketing research. John Wiley & Sons, Inc., New York (1995)
20. Eagly, A.H.C.: The psychology of attitudes. Harcourt Brace Jovanovich, Forth Worth (1993)
21. Mathieson, K.: Predicting users intentions: comparing technology acceptance model with the theory of planned behavior. Information Systems Research 2(3), 173–191 (1991)
22. Robey, D.: Theories that explain contradiction: accounting for the contradictory organizational consequences of information technology. In: Proceedings of the International Conference on Information Systems, Amsterdam, Netherlands (1995)
23. Gentry, L., Calantone, R.: A comparison of three models to explain shop-bot use on the web. Psycology & Marketing 30(3), 184–202 (2002)
24. Hair Jr., J.F., Babin, B., Money, A.H., Samouel, P.: Fundamentos de métodos de pesquisa em administração (Foundations of research methods in management). Bookman, Porto Alegre (2005)
25. Bentler, P.M.: EQS – structural equations program manual. Multivariate Software, Inc., Encino (1995)
26. Jöreskog, K.G., Sörbom, D.: LISREL 8: structural equation modeling with SIMPLIS command language. Scientific Software, Mooresville (1993)
27. Mick, D.G., Fournier, S.: Paradoxes of technology: consumer cognizance, emotions, and coping strategies. Journal of Consumer Research 25(2), 123–143 (1998)
28. Churchill Jr., G.A.: Marketing research: methodological foundation, 7th edn. The Dryden Press, Orlando Fla (1999)
29. Adams, D., Nelson, R., Todd, P.: Perceived usefulness, ease of use, and usage of information Technology: a replication. MIS Quarterly 16(2), 227–248 (1992)
30. Agarwal, R., Prasad, J.: The role of innovation characteristics and perceived voluntariness in the acceptance of information technologies. Decision Sciences 28(3), 557–582 (1997)
31. Chen, P., Hitt, L.: Measuring switching costs and the determinants of customers retention in internet-enabled businesses: a study of the online brokerage industry. Information Systems Research 13(3), 255–276 (2002)
32. Curran, J., Meuter, M.L., Suprenant, C.F.: Intentions to use self-service technologies: a confluence of multiple attitudes. Journal of Service Research 5(3), 209–225 (2003)
33. Hair Jr., J.F., Anderson, R.E., Tathan, R.L., Black, W.C.: Multivaried data analysis, 5ath edn. Bookman, Porto Alegre (2005)
34. Hauser, J.R., Shugan, S.M.: Intensity measures of consumer preference. Operation Research 28(2), 278–320 (1980)
35. Hitt, L.M., Frei, X.F., Harker, P.: How financial firms decide on technology. In: Robert, E. (ed.) Brookings-Wharton Papers on Financial Services, pp. 93–146. Financial Institutions Center, Philadelphia (1999)
36. Hitt, L.M., Frei, X.F.: Do better customers utilize electronic distribution channels? The case of PC Banking. Management Science 48(6), 732–748 (2002)
37. King, W.R., He, J.: A meta-analysis of the technology acceptance model. Information & Management 43(6), 740–755 (2006)

38. Larcker, D.F., Lessig, U.P.: Perceived usefulness of information: a psychometric examination. Decision Sciences 11(1), 121–134 (1980)
39. Ma, Q., Liu, L.: The technology acceptance model: a meta-analysis of empirical findings. Journal of Organizational and End User Computing 16(1), 59–72 (2004)
40. Moore, G.C., Benbasat, I.: Development of an instrument to measure the perceptions of adopting an information technology innovation. Information Systems Research 2(3), 192–222 (1991)
41. Mowen, J.C., Minor, M.S.: Comportamento do consumidor. Prentice Hall, São Paulo
42. Rogers, E.M.: Diffusion of innovation. The Free Press, New York (2003)
43. Swanson, E.B.: Information Channel Disposition and Use. Decisions Sciences 18(1), 131–145 (1987)
44. Swinyard, W., Ghee, L.: Adoption patterns of new banking technology in Southeast Asia. International Journal of Bank Marketing 5(4), 35–48 (1987)
45. Venkatesh, V., Davis, F.D.: Theoretical extension of the technology acceptance model: four longitudinal field studies. Management Science 46(2), 186–204 (2000)

Developing an Instrument to Assess Information Technology Staff Motivation

Fernando Belfo[1] and Rui Dinis Sousa[2]

[1] Polytechnic Institute of Coimbra,
Quinta Agrícola, Bencanta, 3040-316 Coimbra, Portugal
fpbelfo@gmail.com
[2] Algoritmi Research Centre, Information Systems Department, University of Minho
Campus de Azurém, 4800-058 Guimarães, Portugal
rds@dsi.uminho.pt

Abstract. Motivation is a key factor that influences individual effort, which, in turn, affects individual and organizational performance. Nevertheless, motivation at work depends on the organizational rewards and incentives, according to individual goals. This paper reports on the development of an instrument designed to measure the motivation of Information Technology people at their workplace. Psychology theories and work addressing intrinsic and extrinsic motivation have been studied. Some motivation instruments were reviewed and analyzed. Specificities and special characteristics regarding IT workers were evidenced and combined with other more general motivation factors. The instrument has been developed according to the five dimensions of the Worldatwork framework, resulting in a set of 30 scale items addressing 23 variables. Besides measuring the IT motivation levels, the tool may also help any organization to understand the weaknesses and strengths regarding incentive policies, and therefore, assist on the definition of new ones.

Keywords: motivation, IT management, IT human resources, incentive policy, reward, instrument.

1 Introduction

Motivation is related with activation and intention. It concerns energy, direction, persistence and equifinality. Its importance in the real world is based on its tangible consequences. Ryan and Deci clearly underlined that importance when they said that "Motivation produces" [1]. Motivation is a central concern of the society – to know how to move ourselves or others to act. "Parents, teachers, coaches, and managers struggle with how to motivate those that they mentor, and individuals struggle to find energy, mobilize effort and persist at the tasks of life and work" [2].

Driving human behavior may vary. People can be oriented to engage in work primarily for its own sake, because the work itself is interesting, engaging, or in some way satisfying. If so, it is usually called intrinsic motivation. It may also be associated to motivation to work primarily in response to something apart from the work itself, such as reward or recognition or to the dictates of other people. This is usually called

M.M. Cruz-Cunha et al. (Eds.): CENTERIS 2011, Part II, CCIS 220, pp. 230–239, 2011.

extrinsic motivation [3]. Ryan and Deci presented definitions about intrinsic and extrinsic motivations and some new directions [4]. Among other approaches, these authors contributed with the Self-Determination Theory (SDT), distinguishing between different types of motivation based on the different reasons or goals that give rise to an action. They argued that the most basic distinction between them is that intrinsic motivation refers to doing something because it is inherently interesting or enjoyable, and extrinsic motivation refers to doing something because it leads to a separable outcome. Their review supported that experience quality and performance can be very diverse when one is behaving for intrinsic versus extrinsic reasons [1, 5].

WorldatWork, an association representing professions comprising total rewards, proposed an exhaustive reward model composed by five dimensions which are Compensation, Benefits, Work-Life, Performance and Recognition, Development and Career Opportunities [6]. Although it is not an assessment instrument, this model helps to extensively structure motivational dimensions. According to WorldatWork, compensation is a payment provided by an employer to an employee for services rendered (i.e., time, effort and skill) and comprises fixed payment, variable payment, short-term incentive payment and long-term incentive payment. Benefits are programs used to complement the cash payment, usually designed to protect the employee and his or her family from financial risks and can be classified into social insurance, group insurance and payment for time not worked. Another proposed dimension is the Work-life. It consists in a particular group of organizational practices, policies, programs, combined with a attitude which actively supports efforts to assist employees reach success either at work or at home, like workplace flexibility, paid and unpaid time off, health and well-being, caring for dependents, financial support, community involvement or management involvement/culture change interventions. Performance and Recognition, the fourth dimension, promotes the alignment of the organizational, by team and individual performance assessment in order to understand what was accomplished, and how it was accomplished. Performance and Recognition is composed by performance planning, linking individual, team and organizational goals, performance, showing a skill or a capacity and performance feedback, communicating how well worker play a job compared to expectations and recognition that acknowledges or underlines employee actions, efforts, behavior or performance. Finally, Development and Career Opportunities dimension is composed by a set of learning experiences planned to improve employees' practical skills and competencies and an employee plan to pursue career goals and evolve into higher responsible positions in the organization. It also includes Learning Opportunities, Coaching/Mentoring or Advancement Opportunities [7]. According to WorldatWork [6], Total Rewards is "the monetary and non-monetary return provided to employees in exchange for their time, talents, efforts and results".

In the following section of this paper, we perform an analysis of several of the most important motivation assessment instruments. Then, in the third section, we analyze IT staff motivational specificities. Having studied the existing instruments and IT staff motivational specificities, the fourth section presents the instrument we have developed using the WorldatWork model as a cognitive reference. The fifth and last section presents the conclusions pointing out future work.

2   Motivation Assessment Instruments

To define an instrument for assessing the maturity of IT staff motivation, we followed the following steps: (a) analysis of motivation assessment instruments; (b) consideration of IT staff motivational specificities; (c) instrument development. An extensive literature review allowed the identification of a relevant set of motivation assessment instruments: General Causality Orientations Scale, Work Preference Inventory, Harter's instrument, Academic Motivation Scale, Human Resources Survey, Work-Life Questionnaire and Intrinsic Motivation Inventory.

2.1   General Causality Orientations Scale

The General Causality Orientations Scale (GCOS) was initially proposed by Deci and Ryan [8]. The strength of three different motivational orientations within an individual are assessed with this scale. These different directions, labeled Autonomy, Controlled, and Impersonal, are understood as relatively enduring facets of personality, and each one is theorized to exist within each individual to some degree. Main scale is composed by three subscales, and a person gets a score on each subscale. The Autonomy Orientation subscale measures the degree to which a person is oriented toward aspects of the environment that stimulate intrinsic motivation. When strong autonomy oriented, people seek opportunities for self-determination and choice. They tend to select jobs that allow greater initiative, have more autonomy and are likely to "organize their actions on the basis of personal goals and interests rather than controls and constraints". The Controlled Orientation subscale measures the degree to which a person is oriented toward being controlled by rewards, deadlines, structures, ego-involvements, and the directives of others. A high controlled orientated person is expected to be dependent on rewards or other controls. These people may be more familiar to what others demand than to what they want for themselves. The Impersonal Orientation subscale measures the degree to which a person believes that attaining desired outcomes is beyond his or her control and that success is mostly a matter of luck. People highly impersonal oriented are likely to be anxious and to "see themselves as incompetent and unable to master situations". They often feel they are not able to affect outcomes or cope with demands or changes [8].

2.2   Work Preference Inventory

Work Preference Inventory (WPI) is a specific instrument developed for adults' motivation assessment. It was designed as a direct, explicit assessment of individual differences in the degree to which adults perceive themselves to be intrinsically and extrinsically motivated toward what they do [3]. One underlying assumption was that intrinsic and extrinsic motives might coexist. Like GCOS [8], WPI was set out for scales to be scored independently. The items considered at WPI wanted to capture major elements of both intrinsic and extrinsic motivation. The intrinsic motivation elements include (a) self-determination (preference for choice/autonomy), (b) competence (mastery orientation and preference for challenge), (c) task involvement (task absorption and flow), (d) curiosity (preference for complexity) and (e) interest (enjoy and fun). The elements for extrinsic motivation include (a) evaluation, (b) recognition concerns, (c) competition concerns, (d) a focus on money or other tangible incentives, and (e) a focus on the dictates of others.

2.3 Harter's Instrument

Harter developed an instrument to assess elementary school children´s general levels of intrinsic versus extrinsic motivation [9]. This instrument was composed of five subscales: (a) Preference for Challenge vs. Preference for Easy Work, (b) Curiosity/Interest vs. Pleasing the Teacher/Getting Good Grades, (c) Independent Mastery vs. Dependence on the Teacher, (d) Independent Judgment vs. Reliance on the Teacher's Judgment, and (e) Internal Criteria for Evaluation vs. External Criteria for Evaluation. It was assumed that intrinsically motivated students would be more likely to look out for challenging and interesting activities and assignments and would prefer to plan and face difficulties. On the contrary, extrinsically motivated children would prefer easy work more likely to be successful at, and for which they could get credit from the teacher. Also, they would prefer to be assigned with work that they could seek out help from the teacher if difficulties arise [9-10]. Harter's research results showed that both intrinsic and extrinsic motivational orientations are perfectly negatively correlated. In addition, intrinsic motivational orientation systematically decreases with the increasing of age or grade level.

2.4 Academic Motivation Scale

Another instrument developed to measure motivation was the Academic Motivation Scale (AMS), originally known as "Echelle de Motivation en Education" (EME) [11-12]. This instrument wanted to assess not only the intrinsic and the extrinsic motivation among students, but also amotivation in education. According to Deci and Ryan, there is a third type of motivational construct that should be considered in order to fully understand human behavior [5]. Reporting to a "why" question like "Why do you go to college?", possible items answers reflect different types of motivation. Some items of this AMS scale are: amotivational subscale, "Honestly I don´t know; I really feel I wasting my time in the college"; external regulation, "In order to get a more prestigious job latter on", Introjected regulation, "To prove to myself that I can do better than just a high-school degree"; identification regulation, "because eventually it will allow me to enter the job market in a field that I like"; Intrinsic Motivational (IM)- to know , "Because I experience pleasure and satisfaction while learning new things"; IM-Accomplishment, "for the pleasure I experience while surpassing myself in my studies"; IM-stimulation, "for the high feeling that I experience while reading on various interesting subjects".

2.5 HR Survey, Work-Life Questionnaire and Intrinsic Motivation Inventory

An interesting embracing employee's attitude assessment is the Employee Attitude Survey (EAS). Developed by Human Resources Survey (HR Survey), a web based

Application Service Provider, EAS wants to offer a picture of organization's needs, providing an understanding of how the employee perceives the organization and work groups. It contains a series of multiple choice items grouped along one or more dimensions of the organization such as creativity, innovation, satisfaction, senior management, interpersonal relations, compensation, mentoring, teamwork and staff development, among others. Its feedback may provide management with employee feedback (both positive and negative) on the internal health of the organization or can be used to motivate employees and improve job satisfaction [13]. Along the same lines, another instrument was studied: the 'University of Pennsylvania Work–Life Questionnaire' (UPWLQ). This questionnaire was designed to provide initial evidence of the usefulness of the Job–Career–Calling distinctions [14]. Finally, it was also analyzed the Intrinsic Motivation Inventory (IMI), a multidimensional measurement device intended to assess participants' subjective experience related to a target activity in laboratory experiments. This instrument assesses six subscale motivation aspects; participants' interest/enjoyment, perceived competence, effort, value/usefulness, felt pressure and tension, and perceived choice while performing a given activity [15].

3 IT Staff Motivational Specificities

Motivation specificities among certain specific practitioners' areas have already been object of study. For instance, health practitioners' incentives performance and motivation studies found that the response of physicians to economic incentives inherent in payment mechanisms seems to pursue the expected theory directions. Yet, there is lacking evidence of the effects of incentives on motivation and performance of other health workers [16]. Sport is another specific case. The work developed by Pelletier et al. wanted to measure the motivation toward sport [17]. The reasons why people practice their sports are explored, organized at seven subscales that measure different types of intrinsic motivation, extrinsic motivation and amotivation.

Job satisfaction among IT staff and some of its components (work, supervision, co-workers, pay and promotion), were studied by Igbaria and Guimaraes. Their study showed that role ambiguity was the most dysfunctional variable for IT employees in relation to job satisfaction. Also, the connection between role ambiguity and some components of job satisfaction were found to be education and age dependent. It was also confirmed the significance of job satisfaction in predicting organizational dedication and intentions to go away [18]. Based on Igbaria and Baroudi instrument to measure career incentives, Hsu, Jiang, Klein and Tang constructed a framework of various job anchors to study how a sample of IS staff consider incentives provided by employers and the importance of these in assessing the employee's intent to leave.

Moreover, motivational behavior seems to depend on each kind of work. Igbaria and other authors also investigated the role of involvement in influencing the quality of work life. They found significant differences in the level of job involvement by IT employees. The discrepancy strength of job involvement suggests that job characteristics play a major responsibility in IS employees' career expectations and quality of work life [19]. According to Amabile et al.; "perhaps stereotypes of the extrinsically oriented businessperson and the intrinsically oriented scientist or "starving artist" have some kernel of psychological truth" [3]. Daniel Pink defends that the majority of IT professionals use "left brain" skills, while tomorrow's job will require "right brain" skills. This job transformation, transitioning from the old skills to the new skills requires IT practitioners to move from technological skills to artistic skills. Furthermore, organizations should support and reward the new skills, in order to be prepared for the future [20]. Michael Lyons personalities' survey of above 1000 IT professionals working at over 100 international companies evidenced twice as many introverts as extraverts, slightly more intuitive than sensing people, a very high percentage (80-90%) of thinking to feeling persons and a 2-1 ratio of judging to perceiving types. Although thinking IT group is typically much more numerous than feeling ones, as systems tend to move towards integration of a variety of communication facilities, such significant supremacy can slowly be changing [21]. Cloud computing or SOA (Service Oriented Architecture) usage contributes to the advantage of having increasingly artistically minded feelers.

The particular knowledge about what IT professionals look for in their working environments was the objective of the 2004 Information Week Compensation Survey. This survey showed some specificities among IT staff, evidencing some differences between general IT staff and IT managers: (a) more than 55% of the IT staff and more than 65% of IT managers believe that their job and responsibilities are not challenging; (b) about 41% of the IT staff consider that they are not fairly compensated, 12% of the respondents believe that they got fewer bonuses in 2004 than they got in 2003 and 63% of the respondents said that higher compensation is the prime reason that they are interested in changing jobs; (c) 50% of IT staff and 40% of IT managers appreciate flexible work schedules; more than 40% are dissatisfied with their company's management or culture; nearly 50% of IT professionals think they do not have job security; 88% declare their jobs are stressful [22].

A systematic literature review about specificities among software engineers was recently made by Beecham, Baddoo and Robinson. Despite there are other important IT jobs and that software engineers activity specification is not consensual, this job is still one of the most popular at the IT universe. According to these authors, results indicate that software engineers are likely to be motivated according to their 'characteristics' (e.g., their need for variety); internal 'controls' (e.g., their personality) and external 'moderators' (e.g., their career stage) [23]. Nevertheless, this review stresses that motivation models in Software Engineering are disparate and do not reproduce the complex needs of software engineers. The software engineers' motivation question was analyzed at 62 papers which allowed the creation of a list of 22 different motivators. The most frequently cited motivators are, 'the need to identify with the task' and so, having clear goals defined, "a personal interest", "understanding the purpose of a task", understanding its fitness with the whole, having "job satisfaction"; and "working on an identifiable piece of quality work". Some of these papers also stress the importance of having a "clear career path", having a "variety of tasks", "involving the engineer in decision making" and to "participate and work with others" [23]. Supported at this systematic literature review, a new motivation model with detailed factors in software engineering was proposed, classifying factors as extrinsic or intrinsic motivators, some of these inherent at software engineering. Beyond the other intrinsic factors, the identified inherent motivators are: challenging, changing, problem-solving, beneficial, lifecycle models, scientific, experimental, team working, and development practices [24].

Even there were some essays about motivators for IT staff, there is still no specific instrument to measure general and particular IT staff motivation. The instrument proposed in this work will consider typical human motivators and specific IT ones.

4   Instrument Development

From the instruments introduced in the previous sections, over 200 items have been analyzed regarding the potential contribution for the instrument. Taking the five dimensions from the reward model [6] to structure variables regarding either general or IT specific motivators, Table 1 and Table 2 present the resulting instrument comprising 30 items across 23 variables. Some of the 30 items come directly from one of the analyzed instruments, others have been adapted and some are new.

Table 1. Variables and scale items for compensation, benefits and perf./recognition dimensions

Dimension	Variable	Scale Items	Source *
Compensation	Base Wages	I receive fair base wage for my job compared to others doing similar work at other companies	2
	Premium Pay	My company offers a generous premium increases in payment for on-call work or valued special skills	2
	Variable Pay	I am pleased because I'm earning more for what I do if I largely exceed the objectives	4
		I understand how my variable payment is determined	2
Benefits	Legally Required	I feel my company do not meet legal obligation benefits to each employee (R)	2
	Health & Welfare	My company's offers medical plans or other health or welfare benefits that meet my needs	2
	Retirement	I feel the retirement benefits offered by my company meet employees needs	2
	Pay for Time Not Worked	To me, it is very important the company payment for time not worked, like when I get sick or by other weighty reasons	8
Performance & Recognition	Performance	I understand the measures used to evaluate my objectives	1
		I regularly participate in the company's decision making and on the performance management system	2
	Job Assignment	I enjoy doing my activity very much.	6
		My skills are effectively used on the job	1
	Recognition	At my company, I am recognized for my accomplishments	1

Table 2. Variables and scale items for work-life, develop. and career opportunities dimensions

Dimension	Variable	Scale Items	Source *
Work-life	Workplace Flexibility / Altern. Work Arrangements	My current position permits me to experience the chance to do things my own way and not to be constrained by the rules of an organization	5
		I can arrange my work schedule to meet my personal and/or family needs	1
	Paid & Unpaid Time Off	It is difficult for me to get time off because of maternity/paternity or sabbatical reasons (R)	8
	Health and Wellness	It is important for me to have health or wellness initiatives and services, like on-site fitness facilities, that are offered by my company	8
	Community Involvement	I am proud to be working at my company because my work and my company makes the world a better place	7
		My current position permits me to experience a career in which I can be committed and devoted to an important cause	5
	Caring for Dependents	My company helps employees caring for their child and dependents	8
	Financial Support	My company offers financial support to meet my family needs, like education ones	8
	Voluntary Benefits	I don´t give so much importance to benefits offered like parking, employee discounts or car/home insurance (R)	8
	Cultural Environment	My company values team work and diversity	2
		Senior managers listen to me and care about my ideas	1
	Workplace Stability	My current position permits me to experience remaining in my area of expertise throughout my career	5
Development & Career opportunities	Available Equip. & Data	My company provides me with the necessary data and technological resources to do my job well	2
	Learning Opportunities	My work allow me with opportunities for increasing my knowledge and skills.	4
	Coaching / Mentoring	My supervisor is an effective role models for me	1
	Advancement Opportunities	My current position permits me to develop a career that permits to continue to pursue my own lifestyle	5
		My current position permits me to success by being constantly challenged by a tough problem or a competitive situation	5

* 1-HRSurvey; 2-HRSurvey adaptation; 3-WPI; 4-WPI adaptation; 5-Hsu et al.; 6-IMI adaptation; 7-UPWLQ adaptation; 8-New

Carefully observed when developing, adapting or using an existing item was the guarantee that a particular assessment of personal motivation was asked according to what was offered by the respondents' particular company and not about general intrinsic or extrinsic motivation out of organizational context. This was particular important for the adaptation of items from WPI and not so with items coming from IMI or HRSurvey. Moreover, each item assesses one Worldatwork dimension and sub-dimension (variable). As there are 23 sub-dimensions (grouped in 5 dimensions), there are one or two items for each variable. Furthermore, this instrument scores each answer on a 5-point Likert-type scale anchored by the extreme points "1 = strongly disagree" to "5 = strongly agree". It also does allow a middle placement. Although the middle point is sometimes selected by responders who are either indecisive or not concerned, which can cause bias in the measurement of satisfaction levels, it also can be applied to questions requiring a middle position, such as when respondent has no strong opinion one way or the other. So, it was decided to have a middle point "3 = neither agree nor disagree". Three of the questions were reverse coded. This is a procedure where a few number of questions in the questionnaire are worded such that high values for the construct are valued by low scores on the item. The objective in implementing this procedure is to force respondents to really pay attention to the questions they are answering.

5 Conclusions

This work was just a first step for the development of an instrument to assess IT staff motivation. We started with existing motivational instruments having reviewed over 200 items in the light of the WorldatWork reward model. Taking into consideration IT staff motivation specificities, we added a few variables to the reward model. Then, either adopting or adapting existing or developing new items, we have come up with a first representative set of 30 items for the variables that comprise now the five dimensions of our reward model for IT staff. Future work should look into the content validity of the proposed instrument by pre-testing it in IT settings. To ensure later the construct validity of IT staff motivation, we are planning to use the developed instrument in the context of business-IT alignment research. Organizations that have motivated IT employees should be particularly better positioned to pursue and keep business-IT alignment.

References

1. Ryan, R., Deci, E.: Self-determination theory and the facilitation of intrinsic motivation, social development, and well-being. American Psychologist 1, 68–78 (2000)
2. Deci, E., Ryan, R.: Self-Determination Theory,
   http://www.psych.rochester.edu/SDT/
3. Amabile, T., Hill, K., Hennessey, B., Tighe, E.: The work preference inventory: Assessing intrinsic and extrinsic motivational orientations. Journal of Personality and Social Psychology S3 (1994)
4. Ryan, R., Deci, E.: Intrinsic and Extrinsic Motivations: Classic Definitions and New Directions* 1. Contemporary Educational Psychology 1, 54–67 (2000)
5. Deci, E., Ryan, R.: Intrinsic motivation and self-determination in human behavior. Springer, Heidelberg (1985)
6. WorldatWork, T.T.R.A.: Total Rewards Model. WorldatWork Association (2008)
7. Belfo, F.: Influence of incentive policy in strategic alignment of information technology and business. In: Quintela Varajão, J.E., Cruz-Cunha, M.M., Putnik, G.D., Trigo, A. (eds.) CENTERIS 2010, Part I. CCIS, vol. 109, pp. 421–430. Springer, Heidelberg (2010)

8. Deci, E.L., Ryan, R.M.: The general causality orientations scale: Self-determination in personality* 1. Journal of Research in Personality 2, 109–134 (1985)
9. Harter, S.: A new self-report scale of intrinsic versus extrinsic orientation in the classroom: Motivational and informational components. Developmental Psychology 3, 300–312 (1981)
10. Lepper, M., Sethi, S., Dialdin, D., Drake, M.: Intrinsic and extrinsic motivation: A developmental perspective. Developmental Psychopathology: Perspectives on Adjustment, Risk, and Disorder, 23–50 (1997)
11. Vallerand, R., Pelletier, L., Blais, M., Briere, N., Senecal, C., Vallieres, E.: On the assessment of intrinsic, extrinsic, and amotivation in education: Evidence on the concurrent and construct validity of the Academic Motivation Scale. Educational and Psychological Measurement 1, 159 (1993)
12. Vallerand, R.J., Pelletier, L.G., Blais, M.R., Briere, N.M., Senecal, C., Vallieres, E.F.: The Academic Motivation Scale: A measure of intrinsic, extrinsic, and amotivation in education. Educational and Psychological Measurement 4, 1003 (1992)
13. HR-Survey, L.: Employee Attitude Survey, http://www.hr-survey.com/
14. Wrzesniewski, A., McCauley, C., Rozin, P., Schwartz, B.: Jobs, careers, and callings: People's relations to their work. Journal of Research in Personality, 21–33 (1997)
15. McAuley, E.: Psychometric Properties of the Intrinsic Motivation Inventory in a Competitive Sport Setting: A Confirmatory Factor Analysis. Research Quarterly for Exercise and Sport 1, 48–58 (1989)
16. Adams, O., Hicks, V.: Pay and non-pay incentives, performance and motivation (2000)
17. Pelletier, L.G., Blais, M.R.: Toward a new measure of intrinsic motivation, extrinsic motivation, and amotivation in sports: The Sport Motivation Scale (SMS). Journal of Sport and Exercise Psychology, 35–35 (1995)
18. Igbaria, M., Guimaraes, T.: Antecedents and consequences of job satifaction among information center employees. In: Proceedings of the 1992 ACM SIGCPR Conference on Computer Personnel Research, vol. 2 (1992)
19. Igbaria, M., Parasuraman, S., Badawy, M.K.: Work experiences, job involvement, and quality of work life among information systems personnel. MIS Quarterly ,175–201 (1994)
20. Pink, D.: A whole new mind. Riverhead Books (2005)
21. Kaluzniacky, E.: Increasing the Effectiveness of IT Management through Psychological Awareness, In: Yoong, P., Huff, S.L. (eds.) Managing IT Professionals in the Internet Age, pp. 191–232. Idea Group Publishing, USA (2006)
22. Luftman, J., Kempaiah, R.: IT Professionals: Human Resource. In: Yoong, P., Huff, S.L. (eds.) Managing IT Professionals in the Internet Age, pp. 159–190. Idea Group Publishing, USA (2006)
23. Beecham, S., Baddoo, N., Hall, T., Robinson, H., Sharp, H.: Motivation in Software Engineering: A systematic literature review. Information and Software Technology 9-10, 860–878 (2008)
24. Sharp, H., Baddoo, N., Beecham, S., Hall, T., Robinson, H.: Models of motivation in software engineering. Information and Software Technology 1, 219–233 (2009)

Analysing People's Work in Organizations and Its Relationship with Technology

António Gonçalves[1], Marielba Zacarias[2], and Pedro Sousa[3]

[1] Instituto Politécnico de Setúbal, Portugal
antonio.goncalves@estsetubal.ips.pt
[2] Universidade Algarve, Portugal
mzacaria@ualg.pt
[3] Instituto Superior Técnico, Portugal
pedro.sousa@link.pt

Abstract. We do believe that it is possible to describe the people work in an organization and its relationship with Information Technology. For this purpose we build an analysis of the people work, using some principles derived from the Activity Theory and the Structuration Model of Technology. We propose an analytic framework and a method that allows us to watch work made by people and understands how Technologies is used in organization and how the organization can influence the use of technologies. The analytical framework and the method cover the different functions people play in the work, how changes in the work occur over time, and the role played by information technologies after each change. It is our faith that this method can increase the alignment between people, their work and the information technologies in an organization. To test the operational effectiveness of the method and analytical framework, these were applied to a case study. The example chosen is the work within a recruitment organization specialized in finding experts to technological areas. The description was obtained through interviews and on the observation on the work performed by people.

Keywords: activity theory, organization, mediation.

1 Introduction

For organizations to be effective, IT must provide proper support to its activities. A better IT framework offers great opportunities for organizations to leverage the benefits offered by its use, but also poses challenges for IT management, of which organizations are dependable and which present particularities in their operation [3]. Therefore, IT use, development and configuration, cannot be done haphazardly and independently of organizations' reality.

According to Jonassen [40], understanding all human work and its practices, entails analyzing the context in which it occurs. Thus, when analysing human activities we must take into account not only the actions of individuals, but also what are their motives and goals, results or products that originate, what tools (technological or psychological), which rules and procedures (standards) and existing community where the activity occurs.

M.M. Cruz-Cunha et al. (Eds.): CENTERIS 2011, Part II, CCIS 220, pp. 240–259, 2011.
© Springer-Verlag Berlin Heidelberg 2011

The introduction of new IT changes people's work. According to Carroll [2], the work of people in an organization implicitly sets requirements for IT development on one side, but in the other, the use of IT redefines the job for which the IT was originally adopted. Therefore, the introduction of new IT should be considered for these results, in fact, a help, instead of being able to turn into loss.

Organizational modelling is an essential means to communicate perceptions of the organization "reality". However, the representation of an organization is a complex task since it should be accomplished in an integrated and consistent way. Hence, if not supported on a structured and comprehensive approach, it will translate into different and uncoordinated perceptions that will manifest themselves both internal (i.e. organization process, the way that IT is used) and externally (i.e. service offered to clients) [4].

In this scenario, the challenge is to know how to use IT in a given business and how to maintain IT aligned with the business, or how to take advantage of IT so that organizations become more efficient [5]. At the outset are identified the aspects that are always present: administrative automation, streamlining the organization and process reengineering [6].

A possible approach, to understand this aspect, is provided by the theoretical frameworks of the Activity Theory [10] and the structuration model of technology proposed in [7]. Those theories used in combination with other techniques such as Ethnography [11], an observational technique that can be used to understand social and organisational aspects of an enterprise.

Activity Theory is a theory and research of the concept of activity, defined as a systemic collective, building, with a structure that aims to promote mediation. In addition, it takes into account the interaction between people in the socio-cultural context in which they operate. Engeström [10] deepened his studies of mediated activity. For him, the activity evolution occurs by the multiple forms of interaction between people and the environment. Engeström then proposes a system of representation of human activity, which encompasses the various components of the system's activity in a social system, which allows modelling of different forms of human practices through the use of the activity as the basic unit of analysis.

The structuration model of technology by Orlikowski [7] adapts the ideas of Giddens [1] to the field of Information Systems, and defines the term "duality of technology".Orlikowski interprets IT as the result of human coordinated actions and therefore inherently social. That is, the interaction between technology and organizations is a function of the different actors and socio-historical context. In this sense, technology is structural, so it is both "physically constructed by actors working in a given social context as is socially constructed by actors through the different meanings that they embody and the devices that emphasize and use".

This paper proposes an analytical framework that allows analysing the work done by people, as well as the contexts in which that work is performed. This framework is derived from Activity Theory and structurational model of technology. We believe that this analytical framework allows an easier maintenance of the alignment between work, IT and people in their activities. The framework includes the description of the different roles of people who collaborate and work together for a common purpose, and describes the different roles that IT have over the dynamics of work.

The next sections of this paper are organized as follows: Section 2.1 presents Structurational Model of Technology, section 2.2 presents Activity Theory, Section 3, we present a summary of the principles derived from Activity Theory and structurational model of technology that framework the activities, actions and operations at different levels of collaborative activities, in Section 4 and 5, a proposal for an analytical framework that attempts to describe the relationship of IT with the work done by people in transformations between different levels of collaboration and a method. Section 6 shows an example of the usage of the analytical framework on a case study and finally, Section 7 presents our research conclusions and future work.

2 State of the Art

2.1 Structuration Theory

2.1.1 Structuration Theory Historical Background

The Theory of Structuration is a benchmark not only for the history of social theory but also for the journey of Anthony Giddens. In fact, considering as reference the former important social theories namely the structuralism, functionalism, neo-Marxism and the symbolic interactionism among otters, we observe that Giddens managed to present a new theory that though based on the former ones, the theory itself is regarded as revolutionary.

In any case, it is important to consider the evolution of this process that can be divided in two distinct phases. First, he began with a reflection about the classic authors such as Marx, Weber, Durkheim, Mead, Parsons, Merton, Althusser, Lukács, Kant and Heidegger. This phase allowed him to comprehend all these theories and culminated with the work Capitalism and Modern Social Theory (1971). In the second phase, Giddens presents the main lines of the Theory of Structuration and publishes his book New Rules of Sociological Method (1976). This book was the base for a new social theory and was followed by others , such as the Central Problems in Social Theory (1979) and The Constitution of Society (1984) that consolidated the way of thinking defended by him.

Giddens considered that the ascendancy of his theory was linked to the fact the former social theories underestimated certain problems social sciences had such as the case of institutional analysis, and power and social change. Giddens gathered concepts of others theories – structuralist, functionalist and actionalist - , and carried out a critical reflection. This was the foundation of the Theory of Structuration.

2.1.2 Structuration Theory Concepts

The main aspects of the Theory of Structuration are the concepts of agent, structure, duality of structure and space-time. For Giddens, the theory of Structuration has as main principle the duality of structure. This principle considers that on one side, structure limits and enables actions and on the other, actions mould and are moulded up by the structure. Structuration Theory also advises the analysis situated in time and space of aspects related to social practices in organisations. For Giddens, social activities are not created but recreated by the agents throughout their own ways by which they express themselves [1]. Table 1 presents a description of the main concepts aforementioned.

Table 1. Hierarchical levels of activity proposed by Leontiev [24]

Concept	Description
Agent	Giddens included in his theory a notion on an active agent essential to social life. Agents have the knowledge and ability to act in accordance to a model of stratification of the action, being this model kept by a reflexive monitoring of the action and having subjacent the rationalization and motivation of the action itself.
Structure	The structure may be defined as a set of rules (interpretive and normative) and resources (allocative and authority ones).
Duality of Structure	There is dialectic between action and structure. Each action of an agent is supported on a structure that makes it viable but, at the same time, it sets some rules that limit the possibilities of said action. The agents relate themselves with the structures by producing or reproducing them throughout space and time. As such, the social structure exists but its existence depends on the actions of the agents. If there's a change in the actions it is possible that a change or sequence also occurs in the structure. Thus, the structures are the means and the result of the action. This inter-relation between action and structure is called the duality of the structure.
Time-Space	There is an inter-relationship between space and social life repetition as social development is unrolled in time and space (1979, pp. 198-206). The concept space-temporality places and adds the interdependency structure/action in time and space. The social reality and the structure only exist within a space-time dimension

In the Theory of Structuration, Giddens considers that human action involves a reflexive monitoring. This implies the recognition that human behaviour has an intentional character. This means that each action of an agent has a practical though not verbalized conscious. Besides, it is also recognised the existence of a rationalization of the action through which the agent justify his actions. But there is more. The rationalization of the action is perceived as making part of social reproduction. As such there are factors conditioning the action: (1) the unconscious factors that work on the action; (2) the context of the action. Additionally, Giddens points out the existence of a common knowledge that he considers as a set of interpretative schemes controlled by the agents holding the interaction and where the practical sense prevails.

This way, the social action may be defined as a set of reproduced practices that can be studied as a series of acts, forms of interaction creating meaning and as structures [1]. Considering that the production of interaction has three main elements: (1) to create meaning; (2) to establish power; (3) and power relationships, we are forced to admit that the "agency" fits in the "power". Summarizing, while the action implies the usage of some means to reach certain goals, power represents the capacity of the agent to mobilise the resources to use that same means. Using other words, we can say that for Giddens "power is the capacity to transform the action, the ability the agent has to intervene on events and change their way. As such, power is used to assure results when they depend on the "agency" of others, allowing identifying "power" with "domination" upon the asymmetry of the distribution of resources.

Considering that there is an inextricably connection between "agency" and "power" it is prudent to consider that "power" has two sides: (1) the capacity to transform; (2) the capacity of the agent to obtain his desires. Further to this line of thought we see that social interaction is supported by rules and resources that articulate themselves through different combinations. In summary, the concept of agency lays on the practical conscious, rules, resources and routines. The routine is one side of the action and has an important role in reproducing practices. It is also fundamental for reproducing social continuity and whenever ratified or legitimate shows its deeper roots. This "routine" has an indispensable value to the theory of Structuration as it is vital to the agent continuity, its ontological safety and even more to the reproduction of the institutions. In a way, we may consider that Giddens uses the term "non-routine" as an important factor to stimulate social change and also as a way to go against what is taken for granted and that is present in daily interaction. For him social change includes: (1) the relations of autonomy and dependency (relations of power); (2) the development of sectors distinct from social systems; (3) the phases of a radical social change; (4) a concept of change where a development at a certain moment may cause the inhibition of future changes [1].

2.2 Activity Theory

2.2.1 Activity Theory Historic Concept

Under the heading of Activity Theory [13-15] there is a clustered set of concepts that underline a model of individual and social practice as a developmental process. The study of human activity is crucial to the identification of changes and contradictions in the context in which the activity is developed. These contradictions serve as a foundation to the emergence of new knowledge (learning) related with the activity concerned. Activity Theory has been used over time in different areas of development of information systems, including the analysis of requirements, the study of human-machine interfaces for the development of new software tools, in understanding the role of Technology on human work [16-21].

The concept of activity encompasses the following concepts: Participants (subjects), relations of mediation (tools, rules and labour division) and the particular environment (community) in which the activity takes place. The community consists of all individuals who share a given object. The first, more general, interpretation is that an object can be understood as anything, material or mental, that is manipulated, accessed or processed during the activity: "an object can be a material thing, but can also be something less tangible (a plan) or totally intangible (like a common idea). An object must be at least shareable to be manipulated and transformed by the participants of the activity ".

Leontiev [22] argued that human activity is always social and cooperative, and as such, collective, occurring within the division of labour. The collective activity is linked to the object and motive that the community members (individually) are often not aware off. The concept of object is already subsumed in the concept of activity.

Therefore, there is no activity without purpose. One thing or a phenomenon may become in an object of the activity if it satisfies a human need. In this context, Leontiev [24] proposed a three levels structure for an activity (Table 2).. An activity system produces actions and is driven by them. Nevertheless, the activity cannot be reduced to mere actions, which are temporary and have clearly defined beginning and end. Activity systems thrive through a socio-historical process. Vygotsky said that individual actions are linked to goals more or less conscious [23], which, in turn, bind to specific actions and cannot explain the emergence of the actions. Rather, as someone acts, the goals are set and reviewed. Operations depend on the conditions in which actions are performed.

Table 2. Hierarchical levels of activity proposed by Leontiev [24]

Level	Oriented	Composition	Performed by
Activity	Objects that satisfy a need or desire (motive)	Made by actions	Community
Action **Can only be understood in the context of the activity to which it belongs**	Directed towards a conscious goal	Composed of other actions or operations	Individual or group
Operation **The means used to implement the actions**	Instrumental conditions	Are initiated by specific environmental situations	Individual or automated machines

2.2.2 Theory Activity Key Concept

Engeström [10] departed from the theoretical basis of Vygotsky and deepened his studies of mediated activity. For him, the evolution of activity occurs by various forms of interaction between organism and environment (man and society) [10]. For Engeström, the Activity theory considers the human ability from the following:

- Physical (as we are constituted and what sensory-motor skills we have);
- Cognitive (how we think, how we learn and what cognitive abilities we have);
- Social (how we relate socially).

The author then proposes a system of representation of human activity that encompasses the various components of the activity system and its relations of connection and interdependence. What distinguishes one activity from another is its object. For Leontiev [24], the object of an activity is its true motive. Hence, the concept of activity is necessarily linked to the concept of motive. Under the conditions of labour division, the individual participates in activities, even without being fully aware of its objects and motives. Activities are carried out by actions directed to the object subordinate to conscious motives or purposes ([10] and are normally mediated by instruments, tools or signs. Engeström then proposed a model to represent the structure of an activity

The model developed by Engeström suggests the possibility of analysis of various relations within the triangular structure of the activity, however, the main task is always to understand the whole and not its connections separately [10]. Specifying each of the elements contained in the table above:

Concept	Description
Object	An object can be understood as anything, material or mental, that is manipulated, accessed or processed during the activity: "an object can be a material thing, but can also be something less tangible (like a plane), or fully intangible (such as a common idea), but it must be at least shareable to be manipulated and transformed by the participants of the activity." This component reflects the nature of human activity, which allows the control of the behaviour in order to meet identified objectives.
Subjects	Participants in the process. Component that represents the individual and social nature of human activity. Include collaboration and discussion to reach a common goal. The subject is the activity of any individual or group of individuals involved in activities and actions oriented for the object or motive. The relationship of subject and object or motive of the activity occurs by the use of tools. The subject(s) of an activity shape a community that shares the same general subject and which is constituted as a distinct community of any other. It is this component that enters the analysis of activity in the investigated socio-cultural context in which subject (s) operate.
Tools	Act as mediators between the subjects and objects. May be conceptual (with influence over the behaviour) and physical (related to the manipulation of objects). The tools are the resources used to transform the object and to reach a result. They can be any resource used during the transformation process - hammers, computers, mental models, methods, and theories. The tools change and are, in turn, altered by the activity, since they mediate the relationship between subject and object. The physical tools or materials are used to manipulate the object(s), the psychological tools are used to influence behaviour.

Concept	Description
Community	Social and cultural context in which the activity of the subjects is developed. Important in the study of human practice in the context of an organization.
Rules	Boundaries (rules and regulations) affecting the direction of development activities. The rules may be explicit or implicit (e.g., norms of social behaviour within a specific social community). Rules, norms and sanctions specify and regulate, both explicitly and implicitly, the correct procedures and acceptable interactions among participants within the activity system. These are rules that mediate relations between individuals and the community.
Labour division	Refers to the allocation of responsibilities. Framing the role played by each subject in the development of a community activity. Both the horizontal task division between the members of the community as well the vertical division of power and status, mediate the continuously negotiated distribution of tasks, possession of power and responsibilities between the community and the object of the activity system.

3 Directives Derived from the Activity Theory and Structuration Theory

This section presents a set of guidelines, which represent an interpretation of organizational work practices and IT, based on the central themes of the Activity Theory and Structuration Theory (described both in Section 2). The directives derived from Activity Theory were based on work done by Leont'ev [24], Engeström [10], Kaptelinin [14], Kutti [20] and Bodker [21]. The directives derived from Structuration Theory was based on work done by Orlikowski e others and is knows as Structuration Model of Technology [12, 42, 43].

- Directive 1 (D1) - **Activities have a hierarchical structure:** The activities are conducted through a series of conscious steps - the actions - that have defined goals. The actions, in turn, cannot be decomposed into other actions and so on. In the end we have a routine set of unaware operations, which may be physical or mental acts, adapted to the specific context (Figure 1);
- Directive 2 (D2) - **Activities are contextual:** A set of actions and operations is created, maintained and made available in an activity that can be accomplished through contextual choices; Operations can be seen as a means to implement actions. Depending on conditions (physical and socio-cultural), an action will be performed by one or another assembly of operations. Because the operations are unconscious and depend on the specific conditions of each scenario it is unlikely to describe, a priori, what operations will be part of the actions that the subject has planned? Still, from an afterthought and from the observation of actual activities, it becomes possible to survey the most common operations used by the subject during the activity;

- Directive 3 (D3) - **Activities are dynamic:** The activities are not static entities; systems are dynamic and constantly changing. The scripted task is not a business plan or a prescription of work to be performed, but only a script that is modified depending on the context in which it runs. People work with tools, develop new objects and tools. In this case, there is a change in the person and his environment. Finally, this transformation leads to new needs and desires, so that the activity is constantly evolving;
- Directive 4 (D4) - **The concept of mediation in Activities:** According to the Activity Theory, the vast majority of the iterations of the individual with the environment (people and objects) are mediated by tools (physical or mental), rules and labour division. According to the Activity Theory mediation tools are used in the transformation of the object on the result and evolve over time with the practice of the activity, therefore the tools aggregate the development of human history;
- Directive 5 (D5) - **Collaborative activities:** In the analysis of collaborative activities, the activity theory emphasizes that the activity cannot be said to exist on one level, but in many: coordination, cooperation and co-construction. These are analytical distinctions of the same collaborative activity, and compete in different times and ways for its development. At the level of coordination (D5.1), the use of IT can support the automation of operations. At the level of cooperation (D5.2), IT serves as an instrument for the manipulation of objects, i.e., as a technical artefact. It can also be used as psychological artefact, assisting in activities aimed at understanding things (making sense), such as creating reports and viewing process as well as in actions for the communication between the participants of the activity. At the level of co-construction (D5.3), IT can help so that an activity is made possible and feasible (linking participants, streamlining operations).
- Directive 6 (D6)- IT **as a product of human action:** ITs emerge through the creative action of human action and are used in performing the tasks in the workplace and are kept alive by such measures as adaptation and adaptations;
- Directive 7 (D7)- **Conditions of interaction with IT:** Institutional properties influence people in their interactions with IT, for example, intentions, professional standards, state of the art materials and knowledge, patterns of structure and resources;
- Directive 8 (D8)- **Institutional consequences of interaction with IT:** IT influences the institutional properties of an organization through strengthening or transformation of structures of signification, domination and legitimation.

Based on the principles presented, we propose an analytical framework that allows us to capture and represent activities, their evolution and to understand the mediating role of IT in human practices. This analysis gives an important role to the IT support in the contradictions underlying the structure of activities and it is the way in which it is conceived the development and evolution of an activity.

4   Proposal for an Analytical Framework

There isn't a standard and comprehensive method that allows us to render operational the use of Activity Thory despite the availability of several approaches and principles aiming in providing an operational use of Activity Theory among which stand out the principles enumerated by Engeström [34], Korpela -Activity Analysis and Development (ActAD) [38], Activity CheckList [39], Jonassen & Rohrer Murphy - "design of constructive learning environments (CLE) [40] and Martin & Daltrini approach [19]. Each approach proposes a method that will focus on some aspects of people's work. A comparison of the different approaches can be found in [41].

Our proposal consists of an analytical framework (Table 2) and a method. This section describes the analytical framework. Section 5 describes the method proposed. The analytical framework itself is not intended to be a solution that can be applied directly to the resolution of specific problems. Rather, we see its potential in guiding people in their own search for solutions, in particular helping them to focus their attention on how people interact and use technology. Hence, it is our belief that it can help in making significant questions. Moreover, if combined with other techniques it could provide a solution to understand breakdowns, without necessarily having a thorough knowledge of Activity Theory on Stucturation Theory.

Table 3. Proposal for an analytical framework

Means	Level	People (Group)	Resources	IT
Reflexive	Co-construction	Expansive: learn and understands	Construction of new objects	Construction of new tools to capture the sense of things **SOCIAL ASPECT:** IT is a product of human action. IT arise based on the creative action of people
CONTRADICTIONS: REFLECTIONS ON THE SUBJECT OF WORK, WORKING DEFINITION OF OBJECT				
Adaptative	Cooperation	Active: information search, seeking mutual adjustment to achieve a level of satisfactory cooperation	Allows the manipulation of objects	Improves the object handling; models the work processes. **SOCIAL ASPECT:** The interactions with ITs influence the properties of the organization allows the strengthening or transformation of systems of signification, domination and legitimation
CONTRADICTIONS: REFLECTIONS ON THE MEANS OF LABOR, AUTOMATION OF WORK MEASURES				
Communicative	Coordination	Passive: Performs tasks, repetitive work.	Accesses data on the object	Automation of procedures, manages the exchange of messages in time and space, removes people from coordination efforts. **SOCIAL ASPECT:** The conditions of interaction with IT are influenced by the properties of the organization (rules, division of labour).

Reading the table above, we have a division by lines that correspond to different analytical distinctions of collaborative activity, respectively, coordination, cooperation and co-construction (corresponds to the implementation of directives D1, D2 and D3). The columns indicate the issues to be analyzed in an activity (as presented in Section 2.1), the type of involvement that people have at work, how they act on resources and the role that IT has (equals an application of the Directive D4).

Regarding the level of coordination of an activity, the work that is needed is divided into disjoint functions (corresponding to the Directive D5.1). The way people perform their actions is communicative, this involves choosing a set of words, images and behaviours and their transmission through a suitable media so that information is received and understood by other group members. People have a passive attitude, perform the preconceived tasks on an automatic mode, depending on the conditions at the moment they are performed (e.g., if a person has to communicate with another, you can use phone, email, the media will depend on availability when they will have to perform the task). The work is performed with freedom of choice, in view of convenience, opportunity and manner of completion (i.e. discretionary). This does not mean that the work, by giving a certain degree of freedom to people, will be held outside of the principles. It follows the same parameters of other tasks, because the community shares the acts.

The resources used by humans, are seen as administrative data, and the role of the IT artefact, is on one hand to assist / promote the automation of procedures and on the other, to allow for the choice of the means by which people wish to perform their tasks. Since people are focused on carrying out their tasks, some sort of division of labour is imposed by IT, although by people in a transparent manner

The level of cooperation (corresponds to the Directive D5.2); aims at understanding how each person's actions can influence the actions of other people. The access to information involves finding information that group members need to support their actions. At this level the object on which people act in a conscious way is shared, and that will guide decision-making. The role of IT in this scenario should be to enable the process and manipulation of the object. Since people need to share the object to reach consensus, people, although it may be imposed by IT, see the division of labour. About the work, you can say that people cooperate in some way, to be able to break the work in units, and divide it among them.

The level of co-construction (corresponds to the Directive D5.3), people conduct their actions in a reflective way, it is questioning the very object that is manipulated, as a result of a reflection on the objectives, and on the results they seek. The result of this action will create new objects, and then build new routines and new IT tools. It promotes the study and learning, the formation of new communities, as well as new divisions of labour.

This framework includes the social relations embedded in the organization and IT, according to Structuration Model of Technology. Thus the D6 is present in the reflexive level (ie, IT as a product of human action). The D7 is this level of communication (ie conditions of interaction with ITs). Finally, the D8 is present in the adaptation level (ie the institutional consequences of interaction with ITs).

5 Proposed Method

In addition to the analytical framework, a method proposed a (Table 4) This method is composed of a set of steps and is an interpretation of the principles enumerated by Engeström [34] and the principles enumerated by the structurational model of technology [42], and aims to help: 1) capturing the activity system, comprising the set of activities that will be the aim of the study, 2) focuses on contradiction study and finally, via an historical analysis of the development activity, it intends to identify the contradictions (and propose resolutions) and 3) focuses on improvements in the execution of operations. The focus on operations automation, in turn examines three areas: the automation proposal, the impact that automation has on the organization and how the automation could influence an organization (constitutes the steps 9, 10 and 11). The method is presented in Table 4.

Table 4. Proposed Method

PHASE	STEP	DESCRIPTION
Activity System Build	Step 1	Activities of Interest in the problem
	Step 2	Purpose of each activity and expected outcome
	Step 3	Actions of each activity
	Step 4	Operations of each action
	Step 5	Tools used to access objects
	Step 6	Rules and Community
Contradiction Analysis	Step 7	Study of the contradictions at the level of coordination and resolution proposals at the level of coordination or cooperation
	Step 8	Study of the contradictions at the level of cooperation and resolution proposals at the level of cooperation or the co-construction
Operation Automation	Step 9	Automation of operations proposal from Human
	Step 10	How the automation could influence an organization (change or reinforce the organization rules)
	Step 11	The impact of organization in the proposed automation

6 Example Application

With the purpose of experimenting the operational effectiveness of the method and analytical framework, these were applied to a case study, presented here. The example chosen is the work within a recruitment organization specialized in finding experts to technological areas. The description was obtained through analysis BPM diagrams, interviews and on the observation on the work performed by people and includes part of the work involved in recruiting activities.

Recruitment begins with the arrival of a customer request (which is known internally by opportunity). Generally, requests are sent to an email, which is distributed to an internal contact list, which include the members of the team responsible for recruitment.

Upon receipt of the opportunity, it is recorded and monitored in one or more tools. For each opportunity, it chose a team member that becomes responsible for monitoring the customer's request. The choice of the element that accompanies the request is made in accordance with the technology mentioned in the request.

After analyzing the requirements of the application, the controller performs a search in the list of available curriculums of potential candidates. The quest results in the selection of a set of possible candidates. Then, each candidate is contacted (by email, phone or through a scheduled interview) to validate a set of information that may elect him as a possible solution to the opportunity (exp: availability, desired salary, to confirm some skills, etc...)

With the selection of candidates completed, their resumes are then sent to the customer for evaluation. After the evaluation by the client of the candidates, they will then indicate those who they intend to interview.

The responsible for the request will then contact the selected candidates to schedule interviews at the client. Finally, with the chosen candidate, it is made then signed the employment contract on customer site.

Figure 1 illustrates the model of activities corresponding to the two activities identified by the observation: customer's request and opportunity management. The identification of activities corresponds to the application of the 1st rule of the proposed analytical framework: definition of the activity system.

For each activity we have listed the elements that structure them through the systemic model defined by Engestrom. It is observed, for example, that the activity "request from client" is motivated by the transformation of the customer request into a business opportunity. It contains one rule: there must be a commitment to the customer that the request will be answered with the desired speed, this commitment is made trough the confirmation of receipt. It also submitted to labour division in which it is indicated that there is a person responsible for the request. Then, each activity is detailed in its division into actions and operations. The level of detail to be specified depends on the wealth of information required for the purpose it was intended. Table 4 illustrates the actions and operations for the activity "opportunity management".

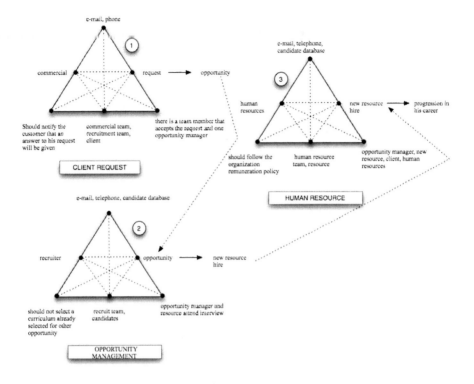

Fig. 1. Recruitment Activities

The next step consists on the study of contradictions from the analytical framework proposed in Section 7. The result consisted on the identification of a set of contradictions (which resulted in a number of proposed changes in operations, activities and the creation of a new activity). This work is illustrated for the activity "application management." Table 5 illustrates the contradictions encountered and possible proposed solutions. The last phase consisted in improving the operations automation, the inclusion and enforcement of rules to be followed by people, and strengthen the labour division to be followed. Table 6 illustrates some of the proposals for operations automation.

Table 5. Decomposition of one activity in Actions and Operations

ACTIONS		OPERATIONS	
DESCRIPTION	**PERSON/GROUP**	**DESCRIPTION**	**IT**
Select curriculums from database	Recruitment	Extract competences that candidates must have from customer's request	Client management database
		Find the candidates in the database based on a query in accordance with the competences of the request	Applicant database
		Validate valences and other characteristics of applicants, update the curriculum of the candidate	e-mail, telephone, interview, pdf and Word processing editor
DESCRIPTION	**PERSON/GRUP**	**DESCRIPTION**	**IT**
Management of the applicant contract	Human Resources	Do the draft contract of the selected candidate	word
		Send the draft contract to the successful candidate	E-mail or fax
		Schedule contract signature	E-mail or fax

Table 6. Set of Contradictions and change proposals to the Activity "Opportunity Management"

CONTRADICTION		CHANGE PROPOSAL	
LEVEL	**DESCRIPTION**	**LEVEL**	**DESCRIPTION**
COORDINATION	In the operation "Send the curriculum of the candidates to the client", it was found that sometimes the curriculum was sent with contact details, which sometimes led to direct contact between the client and the candidate	COORDINATION	It was extracted from the candidate's resumes their contact details. They became part of the attributes that qualify the candidate.
LEVEL	**DESCRIPTION**	**LEVEL**	**DESCRIPTION**
COORDINATION	Selection of candidates who were already selected for other opportunities	COORDINATION	In terms of the curriculum selection action it will be indicated the candidate state, which will allow us to know if he is in another selection process
LEVEL	**DESCRIPTION**	**LEVEL**	**DESCRIPTION**
COOPERATION	Constant problems arising from contract negotiations with the candidates: too many different contracts in the same client for candidates with identical valences	CO-CONSTRUTION	Introduction of a new activity that is responsible for the relationship with the contract signature with the candidates and their follow up

Table 7. Automation proposed study to the activity "Opportunity Management"

OPERATION	AUTOMATION	REASONING	IT ORGANIZATION IMPACT	ORGANIZATION ALLOWS AUTOMATION
Identify the candidates in the database based on a query in accordance with the competences of the request	Store the Query	Allows for similar requests to reuse the same queries, that are rather complex	Change Organization	yes
Send the resume of candidates to client	Via Templates	Allows you to standardize the information that each customer requires on the candidates	Reinforce Rules	yes
Schedule interviews with the selected candidates in the customer	Automatically sending an email to the candidate and to the client after scheduling on the agenda of the recruiter	Allows to keep the recruiter calendar in sync with his tasks	Reinforce Rules	no
Do the draft contract of the selected candidate	Via Templates	Allows you to standardize the type of contract used in recruitment	Reinforce Rules	yes

7   Conclusion and Future Work

This paper proposes an analytical framework and a method to analyse people's work in organizations and suggest improvemens. For that purpose two theories were used: activity Theory and Structuration Model of Technology. From activity theory, it was possible to identify hierarchical levels that define the structure of work: coordination, cooperation and co-construction.   From Structuration Model of Technology it was possible to Look IT as artefacts, that result as the outcome of coordinated human action and hence as inherently social, that mean that Technology is not an external object, but a product of ongoing human action, design and appropriation.

That allows obtaining an explanation for the role of IT in this context: flexibility, consistency and simplicity. Flexibility has to do with the ability to change focus between objects and subjects, but also with the possibility of achieving the same goal with different paths (different actions and operations).

The working results obtained here are being used for the analysis and development of a system supporting the process of capturing and analyzing the work done by people in organizations and their relationship with IT. This system is being developed based on the capture model proposed.

To test the operational effectiveness of the method and analytical framework, these were applied to a case study. The example chosen is the work within a recruitment organization specialized in finding experts to technological areas. The description was obtained through interviews and on the observation on the work performed by people.

From the results of the test case it as possible to know which aspects should be improved, in the future, by challenging us to develop a tool in order to be able to ensure the improvement of the capture of method information, through the collaborative evaluation of the process by the people who participate in the activities.

Bringing people together to work effectively, and collectively, is a challenge in today's organizations. It is necessary to achieve a way of attracting the active participation and commit to support teams whose members have other activities and/or concerns in parallel which divert their attention.

One of the ways that can be explored in future will be the use of the concept of facilitation, known as the art of bringing people together and put them to work effectively [44]. Here arises the role of facilitator, whose action consists in helping people to determine the conclusions given an initial scenario. The facilitator is characterized as having an action that achieves a conclusion [44]. In choosing the level of knowledge that the facilitator may have, there is the scenario where the facilitator can be experienced or not, and in this latter case is explored in engineering collaboration [45, 46].

References

1. Giddens, A.: The constitution of society: outline of the theory of structuration. University of California Press, Berkeley (1986)
2. Carroll, J.M., Kellogg, W.A., Rosson, M.B.: The task-artifact cycle. Cambridge University Press, Cambridge (1991)
3. Lankhorst, M.: Enterprise Architecture at Work: Modelling, Communication and Analysis. The Enterprise Engineering, p. 352. Springer, Heidelberg (2009)
4. Nadler, D.A., Gerstein, M.S., Shaw, R.B.: Organizational Architecture: Designs for Changing Organizations (J-B US non-Franchise Leadership), p. 304. Jossey-Bass (1992)
5. Luftman, J.: Assessing Business-IT Alignment Maturity. In: Strategies for Information Technology Governance, vol. 4, p. 99. Igi Global (December 2004)
6. Davenport, T.H.: Process Innovation: Reengineering Work Through Information Technology, p. 352. Harvard Business Press, Bston (1992)
7. Orlikowski, W.J.: Using technology and constituting structures: A practice lens for studying technology in organizations. Resources, Co-Evolution and Artifacts 11(4), 255–305 (2008)
8. Bardram, J.: Designing for the dynamics of cooperative work activities. In: Proceedings of the 1998 ACM Conference on Computer Supported Cooperative Work - CSCW 1998, pp. 89–98. ACM Press, New York (1998), doi:10.1145/289444.289483
9. Damon, W.: Critical distinctions among three approaches to peer education. International Journal of Educational Research 13(1), 9–19 (1989), doi:10.1016/0883-0355(89)90013-X

10. Engeström, Y.: Learning by expanding: An activity-theoretical approach to developmental research (1987)
11. Viller, S., Sommerville, I.: Social analysis in the requirements engineering process: from ethnography to method. In: Proceedings IEEE International Symposium on Requirements Engineering (Cat. No.PR00188), pp. 6–13. IEEE Comput. Soc., Los Alamitos (1999), doi:10.1109/ISRE.1999.777980
12. Orlikowski, W.J., et al.: Information technology and the structuring of organizations. Information Systems Research 2, 143–169 (1991)
13. Engeström, Y.: Activity theory as a framework for analyzing and redesigning work. Ergonomics 43(7), 960–974 (2000)
14. Kaptelinin, V.: Activity theory: Implications for human-computer interaction. Context and Consciousness: Activity Theory and Human-Computer Interaction 1, 103–116 (1996)
15. Nardi, B.A.: Activity theory and human-computer interaction. In: Context and Consciousness: Activity Theory and Human-Computer Interaction, pp. 7–16. MIT Press, Cambridge (1996)
16. Collins, P., Shukla, S., Redmiles, D.: Activity theory and system design: A view from the trenches. In: Computer Supported Cooperative Work (CSCW), vol. 11(1), pp. 55–80. Springer, Heidelberg (2002)
17. Mwanza, D.: Where theory meets practice: A case for an Activity Theory based methodology to guide computer system design. Human-Computer Interaction (February 2001)
18. Turner, P., Turner, S.: From description to requirements: an activity theoretic perspective. Proceedings of the International ACM (1999)
19. Martins, L.E.G., Daltrini, B.M.: An approach to software requirements elicitation using precepts from activity theory. In: 14th IEEE International Conference on Automated Software Engineering, pp. 15–23. IEEE Comput. Soc., Los Alamitos (1999), doi:10.1109/ASE.1999.802088
20. Kutti, K.: Activity Theory as a Potential Framework for Human-Computer Interaction, pp. 17–44 (1996)
21. Bodker, S.: Through the Interface: A Human Activity Approach to User Interface Design, p. 187. CRC Press, Boca Raton (1990)
22. Leontév, A.N.: Activity, consciousness, and personality, p. 186. Prentice-Hall, Englewood Cliffs (1978)
23. Vygotsky, L.S.: Mind in Society: The Development of Higher Psychological Processes, p. 159. Harvard University Presssss, Cambridge (1978)
24. Leontiev, A.A.: Psychology and the Language Learning Process. Elsevier Science Ltd., Amsterdam (1981)
25. Ure, A.: The philosophy of manufactures: or, an exposition of the scientific, moral... Charles Knight (1835)
26. Beamish, R.: Marx, method, and the division of labor, p. 196. University of Illinois Press, US (1992)
27. Bardram, J.: Designing for the dynamics of cooperative work activities. In: Proceedings of the 1998 ACM Conference on Computer Supported Cooperative Work - CSCW 1998, pp. 89–98. ACM Press, New York (1998), doi:10.1145/289444.289483
28. Dahrendorf: Class and class conflict in industrial society (1959), http://www.getcited.org/pub/101189591 (retrieved May 2, 2011)
29. Ebner, H.: Facetten und Elemente didaktischer Handlungsorientierung. In: Pätzold, G. (ed.) Handlungsorientierung in Der Beruflichen Bildung, Frankfurt a.M., pp. 33–53 (1992)

30. Mickleret, O., et al.: Technik, Arbeitsorganisation und Arbeit. Eine empirische Untersuchung in der automatischen Produktion Aspekte Verlag, Frankfurt am Main (1976)
31. Davidson, N.: Cooperative learning in mathematics: a handbook for teachers, p. 409. Addison-Wesley Pub. Co., Reading (1990)
32. Raeithel: Tätigkeit, Arbeit und Praxis: Grundbegriffe für eine praktische Psychologie. Frankfurt/M (1983)
33. Fichtner, B.: Co-ordination, co-operation and communication in the formation of theoretical concepts in instruction. In: Hedegaard, M., Hakkarainen, P., Engeström, Y. (eds.) Learning and Teaching on a Scientific Basis: Methodological and Epistemological Aspects of the Activity Theory of Learning and Teaching. Technical Report, Psychology Dept., pp. 207–227. Aarhus University (1984)
34. Engeström, Y.: Developmental studies of work as a testbench of activity theory: The case of primary care medical practice. In: Chaiklin, S., Lave, J. (eds.) Understanding Practice: Perspectives on Activity and Context. Cambridge University Press, Cambridge (1993)
35. Cole, M., Engeström, Y., Vasquez, O.A.: Mind, culture, and activity: seminal papers from the Laboratory of.., p. 501. Cambridge University Press, Cambridge (1997)
36. Bødker, S.: Activity theory as a challenge to systems design. In: Nissen, H.-E., Klein, H.K., Hirschheim, R. (eds.) Information Systems Research: Contemporary Approaches and Emergent Traditions, pp. 551–564. North-Holland, Amsterdam (1991)
37. Zuboff, S.: In The Age Of The Smart Machine: The Future Of Work and Power, p. 490. Basic Books, New York (1989)
38. Korpela, M.: Activity Analysis and Development in a Nutshell (1997)
39. Kaptelinin, V., Nardi, B.A., Macaulay, C.: Methods & tools The activity checklist a tool for representing the space of context. Interactions 6(4), 27–39 (1999)
40. Jonassen, D.H., Rohrer-Murphy, L.: Activity theory as a framework for designing constructivist learning environments. Educational Technology Research and Development 47(1), 61–79 (1999), doi:10.1007/BF02299477.
41. Quek, A.: A comparative survey of activity-based methods for information systems development. In: Proceedings of 6th International Conference on Enterprise Information Systems (2004)
42. Orlikowski, W.J., et al.: Shaping electronic communication: the metastructuring of technology in the context of use. Organization Science, 423–444 (1995)
43. Orlikowski, W.J., Baroudi, J.J.: Studying Information Technology in Organizations: Research Approaches and Assumptions. Information Systems Research 2(1), 1–28 (1991)
44. Nunamaker Jr., J.F., et al.: Lessons from a dozen years of group support systems research: a discussion of lab and field findings. J. Manage. Inf. Syst. 13(3), 163–207 (1996)
45. Briggs, R., et al.: Defining key concepts for collaboration engineering. Proceedings of the AMCIS, 17 (2006)
46. Briggs, R.O., De Vreede, G.J., Nunamaker Jr, J.F.: Collaboration engineering with ThinkLets to pursue sustained success with group support systems. Journal of Management Information Systems 19(4), 31–64 (2003)

Autonomic Arousal during Group Decision Making Consensus Rules versus Majority Rules: Pilot Study

Alana Enslein, Chelsea Hodges, Kelsey Zuchegno, Tadd Patton, Reeves Robert, Stephen H. Hobbs, Joseph C. Wood, and W.F. Lawless

Augusta State University, 2400 Walton Way, Augusta, GA 30904
{aenslein,chodges2,kzuchegn,tpatton1,rreeves,shobbs}@aug.edu,
joseph.c.wood@us.army.mil, wlawless@paine.edu

Abstract. Organizational theory is in a poor state today. Supporting this claim, an article in *Nature* in 2011 listed the top challenges, including at fifth, the inability by social scientists to aggregate individual data to group, organizational and system levels. We have proposed that this failure derives from treating interdependence as a hindrance to experimental replications rather than the primary characteristic of social behavior. Recent studies have shown that bistability can be used theoretically to explain states of interdependence common to group debates preceding a decision (e.g., interdependently speaking and listening, and reacting). The goal of this study is to investigate interdependence in groups in the laboratory when specific parameters are placed on debate outcomes. Participants are instructed to engage in debate with one another over various topics (i.e., business, abortion, and race) and placed under one of two decision rules as instructed: consensus or majority rule. The degree to which participants remain "engaged" in the debate is of particular interest in this study. Prior to the test trial each participant completes a pre-discussion questionnaire designed to ascertain personal beliefs regarding each of the topics discussed. Participants complete a similar questionnaire immediately following the test trials. In addition, galvanic skin responses (GSR) and utterance counts over time are being obtained from randomly selected participants as a measure of autonomic arousal. We plan to analyze with time series. We expect that time-series data from groups, teams and organizations can augment self-reported data collected from individuals. Preliminary findings will be reviewed.

Keywords: interdependence, bi-stability, organizations.

1 Introduction

Pfeffer and Fong [17] concluded that the state of theory for organizations had failed to account for any of the observed behaviors of organizations. Bloom and colleagues [6] found no relationship between the perceptions of managers and the performance of their business firms. Supporting these claims, Giles [8] listed the aggregation of individual data into group, organizations or systems data as one of the top challenges for social sciences, with Bonito and colleagues [7] arguing that aggregation was an unsolved problem. As part of a special issue of *Science* that focused on interdependence and the

M.M. Cruz-Cunha et al. (Eds.): CENTERIS 2011, Part II, CCIS 220, pp. 260–269, 2011.
© Springer-Verlag Berlin Heidelberg 2011

theory and data for human behavior, including game theory, the need was widely articulated among the reviewers for new social theory [9]. We have proposed that interdependence, usually treated as a hindrance to the replication of traditional social psychological experiments [10], was not a hindrance to theory and experimental replications, but instead the key phenomenon characteristic of all social behavior [14].

1.1 Review of Our Prior Research

US Department of Energy (DOE). In our studies of citizen advisory boards helping the DOE to cleanup and to better manage its nuclear waste sites, we have found that majority rule produces more open conflict, more success in achieving concrete actions and goals, often results in quicker decisions, and more acceleration in nuclear waste cleanup [12]. In contrast, we have found that consensus rules generate more hidden conflict, less concrete action, more unchallenged conspiracy theories, slower decisions, and with the bottom line being the increased potential for gridlock. For example, the justification given by the European Union for its departure from consensus rule:

> The requirement for consensus in the European Council often holds policy-making hostage to national interests in areas which Council could and should decide by a qualified majority. (p. 29, in [4])

US Army Department of Clinical Investigation (DCI). Individuals are poor at multi-tasking [18]. Organizations are designed to multi-task. To be optimally effective for the multitasking required to be organized [1], organizations need high levels of cooperation to reduce fragmentation [11]. However, peer review requires that scientists need to be highly competitive. Organizations, such as the Army's Departments of Clinical Investigation (DCI), which train physicians to perform as research scientists, create a tension between these two functions. We proposed a system of metrics to track the Army's performance. It led to the adoption by the Department of Defense of an electronic Institutional Review Board (eIRB; in [20]).

While at this point, we have no mathematics for metrics to display, we do have an example of what we have accomplished with metrics in the past. Organizations, such as the Army's DCI to train physicians as research scientists, create a tension between the cooperation necessary to be effective organizational multi-taskers (but generally when solving well-defined problems), and competition to stay to help individuals (i.e., scientists) and organizations stay ahead of their competitors (but generally when solving ill-posed problems). We proposed in 2006 to the Army's DCI at Fort Gordon a system of metrics to track DCI's scientific performance as part of an electronic Institutional Review Board (eIRB; [11]). However, before the first year's data was analyzed, the Department of Defense (DoD) adopted the eIRB DoD-wide [19].

The eIRB system proposed for DCI has been successful. Per Wood [19], one of our co-authors (see [14]), as program manager and team leader for the Defense Medical Research Network (DMRN) and IRBNet, he successfully secured funding from Health Affairs to expand the program to all DoD medical research facilities. This resulted in a savings to DDEAMC of approximately $30,000 annually.[1] Total project

---

[1] Acronyms: DDEAMC is Dwight D. Eisenhower Army Medical Center; TATRC is Telemedicine & Advanced Technology Research Center.

costs secured for DDEAMC and other DOD sites for the program management to date $1.6 million. What began as a TATRC funded business process improvement research project for DDEAMC/SERMC has met our working group's Vision Statement goals since this system has now become the DOD standard: "The product our team develops will be the standard for the DoD by easily allowing all research proposals, supporting documents, and scholarly products to be submitted and managed by a secured web based electronic system that will calculate real time metrics of research workload, productivity, and quality." His organization completed the MEDCOM required CONOPS documentation for DMRN/IRBNet to become recognized as an Army enterprise system, with the required certifications (e.g., AKO/SSO, DIACAP, IA, ATO, Army Certificate of Net worthiness and others). For the past six months, he and his team have been working to complete the Defense Business Transformation documentation process.

Table of Results for eIRB (as of 1/31/11; from [19])

Current user sites (as of 1/31/11):	Network Metrics:	Other Data
Dwight D. Eisenhower Army Medical Center, Walter Reed Army Medical Center, National Naval Medical Center ,Uniformed Services University, Madigan Army Medical Center, Naval Medical Center-San Diego, Wilford Hall, Brooke Army Medical Center, William Beaumont Army Medical Center, Tripler Army Medical Center, Womack Army Medical Center, Walter Reed Army Institute of Research, US Army Research Institute of Environmental Medicine, United States Army Medical Research Institute for Infectious Diseases, Army Medical Research and Materiel Command HQ, Clinical Investigation Regulatory Office.	Total research sites and boards: 123 Total users: 2,785 (CONUS and OCONUS) Total projects: 3,985	Total electronic submissions securely processed: 13,147; Total electronic documents securely processed: 44,772; Total decision letters and other board documents securely issued: 4,750. DMRN/IRBNet successfully migrated to fhpr.osd.mil servers; a project report has been sent to TATRC. Classification: UNCLASSIFIED. Caveats: NONE

Businesses, organizations and systems. Mergers between competitors across a market often lead to consolidation that reduces costs, but also increases cooperation [13]. Our findings and theory indicated that the variance in one paired bistable factor is inversely orthogonal to the variance in the other paired factor (e.g., market size and volatility). Evidence from multiple regressions using data on market size and stock volatility collected from across the stock market was supportive. In the future, we plan to develop transformations between four sets of mathematically equivalent solutions: for planning and execution; organizational center of gravity and spatial frequency; size and volatility; and power and time.

We have also theorized and found support for the existence of dark social networks (DSN) in two broadly different categories of businesses [16]: Normal businesses that become very successful but are not yet mature (e.g., Wal-mart and Southwest Airlines about a decade ago); and businesses engaged in violent behaviors and activities (e.g., Mara Salvatrucha, or MS-13, the most feared gang enterprise in the US). A very successful business becomes dark to outsiders and to itself because it is generating low levels of entropy; in contrast, a violent gang in its attempt to stay hidden to outsiders purposively expends energy to become dark, but in the process, generating a skewed form of information.

Government. We have theorized and found that, as part of command decision-making, autocracies promote corruption [14]. Autocracies usually work with consensus rules (minority rules). The problem is that government run by command decisions reduces the information generated by checks on management excesses, increasing the likelihood of corruption.[2,3]

2 Theory

Our theory of social interdependence is similar to quantum entanglement. Both social interdependence and quantum entanglement are fragile, both replace independence with communication among interacting units, and both produce counterintuitive results, especially under measurement conditions. For both interdependence and entanglement, the measurement of their non-independent and conjugate properties precludes exactness in two coupled properties simultaneously, producing exactness in one property (e.g., a business plan or a quantum particle's position, respectively) as a tradeoff with the conjugate coupled property (e.g., plan execution or particle velocity,

---

[2] From *The New York Times* (2011, 3/24), Shady Dealings Helped Qaddafi Build Fortune and Regime: "The episode and others like it, the officials said, reflect a Libyan culture rife with corruption, kickbacks, strong-arm tactics and political patronage since the United States reopened trade with Colonel Qaddafi's government in 2004. As American and international oil companies, telecommunications firms and contractors moved into the Libyan market, they discovered that Colonel Qaddafi or his loyalists often sought to extract millions of dollars in "signing bonuses" and "consultancy contracts" — or insisted that the strongman's sons get a piece of the action through shotgun partnerships. "Libya is a kleptocracy in which the regime — either the al-Qadhafi family itself or its close political allies — has a direct stake in anything worth buying, selling or owning," a classified State Department cable said in 2009, using the department's spelling of Qaddafi."

[3] *The Washington Post* (2011, 5/27), "In China, a long path of writing the Communist Party's history": As an example of corruption and its coverup, for its 1958-61 "Great Leap Forward", millions of Chinese died from malnutrition and starvation and cannibalism. The official version from the Communist Party's new history: "Extreme shortages of grain, oils, vegetables and no-stable foodstuffs gravely damaged the health and lives of the masses. Edema occurred among village residents in many areas and the number of people suffering from hepatitis and gynecological diseases also rose." In contrast, the consensus view of Western and independent Chinese historians is that: "Starvation, disease and brutal repression by party officials killed tens of millions of Chinese, with some villages resorting to cannibalism. Hepatitis was a problem but afflicted mostly privileged urban residents. All forms of disease--from leprosy to malaria--skyrocketed. Mao Zedong's policies claimed more victims that the Holocaust or Ukraine's famine under Stalin."

respectively), reflecting bistable uncertainties (see Figure 1 below). As examples of a measurement problem in the social realm, first, Baumeister and colleagues [3] found a negligible association in a 30-year meta-analysis between self-esteem and academic or work achievement. Second, the traditional theory of organizational interdependence has failed [17]; Pfeffer speculated that interdependent illusions between members offer a possible way to revise organizational theory. And, third, social psychology considers interdependence a hindrance to the independence between subjects so necessary for experimental replication [10], keeping the theory of interdependence from advancing.

Fig. 1. Example of Bistability (multiple interpretations of a single data set; in [14]): Figure 2A. On the left is an image of an Abrams M1A1 Main Battle Tank that generates a stable interpretation (e.g., www.army-technology.com/projects/abrams). All who view the tank reach the same interpretation. Figure 1B. On the right is a bistable illusion of two women that creates an interdependent interpretation (an older woman facing downward and to the observer's left; or a younger women looking away and over her right shoulder). In a bistable illusion, an observer is incapable of "seeing" both interpretations of its single data set at the same time (Cacioppo et al.; see [14]).

The *closest* alternative to a new theory of interdependence was proposed by Bohr (see [14]) who applied his model of quantum interactions to account for the existence of multiple cultures. In addressing Bohr's speculation, we have found that multiple cultures crystallize from different interpretations of social reality, the defining characteristic of human interaction [14]. Different interpretations cause rotations in the minds of neutrals—the undecided—as a debate rotates back and forth. Fuel for debates are the illusions each opponent holds (e.g., husbands and wives; prosecutors and defense attorneys; two scientists debating like Einstein and Bohr). Multiple interpretations can best be modeled as a bistability between two or more coupled centers of competition that combine to become what we have borrowed from game theory and defined as a Nash equilibrium (NE). A typical example is the competition for customers between Apple and Google over the purchase of their mobile phones;[4] another is the discord in the editorials discussing the climate-gate scandal created by emails from among pro-climate warming

---

[4] *The New York Times* (2010, 1/20), "The war between Apple and Google has just begun", retrieved 2/10/11 from nytimes.com.

scientists indicating their significant data interpretation biases against anti-climate warming scientists (see our case study below).[5]

Discord is common in human affairs, with illusions driving oscillations in the minds of those who are neutral to a debate, if they are attentive to or engaged by it. The competition is over control and it occurs broadly among multiple cultures to produce the oscillations between alternating periods of dominance by a single competitor's culture (e.g., [5]), modeled with limit cycles mathematically characterized by a 90-degree separation (orthogonal) in the periods of dominance over time. Another example of a limit cycle in politics was the competition in 2008 between Clinton and Obama to win the Democratic nomination for President of the United States, reflected as overlapping oscillations in the support for each competitor [14]. Our goal in this paper is to better establish a path with theory toward a mathematical structure for this new theory.

2.1 Experiment

Why is an experiment needed? Primarily because the effects of interdependence are poorly known and studied (e.g., [10]). Having a better grasp and control of interdependence will permit a better understanding of businesses, other organizations, and institutions, as well as systems of organizations.

Hypotheses for the experiment that is being piloted: For well-defined problems where the solution is in hand (a widget manufacturer), cooperation from consensus seeking is the optimum decision rule, especially for organizations, to maximize an organization's ability to multi-task [1]. However, for ill-defined problems where the problem solution is unknown or ill-posed, such as openly determining in a democracy the location of a repository for high-level nuclear wastes, competition in the form of majority rule is the optimum decision rule. These hypotheses are predicated on information theory where, in general, cooperation among interdependent agents consumes information, competition generates it.

2.2 Experiment Participants

Participants include undergraduate level college students enrolled in psychology classes from a medium-sized southeastern university. Two methods are used to solicit participants for this study:

1) Flyers which provide a broad description of the experiment and how to volunteer are posted at several locations on the university campus.
2) A brief description of the experiment and directions to sign up are posted on an online registration system specifically designed to place participants in ongoing experiments conducted within the Psychology Department.

---

[5] As an example of two conflicting sets of opinions in the editorial and op-eds over climate-gate, see the *New York Times* (2010 JULY 21), "Weather Bane"; and the *Wall Street Journal* (2010, JULY 12), OPINION: "The climategate whitewash continues. Global warming alarmists claim vindication after last year's data manipulation scandal. Don't believe the 'independent' reviews." A more objective review of the "climate gate" scandal was reviewed by a scientist (Jasanoff, 2010) who spoke of the words used in the emails such as "trick" and "hide" to refer to their climate model practices and to their conspiracy to prevent unfriendly publications, a scandal that has caused alarm among even physicists (APS, 2010).

All participants are 18 years of age or older. As an incentive to participate, participants may receive extra course credit after completing the study.

2.3 Pilot Procedure

Groups of five participants each are recruited and scheduled. Once all five participants have arrived for the experiment they are randomly assigned to one of five seats positioned around a table. Once seated, participants read and sign a form providing informed consent and are instructed to complete a pre-test questionnaire. This questionnaire provides the investigators with each participant's views regarding the topics they will be discussing. After completing the self-report measure, three of the five randomly selected subjects are assessed for changes in sympathetic arousal (i.e., galvanic skin response, or GSR). Specifically, GSR electrodes are applied to the distal phalanges of the index and middle fingers of their non-dominant hand. Once the electrodes are in place a baseline level of sympathetic arousal will be obtained while the group engages in common or everyday "small" talk.

For the small talk, specific pre-scripted questions designed to produce minimal if any arousal are asked of the participants (e.g., "Where did you attend high school?"). Although electrodes are not applied to the remaining two subjects, they are instructed to not only participate in each debate but to serve, first, as debate leaders and, second, as group facilitators. As debate leaders, these two subjects are to argue for or against positions on each topic. After gaining assent and before each topic is presented, a coin is tossed to determine which of the two participants is to debate the pro or con position. Once a sufficient amount of baseline data are gathered, the test trial begins by presenting sequentially the subjects with three separate topics via PowerPoint slides. The order of topics is randomly predetermined for each trial. Participants are then asked to follow directions on the slides and debate each topic. After the participants have debated the first topic presented for approximately 12 minutes, the three participants attached to electrodes are asked to anonymously write down which side of the argument (pro or con) they felt was the strongest. Answers are collected and later discarded (avoiding the need for confidentiality). This part of the protocol is performed in order to reinforce the importance of a quality debate and affects the decisions. The same procedure is repeated for the next two topics. Pro and con positions for the two group leaders are randomly determined just prior to the presentation of a new topic by the toss of a coin. In addition to debating the selected three topics, participants re-discuss one of the topics, randomly predetermined, and decide on a policy for the topic assigned. The two participants not attached to electrodes are re-assigned to act as group facilitators, encouraging conversation and assisting the group to seek a consensual policy. All participants are instructed to actively participate in the discussion. Upon completion of the debate, electrodes are removed and participants are given a post self-report measure to fill out. Participants are debriefed and thanked for their participation. This study is completed in approximately 45 minutes.

2.4 Pilot Measures

Participants are measured on a pre-Likert and post-Likert scale self-report measure to assess their initial and post positions on each topic presented. GSR is recorded from instrumentation and software specifically designed for psycho-physiological measures (Biopac Systems, Inc.; see Figure 2). This system allows for the data to be manipulated and analyzed. Here, we analyze variability in the amplitude and frequency of GSR variability in the data collected for each participant are analyzed at a later time with time series and Fourier transforms. Finally all data are aggregated by summing within experimental groups and across experimental conditions (consensus or majority rules, topics, GSR monitored or not, and number of utterances) and the means and standard deviations are compared.

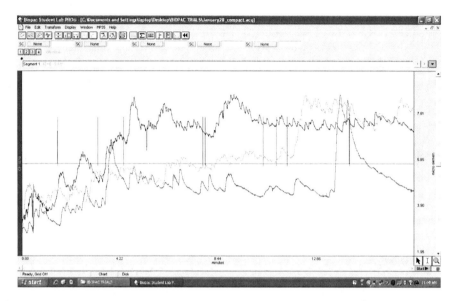

Fig. 2. Data collection has recently begun. A screenshot of unanalyzed GSR data collected from three subjects participating in a group of five subjects is shown below with different colors for each subject. The red vertical lines represent different events controlled by the research assistant (e.g., switching between debate topics), with double vertical lines representing a prompt ("please engage the topic more forcibly").

3   Future Research

Laboratory. Additional Biopacs will be purchased and brought into service to permit us to collect GSR data from up to seven subjects at one time.

Mathematics. In the future, we also plan to develop the transformations between four sets of mathematically equivalent solutions: for planning and execution; organizational center of gravity and spatial frequency; size and volatility; and power and time.

4   Conclusions

Traditional social science research has been unable to satisfactorily aggregate individual level data to group, organization and systems levels, making it one of social science's most fundamental challenge, if not the most important (Giles, 2011). We believe that the fault can be attributed to the normative ordering of elements for the mathematics in game and social theory. As an alternative, we offer a theory of Nash equilibria with countable distances based on bistable or multi-stable perspectives patterned after quantum information theory. The available evidence is supportive. It indicates that meaning is a one-sided, stable, classical interpretation, making the situational awareness of a social situation incomplete, sweeping aside static theories from earlier eras (e.g., Axelrod's evolution of cooperation; Simon's bounded rationality; Kripke's theory of truth claims[6]). This indicates that in democracies, interpretations across a system evolve to become orthogonal (Nash equilibria), that orthogonal interpretations generate the information that uniquely promotes social evolution, but that in dictatorships, dependent as they are on enforced social cooperation along with the suppression of opposing points of view, social evolution stops or slows, such as in China, Iran or Cuba, misallocating capital and energy as government leaders suppress interpretations that they alone have the authority to label.

For hybrid agents, despite its high-risk nature, our program of research suggests even at this early stage that interdependence can be controlled, that a science of interdependence can be developed mathematically, that mathematics can be applied in the field, and that organizational and system performance metrics can be developed.

Acknowledgements. This material is based upon work supported by, or in part by, the U. S. Army Research Laboratory and the U. S. Army Research Office under contract/grant number W911NF-10-1-0252.

References

1. Ambrose, S.H.: Paleolithic technology and human evolution. Science 291, 1748–1753 (2001)
2. APS, Message from the APS President (Am. Physical Society) (2010),
   http://www.aps.org/publications/apsnews/200910/climate.cfm
3. Baumeister, R.F., Campbell, J.D., Krueger, J.I., Vohs, K.D.: Exploding the self-esteem myth. Scientific American (January 2005)
4. WP, White Paper. European governance (COM, 428 final; Brussels, July 25, 2001), Brussels, Commission of the European Community, p. 29 (2001),
   http://ec.europa.eu/governance/white_paper/en.pdf (retrieved 2002)
5. Benincà, E., Jöhnk, K.D., Heerkloss, R., Huisman, J.: Coupled predator-prey oscillations in a chaotic food web. Ecology Letters 12, 1367–1378 (2009)
6. Bloom, N., Dorgan, S., Dowdy, J., Van Reenen, J.: Management practice and productivity. Quarterly Journal of Economics 122(4), 1351–1408 (2007)
7. Bonito, J.A., Keyton, J., Sanders, R.E.: The Grand Challenge of Understanding Group Effectiveness. NSF SBE 2020 (2010),
   http://www.nsf.gov/sbe/sbe_2020/all.cfm.ID#220
8. Giles, J.: Social science lines up its biggest challenges. 'Top ten' crucial questions set research priorities for the field. Nature 470, 18–19 (2011)

---

[6] For a review of Kripke's modal logic and his theory of truth claims, see Menzel, C., "Actualism", *The Stanford Encyclopedia of Philosophy (Summer 2010 Edition)*.

9. Jasny, B.R., Zahn, L.M., Marshall, E.: Connections: Introduction to the Special Issue on Complex systems and networks. Science 325, 405 (2009)

10. Kenny, D.A., Kashy, D.A., Bolger, N.: Data analysis in social psychology. In: Gilbert, D.T., Fiske, S.T., Lindzey, G. (eds.) The Handbook of Social Psychology, vol. I, pp. 233–268. McGraw-Hill, Boston (1998)

11. Lawless, W.F., Bergman, M., Louçã, J., Kriegel, N.N., Feltovich, N.: A quantum metric of organizational performance: Terrorism and counterterrorism. Computational & Mathematical Organizational Theory 13, 241–281 (2007)

12. Lawless, W.F., Whitton, J., Poppeliers, C.: Case studies from the UK and US of stakeholder decision-making on radioactive waste management. ASCE Practice Periodical of Hazardous, Toxic, and Radioactive Waste Management 12(2), 70–78 (2008)

13. Lawless, W.F., Sofge, D.A., Goranson, H.T.: Conservation of Information: A New Approach to Organizing Human-Machine-Robotic Agents under Uncertainty. In: Bruza, P., Sofge, D., Lawless, W., van Rijsbergen, K., Klusch, M. (eds.) QI 2009. LNCS, vol. 5494, pp. 184–199. Springer, Heidelberg (2009)

14. Lawless, W.F., Rifkin, S., Sofge, D.A., Hobbs, S.H., Angjellari-Dajci, F., Chaudron, L.: Conservation of Information: Reverse engineering dark social systems. Structure and Dynamics: eJournal of Anthropological and Related Sciences (2010a), http://www.escholarship.org/uc/item/38475290;jsessionid=26B6 D90CDDDF7EA3381780C60C2B8490#page-1

15. Lawless, W.F., Angjellari-Dajci, F., Sofge, D.: EU Economic Integration: Lessons of the Past, and What Does the Future Hold?, Dallas, TX, Federal Reserve Bank of Dallas (March 18, 2010b), http://www.dallasfed.org/institute/events/10eu.cfm

16. Lawless, W.F., Angjellari-Dajci, F., Sage, D.A., Grayson, J., Rychly, L.: A new approach to organizations: Stability and transformation in dark social networks (DSN). Journal of Enterprise Transformation (Taylor & Francis) (2011) (forthcoming)

17. Pfeffer, J., Fong, C.T.: Building organization theory from first principles. Organization Science 16, 372–388 (2005)

18. Wickens, C.D.: Engineering psychology and human performance, 2nd edn. Merrill Publishing, Columbus (1992)

19. Wood, J.: EIRB Status (UNCLASSIFIED), personal email (January 31, 2011)

20. Wood, Stachura, Astapova, Fjorentina, Tung, Lawless (Corresponding Author): Review of electronic research in Georgia: Telemedicine, eHealth and e-IRBs. In: Miranda, M., Cruz-Cunha, M.M. (eds.) Handbook of Research on ICTs for Healthcare and Social Services: Developments and Applications. IGI, Hershey (2011) (in preparation, tentatively accepted)

Exploring a Framework for a New Focus in Information and Communications Technology Education

Arturo Serrano Santoyo

Centro de Investigación Científica y Educación Superior de Ensenada, CICESE
Ensenada, Baja California. México
serrano@cicese.mx

Abstract. This paper discusses the importance and urgency of developing educational and training programs in the areas of Information and Communications Technologies (ICT) with a sustainable development vision and service to society focus. We suggest the development of ICT curricula emerging from a framework that includes those disciplines, that in our view, constitute a comprehensive educational platform aiming to provide ICT students with the necessary skills, empowerment, insights and vision to face the challenging requirements and complexity of a globalized and converging world.

Keywords: Technology education, moral leadership, human development.

1 Introduction

We live in an age in which technological innovation has a great effect on the way individuals organize and carry out their endeavours. Information and Communications Technologies (ICT) systems play a pivotal role in the current information age providing the tools needed for the transport and processing of information. ICT have become potential vehicles contributing to socioeconomic development of a country. In this context, it is widely accepted that there is a strong correlation between the socioeconomic condition of a country and its telecommunications infrastructure. Furthermore, the concept of the global village has become popular as well as apparent through the use of telecommunications technology for the transmission and reception of voice, data and images using the most sophisticated devices ever created. Unfortunately, although the idea of a global village has, to a certain extent, captured the imagination of many people in recent years, it has yet to be transformed into reality; we still have a long way to go. While advanced and sophisticated ICT systems and equipment have already been developed, its potential to contribute to the goal of a more unified, integrated society remains elusive due in part to a lack of a human development vision of individuals and agencies involved in design and deployment of ICT infrastructure and services. As it was mentioned above, ICT have become important tools for contributing to solutions of innumerable areas of human concern, at the same time, they are powerful instruments for harmful applications in absence of moral leadership and ethical values centred on the spiritual nature of individuals.

M.M. Cruz-Cunha et al. (Eds.): CENTERIS 2011, Part II, CCIS 220, pp. 270–275, 2011.

The obstacles we face in the process of creating a global village conducive to a more integrated society are not only financial or technical but of human and moral nature that require a great deal of community building and participation. ICT have the potential to be transformed into an effective development tool contributing to a more unified, integrated society, by incorporating a sustainable development vision and a service to society focus in the ICT curricula of universities. Within the framework of this "new vision", those concerned with the application of ICT would not focus only on applications in segments of the economy such as the corporate and industrial sectors, but would also seek to improve the condition of the less well-off or of those who live in remote, isolated and underserved areas. To date, most ICT curricula are generally oriented to solving needs oriented towards corporate needs or to satisfy the "consumer" needs. An educational effort in the area of ICT that takes into account factors of moral leadership could produce engineers and scientists committed to creating instruments and means for integrating the world, for establishing universal education and eventually for contributing to world peace and to effectively reducing the digital divide [1].

The motivation of this paper is to emphasize that in the current globalized context, the development of human capital goes far beyond I.Q., degrees and professional skills, those are all important. However, there are other talents and skills that must be included in ICT curricula to thrive in a collaborative and interrelated world.

2 Education as an Instrument of Social Transformation

In preparing the individual and society for a new world order and an attitude of global consciousness, it is necessary to incorporate human development subjects in the ICT educational processes and programs, no longer viewing them as being merely the act of transmitting a collection of facts and figures through repetitive and sometimes mechanical procedures. Education should be seen as a continuous and creative process. Its aim is to develop the capacities latent in human nature and to coordinate their expression for the enrichment and progress of society [2]. With this concept in mind, it is particularly important to incorporate those factors that shape and stimulate attitudes conducive to the conception of harmonious, tolerant and balanced communities. In such an educational strategy, the individual would be encouraged to foster a society in search of cooperation and the betterment of the social, economic and moral condition of its individual members. Under this scenario, education would not be seen only as means to improve the individual's own economic situation, but the society's situation as a whole.

If the objective and purpose of education in ICT were placed in a framework of service to society, the future engineers and scientists would be able to make a greater contribution to society. This contribution would be backed by moral forces, enabling scientific and technological development to promote the prosperity and happiness of all sectors of the population and in general to contribute to a higher quality of life, not only materially, but also intellectually, morally and socially. This paper proposes that if education in high technology areas is not oriented towards producing a radical change in our vision and purpose of life, an opportunity for global cooperation, development and progress will be lost, and the fundamental inequities afflicting society and the family of nations will only worsen. Furthermore, we would miss the opportunity of using ICT to support the prevention, mitigation and elimination of social deviations. All these aberrations of human behaviour are extremely pervasive and represent a serious challenge for society. Unfortunately, individuals with significant ICT skills with a lack of service to society vision, and in many cases experiencing mental and emotional challenges, orient their efforts and capacities to develop ICT applications of negative impact for the wellbeing of society. The idea is not only to design strategies to stopping the potentially harmful deviations, but to develop an educational framework that could contribute to reorienting their focus toward applications for the improvement of social condition. Education in the right context and time may prevent unfortunate and harmful attention to negative and destructive ICT tools and applications.

There have been recent important contributions from different researchers in both developing and developed countries who give emphasis to the creation of a new vision in the educational process of future generations of knowledge workers. Given the conditions and impact of globalization and digitalization of society, it is fundamental to develop cadres of engineers and scientists with a new sense of purpose that goes beyond the economic and intellectual incentives of obtaining a degree. According with Gardner [3], in order to survive and advance in a connected world, five kinds of minds are necessary to be nurtured in the new generation of learners: the disciplined mind, the synthesizing mind, the creative mind, the respectful mind and the ethical mind. These five minds are strongly related to the human factors required in ICT education.

Today, market oriented or technology centric concepts focused on capturing the minds and needs of potential consumers are key forces that stimulate the development of high technology disciplines. One vivid example of this fact is the proliferation of social networks applications focused in intensifying the interactions between members of such social network for commercial purposes. The proposal presented in this paper is that other elements be incorporated into this picture: the concepts of human development, the importance of the arts, innovation for socioeconomic development and job creation and the moral and ethical basis of human advancement (service to society). Such an educational strategy would focus on fulfilling the needs of a specific social group, striving to use technology for educating individuals, for awakening their human potential, providing the communities of learning with the basic elements for social and economic development and instilling in them a better understanding of their responsibility as members of a common environment, planet earth.

An understanding of ICT development and education as disciplines oriented towards service to society would assure social progress in the fields of health, disaster communications, agriculture, and rural and urban education, to name just a few of the possible applications. In this way, ICT would have a direct impact on the lives of individuals around the globe, contributing to their ability to secure their means of existence with dignity and honour and helping them to realize the negative influence of irresponsible use of technology to facilitate harmful aberrations of human behaviour.

3   Elements of an Integral Curricula

It is proposed that a general framework for the development of comprehensive ICT educational programs of future ICT engineers, scientist and practitioners must include the disciplines described in Fig. 1.

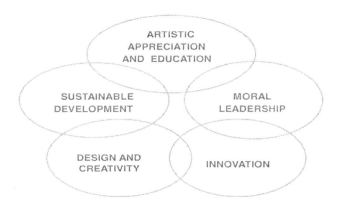

Fig. 1. Elements of an Integral Curricula

The impact of global warming in the future of our planet is being widely accepted. Sustainable development for a more balanced, collaborative and interrelated communities becomes a fundamental discipline if we conceive our planet as one country with common concerns for its survival and harmonious growth. A vision of service to our society in ICT education is central to achieve not only to understand our interrelatedness as human beings, but also to concentrate efforts in developing technologies that can mitigate the effects of socioeconomic disparities, address the lack and access to quality health services in all sectors of the population, or to support communities afflicted by natural disasters, among others. In this scenario, moral leadership provides the insight and human perspective needed to respond to priorities for the integral development of our society. An Innovation focus that incorporates concepts such as collaborative work, value creation and entrepreneurship provides necessary skills for socioeconomic development projects in key areas like "green technology development" or Green ICT. Design and Creativity have been recently considered to be priority areas in major universities and research centres in the world. Knowledge and skills required in the design of systems and devices focused on the needs of the population are in great demand all over the world. Artistic appreciation and education is an integral element conducive to stimulate the creative mind incorporating beauty and simplicity to products with potential of application in diverse areas of the economy.

The above mentioned disciplines are interrelated and can not be isolated from each other or placed out of context from the cultural, social, intellectual and economic needs of the population. This interrelation is needed to create a transdisciplinary [4] environment that stimulates collaborative work relevant to the pressing needs of our society. In order to successfully integrate these five disciplines in the curricula of engineers and scientist involved in ICT, unity of vision and leadership among academics and administrators about the scope and purpose of the educational program must be accomplished.

Regarding the responsibilities of our universities in our time, Ernst [5] explains that it is not only the training of the specialists that is important, but the formation of responsible leaders for leading institutions in society. The fostering of personalities who have a broad vision and a critical sense paired with compassion and understanding of the neediness of others is the ultimate goal of academic education. Dr. Ernst further emphasizes the importance of creating life-long-learning educational programs for professionals and the public as key elements to achieve the extension purposes and relevance of academic institutions This is particularly important in ICT disciplines because they are tools of great value, with transversal nature and great potential for reducing the Digital Divide in the one hand and for providing opportunities of further development and education to individuals with work and family responsibilities on the other. At the end technology is only a vehicle to achieve the social transformation the world requires. The human dimension and the purpose of creating a more unified and integrated society in the ICT educational context need urgent attention.

There are more elements to add in this proposed framework, those related for example to psychology, sociology and behavioural economics [6]. However, we wanted to rely in those that we consider significant to understand the role of ICT as potential contributors to community development and progress. Examples of curricula with focus on sustainability have been developed in different parts of the world, one that is worth mentioning is the one existing at the School of Sustainability at Arizona State University [7], where many disciplines converge to provide an integral approach to serve the Arizona region. The basic idea regarding this approach is that Sustainability is the axis of projects and University outreach in order to create an educational system immersed and integrated with the development requirements of society. Another example is the approach of the Universidad del Desarrollo in Chile where the elements of entrepreneurship and development converge to provide a holistic context to their educational programs [8]. Gender issues regarding the increasing role of women in engineering have arisen as focal themes for discussion in different educational programs, projects and meetings. The participation of women is crucial to take full advantage of ICT as a vehicle for development, the Helena Project developed under the auspices of the European Union FP7 strategy stresses the importance of women in engineering and technology [9]. There are other educational instances in Africa and Asia where culture and community participation become pillars when applying ICT to accomplish development goals [10]. In all the above-mentioned examples a trend and enfoldment of educational initiatives where convergence of the elements described in Figure 1 is observed. However, it is fundamental to develop a transdisciplinary approach where such elements are not isolated, but immersed and interrelated with the vision and objectives of ICT education and training in search of human and sustainable prosperity. Our future work will focus on the structure and detailed curricula of the proposed framework in order to expand its reach and short-term impact in both rural and urban contexts.

4 Conclusions

It is proposed that creating special educational and training curricula focused on the development of a consciousness geared to direct our lives and our work to human development and service to humanity is a key element and priority in the process of educating engineers, scientists and in general users of high technology systems. This would contribute to the development of a different attitude and vision in the mind of the students and professionals. The benefits would not only be of importance to the students themselves, but to the schools, development agencies or governments and in the long run for society, for it would cause a new kind of leadership to come into being. With this in mind, telecommunications and information processing can be viewed as tools to shape a new society in which the human factor is fundamental and where cooperation rather than contention or competition motivate the individual to excel in a challenging and changing world.

References

1. Serrano, A., Martínez, E.: La Brecha Digital: Mitos y Realidades, Fondo Editorial de Baja California, Segunda Edición (2008)
2. Baha'í' International Community Statement for the first session of the UN Preparatory Committee of the World Summit on Sustainable Development, Sustainable Development: The spiritual dimension (2000)
3. Gardner, H.: Five minds for the future. Harvard Business School Press, Boston (2006)
4. Max-Neef, M.A.: Foundations of Transdisciplinarity. Ecological Ergonomics 53 (2005)
5. Ernst Richard, R.: The responsibility of universities in our time, Economía Ética y Bienestar Social, Ediciones Pirámide (2003)
6. Brooks, D.: The new humanism (May 7, 2011), http://www.nytimes.com
7. Global Institute for Sustainability Arizona State University,
   http://schoolofsustainability.asu.edu
8. Universidad del Desarrollo, Chile, http://www.udd.cl
9. Helena Consortium: Framework Programme 7, Collaborative Project. Project no. 230376
10. http://www.fp7-helena.org
11. Development Gateway: Reflections, Milestones and Transformations, Annual Report (2009),
    http://www.developmentgateway.org/
    news-events/2008-annual-report.html

Interoperability on e-Learning 2.0:
The PEACE Case Study

Ricardo Queirós, Lino Oliveira, Cândida Silva, and Mário Pinto

DI-ESEIG/IPP & KMILT, Porto, Portugal
{ricardo.queiros,linooliveira,
candidasilva,mariopinto}@eu.ipp.pt

Abstract. The confluence of education with the evolution of technology boosted the paradigm shift of the face-to-face learning to distance learning. In this scenario e-Learning plays an essential role as a facilitator of the teaching/learning process. However new demands associated with the new Web paradigm require that existent e-Learning environments characterized mostly by monolithic systems begin interacting with new specialized services. In this decentralized scenario the definition of a strategy of interoperability is the cornerstone to ensure the standardization communication among systems. This paper presents a definition of an interoperability strategy for an e-Learning environment at our School (ESEIG) called PEACE – Project for ESEIG Academic Content Environment. This new interoperability model relies on the application of several coordination and integration standards on several services, controlled by teachers and students, and included in the PEACE environment such as social networks, repositories, libraries, e-portfolios, intelligent tutors, recommendation systems and virtual classrooms.

Keywords: Interoperability, E-Learning, Web2.0.

1 Introduction

In the last decades the evolution of e-Learning systems was impressive. In the early times the e-Learning environments were characterized by silo applications developed for specific learning domains and with no support for content and interoperability standards. Then, new systems appeared featuring reusable tools that can be effectively used virtually in any e-Learning course. This is the case of the Learning Management Systems (LMS) that, nowadays, plays a central role in any e-Learning architecture. These systems based around pluggable components, led to oversized systems that are difficult to reconvert to new trends such as the integration of heterogeneous services based on semantic information or the automatic adaptation of services to users (both teachers and learners). These new demands triggered the appearance of a new generation of e-Learning platforms based on services aiming to facilitate the systems' integration in different scenarios [1]. This new approach provides the basis for Service Oriented Architectures (SOA).

The motivation for this work comes from research made by the PIGeCo (Integrated Projects for Content Management) research group at ESEIG and reinforced by a survey [2] conducted by a group of teachers of several schools of the Polytechnic

M.M. Cruz-Cunha et al. (Eds.): CENTERIS 2011, Part II, CCIS 220, pp. 276–285, 2011.
© Springer-Verlag Berlin Heidelberg 2011

Institute of Porto (where ESEIG belongs) within a study to gauge the Internet usage habits of our students. The aim of this study was to know the Internet usage habits of the Portuguese Higher Education students, in order to select the suitable tools and techniques in the teaching-learning process. Based on the survey and in several case studies [3], [4] and [5] of ESEIG and others educational institutions we obtained the basis for the PEACE system architecture [6]. The objective of the PEACE environment is to integrate a set of services such as repositories, social networks, intelligent tutors and recommendation systems to potentiate the learner experience and to improve the process of teaching/learning in ESEIG.

This paper presents our interoperability strategy to face the heterogeneity of services proposed in the PEACE environment. The purpose of this paper is to present our approach to address the issues underlying the communication and information sharing and to share specific good practices and recommendations, based on standards-based solutions.

The remainder of this paper is organized as follows: section 2 focuses on the interoperability levels regarding the communication and information sharing among services in an educational environment. In the following section we present the system architecture for our e-Learning environment at ESEIG, more precisely, its main components and interoperability model. Finally, we conclude with a summary of the major contributions of this paper and future work in this project.

2   Interoperability Levels

In recent years customers demand for interoperability solutions, driven mostly by the need to cut costs and to maximize return on investments given the current economic situation [7]. At the same time, education practitioners increasingly prefer the adoption of new standards for the interchange of learning objects and learners' information boosting content sharing, interoperability and reusability in e-Learning systems. Based on this assumption, several organizations (e.g. ADL, IMS GLC, IEEE) have been developing recently specifications and standards [8] for e-Learning content [9], [10] and [11] and communication [12] and [13].

Regarding the **standardization of e-Learning content**, the concept of learning object is indisputable. Learning Objects (LO) are units of instructional content that can be used, and most of all reused, on web based e-Learning systems. They encapsulate a collection of interdependent files (HTML files, images, web scripts, style sheets) with a manifest containing metadata. This metadata is important for classifying and searching LO in digital repositories and for making effective use of their content in LMS and other e-Learning systems.

The most widely used standard for LO is the IMS Content Packaging (IMS CP). This content packaging specification uses an XML manifest file wrapped with other resources inside a zip file. The manifest includes the IEEE Learning Object Metadata (LOM) standard to describe the learning resources included in the package. The LOM standard is being used in several e-Learning projects all over the world [14]. IMS CP was designed to be straightforward to extend, meeting the needs of a target user community through the creation of application profiles. When applied to metadata the term *application profile* generally refers to "the adaptation, constraint, and/or augmentation of a metadata scheme to suit the needs of a particular community" [15]. A well know e-Learning application profile is SCORM [16] that extends IMS CP with more sophisticated sequencing and Contents-to-LMS communication.

Recently, IMS GLC proposed the IMS Common Cartridge [17] that bundles the previous specifications and its main goal is to organize and distribute digital learning content.

Regarding the **standardization of communication** appeared in recent years, initiatives often called e-Learning frameworks, to adapt SOA to e-Learning and aiming to provide flexible learning environments for learners worldwide. They are characterized by providing a set of open interfaces to several reusable services organized in genres or layers and combined in service usage models. Other e-Learning interoperability initiatives (e.g. NSDL, POOL, OKI, EduSource, IMS DRI, IMS LTI) also appeared in the last decade to fulfill the specific need of e-Learning systems.

The IMS Global Learning Consortium (IMS GLC) has been a very active organization in this context. Two of the most popular communication specifications are the IMS Digital Repositories Interoperability (IMS DRI) specification for repositories and the IMS Learning Tools Interoperability (IMS LTI) specification for manage links between general e-Learning systems. The IMS DRI provides general recommendations for repository functions, namely the submission, search and download of LOs. It recommends the use of web services to expose the repository functions based on the Simple Object Access Protocol (SOAP) protocol, defined by W3C. Due to their growing popularity other web service interface flavours such as Representational State Transfer (REST) since it will improve interoperability with systems that adhere to a more simple and informal style of development.

The IMS LTI provides a uniform standards-based extension point in LMS allowing remote tools and content to be integrated into the LMS. The main goal of the LTI is to standardize the process for building links between learning tools and the LMS. There are several benefits from using this approach: educational institutions, LMS vendors and tool providers by adhering to a clearly defined interface between the LMS and the tool, will decrease costs, increases options for students and instructors when selecting learning applications and also potentiates the use of software as a service (SaaS).

3   PEACE Architecture

In this section we present the design of the e-Learning environment called PEACE. The objective of the PEACE environment is to integrate a set of services such as repositories, social networks, intelligent tutors and recommendation systems to potentiate the learner experience and to improve the process of teaching/learning in ESEIG, a school of the Polytechnic Institute of Porto. The architecture of the system is depicted in figure 1.

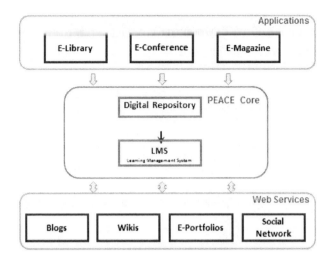

Fig. 1. PEACE system architecture (adapted from [6])

In the following subsections we detail the PEACE Core components and the Social Services of the architecture since they are in a more advanced phase of the project. We also present our interoperability strategy for these components exposing the specifications and standards adopted.

3.1 PEACE Core

The LMS occupies a central position in the proposed architecture, since is currently the natural place where students and teachers communicate. The LMS provides a web-based environment that enables communication and interaction with and among students. Teachers play the role of facilitator and mentor of the learning process through the educational content publication, monitoring and analysis of student's progress, who can plan their learning and collaborate between them [18].

The LMS is fed by a digital repository that gathers information of several other systems such as libraries, e-Conference systems, intelligent tutors, recommendation systems, and others. The set of applications that fed the repository have contributions of many different players like teachers, researchers, students, academics, librarians, professionals, etc. Teachers can also add new content directly to the repository focusing to their specific courses.

A repository of learning objects (LO) can be defined as a system that stores electronic objects and meta-data about those objects [19]. The need for this kind of repositories is growing as more educators are eager to use digital educational contents and more of it is available.

The appropriated metadata descriptions of the LOs permits assembled them together to form lessons and courses, as modular units, interoperating at different levels of granularity. The LO can be a simple text document, a photograph, a video clip, a simulation, a three dimensional image, a Java applet or any other object that might be used for online learning.

The Jorum Team made a comprehensive survey [19] of the existing repositories and noticed that most of these systems do not store actual learning objects, they just store meta-data describing LOs, including pointers to their locations on the Web. This repository collects the LOs and the correspondent describing meta-data.

To exploit the new web paradigm, the LMS interacts also with new Web 2.0 services. These services are well known by the students as they use it quite often in other contexts [3].

3.2 Social Services

The use of Web 2.0 applications in Education enables improvements in several areas [20]:

- More interaction between teachers and students, without the usual constraints in face-to-face relationships;
- More students' participation in course units (CU) activities available in LMS;
- Improvement in research, stud, writing and discussion of subjects.

These benefits were confirmed through an educational experiment carried out which followed the work methodology presented in Fig. 2 [18].

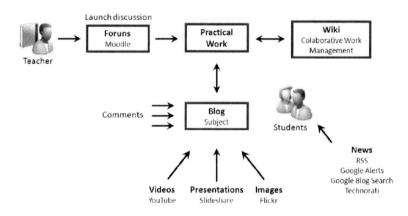

Fig. 2. Methodology used in carrying out activities in Moodle

This strategy also promotes a regular exchange of experiences, creating an ad-hoc learning community or community of practice [21] and [22].

But the use of web-based services poses difficulties in learning and teaching, especially assessment, because it is not possible to ensure the availability of the services and the content created [23]. These are some of the problems that may occur [24]:

- The service can be stopped at any time (possibly without any announcement) and this result in the loss of the content published an not backed up;
- The service that was free become charged;

- Reduced regulation by the teacher;
- Possible dispersion of the content.

To reduce this inconvenient, PEACE architecture include the implementation of Web 2.0 applications, as Fig. 1 shows, inside the infrastructure of ESEIG and, in this way, ensures the preservation of the content published. The PEACE Social Services provide an environment that allows students to create and configure their personal learning environments (PLE) and e-portfolios, according to each of the CUs attended (interaction with LMS Moodle, created content in CU activities, relationship with peers and teachers, etc.). The student can enrich his/her PLE with external content from Internet and with material not necessarily related with academic activity (e.g. personal data, resume, etc.) thus preparing the process of entering the labor market. The activity between these Social Services and the Core can be represented by Fig. 3.

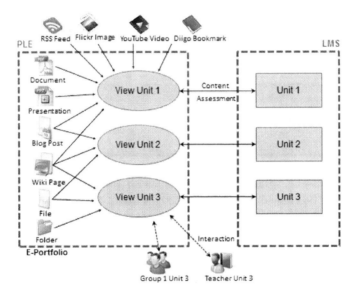

Fig. 3. Integration of PLE, E-Portfolio and LMS [23]

These PEACE Social Services are based in a Mahara implementation, integrated with LMS Moodle. This integration is done through the Moodle Portfolio API.

The completed environment created by the student can be exported and integrated into other platforms since Mahara includes an import/export facility that supports LEAP2A protocol [25].

3.3 Interoperability Strategy

In order to face the heterogeneity of services proposed in the PEACE environment it is important to define, in the design/model phase, an interoperability strategy for the underlying systems. These strategies will beneficiate:

- The selection of the appropriate tools based on the support of emergent standards;
- The communication and information sharing among systems;
- The adoption of good practices by readers facing similar problems.

The interoperability strategy is organized at two levels: content and communication. For each level a set of specifications/standards is presented and based on their support a set of tools is identify as good candidates to be included in the PEACE environment. Notice that other criteria will be used to select tools and to potentiate communication among systems such as availability, cost, maturity, security, development effort and communication type. However due to page size limitations only the standardization study is presented on this paper. In Table 1 we present some of the content standards select to base the communication among the LMS and the repository and the social services.

Table 1. Content level interoperability

System types	LMS	Repository	E-Portfolio	Social Network	Blog/Wiki
LMS		IMS CC	Leap2A	RSS/Atom	RSS/Atom
Repository	IMS CC				
E-Portfolio	Leap2A				
Social Network	RSS/Atom				
Blog/Wiki	RSS/Atom				

The communication between the LMS and the repository will rely on the IMS CC specification. Its main goal is to organize and distribute digital learning content. The IMS CC package can be organized hierarchically in four levels as depicted Fig. 4.

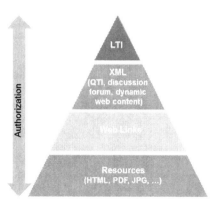

Fig. 4. Common Cartridge Content Hierarchy

In the lower layer the content is distributed within the cartridge and stored in the LMS database. Examples of such resources are HTML or PDF files or even image files with the JPG/PNG/GIF formats. Moving up the pyramid follows the content accessed at runtime though an URL (weblinks). This approach allows the cartridge to minimize its storage space and to have content updates after distribution. The next level is occupied by the XML content. In this layer we stress the use of QTI to describe specialized questions and tests. In the top of the pyramid comes the IMS LTI specification. In this context, the content can be an application still supporting results for tracking. In Table 2 we present some of the communication standards select to base the communication among the LMS and the repository and the social services.

Table 2. Communication level interoperability

System types	LMS	Repository	E-Portfolio	Social Network	Blog/Wiki
LMS		Repository API	Portfolio API	OpenSocial	OpenSocial
Repository	IMS DRI/LTI				
E-Portfolio	IMS Portfolio				
Social Network	OpenSocial				
Blog/Wiki	OpenSocial				

The communication between the LMS and the repository and the e-Portfolio system relies on the APIs (Fig. 5) founded in the new Moodle version (v. 2.0 released in November 2010) that aims to enable the development of plug-ins by third parties to access repositories and portfolios, such as: **Repository API** for browsing and retrieving files from external repositories; **Portfolio API** for exporting Moodle content to external repositories.

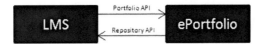

Fig. 5. Moodle Repository and Portfolio APIs

These two APIs are based on the File API - a set of core interfaces to allow Moodle to manage access control, store and retrieve files. The new File API aims to enhance file handling by avoiding redundant storage, when the same file is used twice. Using Moodle 2.0 File API every file is saved into a file pool (a directory in moodle data) with a filename that is calculated as a SHA1 hash of the file content. If a file is copied (e.g. course cloning) no file duplication happens, just a new record in a special table of files is created.

Two other emergent specifications stress in Table 2: the IMS LTI and the OpenSocial API. The IMS Learning Tools Interoperability provides a uniform standards-based extension point in LMS allowing remote tools and content to be integrated into LMSs. This approach is a good alternative to the Repository/Portfolio APIs since it is not tightly connected to the Moodle adoption. The OpenSocial API is the new trend for connecting social networks to other systems and defines a common API for social applications across multiple websites. With standard JavaScript and HTML, developers can create apps that access a social network's friends and update feeds. Several social network support this API such as HI5, LinkedIn, MySpace, Netlog, Ning, orkut, and Yahoo! Some of these social services can be usefulness in the educational context to gauge student's attention and potentiate the teaching/learning process.

4 Conclusion and Future Work

This paper presented an e-Learning environment called PEACE, whose aim is to integrate a set of applications (such as repositories, intelligent tutors, recommendation systems and virtual classrooms) and social services (such as social networks, blogs, wikis and e-portfolios), to potentiate the learner experience and to improve the process of teaching and learning. The paper focused on the PEACE architecture, its components and interoperability strategy to face the heterogeneity of services proposed in the PEACE. The interoperability strategy outlined in this study is guided by the recently specifications and standards for e-Learning content and communication interoperability levels, providing a set of recommendations to base the design and modeling phase of the PEACE project. For each interoperability level, a set of specifications and standards was presented and a set of tools was identified as potential candidates to be included in the PEACE environment.

This study will help the authors to select the appropriate tools based on the support of emergent standards and to potentiate the communication and information sharing among systems.

Future work will focuses on the modeling and implementation phases of PEACE environment, followed by the system evaluation.

References

1. Leal, J., Queirós, R.: e-Learning Frameworks: a survey. In: International Technology, Education and Development Conference, Valencia, Spain (2010)
2. Babo, R., Lopes, C., Rodrigues, A., Pinto, M., Queirós, R., Oliveira, P.: Gender Differences in Internet Usage Habits – A Case Study in Higher Education. In: 14th IBIMA Conference - International Business Information Management Association, Istanbul, Turkey (2010)
3. Gras, M.: Internet Usage and Digital Divide Among Spanish University Students. Revista Media e Jornalismo 14(8(1)) (2005)
4. Misko, J., Choi, J., Hong, S., Lee, I.: E-learning in Australia and Korea: Learning from Practice, Korea Research Institute for Vocational Education & Training (2004), http://www.ncver.edu.au/research/core/cp0306.pdf
5. Oliveira, L., Moreira, F.: Teaching and Learning with Social Software in Higher Education - Content Management Systems integrated with Web-based applications as a key factor for success. In: Proceedings of International Conference of Education, Research and Innovation, ICERI 2008, Madrid, Spain (2008)
6. Queirós, R., Oliveira, L., Pinto, M., Silva, C.: Towards e-Learning 2.0: Case Study of an e-Learning Environment. In: Proceedings of the 9th European Conference on e-Learning, pp. 812–815 (2010)
7. [IAC] Interoperability Strategy: Concepts, Challenges, and Recommendations. Industry Advisory Council (IAC) Enterprise Architecture SIG. Concept Level White Paper Developed for the Federal Enterprise Architecture Program Management Office, FEA-PMO (2003)

8. Friesen, N.: Interoperability and Learning Objects: An Overview of E-Learning Standardization. Interdisciplinary Journal of Knowledge and Learning Objects (2005)
9. IMS-CP – IMS Content Packaging, Information Model, Best Practice and Implementation Guide, Version 1.1.3 Final Specification IMS Global Learning Consortium Inc. (2010), http://www.imsglobal.org/content/packaging
10. IMS-Metadata - IMS MetaData. Information Model, Best Practice and Implementation Guide, Version 1.2. Final Specification IMS Global Learning Consortium Inc., http://www.imsglobal.org/metadata
11. IMS-QTI - IMS Question and Test Interoperability. Information Model, Best Practice and Implementation Guide, Version 1.2.1. Final Specification IMS Global Learning Consortium Inc., http://www.imsglobal.org/question/index.html
12. IMS DRI - IMS Digital Repositories Interoperability - Core Functions Information Model, http://www.imsglobal.org/digitalrepositories/driv1p0/imsdri_infov1p0.html
13. Simon, B., Massart, D., van Assche, F., Ternier, S., Duval, E., Brantner, S., Olmedilla, D., Miklos, Z.: A Simple Query Interface for Interoperable Learning Repositories. In: Proceedings of the WWW 2005 Conference (2006), http://nm.wu-wien.ac.at/e-learning/interoperability/www2005-workshop-sqi-2005-04-14.pdf
14. Godby, C.: What Do Application Profiles Reveal about the Learning Object Metadata Standard? Ariadne Article in e-Learning Standards (2004)
15. IMS Application Profile Guidelines Overview, Part 1 - Management Overview, Version 1.0., http://www.imsglobal.org/ap/apv1p0/imsap_oviewv1p0.html
16. ADL SCORM, http://www.adlnet.gov/Technologies/scorm
17. IMS Common Cartridge Profile, Version 1.0, Final Specification, http://www.imsglobal.org/cc/ccv1p0/imscc_profilev1p0.html
18. Oliveira, L., Moreira, F.: Use of Web Social as a Supplement to Learning in Higher Education - a Case Study. In: Cota, M.P. (ed.) Proceedings of the IIIrd Iberian Conference on Information Systems and Technologies, vol. I, pp. 51–62 (2008)
19. Holden, C.: What We Mean When We Say "Repositories". User Expectations of Repository Systems, Academic ADL Co-Lab (2004)
20. Oliveira, L., Moreira, F.: Integration of Web 2.0 applications and content management systems on personal learning environments. In: Rocha, A., Sexto, C.F., Reis, L.P., Cota, M.P. (eds.) Sistemas y Tecnologías de Información - Actas de la 5ª Conferencia Ibérica de Sistemas y Tecnologías de Información, CISTI 2010, pp. 45–49 (2010)
21. Downes, S.: E-learning 2.0. eLearn Magazine (2005), http://www.elearnmag.org/subpage.cfm?section=articles&article=29-1
22. O'Hear, S.: e-learning 2.0 - how Web technologies are shaping education (2006), http://www.readwriteweb.com/archives/e-learning_20.php
23. Oliveira, L., Moreira, F.: Personal Learning Environments: Integration of Web 2.0 Applications and Content Management Systems. In: Proceedings of 11th European Conference on Knowledge Management, ECKM 2010, vol. 2, pp. 1171–1177 (2010b)
24. Franklin, T., Van Harmelen, M.: Web 2.0 for content for Learning and Teaching in Higher Education. JISC (2007), http://www.jisc.ac.uk/media/documents/programmes/digitalrepositories/web2-content-learning-and-teaching.pdf
25. JISC-CETIS. PIOP Mahara – CETISwiki (2010), http://wiki.cetis.ac.uk/PIOP_Mahara

ALBIS - ALigning Business Processes and Information Systems: A Case Study

Lerina Aversano, Carmine Grasso, and Maria Tortorella

Department of Engineering University of Sannio
Via Traiano 1
82100 Benevento Italy
{aversano,carmine.grasso,tortorella}@unisannio.it

Abstract. The relationships existing between a business process and the supporting software systems is a critical concern for the organizations, as it directly affects their performance. The research described in this paper is concerned with the ALBIS Environment – ALigning Business processes and Information Systems, designed to support software maintenance tasks. In particular, the proposed environment allows the modeling and tracing between business and software entities and the measurement of their alignment degree. An information retrieval approach is embedded in ALBIS based on two processing phases including syntactic and semantic analysis. The usefulness of the environment is discussed through a case study.

Keywords: software evolution, business process evolution, maintenance tasks.

1 Introduction

Alignment of business processes and software systems was conceptualized in the literature in many ways [1]. Actually, a precise definition of the alignment concept misses, even if the concept is clear. It is described at two different abstraction levels, i.e. strategic and functional [2], and involves different aspects, such as enterprise goals, business entities, strategies and processes, information system and data. This paper deals with the links existing between business processes and software systems at the functional level.

In general terms, a view of business and technological alignment defines at which extent the information technology mission, objectives, and plans, support and are supported by the business mission, objectives, and plans [20].

The alignment measure between software system and business process entails an evaluation of the software systems and their components used for supporting a business process when it is executed.

In an operative context, it can happen that a business process and the supporting software systems appear to be aligned, but modifications may cause their misalignment. This can be due to either technological and/or management innovations, or unchecked change of the way the activities are executed or the supporting software systems are exploited. Furthermore, a modification does not only regard the considered objects but also impacts on other objects having a dependence relation

M.M. Cruz-Cunha et al. (Eds.): CENTERIS 2011, Part II, CCIS 220, pp. 286–296, 2011.
© Springer-Verlag Berlin Heidelberg 2011

with the modified ones. All this causes the decreasing of the performance of the business process and requires the execution of evolution activities. In this context, knowing the business process and monitoring its alignment and links existing with the supporting software systems are very helpful. Monitoring the alignment implies the characterization of all the items it involves and definition of measures for evaluating it. This is a complex task and the availability of automatic tools for supporting evaluation and evolution activities may be precious.

This paper proposes a software environment named ALBIS – ALigning Business processes and Information Systems. It supports an alignment strategy including modeling, tracing and evaluation tasks. In particular, ALBIS can also be applied for understanding the software system and business activities it supports.

The next section describes the ALBIS strategy. Section 3 presents ALBIS architecture. Section 4 applies ALBIS in a case study. Section 5 discusses related work, while, concluding remarks and future work are outlined in Section 6.

2   ALBIS Strategy

The ALBIS alignment strategy includes activities for modeling business processes and software systems, tracing business and software assets and measuring the degree of alignment existing between the considered business process and supporting software systems. The main phases of the strategy map the component of the ALBIS architecture depicted in Fig. 1. In particular, the main phases are:

1. **Modelling.** The models of the business process and supporting software systems are defined. A business process model includes all the components involved in its execution. In particular, a business process may be modeled by using the UML activity, use case and class diagrams. [6]. The UML software model is either recovered by applying reverse engineering techniques or designed by using UML.

2. **Analysis and Semantic Matching.** Syntax and semantic analyses of the terms and descriptions, are used for finding the connections existing between business and software concepts. To this aim, the approach proposed in [8], applying information retrieval techniques is applied. The result is a traceability matrix linking the business activities with the software components supporting its execution.

3. **Alignment Evaluation.** The alignment degree between a business process and supporting software system is measured evaluating the Technological Coverage, measuring at which extent the business process is technologically supported, and Technological Adequacy, evaluating how adequate is the technological support [6].

3   ALBIS Architecture

The ALBIS environment aims at automatically supporting the strategy discussed above. Fig. 1 shows that the ALBIS architecture is composed of three macro-components: Modeling, Traceability Recovering and Alignment Evaluation.

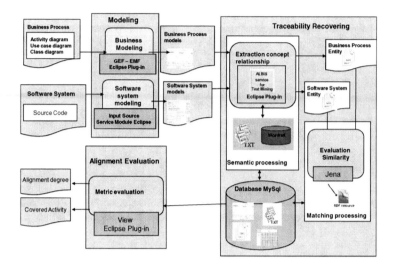

Fig. 1. ALBIS Strategy overview

The figure also shows the technologies used for developing each component. In particular, ALBIS was developed in Java as a plug-in of the Eclipse environment. The Eclipse Modeling Framework – EMF (http://www.eclipse.org/ modeling/emf/), a personalization of the OMG's MOF Object Management Group MetaObject Facility (http://www.omg.org/mof/), was used for its implementation. The Graphical Editing Framework – GEF (http://www.eclipse.org/gef/), was used on the basis of EMF, for creating the modeling components. All the components were developed by using SWT/JFACE , and the MySql Database was used for data storage. The semantic analysis is performed by using the Wordnet Semantic DataBase [7].

The next subsections will give a description of each macro-components.

3.1   ALBIS Modeling

The **ALBIS Modeling** component aims at producing the models of the business process to be analyzed and a software system supporting it. It consists of two main modules: ALBIS Business Modeling and ALBIS Reverse Engineering Modeling. The first module uses the business documentation and process owner's knowledge for defining the business model. It is an Eclipse graphical editor plug-in, developed for extending the UML notation. ALBIS permits the definition of both standard UML diagram, and new diagrams, indicated as ALBIS diagrams and shown in Fig. 2 and Fig. 3, added for representing additional business details [6]. The two figures are referred to the Santaclaus case study, discussed in Section 4. Fig. 2 shows an ALBIS screenshot with a diagram drawing the actors involved in the process activities, and set of operations performed by each activity on the business artifacts. For example, Fig. 2 shows that the Santaclaus business process, involves the actor *Operator* for performing the activity *Selection of goods to donate*. This activity performs operations *index*, *search*, *assignation* and so on, for managing the *Article* artifact. The diagram included in Fig. 3 is automatically elaborated for synthesizing the interaction of each activity with the artifacts during its execution. Specifically, Fig. 3 just shows which activity interacts with which artifacts. For example, the *Selection of goods to donate* activity manages only the artifact *Article*, together with other activities.

ALBIS Reverse Engineering Modeling is the input source service module inherited from Eclipse. If a software system supporting the business process already exists, it receives in input the software system source code and performs reverse engineering activities for obtaining the UML model of the software system. If this operation is not feasible, the system supports to model the software system. The obtained model consists of classes and methods. Both business and software models are represented in XML files and their terms are used in the next Traceability Recovering module.

3.2   ALBIS Traceability Recovering

The ALBIS Traceability Recovering component consists of two main modules: **Semantic Processing** and **Matching Processing** [8]. They are realized by using Java, while XML is used for representing the input Data. The Semantic Analysis uses the Wordnet Database and communication is made between the JENA Semantic Framework API (http://jena.sourceforge.net/), that produces the RDF – Resource Description Framework – descriptor of all the analyzed components. The Semantic Processing consists in the identification of all the relevant business and software terms enriched with semantic information and descriptions. The Matching Processing module evaluates the similarity level existing between the components of each couple of identified business and software terms and selects those couples of terms that are very similar on the basis of Jaccard and Dice similarity measures [9, 10]. The couples of terms that are highly similar indicate business and software concepts interacting in the analysed business process and useful for evaluating the alignment degree. In particular, the **Semantic Processing** regards the extraction of semantic information from both business process model, software system model and source code. The output of this module consists of semantic information regarding both business domain and software components, represented in such a way to permit their automatic processing performed by the next component. The execution of this processing is made of following three independent path:

Path 1 analyses the business process model and its activities, extracts all the identifiers and enriches them of semantic information. In the first step named *Text Processing*, each string is subjected to a text normalization. The *Semantic Enhancement* step aims at improving and completing the description of each business process activity, enhancing it with additional information extracted from a lexical ontology. This path generates a document containing the enhanced description of each business process activity.

Path 2 receives as input the model of the considered software system and performs an analysis for identifying the entities it uses for modeling the business process domain. Then, the software system components are indexed and explored for finding and extracting the reciprocal dependence and use relationships. The business process entities modeled by the software components and list of the related entities, are stored in a document, that will represent a vocabulary for the business process domain, BP vocabulary.

Path 3 receives as input the source code of the considered software system and extracts the list of the sub-components of each software component. A Text Processing of all the components and extracted subcomponents name identifiers follows with the aim of removing the useless parts that are next processed in the Components and Subcomponents indexing. The output of this path is represented by a document containing a normalized index, named map, of software components and subcomponents, Software Entities Index.

The *Matching Processing* looks at the correspondences existing between the business and software information obtained by the previous phases, verifies the similarity between the extracted syntactical and semantic information, and extracts and classifies links between business process activities and software system components. The result of this phase is a traceability matrix highlighting the software components (i.e., classes and methods) potentially used during the execution of each business process activity. The *Matching Processing* includes the following three steps:

Step 1 computes the similarity level existing between the identifiers included in the business enhanced index and those composing the BP Vocabulary. The BP Vocabulary includes the identifiers representing the entities of the business process domain modeled in the software system.

Step 2 computes the similarity level between the identifiers composing the BP Vocabulary and those of the software entities Index, regarding the identifiers extracted from the index document of the software components and subcomponents.

Step 3 analyses the extracted links and related similarity level and merges the intermediate results of the previous steps to obtain a complete map of traceability.

It is worthwhile noticing that the BP vocabulary is just a mean to discover links between business activities and software system components. This link could not be retrieved if a simple syntactical matching criteria is applied directly to the set of initial identifiers composing the business process and software components description. Evaluating the similarity between couples of terms related to business activities and software components identifiers depends on the adopted Information Retrieval – IR – model. The proposed approach uses a vector space IR model, considering the elements of the business process model and software system components organized as vectors in a n-dimensional space, where n is the number of the indexing features, that are identifiers of the entities extracted from the BP Vocabulary. The similarity criteria are used for linking business process activities with software model entities, and software model entities with software source code components. Actually, it is used for computing the product of the probabilities that each identifier contained in an entity node of the BP Vocabulary appears in a business activity name; and, for evaluating the product of the probabilities each identifier in an entity node of the BP Vocabulary is also included in the identifier of a source code components.

The cited probabilities will be referenced in the following as weights. They are computed by using the IR metric called *term frequency–inverse document frequency* (*tf–idf*) [11]. According to this metric, the vector of weights of BP Vocabulary terms over BP activities, w_a, is made of the weights $w_{i,j}$, indicating how much important the *i*-th term of the BP Vocabulary is for the *j*-th activity. It is derived from the *term frequency* measure, $tf_{i,j}$, of the i th term of the BP Vocabulary in the j-th activity, and the *inverse activity frequency, idf_iJ*, of the *i*-th term in the whole set of activities. In the same way, the weights vector of BP Vocabulary terms over software components, $w_k = [w_{i,k}]$, is build by computing the frequency, $tf_{i,k}$, of the *i*-th term of the BP Vocabulary in the *k*-th software component, and the *inverse activity frequency, idf_iK*, of the *i*-th term in the entire set of software components. The term frequency $tf_{i,j}$ is the ratio of the number of occurrences of the i-th word over the total number of terms contained in the A_j activity. The inverse activity frequency idf_{iJ} is defined as follows:

$$idf_{iJ} = \frac{\#\,Activities}{\#\,Activities\_Containing\_Term_i}$$

The vector element w_{ij} (respectively w_{ik}) is represented as: $w_{ij} = tf_{i,j} * log(idf_{iJ})$.

The term $log(idf_{iJ})$ represents a weight of the frequency of an entity identifier in an activity/software component: a higher weight means that an entity identifier is more specific to that activity/software component. We derived that an entity identifier which reaches a weight equal or greater than the established threshold against an activity/software component description can be considered as related to that activity/software component. This evaluation is performed by calculating the Jaccard and Dice similarity measures [9, 10] of each couple of terms and selecting those with a high similarity for defining the Traceability Matrix.

3.3 ALBIS Alignment Evaluation

Albis Alignment Evaluation is developed in Java and presents the outcomes as a View of Eclipse, as shown in Fig. 3. This component evaluates the degree of alignment existing between the analyzed business process and supporting software system. It gets in input the traceability matrix defined by the Traceability Recovering Module and stored in the ALBIS database and calculates the Technological Coverage and Technological Adequacy existing between the two analysed entities. Fig. 3 highlights the outcomes of this component and shows that the evaluation of the two parameters is obtained by analyzing a set of lower level metrics, such as AC, ActorC, ArtfC, ActorA, ArtfA and so on, measuring the technological coverage and adequacy at the level of the business activities, actors and artifacts. A greater detail of the metrics used for the evaluation of the alignment is provided in [6]. The assessment of the alignment parameters helps to identify the business and software components causing a misalignment and requiring the evolution for re-establishing the alignment. In particular, for each metric is displayed the name, a brief description, the numerator and denominator of the mathematical formula and the synthetically value of the metric. It is also possible to visualize the analytical data of each metric.

4 Case study

As an example of the environment application, the software system, named SANTACLAUS, is considered with the business process using it. SANTACLAUS (http://santaclaus.beneslan.it/santaclaus/) is a web application written in PHP and Java.

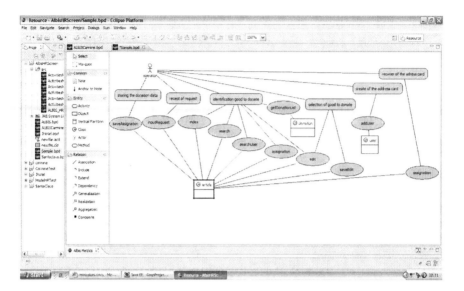

Fig. 2. Example of detailed metric

It was developed for supporting the business process executed by a voluntary association, named Beneslan, to manage object donations for needy children. Fig. 2 and Fig.3 provide some of the diagrams modeling the *goods assignation* business process executed by the voluntary association. For reason of space, the screenshots include just the activities of the business process executed by the *Operator* actor. In particular, the *Operator* executes activities regarding the *receipt of a request*, *identification of good to donate*, *selection of good to donate* and so on. In the models, every activity is linked to an artifact through the operations. For example, Fig. 2 shows that the *Operator* is linked to *selection of good to donate* through the operations *edit* and *saveEdit* of artifact *article*. The diagram of Fig.2 is automatically synthesized into a new model, where the links between actors, activities and classes including the set of operations is depicted. For example, Fig. 3 shows that the activity *Selection of good to donate* is linked to classes *category, donation* and *article*. The analysis of the business process model and software system by using the ALBIS Traceability Recovering, brought to the identification of a set of links existing between these two entities. This analysis permits the restriction of the software components space, while recovering all the software components relevant for each process activity. This was of big help for software maintainers as they did not have to analyze all the software components before identifying the components impacted by the change, but they could consider just a restricted component space.

The found traceability links appeared to be valid. For proving their validity, two widely accepted information retrieval metrics were used, *Recall* and *Precision*. The *Recall* is the percentage of the number of the retrieved relevant software components for the business process activities over the total number of relevant software components for those activities. The *Precision* is the percentage of the number of relevant software components retrieved over the total number of software components retrieved. In the considered context, a software component is relevant for a business activity if it is executed when the activity is performed.

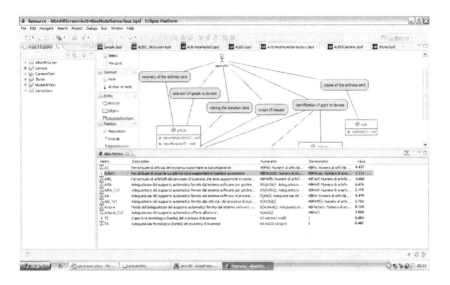

Fig. 3. View of calculed metrics

The evaluation was performed with reference to an oracle that correctly related software components and business activities. The obtained values of the Recall reached the maximum value of 100%, indicating that the tool correctly identified all the relevant software components for each considered business activity. On the contrary, Precision scored lower than the 50%. Showing a high number of retrieved software subcomponents against a lower number of relevant ones. Actually, the automated process found links of the activities with methods not yet implemented. In any case, the results permitted shown that the automatically recovered links could help to cut the whole set of components to be consider in the evolution processes. The automatically identified links were, then, adjusted on the basis of the software engineer knowledge, so that the alignment degree could be evaluated. With this aim, Fig. 3 shows the outcomes of that evaluation. In particular, the Technological Coverage was evaluated 0.465, and Technological Adequacy assumed the value 0.406. This indicated that the business process was not adequately supported by the software system, and some software changes were required. For example, the value of the metrics ActorC and ActorA, regarding the technological coverage and adequacy with reference to the actors, suggested new functionality for including other business process actors in the system.

5   Related Works

Several works deal with the alignment process management in the literature, for easily evaluating and identifying the software components impacted by a business and/or software change. In [5], the authors argue that understanding the code and locating the portion of the code to be changed is a time-consuming process, if the developer does have not the support of automatic tools. Therefore, they present the BPE – Business

Process Explorer – tool integrated in Eclipse. It supports the evolution of a business application, automatically recovers business processes from the User Interface and business logic tier of a business application and establishes the links between the recovered processes and their implementation.

In [3], the alignment between Business and Software Services is considered and the tool "Efficient" is used as automatic support. The presented tool uses an UML activity diagram for representing the choreography of business activities and information exchanged between them, while UML class diagrams are used for representing the structure of this information. The alignment between high-level business specifications and lower-level technological information is debated in [4], where the MDA – Model Driven Architecture – tool is presented. It is developed by using the Eclipse framework for supporting SOD-M – Service-Oriented Development Method.

With reference to the traceability recovering, Antoniol et al. [12] used IR methods for recovering traceability links between software artifacts. They applied and compared the probabilistic and vector space models [12] to recover traceability links between code and documentation in two case studies. The achieved results revealed that the two methods had similar performances when a preliminary morphological analysis (stemming) of the software artifacts is performed. Other authors used enhancing strategies to improve the tracing performance of these basic models. Examples of enhancing strategies for the probabilistic model are hierarchical modeling [13], logical clustering of artifacts [13, 14], semi-automated pruning of the probabilistic network [13, 16], and query term coverage and phrasing [15]. In [17, 18], the authors considered a case studies whose main drawback was the difficulty of comparing the usefulness of different methods and/or tools, and a semantic approach was introduced in [19] for improving the results of the application of a traceability recovery tool in terms of performance metrics applying IR methods.

6   Conclusions

This paper deals with the alignment between business process and software system, and presents the ALBIS supporting environment. It is very important to automatically manage the alignment processes, for easily evaluating its degree and identifying the software components impacted by a business and/or software change. The ALBIS environment supports the management of the alignment between business processes and software systems. Differently from the other tools, ALBIS is a software environment integrating different capabilities, such as modeling, tracing and evaluating. In particular, it allows the formalization of the information regarding business processes and software systems by using a similar notation that permits their direct comparison. Moreover, it applies semantic analysis and information retrieval techniques for automatically recovering the coupling between business and software concepts. Finally, ALBIS uses the extracted information for providing a quantitative evaluation of the alignment degree.

The future work will concern a better investigation of semantic analysis techniques for comparing the   different similarity measure. Moreover, the ALBIS environment will be experimented in different operative contexts.

References

1. Henderson, J.C., Venkatraman, N.: Strategic Alignment: Leveraging information technology for transforming organizations. IBM Systems Journal 32(1), 4–16 (1993)
2. Chan, Y.E., Reich, B.H.: IT alignment: what have we learned? Journal of Information Technology 22, 297–315 (2007)
3. Ramel, S., Grandry, E., Dubois, E.: Towards a Design Method Supporting the Alignment between Business and Software Services. In: Proc. of the 33rd Annual IEEE International Computer Software and Applications Conference, Compsac 2009, pp. 349–354. IEEE Press, New York (2009)
4. De Castro, V., Marcos, E., Vara, J.M.: Applying CIM-to-PIM model transformations for the service-oriented development of information systems. Information and Software Technology 53(1), 87–105 (2011)
5. Zou, V., Guo, E.J., Foo, K.C., Hung, M.: Recovering business processes from business applications. Journal of Software Maintenance and Evolution: Research and Practice 21(5), 315–348 (2009)
6. Aversano, L., Grasso, C., Tortorella, M.: Measuring the Alignment between Business Processes and Software Systems: a Case Study. In: SAC 2010, pp. 2330–2336. ACM, New York (2010)
7. Pedersen, T., Patwardhan, S., Jason, M.: WordNet:Similarity - Measuring the Relatedness of Concepts. In: Proc. HLT-NAACL—Demonstrations, pp. 1024–1025 (2004)
8. Aversano, L., Marulli, F., Tortorella, M.: Recovering Traceability Links between Business Activities and Software Components. In: Quintela Varajão, J.E., Cruz-Cunha, M.M., Putnik, G.D., Trigo, A. (eds.) CENTERIS 2010, Part I. CCIS, vol. 109, pp. 385–394. Springer, Heidelberg (2010)
9. Tan, P.N., Steinbach, M., Kumar, V.: Introduction to Data Mining. Pearson, London (2005)
10. Rijsbergen, V., Joost, C.: Information Retrieval. Butterworths, London (1979), http://www.dcs.gla.ac.uk/Keith/Preface.html ISBN 3642122744
11. Salton, G., McGill, M.J.: Introduction to modern information retrieval. McGraw-Hill, New York (1983)
12. Antoniol, G., Canfora, G., Casazza, G., De Lucia, A., Merlo, E.: Recovering Traceability Links between code and documentation. IEEE Transactions on Software Engineering 28(10), 970–983 (2002)
13. Cleland-Huang, J., Settimi, R., Duan, C., Zou, X.: Utilizing Supporting Evidence to Improve Dynamic Requirements Traceability. In: Proc. of 13th IEEE Int. Requirements Engineering Conference, pp. 135–144. IEEE Press, New York (2005)
14. Duan, C., Cleland-Huang, J.: Clustering Support for Automated Tracing. In: Proc. Of 22nd IEEE/ACM International Conference on Automated Software Engineering, pp. 244–253. ACM Press, New York (2007)
15. Zou, X., Settimi, R., Cleland-Huang, J.: Term-based enhancement factors for improving automated requirement trace retrieval. In: Proc. of Int. Symposium on Grand Challenges in Traceability, pp. 40–45. ACM Press, New York (2007)
16. Hayes, J.H., Dekhtyar, A., Osborne, J.: Improving Requirements Tracing via Information Retrieval. In: Proc. of 11th IEEE Int. Requirements Engineering Conference, pp. 138–147. IEEE Press, New York (2003)
17. De Lucia, A., Oliveto, R., Tortora, G.: IR-based Traceability Recovery Processes: an Empirical Comparison of "One-Shot" and Incremental Processes. In: Proc. of 23rd IEEE/ACM Int. Conference on Automated Software Engineering, pp. 39–48. ACM Press, New York (2008)

18. De Lucia, A., Fasano, F., Oliveto, R., Tortora, G.: Recovering Traceability Links in Software Artifact Management Systems using Information Retrieval Methods. ACM Transactions on Software Engineering and Methodology 16(4) (2007)

19. Marcus, A., Maletic, J.I.: Recovering Documentation to Source-Code Traceability Links Using Latent Semantic Indexing. In: Proc. of ICSE 2003, pp. 125–135. IEEE Press, New York (2003)

20. Reich, B., Benbasat, I.: Factors that Influence the Social Dimension of Alignment Between Business and Information Technology objectives. MIS Quarterly 24(1) (2000)

Challenges of Teams Management: Using Agile Methods to Solve the Common Problems

Mariana de Azevedo Santos, Paulo Henrique de Souza Bermejo,
Adriano Olímpio Tonelli, and André Luiz Zambalde

Computer Science Department – Federal University of Lavras (DCC/UFLA)
DCC - Department of Computer Science
P.O. Box 3037 - Campus da UFLA 37200-000 - Lavras (MG) - Brazil
mariana@bsi.ufla.br, {bermejo,zamba}@dcc.ufla.br,
adrianotonelli@gmail.com,

Abstract. The software development using dynamic and creative teams has become a strategic advantage to improving the performance of software projects. Faced with the problems noted on team management, organizations are seeking less expensive solutions and suitable for the rapidly changing market requirements. The present study aims to identify these challenges related to the management team on software projects and evaluate which and how these challenges can be addressed by promoting continuous improvement of the management of organizations. The adoption of Scrum practices in the studied project proved to be a positive solution, providing greater scalability in terms of manageability and development projects of the organization.

Keywords: Management of teams, enterprise software development, agile method, Scrum.

1 Introduction

The appropriate management and selection of teams is a crucial factor in the success of software development projects.

This idea is complemented by Sommerville [1], stating that people are the intellectual property of an organization and its effective management is likely to ensure a positive return on organization investments.

One of the major challenges being faced in managing a team is that they are often consist of people who barely know each other, never worked together, have no knowledge about the project, neither about the methodology used [3, 4].

Conflicts even bigger arise due to the differences in objectives that may be caused by disagreements on fundamental parts of the project as meeting the schedule, sequencing of project priorities, balancing opinions on technical level, the estimated costs and interpersonal differences [4].

According to Heldman [3], these conflicts can be resolved with the creation of effective teams, teams that are energetic, mature, dynamic and enthusiastic self-sufficient, and that generate creativity and resolve project problems.

M.M. Cruz-Cunha et al. (Eds.): CENTERIS 2011, Part II, CCIS 220, pp. 297–305, 2011.

The IT organizations, eager to reach the stage of implementation and maturity of their development teams, have sought solutions on agile software management to create management enterprise softwares with quality, speed, transparency and flexibility, especially in the Scrum methodology [5].

Agile methods are a group of development and management practices, which were consolidated in 2001 and emphasize principles associated with communication, objectivity, and greater focus on customer interaction in order to provide flexibility and efficiency in development [6].

The Scrum method proposes a multi-functional development team should have a maximum of 10 members to become more effective [7]. This characteristic tends to quickly increase the development process, aligned of the technical skills with the company goals, creating a culture of value between the client and development team and achieve stability in team communication during the project [8-10].

Considering the importance of management of teams in software projects as mentioned and the assumption that agile practices can help to treat the difficulties in managing teams in software projects, this work has the following research question: what and how are addressed the challenges related to management teams on software projects?

The present study aims to identify these challenges related to the management of teams on software projects and evaluate which and how these challenges can be addressed to promoting continuous improvement of the management of organizations.

2 Methodology

The approach of the research problem is defined as qualitative with exploratory objective.

An exploratory research is particularly useful when one has little information and there is a need for deep surveys about a particular process or phenomenon [11].

According to Jung [12], the case study is an important tool for researchers and aims to understand "how" and "why" the "things" work.

From the perspective of technical procedures, the research used multiple case studies were evaluated in three separate projects in two software development companies. There are three reasons why the case studies are a viable strategy for research in information systems areas [13, 14]:

- The researcher can study the field of information systems in a natural environment, learn about the state of the art and generate theories from practice.
- The case method allows researchers to answer questions on techniques and motivations, that is, understand the nature and complexity of ongoing processes.
- Questions that prompt the way the developed processes are critical for researchers to continue with their arguments.

For this purpose, the use of a qualitative approach fits the research proposal that aims to analyze how the agile method Scrum allows developers to self-organize into high performance teams of enterprise software development.

The first stage of the research is characterized by a literature review. A comprehensive literature review can be helpful for better understanding of an issue to be investigated [11]. In that sense, this phase aims at raising: (i) problems and challenges encountered in managing teams in software projects, and (ii) the practices described in the literature to address the barriers faced by a query in 5 databases accessed via a Brazilian portal of search (journals portal) from CAPES - Brazilian Agency for Support and Development of Researches.

To identifying the challenges related to management teams in software projects were found seven articles, which culminated on 13 issues related to management of teams.

The second stage of the research consisted of a review of the literature on agile methodologies which have been pre-selected a group of practices that are presented as possible solutions to problems and challenges raised in the previous step.

The application of these practices has been investigated by performing a case study in three teams of two organizations of software development.

3   Results

Based on this investigation we obtained a list of common problems and challenges faced by these teams, proceeded by the identification and implementation of solutions pre-selected in the literature review for handling the problems and challenges in the teams studied.

With this application had been possible proceeded with an analysis on the efficiency and effectiveness of these solutions are most appropriate to the problems and faced challenges.

We now describe the cases studies, describe the teams behavior without Scrum implementation and the results forwarded of the Scrum practices application.

3.1   Organization A

The organization studied is a software development laboratory, with emphasis on forestry area, which they produced solutions for the public environmental sectors of the government.

The software project was a software inventory on of industrial wastes. Initially, the team analyzed used the methodology development cascade, which is a classical approach, systematic and sequential, beginning on the customer requirements specification, project planning, modeling, development and deployment of software and culminating in the ongoing maintenance of software [1], using as support some concepts of project management PMBOK [15], which is a reference guide which contain a set of best practices to managing projects.

The manager reported that the project was 60% complete and the requirements are not completed at all. Moreover, the team communication it's bad, which makes the estimate tasks of the teams a failure point.

So, in an attempt to complete the project, has started implementation of Scrum with a basic training of the team. In this phase of deployment, according to the Product Owner of the project, the increments started to be more successful, with minimum exceeded in the tasks estimated.

3.2 Organization B

This organization studied is a software development laboratory, with emphasis on IT governance area, which provides enterprises solutions for public and private organizations.

The first team analyzed on the Organization B, Team A, is composed of seven members: three analysts developers, a project leader, a graphic designer and a business analyst. Currently this team is fully involved in a software project to develop a product for management of enterprise performance to a public sector organization based on the concept of strategic management tool Balanced Scorecard.

The software project already existed in the laboratory and already been implemented without success and with many errors. Thus, the organization proposed a restructuring of the project, and building a new development team and using the Scrum methodology to manage the project process.

For being a newly formed team, the first challenge faced by the team was a the reengineering for designing the new goals previously developed seeking the rules of Scrum. The team was charged with studying the old system, along with project leader, to propose a new architecture and design standards, appropriate to the needs of new customer and ensuring software quality.

The faced problems were related to this first contact of team with the methodology and their difficulty of leaving old concepts. The project leader reported the difficulty of covering many roles inside the project and those even possessing well-defined schedules to alter functions, it ends up affecting productivity. The team's lack of experience implies the variations suffered on estimates task completion times.

Another important topic that was brought up by the IT chief was the difficulty of demanding the daily duties from the staff, because he travels very often, and this makes it harder to monitor the team's practices and values.

We can characterize this team on stage of training and confrontation, where the team members are aware of project objectives and initiate actions to gain position and control of the project functions [2].

The second team analyzed in the Organization B, Team B, is composed of five members: two analysts developers, a project leader, a graphic designer and a business analyst. Currently this team is involved in a software project to develop a plugin for the management of enterprise performance software, where the high management could be evaluates the business plan using strategic management concepts of Balanced Scorecard.

The Team B is a newly formed team too, and, the challenge faced by the team was studying the new system developed by Team A and suit the new demands in the software. The project leader on this project is the same person of the Team A and proposed the architecture and design standards similar to the first project, which will be integrate with the original software.

The most faced problems on this project were related with lack of experiences of the team, compounded by the reported disagreement about in relation to the design specifications and performance, once with the software of the Team A still are in implementation and the scope of the project still suffers with the many changes.

3.3   Problems and Challenges Verified in Teams

According to performed the literature review, Table 1 illustrates the main problems and challenges found in management of teams.

Table 1. Problems verified in management of teams on the literature review

Problems and challenges verified in management of teams	References
Disagreements over the project schedule	Valeriano (1998); Phillips (2003).
Disagreement about the sequence of project priorities	Heldman (2005).
Conflicts in relation to the formation of teams	Tellioglu & Wagner (1997); Heldman (2005)
Conflicts over the cost estimate	Valeriano (1998); Heldman (2005).
Lack of motivation of members	Heldman (2005); Fan (2010).
Insatisfaction about the job or role in the project	Tohidi (2010); Fan (2010).
Extensive meetings and misguided	Heldman (2005).
Disagreements in relation to the design specifications and performance	Valeriano (1998); Phillips (2003); Pressman (2005); Tohidi (2010)
Lack of trust and leadership of project manager	Sarin & McDermott (2003); Fan (2010)
Conflicts about the management style	Linden & Parker (1998); Valeriano (1998); Heldman (2005)
Ineffective communication	Heldman (2005); Bstieler & Hemmert (2010); Fan (2010)
Inappropriate workplace environment	Heldman (2005); Tohidi (2010)
Interpersonal differences between the team	Bstieler & Hemmert (2010)

Based on the problems and challenges raised in the literature, described in the methodology section, in this section analyses what these problems and challenges listed could be found in the teams studied.

Table 2 illustrates the main difficulties faced by the team investigated, the group of problems and challenges found in literature review along with agile practices associated with the solution of these difficulties.

Table 2. Problems verified on the case study and the agile practices suggest to solving the problems

Problems and challenges in management of software teams	Related problems listed in the literature	Agile practices to solve the problems and challenges in management of teams
Requirements and project scope changing constantly	Disagreements in relation to the design specifications and performance Disagreements over the project schedule	Adoption of an Agile methodology (Scrum).
IT Chief had difficulties in managing the team and their results	Conflicts about the management style Ineffective communication	Formation of a small team, with self-managed behavior, led by a Scrum Master.
Lack of control and order in performing crucial tasks to the project	Disagreement about the sequence of project priorities Disagreements over the project schedule	With incremental development, the team define together with the stakeholders, the priorities specified in the Sprint (working cycle), documented in the Sprint Backlog.
Lack of control on the estimation task	Disagreements in relation to the design specifications and performance Disagreements over the project schedule	Use of Kanban and estimation of tasks arranged in an Excel spreadsheet to keep track of items Backlog (task list).

4   Discussion

Faced with problems noted on team's management, organizations are seeking less expensive and suitable solutions for the rapidly changing requirements on market [5].

Agile methodologies, particularly Scrum, have attracted the attention of companies that develop software for its flexibility, adaptability and effectiveness.

The Agile manifesto considers two important points for a good performance of managed team's by the agile philosophy [6]:

- Build projects around motivated people, providing a good working environment, support in addressing their needs and confidence in their work. When you have a self-organized team, they pass confidence to the leader and project manager, and they inspire the same confidence to the team.

- The most efficient and effective way to pass information to a development team is talking face to face. The best way to understand the business is discussing with the team. When these meetings happen more frequently are easier to understand what the customer expects the deal to avoid unnecessary gaps and implementations.

The Scrum practices as planning and the daily meetings are intended to reduce the difficulty of understanding the client on what is developed and, for developers helps in better defining the scope of work and estimating tasks [16].

In the studies of Ilieva et al. (2004), Svensson & Host (2005), Sillitti et al. (2005), Mann & Maurer (2005) reported that the adoption of Scrum methodology helps to simplify communication with the rest of the company, the development of professional and interpersonal skills of staff, reduction of cost overruns, provides a more flexible and objective documentation and maintenance a more satisfying relationship with the client [16-19].

The biggest challenge facing the projects was that little disciplinary team to meet the principles of Scrum. The most difficult aspect was to motivate them to actively participate in meetings, properly update the Kanban and commitment to the releases. The training on the methodology is valid, but the charging for these practices being sedimented must be constant.

However, the engagement in practices and agile principles was a positive decision by the organization, which left the stage ad-hoc, where their cases were not properly designed because of the time and the client's needs, promoting greater scalability in terms of capacity management and project development of the organization.

Schwaber and Beedle, the methodology co-creators, says that Scrum exposes dysfunctions of the development practices and the product so that these can be corrected [16]. With a list of problems and challenges encountered in management of teams, aligned the adoption of Scrum, it is expected that the team reach the norming, and performing stage, where the team is productive, efficient and effective.

5   Conclusion

Developing strong teams, agile and effective on problem solving is the key to successful project management. Considering the importance of management of teams in software projects, the discovery of the main problems and solve them directly contributes to the improvement of process performance management and development of software products.

The purpose of this study was to identify challenges related to the management of teams on software projects and evaluate how these challenges can be addressed to promoting continuous improvement of the management process of organizations.

The Scrum practices adopted in the project proved to be a positive solution, since it promoted maturity in their processes, control of time and priorities, improving the technical and interpersonal skills of the team, encouraging greater scalability in terms of manageability and development projects of the organization.

Thus, it is expected that research will guide practitioners in the management of software projects and organizations to identify which problems can be tackled and what possible solutions recommended in front of the main challenges in software development.

In terms of theory and science, this work contributes to classification of the most commons problems in management of teams reported in studies in the IT area.

This article has given a first analysis of the problems and challenges of management of teams which could be solve by using agile methods principles.

Because the sample size limited the study, we plan to expand our data with survey responses about agile methods practices, finding difficulties not mentioned in literature review, based of market experiences.

6 Future Work

Thus, it is expected that with the increase of the samples, we can turn the research on a quantitative research to identify that problems can be tackled and what are possible solutions with other agile methods.

Acknowledgments We would like to thank the Fundação de Amparo à Pesquisa do Estado de Minas Gerais (FAPEMIG) and the Conselho Nacional de Desenvolvimento Científico e Tecnológico (CNPq), which provided support for the work in this paper.

References

1. Sommerville, I.: Engenharia de Software. Pearson, 8ª edição (2006)
2. Phillips, J.: Gerência de projetos de tecnologia de informação. Editora Campus (2003)
3. Heldman, K.: Gerência de Projetos PMP- Project Management Professional. Editora Campus (2005)
4. Valeriano, D.: Gerência em projetos. Makron Books (1998)
5. Santos, M.A., Greghi, J.G., Bermejo, P.H.S.: The Impact of Scrum in Software Development: A Case Study using SWOT Analysis. INFOCOMP Journal of Computer Science. Special 2, 65–71 (2010)
6. Beck, et al.: The Agile Manifesto (2001), http://www.agilealliance.org/the-alliance/the-agile-manifesto/ (accessed in: 01/06/11)
7. Rising, L., Janoff, N.S.: The Scrum Software Development Process for Small Teams. IEEE Software 17(4), 11–13 (2000)
8. Schwaber, K.: Agile Project Management with Scrum. Microsoft Press (2004)
9. Ceschi, M., Sillitti, A., Succi, G., De Panfilis, S.: Project Management in Plan-Based and Agile Companies. IEEE Software 22(3), 21–27 (2005)
10. Marchenko, A., Abrahamsson, P.: Scrum in a Multiproject Environment: An Ethnographically-Inspired Case Study on the Adoption Challenges. In: Proceedings of the Agile 2008 (AGILE 2008), pp. 15–26. IEEE Computer Society, Washington, DC, USA (2008)
11. Hair Jr., J.F., Black, W., Babin, B.J., Anderson, R.E.: Multivariate Data Analysis, 7th edn. Prentice-Hall, Englewood Cliffs (2009)
12. Jung, C.F.: Metodologia para pesquisa & desenvolvimento aplicada a novas tecnologias, produtos e processos, vol. xvi, p. 312. Axcel Books, Rio de Janeiro (2004)

13. Benbasat, I., Goldstein, D.K., Mead, M.: The Case Research Strategy in Studies of Information Systems. MIS Quarterly (11;3), 369–386 (1987)
14. Yin, R.K.: Estudo de caso: planejamento e métodos, 4th edn. Bookman, Porto Alegre (2010)
15. PMBOK. A Guide to the Project Management Body of Knowledge, 4th edn., Project Management Institute (2008)
16. Schwaber, K., Beedle, M.: Agile Software Development with Scrum. Prentice Hall, Englewood Cliffs (2002)
17. Ilieva, S., Ivanov, P., Stefanova, E.: Analyses of an agile methodology implementation. In: Proceedings 30th Euromicro Conference, pp. 326–333. IEEE Computer Society Press, Los Alamitos (2004)
18. Svensson, H., Höst, M.: Views from an organization on how agile development affects its collaboration with a software development team. In: Bomarius, F., Komi-Sirviö, S. (eds.) PROFES 2005. LNCS, vol. 3547, pp. 487–501. Springer, Heidelberg (2005)
19. Sillitti, A., Ceschi, M., Russo, B., Succi, G.: Managing uncertainty in requirements: a survey in documentation-driven and agile companies. In: Proceedings of the 11th International Software Metrics Symposium, METRICS (2005)
20. Mann, C., Maurer, F.: A case study on the impact of scrum on overtime and customer satisfaction. In: Agile Development Conference, pp. 70–79. IEEE Computer Society, Los Alamitos (2005)
21. Tellioglu, H., Wagner, I.: Negotiating Boundaries: Configuration Management in Software Development Teams. Computer Supported Cooperative Work: The Journal of Collaborative Computing 6, 251–274 (1997)
22. Tohidi, H.: Human resources management main role in information technology project management. Elsevier, Procedia Computer Science 3, 925–929 (2011)
23. Fan, D.: Analysis of Critical Success Factors in IT Project Management. In: Proceedings of 2nd International Conference on Industrial and Information Systems (2010)
24. Pressman, R.S.: Engenharia de software, 6th edn., vol. xxxi, p. 720. McGraw-Hill, New York (2006)
25. Sarin, S., McDermott, C.: The Effect of Team Leader Characteristics on Learning, Knowledge Application, and Performance of Cross-Functional New Product Development Teams. Decision Sciences 34(4) (2003)
26. der Linden, G.V., Parker, P.: On paradoxes between human resources management, postmodernism, and HR information systems. Accounting, Management & Information Technology 8, 265–282 (1998)
27. Bstieler, L., Hemmert, M.: Increasing Learning and Time Efficiency in Interorganizational New Product Development Teams. Journal of Product Development & Management Association 27, 485–499 (2010)

Risk Management Model in ITIL

Sarah Vilarinho and Miguel Mira da Silva

Instituto Superior Técnico, Av. Rovisco Pais, 1
1049-001 Lisbon, Portugal
{sarah.vila-real,mms}@ist.utl.com

Abstract. ITIL is considered a framework of Best Practice guidance for IT Service Management and it is widely used in the business world. In spite of this, ITIL has some gaps in Risk Management specification. This paper approaches this problem in ITIL and compares IT risk management in ITIL to other IT Governance Frameworks. Despite ITIL stating that risk should be identified, measured and mitigated, it is not clear on how to proceed (no concrete process is defined on how to deal with risk). To solve this, we propose to map the M_o_R risk management framework in ITIL, mapping every M_o_R process in ITIL, therefore adopting a strong risk management in ITIL, based on concrete guidelines, without changing the framework. Here in this paper we will summarize the necessary guidelines. Finally, we will show a planning for future work.

Keywords: risk management, ITIL, M_o_ R, IT governance frameworks.

1 Introduction

Nowadays, managers need to balance risk and control their business in an often unpredictable IT environment, so fitting risk management in organizations can be a real challenge. The standards can offer a control sensation. For that reason, it is important to implement the frameworks according to the organization's goals and integrate all business elements.

IT Governance is one of the most important classes of frameworks in the IT Business and it is supposed to support management in order to aid the organization in achieving its goals and preventing or detecting undesired events. Some of these frameworks have an IT risk management component in their implementation but this process is sometimes an abstract and unclear one. The ITIL framework, despite stating that risk should be identified, measured and mitigated, does not clarify what concrete method is to be used in dealing with risk. The one million dollar question is: How does best-practice risk management relate to best-practice corporate governance? [1]

In any IT Governance Framework, one expects to find a set of risk management guidelines to deal with the organization's opportunities and threats. In the COBIT framework, for instance, there is a strong risk management component that is based on the control of all organizational processes.

The ITIL IT Governance framework is a less comprehensive one. The risk management component is implicit in the process but in a very abstract, unobvious way and not as specified as desired in the actual business scenario.

M.M. Cruz-Cunha et al. (Eds.): CENTERIS 2011, Part II, CCIS 220, pp. 306–314, 2011.
© Springer-Verlag Berlin Heidelberg 2011

In this paper we will first address the risk management in ITIL problem in section 2; then, we will compare it with risk management in other IT Governance Frameworks and analyze the current proposals for implementing risk management in ITIL in the related work section (section 3). In sections 4 and 5 we will examine the mapping of M_o_R in ITIL and how to implement it. At last, in section 6 we will conclude and propose some future work.

2 Problem

All organizations want some standards that alert their clients to the organization's quality processes. In the case of risk management and IT Governance we have the ISO 31000 and 20000. To implement ISO 20000, ITIL is usually the option. However, risk management is not clearly shown because there is not an obvious way to implement risk management in ITIL.

Despite risk management being referenced in some of the ITIL books [2], mainly in Operation [3] and Continual Service improvement [4], **this approach is not explained enough for the organizations to implement risk management without following specialized guidelines for it**.

So an issue comes up:

> How to adopt a strong risk management in ITIL, in an integrated, effective and efficient way, without changing the framework, so that organizations do not have to use another mechanism for risk management?

3 Related Work

History tells us that many fatal IT risks in organizations are associated to business strategies. For this reason it is not really possible to separate best-practice risk management from best-practice IT governance [1]. There are some IT governance frameworks that have a very strong risk management component, such as COBIT and OCTAVE [5], and, despite ITIL not having a very clear risk management approach, some ITIL processes obviously incorporate it.

IT Governance

There are a lot of frameworks that implement IT Governance. One of the most well-known is COBIT.

The COBIT framework is a process model subdivided into 4 domains (applications, information, infrastructure, and people) and 34 processes aligned with the responsibility areas of planning, building, running and monitoring, providing an end-to-end view of IT [5]. The goal of COBIT is to ensure that business objectives are achieved and undesired events are prevented or detected and corrected.

Despite using a different vocabulary, ITIL and COBIT cover the same problem. It is only for Incident Management in ITIL that there is no equivalent in COBIT. While ITIL is stronger in strategy, plans and processes, COBIT has advantages in the specification of metrics benchmarks and audits. In addition, COBIT uses ISO/IEC27002 to address security issues so as to mitigate risk and specifies how to act against risk [6].

ITIL is considered the best practices in IT Governance but, in fact, this framework has been developed throughout the years. In May 2007, following a major refresh project, ITIL version 3 was published. The new version gives recognition to the idea that delivering IT services can be considered of strategic value to a business. ITIL Version 3 highlights the importance of managing corporate risk and the Service Strategy publication includes information on strategic risks across the ITIL service lifecycle [7].

Risk and ITIL

ITIL Version 3 highlights the importance of managing corporate risk. While the Service Strategy [2] and Continual Service Improvement [4] books define what risk and risk management are, the Service Operation [3] book defines how risk is integrated in ITIL. Nevertheless, there is a gap in the definition of risk in ITIL: the lack of a concrete process to deal with risk [8] [9].

In the Continual Service Improvement book there is an attempt to clarify what is risk management in ITIL. According to this publication, risk management should take place during the design and transition stages of the service lifecycle. Yet, in this book, it is held that a good Continual Service Improvement (CSI) programme will assess the results of Risk Management activities and identify service improvements through risk mitigation, elimination and management. In order to achieve this they suggest the use of a SWOT analysis. One thing that all related work has in common, is the focus on the definition of mitigation strategies for risks and the identification of the best ways to overcome the challenges that an organization may encounter. Knowing the critical success factors before undertaking CSI implementation will help manage the risks and challenges.

In the Service Operation book every activity has a sub-section with some well-known risks (Section Challenges, Critical Success Factors and Risks Subsection risk).

Besides the ITIL Books there are some publications from OGC that deal with Risk and ITIL. According to OGC [7] 5 main ITIL processes have the risk management covered. Below there is a table with a summary of OGC descriptions about the risk management coverage and a column on criticism about it.

Table 1. Risk management coverage according to OGC and critical analysis

Process	*OGC*	*Critical Analysis*
Problem Management	There is a proactive and reactive management, with the goal of reducing the impact of service outages	They do not specify how the actions to do (e. g. disaster covered plan) are predicted and implemented
Change Management	Good change management techniques and approach help reducing risks, minimize the potential negative impact of change, and reduce the risk of an undesirable outcome	What techniques and approaches should be implemented? [9] They do not say a specific one

Table 1. (*continued*)

Service Delivery	Services must be maintained, so it is important to have a careful design	Besides the careful design, how to maintain service delivery must be specified as well as plans to recover from threats
Availability Management	Focuses on reliability and on how to put in place alternative options to ensure service availability	
IT service Continuity	Assesses risk to ensure overall continuity for the business	They do not specify how to implement risk management across all modules

In the Wickboldt article [9] they propose an representation model in order to obtain feedback from the execution of changes over an IT Infrastructure in which the process of record changes should be automated.

On the one hand, risk analysis would allow human operation to be more precise and quick and to react more efficiently, but, on the other hand, the change management is just a part of the risk management gap in ITIL and it is not possible to automatize all the process.

4 Proposal

Our proposal is to integrate M_o_R with ITIL.We choose M_o_R for this mapping because, besides the obvious common origin with ITIL (OGC framework), M_o_R considers risk from different perspectives within an organization: strategic, programme, project and operational. While it links to other OGC Best Practices, such as ITIL, it respects the roles, responsibilities and terminologies used outside the fields of programme and project management [10]. Actually, despite M_o_R being intuitively the risk management framework in ITIL, nothing is explicitly said in the ITIL books.

M_o_R is based on 4 concepts [11]:

- **Principles** – the best principles based on corporate governance principles
- **Approach** – the approach for the implementation of the principles
- **Processes** – describe the inputs, outputs and all the workflows of the organization in the risk management processes (identifying risks, assessing and controlling them)
- **Embedding and reviewing M_o_R** – incorporate in the organization its principles, using specific approaches and processes

The most desirable option would be to map M_o_R in ITIL, relating the M_o_R processes to the ITIL ones. It is preferable to have all M_o_R processes integrated in ITIL, for an organization could then be capable of using this conceptualization to implement risk management without another mechanism.

The following conceptual map outlines the desired integration between ITIL and M_o_R.

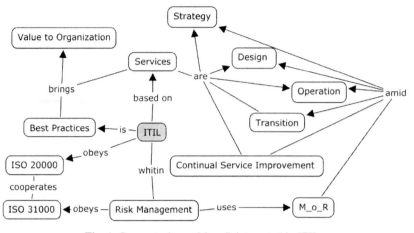

Fig. 1. Conceptual map M_o_R integrated in ITIL

The principles of M_o_R must be integrated in the ITIL Strategy and Design Module. These guidelines should be followed according to ISO 20000.

All ITIL modules should be linked at least to 1 of 4 M_o_R perspectives (Strategy, Project, Program, and Operation) and 1 of M_o_R Concepts (principles, approach, process and review and embedding).

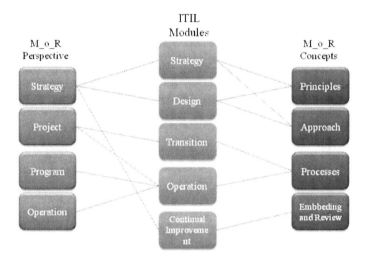

Fig. 2. Main relationship between M_o_R concepts, Perspectives and ITIL

The implementation of the principles must vary from organization to organization. The sequence in which an organization adopts the principles depends on how long it has been established, its size, organization structure, management culture and current_risk maturity. Nonetheless, in this approach, the main concerns must be policy communication, strategy (what the organization's goals are and how risk management will help achieve them), documentation of the organizational process, according to ITIL polices, and the maintenance of a satisfying service level.

For the implementation, we suggest that risk management in IT must be done in accordance with the risk management main processes: identify risk, assess, plan and implement. All of the M_o_R processes must be mapped in the ITIL processes so that the organization does not have any unmapped M_o_R process.

During this, it is important to identify the inputs, outputs and the organization's main activities. For this, we recommend the use of standard documentation to help the process.

The ITIL policy has risk management embedded in the process so this is a common point between ITIL and M_o_R and it is easily implemented. Nevertheless, it is important to prepare the organization for it and for identifying and describing the benefits that need to be accomplished and how the effectiveness will be measured. These should be defined in advance and continuously assessed to determine whether these benefits are being delivered as part of the programme. Risk management review should include regular assessments on the development of awareness and understanding within the organization.

5 Implementation

The implementation of risk management in ITIL must follow the Modules sequence: Principles, Approach, Processes, and Embedding and Reviewing.

Principles

In accordance to ISO31000, there are 8 principles [11]. In ITIL we propose their application as follows:

- **Aligns with objectives:** The threatening situations must be documented, measured (mathematically and based on previous experiences) and analyzed by risk experts that have the organization's goals in mind.
- **Fits the context:** For this analysis we need experts and a well-documented process. Some risk management tools can be used such as surveys and observations of the business environment, depending on the organization.
- **Engages stakeholders:** Adopt appropriate level and style of communication which can be created by standard documentation, like common communication channels or through the use of ITIL tools (Easyvista, HP ITIL software, CA, etc.).
- **Provides clear guidance:** ITIL processes must be communicated according to the 4 perspectives of M_o_R, helping the different stakeholders to deal with them.
- **Informs decision-making:** Risk management must influence every decision. The identified risks should influence the decision-making process.
- **Facilitates continual improvement:** Uses historical data and facilitates learning and continual improvement by collecting incidents and requesting statistics of identified errors and their impact.
- **Creates a supportive culture:** Risk must be understood and recognized by the organization's members.
- **Achieves measurable value:** Measurable techniques, like KPIs or KRIs,[1] can be used.

---

[1] KPI - *Key Performance Indicator.*
  KRI - *Key Risk Indicator.*

Below, we can see the corresponding principles and its related modules in ITIL.

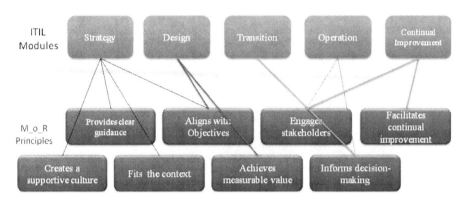

Fig. 3. Relationship between ITIL Modules and M_o_R principles

Approach

As previously mentioned, the approach will vary from organization to organization, according to size, policy and the organization's plans, but it will always be based on M_o_R principles. These principles will be supported by the creation of a set of documentation, comprising: risk management, risk management process guide, and risk management strategies for each organization. Documentation of all processes is fundamental. The plan must be implemented in the ITIL Strategy module and must describe the process sequence, metrics, plan communication and the standard documentation, such as records (Risk register, Issue register), plans (risk improvement plan, risk communication plan, and risk response plan) and reports.

Below we present a relationship between documents and the ITIL modules.

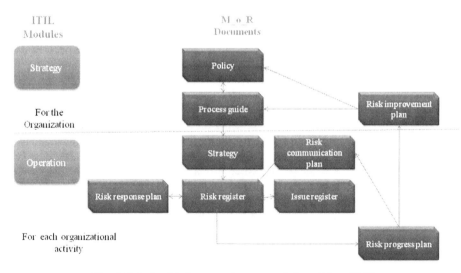

Fig. 4. Relationship between documents (adapted from [11])

Processes

During the implementation, it is important to map all M_o_R processes in the ITIL framework in order to guarantee that no M_o_R process is missing.

This is composed by 4 steps: **identify risk, assess, plan** and **implement** the ITIL process. These must be carried out in sequence since no step can be undertaken until the preceding one has been completed according to ISO31000 standards. The process can be revisited as a cycle (several times).

Besides **identifying** risk in ITIL process, it is important to identify risk based on SLA, incidents, requested statistics and experts experience and organization's goals. We can achieve this by using stakeholder analysis, PESTLE analysis, SWOT analysis, horizontal scanning or by defining the probability impact grid [11].

During the **assessment** an estimation of goals, inputs, outputs, techniques and tasks must be carried out. All these activities must be evaluated according to the organization's goals and the best practices of ISO20000.

In the **planning** step, the goal is to prepare specific management responses to the identified threats and opportunities, ensuring that the staff is not taken by surprise if a risk becomes a problem.

The last step, **implementation**, must ensure that the prearranged risk management actions are implemented and monitored according to their effectiveness and that corrective actions are taken when responses do not match expectations. All ITIL processes must have this implementation ideal. Furthermore, these operations are made in the Operation module in parallel with the processes of implementation

Embedding and Review

Embedding risk management must be done in parallel with ITIL continual service improvement module and we must start with the M_o_R principles in mind. The values must be presented and communicated to stakeholders throughout all processes. Regular assessment on the development of awareness and understanding within the organization must be made. All M_o_R processes have to be present in ITIL processes.

6   Conclusion

In ITIL there are some clues about how to implement risk management across the framework and about the tools and the already known risks. However, the information in the ITIL Library is still unsatisfactory and compared to other IT governance frameworks, ITIL is weak in the risk management field.

Despite M_o_R being a reference, it is unclear if this is the official way to treat risk in ITIL and how to implement this risk management framework in it. The tool list for risk assessment is not complete and the information is too vague.

The best option would be to map the ITIL processes in the M_o_R processes in order to have a strong risk management approach in the organization and avoiding missing any process in risk management. For future work, it is important to develop a model with the mapping of M_o_R in ITIL and to clarify the techniques, tools, and metrics to use within all processes. To validate this new "model", it is important to make a comparison with other guidelines involving ITIL, other IT governance frameworks and/or to validate it with experts in ITIL and Risk Management.

References

1. Crouhy, M., Galai, D., Mark, R.: The Essentials of Risk Management. McGraw-Hill, New York (2005)
2. Office of Government Commerce: ITIL - Service Strategy. TSO, London (2007)
3. Office of Government Commerce: ITIL - Service Operation. TSO, London (2007)
4. Office of Government Commerce: ITIL - Continual Service Improvement. OGC, London (2007)
5. Kouns, J., Minoli, D.: Information Technology Risk Managemen In Enterprise Environments. Willey, Canada (2010)
6. Sahibudin, S., Sharifi, M., Ayat, M.: Combining ITIL, COBIT and ISO/IEC 27002 in Order to Design a Comprehensive IT Framework in Organizations, pp. 749–753. University Teknologi Malaysia 81310 UTM, skudai (2008)
7. Faber, M., Faber, R.: ITIL® and Corporate Risk Alignment Guide An introduction to corporate risk and ITIL, and how ITIL supports and is assisted by Management of Risk (M_o_R®). Whitepaper, The Stationery Office (TSO), London (2010)
8. Feglar, T.: ITIL based Service Level Management if SLAs Cover Security, pp. 61–71. Czech Republic (2004)
9. Wickboldt, J., Machado, G., da Costa Cordeiro, W., Lunardi, R., dos Santos, A., Andreis, F., Both, C., Granville, L., Paschoal Gaspary, L.: A Solution to Support Risk Analysis on IT Change Management, Piscataway, NJ, USA, pp. 445–452 (2009)
10. OGC. In: M_o_R - Management of Risk. http://www.mor-officialsite.com/
11. OGC: Management of risk: Guidance for Practitioners, 3rd edn. TSO, United Kingdom (2010)
12. Office of Government Commerce: ITIL - Service Transition. TSO, London (2007)

What Service?

Ana Cardoso[1], Isabel Ferreira[1], João Álvaro Carvalho[1,2], and Leonel Santos[1,2]

[1] Centro Algoritmi, [2] Information Systems Department of University of Minho
Universidade do Minho, Campus de Azúrem, 4800-058 Guimarães
{anachcardoso,iferreiragisa}@gmail.com,
{jac,leonel}@dsi.uminho.pt

Abstract. Technology is changing society, organizations, and interactions between service organizations and customers at a fast pace. Moreover, technology is transforming the nature of services and, in academia, multidisciplinary research is trying to make sense of these changes and leverage the opportunity of service innovation in different fields. After a brief review of the literature focused on services, we found that the term "service" is often used to mean many different things. This paper explores the meaning and scope of services in technological and managerial domains. As a final result, we summarize the concepts of services in the broad areas of management and technology that we found in the literature. Management refers to the concepts that are often used in the fields of marketing and operations management, whereas technology includes the service-like concepts from the fields of software engineering and information systems.

Keywords: services, service science, service concept, and taxonomy.

1 Introduction

In recent past, there has been a renewed interest in the concept of service. In different areas, such as marketing, operations management (OM), software engineering (SE) and information systems (IS), the term "service" is used to refer to different things. For example, in marketing, services refer to the provision of intangible goods that are valued and traded in the market. In SE this term usually nominates an abstraction useful for implementing software applications for open environments in a productive and scalable manner [1]. In IS we can find the word in different contexts, either to refer to electronic or digital services or to the infrastructure layer of organizations that provides the computing capabilities that help organizations achieving their goals.

Many agree that services have been at the core of economic activity in the past years [2, 3, 4, 5]. There seems to be a relation between the dominance of services in world economy and the growing phenomenon of outsourcing. Information technology (IT) and Internet facilitate the creation of a commoditization-logic of services and knowledge work, as for example payroll transactions, programming, and help desk services, that are increasingly being outsourced [6]. Despite the economic stagnation of the last years and the growing unemployment in many industries, there has been a

M.M. Cruz-Cunha et al. (Eds.): CENTERIS 2011, Part II, CCIS 220, pp. 315–324, 2011.
© Springer-Verlag Berlin Heidelberg 2011

growing demand for labor in the sector of services, in both developed and developing countries, thus confirming this outsourcing trend [7, 8].

Researchers in the aforementioned disciplines have been refocusing their interests in services, given the complex transformations occurring in society and the belief that the future of global economy is deeply related to growth in the services sector [9]. The recognition of the growing importance of services in today's world and the interdisciplinary and complex nature of today's services led to the emergence of a new discipline - Service Science Management and Engineering (SSME) [4]. This new discipline intends to tackle emergent service research problems with interdisciplinary approaches and is expected to grow as a meeting place and forum for discussion of service related problems, regardless the original field of study of researchers and practitioners.

The multiple uses of the term "service" in different disciplines sometimes introduces confusion. Therefore, a clarification is needed. Services as a general category of products that involve deeds, acts or performances [10] - a classical and well-known definition from OM and marketing – does not reflect anymore the complete set of possible entities or situations currently presented as services. The distinction among different types of services, can lead to multiple perspectives, each with its own narrow focus, such as IT-enabled services or electronic services, services infrastructure of organizations, or service-oriented design of software. Such line of development is contrary to what is being suggested by the proposers of SSME that aim at an interdisciplinary and integrative approach to the study, management and engineering of services.

This paper is organized as follows. Section 2 is a discussion of literature with focus on the services concept in different areas. Section 3 presents examples of services taxonomies found in the literature. Conclusions and future work are discussed in Section 4.

2 A Review of the Concept of Services

The usage of the word "service" by different disciplines is often confusing because of the multitude of meanings that are involved. Even when the word is used in the context of a single discipline, ambiguity still persists. For example, in management literature, there is inherent ambiguity with the concept of services because it can mean, "an industry, an output or offering, or a process, (...) core service delivery, interpersonal interaction, performance in a wider sense of drama and skill, or the customer's experience of service" [11].

In order to clarify the meanings given to this word, we conducted a literature review that aimed at answering following questions.

Question 1. Which knowledge fields use the term "service"?
Question 2. What is the meaning of service in each of these fields?

The search focused first on the combination of words on title and abstract, and second, full text of selected papers. The initial queries submitted to databases used the keywords: service(s) taxonomy, service(s) management, service(s) concept, service(s) and information technology, and service(s) and information systems.

2.1 Concept of Services in Services Marketing

The well-known definitions of services are historically linked with the services marketing field. The dominant view is that services are opposed to goods. One of the earliest considerations about this matter is presented by Rathmel [12]: "... to consider a good to be a noun and a service a verb – a good is a thing and a service is an act".

In general, goods are defined as "objects, devices or things", while services are "actions, efforts or performances" [13]. Other definitions are also current and popular. For instance, Lovelock [14], and Zeithaml and Bitner [15] agree in the definition of services as deeds, processes, and performances. A similar definition is contended by Berry [10] that defines services as deeds, acts, or performances. Vargo and Lusch [16] elaborate further, and define services as the "application of specialized competences (knowledge and skills) through deeds, processes, and performance for the benefit of another entity or the entity itself". In the same line, Spohrer and Maglio [4] define services as "clients and providers working together to transform some client-controlled state".

The following characteristics of services are commonly used to distinguish them from goods: *intangibility*, *heterogeneity*, *inseparability*, and *perishability* [17]. These characteristics form the *IHIP paradigm*, which is a unifying framework that has guided research in the fields of services marketing and OM for the past decades.

However, the boundaries between what are services and goods have become increasingly fuzzy and unclear. Services are often provided through tangible goods and, conversely, goods are applied in the provision of services [18]. Other important aspects, as for example the differences among services and the differences among services firms [17] (rather than the differences between goods and services), have been neglected and are even more poignant today. Thus, there has been an effort to introduce alternative paradigms that can reflect better the present situation.

One example is the services-dominant logic [16] that emphasizes the non-mutual exclusion of goods and services, and "implies that the goal [of marketing] is to customize offerings, to recognize that the consumer is always a co-producer, and to strive to maximize consumer involvement in the customization to better fit his or her needs". Service-dominant logic is argued to constitute the adequate philosophical foundations for SSME [19, 20], and has created large discussion in marketing literature, still not being consensual. A common criticism is the extremism of their conceptualization, with their services-centric view implying that everything (and anything) can be a service.

Other example is the rental/access paradigm proposed by Lovelock and Gummesson [18]. This paradigm builds on the importance of the characteristic of non-transfer of ownership in services emphasizing that, "marketing transactions that do not involve a transfer of ownership are distinctively different from those that do". Thus, services consist of offerings that benefit users through access or temporary possession, having payments of rental or access fees as their counterpart [18].

2.2 The Concept of Services in Operations Management

Most services involve working together with the customer. Hence, in the area of OM the customer is seen as a basic input for the operations system, with important consequences for the criteria used to evaluate and define services. This characteristic has caused a strong connection between marketing, that creates and manages the expectations of the service to be provided, and operations, that generate the perception of service for customers, thus creating an integrated perspective of services management [21].

In the area of OM, the IHIP paradigm is widely used as the basis for defining services [22]. Spring and Araujo observe that this conception is changing, essentially influenced by the unified service theory (UST), which seems to be the "most radical break with IHIP thinking" in OM [23]. According to this theory, customer inputs, being distinct from customer involvement, are essential for defining services processes.

In services process, the role of customers is different as they "provide significant input" [23]. These inputs are of 3 types: (i) customer self-inputs, (ii) tangible belongings, and (iii) customer-provided information. Customers provide self-inputs either with co-production or when their body is acted upon, as for example with healthcare and transportation services. Sometimes, the customer's tangible belongings are the ones that are acted upon, as for instance reparation services, and other times the customer provides information for the provision of service, as for example fiscal and accounting services [22].

According to Sampson and Froehle [23], UST helps to explain all schemes of classification of services, including the aforementioned IHIP. However, in some cases the rental/access approach [18] to service provision is more helpful as apparently it is more useful to explain the servitization of many manufacturing firms that have "gone downstream", integrating further in the value-chain [24]. Hence, both UST and rental/access approaches are useful alternatives to IHIP classification.

However, the passive conception of customer role, according to the UST, is somewhat limited and does not reflect the contemporary view of customers as co-producers [22]. Moreover, the increasing trend to combine goods and services in offerings, rather than any single of them, and the augmented capabilities of service industries boosted by IT, demand that the field of OM to be directed to the following emergent approach: operations management to operations services through the use of business models that provide added value to customers [22]. This approach expands the OM way of thinking that has traditionally concerned with intra-firm capabilities, namely the control of the flow of materials or information through a sequence of process steps. The integration of the corresponding business models requires that OM also consider inter-firms capabilities, transactions, revenue models, incentives, and the transfer of provider's capabilities [22].

2.3 The Concept of Services in Public Administration

The term "service" is often used in the context of public finance as a result of the state public intervention, to ensure one of its fundamental functions: allocation [25]. This function is reflected in the provision of public goods and services [26]. The citizens, in the scrutiny process, ultimately do the choice of public goods and services, and thus legitimate the government decisions reflected in public policies. In Portugal, the implementation of these public goods and services is done with the annual budget, approved by the parliament [25, 27].

In administrative science, the term "public service" has two meanings: as functional units, grouped on functional consideration, distinguished according to their purposes (e.g. education services, health services); or as working units, according to a structural perspective depending on the type of activity that is developed (e.g. finance services, administrative services) [27]. This view of the public service may, to some extent, be analyzed from the standpoint of organizational design [28].

Finally, in the scope of public economics, the term "public service" is associated with the function allocation, which will be ensured by the administrative machinery structured according to different models of service management, both from the perspectives of services operations and marketing [29]. Moreover, the result of this function can be the provision of a good or a service to citizens [26]. The state, viewed as the provider of public service through public administration, is thus a service organization [30].

2.4 The Concept of Services in Software Architectures and Software Development

Software engineering adopted the concept of service to offer an innovative approach to software development, thus resulting the idea of web services. Services, in this context, are an effective means of building distributed applications, "providing higher-level abstractions for large-scale, open environments" [1]. Thus, services are software components that interact in request-fulfill logic, as opposed to the bureaucratic and conventional logic of command and control.

As a result, software components are articulated with a loose coupling that brings clear benefits to the development and maintenance of software, especially in software distributed over platforms. However, the issues of authentication of client applications and security of data transmission are critical and pose challenges to the development and deployment of services oriented architectures [1].

2.5 Services in Information Systems and Information Services

Information systems researchers are positioned at the nexus of organizations and people, where IT helps people's work within organizations. Therefore, they are often concerned with the efficient provision of IT capabilities that helps organizations achieving their goals.

Outsourcing of organizations' IT needs is a growing phenomenon. Researchers in IS are concerned with the effects of outsourcing in organizations and IT projects [31, 32, 33]. It is argued that outsourcing is changing work practices and demanding innovative approaches to management of inter-regional teams. At the same time, outsourcing challenges the future of IT job market in developed countries and increases specialization of the workforce [6].

On the other hand, the distribution of information goods is nowadays done via Internet with the rental/access paradigm [18] being the major form of delivery. The intangible nature of information makes it easy to change its form without affecting its content. Thus, the dematerialization of information business (mostly publishing industry) has led to the provision of information as a service. Hence, the term "information services" is often used when referring to the provision of information goods via Internet.

2.6 Implications of Information Technology to the Conceptualization of Services

Organizations and businesses are changing, reflecting the impact of IT. Particularly the Internet, known as "one big service vehicle" [34], is altering the way services and goods are delivered and managed, the relations between organizations and customers, and is redefining value chains.

In services, important changes have occurred due to increasing faster communication networks and Internet. Information technology provides significant opportunities for services innovation, superior customer service, and efficiency gains. Moreover, other opportunities such as customers' accessibility and control are also leveraged with self–service technologies (SSTs) [35]. Although technology transforms organization and customers' interaction – shifting from arm's-length relationships to impersonal ones – the customers' expectations of quality are immutable. In fact, customers and employees are not always receptive to technological offers, nor they recognize the associated value [34].

Self-service technologies enable customers to provide their own service and also to take part on the goods acquisition process. The challenges of introducing on-line service technologies are not minor. Often, what works for an organization may not produce the same result in others.

Multi-channel access – the in-person service and the electronic service – is nowadays almost generalized in services sector [36]. Internet-based SSTs and electronic business models created a momentum for services evolve their access strategy, and organizations perceived the increased value of offering services via Internet (e-services). In many cases, e-services are catalyzing service innovation thereby creating competitive advantages. For this reason, benefits of the electronic channel are far beyond providing diverse access options, although in many cases, e-services are indeed a simple expression of multi-channel access [36].

2.7 Summary

In this section, we summarize the different conceptualizations of services of the previous sections. In Table 1, we plot the concepts we have previously referred against the areas of management and technology. Thus, the concepts of service more related with the management field (including marketing and operations management) are identified. The technology side represents both the fields of software engineering and information systems.

Table 1. The concepts of services in the broad areas of management and technology

	Management	Technology
Web services		X
Self-service technologies	X	
Electronic services		X
Deeds, processes and performances	X	
Functional units	X	
Working units	X	
IT outsourcing (or IT as a service)		X
Information services	X	X

3   Classifications of Services

Classifications are instruments that aim at reducing complexity and systematizing knowledge about something. Classification is approachable in two ways: typology and taxonomy. The first one is fundamentally conceptual, whereas the second is essentially empirical [37]. The idea of a typology is that through a combination of variables we can reduce the complexity of a concept, and thereby explain its dimensions [30]. A taxonomy consists on "a scheme that partitions a body of knowledge and defines the relationships among the pieces" [38].

The distinction between these 2 classification approaches is often overlooked in the literature. Several authors refer only to classification schemes, thereby disregarding the dichotomy between taxonomy and typology.

In marketing and management research, typological classifications of services are more abundant. Bowen refers to 16 known typologies for services [39]. He proposes an empirical-based classification scheme based on 7 characteristics that he illustrates by applying it to 10 services business that were representative of 4 different services industries. The characteristics are: (1) importance of employees; (2) customization; (3) ability to switch firms; (4) employee / customer contact; (5) services directed at people or things; (6) continuous benefits; and (7) difference. The objective was to assess if this scheme "would group services from the same industries together or (...) producing groups that would transcend industry boundaries".

Data was collected with a mail survey of consumers, and a review of services marketing literature identified the conceptual classification schemes. After statistical analysis with ANOVA and clustering, services were grouped in 3 clusters: (1) High-Contact, Customized, Personal Services, (2) Moderate Contact, Semi-Customized, Non-Personal Services, and (3) Moderate Contact, Standardized Services.

Since its early beginnings, the field of Services Marketing has sought for a generalizable classification scheme for services. Bowen's empirically based classification work is pioneer in the creation of groups of services based on consumer's perceptions. However, there are some limitations in terms of generalizability because of the number of industries and firms selected and some bias toward upper-lower and middle classes consumers in the sample.

More recently, Lee and Park develop a taxonomy of South-Korean electronic commerce sites [40]. Their objective is to create a taxonomy for online service goods. They identify 11 characteristics of online commercial services, namely (1) criticality for customer, (2) importance of professional knowledge, (3) degree of labor intensity, (4) degree of interaction, (5) degree of customer contact, (6) necessity of membership relation, (7) frequency of purchase, (8) features of search goods, (9) price, (10) degree of customization, and (11) necessity of offline. Forty-five electronic commerce sites were selected for their project. This selection was made through the lists of Korean portal sites and a further refinement with the introduction of the North American Industry Classification System.

Perceptions about the characteristics of services were gathered through a questionnaire to consumers, which had 164 respondents. First, data was statistically analyzed, resulting in six clusters of services: (1) mass, (2) professional, (3) intellectual, (4) credit, (5) support, and (6) facility services [40]. Next, they examine the characteristics of each group and propose marketing and operational strategies for each. Despite the meaningful contributions of this research, the classification is biased and context-sensitive because of the sample used.

The opportunity for an empirically based classification scheme of services is still urgent. The different ways we see the word "services" being used demand a clarification of its meaning in context. The service-dominant logic [16] that SSME has cherished [41, 42] further increases this need because that theorization has not yet been empirically validated. Moreover, service innovations depend on interdisciplinary research and skills and, thus, a coherent and comprehensive classification scheme for service scientists and practitioners with different backgrounds is certainly helpful.

4 Conclusions and Future Work

This paper focuses on the concept of services from the point of view of marketing, operations management, and the changes introduced in these fields by the widespread use of information technology (IT). Moreover, the appropriation of service's concept in software engineering and the phenomenon of IT-outsourcing, which is increasingly relevant for information systems research, are also explored.

The objective is to clarify the meaning of the concept of service, with the aim of contributing to the literature in the field of service science management and engineering (SSME), based on a transversal perspective. At the end of this exploratory phase, we discuss existing classification schemes and argue that an empirically based classification of services is useful for evolving the field of SSME. As future work, we intend to develop a project with a multidisciplinary team to work on an empirically based taxonomy of services. This project will evolve in two stages. The first will clarify which characteristics underlie the different concepts in the areas of study, and the second will identify the differing and approximating characteristics among the different areas.

Acknowledgments. This research was partially supported by Fundação para a Ciência e Tecnologia via Bolsa de Doutoramento SFRH/BD/60838/2009.

References

1. Huhns, M.H., Singh, M.P.: Service-Oriented Computing: Key Concepts and Principles. IEEE Internet Computing 9(1), 75–81 (2005)
2. Chesbrough, H., Spohrer, J.: A Research Manifesto for Services Science. Communications of ACM 49(7), 35–40 (2006)
3. Spohrer, J., Maglio, P.P., Bailey, J., Gruhl, D.: Steps Toward a Science of Service Systems. Computer 40, 71–77 (2007)
4. Spohrer, J., Maglio, P.P.: The Emergence of Service-Science: Towards Systematic Service Innovations to Accelerate Co-Creation of Value. Production & Operations Management 17(3), 238–246 (2008)
5. Bitner, M.J., Brown, S.W.: The Service Imperative. Business Horizons 51(1), 39–46 (2008)
6. Hirschheim, R.A.: Offshoring and the New World Order. Communications of ACM 52(11), 132–135 (2009)

7. International Labor Organization: Global Employment Trends. Report, Geneve (2009)
8. International Labor Organization: Global Employment Trends. Report, Geneve (2010)
9. Ostrom, A.S., et al.: Moving Forward and Making a Difference: Research Priorities for the Science of Service. Journal of Service Research 13(1), 4–36 (2010)
10. Berry, L.L.: Services Marketing is Different. Business 30(3), 24–29 (1980)
11. Johns, N.: What Is This Thing Called Service? European Journal of Marketing 33(9/10), 958–974 (1999)
12. Rathmel, J.M.: What Is Meant By Services? Journal of Marketing 30, 32–36 (1966)
13. Hoffman, J.M., Bateson, J.E.: Essentials of Services Marketing. Dryden Press, Forth Worth (1997)
14. Lovelock, C.: Services Marketing, 2nd edn. Prentice Hall, Englewood Cliffs (1991)
15. Zeithaml, V., Bitner, M.J.: Services Marketing: Integrating Customer Focus Across The Firm, 2nd edn. Mc-Graw Hill, Boston (2000)
16. Vargo, S.L., Lusch, R.F.: Evolving to a New Dominant Logic for Marketing. Journal of Marketing 48(1), 1–17 (2004)
17. Zeithaml, V., Parasuraman, A., Berry, L.L.: Problems and Strategies in Services Marketing. Journal of Marketing 40, 33–46 (1985)
18. Lovelock, C., Gummesson, E.: Whither Services Marketing? In Search of a New Paradigm and Fresh Perspectives. Journal of Service Research 17(1), 20–41 (2004)
19. Maglio, P.P., Spohrer, J.: Fundamentals of Service Science. Journal of the Academy of Marketing Science 36(1), 18–20 (2008)
20. Vargo, S.L., Lusch, R.F.: A Service Logic for Service Science. In: Hefley, Murphy (eds.) Service Science, Management and Engineering: Education for the 21st Century, pp. 83–88. Springer, New York (2008)
21. Gianesi, I., Corrêa, H.: Administração Estratégica de Serviços: Operações para a Satisfação do Cliente, Atlas, São Paulo (2000)
22. Spring, M., Araújo, L.: Service, Services, and Products: Rethinking Operations Strategy. International Journal of Operations & Production Management 29(5), 444–467 (2009)
23. Sampson, S.E., Froehle, C.M.: Foundations and Implications of a Proposed Unified Services Theory. Production and Operations Management 15(2), 329–343 (2006)
24. Wise, R., Baumgartner, P.: Go Dowstream: the New Profit Imperative in Manufacturing. Harvard Business Review, 133–141 (September-October 1999)
25. Pereira, P.T., Afonso, A., Arcanjo, M., Santos, J.: Economia e Finanças Publicas 2.a Edição. Escolar Editora, Lisboa (2007)
26. Musgrave, R.: Public Finance in Theory and Practice, 5th edn. McGraw-Hill, Boston (1989)
27. Amaral, D.F.: Curso de Direito Administrativo, vol. 2. Almedina, Coimbra (2002)
28. Andersen, J.A.: Organizational Design: Two Lessons to Learn Before Reorganizing. International Journal of Organizations Theory and Behavior 5(3,4), 343–358 (2002)
29. Osborne, S.: Delivering Public Service: Time for a New Theory? Public Management Review 12(1), 1–10 (2010)
30. Mills, P.K., Margulies, N.: Toward a Core Typology of Service Organizations. The Academy of Management Review 5(2), 255–265 (1980)
31. Choudhury, V., Sabherwal, R.: Portfolios of Control in Outsourced Software Development Projects. Information Systems Research 14(3), 291–314 (2003)
32. Levina, N.: Collaborating on Multiparty Information Systems Development Projects: A Collective Reflection-in-Action View. Information Systems Research 16(2), 109–130 (2005)

33. Sarker, S., Sarker, S.: Exploring Agility in Distributed Information Systems Developmente Teams: an Interpretive Study in an Offshoring Contexr. Information Systems Research 20(3), 440–461 (2009)

34. Bitner, M.J.: Service and Technology: Opportunities and Paradoxes. Managing Service Quality 11(6), 375–379 (2001)

35. Pujari, D.: Self-service with a Smile? Self-Service Technology Encounters Among Canadian Business-to-Business. International Journal of Service Industry Management 15(2), 200–219 (2004)

36. Rowley, J.: An Analysis of the E-Service Literature: Towards a Research Agenda. Internet Research 16(3), 330–359 (2006)

37. Bailey, K.D.: Typologies and Taxonomies: an Introduction to Classification Techniques. Sage Publications, Thousand Oaks (1994)

38. IEEE, IEEE Standars Taxonomy for Software Engineering Standards. IEEE, New York (1989)

39. Bowen, J.: Development of a Taxonomy of Services to Gain Strategic Marketing Insights. Journal of the Academy of Marketing Science 18(1), 43–49 (1990)

40. Lee, S., Park, Y.: The Classification And Strategic Management of Services in E-Commerce: Development of Service Taxonomy Based on Customer Perception. Expert Systems With Applications 36, 9618–9624 (2009)

41. Spohrer, J., Vargo, S.L., Caswell, N., Maglio, P.P.: The Service System is the Basic Abstraction of Service Science. In: Proceedings of the 41st Annual Hawaii International Conference on System Sciences (2008)

42. Vargo, S.L., Akaka, M.: Service-Dominant Logic as a Foundation for Service Clarifications. Service Science 1(1), 32–41 (2009)

Enterprise Information Systems - Managing I.T. Human Resources from 18 to 70 Years Old (Living with the Conflict of Generations)

Joel Mana Gonçalves and Rejane Pereira da Silva Gonçalves

Independent Media Consultant, Rua Charles Spence Chaplin, 85 – ap. 64,
05642-010 São Paulo, Brazil
{joel.mana,rejane.psg}@uol.com.br

Abstract. The paper presented here addresses the management of IT human resources available in the companies for the development of Enterprise Information Systems, mainly under the social aspect of the conflict between generations that comprise the business population, showing how to get through awareness and training, ensuring confidence in new technologies and overcome the natural resistance to changes. It compares the main positive and negative characteristics of each age group and how to take advantage of the unique strengths of each generation.**Keywords:** Human resources, confidence in new technologies, resistance to changes, conflict of generations, awareness and training.

1 Introduction

This article discusses the management of IT human resources available in the companies for the development of Enterprise Information Systems from the point of view of the generational conflict that is caused by the different age groups within a corporation. This generational conflict has special characteristics within the world of Information Technology. We are going to show how to live with these differences and how to transform them into an asset for us.

The findings and suggestions presented here are the results of verification on the spot with different reactions due to age differences between the various age groups that constitute a business.

A situation that every day is more visible in corporations is the clash of generations. All companies have their share of representatives in at least three significant groups with respect to age distribution, i.e.: The so-called Baby Boomers (born after World War 2 until the mid-60), Generation X (born between 1965 and 1980) and Generation Y (born between 1980 and 1996).

This article looks at how each of these generations work in the development of Enterprise Information Systems and, most important and interesting phenomenon observed in the interaction and complimentarily between the generations, where we can say we have the young and lively "stuck" to older and traditional. And that, properly managed, will provide us with innovative solutions in the market.

M.M. Cruz-Cunha et al. (Eds.): CENTERIS 2011, Part II, CCIS 220, pp. 325–334, 2011.

This paper serves as an alert and gives suggestions for leaders in general. All of this, with a single purpose, namely the operational excellence of companies that develop the Enterprise Information Systems. In the following sections we will discuss the definitions of each generation involved in our business scenario, they are the Baby Boomers and the Generations X and Y. Then we will show the observations concerning the interaction between them in our businesses, ending with specific recommendations for each group and concluding with the results of our observations, suggesting some approaches that can be used successfully in companies.

2 Baby Boomers, Generation X and Generation Y

Our companies have employees in different age groups with their individual and collective characteristics. Each group has its share within the hierarchy and structure of them.

The interaction between different generations leads to surprising results in aspects of corporate governance, operational and even interpersonal.

Leaders and managers, it is knowing how to exploit these differences in age, experience and even outlook on life, with the approach of latent characteristics of each generation which allows reap extraordinary results for our companies and employees, all within a healthy climate.

According to Leandro Fernandes, "in the next few years, the organizations around the world will experience the challenge of integrating three generations, completely different from each other, within the same environment. These are the baby boomers, those who are born until 1964, Generation X, made up of those born between 1965 and 1977 and Generation Y, born after 1978.

The first consists of children of those who lived through the Second World War. They were educated in an environment where corporate leadership is synonymous with command and control, they have value as loyalty to the company they work for, care little for quality of life and have focused on results.

The second consists of children of those professionals who worked hard and had little time for them. Therefore, this generation has little connection with traditional institutions. They are more independent, enterprising and are even more results-oriented. The third and latest generation is more independent, inherited from the previous generation".

For we begin, let us consider the organizational learning in an IT company, relating to the theory of Nolan. Cited by Medeiros [1], Nolan presents the timeline of technology in three eras of organizational learning, which are divided into stages as shown in Figure 1.

In a brief analysis of the timeline of enterprise (represented in Figure 1) shows that throughout history they have adapted to the new realities of technology and especially information technology and communication, noting that alongside the changes in technological field, there is also the development of changes in the profile of professionals in the labor market.

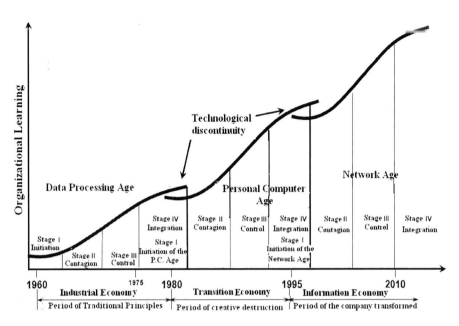

Fig. 1. The ages of organizational learning
Source: Medeiros [1], based on Nolan [2]

The Baby Boomers. As shown in Figure 1, the organizational learning in a company has its beginnings in a first phase called Data Processing, where the use of mainframe featured the companies among 60 and 80. Right now, the performance of the companies was to process the strategic information of them.

The era of data processing was extended from 1960 to about 1980 and was based on the mainframe computer. Minicomputers then existing were administered centrally, just as mainframes. The demand for Enterprise Information Systems was by the automation of factory work and of the administrative assistants. The computer was used to raise the efficiency of organizations, often by automating existing processes and procedures; rarely significantly changing their functional hierarchies. It is noteworthy that time, its use in inventory control, development of the payroll and accounting applications. At this time we had mainly the Baby Boomer generation working into our companies in development activities. The mainframe computer was the "king", and that people that was working with it was something different and special.

Drawing a parallel between the ages of Organizational Learning in a tech company, and the study of the entry of several generations in the labor market, we realized that the generation that lived with the end of the Second World War was the one who worked in that period where the computer has automated the manufacturing work, seeking efficiencies of organizations. This same generation can observe a period of great prosperity of the countries that they needed to rebuild the post war rebuilding their economies. The consequence was the greater stability of homes and a notable increase in the birthrate. This population explosion has created the so-called Baby Boomer Generation, a generation that remained the largest group of people with a unique cultural, political and economic unprecedented, dominating the landscape in all stages of their lives.

The baby boomer generation was the first who grew up on TV. They were able to share events and cultural landmarks with the people in your age group, regardless of where they were. These shared moments helped establish a bond never experienced by any previous generation. When they were young, they saw the man walk on the moon, attended the Vietnam War, and fought for civil rights, sexual freedom and at 20 years old they created the culture of excess. According Helenita Fernandes, the arrival of baby boomers into the labor market brought values as a concern for quality of life, the nonconformity, the search for autonomy and loyalty to themselves. This was quite revolutionary for its time. For Karim Khoury they were accustomed to the leadership style of command and controls of their leaders, this generation tends to work hard and usually makes no claims, although a relationship of distrust with his leadership. They expect to remain several years in the same job [5].

The Generation X. Returning to the theory of Nolan, and into the second age (cited in [1], p.42), as seen in Figure 1, into the second age, the Age of Microcomputers, we realized that a new concept was introduced in the design of technology applied to the companies, a new paradigm that is originally not trying to replace professional by computers, but they enable greater efficiency in their tasks.

In the 90s, the companies lives with two generations: the baby boomer generation who, with the need to use microcomputers and the emergence of new forms of systems development prompted the organization to sensitize professionals to a new way of working, a new production of logical thinking and a new generation, Generation X (born between 1965 and 1979), which began to reach the labor market bringing with them the experience of a new social reality.

Generation X saw the start of the decay of old social patterns. Many were children of divorced parents, lived in homes where men and women employed outside the home. In personal life, this generation is not particularly a fan of rules, but at work they think should be met. It tends to focus on results, has developed an entrepreneurial vision and the ability to learn new technology to stay on the market. Although this generation worries about having more balanced relationship between the personal and professional life, it tends to perform tasks for her instead of working in teams.

They are part of that generation responsible for the invention of various communication tools in today's world. Companies that have revolutionized the Internet, like Google, Amazon and YouTube, the Web 2.0 icons were created by people of this generation.

Following on from this explanation, we have the third age, the Age of the Network. As shown in Figure 1, we have a milestone in the scheme of Ages Learning IT in 1995.

The era of networks arises from investments in the three areas mentioned - automation of manufacturing tasks and clerks, support for professionals in the media organizations and the incorporation of microcomputer products and services - that form the basis for the demand for computer networks.

The companies assume the functionality of IT as a management tool. The information becomes a strategic resource of organizations and IT's role is to assist with tools to develop new products and services, including the EIS – Enterprise Information System:

The evolution of computing has enabled organizations to increase their own capacity to collect and store data. Many of these data hold valuable information that can be used to improve business decisions. With this, organizations are undergoing constant restructuring to strengthen its competitiveness, and are finding projects in information technology (IT) support to develop new products better or provide better services.

The Generation Y. As we see, initially, the technology is responsible for generating automated data and then with the advent of microcomputers, these data are being worked out, and generating contextual information. And now, living in what was called the Age of the Network, we realize that information management is crafted for the creation of knowledge by making use of established network.

Just as technology is replaced by features of the Age of the Network, his own life in society now receive the impacts of new communication technologies and information. Those born in this scenario, i.e., the generation born between 1980 and 2000, is a generation that was born acquainted with the great flow of information, although already childhood living with the internet and the many new ways to communicate. This is the first generation where children have more access to information and knowledge than their parents.

This is Generation Y, a generation of better protected by parents, has grown accustomed to being valued, to feel special. Exposed to diseases such as AIDS, has seen terrorism become a worldwide phenomenon, played video games with increasingly violent and increasingly saw the advertisements with sex appeal.

The result is an optimistic generation, proactive, ambitious, demanding, self centered, who value teamwork and the relationship with the leadership and employees, confident, "wants to make a difference" and believes he can change the world. Globalization, the rapid pace of constant change and the large volume of information is part of everyday life in this new generation. It is the generation that communicates with new technologies: SMS, email, Twitter, blogs. Learn to enjoy using technology, networks, groups and collaboration. At work have focused on personal success, career outlook in the short term; see no clear boundary between life and work, hope to work anytime, anywhere, virtually and with greater flexibility, value autonomy and optimism, like teamwork and expect results quickly.

This generation, as mentioned in "social networking", already has his first contact with the Internet through new ways to communicate, the majority has a profile on several social networks.

Table 1. The mainly Characteristics of the Generations in an Enterprise

Baby boomers	Generation X	Generation Y
(born between 1945 and 1961) Occupy the top position in the hierarchy or are senior level professionals.	(born between 1965 and 1980) Occupy an intermediary position on hierarchy or are medium level professionals	(born between 1980 and 2000) Occupy initial position in the hierarchy or are senior level professionals. At IT companies they can be in leadership positions.
•These people are totally focused on the job, which is its priority. •Oriented to results they are competitive. •More difficult is the loss of status and power. •Leadership means to command and control. •Do not worry much about quality of life. •They have a difficult relationship with digital technologies; they have learned to use it as adults.	•Have lots of experience and dedication. •They have an unconscious fear of being fired and being threatened by someone from Generation Y. •They are also focused on the job, with a focus on results. •Strive to balance personal life with professional. •They are "digital immigrants" have learned to digital technologies in adolescence. •They often have high levels of stress.	•Have strong self-esteem and non-negotiable commitment to values. •They are fascinated by challenges and want to do everything his way. •They are impulsive and fearless face positions of power and authority. •They are "multitasking." •They are "digital natives". •Have online meetings with ease. •They want flexible hours and prefer casual clothes. •Difficulties with hierarchy, •They live in network and hate bureaucracy, control and routine activities.

3   The Three Generation Living Together and Developing Enterprise Information Systems

This is the scenario that confronts us in our companies. Are these companies located anywhere in the world is having the typical composition of the staff made up of three generations as described in previous item.

So how can we to ensure synergy between these disparate groups to ensure us a homogeneous outcome and quality?

This is a major challenge that managers of companies developing the Enterprise Information System is facing today and the answer to achieving the goals described and synergy so sought after and desired, is the behavioral training and constant awareness of the three groups, highlighting the virtues specific and mitigating (or eliminating) the flaws inherent in each group!

Technically the groups (and the individuals) are capable, this is an assumption that we made, otherwise they would not be developing our EIS, and therefore we will leverage this technical component with behavioral self-empowerment group.

In this situation, the behavioral differences have a great weight: initially we found that the older accused the younger generations (especially the Y) have no business ethics. The youngest is at odds with the generation X to identify resistance to change. The youngest is at odds with the generation X to identify resistance to changes. So, the firms need managing the conflicts and adapting their workforce according to their market reality.

In Brazil, as well as most of the world, there are not many options. The shortage of skilled professionals makes all the relevant people to find their place, whatever their generation. Without being able to choose too, companies are forced to become flexible enough to accommodate all types of professionals.

The difficulties start with the expectations that employees have with respect to companies and vice versa. The youth of Y see the need to always have new challenges, share knowledge with colleagues and feel very frustrated if they do not receive a promotion after one year of home. The X, not accustomed to this dynamic, does not give due attention to the demands of Generation Y and the relationship deteriorates. The Baby Boomer sees this attitude as a lack of dedication and ethics. The result is that everyone can come out unmotivated.

The issue of collaborative work is also a major source of conflict. Professionals from Generations X and Baby Boomers are not very flexible in this regard. They do not like to share their knowledge and their results and think that if this happens, most youngsters will take ownership of knowledge to take their place. Thus, the Y can have two professional attitudes: either leave the company because I believe that is not learning anything from their managers or use other ways to achieve the same goals, sometimes even more efficient way, a situation that will make the manager feel it is even worse.

4   What to Do with the Older People

A clever and profitable strategy, not to lose sight of the talent about to retire, is to create networks of former employees. The California state government, for example, created the Boomerang, a site that acts as a database those who have retired and are interested in reenter the state agencies to work in positions of half period.

Penelope Trunk, author of Brazen Careerist: the New Rules for Success (ed. Warner Books)[20], advises organizations to adopt three measures to avoid losing talent:

Recruit constantly. Younger people are not loyal one company, but to a set factors that make them feel good, which is why they never fail to seek new opportunities to contribute for their personal development.

Use branding as a strategy seduction. It takes more than talk corporate culture and commitment social and less description task.

Go in search of talent. Younger people are online, and the "blogosphere" represents the more committed sector of this talent. Writing a blog requires time and dedication and bloggers only write about what matters to them: his career.

Communication, motivation and building bridges between generations are to Lynda Gratton, professor of Administration at London Business School, three others key elements of any management strategy staff. Therefore, we suggest encouraging people to communicate using all styles. Motivation requires all kind of approaches. While bonuses may arouse interests of boomers, generations X and Y are inclined to privilege of having a flexible agenda. Leaders also should make sure to capture the corporate memory and transfer this knowledge to younger generations.

5   What to Do with the Younger People

A survey of U.S. companies conducted by Lee Hecht Harrison, a consulting firm in talent management, said the disagreements existing in labor relations. Check out this example: 70% of older executives downplay the skills the young, and almost 50% of staff ensures that young people do not value the skills of their older colleagues. Employers do not believe that the situation will improve and in fact more than 60% expect to increase the tension.

Generation Y grew up in a world dominated by the speed and immediacy. The office is to Y a straitjacket that limits its productivity. Young companies recognize the importance to offer their workforce flexibility and freedom of action necessary for the stimulation of creativity.

At Google offices, for example, among other peculiarities, there are open spaces for interaction and private places of work, which are assembled and disassembled quickly, by a system of collapsible panels. They work in Teams and times that suit them best.

Xerox is not as young as Google (has more than one hundred years), but considers itself a modern enterprise. With its slogan "Express Yourself", whose aim is the generation Millennium, recruits graduates from MIT and Cornell University. Anne Mulcahy, CEO says in the Xerox website that summarizes the slogan the essential values of the organization, a place where "creative people thrive, find unique solutions and boost their careers through of an express way.

The younger executives are not impressed by status or the rise. Directing a company not bring prestige, if the price is life devoted to work. Once again, companies have to adapt and develop systems of clearing and personalized benefits.

As the younger generations prefer a culture that measure the performance to one that prioritizes the seniority the short-term variable should have more weight than long term

6   Conclusion

Today we have working on our companies the three generations described here, they are developing and maintaining our Enterprise Information Systems.

This is a social reality of which we should take all the positives and minimize the most negative points. This is the challenge for managers of companies that will help organizations create work systems that comply with them.

It is important to note that our work continues, since it is mainly based on practical observation and constant monitoring of the business environment that has the characteristic of being very dynamic. Another point to consider, at short or medium term, is the entering in the job market of a new generation, the Z (born from the mid 90s), with its characteristics and peculiarities. The consultant Gilberto Wiesel, from the area of competence development, explains that, by being directly with the new digital tools like social media, the Z's are fast and deeply anxious for change. Also, usually, members of this generation are critical, dynamic, technological and concerned with environmental issues. They are also demanding for products and services: "These characteristics are positive and would benefit business in the future. Knowing the dynamic way in which they deal with many situations, I believe that these future professionals will be, first of all employees multitask".

As a final message we suggest the following precepts that will make easier the task of matching the needs of three generations of information technology companies to enable the best possible performance for the development of the EIS:

Rethinking authority. Sometimes the leader will be the student, the young teacher.
Being a facilitator. Provide coaching and constant feedback.
Redesigning the recruitment strategy. Start long-term relationships.
Redesigning the capacity strategy. Commit to continuous learning.
Taking advantage of social networks. No Facebook ban. Instead, redefine management processes and the layout of office to facilitate collaborative work.
Redesigning the strategy of talent retention. Fostering a relationship of long term, also with the employees who leave the company.
Releasing the power of youth. Listen to them.

References

1. de Medeiros Jr., A.: Integrated management systems: proposal for a decision procedure for Advanced Strategic Review - Doctoral Thesis – Polytechnic School of São Paulo University. Department of Industrial Engineering. São Paulo (2007)
2. Nolan, R.L.: Dot Vertigo: Doing business in a permeable world, p. 254. John Wiley & Sons, New York (2001)
3. Pocket Learning 4 – Geração Y Perspectivas sobre o ambiente multigeracional (Generation Y Perspectives on multigenerational environment), http://issuu.com/labssj/docs/pocket4_geracaoy
4. Fernandes, H.: Revista Ser Mais. Ser Mais Magazine, year 2, (13)
5. Khoury, K.: Liderança é uma questão de atitude. Leadership is a matter of attitude. SENAC Publisher, São Paulo (2009)
6. Bernoff, J., Schadler, T.: Deixe o pessoal explorar as mídias sociais. Let the staff to explore social media. Harvard Business Review Brazil Magazine (2010)
7. Castells, M.: A sociedade em rede (The network Society), vol. 1. Paz e Terra, São Paulo (2000)
8. Cross, R., Parker, A.: The Hidden Power of Social Networks. Harvard Business School Press, Boston
9. Lévy, P.: Cibercultura. Tradução: Carlos Irineu da Costa. 34 Publisher, São Paulo (2001)
10. Fernandes, H.: – "Revista Ser Mais" ano 2, Nº13, http://www.revistasermais.com.br

11. Tapscott, D.: Grown Up Digital: How The Net Generation Is Changing The World. Mcgraw-Hill, São Paulo (2008)
12. Choque de gerações o desafio de lidar com os diferentes perfis de carreira – COMPUTERWORLD,
http://computerworld.uol.com.br/carreira/2009/06/02/choque-de-geracoes-como-as-empresas-lidam-com-os-diferentes-perfis/
13. UNIFIN (São Francisco de Assis College – Porto Alegre) – Dossiê Choque de Gerações,
http://www.unifin.com.br/gerenciador/_uploads/artigo_arquivo/151/dossie_geracoes.pdf
14. Teixeira Filho, J.: Comunidades Virtuais - Como As Comunidades Virtuais Estão Mudando Os Negócios. SENAC Publisher, Rio de Janeiro (2009)
15. Gravett, L., Throckmorton, R.: Bridging the Generation Gap: How to Get Radio Babies, Boomers, Gen Xers, and Gen Yers to Work Together and Achieve More. The Career Press Inc., New Jersey (2006)
16. Burmeister, M.: From Boomers To Bloggers: Success Strategies Across Generations. Synergy Press, Fairfax (2008)
17. Fernandes, L.: Para integrar baby boomers e as gerações X e Y, empresas precisam reduzir hierarquias,
http://www.canalrh.com.br/mobile/artigo.asp?o=%7BE3A54183-4D5A-4CB8-AD75-E184E6C1FF22%7D&a=1
18. Wiesel, G.: Geração Z mudará rumos do mercado de trabalho -,
http://vilamulher.terra.com.br/geracao-z-mudara-rumos-do-mercado-de-trabalho-5-1-37-605.html
19. American workers no longer see their jobs as a "Labor of Love" - Lee Hatch Harrison,
http://www.lhh.com/aboutus/pressreleases/Pages/American-workers-no-longer-see-their-jobs-as-a-Labor-of-Love.aspx
20. Trunk, P.: Brazen Careerist: the New Rules for Success. Warner Books, New York (2007)
21. Boomerang State of California Retires Job Connection. California Government,
https://boomerang.ca.gov/
22. Gratton, L.: The Democratic Enterprise. FT Press, London (2004)

An Analysis of MoReq2010 from the Perspective of TOGAF

Ricardo Vieira, Francisco Valdez, and José Borbinha

INESC-ID, Information Systems Group
Rua Alves Redol, nº 9 1000-029, Lisbon
{rjcv,francisco.valdez,jlb}@ist.utl.pt

Abstract. The practice of Records Management in organizations is becoming a subject of research as organizations increasingly face the dematerialization of their processes. Standards and requirements have emerged in order to assist organizations to manage digital records with the purpose of streamlining their processes and ensuring accountability and evidence of their actions. However, there is still no guidance on how to embody these requirements into the organization's Enterprise Architecture. As a result, this paper explores and analyzes a requirements specification for records management (MoReq) from the perspective of an enterprise architecture framework (TOGAF). It intends to give the basic insights about how to incorporate such requirements into the development process of building an Enterprise Architecture by matching them with the corresponding architecture specification element or domain.

Keywords: Records Management, Enterprise Architecture, MoReq, TOGAF, Architecture Requirements Specification.

1 Introduction

Organizations are facing new emerging challenges due to the rapid change of their business and technological environment, so Enterprise Architecture has emerged as a valuable concept to help them dealing with the increasing complexity of their information systems [1] [2]. Although these governance techniques are responsible for handling the relevant information of an organization, it is also essential to properly manage the records created within business processes. As such, the principles, standards, and requirements related to Records Management must also be embodied in these architectures. Apart from constituting an essential part of any organization and being considered a good business practice, the management of records can also bring benefits in terms of transparency, compliance, legal pursuance and process efficiency.

An actual important reference in the area of Records Management is the Model Requirements for Electronic Records (MoReq)[1]. However, there is still no comprehensive knowledge about how to incorporate those requirements into an organization's Enterprise Architecture. That is the motivation of this paper, where we

---

[1] http://www.dlmforum.eu/

M.M. Cruz-Cunha et al. (Eds.): CENTERIS 2011, Part II, CCIS 220, pp. 335–344, 2011.

present an analysis of MoReq from the perspective of The Open Group Architecture Framework (TOGAF) [3], an intensive documented approach for developing Enterprise Architectures.

2 Records Management and MoReq2010

The ISO 15489 defines **Records Management** as "the field of management responsible for the efficient and systematic control of the creation, receipt, maintenance, use and disposition of records, including the processes for capturing and maintaining evidence of and information about business activities and transactions in the form of records" [4].

In this context, an **Electronic Records Management System** (ERMS) is "an automated system used to manage the creation, use, maintenance and disposal of electronically created records for the purposes of providing evidence of business activities" [5]. In order to complement this concept it is also essential to define a **record** as the consequence or product of an event or a business transaction, which can exist in any format.

Within this domain, MoReq stands for "Model Requirements for Electronic Records" and is a requirements specification for ERMS that has been developed by DLM Forum and strongly supported by the European Commission. Its first version was published in 2001 and revised in 2008, resulting in the untitled MoReq2. The major changes in this second version were the inclusion of an independent MoReq-based XML Schema, as also of a test framework and the addition of a "Chapter Zero" section to provide guidance on legislative and regulatory requirements [6].

Since the publication of MoReq2 the MoReq Governance Board, responsible for monitor and plan new developments for this specification, has received considerable feedback. As a consequence it was decided to undertake two fully public consultation phases as part of the development of a third version, named MoReq2010. By the time of this paper the consultation phases are already closed, and a stable MoReq2010 draft is available for public consultation, on which this paper writes about (the final version is expected for May 2011). MoReq2010 contains 475 mandatory requirements (9 more than MoReq2), which are divided in 16 sections and 6 modules.

MoReq2010 brought a big change in the structure of the requirements from the earlier versions, now grouped in modules of functionality surrounding a reduced set of core requirements. Those modules are conceived to be easily combined to specify a specific MoReq compliant ERMS according to the needs of an organization, resulting in multiple possible shapes of ERMS [7]. This new approach also allows evolutionary revision and upgrade, enabling MoReq2010 to adapt to new innovations and new practices in both the technology and in the field of records management.

3 TOGAF

The emerging requirements related to the access of information are increasingly becoming a critical part of any organization as its size and complexity growths. This is precisely where Enterprise Architecture comes into play by providing rigorous descriptions of complex systems with diverse concerns.

In this context, **Enterprise Architecture** is defined as "a set of principles which guide design, selection, construction, implementation, deployment, support, and management of information infrastructure" [8]. More specifically, Enterprise Architecture describes the structure of an enterprise by exposing the composition of the enterprise components and their relationships with the environment. It aligns enterprise goals and drivers, business processes, organizational structures and behaviors, information, software applications, computer systems and technological infrastructure [1]. As a result, Enterprise Architecture is also a tool for identifying opportunities to improve the enterprise and the business itself by pursuing its future effectiveness and efficiency.

In order to realize these architectural descriptions, architects rely on frameworks that offer the tools, methods, techniques, descriptions, views, models and guidelines which are able to support the production of enterprise architectures.

TOGAF stands for "The Open Group Architecture Framework", and it was developed by the Architecture Forum of the Open Group[2] with the purpose of defining a framework for developing an Enterprise Architecture. It is based on an iterative process that supports four architectural domains [3]:

- **Business Architecture:** defines the business strategy, governance, organization, and key business processes.
- **Data Architecture:** describes the structure of an organization's logical and physical data assets and data management resources.
- **Application Architecture:** provides a blueprint for the individual application systems to be deployed, their interactions, and their relationships to the core business processes of the organization.
- **Technology Architecture:** describes the logical software and hardware capabilities that are required to support the deployment of business, data, and application services.

These domains are developed through a repeatable and iterative process that supports their development in terms of content, transition, and governance, according to business goals and opportunities. This method is called "Architecture Development Method" (ADM) and as represented in Fig 1 is understood as in the core of TOGAF [3].

In the preliminary phase of TOGAF, the organizational context is reviewed as well as relevant principles, standards and guidelines that will impact the architecture.

The process begins with the development of an architecture vision (phase A) in which the stakeholders are defined together with their own concerns. Also, business requirements, goals, drivers and constrains are identified and confirmed. This architecture vision guides the development of the business architecture (phase B), information systems architecture (phase C), and technology architecture (phase D).

Based on these architectures, solutions and opportunities are identified (phase E) in order to derive "Transition Architectures" that deliver continuous flow of business value in support of enterprise goals. This phase takes both a business and technical perspective to address IT governance activities. Next, a migration plan is created (phase F) to ensure that the adequate resources are allocated and that business value is delivered to each project.

---

[2] http://www.opengroup.org/

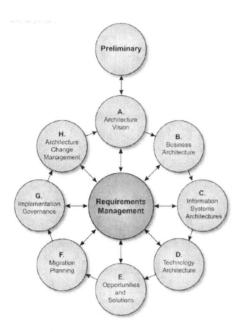

Fig. 1. TOGAF – The phases of ADM [3]

The architectures produced are then implemented (phase G) through an organizational-specific development process. Finally, these are subject of an architecture change management (phase H) which aims to ensure that the architecture continues to fit-for-purpose and still delivers business value.

TOGAF also provides the concept of Enterprise Continuum which explains "how generic solutions can be leveraged and specialized in order to support the requirements of an individual organization" [3]. In this sense Enterprise Continuum includes both the Architecture Continuum and the Solution Continuum. While the former specifies methods for classifying architectures assets as they evolve from generic to more specific ones, the latter describes the realization of Architecture Continuum through reusable building blocks and vice-versa.

4   Requirements on TOGAF

Requirements management is the central process of the TOGAF ADM, as shown in **Fig 1**, and is crucial to the entire framework since it clarifies some of the uncertainty and the need of managing changes during EA processes. The objective of this phase is to "identify requirements for the enterprise, store them, and feed them in and out of the relevant ADM phases, which dispose of, address, and prioritize requirements"[3]. It's also important to state that the requirements management process is designed to be a dynamic process that reacts to, and encourages, changes by adding, removing and updating requirements continuously.

TOGAF recognizes that the world of requirements engineering is very rich so they don't mandate any process or tool to perform the requirements management process. Rather, they prefer to describe what outputs a process like this should have and recommend some resources for the process.

One of those resources is the Business Scenario – a technique to discover and document business requirements for the architecture and the implied technical requirements. A Business Scenario "represents a significant business need or problem, and enables vendors to understand the value to the customer organization of a developed solution" [3]. The depth of the description given in the technique depends on the scenario being described but typically it should have references to the business process, or the application that can be supported by the architecture, the technology environment, the actors of the scenario and the expected results from the execution of the EA process.

With a good Business Scenario it is possible to derive a set of requirements that describe the whole problem description, or to clearly understand the value of the problem and the relevance of potential solutions. It's also essential to understand that the creation of a scenario is a task not only for the architect but also for all the stakeholders involved in the business problem being described [3]. That involvement is crucial to ensure that the problem, goals and requirements are properly captured.

Another recommended source suggested by TOGAF is the Volere[3], a trademark brand owned by Atlantic Systems Guild that offers a collection of requirements resources which include courses, templates, books, processes, etc. One of the most known resources is the Volere Requirements Specification Template [9], a useful template to use as a foundation for requirements specification. It provides a structured template that describes the most appropriate requirements types that should be used in the business, scientific and software systems domains providing a checklist, structure, and traceability paths for the requirements. Another important resource provided by Volere is the Requirements Tools section[4] that offers a large, and increasing, number of Requirements Management tools.

Therefore, according to TOGAF, after finishing the Requirements Management process, one should produce two major outputs: the Requirements Impact Assessment and the Architecture Requirements Specification. The first one is used to assess how the architecture requirements imply the current state of the architecture by identifying the changes that should be made and their implications. It is typically identified over requirements by exploring the stakeholders, the importance or given priority, the phases that need to be reviewed, new requirements priority according to new requirement(s), recommendations on how to manage the impact of the modifications, and a repository reference number.

On another hand, the Architecture Requirements Specification "provides a set of quantitative statements that outline what an implementation project must do in order to comply with the architecture" [3]. It addresses success measures; architecture requirements; service contracts; implementation guidelines, specifications and standards; interoperability requirements; constrains and assumptions.

---

[3] http://www.volere.co.uk
[4] http://www.volere.co.uk/tools.htm

Table 1. Definition of the sections that an architecture requirements specification must contain

Section	Definition
Success Measures	Lists "indicators or factors that can be tracked, usually on an ongoing basis, to determine success or alignment with objectives or goals" [3].
Architecture Requirements	Section divided in three architecture requirements types: Business, Information System and Technology. Definitions below.
Business Architecture Requirement	Requirement related to all the aspects of the business processes that can be identifiable as a segment of an organization's overall mission [10] [11].
Information System Architecture Requirement	Requirement that reflect a property that is essential for an IT system to perform its function.
Technologic Architecture Requirement	Requirement with concerns about the technologic components available from the market or configured within the organization into technology platforms.
Architecture Service Contracts	Describes the joint agreements between development partners and sponsors on the deliverables, quality and fitness-for-purpose of an architecture. The contracts can be about business or application services [3].
Implementation guidelines, specifications and standards	Describes the guidelines, specifications and standards recommended or mandated for achieving success.
Interoperability Requirements	Lists the requirements that define or relate to the ability to share information and services.
Constrains	Requirements that place a condition on the achievement of a goal describing a restriction or a limitation [12].
Assumptions	Requirements where we assume something to be true in order to achieve it.

5   MoReq2010 as an Architecture Requirements Specification

MoReq2010 is a requirements specification for ERMS resulting from a requirements management process that gathers, analyzes, and categorizes requirements for that kind of systems. But is this specification broad enough to be used as an Architecture Requirements Specification? Does the specification address all of the sections defined in TOGAF? To answer these questions one should define what an Architecture Requirements Specification must be according to TOGAF. This is given by **Table 1**, from where we can compare MoReq2010 specification with the elements listed in Table 2 and match the corresponding requirements.

Table 2. Number of Architecture Requirements present in the non-functional requirements chapters of MoReq2010

MoReq2010 Non- Functional Requirements Chapter		Business Requirements	Information System Requirements	Technologic Requirements
1.16	Business Continuity	1	9	5
1.17	Performance and Scalability	1	15	2
1.18	Operation Compliance	0	15	0
101.4	Graphical User Interfaces	0	12	0
102.4	Application Programming Interfaces	2	0	5
202.4	Monolingual Thesauri	0	1	0
301.4	Managed Components	0	2	4
302.4	Unmanaged Components	5	3	0
	Total	9	55	16

Table 3. Possible Architecture Service Contracts found on MoReq2010

Architecture Service Contract	Stakeholders Involved	MoReq2010 Requirements	Goal of the contract
Business	ERMS Developer	R1.5.11 N1.6.2-9 N1.18.8-15 N102.4.4-5	- Schedule periodic updates and backups of the ERMS - Define system maintenance and support- Define costs - Define Documentation to be provided - Schedule API updates
Application	Authentication Service Developer	R1.7.1 N1.18.2	- Provide secure access to the ERMS user
Application	Directory Service Developer	R1.7.4 N1.18.3	- Provide user information to the ERMS

Analyzing MoReq2010 we couldn't find any requirement that can be understood as a possible *success measure*. However, like his ancestor MoReq2, the specification is going to have a framework test that intends to provide a way of determining the alignment of a system with MoReq2010, so in that sense achieving the same goal as the success measures.

Since MoReq2010 is a requirements specification for an information system (an ERMS) it was not strange to realize that all the functional requirements described fall in the category of Information System *Architecture Requirements*. However it also was possible to identify some business and technologic requirements in the non-functional requirements of MoReq2010, as the **Table 2** shows.

In what concerns *Architecture Service Contracts* there isn't any section in MoReq2010 that list them but it's possible to find references to three possible contracts, described in **Table 3**, on the requirements of the specification.

Regarding guidelines, specifications and standards, MoReq2010 states that:

- ISO 15489 and the emerging ISO 30300 are solid internationally recognized resources for organizations to refer to when planning their wider business objectives around MoReq2010 compliant records systems.
- The ERMS must generate universally unique identifiers (UUID) and recommends using the approaches listed in RFC4122 for the process.
- The ERMS must use valid language identifiers compliant with RFC5646 and the IANA Language Subtag Registry.
- The ERMS must be able to capture, store and export Unicode text and must use it for all textual metadata elements.
- The ERMS must keep timestamps that are compatible with W3C XML dateTimeStamp formats.
- The ERMS must support the export of entities, their metadata and their components using the W3C EXI (Efficient XML Interchange) standard.
- When the GUI of the ERMS is hosted within a web-browser interface the ERMS must meet the W3C Web Content Accessibility Guidelines (WCAG) 2.0 and the W3C Accessible Rich Internet Applications (WAI-ARIA) 1.0 to at least conformance level A.

Interoperability in MoReq2010 is restricted to the XML Schema that underpins the specification. Using that schema, the ERMS is compliant with MoReq2010 which enables the transfer of records between systems without losing contextual data and providing the ability to maintain the record's lifecycle after transfer. Moreover, in order to achieve the goal of interoperability, MoReq2010 is much more prescriptive than its predecessors in the sense that it can provide a way of interpreting the metadata of another system.

Interoperability is also another subject that DLM Forum wants to continually address in future versions of the specification so that real-time collaboration between records and archival systems, live transfers, and accessibility can also be possible. Concluding on this, MoReq2010 can be seen as a starting point for that goal.

When looking for *assumptions and constrains* we realize that almost all MoReq2010 requirements are constrains in the sense that they are so specific that avoid other interpretations or implementations. This complies with the DLM-Forum objective of making the specification as precise as possible to improve the interoperability of

MoReq2010 systems. In what concerns the assumptions, the requirements that are related to the architecture application service contracts previously described are the only ones that can be seen as assumptions since they depend on the supposition that the authentication and directory services work correctly.

6 Conclusions and Future Work

By the results observed in the previous section we can conclude that MoReq2010 is not complete enough to be used as an Architecture Requirement Specification in the scope of an Enterprise Architecture framework as TOGAF. Mostly it lacks on success measures and on insufficient number of Business and Technologic Architecture Requirements. However the requirements specification address almost all the concerns that an Architecture Requirements Specification must have, so it should be considered at least as a good starting point for further research in this area.

Another conclusion that we can extract from our analysis is that are concerns that maybe MoReq2010 fails to properly address. We could agree that some of them may be out of the scope of the specification, but other relevant requirements may be really pointed as missing. For example the lack of technologic architecture requirements can be seen as a valid approach since it brings less constrains to the information system architecture, meaning that the ERMS doesn't depend on specific technology to be implemented. But that's only one viewpoint since others may say that some functions of the system fully depend on technologic requirements. In fact this can be an issue to explore in upcoming work.

In the same topic, we pretend in the future to use the same methodology to analyze and adapt other records management resources besides MoReq, so that in the end we can achieve a complete records management profile that fits the TOGAF framework. We also expect that this work will be relevant for the future development of MoReq.

Acknowledgments. This work was supported by FCT (INESC-ID multiannual funding) through the national PIDDAC Program funds and by the European Commission through the SHAMAN project (contract FP7-ICT-216736).

References

1. Lankhorst, M.: Enterprise Architecture at Work: Modelling, Communication, and Analysis. Springer, Heidelberg (2005)
2. Borbinha, J.: It Is the Time for the Digital Library to Meet the Enterprise Architecture. In: Goh, D.H.-L., Cao, T.H., Sølvberg, I.T., Rasmussen, E. (eds.) ICADL 2007. LNCS, vol. 4822, pp. 176–185. Springer, Heidelberg (2007)
3. The Open Group: TOGAF Version 9: The Open Group Architecture Framework. Van Haren Publishing, Zaltbommel (2009)
4. International Organization for Standardization: ISO 15489: Information and documentation - Records management - Part 1: General. ISO Std. (2001)
5. National Archives of Australia: Digital Recordkeeping: Guidelines for Creating, Managing and Preserving Digital Records. Exposure draft, Commonwealth of Australia (May 2004) ISBN 1 920807 08 X

6. DLM-Forum: MoReq2010 - a new world standard for compliance & the best practice information management for all sectors (2010)
7. Fresko, M.: MoReq2010 - on the track or off the rails? (2010)
8. Spewak, S.: Enterprise Architecture Planning: Developing a Blueprint for Data, Applications, and Technology. John Wiley & Sons, New York (1995)
9. Robertson, J., Robertson, S.: Volere Requiremens Specification Template (2006)
10. Kazhamiakin, R., Pistore, M., Roveri, M.: A framework for integrating business processes and business requirements. In: EDOC 2004, Monterey, USA (2004)
11. Lavoie, B., Henry, G., Dempsey, L.: A service framework for libraries (2006)
12. Antón, A.: Goal-based Requirements Analysis, Colorado (1996)

Strategic Alignment: Comparison of Approaches

Karim Doumi, Salah Baïna, and Karim Baïna

ENSIAS, Mohamed V - Souissi University, Morocco
Kdoumi@fsjesr.ac.ma, {sbaina,baina}@ensias.ma

Abstract. Nowadays, the strategic alignment of information systems has become a priority in most large organizations. It is a question of aligning the information system on the business strategies of the organization. This step is aimed at increasing the practical value of the information system and makes it a strategic asset for the organization. In the literature several approaches have been developed to solve the problem of alignment. For example the approach of alignment between architecture and the business context, the approach needs oriented, approach alignment between process and information system...etc. In this paper we propose a detailed study of each approach (benefits and limitation) and we propose a comparison between these different approaches.

Keywords: strategic alignment, Enterprise architecture, goals modeling, strategy, Business process, information system.

1 Introduction

The strategy of the enterprise is to set up the long-term commitments to reach the explicit objectives. It is a question of studying, via real cases, how an enterprise can position itself in an international competing. The alignment of this strategy with the evolution of information system requires an alignment allowing the perfect coherence of all the actions and the decisions with the strategic objectives of the enterprise. This alignment will transform strategic objectives into operational actions to align them in the information system.

Many authors have shown the importance of alignment in the evolution of the enterprise [1-2] and according to [3-6], this alignment has a great influence on the performance of the organization and any rupture in the process of alignment causes a fall of the organization's performance.

If the interest of alignment is greatly recognized, its implementation remains very limited. According to [1,7], few leaders consider that the strategy and the information systems are aligned. Thus, this implies that actors of the organization are not able to distinguish between alignment and non-alignment.

Also, the absence of methods of maintenance of alignment makes the task extremely difficult at the decisional level.

In the literature several approaches have been developed to solve the problem of alignment. In this paper we present an evaluation of 8 approaches to alignment, which we felt were relevant, applicable and representing the state of the art.

M.M. Cruz-Cunha et al. (Eds.): CENTERIS 2011, Part II, CCIS 220, pp. 345–355, 2011.

This document is structured in four parts. In Section 2, we present a set of approaches to strategic alignment. Each approach is briefly presented. In Section 3, we present a comparative study between these approaches. We conclude and present our work in progress in Section 4.

2   Approaches of Strategic Alignment Business /IT

2.1   Approach of Enterprise Architecture

Approach:
Several studies have shown that enterprise architecture is practiced in major international organizations and governmental institutions that have adopted it as a tool of strategic governance.

ZACHMAN proposes a framework in which there are 36 models distributed according to six prospects and six aspects of the enterprise and system.

In this framework there are three categories of model:

(1) Business models
(2) System information models
(3) Technological models (IT)

The first type of models is present in the first two rows of the matrix and is interested in the enterprise and its environment (strategy, objectives, activities ...). The 2nd type on the 3rd line and describes the architecture of information systems. Finally the last type of model is on the last two lines that describe the technical architecture of the enterprise.

Limits:
Real experiments have shown interest of the ZACHMAN Framework [15] to help manage change and improve the availability of enterprise documentation. However, several practical issues were raised [16],[17]. We can cite for example the lack of methodological process to guide a process of alignment, lack of dynamics and lack of integration of different views.

2.2   Approach of Enterprise Architecture (French): Urbanization of Information System [9]

Approach:
If it has been usual for a long time to speak about architecture of the information systems, the concept of town planning is more recent but spreads quickly. It rests on the report that it is impossible to rebuild entirely an information system by making a clean slate of what exists, but that on the contrary the reorganizations and modernizations are permanent.

The problems thus consist in making the information system most reactive possible (i.e. able to evolve quickly to answer the new requests) while preserving the informational inheritance of the enterprise. The urbanization of the information systems aims at bringing an answer to this need.

The approach of urbanization of information system was studied by many authors [9, 18]. The works of these authors supplement the works relative to the enterprise's architecture (Zachman) [8]. All these authors use the metaphors to found the concept structures and urbanization of information system, in particular the metaphor of the city is used like base of urbanization of information system. Methods of urbanization of information systems have all in common eight essential steps:

- Model business processes
- Document the current (As-Is)
- Define the target « future » (To-Be)
- Define a migration plan
- Use a modeling tool for documenting the EA
- Set rules
- Assist projects
- Manage projects

Limits:
Urbanization Information System provides a guide to manage the strategic alignment to define future Information system.

However, the method of this approach does not say how to ensure an evolution of enterprise strategy, its business processes and its information system and how to measure and improve the alignment between these elements.

2.3 Approach of Modeling and Construction of Alignment Oriented Needs [10]

Approach:
Bleistein [10] seeks to align enterprise strategy to the system. For this they propose requirements engineering approach that brings in the same model (1) the strategic objectives of the organization and (2) the activities and processes to which these objectives are achieved.

This approach uses goals modeling for modeling the enterprise strategy. Bleistein use the model BRG (Business Rules group) to organize enterprise strategy. This model is a conceptual framework consists of two concepts: (1) Ends: that are the things the enterprise wants to reach as (goal, objective, vision) (2) Means: the things that the company uses to achieve those purposes as (strategy, tactics, mission).

This model does not use specific language of representation that is why Bleistein uses the modeling language I * [20]. He proposed to match the model I * with BRG to make it operational.

This approach allows building a system aligned with enterprise strategy and business processes. It is based on:

- Modeling strategy using the model I *
- Defining the business context using problem fram (jackson)[19]. This step is based on the clear separation between the context of existing problems and solutions to build.
- The modeling of business processes through diagrams roles activities.

Limits:

The approach of Bleistein is interesting in the sense that it takes into account the strategic level in the presentation of the alignment but is impractical and very complicated to master it. Is an approach to building alignment and not the evaluation and evolution of the alignment.

The guide is not defined, the method proposes to use the fram problem of Jackson and match the BRG model with elements of model I * but there is no clear guide to construct the alignment.

2.4   Approach of Evaluation and Evolution of Strategic Alignment [2]

Approach:

Luftman [2] proposes a framework for measuring the alignment between two entities: the enterprise strategy and IT strategy. This framework incorporates the fundamentals of the CMM model *(Capability Maturity Model).*

The approach aims to assess and improve the relationship of alignment between enterprise strategy and IT strategy.

The approach does not define any relationship between the elements of the alignment. Luftman tries to explain the "understanding of IT by the business".

To identify the level of alignment of an organization, six criteria were identified:

- The degree of maturity of communication.
- The maturity of the ability to measure.
- The maturity to lead (steering).
- The maturity of the partnership between business and IT.
- The degree of maturity of the architecture.
- The maturity of knowledge.

Guidance is proposed through six steps:

(1) Define goals and develop a team of managers and engineers from functional entities. The team must assess the maturity of the alignment between enterprise strategies and IT strategies

(2) Understanding the link between business and IT. The team assesses each of the six criteria with the objective of converging towards a single vision.

(3) Analyze gaps: this step aims to analyze the actions needed to improve alignment. For each criterion, the differences are fixed between the current situation of organization and the situation that the team has set. The high level of maturity serves as a guideline to identify actions to put in place.

(4) Specifying actions: knowing the maturity level of alignment helps identify actions to improve alignment. This step aims to assign tasks to each of the gaps identified in the previous step in precisely defining the documentation, resources, risks, measures to ensure that the problem of the gap has been resolved.

(5) Choose and evaluate success criteria: this step requires review the goals and revisit regularly measurement criteria identified to assess the implementation of projects.

(6) Maintain alignment. This step is, according to Luftman [2], the most difficult.

Limits:
The approach of Luftman gives guidance for the construction of the alignment. The approach does not seek to change the alignment of the elements but to achieve a higher maturity level of alignment between strategic objectives and IT strategy.

2.5 Approach of Modeling and Construction of Alignment between the Environment, Processes and the Systems [11]

Approach:
The SEAM approach ("Systemic Enterprise Architecture Method") aims to build a future situation in which the company and its system are aligned [11].

The SEAM method focuses not only on the alignment between the system and the company but also a managerial view "between the enterprise and its environment, the market...)

In SEAM, the company is represented by a hierarchical model. Each level contains systems. A system may be an information system, department, enterprise or corporate of enterprise or even a market.

A SEAM enterprise model has three levels: (1) the business level representing enterprise, (2) the operational level and (3) the level of information technology

In SEAM, the alignment is defined as follows:

- Alignment of sets of entities from different organizational levels: two representations of a set of entities in two adjacent levels of the organization are aligned if it is possible to identify the conduct described in the highest level in the conduct described in the lowest organizational level.
- Alignment of sets of entities of different functional levels: two representations of entities with two different functional levels are aligned if it is possible to identify in the conduct described above in the functional behavior described at the functional level as low.
- Alignment of business and information technology: the alignment of business and IT requires alignment of sets of entities from different organizational levels and alignment of sets of entities of different functional levels.

Limits:
The SEAM method uses the same notations in different levels and thus between the different elements of alignment. The SEAM method does not take into account the particularity of each level of abstraction.

2.6 Approach of Evaluation of the Degree of Alignment of the Business Process and Information System [12]

Approach:
The method ACEM (Alignment Correction Method and Evolution) focuses on the alignment between two entities, business processes and information system (functional level).

The method proposes to adapt the model business processes with the system information model in order to restore the alignment between these two entities.

ACEM method proposes an approach that allows an organization to move from a present situation to a future situation.

The present situation is characterized by the As-Is models PM (Process Model) and As-Is SM (System Model) that represent business processes and system functionality. The future situation is characterized by the models To-Be PM and To-Be SM representing respectively the state of business and system, after evolution.

The methodology proposes three steps ACEM, presented and detailed in [12].

The three steps are:

(1) Obtaining the pivot model for a unified view of the process model and system.

(2) The evolution of the pivot model with the identification of gaps that can express a change or improvement in the alignment.

(3) Analyze of the gaps identified in the pivot model system models and processes.

The pivot model uses the formalism of the Map [21].

A map is represented graphically as a directed graph where nodes are goals and arcs of ways to achieve the target goals from the goals sources.

ACEM method takes into account requirements changes respectively from (1) dysfunction of the system or process (2) breaks the relation of alignment.

The requirements of change are expressed as differences between the model pivot As Is and model pivot To Be. Evolution is the common model, pivot, and then there is an impact on entities to align, so it is a method of evolution interdependence type.

Limits:

This approach allows to model and evolve the alignment between business process and information system but do not take into consideration the strategic level in the representation of the alignment.

2.7 Approach of Evaluation of the Degree of Alignment between the Couple Strategy of the Enterprise and (Business Process, Information System) [14]

Approach:

The INSTAL (Intentional Strategic Alignment) method focuses on the alignment between two levels, strategic and functional level.

The operational level includes business processes and information systems. The strategic level involves the enterprise strategy and needs at high level.

This method proposes first to document the strategic alignment by: (1) the intentional model representing the two levels and (2) the definition of alignment links between this model and the elements of the enterprise (documents, methods, procedures) from the strategic and operational level.

The approach uses the formalism maps [21] to represent elements of the two levels.

Links strategic alignment, which are attached to the intentions of MAPs, defines all the elements justifying strategic intentions and all operational elements contributing or not to them.

Then INSTAL offers metrics and measures. Metrics provide quantitative or qualitative view of the alignment. Each metric or measure is defined by a specific method. The methods may be objective (based quantification of numerical rules) or subjective.

INSTALL adopts a typology to organize the metrics / measures. This typology has four categories: efficiency, effectiveness, accessibility and accountability. Each category has the characteristic dimensions. For example, efficiency on the number of resources required for the provision of a service has two dimensions: time and economic.

The evolution guided by INSTAL takes place at the operational level, and simultaneously on business processes and information systems. As such, INSTAL can be seen as a methodological approach that guides the co-evolution of business processes and information system with respect to strategy.

The methodological approach INSTAL consists of three steps:

(1) Diagnosis of strategic alignment.
(2) Discovery and analysis of requirements evolution.
(3) Propagation and validation of requirements of evolution.

(1) INSTALL proposes for diagnosing alignment As-Is from the modeling alignment. The model establishes a mapping which aims to produce a model of strategic alignment.

(2) The requirements of change can occur when developing models of strategic alignment or in their analysis. The requirements of evolution are either corrections from the previous step or new requirements, known alignment requirements which are derived from the strategy or operational level.

(3) Different requirements evolution can be produced following the analysis of patterns of alignment. These requirements might involve changing the same elements, they can be combined or mixed. This step can again check the consistency of the requirements of development and analyze their impact on the operational elements.

Limits:
The method takes into consideration the INSTALL strategic level in representing the strategic alignment but impractical because it uses formalizes card that does not include all elements of the strategic level.

2.8 Approach Oriented Values: E3 Values

Approach:
The approach E3 values [22] examine the alignment between strategy and business processes and IT. This approach combines the goals models and Business model [23]. The Model E3 values focuses on the transfer of items of economic value between a networks of actors.

Other work has been based on E3 values, for example the Framework approach E 3 alignment [24]. This approach is a model that explores the issue of inter-organizational alignment on the interaction between organizations in network of values (value Web).

To create alignment, coherence between the various organizations within the value network, the approach E3 alignment is interested to the alignment of interactions between these organizations. By aligning the interactions between organizations, E 3 alignment creates a network of viable and sustainable value in 4 perspectives :

- Strategic perspective: to understand the strategic influence of organizations on other organizations (This perspective uses E3 values).
- value perspective to understand the things of economic value that is exchanged between organizations in a value network (This perspective uses E3 values)
- Process perspective: to understand the order and activities behind the interactions (this perspective uses UML activity diagrams)
- SI perspective to understand IT for the exchange of information between organizations. (This perspective uses technical architecture diagrams)

Limits:
The e3-value framework particularly interested in the value stream, the creation, exchange and consumption of objects in network multi-actor that includes the company itself and its environment (customers, partners) . According to Bleistein missing a crucial point in the e3-value is the distinction between value analysis and business strategy. Moreover, the link between the creation of economic value and goals of low-level system is unclear.

Tools and guidance to change are not defined.

3   Comparison of Approaches

In all these approaches, the concept of alignment of information system is traditionally treated through the results obtained after alignment. Thus, according to [25], alignment exists when the information system is consistent with the purposes and activities selected to position the enterprise in its market. [12] defines alignment as the set of linkages between elements of the model business processes and elements of the model of the information system support. [26] defined alignment as the degree to which the mission, goals and plans contained in the competitive strategy is shared and supported by the IT strategy. According to the report CIGREFF 2002 the term "alignment" expresses the idea of the consistency of the information system strategy with business strategy. This alignment requires constant maintenance throughout its life cycle.

In other words, the classical vision of alignment involves two main areas: the area of Business (competitive strategy and activities of the organization) and the field of IT (IT strategy and IS support) that it is to ensure consistency.

The issue of business IT alignment must necessarily pass through the life cycle of alignment: (1) identification of elements that will contribute to the construction of the alignment and (2) the evaluation, and (3) necessary actions to correct this alignment (figure 1).

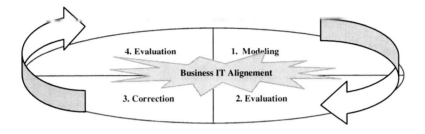

Fig. 1. Cycle of strategic alignment

Our evaluation criteria are related to this cycle of alignment: modeling (alignment entity, modeling language), evaluation and correction of alignment.

Alignment entity: (levels supported by the alignment) as the table shows it, the majority of the approaches of alignment connect 3 entities at the maximum only the approach of [8] has seven entities.

In the whole of these approaches, alignment passes between a pair of entities. [2] is interested in the alignment of enterprise strategies and IT strategies. [11] in alignment between the system, the processes and the environment, [14] alignment between the couple strategy of the company/business process, information system.

Modeling: (modeling language used) the modeling or the documentation of alignment is based on the modeling of the objectives for [11], while [12] uses the intentional approach based on ontology of WWB. [8] uses a modeling based on a matrix according to 6 prospects and 6 aspects.

Evaluation: (valuation method used) [11] proposes an approach of evaluation which rests on interpretation, judgment. These are the interpretations which make it possible to show if there is alignment or not without evaluating a degree of this alignment. Other approaches propose criteria of evaluation associated with quantitative measurements. For example, to count to accounting) the number of activities dealt with by the system [12,13].

Correction: (correction method used) several approaches were interested in the correction of strategic alignment. For example [12, 14] are based on the results of the evaluation of alignment to define the evolutions to be implemented. The correction is done step by step by evaluating alignment after each change [12]. In all these approaches, actions proposed for the corrections are very difficult to implement and very poor at detail provided.

4 Conclusion

This paper presents a state of art and a comparison between some approaches of alignment. The objective is then to propose a model for representation of the alignment that takes into account three entities: enterprise strategy, business processes and information system.

Table 1. Comparative table of the approaches of strategic alignment

Study ⟍ Criterion	Luftman 2000	Zachman 2003	Bodhuin 2004	Bleinstein 2005	Wegmann 2005	Etien 2006	Longépé 2006	Gordijn 2006	Thevenet 2009
alignment entity	strategy/ IT	Enterprise strategy& IT BP, System, environment, organisation, architecture.	Business process/ IS	Strategy/ Business Process	Environment/ Business process	Business process/IS	Strategy/ IS	Straategy/business Process , IT	strategy/ (business process, IS)
Modelling levels	---	---	functional	strategy	functional	functional	functional	Strategy/functional	Strategy/functional
Construction of alignment	—	——	Top-Down	Top-Down	Top-Down	Top-Down	Top-Down	Top-Down	Top-Down
Modelling	--	Artifact classification	---	Goals modeling (I*)	---	Ontology	---	Goals modeling/ Business Model	card formalism
Evaluation of alignment	No	No	yes	No	No	yes	NO	NO	yes
Correction of alignment	No	No	No	No	No	NO	No	No	No

We consider that the strategic level defines the intentions of the enterprise. Its implementation is done through the conduct of business processes and thus the treatment of strategic alignment between business strategy and information system does can be done without going through the business processes that support enterprise activities.

References

1. Luftman, J., Maclean, E.R.: Key issues for IT executives. MIS Quarterly Executive 3, 89–104 (2004)
2. Luftman, J.: Assessing business-IT alignment maturity. Communications of the Association for Information Systems 4(14), 1–50 (2000)
3. Baïna, S., Ansias, P., Petit, M., Castiaux, A.: Strategic Business/IT Alignment using Goal Models. In: Proceedings of the Third International Workshop on Business/IT Alignment and Interoperability (BUSITAL 2008) Held in Conjunction with CAISE 2008 Conference Montpellier, France, June 16-17 (2008)
4. Chan, Y., Huff, S., Barclay, D., Copeland, D.: Business Strategic Orientation: Information Systems Strategic Orientation and Strategic Alignment. Information Systems Research 8, 125–150 (1997)
5. Croteau, A.-M., Bergeron, F.: "An Information Technology Trilogy: Business Strategy", Technological Deployment and Organizational Performance. Journal of Strategic Information Systems (2001)
6. Tallon, P.P., Kraemer, K.L.: Executives' Perspectives on IT: Unraveling the Link between Business Strategy, Management Practices and IT Business Value. In: Americas Conference on Information Systems, ACIS 2002, Dallas, TX, USA (2002)
7. Renner, A.R., Latimore, D., Wong, D.: Business and IT operational models in financial services: Beyond strategic alignment. IBM Institute for Business Value study (2003)

8. Zachman, J.A.: A Framework for Information Systems Architecture. IBM Systemps Journal 26, 276–292 (1987)
9. Longépé, C.: Le projet d'urbanisation du SI. Collection Informatique et Entreprise, Dunod (2001)
10. Bleistein, S.J.: B-SCP: an integrated approach for validating alignment of organizational IT requirements with competitive business strategy, the university of new south wales, phD thesis, Sydney Australia (January 3, 2006)
11. Wegmann, A., Regev, R., Loison, B.: Business and IT Alignment with SEAM. In: Proceedings of REBNITA Requirements Engineering for Business Need and IT Alignment, Paris (August 2005)
12. Etien, A.: L'ingénierie de l'alignement: Concepts, Modèles et Processus. In: La méthode ACEM pour la correction et l'évolution d'un système d'information aux processus d'entreprise, thèse de doctorat. Université Paris 1 (mars 16, 2006)
13. Etien, A., Salinesi, C.: Managing Requirements in a Co-evolution Context. In: Proceedings of the IEEE International Conference on Requirements Engineering, Paris, France (September 2005)
14. Thevenet, L.H., Rolland, C., Salinesi, C.: Alignement de la stratégie et de l'organisation: Présentation de la méthode INSTAL, Ingénierie des Systèmes d'Information (ISI). In: Revue Ingénierie des Systèmes d'Information Special Issue on IS Evolution, Hermès, pp. 17–37 (June 2009)
15. Brown, T.: The Value of Enterprise Architecture, ZIFA report (2005)
16. Meersman, B.: The Commission Enterprise Architecture cadre., Presentation to European Commission Directorate Genral Informatics (2004)
17. Khory, R., Simoff, S.J.: Enterprise architecture modelling using elastic metaphors. In: Proceedings of the First Asian-Pacific Conference on Conceptual Modelling, vol. 31 (2004)
18. Bonne, J.C., Maddaloni, A.: Convaincre pour urbaniser le SI. Hermes, Lavoisier (2004)
19. Jackson, M.: Problem Frames: Analyzing and Structuring Software Development Problem. Addison-Wesley Publishing Company, Reading (2001)
20. Yu, E.: Towards Modeling and Reasoning Support for Early-Phase Requirements Engineering. In: Proceedings of the 3rd IEEE International Symposium on Requirements Engineering, p. 226 (1997)
21. Rolland, C.: Capturing System Intentionality with Maps. In: Conceptual Modeling un Information Systems Engineering, pp. 141–158. Springer, Heidelberg (2007)
22. Gordijn, J., Akkermans, J.: Value-based requirements engineering: Exploring innovative e-commerce ideas. Requirements Engineering 8(2), 114–134 (2003)
23. Gordijn, J., Petit, M., Wieringa, R.: Understanding business strategies of networked value constellations using goal- and value modeling. In: Glinz, M., Lutz, R. (eds.) Proceedings of the 14th IEEE International Requirements Engineering Conference, pp. 129–138. IEEE CS, Los Alamitos (2006)
24. Pijpers, V., Gordijn, J., Akkermans, H.: Exploring inter-organizational alignment wit e3alignment – An Aviation Case. In: 22nd Bled eConference eEnablement: Facilitating an Open, Effective and Representative eSociety, BLED 2009, Bled, Slovenia, June 14-17, (2009)
25. McKeen, J.D., Smith, H.A.: Making IT Happen: Critical Issues in IT Management. Wiley, Chichester (2003)
26. Reich, B.H., Benbasat, I.: Measuring the Linkage between Business and Information Technology Objectives. MIS Quarterly, 20(1), 55–81 (1996)

Experimenting a Modeling Approach for Modeling Enterprise Strategy in the Context of Strategic Alignment

Karim Doumi, Salah Baïna, and Karim Baïna

ENSIAS, Mohamed V - Souissi University, Morocco
kdoumi@fsjesr.ac.ma, {sbaina,baina}@ensias.ma

Abstract. Nowadays, the business IT alignment has become a priority in most large organizations. It is a question of aligning the information system on the business strategies of the organization. This step is aimed at increasing the practical value of the information system and makes it a strategic asset for the organization. Many works showed the importance of documentation, the analysis and the evaluation of business IT alignment, but few proposed solutions applicable to the strategic and functional level. This paper aims has to fill this gap by proposing a simple approach for modeling enterprise strategy in the context of strategic alignment. This approach is illustrated by case study of a real project in a Moroccan public administration.

Keywords: strategic alignment, goals modeling, Enterprise architecture, Business process, information system.

1 Introduction

The strategy of the enterprise is to set up the long-term commitments to reach the explicit objectives. It is a question of studying, via real cases, how an enterprise can position itself in an international competing. The alignment of this strategy with the evolution of information system requires an alignment allowing the perfect coherence of all the actions and the decisions with the strategic objectives of the enterprise. This alignment will transform strategic objectives into operational actions to align them in the information system.

Today, it is not quite enough to build powerful information systems. In order for the enterprise to be performing and be able to compete and evolve, its information systems and business processes must be permanently aligned and in perfect coherence with its strategy.

Many authors have shown the importance of alignment in the evolution of the enterprise[1, 2] and according to [3-6], this alignment has a great influence on the performance of the organization and any rupture in the process of alignment causes a fall of the organization's performance.

If the interest of alignment is greatly recognized, its implementation remains very limited. According to [1, 7], few leaders consider that the strategy and the information systems are aligned. Thus, this implies that actors of the organization are not able to distinguish between alignment and non-alignment.

M.M. Cruz-Cunha et al. (Eds.): CENTERIS 2011, Part II, CCIS 220, pp. 356–368, 2011.
© Springer-Verlag Berlin Heidelberg 2011

Also, the absence of methods of maintenance of alignment makes the task extremely difficult at the decisional level.

There exist a number of models of strategic alignment. A well known model is Henderson's and Venkatraman's Strategic Alignment Model which give a rather total vision of strategic alignment. However, this kind of model remains very related to the field of management.

According to [17], a step of engineering is necessary to analyze the strategic alignment of the information system. This vision is also supported by the approaches of enterprise architecture [10] as well as the leaders of information system [9].

In the literature several approaches have been developed to solve the problem of alignment:

- Approach of Enterprise architecture (French): urbanization of Information System [9]. This approach provides a guide to manage the strategic alignment to define future Information system.

However, the method of this approach does not say how to ensure an evolution of enterprise strategy, its business processes and its information system and how to measure and improve the alignment between these elements.

- Approach of modeling and construction of alignment oriented needs [10]: The approach of Bleistein is interesting in the sense that it takes into account the strategic level in the presentation of the alignment but is impractical and very complicated to master it. Is an approach to building alignment and not the evaluation and evolution of alignment.

- Approach of evaluation and evolution of strategic alignment [2]: The approach of Luftamn gives guidance for the construction of the alignment. The approach does not seek to change the alignment of the elements but to achieve a higher maturity level of alignment between strategic objectives and IT strategy.

- Approach of modeling and construction of alignment between the environment, processes and the systems [11]: for example the SEAM method uses the same notations in different levels and thus between the different elements of alignment. The SEAM method does not take into account the particularity of each level of abstraction.

- Approach of evaluation of the degree of alignment of the business process and Information system [12, 13]. This approach allows to model and evolve the alignment between business process and information system but do not take into consideration the strategic level in the representation of the alignment.

- Approach of evaluation of the degree of alignment between the couple strategy of the enterprise and < Business process, information system> [14]. The INSTALL method takes into consideration the strategic level in representing the strategic alignment but impractical because it uses formalizes card that does not include all elements of the strategic level.

- Approach oriented values [22]. The e3-value framework particularly interested in the value stream, the creation, exchange and consumption of objects in network multi-actor that includes the company itself and its environment (customers, partners) . According to Bleistein missing a crucial point in the e3-value is the distinction between value analysis and business strategy. Moreover, the link between the creation of economic value and goals of low-level system is unclear. Also tools and guidance to change are not defined.

In all these approaches, the concept of alignment of information system is traditionally treated through the results obtained after alignment. Thus, according to [25], alignment exists when the information system is consistent with the purposes and activities selected to position the enterprise in its market. [12] defines alignment as the set of linkages between elements of the model business processes and elements of the model of the information system support. [26] defined alignment as the degree to which the mission, goals and plans contained in the competitive strategy is shared and supported by the IT strategy. According to the report CIGREFF 2002 the term "alignment" expresses the idea of the consistency of the information system strategy with business strategy. This alignment requires constant maintenance throughout its life cycle.

In other words, the classical vision of alignment involves two main areas: the area of Business (competitive strategy and activities of the organization) and the field of IT (Information System support) that it is to ensure consistency.

The issue of business IT alignment must necessarily pass through the cycle of alignment: (1) identification of elements that will contribute to the construction of the alignment and (2) the evaluation, and (3) necessary actions to correct this alignment (figure 1).

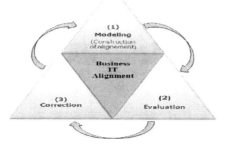

Fig. 1. Cycle of strategic alignment

In this paper we propose a model driven approach to (1) represent and (2) evaluate the business IT alignment. This approach allows to construct the alignment from the elements belonging to different abstraction levels (strategic & operational).

The paper is organized as follows: Section 2.1 presents a brief introduction of our approach. Sections 2 and 3 present our approach in strategic and functional level. Finally, Section 4 presents primary conclusions of the work presented in this paper and gives short term perspectives for ongoing research work.

2   Modeling of Business IT Alignment

2.1   Related Work

One of the most recurrent problems lately is the lack of strategy in strategic alignment [26], and even when it is taken into account, it remains ambiguous and very difficult to adapt. Indeed in the industry can find a set of techniques dedicated to the strategy. Each has its own concepts, methods and tools (eg, BCG matrix, the method MACTOR, SWOT analysis, the McKinsey 7S, internal value chains ... etc). These techniques are often used to plan and coordinate the business decision process with the Business Strategy. They are often used by business leaders and strategy consulting firms. They are thus based on measurements and performance values, but these approaches are rarely used in a process of alignment with the operational level.

At most research approaches alignment does not always specify explicitly which elements of the business that are involved in strategic alignment. For example, Bleistein & al. [10] in trying the method of using B-SCP requirements engineering for linking high-level requirements (strategic) with those of lower level, and focusing on the alignment of strategy business and information system components. Yu & al. [20] look at the reasons and contexts (including strategic goals) that lead to system requirements.

The approach e3 values interest in values exchange between the network actors. The approach e3-alignment focuses on the alignment within and between organizations with respect to: (1) business strategy, (2) values, (3) business processes, and (4) Information System.

In all these approaches, there is little explicit links with the elements of the enterprise to align (strategic and functional level). These models use either intermediate or dependencies between the elements, or the decomposition of high level goals into low-level goals.

Approaches ACEM (Alignment and Evolution Correction Method) [12] and INSTALL (Intentional Strategic Alignment) [14], fit into the type methods that use an intermediate model to represent alignment. Note however that the first (ACEM) addresses the alignment of IT and business process but do not take into account the strategy.

Approaches of the dependence that propose to define dependencies between high-level goals (strategic) and operational goals. Approaches based on i * models [10], [20] and the approach of urbanization Longépé [9] fall into this category.

Decomposition approaches propose to decompose high-level goals into lower level goals (operational). Among these approaches, we find KAOS or approaches of Enterprise Architecture (eg Zachman).

2.2 Our Approach

The approach we propose for modeling strategic alignment is an approach oriented models. This approach ensures that the models of the strategy are linked with models of the functional level through a study of alignment between these 2 levels. Modeling in the two levels is traditionally expressed in different languages, and in separated documents. At the strategic level, one may find concepts like goal, task, actor, role and indicator. Whereas at the functional level, one may find object, operation, function, application etc.

The concept of alignment that we adopt in our approach is defined as the set of links (impact of element of model on an element of another model) between the strategic model and the IS model. Thus, the degree of alignment is measured by comparing: (i) the set of linkages between elements of the IS model and elements of strategic model and (ii) the aggregate maximum possible links between these models (figure 2).

For modeling the alignment, our approach allows:

- Represent elements of the fields of Business (enterprise strategy) and IT (information system) by the models.
- Measuring the degree of alignment by checking similarities between elements of these models.

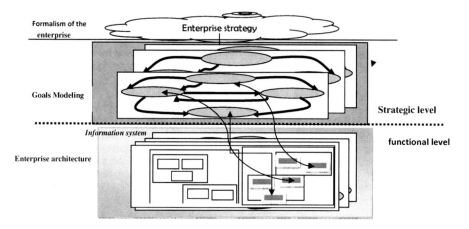

Fig. 2. Framework of our approach

2.3 Strategic Study

In this paper we consider the use of a goal model approach that supports analysis of strategic business goals such as I* [22] or the Business Motivation Model (BMM) [10]. The I* technique focuses on modeling strategic dependencies among business agents, goals, tasks and resources.

The I* model adopts an agent-oriented approach to model information system requirements. The intentional elements are the task and the soft goals, hard goals and can be related the ones to the others with relations of the type "means ends" and relations of the decompositions type of spots.

The following figure 3 illustrates the elements of formalism I * adapted:

Hard goals: Represents and intentional desire of an actor, the specifics of how the goal is to be satisfied is not described by the goal. This can be described through task decomposition

Soft goals: are similar to (hard) goals except that the criteria for the goal's satisfaction are not clear-cut, it is judged to be sufficiently satisfied from the point of view of the actor. The means to satisfy such goals are described via contribution links from other elements.

Task: The actor wants to accomplish some specific task, performed in a particular way. A description of the specifics of the task may be described by decomposing the task into further sub-elements.

Contribute to: A positive contribution strong enough to satisfy a soft goal.

Means end link: These links indicate a relationship between an end, and a means for attaining it. The "means" is expressed in the form of a task, since the notion of task embodies how to do something, with the "end" is expressed as a goal. In the graphical notation, the arrowhead points from the means to the end.

Target: target or indicator is information to help an actor, individual or collective, to drive action toward achieving a goal or to enable it to assess the result. It is that which makes it possible to follow the objectives defined at the strategic level related to a high level orientation.

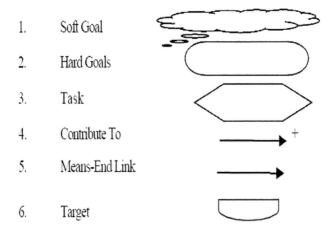

1.	Soft Goal
2.	Hard Goals
3.	Task
4.	Contribute To
5.	Means-End Link
6.	Target

Fig. 3. I* legend adapted

Several authors used the formalism of I * for strategic modeling due to its flexibility and the possibility to be used in different contexts. In order to let this formalism become more adapted to our approach, we added another element "target». Indeed, once the objectives are clearly definite, it is necessary to associate the indicators (target) for the regular follow-up of the actions implemented at the functional level. In the figure 3, elements 1, 2, 3 ,4, 5 are fundamental elements of formalism i* and the element 6 (target) is the element added.

This indicator one finds it at the strategic level (for example in a score board) and operational level has through its execution.

For this reason one chose approaches based on models I * [22] and approaches of enterprise architecture [10] and which belong to the approaches which propose to define bonds of the dependence between the goals.

2.4 Functional Study

At the functional level we have been inspired by the approach of urbanization (enterprise architecture) for several reasons:

(i) In the context of urbanization, the functional view is generally deducted from the business view. (ii) This functional view is designed to meet the needs of the strategy (iii) the link between the two views is realized by evaluating their alignment.

This architecture at the functional level use the metaphors to found the concept structures, in particular the metaphor of the city is used like base of information system [9].indeed Any functional architecture comprises several Business areas. A business area is broken up into several neighborhoods (district in notation city). Each neighborhood is composed of several blocks. This last belongs has only one and only one neighborhood. A block should never be duplicated and 2 blocks should never have of exchange direct (figure 4).

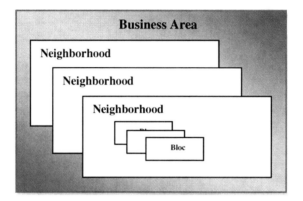

Fig. 4. Structure of a business area

The problems thus consist in making the information system most reactive possible (i.e. able to evolve quickly to answer the new requests) while preserving the informational inheritance of the enterprise. The urbanization of the information systems aims at bringing an answer to this need.

2.5 Alignment Study

It is the most important step in our approach or one puts in correspondence the strategic indicator with bloc of plan of urbanization. For this our approach proposes a projection of the indicators of the strategic level with the blocks of the urbanization plan. This confrontation thus will enable us to align this last with the objectives of the organization (table 1).

In this level of the possible dysfunctions of alignment will be detected. For example it will be noted can be that such a function is covered by several application different or a strategic indicator is supported by no block.

Table 1. Correspondence between the blocks and strategic indicators

Correspondance	Bloc1	Bloc 2	Bloc3	Bloc 4	Bloc 5
Indicator 1				X	
Indicator 2			X		
Indicator 3					
Indicator 4					X

3   Case studies: Project of the Ministry of Higher Education (Morocco)

The project we have chosen is very important for the Moroccan government, which is part of a national program to improve the situation in higher education. The study of the alignment of this project will help actors to decide if information system is aligned with this project. The case study is inspired from a real project at Rabat University, Morocco.

3.1   Description of the Case

In the context of the reform of higher education in Morocco, a reorganization of the university cycles based on LMD System (License - Master - Doctorate) took place.

Also, important efforts were made to develop the technical and professional options in each University.

The objectives of studied project are:

- To improve the internal output of higher education and the employability of the award-winnings who arrive on the job market.
- To offer to the students good conditions of training and lodging.

Some of the awaited results are:

- Creation of almost 124,000 places at the University;
- Multiplication by 2 of the capacity of reception of university.
- Registration of the 2/3 of all students of higher education in technical, scientific and professional options.
- Creation of almost 10,000 places in the halls of residence.

3.2   Strategic Study

In our project we have main strategic goals (1) "To improve the output interns and the employability of the award-winnings who arrive on the market" and (2) "To offer to the students' good conditions of training and lodging". Instead of customer the university aims to satisfy its users: students, teachers and administrative staff.

The internal axis process is organized around four strategic topics:

- To extend the capacity of reception
- To define the university components of tomorrow
- To accelerate the development of technical and vocational trainings
- To set up an orientation system and devices of council.

In order to apply our approach for strategic alignment to the university Mohamed 5, the first step consists in the translation of all objectives of the project into goal model formalism. (figure 5)

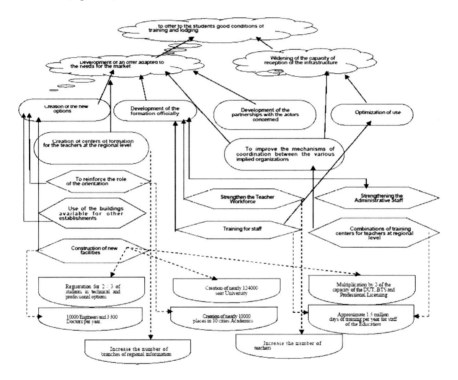

Fig. 5. Modeling Strategic of the project with the formalism I *

3.3 Functional Study

At this level, all applications and databases of the university are listed. After analyzing the existing we identified three major areas: an area for the activities of education, area of management of the library and the archive and the last for the management of human resources.

For example the area of education we identified three Neighborhoods that correspond to three major information systems: information system for student registration, another for the management of reviews and deliberations and the last for the management of cycle master.

In each area we identified a set of blocks that match a set of application. For example in the neighborhood "Reviews & Deliberations" we identified two blocks. one for the management of reviews and the other for deliberations. (figure 6)

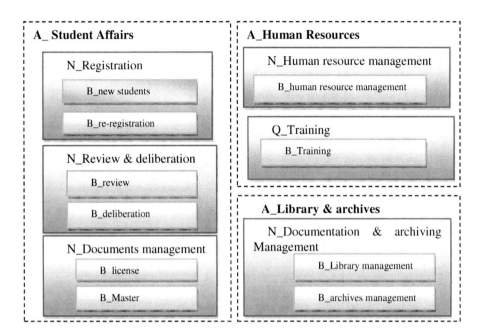

Fig. 6. Cutting areas of the system of information

This step consists in reorganizing the information systems in order to make them modular (via the blocks). The block is owner of its data and treatments; it is in relation with different blocs. For example in the area of student affairs the neighborhood of the registration constitutes several blocks, The block of registration which is dedicated to the management of the procedure of the registration of the new students and which is in relation w the block of management of documents (license).

3.4 Alignment Study

In the order to link the strategic objectives as define in the figure 1 to the existing information system as depicted by figure 6. The aim of this step is to establish the relation between the indicators with the neighborhood and blocks in functional level. This step permits to verify that the university meets the objectives, and to reorganize these business processes to meet the expected indicators.

In the table below we present all indicators related to our case study and its projections on the areas and blocks of functional level.

Table 2. Table of correspondence of the strategic indicators with the blocks

Indicator	Target	Area	Bloc
Increase the number of students at the University	Creation of nearly 124000 seats in the university	Unsupported	Unsupported
% enrollment in technical and professional option.	Registration for 2 / 3 of the students in technical options	A_ Student Affairs	B_new students
Capacity in technical options.	Multiplication by 2 of the capacity of the technical option	A_ Student Affairs	B_new students
Number of student in technical options.	10 000 Engineers and 3 300 Doctors per year.	A_ Student Affairs	B_new students
Number of places in university cities	Creation of nearly 10000 places in 10 Cities hosting university	unsupported	unsupported
Number of training days for university staff.	Approximate 1.5 m i l l i o n d a y s o f training per year for staff of the Education	A_Human Resources	B_human resource management

This confrontation will therefore enable us to align the elements of information systems with strategic objectives. At this level, some failures of alignment will be detected. We might find that to be such an indicator is covered by several different blocks or a strategic level indicator is not supported by any block of information system.

For example the indicator "Number of places in university cities" is not supported by any block, which shows that there is an alignment problem between the two levels of abstraction' functional and strategic.

After this step any corrections may be made to resolve the alignment problem. There are two distinct approaches: (1) adaptation of the objectives of the strategic level with the functional level "top down» or (2) adapting elements of the functional level so as to cover the strategic objectives "bottom up".

4   Conclusion and Discussion

In this paper we presented an approach to strategic alignment convenient and easy to apply. It is an approach with two levels of modeling (1) a strategic level model in a formalism for I * (2) a functional level, based on the approach to enterprise architecture. The main contribution is to show that a process of strategic alignment can be implemented in practice by adapting the model in two levels of abstraction.

Our approach allows to build the alignment based on elements belonging to the two abstraction levels (strategic and functional). The correspondence between strategic indicators and the blocks of the information system has allowed us to assess the alignment.

Our goal then is to improve the quality assessment of alignment, to determine the degree of alignment and to locate the level of dysfunction. Also among our research objectives is to develop a procedure to correct the alignment. In this way to develop a procedure that affects the set of step of construction, evaluation and correction of strategic alignment.

References

1. Luftman, J., Maclean, E.R.: Key issues for IT executives. MIS Quarterly Executive 3, 89–104 (2004)
2. Luftman, J.: Assessing business-IT alignment maturity. Communications of the Association for Information Systems 4(14), 1–50 (2000)
3. Baïna, S., Ansias, P., Petit, M., Castiaux, A.: Strategic Business/IT Alignment using Goal Models. In: Proceedings of the Third International Workshop on Business/IT Alignment and Interoperability (BUSITAL 2008) Held in Conjunction with CAISE 2008 Conference Montpellier, France, June 16-17 (2008)
4. Chan, Y., Huff, S., Barclay, D., Copeland, D.: Business Strategic Orientation: Information Systems Strategic Orientation and Strategic Alignment. Information Systems Research 8, 125–150 (1997)
5. Croteau, A.-M., Bergeron, F.: "An Information Technology Trilogy: Business Strategy", Technological Deployment and Organizational Performance. Journal of Strategic Information Systems (2001)
6. Tallon, P.P., Kraemer, K.L.: Executives' Perspectives on IT: Unraveling the Link between Business Strategy, Management Practices and IT Business Value. In: Americas Conference on Information Systems, ACIS 2002, Dallas, TX, USA (2002)
7. Renner, A.R., Latimore, D., Wong, D.: Business and IT operational models in financial services: Beyond strategic alignment. IBM Institute for Business Value study (2003)
8. Zachman, J.A.: A Framework for Information Systems Architecture. IBM Systemps Journal 26, 276–292 (1987)
9. Longépé, C.: Le projet d'urbanisation du SI. Collection Informatique et Entreprise, Dunod (2001)
10. Bleistein, S.J.: B-SCP: an integrated approach for validating alignment of organizational IT requirements with competitive business strategy, the university of new south wales, phD thesis, Sydney Australia (January 3, 2006)
11. Wegmann, A., Regev, R., Loison, B.: Business and IT Alignment with SEAM. In: Proceedings of REBNITA Requirements Engineering for Business Need and IT Alignment, Paris (August 2005)
12. Etien, A.: L'ingénierie de l'alignement: Concepts, Modèles et Processus. In: La méthode ACEM pour la correction et l'évolution d'un système d'information aux processus d'entreprise, thèse de doctorat. Université Paris 1 (mars 16, 2006)
13. Etien, A., Salinesi, C.: Managing Requirements in a Co-evolution Context. In: Proceedings of the IEEE International Conference on Requirements Engineering, Paris, France (September 2005)
14. Thevenet, L.H., Rolland, C., Salinesi, C.: Alignement de la stratégie et de l'organisation: Présentation de la méthode INSTAL, Ingénierie des Systèmes d'Information (ISI). In: Revue Ingénierie des Systèmes d'Information Special Issue on IS Evolution, Hermès, pp. 17–37 (June 2009)
15. Brown, T.: The Value of Enterprise Architecture, ZIFA report (2005)
16. Meersman, B.: The Commission Enterprise Architecture cadre., Presentation to European Commission Directorate Genral Informatics (2004)

17. Khory, R., Simoff, S.J.: Enterprise architecture modelling using elastic metaphors. In: Proceedings of the First Asian-Pacific Conference on Conceptual Modelling, vol. 31 (2004)
18. Bonne, J.C., Maddaloni, A.: Convaincre pour urbaniser le SI. Hermes, Lavoisier (2004)
19. Jackson, M.: Problem Frames: Analyzing and Structuring Software Development Problem. Addison-Wesley Publishing Company, Reading (2001)
20. Yu, E.: Towards Modeling and Reasoning Support for Early-Phase Requirements Engineering. In: Proceedings of the 3rd IEEE International Symposium on Requirements Engineering, p. 226 (1997)
21. Rolland, C.: Capturing System Intentionality with Maps. In: Conceptual Modeling un Information Systems Engineering, pp. 141–158. Springer, Heidelberg (2007)
22. Gordijn, J., Akkermans, J.: Value-based requirements engineering: Exploring innovative e-commerce ideas. Requirements Engineering 8(2), 114–134 (2003)
23. Gordijn, J., Petit, M., Wieringa, R.: Understanding business strategies of networked value constellations using goal- and value modeling. In: Glinz, M., Lutz, R. (eds.) Proceedings of the 14th IEEE International Requirements Engineering Conference, pp. 129–138. IEEE CS, Los Alamitos (2006)
24. Pijpers, V., Gordijn, J., Akkermans, H.: Exploring inter-organizational alignment wit e3alignment – An Aviation Case. In: 22nd Bled eConference eEnablement: Facilitating an Open, Effective and Representative eSociety, BLED 2009, Bled, Slovenia, June 14-17, (2009)

How and Why
Do Top Managers
Support or Not Support
Strategic IS Projects?

Albert Boonstra

University of Groningen,
Faculty of Economics and Business
P.O. Box 800
9700 AV Groningen, The Netherlands
albert.boonstra@rug.nl

Abstract. There is much evidence that top management support is the single most important determinant of IS project success. This is especially the case in complex and large-scale IS projects. Surprisingly however, despite its crucial importance there is only limited knowledge of the types of behaviour associated with top management support and the reasons for low support levels. This research aims to address this gap by focussing on two questions: (1) Which types of behaviour constitute the top management support for strategic IS projects? and (2) Why do managers sometimes fail to provide this support? To answer these questions, we analyzed the top management support during enterprise system implementations in five different organizations. We conducted cross-case analyses to determine the range of behavioural approaches associated with this concept. Based on our research questions, we propose a taxonomy that includes six categories of supportive behaviour of top management, from which potential reasons can be derived to either support or non-support strategic IS projects.

Keywords: strategic IS, top management support, implementation, management of change.

1 Introduction

One of the main recommendations for a successful management of large-scale strategic IS projects is top management support [1,2,3,4]. Top management support is considered to enhance the understanding and perception of a project among its users, and thus stimulate better outcomes. Surprisingly however, only little research has been conducted on the essence of the top management support concept [5,6]. We do not know much about what top management support entails in practice or which types of behaviour are associated with it, while we know even less about why top managers sometimes choose not to support a project, given that it is such a well-known success factor. The general advice for top managers who are planning to support an IS project

M.M. Cruz-Cunha et al. (Eds.): CENTERIS 2011, Part II, CCIS 220, pp. 369–379, 2011.
© Springer-Verlag Berlin Heidelberg 2011

is often mainly rhetorical and not research-based. Mostly the suggestions do not go beyond obvious recommendations such as promoting communication, expressing enthusiasm and demonstrating a true interest in a project [7].

Therefore, this paper aims to examine the concept of top management support by focussing on two main questions: 1) What behaviour is associated with top management support in relation to strategic IS projects? and 2) Why do managers sometimes fail to provide this support? These questions will be addressed through an explorative study of the implementation of strategic IS projects in five different organizations. We will identify the behaviour of these companies' top managers throughout the IS projects, thereby categorizing several types of potential support behaviour. This study contributes to the existing body of knowledge by its focus on increasing the understanding of the determinants of top management support and the possible reasons for and solutions to low levels of this support.

We have particularly concentrated on strategic IS projects because here top management support is especially critical [5]. By strategic IS projects we mean system projects that affect a firm's strategic interests, e.g. the integration of departments, the performance of core business processes, and the relations with suppliers or customers [4]. Generally, strategic IS projects affect the interests of many stakeholders, including those of parties outside the organization. Furthermore, these projects involve high investments since their organizational and technical complexities are often large and their duration is normally more than a year, which can easily extend to four years or more [8]. We selected projects that met these criteria, including the following applications: ERP, CRM, e-commerce, e-government and electronic patient records.

The remaining part of this paper is organized as follows. In the next section we present the theory on top management support, in particular in relation to IS projects. Next, we discuss our method and describe the case studies. Finally, in the discussion section we present the categorization of the top management support concept in the various cases and address the reasons for support or non-support.

2 Theoretical Perspectives

Top managers have a crucial position in creating the conditions that promote project success. Generally they play an important role in the project definition and the composition of the project team. They can structure the organizational context of the IS project and facilitate the resource provision. This is why the general management and change management theories make a strong case for the importance of top management support [9,10]. For example, a study of Green [11] on the top management support for 213 R&D projects indicated that projects with this kind of support were less likely to be terminated. The IS literature [7, 12, 13, 14, 15] confirms these findings in relation to large-scale IS projects. Also here top management support is associated with effective application [1], perceived usefulness [3], system use [16] and assimilation [17].

Top management support can be defined and measured in both attitudinal and behavioural terms. Most authors emphasize the attitudinal elements. Guimaraes and Igbaria [16] for example, suggest that 'top management understanding, interest and encouragement´ are important determinants. Gottschal [18] measures top management support by ´enthusiasm and vision for IT´. Liang et al. [17] base top management support on the view that ´ERP will create competitive advantage´ and ´articulates a vision for IS´. In a survey, Ragu-Nathan, Apigian and Tu [19] measure top management commitment on the basis of the following attitudinal statements: 1) top management is strongly committed to IS, 2) top management is interested in the IS function, 3) top management understands the importance of IS, 4) top management supports the IS function, 5) top management considers IS as a strategic resource, 6) top management understands IS opportunities.

Within the context of these attitudinal interpretations of top management support, the creation of a supportive climate towards the IT project is seen as the main role of the top managers. Some authors go even further, suggesting that top managers should promote a successful implementation by positioning themselves as project champions. Project championing is considered to refer to a very clear communication of the crucial importance of the project, the resolvement of conflicts, and support for the project team in unequivocal ways [20,21]. While acknowledging that these attitudinal elements can be important, we will specifically focus on the top management behaviour that either supports or does not support the IT project. In the literature the most specific supportive behaviour of the top management is resource provision [2,3]. In this research we will seek a more coherent view on the several types of behaviour associated with the top management support throughout strategic IS projects and the motives that drive this behaviour.

3   Methodology

We used a multiple case study design, following a replications logic [22]. To attain robustness five case studies of strategic IS implementations were conducted, while five different types of organizations were chosen to obtain sufficient information richness. Since our focus was on top managements, organizations employing more than 500 employees were selected. The IS projects had to be company-wide and strategic in nature. In addition, in order to review the degree of top management support throughout the projects, they had to be in their implementation, roll-out or use phase [23]. Next, we chose a variety of industries in order to reduce contextual bias. Finally, to compare the projects and address the research questions we looked for projects with various degrees of top management support.

Based on the strategies recommended for grounded theory development [24, 25] we conducted a qualitative investigation of the top managements' commitment to the projects by addressing multiple sources of data. The author conducted semi-structured interviews while a research assistant assisted in sorting, coding and analyzing the data. Robustness was maintained by interviewing informants with different roles within the project (top managers, project managers, project members, and business managers). This approach allowed us to compare the perceptions of top management support from different perspectives.

The interviewees checked the interview reports and parts of the case descriptions, which sometimes resulted in additional information and further insights. Sometimes we had the opportunity to conduct follow-up meetings for a clarification of or further updates on new developments, which led to a total of 36 interviews. The researchers reviewed the transcribed interviews and other sources of data, and coded the quotations and citations about the (un)supportive behaviour of the top managements, any changes in the degree of support, and the motives for the support or non-support. Table 1 lists the characteristics of the companies, the projects, and the numbers and types of the respondents.

Table 1. Characteristics of participating companies and strategic IS projects

Organization					
Industry	Manu-facturing	Financial services	Dairy Food	Govern-ment	Healthcare
Turnover (x 1 mln euro)	95	n.a.	8,200	150	250
# employees	457	59,536	21,367	689	2275
Project					
Type of IS project	ERP	CRM	ERP	e-gov	EPF
Duration (months)	10	62	12	38	18
Budget (x 1 mln euro)	4,1	65	3,4	8,1	3,4
Customer or suppliers involved?	No	Yes	Yes	Yes	Yes
Number of project members	16	45	23	9	12
# users	200	9520	1129	354	210
Data collection					
Respondents					
Top mngmnt	1	2	1	2	1
Project mngmnt	1	1	1	1	1
Project members	-	1	1	-	1
Business mngmnt	2	1	3	2	2
Total # of respondents	4	5	6	5	5
Total # of interviews	6	7	9	8	6

4   Case Descriptions

This section introduces the companies and the projects, and deals with the degree of top management support.

Project of a Manufacturer - The ERP implementation of a manufacturer of high tech safety equipment concerned the introduction of a range of SAP-modules. The main goal of implementing these modules was to improve the structure and quality of the management information. It was a major operation that covered all fourteen departments of the company. The organization had had a long tradition of using complex information systems and was used to dealing with the management of large projects. Its top management hired a high profile consultancy firm to determine which resources in terms of finance and people were needed for a project of this size and nature. Based on their suggestions, an adequate but tight budget was made available, together with a competent project team facilitated by the consultancy firm. The resources were tight but realistic and the time scope was deliberately kept limited. After the module selection, eight working groups were established, coordinated by the project team.

Project of a Financial Services organization – Another major project was a CRM implementation at a large bank, directed at improving the relations with target customers. More than 9,000 potential account managers in many branches had to use this system. The project duration was more than five years, while the budget exceeded 65 million euros, which was still perceived as fairly tight given the scope of the project. The project structure was complex, including a steering group, project groups and working groups, of which the first two consisted of a maximum of 45 members. The groups included business unit managers, IT developers and implementers. Apart from the involvement of a consultant experienced in CRM implementations, the project management was kept in-house.

Project of a Dairy Food company - An ERP project at a dairy food company was perceived by the board as crucial for the system integration of the firm. The board member responsible, who had ERP-expertise, was given a major role in the project. In a previous position elsewhere he had been responsible for an effective ERP implementation, and he was surprised that the IT of this firm was not integrated. He therefore convinced the other board members of the advantages of ERP. After the initiation of the project he relied on the project manager to realize the implementation. This delegation was based on a strong relationship and mutual trust. The project was adequately funded and also the time schedule appeared to be realistic. The project group consisted of representatives of the business units together with a project leader, the senior manager who initiated the project, and an external consultant. In each of the three business units, project groups were responsible for the modification and implementation of the system.

Project of a City Council - An e-government project at a city council started as a departmental initiative to digitalize and streamline requests for licenses, permits and passports. The resources to develop and realize this initiative were limited. The initiators tried to modify the e-government formats used by other municipalities. The project was started by a small project group of volunteering and enthusiastic civil servants. After some months, the minister of internal affairs, responsible for the regional governance, announced that city councils had to modernize their services by providing 80% of them online via web 2.0 interactive websites.

Project of Health Care organization - The IT department of a medium-sized hospital maintained 24 different electronic patient record systems. These different systems were used by various medical specializations, as well as by the pharmacy unit and some nursing departments. They were incompatible and hard to operate and maintain in a responsible manner. The head of the IT department proposed to integrate these systems in a hospital-wide patient record. Additional financial resources were not available.

5 Discussion

This discussion addresses the research questions via a cross case analysis. The first question was: *which determinants and types of behaviour constitute the top management support in the various projects?* During the qualitative data analysis six groups of supportive types of top management behaviour were identified, including 1) resource provision, 2) establishing structural arrangements, 3) communications, 4) expertise and interest, 5) using power and giving trust, 6) alignment with company policies.

Resource provision – Most participants in the five projects agreed that sufficient financial, technical and human resources are critical to the success of strategic IS projects. The respondents also emphasized that securing these resources is a key responsibility of the senior managers. An adequate supply of financial resources enables the acquisition of appropriate technical equipment and the necessary external expertise. Sufficient resources also function as a form of mental support for the project team managers. It demonstrates to all members of the organization that the top management has given the project a high priority among the other business objectives. It also tells us something about the potential non-support: in the struggle for resources IS projects compete for priority. In this context, top management support is not a free but a scarce means, for which several parties compete that have different views on the use of resources. According to our data, the projects at the manufacturing, financial services, and dairy food companies received adequate financial resources, whereas the government and healthcare trajectories suffered from limited financial resources, both absolutely and relative to other policy areas.

Establishing structural arrangements – According to the respondents, another indication of top management support is the establishment of clear and well communicated project structures, such as steering as well as project groups and the determination of group roles and responsibilities. The degree to which these structural arrangements are realized can be measured by the way in which they are communicated to the rest of the organization and by the actual functioning of these groups. We analyzed agendas, minutes, attendance and the frequency of meetings to assess the relative importance of these project structures. The financial services, dairy food, and health care projects had a steering group with at least one senior executive. Manufacturing had a project group chaired by a senior executive. The e-government project was organized by a temporary and ad-hoc set of project and working groups. The dairy food project had a strong formal structure, but due to personnel changes in the top management team this changed during the course of time.

Communications – Many respondents mentioned that frequent formal and informal communication between the project team and the top management is important. During the ERP project in the manufacturing firm there were weekly team meetings chaired by a top manager. These sessions were perceived as a very strong form of top management support. Additionally, frequent e-mails, phone calls and face-to-face meetings complemented the communication needs of the project members. Some project members argued that the top management support was sometimes too strong, lacking 'a healthy degree of delegation and trust'. In the case of the CRM project at the bank the communication with the top management mainly took place via the project leader. The project leader and the senior executive met regularly to make sure that the management was well informed. In the dairy food project the communication was very intensive at the start but decreased after the departure of the responsible executive. Both the e-government and the healthcare projects can be characterized by infrequent communication between the project management and the top management. Here the top management preferred to communicate only in the case of problems or incidents.

Expertise and interest – The respondents indicated that they perceived an adequate degree of knowledge of and interest in the project on the part of the top managers as an important form of top management support. This knowledge included a sufficient understanding of both the content and the implications of the system proposed. Both in the financial services and in the manufacturing project the expertise was assessed as adequate. In the latter the senior executive read all relevant documents. In the e-government trajectory and the hospital's project, however, the knowledge of the top managements (the council's highest officials, the alderman, and the hospital board) was very limited. Here basic documents were often not read properly. The interviewees of the dairy food, government, and health care projects mentioned that the documents produced by the project groups were often too elaborate and difficult to understand. As a result these projects were largely left in the hands of the project group members.

Using power and giving trust - An important example of top management supportive behaviour is the use of formal power to serve a project. Top management's role is to resolve conflicts and protect the project team during political battles. In the manufacturing project there was a great deal of compliance on all levels of the organization. This was partly the result of the clarity with which top management had defined the project as a business priority. In the healthcare project the other side of the spectrum could be observed. Here top management did not instill compliance. Autonomous units felt the freedom to decide individually whether or not to participate, which led to varying degrees of cooperation. Also to the dairy food trajectory applied that the top management no longer used its formal power after the project promoter had gone. By then, the different business units had already been adopting their own approaches.

Alignment with company policies - Support tends to be larger if the IT project fits the general policy of the organization. Many respondents indicated that the degree of support is reflected by the extent to which the top management demonstrates the project's relation to the wider organizational policies. An organization's employees will be more willing to support critical than marginal projects. In the manufacturing and financial services projects, the alignment with the wider company policies was high. In the dairy food company, this fit reduced during the project. In the e-government project the connection was erratic. At times the municipality indicated that the project was crucial, whereas at other times it did not emphasize its strategic importance at all. In the healthcare project there was a difference between words and deeds. In the policy documents, including the strategic plan, the board indicated that an organization-wide electronic patient file is of vital importance, whereas in reality this appeared not to be the case.

Motives for support or non-support – Since top management support is the most important success factor of strategic IS projects, senior managers have obvious reasons to adopt this approach. Moreover, failure generally leads to a loss of resources and potentially damages the reputation of the organization as well as that of the top managers responsible. However, the case studies also demonstrate that the top management can choose between different forms of interrelated support. Some respondents, especially from the manufacturing project, argued that top management support can also be too strong and thereby dysfunctional. In this case it could lead a lack of room for the participants to discuss alternative ways to define and execute the project, and even to intimidation. This finding implies that it should be discussed beforehand how top management support can be organized in the most optimal way, given the characteristics of the project, the organization and its context.

There are also reasons for top managers to refrain from providing support. The most obvious one is that top management support is a scarce resource. It cannot cover each organizational issue, which means that IS projects have to compete with other areas that potentially require top management support. According to the e-government respondents this was the main reason for the limited amount of top management support for the project at the city council.

Another reason for decreasing project support relates to changing goals or contexts. During the course of time the ideas about the desirability of a project may change, a situation which can potentially undermine its top management support. In the case of the dairy food ERP project, changes in the composition of the top management caused differences in attitude towards the initial plans. As a result, the project became the subject of a dispute among various divisions.

A third reason for a lesser degree of support concerns the risk profile of the project. If a project has a high risk potential, top management will generally be inclined to adopt a more distant approach and grant more responsibilities to the internal project team and the external consultants who possess the expertise. This was the case in the financial services, dairy food (second phase), and health care projects.

A fourth explanation for a low support level is disagreement within the board. During the ERP project of the dairy food company, there was debate about the degree of control and centralization of the headquarters. Especially when powerful division managers complained about the implications of the project, some board members withdrew their initial support. This situation led to the departure of the responsible top manager, who was replaced by someone with a more critical and distant view on the project.

The final reason why the support for projects is sometimes limited is the top managements' unfamiliarity with information systems. Especially in the government and healthcare cases we observed discomfort and sometimes a lack of interest in information technology and its applications. After a 'yes' by the board, sometimes top managers feel that the project should be left to the experts.

6 Conclusions

Despite the general agreement on the importance of top management support for strategic IS projects, a comprehensive view on the behavioural spectrum that constitutes this concept has as yet not been presented. This research has demonstrated that top management support is not a one dimensional construct but that it involves a set of inter-related types of behaviour that can be measured throughout a project. In this study we identified six types of behaviour: 1) resource provision, 2) structural arrangements, 3) communication, 4) expertise and interest, 5) power and trust and 6) alignment. These categories have partially been identified in other studies but have until now not been depicted as a potentially coherent set of interrelated behavioural types that can be identified throughout a project.

In summary, all six types of behaviour could be observed in the manufacturing project and to a smaller extent in the financial services trajectory. Three of the six types (communications, expertise and interest, power and trust, and alignment) fairly decreased during the dairy food project. In the case of the government and healthcare projects the level of support of the top managers was relatively low during the entire period. This finding illustrates that top management support is not a static but a dynamic construct, which is susceptible to change during the course of a project.

This study has also shed light on the reasons for either providing or refraining from top management support. We emphasize that support is a scarce resource in terms of finance, people, communication, attention, expertise and time, arguing that it cannot be distributed evenly among all topics potentially relevant to a firm. In other words, the top management support for an IS project involves a highly demanding and intensive set of behavioural types, and top managers are often pressurized into making a choice between current organizational activities and new initiatives. Another important explanation for low support concerns the inherent risks of IS projects. In the case of close involvement, failure may damage the top management's reputation and credibility. Furthermore, the dairy food project showed that also a dynamic organizational context affects the degree of top management support. Finally, top management support can also be too strong, which may lead to a waste of scarce resources and increase the possibility of project failure.

As any qualitative study, this paper has its limitations. We collected our data from only five organizations. Therefore, we cannot claim that our findings provide a complete overview of the issues surrounding top management commitment in large IS projects. We sought to use multiple methods to triangulate the findings, while relying the most heavily on the data from our interviews with the top managers, the project managers and the business managers. Interviews with other members of the top management as well as with users, IS-staff, and external consultants might have resulted in more and richer perspectives on this topic. Nevertheless, we hope that these findings will inspire top managers, project managers and others to rethink the concept of top management commitment and to organize it in the best possible way, given the characteristics of the project and the context. We also hope that this explorative study will encourage the realization of additional qualitative and quantitative studies of the role of leadership in IS projects.

References

1. Standish Group: Chaos Report 2009, Boston, Massachusetts (2010)
2. Igbaria, M., Zinatelli, N., Cragg, P., Cavaye, A.L.M.: Personal computing acceptance factors in small firms: a structural equations model. MIS Quarterly 21(3), 279–305 (1997)
3. Bruqué-Cámara, S., Vargas-Sánchez, A., Hernández-Ortiz, M.J.: Organizational determinants of IT adoption in the pharmaceutical distribution sector. European Journal of Information Systems 13(2), 133–146 (2004)
4. Sharma, R., Jetton, P.: The contingent effects of management support and task interdependence on successful information systems implementation. MIS Quarterly 27(4), 533–555 (2003)
5. Dong, F., Neufeld, D., Higgins, C.: Top management support of enterprise systems implementations. Journal of Information Technology 24, 555–580 (2009)
6. Dutton, J.E., Ashford, S.J.: Selling issues to top management. Academy of Management Review 18(3), 397–428 (1993)
7. Young, R., Jordan, E.: Top management support: mantra or necessity? International Journal of Project Management 26, 713–725 (2008)
8. Boonstra, A.: Structure and analysis of IS decision. European Journal of Information Systems 12(3), 195–209 (2003)
9. McComb, S.A., Kennedy, D.M., Green, S.G., Compton, W.D.: Project team effectiveness: the case for sufficient setup and top management involvement, vol. 19(4), pp. 301–311 (2008)
10. Rodgers, R., Hunter, J.E., Rogers, D.L.: Influence of top management commitment on management program success. Journal of Applied Psychology 78(1), 151–163 (1993)
11. Green, S.G.: Top management support of R&D projects: a strategic leadership perspective. IEEE Transactions on Engineering Management 43(3), 223–232 (1995)
12. Bingi, P., Sharma, M.K.: Critical issues affecting ERP implementation. Information Systems Management 16(3), 7–15 (1999)
13. Doll, W.J.: Avenues for top management involvement in successful MIS development. MIS Quarterly 9(1), 17–35 (1985)
14. Ehie, I.C., Madsen, M.: Identifying critical issues in enterprise resource planning implementation. Computers in Industry 56(6), 545–557 (2005)
15. Jarvenpaa, S.L., Ives, B.: Executive involvement and participation in the management of information technology. MIS Quarterly 15(2), 205–228 (1991)
16. Guimareaes, T., Igbaria, M.: Client-server system success: exploring the human side. Decision Sciences 28(4), 851–876 (1997)
17. Liang, H., Saraf, N., Hu, Q., Xue, Y.: Assimilation of enterprise systems: the effect of institutional pressures and the mediating role of top management. MIS Quarterly 31(1), 1–29 (2007)
18. Gottschal, P.: Strategic information systems planning: the IT strategy implementation matrix. European Journal of Information Systems 8(2), 107–118 (1999)
19. Ragu-Nathan, B.S., Apigian, C.H., Tu, Q.: A path analytic study of the effect of top management support for information systems performance. Omega 32(6), 459–472 (2004)
20. Kazanghi, D., Reigh, B.H.: Achieving IT project success through control, measurement, management experience and top management support. International Journal of Project Management 26(7), 699 (2008)
21. Naranjo-Gil, D.: Management information systems and strategic performances: the role of top management composition. International Journal of Information Management 29(2), 104–110 (2009)

22. Yin, R.K.: Applications of case study research. Sage, Thousand Oaks (2003)
23. Markus, I.M., Tanis, C.: Multisite ERP implementations. Communications of the ACM 43(4), 42–47 (2000)
24. Miles, M.B., Huberman, M.: Qualitative data analysis. Sage, Thousand Oaks (1994)
25. Eisenhardt, K.M.: Building theories from case studies research. Academy of Management Review 14, 532–550 (1989)

Defining a Process Framework for Corporate Governance of IT

Alberto Arroyo[1] and José D. Carrillo Verdún[2]

[1] Undergraduate. Facultad de Informática. Universidad Politécnica de Madrid. Campus de Montegancedo. 28660 – Boadilla del Monte Spain
albertoarroyo@alamcia.es
[2] Professor. Facultad de Informática. Universidad Politécnica de Madrid. Campus de Montegancedo. 28660 – Boadilla del Monte Spain
jcarrillo@fi.upm.es

Abstract. IT governance is a discipline of corporate governance. Standard ISO/IEC 38500 set the basis for implementing IT governance. Nevertheless, IT governance is based in a set of best practices. There have been attempts to implement IT governance from different perspectives, none based on processes. This paper defines a process framework to implement IT governance in organizations, regardless of their size and type.

Keywords: IT governance, corporate governance of IT, process framework.

1 Introduction

Corporate governance of IT[1] is, according with the ISO 38.500 standard [1] "the system by which the current and future use of IT is directed and controlled". It is widely accepted that corporate governance of IT is a discipline of corporate governance; in fact, according to Weill and Ross [2], corporate governance of IT is the govern of one of the six key assets: financial, physical, relationships, human resources, intellectual property and, as said, information and its related technology.

Nowadays, information technology importance is getting higher in the organizations worldwide. Its role in not only supporting current business strategies, but also future strategies is indisputable. Moreover, technology is the second important issue for the CEOs [3]. The issue now is how to prepare the organization for controlling and investing in IT.

2 Corporate and IT Governance

Corporate governance is the system by which organizations are directed and controlled. Despite of the general acceptance, corporate governance is not only about complying with rules and regulation, such as Sarbanes-Oxley Act. Literature [4] includes recommendations and suggestions in which, for example, company strategy

---

[1] We refer here corporate governance of IT and IT governance indistinctly.

M.M. Cruz-Cunha et al. (Eds.): CENTERIS 2011, Part II, CCIS 220, pp. 380–387, 2011.

plays an important role in corporate governance, by leveraging and balancing shareholders and management expectations.

This is clear in CIMA [5], which conceives corporate governance as enterprise governance, and divides it in two different areas: compliance and performance, as seen in Figure 1. Performance is the complying part of corporate governance, while performance has to do with the operation of the business.

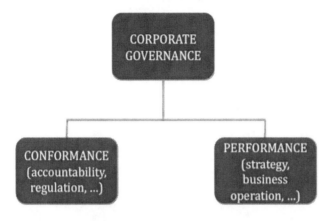

Fig. 1. Corporate governance as conformance + performance

In the last decade, IT governance has been arranged, conceived, analyzed and structured. First, isolated by analyzing its different components: IT investments, alignment between IT and the business, IT governance processes and structures, etc. As said, the conception of corporate governance of IT as a discipline of IT was mentioned first by Weill and Ross [2], and accepted since then,

Researches and practitioners have tried to structure IT governance, from different points of view. The Center for Information Systems Research, from the MIT, has analyze the status of corporate governance of IT in the organizations, and developed a framework with the best practices [2], that has been complemented with different contributions with regard to areas such as governing the risk of IT [6], and IT investments [7]. The IT Governance Institute has also developed frameworks to cover different areas of corporate governance of IT: COBIT for the performance and control area [8], Risk IT for governing the risk of IT [9], and Val IT [10], which is related to the value delivery of IT to the business.

There have been some other attempts to structure corporate governance of IT, or make recommendations about best practices on this subject (Forrester [11], CIGREF [12], etc.) The publication of the standard ISO 38.500 [1] allowed defining the basis regarding corporate governance of IT, as well as its principles.

However, despite of different attempts to implement frameworks for corporate governance of IT based on this standard (i. e. the Calder-Moir framework [13]), that provided useful tools and techniques, there is no attempt to structure a process framework for implement corporate governance of IT in all kind of organizations. Our purpose is this, to define a guide, based in processes, to implement IT governance in the organizations.

3   The Framework

Standard ISO 38.500 [1] set the basis for corporate governance. It is important to consider, first, the role of the governing body in the "direct-monitor-evaluate" cycle. The governing body performs this cycle by establishing mechanisms to assume decisions and to delegate authority. This is what Weill and Ross [2] name "decision rights and accountability", and Toomey [14] calls "delegation of authority". Not only this; it is important also, as Toomey says, to reserve some specific decisions to the governing body.

Taking this into account, the next step is to identify the different levels in the organization for implementing Corporate governance of IT. Calder-Moir [13] establishes three levels: the Board of Directors, executive managers and managers.

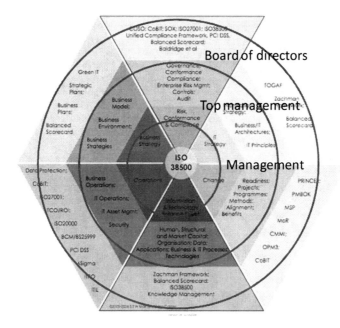

Fig. 2. Organizational levels according to Calder-Moir

In our perspective, there are three layers in the organization to implement Corporate governance of IT: the board, the management, and IT. Each level has a different degree of responsibility: while the board should assume the competencies for what is called the "governing body", that is, the "direct-monitor-evaluate" cycle, the management is responsible for implementing Board decisions, and IT is responsible for implementing decisions regarding IT, as well as best practices.

Corporate governance of IT is present in all the organizations, but in different stages or, as said by Symons et al [11], in different maturity levels. When the organizations begin to be aware of the importance of information and IT, the first thing to do is an evaluation. That is important, for instance, for transitioning from an ad-hoc to fragmented IT governance. Evaluation, or diagnosis, must not only to identify the current status of IT governance and set a roadmap; it must also obtain the commitment of the different elements in the governing body. Evaluation questionnaires that cover that issue are defined, for example, in the Calder-Moir framework [13]. This evaluation is the first phase in the process framework.

There is another prerequisite for out process framework. From our perspective, the six principles of corporate governance of IT are not present from the beginning of the cycle. In fact, the first thing to do is, as said before, establish the decision structure. This is a task for the governing body, and it is embedded in the rest of the principles:

- The strategy principle must be preceded by a clear understanding on who must define the strategy of the company, and who must approve it.
- Regarding acquisition, the organization, through its governing body, has to set investment thresholds, rules, and, of course, the different authorization levels for detecting, analyzing and approving investments.
- The performance principle has, as a prerequisite, what organ in the company should establish what to control and measure, and who needs to make the
- The conformance principle depends on the environment, but also in the risk appetite of the governing body for
- Human behavior, as defined by the ISO 38.500 standard, is about organizational culture and people interactions. This culture and interactions are fitting inside a set of rules that are defined and approved for the governing body.

The consequence is that the responsibility schema is very important in the governance process.

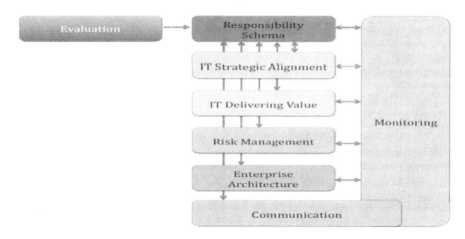

Fig. 3. Processes blocks in the Process Framework

Taking all into account, the framework has two key elements: an initial stage for evaluating the state-of-the-art of corporate governance of IT in the organizations, and the need to define a schema of responsibilities in the whole organization. After that, any decision with regard IT and its governance has to comply with that schema, or the schema will need to include new rules in the organization for assigning responsibilities and ways to control the decision making process.

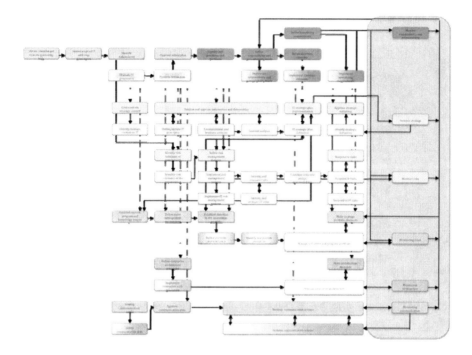

Fig. 4. Process Framework

In this figure, the darker colors are processes associated to the governing body; the mediums darker colors are to the executive management, and the lighter colors are associated to line managers.

The process framework is complemented with its correspondent RACI matrix, which considers the different roles in the organization involved with the process, and the levels of decision and information required. An example for strategic alignment is the matrix shown in Figure 5:

3.1 Implementation

Implementation of this process framework is being performed currently in a big company in Spain, focused on the catering industry. It is a family owned enterprise, with two shareholders holding different portions of the company, and a strong board

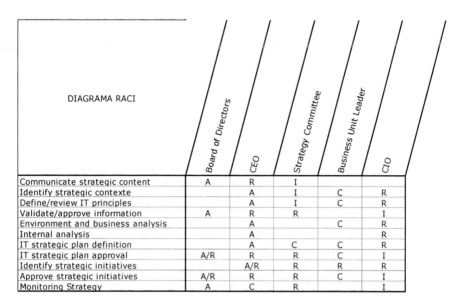

DIAGRAMA RACI	Board of Directors	CEO	Strategy Committee	Business Unit Leader	CIO
Communicate strategic content	A	R	I		
Identify strategic contexte		A	I	C	R
Define/review IT principles		A	I	C	R
Validate/approve information	A	R	R		I
Environment and business analysis		A		C	R
Internal analysis		A			R
IT strategic plan definition		A	C	C	R
IT strategic plan approval	A/R	R	R	C	I
Identify strategic initiatives		A/R	R	R	R
Approve strategic initiatives	A/R	R	R	C	I
Monitoring Strategy	A	C	R		I

Fig. 5. RACI Diagram

of directors, with independent directors. The board was set up recently, in an effort to professionalize the government of the company.

Company structure is as follows.

Fig. 6. Organizational structure for Company analyzed

The board has different skills, but none technical. IT situation in the company was archaic, with an ERP covering only the admin area. The company is experimenting a period of big growth, both nationally and internationally, and IT was not helping in the business aims. Thus, the implementation of a new ERP was a priority, and began shortly.

The hire of a new CIO meant the need to implement Corporate governance of IT mechanisms. The first was to evaluate the state of IT, and the status of the Board of directors regarding this. That allowed embedding a culture of focusing on IT in the business. And, consequently, the setting of a roadmap to this implement corporate governance of IT mechanisms, with the implementation of the new ERP as a high priority.

This roadmap consisted in two types of things: first, a list of IT projects and priorities, and second, the definition of a responsibility schema, in which the board played an important role in setting directions and validating the decisions. The first organizational structure in the responsibility schema was the called "Moving forward Committee", that was comprise by the CEO, CIO, an independent member of the board, Sales Manager (very concerned about regulation) and CFO.

IT strategy was defined according with the process framework defined, and allowed a highly alignment between IT and the business, measured with personal interviews performed with members of the board. Not only this, the board monitored the strategy and the Strategy Committee (comprised by CEO, Sales Manager, COO, CFO and CIO, as well as two independent directors) established a process to incorporate strategic initiatives that could reshape the strategy of the company. The number of initiatives was high due to the potential markets and growing of the company, and all were evaluated from the IT perspective (due to the implementation of the new ERP and the increasing demand on IT developments from the different departments). Most of the initiatives were stopped, due to the accepting criteria:

- Support new markets and clients.
- Provide tools for increasing control of the Operations.

Corporate risk governance (and subsequently IT risk) was another consequence of this process framework implementation. The board structured the management and governs of the risk according to the processes identified, and a risk management structure is implemented, in which the participants are shown in the next figure, according with their roles. Risk management was dependent of the "Moving forward committee", and an extremely consistent information security implementation plan was put in place.

Also, an IT portfolio was set and managed, which project and related priorities were coming from the initial evaluation. The portfolio committee was the Strategy Committee, and reviews in a biweekly manner all the different initiatives. The criteria was described below, and served for both new initiatives and ongoing initiatives.

Currently, the company is tuning these mechanisms, and adjusting processes and the responsibility schema according with the important growth that is having, and also adjusting its organizational (and IT) structure.

4 Conclusion

The process framework makes a contribution in defining the different processes to be implemented in the companies for allowing Corporate governance of IT implementation. Its structure and modularity, based in the evaluation and the responsibility schema, makes it extendable to other Corporate governance of IT areas, such as IT green.

Although the example is a big company, recent experiences are with different type of companies and organizations: from SMEs to NPOs.

References

1. ISO / IEC 38500:2008. Corporate Governance for Information Technology. ISO (2008)
2. Weill, P., Ross, J.W.: IT Governance. How top performers manage IT decision for superior results. Harvard Business School Press, Boston (2003)
3. IBM 2010 Global CEO Study. IBM (2010)
4. Conthe: Código de Buen Gobierno de las Sociedades Cotizadas, Grupo Especial de Trabajo sobre Buen Gobierno de las Sociedades Cotizadas. Comisión Nacional del Mercado de Valores (2006)
5. CIMA Enterprise Governance. Getting the balance right, CIMA, IFAC (2003)
6. Westerman, G., Hunter, R.: IT Risk, turning business threats into competitive advantage. Harvard Business School Press, Boston (2007)
7. IT Governance Institute. Control Objectives for Information and Related Technology, versión 4.1, IT Governance Institute (2007)
8. IT Governance Institute. Enterprise Risk: Identify, Govern and Manage IT Risk. The Risk IT Framework. Exposure draft (2009)
9. IT Governance Institute. Enterprise Value: Governance of IT Investments. The Val IT Framework 2.0. IT Governance Institute (2008)
10. Symons, C., Oliver Young, G., Lambert, N.: IT Governance Framework. Forrester (2005)
11. Institute de la Governance des Systèmes d'Information. The place of IT governance in the Enterprise Governance. AFAI, CIGREF (2005)
12. Calder, A.: IT Governance Pocket Guide. IT Governance Publishing (2007)
13. Cadbury, A.: Report of the Committee on the Financial Aspects of Corporate Governance. G. P. Publishing (1992)
14. Toomey, M.: Waltzing with the elephant. A comprehensive guide to directing and controlling information technology. Infonomics (2009)

Assessing Information Technology Use in Organizations: Developing a Framework

Emre Sezgin and Sevgi Özkan

Middle East Technical University, Informatics Institute, Department of Information Systems
06531 Ankara, Turkey
{esezgin,sozkan}@ii.metu.edu.tr

Abstract. Increasing use of current and developing information technologies (IT) within business and production processes is a required transformation to survive in the market. However, IT should be well-managed to be adapted by an organization as a whole. This study proposes a new model for the assessment of IT use in organizations. The aim is to assist decision making processes in information technology management through exploring strength and weaknesses of organization on IT tools and applications. The model has been developed upon a three-folded structure including *academic studies* in technology management, *best practices* which are developed for control over operations and processes including COBIT, CMMI and ITIL, and *standards* about IT management and IT security. The study assists to reveal benefits and deficiencies of IT use in organizations. It also provides information for decision-makers about IT value within companies, and demonstrates the effects of best practices and standards over IT use.

Keywords: Information technology use, assessment, technology management, model framework, information technology governance.

1 Introduction

In the global market, all organizations are required to process information to produce valuable outputs for keeping competitive advantage and market share, especially in the market having high demand elasticity and rapidly changing demands [1]. To reach desired outputs, information technology has become a necessity for companies which is being used as a tool for business operations. After understanding the importance of IT and its applications, in these days, most companies in the market place use IT as leverage in business. IT utilities, including information and communication technologies (ICT), vary with regards to purpose and needs of a company. But in general terms, it is defined as "development, implementation and management of information systems within business operations" [13]. Deans and Kane put emphasis on the importance of IT by explaining that IT has a remarkable role for success of a company under uncertain economic conditions [8]. Thus, IT management becomes an important role to be capable of effectively using IT.

To maintain effective management for fulfilling duties at desired level of quality and for controlling of IT in competitive level, supportive tools and techniques are needed. In general terms, these tools aim to assist controlling over IT applications and

M.M. Cruz-Cunha et al. (Eds.): CENTERIS 2011, Part II, CCIS 220, pp. 388–397, 2011.
© Springer-Verlag Berlin Heidelberg 2011

increase management capability. For this purpose, standardized procedures, such as best practices and standards, were developed to help the managers to control IT utilities and take measures for the standardized quality in IT operations [11] [25].

Even though the best practices and standards are popular tools in controlling and maintaining IT, they have problems and missing points in practice. The most important problem of best practices and standards is the lack of know-how [17]. Any company, who needs to practice any of those, also needs an experienced person in the field to implement the tools or train employees. This problem reduces availability and applicability of the best practices. In addition, their aggregate cost (i.e. time, training, purchasing license of use, expert) can go beyond affordable boundaries of most of the companies [17]. In our model it was aimed to eliminate such obstacles encountered with current applications, which also become the main issues in other developed practices [15].

In this study, a new method is proposed which is called ITMEM: Information technology management enhancement model. The model is designed to assess IT use in the companies in order to assist the IT managers in decision making. It is argued that ITMEM presents a holistic and valid scope to evaluate IT use in organizations. The scope of the study includes companies in every industry which uses IT as a tool to assist their business processes and to gain competitive advantage.

The aims of this study are as follows: (1) Proposing an assessment framework to literature that is believed to define objectives in which IT use is assessed (2) Gathering information about IT use in companies to assist IT management in decision making processes, (3) Providing a framework to improve the IT structure of companies by exploring their strengths and weaknesses with regards to IT in a practical manner, (4) Providing an auditing tool to industries about IT use as well as IT awareness and knowledge.

2   The Need for Assistance in IT Management

Over the time, not the basics but the scope of the definition of technology management that was expanded. With the advancements in technology, the scope of technology management broadened to include information technology management. But adoption of concept, understanding of information technology and IT management became an issue in its early years. Several major obstacles arose such as training, business integration, poor performance levels and resistance to change [3]. But after all, it was inevitable need to understand and explore IT, because IT became a resource to determine strategic and operational capabilities of the firm for maximizing corporate productivity, profitability and competitiveness [2]. IT management studies were, similarly to technology management, searching for the ways that lead to create effective management approaches and resolve management effects on IT use [4]. The studies are advanced dramatically over the time with the increasing need to IT management by the industries [7]. This progress demonstrates that IT management became an inevitable part of every company as well as the IT itself.

2.1   Current Tools and Techniques

Best practices and standards constitute the most common tools and techniques for organizations which aim to bring solution for specific IT problem domains. A best practice can be defined as method, activity or process that is accepted by authorities and communities as more effective way to reach a particular outcome than any other ways [5]. They are the completion of experiences and procedures which enable users to effectively and efficiently complete the tasks.

Today, best practices are popular tools in the business world especially in the fields of management, software and policy making. They are also used in domains of sustainable development, project management, construction, health care and transportation. Even though best practices are well accepted tools in the business environment, it was observed that the academic studies over best practices are conducted rarely [22]. The confidential issues based on commercial rights set barriers between the private industry and academic studies regarding in knowledge and information sharing. The private companies produce the solutions by in-company studies or through associations, which leads to development of best practices. Today the most explicit examples are Control Objectives for Information and related Technology (COBIT), Information Technology Infrastructure Library (ITIL), Capability Maturity Model Integration (CMMI) and International Organization for Standardization (ISO) standards, which are designed and developed mostly by professionals in private industries and institutions for creating solutions to specific problems. Even though there are variety of best practices and standards developed for IT domain, the most popular and comprehensive tools were selected to be investigated.

Best Practices. Even though there are several best practices in use, the most popular and effective tools were selected to be used in the study. In this context, the first one is COBIT, which is a best practice developed by Information Systems Audit and Control Association (ISACA) in order to provide IT governance to the companies for creating value from IT and understanding the risks [11]. What COBIT brings for IT management is set of objectives that are required to fulfill in order to accomplish best IT governance and minimize IT risks. ITIL, which developed in 1989 by British government, is a collection of defined and published best practice processes for information technology service management [14]. ITIL provides the IT service management key areas to guide IT management for auditing and control. What ITIL brings for IT management is set of tools that include advices and standards in IT service management which is important in service industries. Capability Maturity Model Integration (CMMI) is an approach for process improvement that presents the key items for effectiveness in processes of software engineering and organizational development [26]. What CMMI brings for IT management is set of process control for effective processes in IT management which is important in IT operations.

Standards. According to International Organization of Standardization (ISO), standards provide essential characteristics of products and services which involve quality, safety, reliability, efficiency, interchangeability and environmental care at an affordable level [12]. Standards bring quality to a constant degree for IT use and applications. This provides a guideline to IT management for maintaining control over IT. The followings are the ISO standards developed for IT domain [12]:

- ISO/IEC 38500:2008- Set of principles for effective, efficient, and acceptable use of IT within the organizations

- ISO/IEC 27002:2005- A tool for building guidelines and general principles for applying and maintaining information security management of an organization
- ISO/IEC 12207:2008   Software lifecycle processes standard
- ISO 9000:2005-   Set of quality management systems standards
- ISO/IEC 15288:2008- Standard for systems engineering including stages of life cycle and processes
- ISO/IEC 15504:2004- A framework for the assessment of processes
- ISO/IEC 20000:2005- Standard for IT Service Management (Covered by ITIL)
- ISO/IEC 19770:2006- Standard about Software Asset Management
- ISO/IEC 24762:2008- Guidelines   on   the   provision   of   information   and communications technology disaster recovery services

The needs for the guidelines and practices for IT management led the studies to find the way of how to utilize the standards and best practices more effective. The pros and cons of standards were investigated and evaluated by academic studies to achieve better understandings [24][27]. In this study, standards and best practices were examined in detail to gain comprehensive knowledge about factors affecting IT and its control. The strengths and limitations of best practices (COBIT, ITIL, and CMMI) and standards [11][12][14][18][27] were determined, and they were helpful to conceptualize the limitations and influential aspects of the model [23].

3   Research Methodology

Research methodology is composed of interdisciplinary methods in each steps of development and implementation of the model. The details will be presented in this paper with step-wise. It is believed that the step-wise method would be "reader-friendly" while following the process of model development and implementation. The study will be demonstrated in 6 steps which were grouped into two phases. Phase A contains the steps which represents framework development processes: Literature review on technology management, development of the conceptual framework and development of survey method and questions. Phase B includes the steps which represents practicing processes of the developed framework into the organizations: Implementation, quantification and data analysis and results evaluation.

STEP 1: Literature Review on Technology Management

This step involves in-depth research about technology management studies. Developed frameworks about technology management and assessment, research approaches adopted in IT management studies and techniques were systematically investigated through academic databases including Scopus, Sciencedirect and Google Scholar. The framework of literature review was based on basic principles, thus every finding was recorded step by step, and then they were analyzed, refined and finally evaluated. In addition to that, best practices and standards were researched through same academic channels as well as commercial connections. Similar systematic way in literature review was followed for best practice and standards research. The findings were systematically refined and resources extracted considering the purpose and the scope of this study [23]. Those three sources- best practices, standards and academic researches, which were utilized in literature review, constituted the three-folded structure of the model. This structure established in order to build the model on sound ground literature with three different resources.

STEP 2: Development of the Conceptual Framework

In the lights of findings from the literature review, the conceptual framework of ITMEM was determined to be based on a technology management process assessment model which was developed by M.J. Gregory in 1995 [10]. In his study, Gregory states that very few companies have systematic and comprehensive approaches to the management of technology, and specified that there were few frameworks in technology management which is an important missing link in technology management [10]. Considering this problem, he developed technology management process framework to provide to the companies the ability to audit and improve the technology management processes. In the study, the elements of technology management contributed to the main frame of the model which was identified as identification, selection, acquisition, exploitation and protection. But the scope was modified to fit the IT management domain:

Identification: It includes issues of awareness about information technologies that are significant for business operations. It contains research subjects targeting existing and emerging information technologies.

Selection: Selection involves preferences of information technologies that should be encouraged and promoted within the company.

Acquisition: The acquisition is interested in decisions about suitable ways of selected information technologies' acquisition and embedding them effectively. Selected information technologies may be acquired internally or externally.

Exploitation: Exploitation is concerned with realization of information technologies' value or systematic conversion of information technologies into marketable products. The link among market, technologies and platforms is important. It involves contribution of IT in the final product and to the market share.

Protection: It is concerned with preservation of the expertise and knowledge that are related in products and systems. It also includes legal issues as patenting and licensing. Protection is matters for the operations about all other constructs.

After in-depth researches in literature about the framework of technology management, Gregory's study was selected as a basis for ITMEM framework due to the following reasons:

▪   Gregory's framework was the result of a comprehensive study which involved the influential elements of technology management considering deficiencies in management processes.   This provided a path to receive further insight about technology management and its requirements [6].
▪ It addressed different characteristics of companies in technology management and provided a generic model of assessment. Thus, it helped to create a generic model of assessment in IT use which was applicable to the organizations in different industries [6].

- The established framework helped to understand the current practices and applications of the company about technologies and management. It helped to evaluate current practices, to measure the quality and to identify differences before and after implementation of ITMEM [20].
- Constructs of the Gregory's framework of the model designed comprehensively which were aimed to be clearly apprehended by managers and to be applied effectively through domain-based management process. The scope of the study was considered by ITMEM to provide a useful guide for IT use and management [19].
- The Gregory's framework provided a basis for auditing [19] which is fundamentally an aim of ITMEM through gathering practicable insight about the IT management of companies and assisting to management.

STEP 3: Development of Survey Method and Questions

After development of the framework, the items (factors effecting IT use) which were the subject areas in IT management were determined and allocated under each 5 elements of the model. Three folded structure of literature review constitutes the main source of the items. Under each element, it was aimed to measure factors of IT use through questioning the identified items in an organization. In order to conduct accurate assessment, each item was validated by at least three different sources in order to measure IT use [23].

Once the items were determined for measuring IT use and allocated under constructs of the framework, it was essential to investigate and observe the findings of ITMEM in practice in order to identify strength and weaknesses of the model and effectiveness. Thus, semi-structured survey method was employed to practice the model over the organizations [16]. This method is used to gather qualitative data through the interview that provides scope and time to participant for mentioning about their opinions on a specified subject. The objective is to apprehend participants' point of view instead of making generalizations about their acts. The focus of the interview and flow of the interview are decided by the researcher depending on the level of exploratory needs.

For ensuring validity and reliability during the practice, methodological triangulation was employed. As stated by Denzin, methodological triangulation includes contrasting research methods as a questionnaire and observation [9]. Thus, methodological triangulation fits in our model with the selected data collection methods. With this method, Data collection will be conducted and validated in the triangulation of 3 sources: interview, survey and documents. The findings of interview (which involves recorded data, observations and interview questions) should be matched by results of survey questions (which aim to measure items of IT use) and findings of documents (which involves reports, certificates and written documents of the organization about the questioned item).

In total, 64 questions constituted the questionnaire [23]. Each question had detailed descriptions to ensure that the participants fully comprehend the objective and goal in each question. The type of questions was close-ended and 5-point Likert-type response scales were adapted. This question type was selected due to its ease to complete, efficiency and specificity in measuring attitudes [21]. The respond scale was ranged between 0 and 4. In each question, every answer had also comprehensive description as much as the question itself in order to clarify the requirements of question. Addition to that, each question had a unique weight which aims to identify items with respect to their importance. IT experts took a role in weighting each item. The experts were selected from selected companies in the study considering the degree of knowledge in the domain. By this way, the final score was fairly affected by companies' level of success in important questions. Question weights' scale ranges between one and three (1-Little important, 2-Medium Important, 3- Highly Important). The weight criteria determined by the experts considering current needs and future needs in IT, damage in inefficient and ineffective use of IT specified in the item.

According to weight criteria, if the questioned subject is highly important (level 3), its duties should be fulfilled. Lacks may cause severe damages for the company and its operations. If the questioned subject is medium important (level 2), lacks may cause some damages for the company its operations. If the questioned subject is little important (level 1), lacks may cause little or no damages for the company its operations.

A sample set of questions with the sources of each item were given in the followings but other questions and detailed resource explanations can be found in Sezgin's study [23]:

- To What degree does IT take place in main strategic business goals? {[11][12][14]}
- To what degree IT performance and efficiency are measured in the company? {[11][12]}
- To what extent is IT used in project management? {[12][26]}

STEP 4: In-Company Implementation

In-company implementation is required to effectively conduct the interview and survey. In the first phase of implementation, particular experts of an organization who have comprehensive knowledge about IT and IT operations in the organization will be assigned by authorities. Then, the survey will be implemented on this group of employees. Additional to the quantitative data retrieved from survey, in the context of triangulation, presented documents and interview records will bring qualitative data for validation of the results.

STEP 5: Quantification and Data Analysis

After the data collected by quantitative and qualitative approaches, it needs to be converted meaningful and interpretable values in order to initialize analysis. In our study, the quantitative survey results mathematically calculated to find the success level, which is the aggregated score in percentages for each construct and final score. Data, which were quantified answers and weights of questions, were converted to success level by Equation 1. Calculation is done as: given quantitative answer of survey question (p) is multiplied by the designated weight (w) of the question for all of the questions (m, between 1 and 64, question number). To find the success level (SL), which is the score of a company over 100, total score converted to percentage.

$$SL = \nabla \sum_m w_m p_m \qquad (1)$$

The success level of each company converted to 5 point scale- named as quantitative level to present simple and scalable score to the authorities and decision makers. The quantitative level conversion was inspired from best practices' maturity level scoring framework. The conversion of the success level to maturity level was conducted by the experts who are experienced in best practices and scoring.

The interpretation guide of quantitative level of a company is presented at 5 levels: 1- Initial, 2- Rising, 3- Promising, 4- Manageable, 5- Improved. This guideline was aimed to help authorities understanding the missing points and achievements in IT use through ITMEM. The framework of quantitative levels interpretation table is inspired from COBIT's generic maturity level, which defines maturity levels in levels of IT processes to describe possible current and future states [11]. Similarly, purpose of quantitative level interpretation table is to provide a profile to companies which describe their current status with regards to their quantitative levels. The guide is given in the followings:

1 Initial: There is no evidence or little evidence that the company is aware of IT issues, and they are required to be addressed. Standardized processes do not exist in IT.

2 Rising: IT has developed to the level where employees are responsible of IT tasks which operates similar procedures. The awareness is low. Awareness of standardized processes of IT exists but not implemented. There is a confidence bout IT knowledge of employees at a significant level which causes problems in operations including IT. Low compliance is observed in IT and related approaches.

3 Promising: IT procedures and processes are mostly communicated, documented and standardized. But updating processes and tools are not applicable. IT takes place in long term and short term plans. Continuous improvement is not applied but promising. Compliance is observed in IT and related approaches in a rising trend.

4 Manageable:IT awareness is high. IT Management can monitor and measure IT use and procedures compliance, and brings precautions in problems. IT applications and processes are continuously improving and help for effective and efficient business operations. High compliance is observed in IT and related approaches. Continuous improvement slowly becomes a part of company culture in IT.

5 Improved: IT becomes an inevitable part of company culture and operations. IT processes and level of IT use have been reached to a good practice level, through continuous improvement and effective use of IT in every division. IT is integrated to business processes to automate and control the workflow.

4   Conclusion and Future Studies

IT use takes a significant role in operations of any organization to stay competitive in the market and to be effective. The position of IT brings the IT management concept in considerable states. Studies and developments in IT management field evolved over the time depending on the changing market needs [3]. The emergence of best practices, standards demonstrated the need of assessment and control over operations.

But implementation phase has particular defects. These are mainly: (1) high cost of implementation, (2) focusing on only limited area of IT involved operations, (3) need for training, (4) not guiding for solutions. In our study, those major defects in establishing the framework and developing implementation methods were taken into account. ITMEM framework based on Gregory's technology management assessment model [10], and developed by the contribution of best practices, standards and other studies about technology management

The contribution of this study is primarily to bring a new aspects to assessment of IT use which is, in comparison with other practices, requires comparatively less time, money, and training. It enables the small and medium sized companies to assess their IT use practically, and through this way, enhance IT management practices and approaches. Another contribution is to bring a different model to the literature which is based on academic framework and developed upon three-folded structure of academic studies, best practices and standards. It should be valuable asset considering the fact that other best practices were not academic-based studies. The other contribution to literature is about the validation of the model. Other than the best practices and standards which are only directing several questions on determined fields and seeking only the documentations, ITMEM involves use of semi-structured interview, questionnaire, and documentation. This structure establishes a triangulation for validation which enables the surveyor to retrieve proof of given information, emerging data and comprehensive insight of the companies. From the community perspective, ITMEM provides a tool for IT assessment especially for small and medium-sized enterprises (SMEs) with low budget. It can also be valuable asset for auditing.

The current practices of ITMEM are limited to particular set of companies. Further and much detailed studies on different sectors and different companies are required to establish more comprehensive, accurate and acceptable model. The study results also present promising data in further behavioral studies. The interview results are believed that they provide supportive data for social studies targeting human behavior about understanding employees towards IT.

References

1. Ankeny, J.:
http://www.entrepreneur.com/magazine/entrepreneur/2009/december/204074.html
2. Badawy, M.: Technology Management Education: Alternative Models. California Management Review 40, 94–115 (1998)
3. Benamati, J., Lederer, A.L., Singh, M.: Changing information technology and information technology management. Information & Management 31, 275–288 (1997)
4. Boynton, A.C., Zmud, R.W., Jacobs, G.C.: The Influence of IT Management Practice on IT Use in Large Organizations. MIS Quarterly 18, 299–318 (1994)
5. Camp, R.: Benchmarking: The Search for Industry Best Practices that Lead to Superior Performance. Quality Press, Milwaukee (1989)
6. Cetindamar, D., Phall, R., Propert, D.: Understanding technology management as a dynamic capability: A framework for technology management activities. Technovation 29, 237–246 (2009)

7. Crowston, K., Myers, M.D.: Information technology and the transformation of industries: three research perspectives. Strategic Information Systems 13, 5–28 (2004)
8. Deans, P., Keane, M.: Information systems and technology. PWS-Kent, Boston (1992)
9. Denzin, N.: Sociological Methods: A Sourcebook. Aldine Transaction, New Jersey (2006)
10. Gregory, M.: Technology management: a process approach. Proceedings of the Institution of Mechanical Engineers 209, 347–356 (1995)
11. Information Systems Audit and Control Association–ISACA, http://www.isaca.org
12. International Organization for Standardization–ISO, http://www.iso.org
13. Information Technology Association of America, http://www.itaa.org
14. Information Technology Infrastructure Library–ITIL, http://www.itil-officialsite.com
15. Karabacak, B., Sogukpinar, I.: ISRAM: information security risk analysis method. Computers & Security 24, 147–159 (2005)
16. Lindlof, T., Taylor, B.: Qualitative Communication Research Methods, 2nd edn. Sage Publications, California (2002)
17. Morimoto, S.: Application of COBIT to Security Management in Information Systems Development. In: Fourth International Conference on Frontier of Computer Science and Technology, pp. 625–630. IEEE Press, New York (2009)
18. Ozkan, S., Hackney, R., Bilgen, S.: Process based information systems evaluation: towards the attributes of "PRISE". Journal of Enterprise Information Management 20, 700–725 (2007)
19. Palm, E., Hansson, S.: The case for ethical technology assessment (eTA). Technology Forecasting and Social Change 73, 543–558 (2006)
20. Phaal, R., Farrukh, C.J., Probert, D.R.: Technology roadmapping- A planning framework fo revolution and revolution. Technological Forecasting & Social Change 71, 5–26 (2004)
21. Phaal, R., Farrukh, C., Propert, D.: Technology management tools: concept, development and application. Technovation 26, 336–344 (2006)
22. Scientific Article Database, http://www.sciencedirect.com
23. Sezgin, E.: Information Technology Management Enhancement Model: Assessment Of Information Technology Use In Organizations (Dissertation). Middle East Technical University, Ankara (2010)
24. Solms, B.V.: Information Security-A Multidimensional Discipline. Computers & Security 20, 504–508 (2001)
25. Tranchard, S.: ISO, http://www.iso.org/iso/pressrelease.htm?refid=Ref1135
26. What is CMMI? Software Engineering Institute, http://www.sei.cmu.edu/
27. Yoo, C., Yoon, J., Lee, B., Lee, C., Lee, J., Hyun, S., Wu, C.: A unified model for the implementation of both ISO 9001:2000 and CMMI by ISO-certified organizations. Systems and Software 79, 954–961 (2006)

Information Systems Planning - How to Enhance Creativity?

Vitor Santos[1], Luís Amaral[1], and Henrique Mamede[2]

[1] Universidade do Minho, Guimarães, Portugal
[2] Universidade Aberta, Lisboa, Portugal
{vsantos,amaral}@dsi.uminho.pt,
hsmamede@univ-ab.pt

Abstract. The global competitiveness and the organizations ability to make effective use of information technology and to focus on innovation and creativity are recognized as being important. The perspective of using creativity techniques or some adaptations, to help innovation in the area of information systems seems to be promising.

In this article we propose a strategy for the introduction of creativity in the information systems planning in order to build more agile and efficient information systems, allowing therefore more competitive business.

Keywords: Information Systems Planning, Creative Thinking, Innovation.

1   Introduction

The ability of companies effectively using information technologies and betting on innovation and creativity is recognized today as one important factor on the competiveness and agility of the companies. These take natural benefits through creativity and innovation by restructuring their processes, projects and products [5].

The Information Systems Planning (ISP) is a vital activity for the success and competitiveness of companies [3].

The diversity of the sectors in corporate activity, the different contexts and organizational structures are, along with the growing complexity of the globalized world of business, a huge challenge for the effectiveness of this project.

In this context, the chances of resourcing to known creativity techniques or their adaptations, in order to mediate the spawning of ideas, help produce new combinations, supply unexpected answers, as well as original, useful and satisfactory, in the area of Information Systems is challenging.

In this article, in a more limited aspect, we propose a method for the introduction of creativity and innovation techniques in the Information Systems Planning, regarding the construction of more agile and efficient Information Systems, which consequently allow an enhanced corporate competitiveness.

2   Creativity in the Information Systems Planning

The role of Information Systems Planning (ISP) has become crucial in the development and implementation of effective strategic plans in the organizations [9].

M.M. Cruz-Cunha et al. (Eds.): CENTERIS 2011, Part II, CCIS 220, pp. 398–407, 2011.

The growing uncertainty in the markets has led the companies to be more pro-active and to develop strategies that might allow enhancing their competitiveness. The strategy formula is oriented through company's mission and objectives based on a careful analysis of the involving means and the company itself, as shown in Figure 1.

Fig. 1. Strategy and competitiveness

Information technology allows a set of opportunities to reach a competitive edge and to adjust the Information Systems to the company's benefit. On the other hand, organizations verify that the capacity do provide a quick answer to unforeseeable events is fundamental to its survival [1].

In spite of the importance of the creativity in the Information Systems Planning being acknowledged, and a part of the main approaches to ISP as for instance the three-stage model by Bowman [4] and the multidimensional approach of Earl [7], developed investigation in this area has been scarce. Ruohonen and Higgins analyze the potential of ISP's activity theory application [12]. The analysis is divided into three separate time periods according to an ISP evolutionary perspective, and in each of the time periods the relation of creativity with Information Systems Planning is discussed.

Horton and Dewar propose the use of alexandrine patterns formalism to encapsulate the creative aspects of strategic Information Systems formation [8]. They apply a case-study on a Great Britain police force that allows them to derivate two patterns which demonstrate the use of a creative practice on a micro political level.

In the theoretical review on Information Systems Creativity, in particular in this article's context it stands out, on one hand, the importance of ISP activity in the definition of systems to develop, in order that these be aligned with the organization's strategy, and on the other hand, the need that this activity be creative and innovating thus providing the development of more competitive and adaptable solutions to environmental conditions.

Regarding the revision made on creativity and its techniques, it was possible to come to the conclusion it is a solid area, with about two hundred different creative techniques that can be grouped and used in different situations. Of these, that may support, stimulate, accelerate the creative production, we select for the use in different stages of the method, those that prove more adequate in which case.

Crossing these two areas of study, Information Systems and creative thought, there are various investigation themes, primary ones being: generating computer mediated ideas, creativity in the development of Information Systems, support tools to creativity and creative Information Systems, as well as Information Systems Planning creativity. It is on this last theme of crossing between Information Systems and creative thought that the present proposal fits in. More specifically in the convergence between ISP that, on its own should be creative, with an investigation on creativity and creative thought.

3   A Strategy to Introduce Creativity in ISP

As there are several approaches to ISP, where Alignment and Impact stand out, it is important to understand which the introduction and creative mechanisms are in these. Since Bowman's three stage model and Earl multidimensional are the more representative on Alignment and Impact approaches, and the PRAXIS/a by Amaral [2] an important conjugation of the three stage model and multidimensional approach, we focus our investigation on these three approaches.

The «Three Stage Model» [4] is one of the most relevant ISP approaches. It is based on the alignment of IS with the organization, caring for the analysis and needed information as well as resources rationalization. It follows a top-down strategy and it points out a range of ordained and well defined activities and tasks.

In this approach ISP activities are done in three separate stages. Figure 2 describe these stages according to their main activities, linkage and main results.

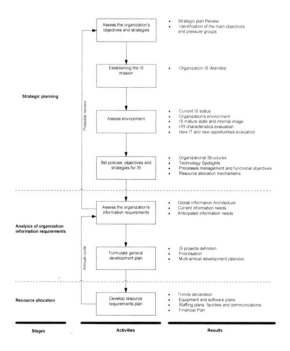

Fig. 2. Three Stage Model

Earl, on his «Multidimensional Approach» [7], defends that ISP must separately seek these three goals: to clarify the needs and strategy of the organization relating to its IS, assess the support to the organization and current IS usage, and Innovate by taking advantage of given strategic opportunities by IT/IS. This demand must be done in separate processes, but they must reflect on each other. The reason the search must be done separately is due to the fact that each goal is totally separate and has unique characteristics. Earl called «legs» to each of these distinct research processes. In Figure 3, the characteristics and main focuses of each «legs» are described.

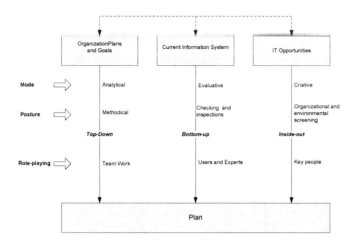

Fig. 3. Multidimensional Approach - adapted from Amaral [2]

The PRAXIS/a approach, as visualized on Figure 4, incorporates simultaneously the «Multidimensional Approach» and «Three Stage Model», and complements them with intention or focus: while the first seeks the alignment and impact of IT/IS in the organization, the second seeks the IT/IS alignment with the organization and linkage of the ISP with the Information Systems Development (ISD).

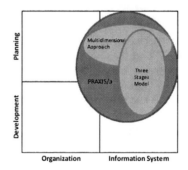

Fig. 4. PRAXIS/a approach – Three Stages Model and Multidimensional Approach relative positioning - adapted from Amaral [2]

The strategy we propose aims at incorporating creative processes and creativity techniques in different moments of main ISP approaches. For that we recognize the differences between approaches and phases, where to each one will make sense to introduce creative processes, as illustrated in the zones identified with «C» on Figure 5.

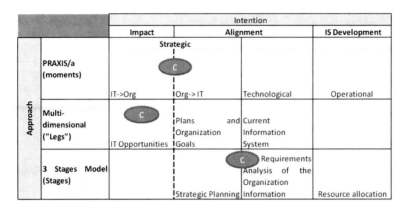

Fig. 5. Creativity in ISP approaches

To turn the creative processes viable, we propose a generic introduction and creativity method, to adapt according to the specifics of each of the three approaches.

This method resorts to several creativity techniques that we think are adequate to the different stages of the method, and in its whole allow it creative power. The method is based on six stages. Figure seven presents a global view on the method, in which stages to execute in sequence are now described:

Stage 1- Building a Team- In this stage we proceed to build a team that will apply the method. It is important to define a team leader and identify the competences and personal experience of each member. Preferably team members should have different personal and professional profiles.

Stage 2- Clarifying the Goal- In this stage the team should, starting with a generic business need (typically new challenge, opportunity, lacking or improvement) clearly identify the objective to be reached by the Information System to develop. Out of the need of the initial business necessity, the goal must be defined in an effective, clear, precise and measurable way.

Stage 3 - Understanding the needs of the Organization- After a clear definition of the goal, we must examine in depth the actual organization situation facing the objective to attain. This analysis means to comprehend which points are condition to success and precise what the ideal solution will be, under the point of view of achieving the goal. On this last subject, using creative techniques, as brainstorming, may be very useful, for instance to «define the ideal goal to reach» in unexpected and innovative ways.

Stage 4 - Focus on primary causes- This stage has for goal identifying the primary causes in the origin of the business. Root cause analysis (RCA) is a class of problem solving methods aimed at identifying the root causes of problems or events. The objective in root cause problem solving is to discover the points of leverage where patterns of behavior originate and can be changed.

This is a fundamental issue, for it will only be possible to think of new approaches and solutions having established the true causes in the origin of business necessities. Here too, resorting to creativity techniques, like brainstorming can prove very useful to identify deeper causes.

Stage 5- Finding Opportunities for Information Systems (OIS) - In this stage, considering the needs of the organization, and the primary causes, one or more creativity techniques are applied, to be selected according to typology in cause (as explained in Figure 6), in the attempt to obtain innovative solutions to address these causes.

		OIS source			
		No Coverage	Improvement	New business	Integration
Creativity Techniques	Idea Box		X		X
	Brainstorming	X		X	X
	Brute Thinking			X	
	Reversal			X	
	SCAMPER		X		X
	White Board			X	

Fig. 6. Application of creativity techniques to identify innovative Opportunities for Information Systems (OIS)

In this stage it is important to think creatively and keep an open mind so it is possible to get the maximum of alternate solutions. Given the foreseeable elevated number of alternate solutions, one should use a formal method to choose the better solution.

Stage 6-Incorporating OIS in the Plan- Finally in the last stage, one will to proceed to incorporate the Opportunities for Information Systems found in Stage 5 in the plan. The plan must be built according to the structure adopted by the organization.

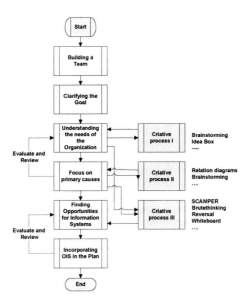

Fig. 7. Overview of ISP introduction and creativity generic method

In order to support the strategy application and the methods described above, we developed a series of tools and templates. In Figure 8, as an example, is one of the *templates* we developed.

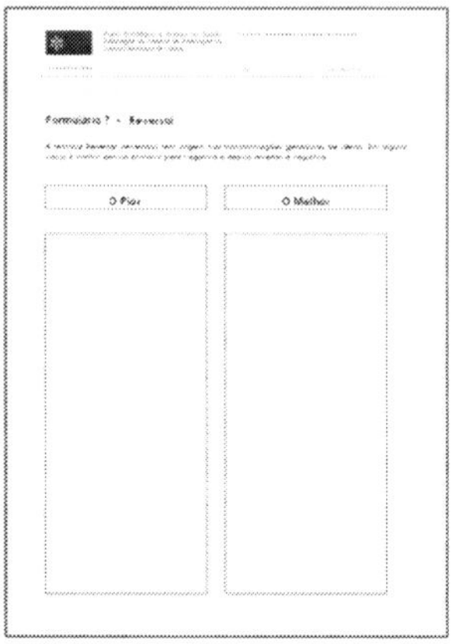

Fig. 8. Template for Reversal technique

Some of the tools have for goal helping to the analysis of the problems, and data collection, others, to support the documentation production.

4   Identification of Information Systems Opportunities in Câmara Municipal de Lisboa

In the context of the Strategic Plan and Strategic Management Project for the Information System of Câmara Municipal de Lisboa (CML), several work sessions were made with the purpose of identifying innovative Information Systems Opportunities (ISO).

The first work session had as goal to identify innovative ISO which could help the Direcção de Património Cultural (DPC) solve one of the problems it faces in its mission. The session was 4 hours long.

The following method was used, as described below:

1- The team was formed by CML before initializing the session. A heterogeneous group was one care, with both experts and non-experts in the area of culture, so that would provide «out of the box» thinking. Apart from the people in the culture area (from DMC), the session was attended by services and informatics people.

2- The Direcção de Património Cultural (DPC) presented the following need of business:

«There is a need to improve the communication on cultural activities with the mayors and reach out to a new public. The media don't care there is dispersion of their means and excess of information».

The problem was broken down by filling a support paper and discussing and defined what the ideal solution would be (goal).

3- There was then a debate in order to identify and list the primary sources. The relations diagram is shown on Figure 9.

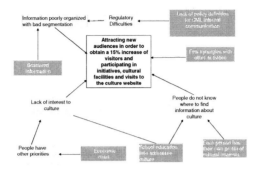

Fig. 9. Relation diagram

4- Based on what the ideal solution would be (goal), there was an identifying and a listing of key-points that would sustain an ideal solution. The primary causes list is shown on Figure 10.

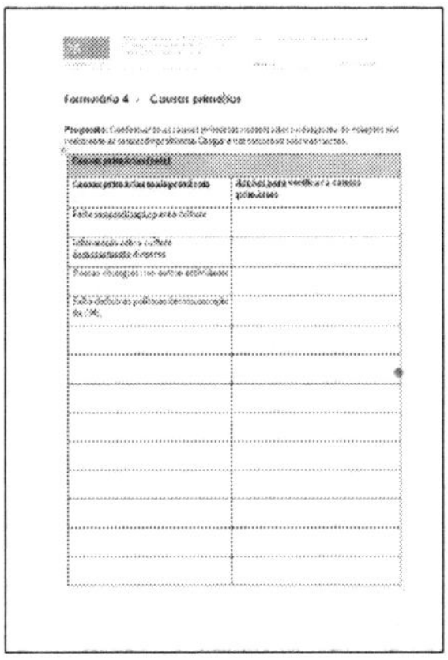

Fig. 10. Root cause list form

5- To approach the problem and according to the typology of the identified primary causes, two creative techniques were chosen and implemented: Brute Thinking and the Reversal.

Brute Thinking by Michael Michalko [10] is a creative and lateral thinking aid technique. It may be used to conceive alternate solutions, but also useful to identify problem causes.

This technique is based on a very simple process that is developed in four steps: to choose a random word; choose things/elements associated to the word randomly obtained; forcing a link between the word and the problem and between the associations and the problem; listing the ideas obtained and analyzing them.

The Reversal technique has its origin in the idea generating transformations included in the verification list of Osborn [11].

In some cases it is best to think first on the negative side then reverse the negatives.

6- From the application of both techniques came the seven following new ISO:

- CRM for Culture
- A publishing tool on City Cultural activities with a senior editor
- Culture and engineering synergy (culture and engineering portal)
- Culture Passport (every citizen can make a virtual collection of the events they attended, by the means of a stamp on their cultural passport- like in expo)
- Cultural offer Virtualization (virtual reality)
- Superculture Portal (all cultural activities information on a single website)
- Cultural program in terms of proximity (Project Unit or City zones)

DMC experts that attended declared that all the ISO found due to the creative techniques application are pertinent and promising.

5 Conclusions

Information Systems Planning is probably one of the most daring areas in Information Systems management. In a market environment characterized by the fast development of technologies and global competition intensification, in our view, the introduction of more creativity in the Information Systems Planning is of growing importance and has a probable impact in the success of Organizations.

The necessity for creative approaches in the design of new systems is both an opportunity and a challenge for Information Systems managers [5].

In this article we present a method for the introduction of creativity in the Information Systems Planning project, by describing it in a macroscopic level, along with a success case in its practical application in the context of information systems opportunities for CML. Applying the method resulted in seven new ISO.

So, in our opinion, it is possible to draw a consistent strategy for creativity and innovation processes in the Information Systems Planning, and make this work with simple and practical methods.

The next stages to be developed, following this work have mainly to do with the developing of theoretical models that support the design and developing of the strategy, perfecting the method, refining validation criteria and applicability analysis, and doing new tests and evaluations, as well as implementing eventual corrections.

References

1. Allaire, Y., Firsitoru, M.E.: Coping with Strategic Uncertainty. Sloan Management Review 30(3), 7–16 (1989)
2. Amaral, L.: PRAXIS: Um referencial para o Planeamento de Sistemas de Informação. In: Departamento de Sistemas de Informação, Universidade do Minho, Guimarães (1994)
3. Amaral, L., Varajão, J.: Planeamento de Sistemas de Informação, FCA - Editora de Informática, Lda, Lisboa, 4th edn., p. 247 (2007)

4. Bowman, B., Davis, G., Wetherbe, J.: Three Stage of MIS Planning. Information and Management 6, 1 (1983)
5. Cooper, R.B.: Information technology development creativity: A case study of attempted radical change. MIS Quarterly 24(2), 245–275 (2000)
6. Couger, J.D.: Ensuring Creative Approaches in Information System Design. Managerial and Decision Economics 11, 281–295 (1990)
7. Earl, M.: Management Strategies for Information Technologies. Prentice Hall, London (1989)
8. Horton, K.S., Dewar, R.G.: Evaluating Creative Practice in Information Systems Strategy Formation: the application of Alexandrian patterns. In: 34th Hawaii International Conference on System Sciences (2001)
9. Lederer, A.L., Sethi, V.: Critical Dimensions of Strategic Information Systems Planning. Decision Sciences 22, 104–119 (1991)
10. Michalko, T.: A Handbook of Creative-Thinking Techniques, 2nd edn. Ten Speed Press, Toronto (2006)
11. Mycoted "Creativity, Innovation, Tools, Techniques, Books, Discussions, Puzzles, Brain Teasers, Training..." (2011)
12. Ruohonen, M., Higgins, L.F.: Application of Creativity Principles to IS Planning. In: Watson, H.J. (ed.) Proceedings of the Thirty-First Hawaii International Conference on System Sciences. Organizational Systems and Technology Track, vol. VI. IEEE Computer Society, Los Alamitos (1998)

Software Solutions Construction According to Information Systems Architecture Principles

Sana Guetat[1] and Salem Ben Dhaou Dakhli[2]

[1] Le Mans University,
Le Mans, France
Sana.Guetat@univ-lemans.fr
[2] Paris-Dauphine University,
Place du Maréchal de Lattre de Tassigny
75775 Paris, France
sdakhli@computer.org

Abstract. Information Systems (IS) play a critical role in modern organizations. They are nowadays a necessary condition for organizations survival within an unstable and continuously changing economic and technology environments. Indeed, organizations need IS which help them reaching various difficult and often conflicting goals. To support innovation processes and, short time-to-market constraints, organization's IS must be agile and flexible. The concept of IS urbanization has been proposed since the late 90's in order to help organizations building agile IS. Nevertheless, despite the advantages of this concept, it remains too descriptive and presents many weaknesses. In particular, there is no useful approach dedicated to urbanized IS construction. In this paper, we propose a development approach of software solutions which is compliant with the IS urbanization rules.

Keywords: Information System, Computer solution, Urbanization, Function, Informational entity, Process, Target Urbanization Plan.

1 Introduction

Information Systems (IS) play a critical role in modern organizations. They are nowadays a necessary condition for organizations survival within an unstable and continuously changing economic and technology environments. Indeed, organizations need IS which help them reaching various difficult and often conflicting goals. To support innovation processes and, short time-to-market constraints, organization's IS must be agile and flexible. The concept of IS urbanization has been proposed since the late 90's in order to help organizations building agile IS. Nevertheless, despite the advantages of this concept, it remains too descriptive and presents many weaknesses. In particular, there is no useful approach dedicated to urbanized IS construction. In this paper, we propose a framework which improves existing work related to IS urbanization and describe a development approach of software solutions which is compliant with the IS urbanization rules. Taking into account the IS urbanization framework while building software solutions is related to the definition of a

M.M. Cruz-Cunha et al. (Eds.): CENTERIS 2011, Part II, CCIS 220, pp. 408–417, 2011.
© Springer-Verlag Berlin Heidelberg 2011

repository containing a set of architecture rule to be respected by software architects and developers. Our paper is organized as follows. Section 2 presents the foundations of IS urbanization based on the "city landscape" metaphor. Three sections are dedicated to the dimensions of IS architecture rules. In section 3, we present the spatial dimension. The communication dimension is presented in section 4. Section 5 describes the informational and functional dimensions. In section 6, we present a layered model which synthesizes and completes the existing contributions to IS urbanization proposed by academics and practitioners. In section 7, we use the concepts and models described previously to present an approach of software solutions construction. Section 8 concludes this paper by listing the encountered problems and the future research directions.

2 Foundations of Information Systems urbanization

IS urbanization has been studied by many authors [7] [10] [14]. The contributions of these authors have enriched the existing work related to the enterprise architecture concept [1] [2] [5] [6] [8] [11] [12] [17] [18]. All these authors use metaphors to define the foundations of enterprise architecture and IS urbanization. In particular, the "city planning" or "city landscape" metaphor has been proposed by many authors as a foundation of IS urbanization [4]. Guetat and Dakhli [19] propose the information city framework which generalizes the use of the "city planning" metaphor by stating that – within a modern organization – an information system may be considered as a city where the inhabitants are the applications belonging to this information system. In this city, called the information city, the common parts are information shared by all the information system applications while the private parts are composed of software artifacts owned by each application. An application belonging to the information city behaves as master of its proper data and artifacts and as a slave regarding shared information. That means that an application can use, update or suppress data and artifacts it owns but can only use a copy of shared information. Comparing an information system to a city extends the use of the "city landscape" beyond the analogy between software and building construction by emphasizing the problem of information system governance. On the one hand, following the example of a city, the relationships between the applications which populate the information city must be managed. That means that a set of architecture principles and rules has to be specified in order to govern exchanges either between application belonging to an information system or between such applications and the external environment like other information systems or end-users. On the other hand, the vast number of application assets in combination with the natural expansion of the application portfolio as well as the increasing complexity of the overall information system, drive a need for the information system governance. Therefore, the "information city" framework permits defining architecture principles and rules which help organizations prioritize, manage, and measure their information systems. The IS architecture rules and principles have five dimensions: a spatial dimension, a communication dimension, a functional dimension, a dynamic dimension, and an informational dimension. The spatial dimension describes the addresses of applications in the information city. This dimension is associated on the one hand, with the Target Information City Plan

(TICP) and on the other hand, with the Current Information City Plan (CICP). The communication dimension describes the rules which govern exchanges either between the applications belonging to the organization's IS or between the organization's IS and the external Information Systems and end-users. The dynamic dimension describes the roadmap which permits integrating each IS application in the TICP. The integration of an application in the TICP is based on a CICP analysis which defines an action plan to make this application compliant with the TICP requirements. The informational (vs. functional) dimension describes data (vs. functions) manipulated and implemented by an IS application. Therefore, the informational and functional dimensions describe the specific characteristics and the portfolio of the IS applications. The roles played by these two dimensions are complementary with the communication dimension role since the exchanges between IS applications or between the organization IS and external IS and end-users are based on the data manipulated and managed by IS applications and the services they offer. The following sections are dedicated to the presentation of the spatial, informational, functional, and communication dimensions of IS architecture rules.

3   The Spatial Dimension of Architecture Rules

Using the "information city" framework makes organizations able to apply a structure for classifying information system applications, functions, or services in a coherent way. It defines responsibility plots from coarse to fine-grained into discrete areas, which together form the complete Target Information City Plan (TICP).

Developing the TICP of an organization's information city is a result of a deep understanding of both the business and IT strategy of this organization. One of the central concepts of the TICP is the desire to eliminate the intricacy of the IT environments through the separation of concerns from the applications. Analysis of the principles behind the organization's and IT strategies leads to the four following architecture principles which help guide the development of the organization's information city TICP.

- Determine Front-office vs. Back-office responsibilities
- Specialize back-office regarding the organization's processes
- Identify the components common to the back-office and the front-office.
- Separate in the front-office the functions related to management of the communication network from those related to management of the relationships with the organization's customers and partners.

The first architecture principle - Determine front-office vs. back-office responsibilities – identifies the responsibilities of the organization's front-office and back-office. The front-office is dedicated to management of the relationships with the organization's external environment while the back-office is dedicated to the development of products and services. For instance, within an insurance company the back-office manages the insurance and services commitments whatever the distribution channels.

The second architecture principle - Specialize back-office regarding the organization's processes – permits identifying a "Business Intelligence" area, a "Support area", and at least one business area. A "Policy and Claims area" is an example of a business area within an insurance company.

The third architecture principle - Identify the components common to the front-office and the back office – refers to either the components that link the front-office and the back-office or the artifacts shared by the back-office and the front-office. Application of this principle results in identifying two areas: an "Integration area" and a "Shared information area". The first area allows exchanges of informational flows and services between the back-office and the front-office applications. The second area contains information shared by all the applications of the organization's information system as well as the applications which manage shared information data. The customers and products repositories are examples of information shared by all the applications of an organization's information system.

The fourth architecture principle - Separate in the front-office the functions managing the communication network from those managing the relationships with the organization's customers and partners – permits identifying two areas: an "Inbound and Outbound flows Management area" and a "Party Relationships area". The "Inbound and Outbound flows Management area" is dedicated to the management of the informational flows exchanged by an organization and its external environment. This area describes the various technology channels used by an organization while exchanging information with external environment. The "Party Relationship area" supports the relationships linking an organization with its customers and partners whatever the communication channel. Let us note that each area of the TICP can be broken down into more discrete areas of functionality. Generally, an area is composed of districts and a district is a set of blocks.

The following schema (Fig. 1) presents an example of TICP which may be used to illustrate the information city in various service-intensive organizations like banks and insurance companies.

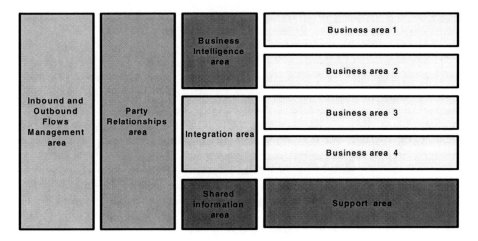

Fig. 1. The Target Information City Plan (TICP)

4 The Communication Dimension of Architecture Rules

The Communication dimension of IS architecture rules describes how intra-SI and inter-SI exchanges take place. The goal of the architecture rules associated with the Communication dimension consists on the one hand, in reducing the point-to-point connection exchanges between the SI applications which belong to different areas of the TICP and on the other hand, in facilitating weak coupling between IS applications as well as the reuse of information contained in the exchanged flows. Therefore, applying the architectural rules associated with the Communication dimension results in reducing development, maintenance, and operation costs of the IS applications. Moreover, exchanges of services and informational flows between applications belonging to different TICIP areas must take place through the Integration area. Concerning the exchanges with applications belonging to external IS, the IS architecture rules associated with the Communication have two goals. The first goal consist in hiding the complexity of an organization's IS for the external applications who consume services proposed by this IS. While the second goal is related to the IS security constraints. Consequently, exchanges with external applications must take place through the Inbound and Outbound Flows Management area.

5 The Informational and Functional Dimensions of Architecture Rules

The informational (vs. functional) dimension of the IS architecture rules describes informational entities or data chunks managed (vs. implemented) by each IS application. Functions and informational entities permit defining the scope of a computerization project (i.e. What?). The informational entity and the function concepts enable the description of the computerization problem by using words and sentences understandable by all the stakeholders.

5.1 The Informational Entities

An informational entity is a set of information chunks manipulated (stored, processed, used,...) by an IS application. An informational entity represents common data, material goods, or concepts used while carrying out organizational processes. A customer and a contract are examples of informational entities within insurance companies and banks. The informational entities and their relationships constitute the business conceptual model which is independent from its implementation in databases. An application is a master of an informational entity if it owns the official copy of this entity. Otherwise, it behaves as a slave of this entity. This means that the creation or the modification of an informational entity must be accepted by the application which is the master of this informational entity. An informational entity has a one and only one IS application master. Each IS application proposes read, modification, integrity control, and publication services of the informational entities of which it is the master.

5.2 The Functions

A function is a use or transformation action (collection, creation, processing, edition, storage) over a set of an IS informational entities. We draw on Porter's typology of organizational processes [13] to identify three types of functions. A function may be a business function, a support function, or a decision-making function. The business functions are manipulated by the organization's business processes. The support functions are manipulated by the organization's support processes while the decision-making functions are related to the organization's decisional processes. Editing an insurance contract information and processing a customer claim are examples of functions within an insurance company or a bank.

Functions describe the use or transformation of information chunks contained in informational entities manipulated by the organizational processes. Inputs and outputs of functions are informational entities. Functions identified at the beginning of a computerization project determine the project scope. They are used during the evaluation of the alternative software solutions of the computerization problem associated with this project.

The organizational actors manipulate informational entities and execute business, support, or decision-making functions while carrying out the activities of organizational processes in which there are involved. An organizational process task executes at least one function. We note that a function may be decomposed into elementary functions according to the organizational context. Organizational processes focus on structuring and executing their steps in order to produce goods and services required by the organization's customers. While activities and tasks describe what the organizational actors do while carrying out organizational processes. From an IS perspective, the inputs and outputs of organizational processes are informational flows. Functions don't describe organizational processes i.e. organizational processes activities and tasks are not decomposed into functions. As stressed by Dakhli [3], functions are orthogonal to organizational processes. They are independent of organizational actors and may be reused by many organizational processes. For instance, business functions related to the customer informational entity are reusable by many organizational processes. We note that there are functions which are specific to a business domain or an organizational process.

The concept of function is independent from information technology i.e. a function is independent of the IS applications which implement and manipulate it. It corresponds to a business, support, or decision-making requirement within an organization. Therefore, the concept of function is independent of software solutions. Functions may be supported by software services offered by IS applications. There are two types of services: applicative services, and end-user services. In order to reduce redundancies between IS applications, an elementary function must be implemented by only one software service. So, only one IS application is the master of this service and offers it to the other IS applications.

The relationships between functions and software services permit identifying the software services implemented by IS applications and evaluating the IS redundancy level. Moreover, these relationships help organizations in impact analysis, definition of services to be modified or created, and determination of reusable services among the existing ones.

6 The Layered Model of Information Systems Architecture

In this section, we draw on the work by Dakhli [3] to propose a multi-layered model of IS architecture based on five interacting layers: the strategy layer, the functional architecture (information system architecture) layer, the applicative architecture layer, and the software architecture layer (Figure 2). The strategic layer defines the organizational problems to be solved and their organizational solutions. Such problems result from the organization's external and internal constraints. External constraints may be economic, political, social, legal or related to the evolution of the technology. Internal constraints reflect the impacts of external constraints on the organization's components: structure, people, production technology, tasks and information technology [9] [15] [16].

The business process layer describes the business processes architecture at the conceptual and the organizational levels. The business processes conceptual architecture models business processes as a nexus of activities exchanging and processing information. The organizational business processes architecture is the projection of the conceptual business processes architecture on the organization. Therefore, it models business processes as nexus of operational activities and tasks carried out by organizational actors in order to create value. The business processes architecture is updated according to the organizational solutions defined by the strategic layer.

The functional architecture layer describes the information system architecture as a nexus of business entities and functions. A business entity is a set of information chunks which define a concept used by the organizational actors while carrying out a business process. A business function is an action which uses and transforms at least one business entity. A business process manipulates business entities through the use of business functions. Business entities are described in a business repository. A business function may be considered as an aggregation of many business sub-functions. Business functions may be used by many business processes. Such business functions are called reusable business functions. Business entities manipulated by many business processes are called shared information. Because of the invariant and stable nature of business entities and business functions, they are independent of the organizational structure and the roles played by actors within an organization. Architecture of an organization's information system is defined as a model describing the organization's business functions and business entities as well as the relationships between these concepts. The business processes architecture is updated by integrating the impacts of the organizational solutions defined by the strategic layer on the business entities and functions.

The applicative layer provides a map which describes the organization's applications as well as the information flows they exchange. An application is a set of software systems which computerizes at least partly a business process. So, an application provides a software support to the value creation behavior of organizational actors. This behavior consists in carrying out business processes activities which manipulate business information by using business functions. An application provides two categories of services: service-to-user and service-to-application. A service-to-user results from an interaction between and end-user and an application and helps an organizational actor who carries out a set of operational activities. A service-to-application is an intermediate service provided by an application to another application while processing information. An application may be considered as a dynamic conjunction of a set of business process activities with business entities and business functions in order to contribute to goods and services production. The applicative layer results from the interaction between the functional layer and the business process layer which supports the problem and operation spaces. The applicative layer delivers a first level description of a software solution as a new or enhanced application which interacts with existing and future applications.

The software layer describes each software solution as a set of software components and connectors distributed according to a software architecture model (e.g. MVC,…). A software solution is either the architecture of a new application which supports at least partly a new business process or the architecture of an existing application which is enhanced in order to take into account the modifications of an existing business process. Despite the richness of the existing definitions of the software component concept, we think that these definitions are note appropriate to take into account all the perspectives of information system architecture. So, we propose in this paper a definition of this concept which refers to business functions. Our definition states that a software component is an autonomous and homogeneous logical unit which implements a business function in order to provide a service either to end users or to other logical units. A software connector is an autonomous and homogeneous logical unit which facilitates interactions between two software components. A software solution is composed of reusable and specific software components and connectors. A reusable software component implements a business function used by many business processes.

We note that a software solution has many facets associated with the layers of the IS architecture model presented previously. Each facet corresponds to an architecture metamodel which describes the main concepts characterizing this facet and the relationships between these concepts.

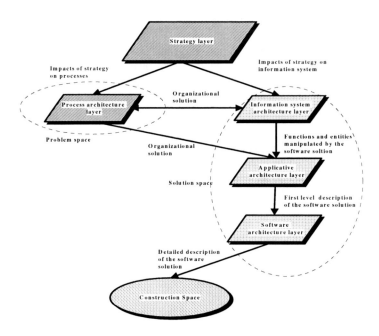

Fig. 2. The layered model of Enterprise Architecture (Adapted from [3])

7 The Construction Approach of Software Solutions

The software solution construction approach proposed in this paper is compliant with IS urbanization requirements and constraints. That the construction of a software solution is guided by the layered IS architecture model results in two complementary interpretations: horizontal and vertical. The horizontal interpretation refers to the systemic nature of the proposed approach since it assumes that a software solution has many facets which may be viewed as levels of abstraction associated with the IS architecture layers. Therefore, the multifaceted description of software solutions facilitates the management of IS applications complexity. The vertical interpretation highlights that a software solution has a lifecycle whose states and transitions are managed by the construction approach. This interpretation points out that a software solution is a sequence of architecture models such as the model M_n is a more formal version of the model M_{n-1} which incorporates the constraints of the architecture layer. In other words, the architecture model M_{n-1} is an abstraction of the architecture model M_n. Furthermore, each architecture model belonging to a software solution is associated with a IS architecture layer and may be considered as a state of this software solution. The software solutions construction approach -proposed in this paper - is composed of the following six phases:

❶ Description of the process architecture;

❷ Description of the functional and informational architecture;

❸ Description of the applicative architecture;

❹ Description of the software architecture;

❺ Description of the alternative software solutions;

❻ Selection of the target software solution.

These phases are not necessarily sequential. For instance, the steps ❶ et ❷ are parallel since the description of the activities and tasks of an organizational process may take place at the same time than the identification of functions and business entities manipulated by this process. In order to build a satisfying software solution which takes into account the organization constraints, many iterations of the six steps listed above may be necessary.

8 Conclusion and Future Research Directions

In this paper, we have presented the main concepts of IS urbanization prior to presenting an approach to build software solutions which are compliant with IS urbanization rules and constraints. Our work has three main contributions. On the one hand, it enriches the existing work related to IS urbanization by defining the concept of architecture rules dimensions which help understand the relationships between the main IS urbanization concepts and resources. On the other hand, our paper stresses that organizations may get value from IS urbanization through adaptation of existing software development, evolution and maintenance processes and methods. Finally, the software solutions construction approach proposed in this work help understanding the IS architecture concept and provides IS architects with a new vision of software artifacts reuse based on IS functional architecture. The validation of our framework within a French insurance company permitted us identifying many problems which may constitute future research directions. Firstly, the difference between the activity, task, and function concepts is not clear. To solve this problem, we think that a set of discriminating criteria must be defined in order to help IS architects and developers understand the difference between these concepts. Secondly, while validating the proposed approach, we noted that IS architects and developers use ambiguous non standard words and expressions to name functions and informational entities. So, the definition of codification and naming standards of functions and informational entities is needed to avoid design errors, redundancies and inconsistencies which may be an obstacle to reuse. Finally, functions reuse requires the definition of a repository which describes reusable functions and offers an efficient tool to search them easily.

References

1. Bernard, S.A.: An Introduction to Enterprises Architecture. Author House, Indiana (2004)
2. Boar, B.H.: Constructing Bluprints for Enterprise Architecture. Wiley Computer Publishing, New York (1999)
3. Dakhli, S.B.D.: The Solution Space Organisation: Linking Information Systems Architecture and Reuse. In: Proceedings of the ISD 2008 Conference, Paphos, Cyprus. Springer, Heidelberg (2008)
4. Dieberger, D., Frank, A.U.: A City Metaphor to Support Navigation in Complex Information Spaces. Journal of Visual Languages and Computing 9, 597–622 (1998)
5. Everden, R.: The Information Framework. IBM Systems Journal 35, 37–38 (1996)
6. Fayad, M., Henry, D., Bougali, D.: Enterprises Frameworks. Software Practice and Experience 32, 735–786 (2002)
7. Jean, G.: Urbanisation du business et des SI. Editions Hermès, Paris (2000)
8. Kaisler, S.H., Armour, F., Valivullah, M.: Enterprise Architecting. In: Proceedings of the 38th HICSS, Hawaï. IEEE Computer Society Press, New York (2005)
9. Leavitt, H.J. (ed.): The Social Science of Organizations, Four Perspectives. Prentice-Hall, Englewood Cliffs (1963)
10. Longépé, C.: Le Projet d'Urbanisation du SI, Editions Dunod, Paris (2006)
11. Maier, M.W., Rechtin, E.: The Art of Systems Architecturing. CRC Press, Boca Raton (2000)
12. Noran, O.: Analysis of the Zachman Framework for EA from the GERAM Perspective. Annual Reviews in Control 27, 163–183 (2003)
13. Porter, M.E.: Competitive Advantage: Creating and Sustaining Superior Performance. Free Press, New York (1998)
14. Sassoon, J.: Urbanisation des SI. Editions Hermès, Paris (1998)
15. Toffolon, C., Dakhli, S.: The Software Engineering Global Model. In: Proceedings of the COMPSAC 2002 Conference, Oxford, United Kingdom (2002)
16. Toffolon, C.: L'Incidence du Prototypage dans une Démarche d'Informatisation. Thèse de doctorat, Université de Paris-IX Dauphine, Paris (1996)
17. Zachman, J.A.: A Framework for Information Systems Architecture. IBM Systems Journal 26, 276–292 (1987)
18. Zachman, J.A., Sowa, J.: Extending and Framework for IS Architecture. IBM Systems Journal 31, 590–616 (1992)
19. Guetat, S., Dakhli, S.B.D.: The Information City: A Framework for Information Systems Governance. In: Proceedings of the MCIS 2009 Conference, Athens, Greece (2009)

Author Index

Abelha, António   III-156, III-223, III-233
Abreu, Jorge Ferraz de   III-40, III-49, III-59
Adão, Telmo   II-51
Afonso, João   III-49
Afonso, José   II-162
Alexandre, Guilherme   II-51
Ali, Mahmood   I-310
Almada-Lobo, Bernardo   III-213
Almeida, Ana Margarida Pisco   III-59, III-337
Almeida, Pedro   III-40, III-49
Alves, Mário   II-62
Alves, Samanta   III-423
Amaral, Cléia M. Gomes   I-228
Amaral, Luís   II-398
André, Marc   III-107
Antero, Michelle   I-147
Arroyo, Alberto   II-380
Assuncao, Pedro   II-111
Aversano, Lerina   II-286
Ayachi-Ghannouchi, Sonia   I-331, III-79

Bacao, Fernando   I-44
Baïna, Karim   II-345, II-356
Baïna, Salah   II-345, II-356
Balloni, Antonio José   III-347
Barão, Alexandre   I-400
Bastião, Luis   III-254
Basto-Fernandes, Vitor   II-120
Bastos, David   III-361
Belaazi, Mehrzia   I-331
Belfo, Fernando Paulo   I-129, II-230
Berg, Jan van den   II-72
Bermejo, Luis B. Pérez   I-351
Bermejo, Paulo Henrique de Souza   II-297
Bessa, Maximino   II-19, II-51
Bjørn-Andersen, Niels   I-147
Boltena, Abiot Sinamo   I-190
Boonstra, Albert   II-369
Borbinha, José   II-335
Borges, José   III-213

Bote, Juanjo   III-136
Botella, Jose Luis Montes   I-351
Brás, Samuel   III-361
Brega, José Remo Ferreira   III-89
Brito, António   III-213
Bruno, Giorgio   II-206

Cabral, Alexandra   III-223
Cáceres, Jesús   III-117
Cal, Bruno   I-248
Calle, Eusebi   III-11
Caran, Gustavo Miranda   I-228, III-21
Cardeal, Simão   II-111
Cardoso, Ana   II-315
Carse, Bruce   III-30
Carvalho, J.A.R. Pacheco de   II-188
Carvalho, João Álvaro   II-315
Carvalho, José P.   II-196
Castela, Eduardo   III-97
Chebil, Maha   III-79
Coelho, Jorge Soares   I-129
Coelho, Pedro Simões   I-158
Corchuelo, Rafael   II-170
Costa, Carlos   III-254
Costa, Ricardo   I-96
Costa, Rui Pedro   II-141
Cotet, Costel Emil   I-410
Cristo, Paulo   II-82
Cruz-Jesus, Frederico   I-44
Cunha, João Carlos da   II-215

Dakhli, Salem Ben Dhaou   II-408
Davarynejad, Mohsen   II-72
de Assis Moura Jr., Lincoln   III-194
Dedene, Guido   I-238
de Pablos, Carmen   I-351
Dias, Albertina   I-73
Dias, Diego Roberto Colombo   III-89
Dias, Ricardo   III-49
Diaz, Javier   III-185
Ding, Yi   III-175
Domingos, Dulce   I-260
Domingues, Patricio   III-317
Doukas, Dimitris   I-300
Doumi, Karim   II-345, II-356

Draghici, Anca   I-270, I-380, I-410
Draghici, George   I-380
Dragoi, George   I-270, I-410
Duarte, Júlio   III-156

Elragal, Ahmed   I-168
Enslein, Alana   II-260

Farkas, Romain   III-107
Fava, Laura   III-185
Fdez-Riverola, Florentino   III-317,
    III-327
Felgueiras, Miguel   III-317, III-327
Felisberto, Filipe   III-317, III-327
Fernandes, Tiago   III-423
Fernández, Joaquin   III-1
Fernandez-Feijoo, Belen   I-54
Fernández-Luna, Juan M.   III-146
Ferreira, Anderson   III-69
Ferreira, Flávio   III-289
Ferreira, Isabel   I-129, II-315
Ferreira, Pedro   I-260
Filho, Bento Alves da Costa   II-215
Filho, Guido Souza   III-69
Francischetti-Corrêa, Moacyr   III-128
Frantz, Rafael Z.   II-170
Freire, Carla S.   III-1
Friedrich, Michael   III-107

Gameiro, Atílio S.   II-196
Garcia, Bruno Paula   I-228
Garrido, Piedad   I-208
Ge, Xiaocheng   I-139
Gelabert, Gemma   III-136
Gkintzou, Vasiliki   III-413
Gnecco, Bruno Barberi   III-89
Goderis, Antoon   I-238
Gomes, Carlos   III-213
Gomez, Jorge Marx   I-190
Gonçalves, António   II-240
Gonçalves, Joel Mana   II-325
Gonçalves, Martinho   II-51
Gonçalves, Rejane Pereira da Silva
    II-325
Grasso, Carmine   II-286
Greaseley, Andrew   I-198
Guetat, Sana   II-408
Guillén, Alberto   III-264
Guillén, José F.   III-264
Guimarães, Marcelo de Paiva   III-89,
    III-128

Haddara, Moutaz   I-168, II-180
Hobbs, Stephen H.   II-260
Hodges, Chelsea   II-260
Hori, Mayumi   I-14, I-22
Hubac, Stéphane   I-118
Huete, Juan F.   III-146
Hustad, Eli   I-290
Huysegoms, Tom   I-238

Iuliano, Pablo   III-185
Ivascu, Larisa   I-270, I-410
Izvercianu, Monica   I-270

Jaklič, Jurij   I-158
Janssen, Maarten   II-72

Kekre, Sham   III-402
Kotb, Mohamed T.   II-180
Kotb, Yehia T.   II-180
Kurata, Noriko   I-22

Lauris, José Roberto Pereira   III-89
Lawless, W.F.   II-260
Leishenring, Carlos   III-204
Lenart, Gregor   I-322
Lima, Joselice Ferreira   I-228, III-21
Lopes, Diogo   II-151
Lopes, Vanda   III-307
López, Francisco Martínez   I-73
Lopez, Jorge L.   I-178
Loudon, David   III-30

Macdonald, Alastair S.   III-30
Machado, Humberto   III-223
Machado, José   III-156, III-223, III-233
Magalhães, Luís   II-19, II-51
Maggiorini, Dario   II-101
Mamede, Henrique   II-398
Mano, Licínio Kustra   III-337
Mansar, Selma Limam   III-402
Mantakas, Marios   I-300
Marcelino, Luís   II-141, II-151
Marchau, Vincent   II-72
Marques, Maria da Conceição da Costa
    I-361
Marques, N.   II-188
Martinho, Ricardo   I-260, II-82
Martins, Henrique M.G.   III-204, III-392
Martins, José Carlos Lourenço   I-129
Martins, Paula   III-97
Martins, Paula Ventura   I-390

Martins, Rui   III-97
Martins, Valéria Farinazzo   III-194
Marzo, Jose L.   III-11
Mathew, Wesley   III-244
McDermid, John A.   I-139
Medeiros, Leonardo Melo de   III-384
Meinecke, Christian   I-218
Melo, Erick   III-69
Melo, Miguel   II-19
Mendes, David   III-297
Méndez, José R.   II-120
Michelini, Rinaldo C.   I-34
Miranda, José   III-423
Mocan, Marian   I-380
Modesto, Fábio   III-89
Modrák, Vladimír   I-63, II-11
Molina-Jiménez, Carlos   II-170
Monguet, Josep M.   III-1
Motta, Gustavo   III-69
Munkelt, Torsten   I-280

Naranjo, Fernando   I-208
Naumenko, Andrey   III-107
Negreiros, J.   II-29
Neves, Filipe   II-111
Neves, José   III-223
Noce, Irapuan   I-129
Nogueira, Ana Filipa   II-130

Ohashi, Masakazu   I-14, I-22
Okuda, Koji   I-14
Oliveira, André   III-289
Oliveira, Lino   II-276
Oliveira, Rita   III-59
Oliveira, Saulo Barbará de   III-347
Oliveira, Tiago   I-44, I-86
Olsen, Dag H.   I-290
O'Neill, Henrique   I-248
Ordaz, Mercedes García   I-73
Orvalho, Verónica   III-423
Özkan, Sevgi   II-388

Pacheco, C.F. Ribeiro   II-188
Pacheco, Osvaldo   III-40
Paige, Richard F.   I-139
Papablasopoulou, Theodora   III-413
Páscoa, Carlos   I-86, I-96, II-1
Passos, Marcello   III-69
Patton, Tadd   II-260
Pedro, Luís M.C.C.   III-392

Pereira, António   III-317, III-327,
     III-361
Pereira, Carlos   III-289
Pereira, Francisco   II-62
Peres, Emanuel   II-19, II-51
Pérez-Vázquez, Ramiro   III-146
Pina, Carla   III-223
Pinto, Joaquim Sousa   II-91, III-289
Pinto, Mário   II-276
Pires, Péricles José   II-215
Plaza, Inmaculada   I-208
Pong, F.   II-29
Popovič, Aleš   I-158
Porfírio, José António   I-106
Portela, Carlos Filipe   III-156, III-223,
     III-233, III-244
Pragosa, Miguel   II-151
Pucihar, Andreja   I-322

Queirós, Cristina   III-423
Queirós, Ricardo   II-276
Quintas, César   III-223

Ramos, Isabel   I-371
Razzoli, Roberto P.   I-34
Reis, António D.   II-188, II-196
Reis, Catarina I.   III-1
Ribeiro, António Miguel   II-141
Rico, Nuria   III-264
Rieken, Matthias   I-190
Riis, Philip Holst   I-341
Rijo, Rui   III-361
Ripamonti, Laura Anna   II-101
Rippel, Daniel   I-218
Robert, Reeves   II-260
Rocha, José F.   II-196
Rocha, Nelson   III-254
Rocha, Tânia   II-19
Rodrigues, Carlos   II-162
Rodrigues, Irene   III-297
Rodrigues, Joel J.P.C.   III-392
Rodrigues, Nuno   III-371
Rodrigues, Pedro   III-272
Rodríguez-Solano, Carlos   III-117
Romero, Silvia   I-54
Rosa-Paz, Darien   III-146
Rosso, Jorge   III-185
Rosu, Sebastian Marius   I-410
Rovira, Mercè   III-11
Roxo, Diogo   III-97

Ruiz, Silvia   I-54
Rusu, Lazar   I-178

Salazar, Maria   III-223
Sampaio, A.Z.   II-40
Santos, Jaime B.   III-97
Santos, João   III-204
Santos, João Correia dos   I-106
Santos, J.P.   II-40
Santos, Leonel   II-315
Santos, Manuel Filipe   III-156, III-223,
    III-233, III-244
Santos, Mariana de Azevedo   II-297
Santos, Milton   III-254
Santos, Pedro   II-1
Santos, Vitor   II-398
Santoyo, Arturo Serrano   II-270
Scholz-Reiter, Bernd   I-218
Seco, Alexandra   III-327
Semančo, Pavol   II-11
Sénica, Nuno   II-91
Sezgin, Emre   II-388
Shahzad, Muhammad Kashif   I-118
Siadat, Ali   I-118
Sicilia, Miguel-Ángel   III-117
Silva, Alberto Rodrigues da   I-400
Silva, Álvaro   III-233
Silva, Augusto   III-254
Silva, Cândida   I-371, II-276
Silva, Catarina   II-62, II-130, II-141,
    II-151
Silva, José Silvestre   III-97
Silva, Julio   III-69
Silva, Leandro Dias da   III-384
Silva, Miguel Mira da   II-306
Silva, Telmo   III-40, III-49
Singhal, Anoop   III-165
Snoeck, Monique   I-238
Soares, Salviano   II-111
Sobrinho, Álvaro Alvares de Carvalho
    César   III-384
Sourla, Efrosini   III-413
Sousa, José   II-19
Sousa, Pedro   II-240
Sousa, Rui Dinis   II-230
Sperandio, Fabrício   III-213
Stavrou, Angelos   III-165
Sudzina, Frantisek   I-322
Sultana, Rabeya   I-178
Syrimpeis, Vasileios   III-413

Targowski, Andrew   I-63, III-282, I-1
Tavares, Filipe   II-111
Tavares, Tatiana   III-69
Teixeira, António   III-289
Teixeira, Cláudio   II-91, III-289
Teixeira, João Paulo   III-272, III-307
Termens, Miquel   III-136
Terzaghi, Maria Alicia   III-185
Thanassoulis, Emmanuel   I-198
Toda, e Favio Akiyoshi   III-347
Tollenaere, Michel   I-118
Tomé, Paulo   II-162
Tonelli, Adriano Olímpio   II-297
Torres-Padrosa, Víctor   III-11
Tortorella, Maria   II-286
Tovar, Carlos   III-264
Trevelin, Luis Carlos   III-128
Tribolet, José   I-86, I-96, II-1
Tsakalidis, Athanasios   III-413
Tzimas, Giannis   III-413

Valdez, Francisco   II-335
Varajão, João   II-19, II-51
Vardasca, Tomé   III-204
Varga, J.   III-165
Veiga, H.   II-188
Verdún, José D. Carrillo   II-380
Vieira, Elenilson   III-69
Vieira, Ricardo   II-335
Vilaça, João L.   III-371
Vilarinho, Sarah   II-306
Vilches, Diego   III-185
Völker, Sven   I-280

Wang, Yucan   I-198
Whitfield, R.   II-29
Wijesekera, Duminda   III-165
Wood, Joseph C.   II-260
Wu, Bing   III-175
Wu, Jianfeng   III-175

Xie, Ying   I-310

Yevseyeva, Iryna   II-120
Yu, Bo   III-165

Zacarias, Marielba   I-390, II-240
Zambalde, André Luiz   II-297
Zhou, Erqiang   III-175
Zuchegno, Kelsey   II-260